A HISTORY OF THE EDWINSFORD and CLOVELLY COMMUNITIES

The Williams, Drummond, Cary, Hamlyn, Fane, Manners, Asquith and Rous Family Owners

by

David TR Lewis

Front cover photo: Edwinsford by Paul Sandby 1776

This book is dedicated to my son Tom Lewis

All proceeds from the sale of this book received by the author will be donated to a Jesus College Oxford charitable trust to fund an annual national prize for the best published book or article on Welsh history in memory of the late Major Francis Jones (1907-1993), Wales Herald Extraordinary, Carmarthen County Archivist and prodigious author and publisher

ISBN 978-0-9571896-2-1

Published in 2017 by David TR Lewis of Erwhen, Cwrt-y-Cadno, Pumsaint, Cynwyl Gaeo, Carmarthenshire SA19 8YP
lewis.erwhen@icloud.com

Design by: stiwdio@ceri-talybont.com
Printed and bound in Wales by Y Lolfa, Talybont

Foreword

This book is the third in a series about some of the gentry and other families whose seats and estates were situated in North Carmarthenshire. *Family Histories and Community Life in North Carmarthenshire (2012)* described the families of over 100 farms and properties and the life of the community in the parish of Cynwyl Gaeo over past centuries. *Dolaucothi and Brunant-A Tale of Two Families in Wales (2016)* described the histories of two Welsh families, the Johnes family of Dolaucothi and the Lloyd family of Brunant, and their estates in and around Pumsaint, Carmarthenshire.

This book contains the histories of (a) their neighbours, the Williams family of Edwinsford (together with the histories of their estates and tenant families in Talley, Llansawel and Caio), (b) the Drummond family of Hawthornden Castle in Midlothian near Edinburgh, who intermarried with the Williams family, and (c) the Cary, Hamlyn, Fane, Manners, Asquith and Rous families of Clovelly in Devon, who intermarried with the Williams family. These gentry families had an extraordinary influence on life in Carmarthenshire, Midlothian and North Devon; many members held high office both nationally and locally over a period of centuries.

This book tells the origin and history of these families over the past 1,500 years and of the background to some of the other seats and houses in which their wider families resided, and of the social, political, military and economic times in which they lived. Those family members who as Lords of the Manor owned and managed their family estates in Carmarthenshire, Devon and Scotland were almost universally respected and admired by their tenants and neighbours; indeed this is still the case in Clovelly, which remains owned by the same family and is now one of the very few remaining privately owned villages in Britain. This book also contains the detailed pedigrees of the families including their English and Scottish Royal bloodlines going back to William the Conqueror and Robert the Bruce.

I am especially grateful to Pat Edwards, Dane Garrod, Janet James, and Tom Lloyd OBE who read and commented on a draft of the book; to Hugh Clifton, Bill Davis, Roger Pike, Hon John Rous (of the Clovelly Estate), and Hon John Vaughan (of the Trawsgoed Estate) who read and commented on sections of the book; and to Janet James, Vincent James and Esme Jones for all their help and remarkable memories of the area and of former residents of several properties. All their comments and corrections were most helpful.

I have visited and received most helpful assistance from the staff at The National Library of Wales (which holds a large number of Edwinsford family muniments), at the Royal Commission on the Ancient and Historical Monuments of Wales, at the National Museum of Wales, at the North Devon Record Office in Barnstaple, and at Clovelly and Hawthornden. I have drawn from and used sources in libraries and on the internet, together with the scholarly books and articles of a number of historians. I have tried to give the correct source and where relevant to obtain the necessary consents; I apologise if I have missed any.

I could not have written this book without the enormous support of many people including current residents to whom I express my sincere thanks for all their assistance and in particular for their family histories and for the use of their photographs. My particular thanks go to David Ashton, Rev Ian Aveson, Neil Callan, Mair Cavanhagh, Professor Thomas Charles-Edwards, Peter and Brenda Christman, Hugh Clifton, Siân and Siobhan Corcoran, Suzy Cushing, Alun and Mairwen Davies, Arwyn Davies, Bill Davis, Cynfyn and Beryl Davies, Sue Davies, Pat Edwards, Christopher Evans, Colin Evans, David and Theresa Ford, Anne Francis, Rev Jeffrey Gainer, Dane Garrod, Glyn George, Brian and Linda Giles, Lloyd and Emily Gregory, Alan and Catherine Griffiths, Angela Hastilow, Colin and Carol Hayward, Andrew Hill, Eric Horley, Dale and Jenni Hudson, David Ince, Janet James, Vincent James, Arwel Jenkins, Esme and Dan Jones, Will Jones, Ieuan Lewis, Ron Lewis, Henri Lloyd Davies, Tom Lloyd OBE, Derek and Jackie Nash, Francis O'Dempsey, Roger Pike, Jamie Philipps, Rhiannon Price, John Rees, Robert Rees, Jack and Gilda Roberts, Hamish Robinson, Hon John Rous, James Somerfield, Liz Spencer, Alfor and Elwyn Thomas, Douglas and Helen Thomas, Hon John Vaughan, John Walford, Robert Walters, Betty Williams, Sion and Claire Williams, Cliff and Georgina Williams, Malcolm Williams, and

Wendy Williams. I am very grateful for the use of photographs provided by Neil Callan, Hugh Clifton, Dane Garrod, Ieuan Lewis, Tom Lloyd OBE, Hon John Rous and Hon John Vaughan, by the Talley History Society, and for those published by permission of The National Library of Wales. I also thank Huw Davies (Llandre) for the enormous help which he has given to me in assembling the photographs for this book.

I have used current spellings for Welsh names in most cases, although where other spellings were used in the past I have adopted them where it seems relevant to do so. All errors and omissions are entirely my own fault and for which I apologise.

I have long admired the scholarly writings of the late Major Francis Jones (1907-1993), Wales Herald Extraordinary, Carmarthen County Archivist and prodigious author and publisher. All proceeds from the sale of this book will be donated by me to a Jesus College Oxford charitable trust to fund an annual national prize for the best published book or article on Welsh history in his memory; I am very grateful to Professor Thomas Charles-Edwards, Emeritus Jesus Professor of Celtic at Oxford, for organising and chairing the prize committee, and to Hugh Charles Jones (son of Francis Jones) for his family's consent.

David Lewis
Erwhen, Cwrt-y-Cadno, Cynwyl Gaeo

Midsummer Day, the Feast of St John the Baptist
24 June 2017

Major Francis Jones (1907-1993)

Major Francis Jones, came from a Pembrokeshire gentry family who held the Brawdy estate for 17 generations and 530 years. His father had been a pioneer rancher in Patagonia for eight years; his mother was a keen Welsh historian. So Francis was brought up with adventurous tales, and his family history, genealogy and heraldry. Aged six, as a wide-eyed boy, he gazed up at a medieval knight's helm in St Mary's Church, Haverfordwest. It was crowned with a circular coloured wreath and topped with a red lion rampant crest. He often said that moment inspired him on a course, leading to a Herald's tabard.

The family were fluent Welsh speakers. Francis was educated in Fishguard and became a schoolmaster. In the early 1930s he was commissioned into the Welch Regiment, later transferring to the Pembroke Yeomanry. He joined the National Library of Wales as a researcher in 1936 becoming renowned for his articles in newspapers and learned journals, and for his lecturing. He often broadcast on BBC radio then in its infancy.

In the Second World War he fought in North Africa, Sicily and Salerno and up to Monte Cassino. He was posted from the front line to become an official War Historian in the Cabinet Office in London. His task was to write the official War History of campaigns in which he had fought. This took nearly fourteen years to 1958. He was seen as remarkable for his intellectual discipline, as well as his stamina, needing very little sleep. Meanwhile he also served with the Surrey Yeomanry (Queen Mary's Regiment T.A.).

In 1958 he returned to Wales as the first county archivist for Carmarthenshire; an office he filled with great distinction until retiring in 1974. His produced learned yet readable essays, articles and books, particularly on families in the three counties of Dyfed in English and Welsh including *The Holy Wells of Wales*, *The Princes and Principalities of Wales*, and the trio of books, *Historic Carmarthenshire Homes and their Families, Historic Pembrokeshire Homes and their Families* and *Historic Cardiganshire Homes and their Families* among others. His archive contains several hundred articles and manuscripts, many unpublished.

Francis was appointed Welsh Herald of Arms Extraordinary when the office was created in 1963 (its forbear being Henry VII's Rouge Dragon Herald), prior to the investiture of the Prince of Wales in 1969, after which Francis was appointed a Commander of the Royal Victorian Order (CVO). He held this office for 30 years until his death, participating in annual State Openings of Parliament and the Garter ceremonies in Windsor amongst other royal events including the State Funeral of Sir Winston Churchill.

He became a Deputy Lieutenant for Carmarthenshire in 1965 and held other appointments included being a member of the Gorsedd of Bards, President of the Cambrian Archaeological Society, a Vice-President of the Hon Society of Cymmrodorion, and a Governor of the National Library of Wales. He was awarded an Honorary M.A. by Bangor University. He was also made an honorary member of learned societies in America and France.

He died in December 1993 and is buried in the tiny Welsh chapel of Rehoboth near his birthplace of Trevine with his wife, Ethel (née Charles), who predeceased him.

Contents

Bibliography

Baker-Jones, Leslie: *Princelings, Privilege and Power, The Tivyside Gentry (1999)*

Bartrum, PC: *Welsh Genealogies AD300-1400 (Cardiff 8 Vols 1974)*

Bartrum, PC: *Welsh Genealogies AD1400-1500 (Aberystwyth 1983)*

Borrow, George: *Wild Wales (1862—new edition 1901)*

Davies, Prof Sir RR: *The Age of Conquest—Wales 1063-1415 (1987, OUP 1991)*

Davies, Prof Sir RR: *The Revolt of Owen Glyn Dŵr (1995)*

Davies, Prof Sir RR: *Owain Glyn Dŵr (2009)*

Dwnn, Lewys: *Heraldic Visitations of Wales and Part of the Marches from 1586 to 1613 (edited Sir Samuel Merrick, Llandovery 1846)*

Ellis, Sheila: *Down a Cobbled Street (1987)*

Gerald of Wales: *The Journey through Wales (1188, English edition 1978)*

Gerald of Wales: *The Description of Wales (1193, English edition 1978)*

Fenton, Richard: *Tours in Wales (1804-1813)(1917)*

Francis Green: *Historical Society of West Wales Transactions (1911)*

Griffiths, Prof Ralph: *Sir Rhys ap Thomas and his Family (1993 reprint 2014)*

Hughes, Lynn: *A Carmarthenshire Anthology (1984 reprint 2002)*

James, Brenda: *Fond Memories of Talley (1994)*

Jenkins, Prof Geraint: *The Foundation of Modern Wales 1642-1780 (1987, OUP 1993)*

Jenkins, Thomas: *The Diary of Thomas Jenkins 1826-1870 (Historia Wales 2010)*

Jones, Major Francis: *Historic Carmarthenshire Homes and their Families (1987)*

Jones, Major Francis: *Treasury of Historic Carmarthenshire (2002)*

Jones, Major Francis: *Historic Cardiganshire Homes and their Families (2004)*

Kennedy, John: *The Clifton Chronicle (1990)*

Llandovery Civic Trust Association: *Llandovery and its Environs (1994)*

Lewis, Sir David: *Family Histories and Community Life in North Carmarthenshire (2012)*

Lewis, Sir David: *Dolaucothi and Brunant—A Tale of Two Families in Wales (2016)*

Lloyd, Prof Sir John: *History of Carmarthenshire (1935 Cardiff)*

Lloyd, Thomas: *The Lost Houses of Wales (1989)*

Lloyd, Thomas, Julian Orbach and Robert Scourfield: *The Buildings of Wales: Carmarthenshire and Ceredigion (2006)*

Mee, Arthur: *Carmarthenshire Notes 1889-1891 (reprinted 1997)*

Morgan, Gerald: *Dinefwr A Phoenix in Wales (2014)*

Morgan, Gerald: *A Welsh House and its Family, The Vaughans of Trawsgoed (1997)*

Nicholas, Thomas: *Annals and Antiquities of the Counties and County Families of Wales (1872)*

Pennant, Thomas: *Tours in Wales (1883)*

Price, Fred: *History of Caio (1904)*

Price, Fred: *History of Llansawel (1898 reprint 2014)*

Price, Fred: *History of Talley and Talley Abbey (1934)*

Prys-Jones, AG: *The Story of Carmarthenshire (2 Vols 1959 & 1972)*

Rees, Dylan: *Carmarthenshire (2006 Cardiff)*

Michael Siddons: *Welsh Genealogies AD1500-1600 (2017)*

Vaughan, Herbert: *The South Wales Squires (1926 reprint 1988)*

Williams, DJ: *Hen Dŷ Ffarm (The Old Farmhouse) (1953 reprint 2001)*

Williams, Prof Sir Glanmor: *Renewal and Reformation Wales 1415-1642 (1987, OUP 1993)*

Williams-Drummond, Sir FD: *Annals of Edwinsford, Clovelly and Hawthornden (1924)*

Worden, Prof Blair: *The English Civil Wars 1640-1660 (2009)*

The source references in the text and footnotes refer, where not otherwise stated, to the above.

Many of the persons mentioned in the text of this book are numbered in the family pedigrees to avoid confusion given the similarity of names.

Abbreviations

ARP	Acres, roods and perches
CASJ	Cardiganshire/Ceredigion Antiquarian Society Journal
CA	Carmarthenshire Antiquary
Cadw	Welsh Government's historic environment service (to protect)
CH	Carmarthenshire Historian
CL	Carmarthen Library
CRO	Carmarthenshire Record Office
FDWD	Sir Francis Dudley Williams-Drummond
HP	History of Parliament
LCTA	Llandovery Civic Trust Association
NA	National Archives
NLW	National Library of Wales
NLWBO	National Library of Wales Welsh Biography online
NLWJ	National Library of Wales Journal
ODNB	Oxford Dictionary of National Biography
RCAHMW	Royal Commission on the Ancient and Historical Monuments of Wales
THSC	Transactions of the Honourable Society of Cymmrodorion
WHR	Welsh History Review
Y Llychau	Newsletter of Parochial Church Council of St Michael and All Angels, Talley

EDWINSFORD FAMILIES OUTLINE PEDIGREE

c= approximately
cb= concubine mistress

(1) Coel Hen (the Old) Godebog (Hawk-beak), High-King of North Britain (c350-c420)
m= Ystradwel ap Coel, Queen of Rheged (c360-) (18th in descent from Beli Mawr)

|

Cynan ap Coel Hen St Ceneu, King of North Britain (c382-c425)

|

Gwrast Lledlwm (the Ragged), King of Rheged (c422-)

|

Meirchion Gul (the Lean), King of Rheged (c438-535)

|

(2) Elidyr Llydanwyn (the Stout and Handsome) (c462-), King of South Rheged

|

(3) Llywarch Hen (the Old) (c534-), the last King of South Rheged

|

Dwywg ap Llywarch (c560-)

|

Caid ap Dwywg (c595-)

|

Tegid ap Caid (c630-)

|

Alcun ap Tegid (c660-)

|

(4) Sanddle ap Alcun (c690-), King of Ynys Manaw

|

Elidyr ap Sanddle (c720-), King of Ynys Manaw

|

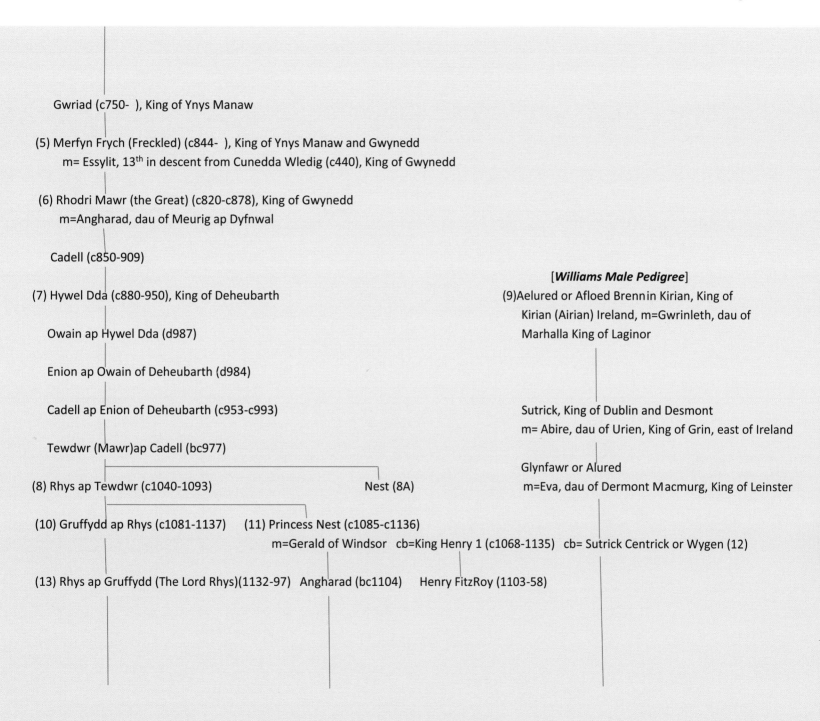

Gwriad (c750-), King of Ynys Manaw

(5) Merfyn Frych (Freckled) (c844-), King of Ynys Manaw and Gwynedd
m= Essylit, 13th in descent from Cunedda Wledig (c440), King of Gwynedd

(6) Rhodri Mawr (the Great) (c820-c878), King of Gwynedd
m=Angharad, dau of Meurig ap Dyfnwal

Cadell (c850-909)

(7) Hywel Dda (c880-950), King of Deheubarth

Owain ap Hywel Dda (d987)

Enion ap Owain of Deheubarth (d984)

Cadell ap Enion of Deheubarth (c953-c993)

Tewdwr (Mawr)ap Cadell (bc977)

(8) Rhys ap Tewdwr (c1040-1093)   Nest (8A)

(10) Gruffydd ap Rhys (c1081-1137)   (11) Princess Nest (c1085-c1136)
m=Gerald of Windsor   cb=King Henry 1 (c1068-1135)   cb= Sutrick Centrick or Wygen (12)

(13) Rhys ap Gruffydd (The Lord Rhys)(1132-97)   Angharad (bc1104)   Henry FitzRoy (1103-58)

[***Williams Male Pedigree***]

(9)Aelured or Afloed Brennin Kirian, King of Kirian (Airian) Ireland, m=Gwrinleth, dau of Marhalla King of Laginor

Sutrick, King of Dublin and Desmont
m= Abire, dau of Urien, King of Grin, east of Ireland

Glynfawr or Alured
m=Eva, dau of Dermont Macmurg, King of Leinster

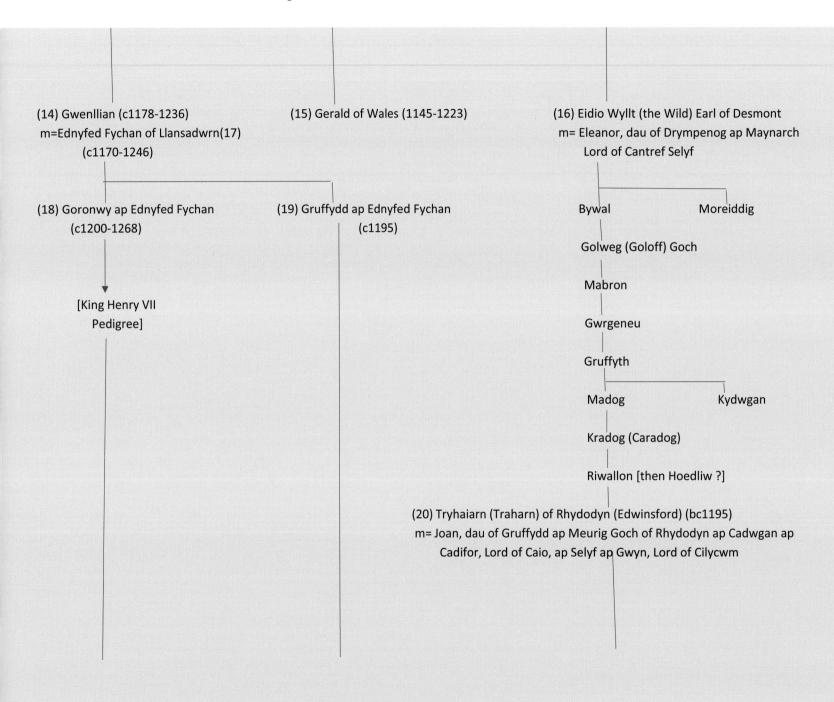

(14) Gwenllian (c1178-1236)
m=Ednyfed Fychan of Llansadwrn(17)
(c1170-1246)

(18) Goronwy ap Ednyfed Fychan
(c1200-1268)

[King Henry VII
Pedigree]

(19) Gruffydd ap Ednyfed Fychan
(c1195)

(15) Gerald of Wales (1145-1223)

(16) Eidio Wyllt (the Wild) Earl of Desmont
m= Eleanor, dau of Drympenog ap Maynarch
Lord of Cantref Selyf

Bywal

Moreiddig

Golweg (Goloff) Goch

Mabron

Gwrgeneu

Gruffyth

Madog

Kydwgan

Kradog (Caradog)

Riwallon [then Hoedliw ?]

(20) Tryhaiarn (Traharn) of Rhydodyn (Edwinsford) (bc1195)
m= Joan, dau of Gruffydd ap Meurig Goch of Rhydodyn ap Cadwgan ap
Cadifor, Lord of Caio, ap Selyf ap Gwyn, Lord of Cilycwm

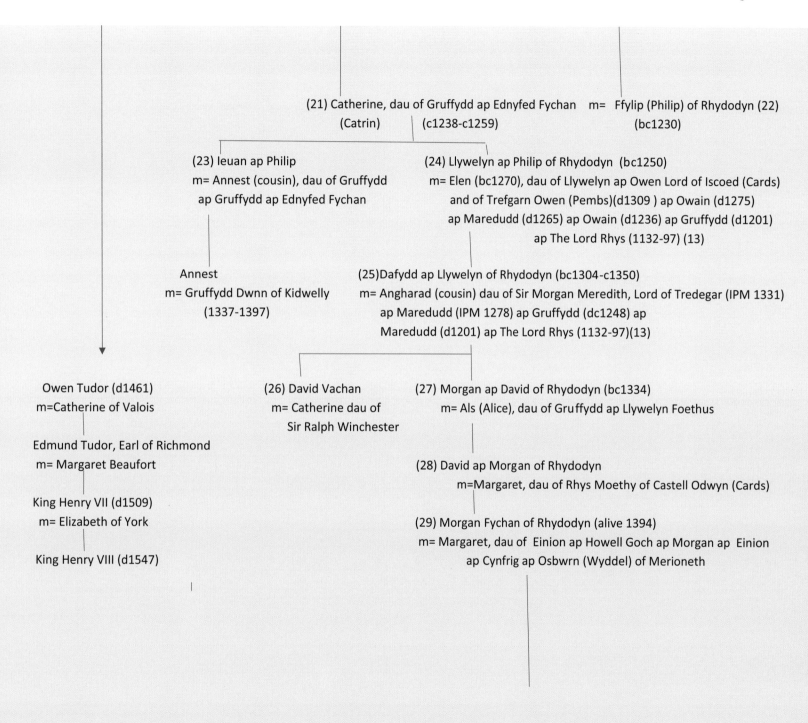

(21) Catherine, dau of Gruffydd ap Ednyfed Fychan m= Ffylip (Philip) of Rhydodyn (22)
(Catrin) (c1238-c1259) (bc1230)

(23) Ieuan ap Philip
m= Annest (cousin), dau of Gruffydd
ap Gruffydd ap Ednyfed Fychan

(24) Llywelyn ap Philip of Rhydodyn (bc1250)
m= Elen (bc1270), dau of Llywelyn ap Owen Lord of Iscoed (Cards)
and of Trefgarn Owen (Pembs)(d1309) ap Owain (d1275)
ap Maredudd (d1265) ap Owain (d1236) ap Gruffydd (d1201)
ap The Lord Rhys (1132-97) (13)

Annest
m= Gruffydd Dwnn of Kidwelly
(1337-1397)

(25)Dafydd ap Llywelyn of Rhydodyn (bc1304-c1350)
m= Angharad (cousin) dau of Sir Morgan Meredith, Lord of Tredegar (IPM 1331)
ap Maredudd (IPM 1278) ap Gruffydd (dc1248) ap
Maredudd (d1201) ap The Lord Rhys (1132-97)(13)

(26) David Vachan
m= Catherine dau of
Sir Ralph Winchester

(27) Morgan ap David of Rhydodyn (bc1334)
m= Als (Alice), dau of Gruffydd ap Llywelyn Foethus

(28) David ap Morgan of Rhydodyn
m=Margaret, dau of Rhys Moethy of Castell Odwyn (Cards)

(29) Morgan Fychan of Rhydodyn (alive 1394)
m= Margaret, dau of Einion ap Howell Goch ap Morgan ap Einion
ap Cynfrig ap Osbwrn (Wyddel) of Merioneth

Owen Tudor (d1461)
m=Catherine of Valois

Edmund Tudor, Earl of Richmond
m= Margaret Beaufort

King Henry VII (d1509)
m= Elizabeth of York

King Henry VIII (d1547)

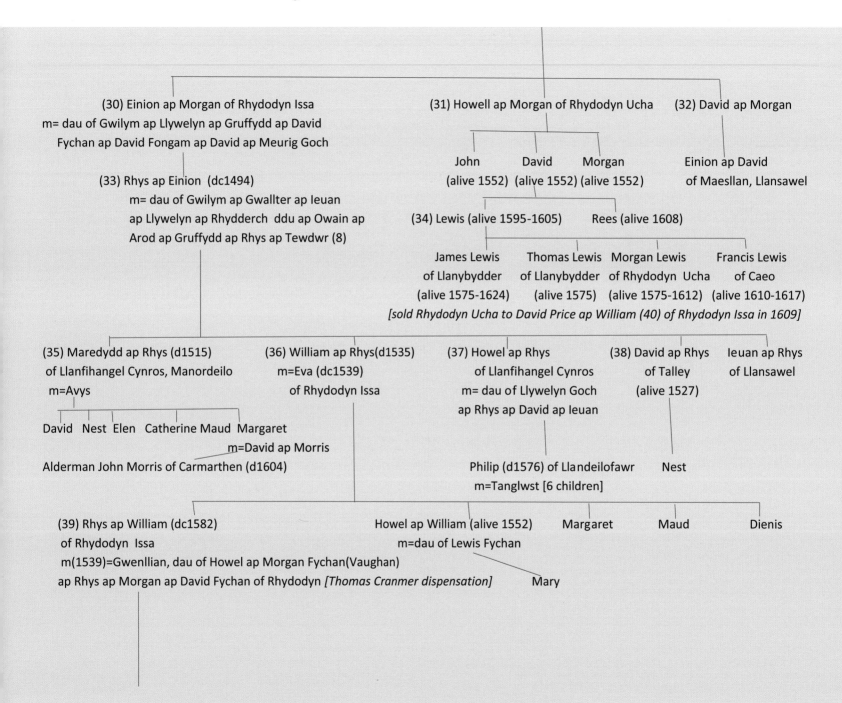

(30) Einion ap Morgan of Rhydodyn Issa
m= dau of Gwilym ap Llywelyn ap Gruffydd ap David
Fychan ap David Fongam ap David ap Meurig Goch

(31) Howell ap Morgan of Rhydodyn Ucha

(32) David ap Morgan

John
(alive 1552)

David
(alive 1552)

Morgan
(alive 1552)

Einion ap David
of Maesllan, Llansawel

(33) Rhys ap Einion (dc1494)
m= dau of Gwilym ap Gwallter ap Ieuan
ap Llywelyn ap Rhydderch ddu ap Owain ap
Arod ap Gruffydd ap Rhys ap Tewdwr (8)

(34) Lewis (alive 1595-1605)

Rees (alive 1608)

James Lewis
of Llanybydder
(alive 1575-1624)

Thomas Lewis
of Llanybydder
(alive 1575)

Morgan Lewis
of Rhydodyn Ucha
(alive 1575-1612)

Francis Lewis
of Caeo
(alive 1610-1617)

[sold Rhydodyn Ucha to David Price ap William (40) of Rhydodyn Issa in 1609]

(35) Maredydd ap Rhys (d1515)
of Llanfihangel Cynros, Manordeilo
m=Avys

(36) William ap Rhys(d1535)
m=Eva (dc1539)
of Rhydodyn Issa

(37) Howel ap Rhys
of Llanfihangel Cynros
m= dau of Llywelyn Goch
ap Rhys ap David ap Ieuan

(38) David ap Rhys
of Talley
(alive 1527)

Ieuan ap Rhys
of Llansawel

David Nest Elen Catherine Maud Margaret
m=David ap Morris

Alderman John Morris of Carmarthen (d1604)

Philip (d1576) of Llandeilofawr
m=Tanglwst [6 children]

Nest

(39) Rhys ap William (dc1582)
of Rhydodyn Issa
m(1539)=Gwenllian, dau of Howel ap Morgan Fychan(Vaughan)
ap Rhys ap Morgan ap David Fychan of Rhydodyn *[Thomas Cranmer dispensation]*

Howel ap William (alive 1552)
m=dau of Lewis Fychan

Mary

Margaret

Maud

Dienis

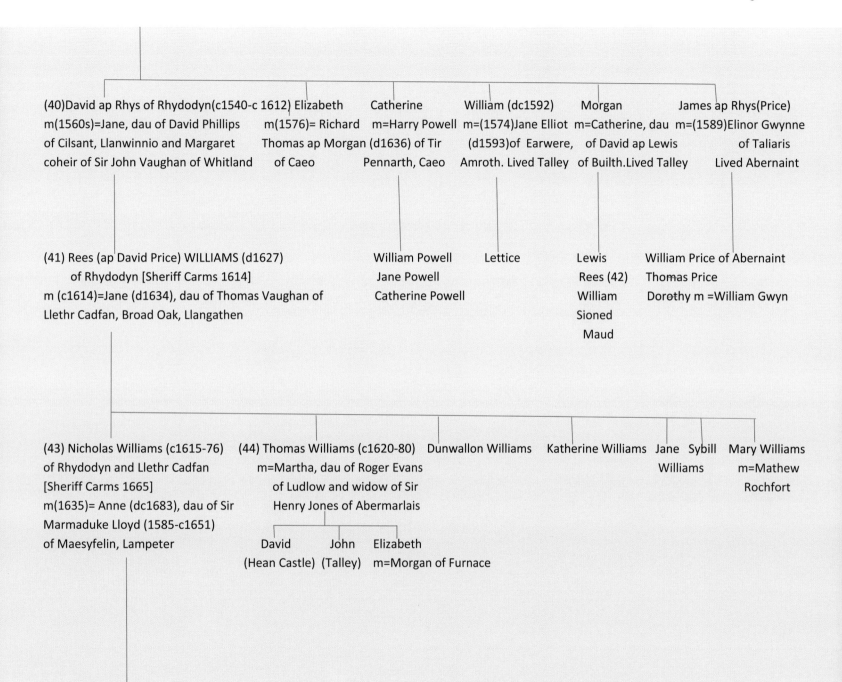

(40)David ap Rhys of Rhydodyn(c1540-c 1612)
m(1560s)=Jane, dau of David Phillips
of Cilsant, Llanwinnio and Margaret
coheir of Sir John Vaughan of Whitland

Elizabeth
m(1576)= Richard
Thomas ap Morgan (d1636) of Tir
of Caeo

Catherine
m=Harry Powell
Pennarth, Caeo

William (dc1592)
m=(1574)Jane Elliot
(d1593)of Earwere,
Amroth. Lived Talley

Morgan
m=Catherine, dau
of David ap Lewis
of Builth.Lived Talley

James ap Rhys(Price)
m=(1589)Elinor Gwynne
of Taliaris
Lived Abernaint

(41) Rees (ap David Price) WILLIAMS (d1627)
of Rhydodyn [Sheriff Carms 1614]
m (c1614)=Jane (d1634), dau of Thomas Vaughan of
Llethr Cadfan, Broad Oak, Llangathen

William Powell
Jane Powell
Catherine Powell

Lettice

Lewis
Rees (42)
William
Sioned
Maud

William Price of Abernaint
Thomas Price
Dorothy m =William Gwyn

(43) Nicholas Williams (c1615-76)
of Rhydodyn and Llethr Cadfan
[Sheriff Carms 1665]
m(1635)= Anne (dc1683), dau of Sir
Marmaduke Lloyd (1585-c1651)
of Maesyfelin, Lampeter

(44) Thomas Williams (c1620-80)
m=Martha, dau of Roger Evans
of Ludlow and widow of Sir
Henry Jones of Abermarlais

David
(Hean Castle)

John
(Talley)

Elizabeth
m=Morgan of Furnace

Dunwallon Williams

Katherine Williams

Jane
Williams

Sybill

Mary Williams
m=Mathew
Rochfort

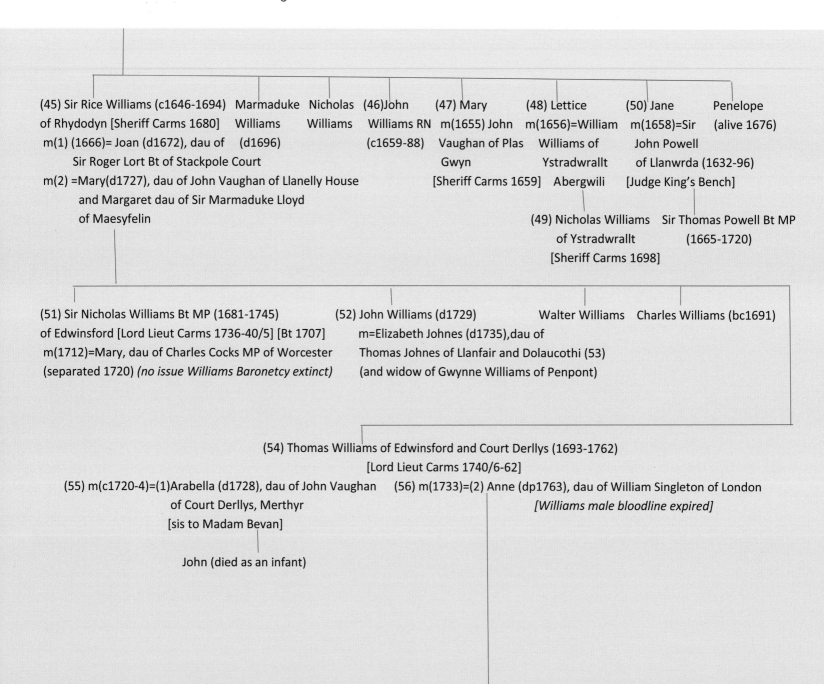

(45) Sir Rice Williams (c1646-1694)
of Rhydodyn [Sheriff Carms 1680]
m(1) (1666)= Joan (d1672), dau of
Sir Roger Lort Bt of Stackpole Court
m(2) =Mary(d1727), dau of John Vaughan of Llanelly House
and Margaret dau of Sir Marmaduke Lloyd
of Maesyfelin

Marmaduke
Williams
(d1696)

Nicholas
Williams

(46)John
Williams RN
(c1659-88)

(47) Mary
m(1655) John
Vaughan of Plas
Gwyn
[Sheriff Carms 1659]

(48) Lettice
m(1656)=William
Williams of
Ystradwrallt
Abergwili

(49) Nicholas Williams
of Ystradwrallt
[Sheriff Carms 1698]

(50) Jane
m(1658)=Sir
John Powell
of Llanwrda (1632-96)
[Judge King's Bench]

Sir Thomas Powell Bt MP
(1665-1720)

Penelope
(alive 1676)

(51) Sir Nicholas Williams Bt MP (1681-1745)
of Edwinsford [Lord Lieut Carms 1736-40/5] [Bt 1707]
m(1712)=Mary, dau of Charles Cocks MP of Worcester
(separated 1720) *(no issue Williams Baronetcy extinct)*

(52) John Williams (d1729)
m=Elizabeth Johnes (d1735),dau of
Thomas Johnes of Llanfair and Dolaucothi (53)
(and widow of Gwynne Williams of Penpont)

Walter Williams

Charles Williams (bc1691)

(54) Thomas Williams of Edwinsford and Court Derllys (1693-1762)
[Lord Lieut Carms 1740/6-62]

(55) m(c1720-4)=(1)Arabella (d1728), dau of John Vaughan
of Court Derllys, Merthyr
[sis to Madam Bevan]

John (died as an infant)

(56) m(1733)=(2) Anne (dp1763), dau of William Singleton of London
[Williams male bloodline expired]

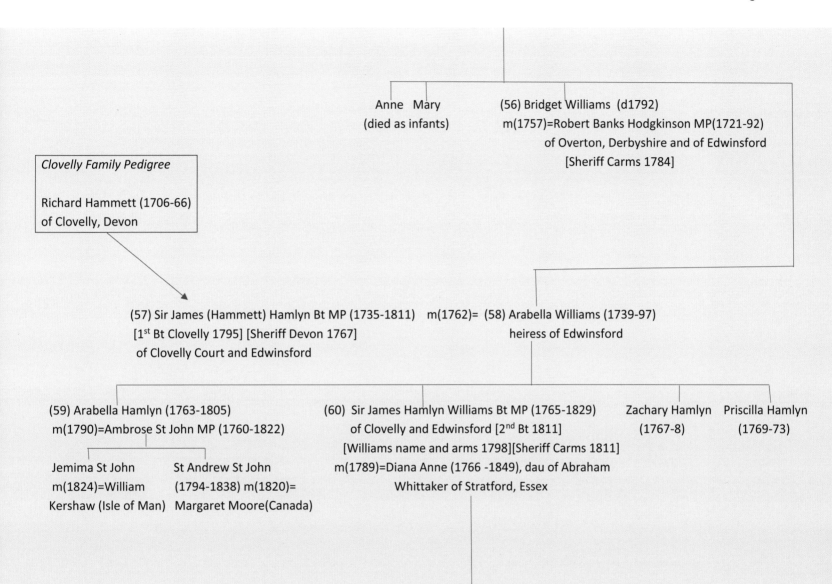

Anne Mary
(died as infants)

(56) Bridget Williams (d1792)
m(1757)=Robert Banks Hodgkinson MP(1721-92)
of Overton, Derbyshire and of Edwinsford
[Sheriff Carms 1784]

Clovelly Family Pedigree

Richard Hammett (1706-66)
of Clovelly, Devon

(57) Sir James (Hammett) Hamlyn Bt MP (1735-1811) m(1762)= (58) Arabella Williams (1739-97)
[1st Bt Clovelly 1795] [Sheriff Devon 1767]
of Clovelly Court and Edwinsford

heiress of Edwinsford

(59) Arabella Hamlyn (1763-1805)
m(1790)=Ambrose St John MP (1760-1822)

Jemima St John
m(1824)=William
Kershaw (Isle of Man)

St Andrew St John
(1794-1838) m(1820)=
Margaret Moore(Canada)

(60) Sir James Hamlyn Williams Bt MP (1765-1829)
of Clovelly and Edwinsford [2nd Bt 1811]
[Williams name and arms 1798][Sheriff Carms 1811]
m(1789)=Diana Anne (1766 -1849), dau of Abraham
Whittaker of Stratford, Essex

Zachary Hamlyn
(1767-8)

Priscilla Hamlyn
(1769-73)

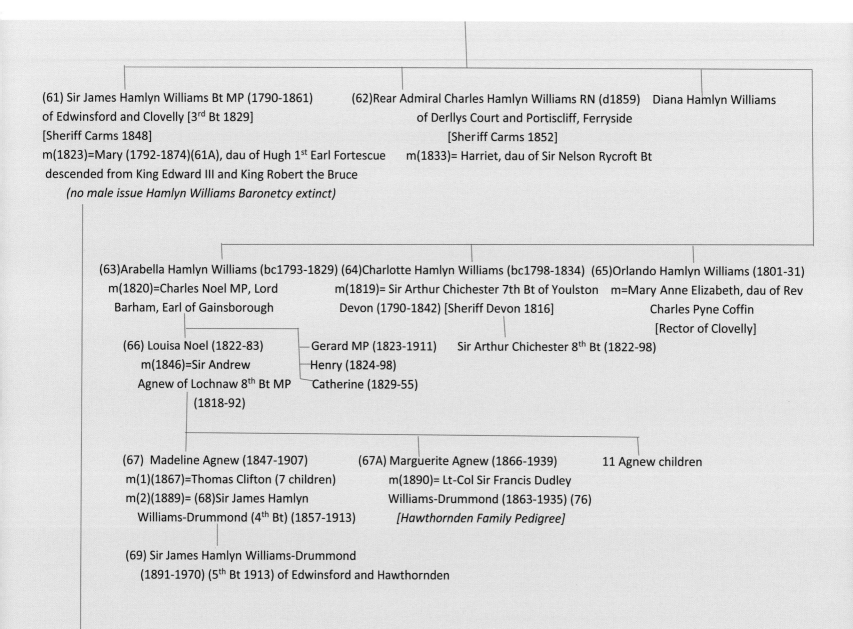

(61) Sir James Hamlyn Williams Bt MP (1790-1861)
of Edwinsford and Clovelly [3rd Bt 1829]
[Sheriff Carms 1848]
m(1823)=Mary (1792-1874)(61A), dau of Hugh 1st Earl Fortescue
descended from King Edward III and King Robert the Bruce
(no male issue Hamlyn Williams Baronetcy extinct)

(62)Rear Admiral Charles Hamlyn Williams RN (d1859)
of Derllys Court and Portiscliff, Ferryside
[Sheriff Carms 1852]
m(1833)= Harriet, dau of Sir Nelson Rycroft Bt

Diana Hamlyn Williams

(63)Arabella Hamlyn Williams (bc1793-1829)
m(1820)=Charles Noel MP, Lord
Barham, Earl of Gainsborough

(64)Charlotte Hamlyn Williams (bc1798-1834)
m(1819)= Sir Arthur Chichester 7th Bt of Youlston
Devon (1790-1842) [Sheriff Devon 1816]

(65)Orlando Hamlyn Williams (1801-31)
m=Mary Anne Elizabeth, dau of Rev
Charles Pyne Coffin
[Rector of Clovelly]

(66) Louisa Noel (1822-83)
m(1846)=Sir Andrew
Agnew of Lochnaw 8th Bt MP
(1818-92)

Gerard MP (1823-1911)
Henry (1824-98)
Catherine (1829-55)

Sir Arthur Chichester 8th Bt (1822-98)

(67) Madeline Agnew (1847-1907)
m(1)(1867)=Thomas Clifton (7 children)
m(2)(1889)= (68)Sir James Hamlyn
Williams-Drummond (4th Bt) (1857-1913)

(67A) Marguerite Agnew (1866-1939)
m(1890)= Lt-Col Sir Francis Dudley
Williams-Drummond (1863-1935) (76)
[Hawthornden Family Pedigree]

11 Agnew children

(69) Sir James Hamlyn Williams-Drummond
(1891-1970) (5th Bt 1913) of Edwinsford and Hawthornden

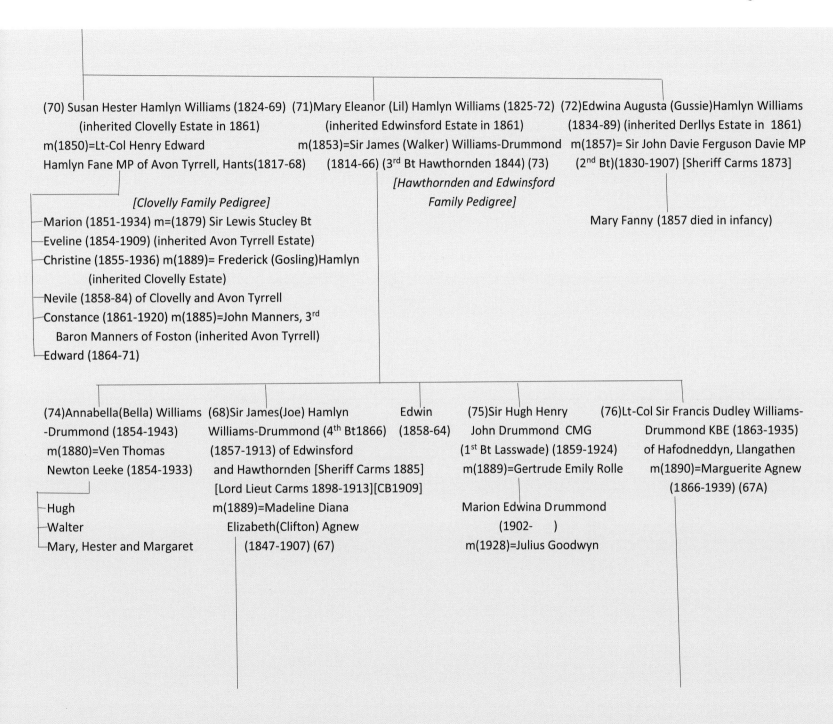

(70) Susan Hester Hamlyn Williams (1824-69)
(inherited Clovelly Estate in 1861)
m(1850)=Lt-Col Henry Edward
Hamlyn Fane MP of Avon Tyrrell, Hants(1817-68)

[Clovelly Family Pedigree]

- Marion (1851-1934) m=(1879) Sir Lewis Stucley Bt
- Eveline (1854-1909) (inherited Avon Tyrrell Estate)
- Christine (1855-1936) m(1889)= Frederick (Gosling)Hamlyn (inherited Clovelly Estate)
- Nevile (1858-84) of Clovelly and Avon Tyrrell
- Constance (1861-1920) m(1885)=John Manners, 3rd Baron Manners of Foston (inherited Avon Tyrrell)
- Edward (1864-71)

(71)Mary Eleanor (Lil) Hamlyn Williams (1825-72)
(inherited Edwinsford Estate in 1861)
m(1853)=Sir James (Walker) Williams-Drummond
(1814-66) (3rd Bt Hawthornden 1844) (73)

[Hawthornden and Edwinsford Family Pedigree]

(72)Edwina Augusta (Gussie)Hamlyn Williams
(1834-89) (inherited Derllys Estate in 1861)
m(1857)= Sir John Davie Ferguson Davie MP
(2nd Bt)(1830-1907) [Sheriff Carms 1873]

Mary Fanny (1857 died in infancy)

---

(74)Annabella(Bella) Williams
-Drummond (1854-1943)
m(1880)=Ven Thomas
Newton Leeke (1854-1933)

- Hugh
- Walter
- Mary, Hester and Margaret

(68)Sir James(Joe) Hamlyn
Williams-Drummond (4th Bt1866)
(1857-1913) of Edwinsford
and Hawthornden [Sheriff Carms 1885]
[Lord Lieut Carms 1898-1913][CB1909]
m(1889)=Madeline Diana
Elizabeth(Clifton) Agnew
(1847-1907) (67)

Edwin
(1858-64)

(75)Sir Hugh Henry
John Drummond CMG
(1st Bt Lasswade) (1859-1924)
m(1889)=Gertrude Emily Rolle

Marion Edwina Drummond
(1902-)
m(1928)=Julius Goodwyn

(76)Lt-Col Sir Francis Dudley Williams-
Drummond KBE (1863-1935)
of Hafodneddyn, Llangathen
m(1890)=Marguerite Agnew
(1866-1939) (67A)

(69) Sir James (Jimmy) Hamlyn Williams-Drummond
(1891-1970) (5th Bt1913) of Edwinsford and Hawthornden
m(1914)=Enid Evelyn Malet Vaughan (1889-1958), dau of
George Vaughan, 6th Earl of Lisburne of Trawsgoed, Cards
[Edwinsford and Hawthornden inherited by Frank Coombs butler and chauffeur (1914-78) in 1970]

Eleanor (1891-1962)
m(1914)=Robert
Barnewell Elliot of
Bryneithin, Talley

Robert Hugh Elliot (1923-99)

Constance (1893-1968)
m(1927)=Francis Stapleton-Cotton
4th Viscount Combermere of
Bhurtpore

(two children)

(77) Sir William Hugh Dudley Williams-Drummond
(1901-76) (6th Bt Hawthornden 1970) of Bryneithin, Talley
(no issue Hawthornden Baronetcy extinct)

CLOVELLY FAMILIES OUTLINE PEDIGREE

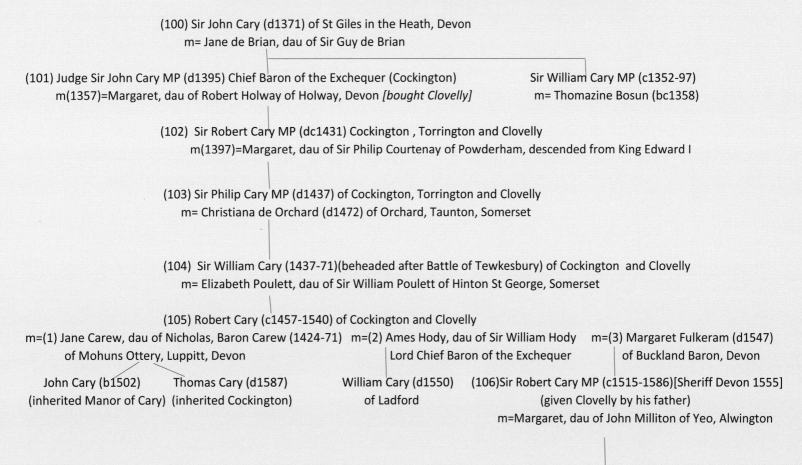

(100) Sir John Cary (d1371) of St Giles in the Heath, Devon
m= Jane de Brian, dau of Sir Guy de Brian

(101) Judge Sir John Cary MP (d1395) Chief Baron of the Exchequer (Cockington)
m(1357)=Margaret, dau of Robert Holway of Holway, Devon *[bought Clovelly]*

Sir William Cary MP (c1352-97)
m= Thomazine Bosun (bc1358)

(102) Sir Robert Cary MP (dc1431) Cockington , Torrington and Clovelly
m(1397)=Margaret, dau of Sir Philip Courtenay of Powderham, descended from King Edward I

(103) Sir Philip Cary MP (d1437) of Cockington, Torrington and Clovelly
m= Christiana de Orchard (d1472) of Orchard, Taunton, Somerset

(104) Sir William Cary (1437-71)(beheaded after Battle of Tewkesbury) of Cockington and Clovelly
m= Elizabeth Poulett, dau of Sir William Poulett of Hinton St George, Somerset

(105) Robert Cary (c1457-1540) of Cockington and Clovelly

m=(1) Jane Carew, dau of Nicholas, Baron Carew (1424-71)
of Mohuns Ottery, Luppitt, Devon

m=(2) Ames Hody, dau of Sir William Hody
Lord Chief Baron of the Exchequer

m=(3) Margaret Fulkeram (d1547)
of Buckland Baron, Devon

John Cary (b1502)
(inherited Manor of Cary)

Thomas Cary (d1587)
(inherited Cockington)

William Cary (d1550)
of Ladford

(106)Sir Robert Cary MP (c1515-1586)[Sheriff Devon 1555]
(given Clovelly by his father)
m=Margaret, dau of John Milliton of Yeo, Alwington

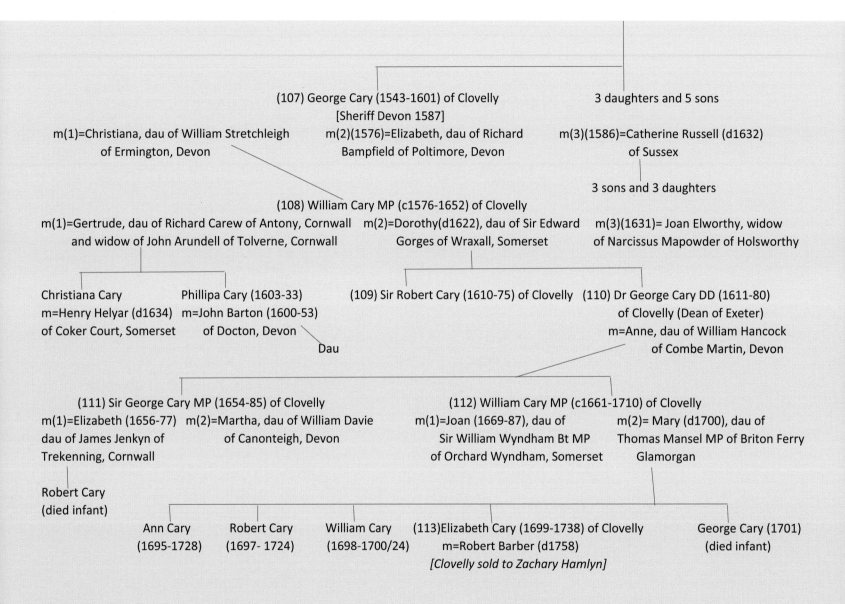

(107) George Cary (1543-1601) of Clovelly
[Sheriff Devon 1587]

3 daughters and 5 sons

m(1)=Christiana, dau of William Stretchleigh
of Ermington, Devon

m(2)(1576)=Elizabeth, dau of Richard
Bampfield of Poltimore, Devon

m(3)(1586)=Catherine Russell (d1632)
of Sussex

3 sons and 3 daughters

(108) William Cary MP (c1576-1652) of Clovelly

m(1)=Gertrude, dau of Richard Carew of Antony, Cornwall
and widow of John Arundell of Tolverne, Cornwall

m(2)=Dorothy(d1622), dau of Sir Edward
Gorges of Wraxall, Somerset

m(3)(1631)= Joan Elworthy, widow
of Narcissus Mapowder of Holsworthy

Christiana Cary
m=Henry Helyar (d1634)
of Coker Court, Somerset

Phillipa Cary (1603-33)
m=John Barton (1600-53)
of Docton, Devon

Dau

(109) Sir Robert Cary (1610-75) of Clovelly

(110) Dr George Cary DD (1611-80)
of Clovelly (Dean of Exeter)
m=Anne, dau of William Hancock
of Combe Martin, Devon

(111) Sir George Cary MP (1654-85) of Clovelly

m(1)=Elizabeth (1656-77)
dau of James Jenkyn of
Trekenning, Cornwall

m(2)=Martha, dau of William Davie
of Canonteigh, Devon

Robert Cary
(died infant)

(112) William Cary MP (c1661-1710) of Clovelly

m(1)=Joan (1669-87), dau of
Sir William Wyndham Bt MP
of Orchard Wyndham, Somerset

m(2)= Mary (d1700), dau of
Thomas Mansel MP of Briton Ferry
Glamorgan

Ann Cary
(1695-1728)

Robert Cary
(1697- 1724)

William Cary
(1698-1700/24)

(113)Elizabeth Cary (1699-1738) of Clovelly
m=Robert Barber (d1758)
[Clovelly sold to Zachary Hamlyn]

George Cary (1701)
(died infant)

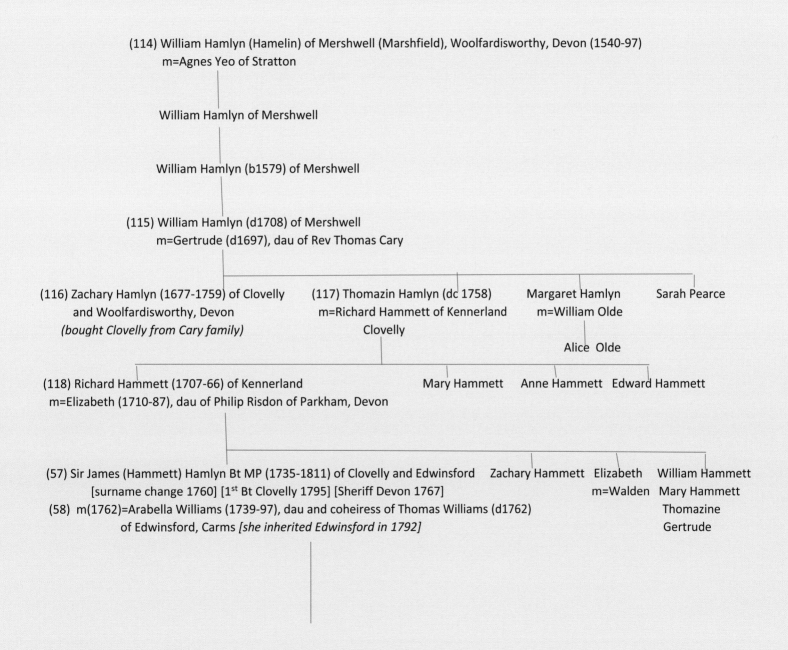

(114) William Hamlyn (Hamelin) of Mershwell (Marshfield), Woolfardisworthy, Devon (1540-97)
m=Agnes Yeo of Stratton

William Hamlyn of Mershwell

William Hamlyn (b1579) of Mershwell

(115) William Hamlyn (d1708) of Mershwell
m=Gertrude (d1697), dau of Rev Thomas Cary

(116) Zachary Hamlyn (1677-1759) of Clovelly
and Woolfardisworthy, Devon
(bought Clovelly from Cary family)

(117) Thomazin Hamlyn (dc 1758)
m=Richard Hammett of Kennerland
Clovelly

Margaret Hamlyn
m=William Olde

Alice Olde

Sarah Pearce

(118) Richard Hammett (1707-66) of Kennerland
m=Elizabeth (1710-87), dau of Philip Risdon of Parkham, Devon

Mary Hammett

Anne Hammett

Edward Hammett

(57) Sir James (Hammett) Hamlyn Bt MP (1735-1811) of Clovelly and Edwinsford
[surname change 1760] [1st Bt Clovelly 1795] [Sheriff Devon 1767]
(58) m(1762)=Arabella Williams (1739-97), dau and coheiress of Thomas Williams (d1762)
of Edwinsford, Carms *[she inherited Edwinsford in 1792]*

Zachary Hammett

Elizabeth
m=Walden

William Hammett
Mary Hammett
Thomazine
Gertrude

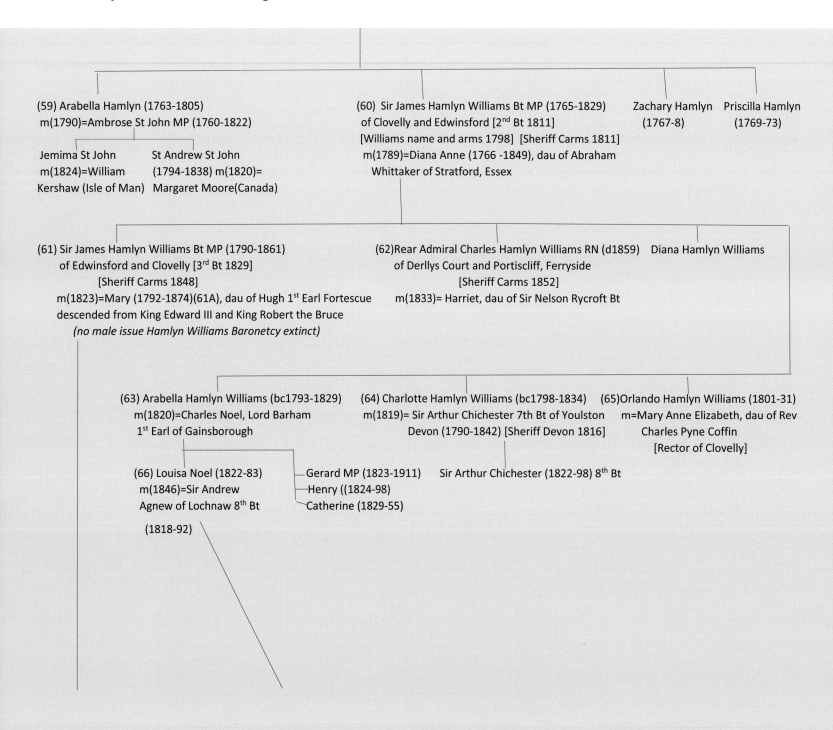

(59) Arabella Hamlyn (1763-1805)
m(1790)=Ambrose St John MP (1760-1822)

- Jemima St John m(1824)=William Kershaw (Isle of Man)
- St Andrew St John (1794-1838) m(1820)= Margaret Moore(Canada)

(60) Sir James Hamlyn Williams Bt MP (1765-1829)
of Clovelly and Edwinsford [2nd Bt 1811]
[Williams name and arms 1798] [Sheriff Carms 1811]
m(1789)=Diana Anne (1766 -1849), dau of Abraham Whittaker of Stratford, Essex

Zachary Hamlyn (1767-8)

Priscilla Hamlyn (1769-73)

(61) Sir James Hamlyn Williams Bt MP (1790-1861)
of Edwinsford and Clovelly [3rd Bt 1829]
[Sheriff Carms 1848]
m(1823)=Mary (1792-1874)(61A), dau of Hugh 1st Earl Fortescue
descended from King Edward III and King Robert the Bruce
(no male issue Hamlyn Williams Baronetcy extinct)

(62)Rear Admiral Charles Hamlyn Williams RN (d1859)
of Derllys Court and Portiscliff, Ferryside
[Sheriff Carms 1852]
m(1833)= Harriet, dau of Sir Nelson Rycroft Bt

Diana Hamlyn Williams

(63) Arabella Hamlyn Williams (bc1793-1829)
m(1820)=Charles Noel, Lord Barham
1st Earl of Gainsborough

- (66) Louisa Noel (1822-83) m(1846)=Sir Andrew Agnew of Lochnaw 8th Bt (1818-92)
- Gerard MP (1823-1911)
- Henry ((1824-98)
- Catherine (1829-55)

(64) Charlotte Hamlyn Williams (bc1798-1834)
m(1819)= Sir Arthur Chichester 7th Bt of Youlston
Devon (1790-1842) [Sheriff Devon 1816]

- Sir Arthur Chichester (1822-98) 8th Bt

(65)Orlando Hamlyn Williams (1801-31)
m=Mary Anne Elizabeth, dau of Rev
Charles Pyne Coffin
[Rectror of Clovelly]

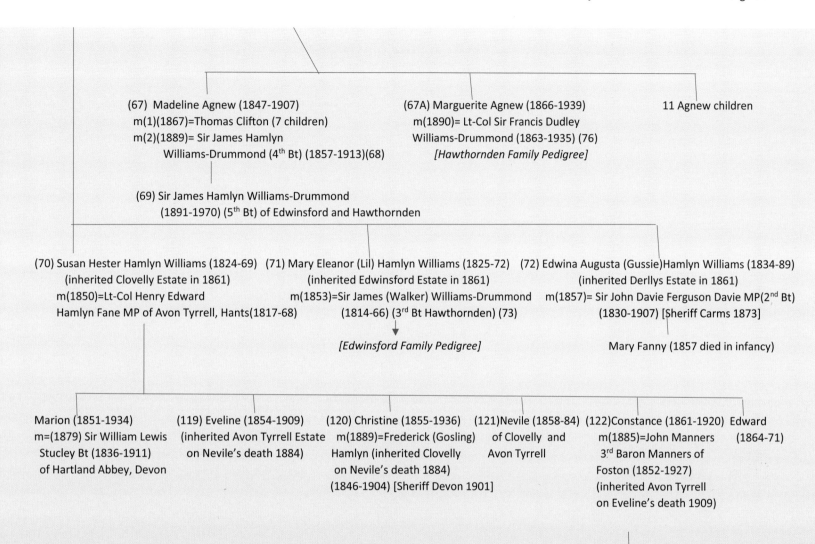

(67) Madeline Agnew (1847-1907)
m(1)(1867)=Thomas Clifton (7 children)
m(2)(1889)= Sir James Hamlyn Williams-Drummond (4th Bt) (1857-1913)(68)

(69) Sir James Hamlyn Williams-Drummond (1891-1970) (5th Bt) of Edwinsford and Hawthornden

(67A) Marguerite Agnew (1866-1939)
m(1890)= Lt-Col Sir Francis Dudley Williams-Drummond (1863-1935) (76)
[Hawthornden Family Pedigree]

11 Agnew children

(70) Susan Hester Hamlyn Williams (1824-69)
(inherited Clovelly Estate in 1861)
m(1850)=Lt-Col Henry Edward Hamlyn Fane MP of Avon Tyrrell, Hants(1817-68)

(71) Mary Eleanor (Lil) Hamlyn Williams (1825-72)
(inherited Edwinsford Estate in 1861)
m(1853)=Sir James (Walker) Williams-Drummond (1814-66) (3rd Bt Hawthornden) (73)
[Edwinsford Family Pedigree]

(72) Edwina Augusta (Gussie)Hamlyn Williams (1834-89)
(inherited Derllys Estate in 1861)
m(1857)= Sir John Davie Ferguson Davie MP(2nd Bt) (1830-1907) [Sheriff Carms 1873]

Mary Fanny (1857 died in infancy)

Marion (1851-1934)
m=(1879) Sir William Lewis Stucley Bt (1836-1911) of Hartland Abbey, Devon

(119) Eveline (1854-1909)
(inherited Avon Tyrrell Estate on Nevile's death 1884)

(120) Christine (1855-1936)
m(1889)=Frederick (Gosling) Hamlyn (inherited Clovelly on Nevile's death 1884) (1846-1904) [Sheriff Devon 1901]

(121)Nevile (1858-84)
of Clovelly and Avon Tyrrell

(122)Constance (1861-1920)
m(1885)=John Manners 3rd Baron Manners of Foston (1852-1927) (inherited Avon Tyrrell on Eveline's death 1909)

Edward (1864-71)

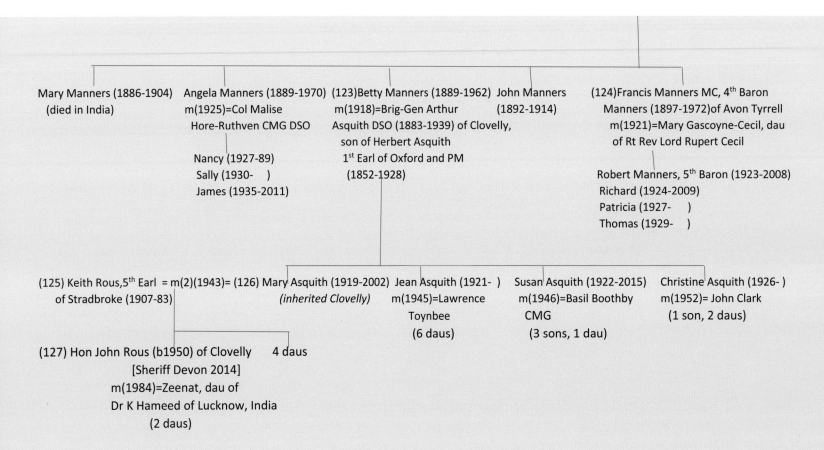

Mary Manners (1886-1904)
(died in India)

Angela Manners (1889-1970)
m(1925)=Col Malise
Hore-Ruthven CMG DSO

Nancy (1927-89)
Sally (1930-)
James (1935-2011)

(123)Betty Manners (1889-1962)
m(1918)=Brig-Gen Arthur
Asquith DSO (1883-1939) of Clovelly,
son of Herbert Asquith
1st Earl of Oxford and PM
(1852-1928)

John Manners
(1892-1914)

(124)Francis Manners MC, 4th Baron
Manners (1897-1972)of Avon Tyrrell
m(1921)=Mary Gascoyne-Cecil, dau
of Rt Rev Lord Rupert Cecil

Robert Manners, 5th Baron (1923-2008)
Richard (1924-2009)
Patricia (1927-)
Thomas (1929-)

(125) Keith Rous,5th Earl of Stradbroke (1907-83) = m(2)(1943)= (126) Mary Asquith (1919-2002)
(inherited Clovelly)

Jean Asquith (1921-)
m(1945)=Lawrence
Toynbee
(6 daus)

Susan Asquith (1922-2015)
m(1946)=Basil Boothby
CMG
(3 sons, 1 dau)

Christine Asquith (1926-)
m(1952)= John Clark
(1 son, 2 daus)

(127) Hon John Rous (b1950) of Clovelly
[Sheriff Devon 2014]
m(1984)=Zeenat, dau of
Dr K Hameed of Lucknow, India
(2 daus)

4 daus

HAWTHORNDEN FAMILIES OUTLINE PEDIGREE

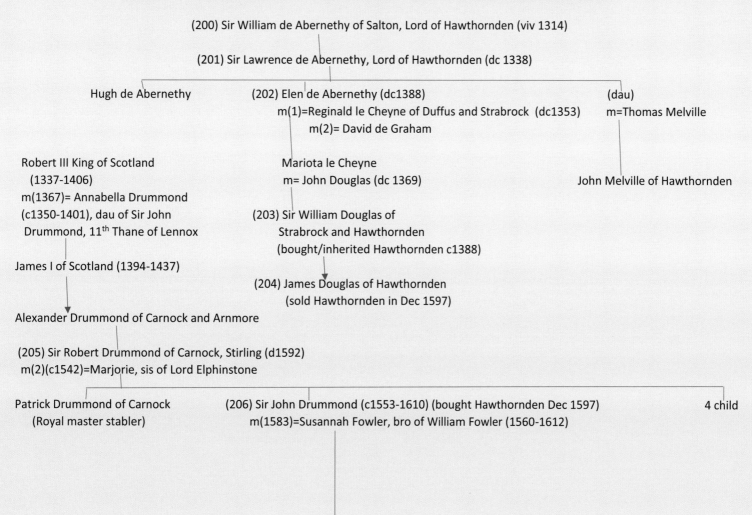

(200) Sir William de Abernethy of Salton, Lord of Hawthornden (viv 1314)

(201) Sir Lawrence de Abernethy, Lord of Hawthornden (dc 1338)

Hugh de Abernethy

(202) Elen de Abernethy (dc1388)
m(1)=Reginald le Cheyne of Duffus and Strabrock (dc1353)
m(2)= David de Graham

(dau)
m=Thomas Melville

Robert III King of Scotland
(1337-1406)
m(1367)= Annabella Drummond
(c1350-1401), dau of Sir John
Drummond, 11th Thane of Lennox

Mariota le Cheyne
m= John Douglas (dc 1369)

John Melville of Hawthornden

(203) Sir William Douglas of
Strabrock and Hawthornden
(bought/inherited Hawthornden c1388)

James I of Scotland (1394-1437)

(204) James Douglas of Hawthornden
(sold Hawthornden in Dec 1597)

Alexander Drummond of Carnock and Arnmore

(205) Sir Robert Drummond of Carnock, Stirling (d1592)
m(2)(c1542)=Marjorie, sis of Lord Elphinstone

Patrick Drummond of Carnock
(Royal master stabler)

(206) Sir John Drummond (c1553-1610) (bought Hawthornden Dec 1597)
m(1583)=Susannah Fowler, bro of William Fowler (1560-1612)

4 child

(207) William Drummond (1585-1649)
of Hawthornden (the poet)
m(1632)= Elizabeth Logan, grandau of
Sir Robert Logan of Restalrig
Edinburgh

James

Alexander

John

Ann
m= Sir John Scot
of Scotstarvet

Jane

Rebecca

(208) Sir William Drummond (d1713)
of Hawthornden
m(2)=Barbara, dau of Sir William Scott
of Clerkington

Robert (d1687)

Elizabeth
m=Dr Henderson
of Edinburgh

3 sons

3 daus

(209) William Drummond (1664-c1735)
of Hawthornden
m=Isabella, dau of Sir John Ramsay Bt of Whitehall

(210) William Drummond of Hawthornden (d1760)
m=Jean, dau of Sir Charles Milne Bt of Banton

Alexander Abernethy of Corskie, Banff

Dr William Drummond
(died in Jamaica)

(211) Mary Barbara Drummond (bc1721-1789) of Hawthornden
m(1)= Robert Macgregor
of Glengarnock
m(2)(1760)= Dr William Abernethy-Drummond, Bishop of Edinburgh
(1720-1809) (took Drummond surname in 1760)(212)
(only dau died aged 13)

(213)Anne Abernethy
m=Robert Forbes
of Corskie, Banff

(214) Mary Ogilvie of Murkle, Angus
(heiress of Hawthornden,
cousin of Barbara Drummond)
m(1785)=(215) Capt Sir John Forbes-Drummond RN
(1746-1829)[1st Bt of Hawthornden 1828]

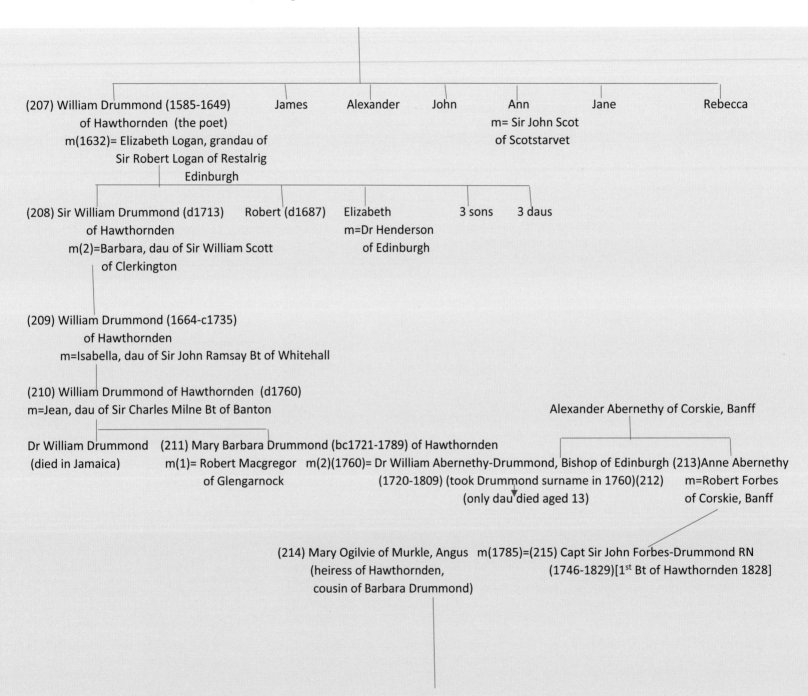

(216) Margaret Anne Forbes-Drummond (d1876) of Hawthornden
m(1810)= Sir Francis (Walker) Walker Drummond [2nd Bt 1829] (217)
(1781-1844), son of James Walker (1743-1817) of Dalry, Midlothian
and Jane Hay Newton (descended from King Robert the Bruce)

(73) Sir James (Walker Drummond) Williams-Drummond of Hawthornden (1814-1866) [3rd Bt 1844][changed surname 1858]
m(1853)=Mary Eleanor(Lil) Hamlyn Williams (1825-72)
who inherited Edwinsford in 1861 (71)
(lived at Edwinsford)

(218) Maj-Gen Francis Walker Drummond
(1817-91) Bengal Cavalry, India
m(1839)=Pauline (d1918), dau
of Charles Mackenzie
(lived in Hawthornden)

- Pauline m(1865)=JW Quinton CSI
- Alice m(1871)= MT Carmichael
- Margaret(d1918) m(1869)= Lt-Gen TM Hazlerigg(1840-1915) (7 child)
- Maj Charles (1840-80) Bengal Nat Inf
- Charles (b1861)

(219)John Forbes Walker Drummond
(1819-96)
m(1866)=Emma (d1920), dau of
Butler Edmund Thornton
of Skerton, Lancs

Annabella (d1936)
m(1889)=Lt-Col Richard
Wilson DSO(1855-1936)
10th Hussars

Richard Hay Walker Drummond

Mary Walker Drummond
m=Francis Thiergartner

Jane Hay Walker Drummond
m=Willam Douglas Dick of
Pitkerro, Forfarshire

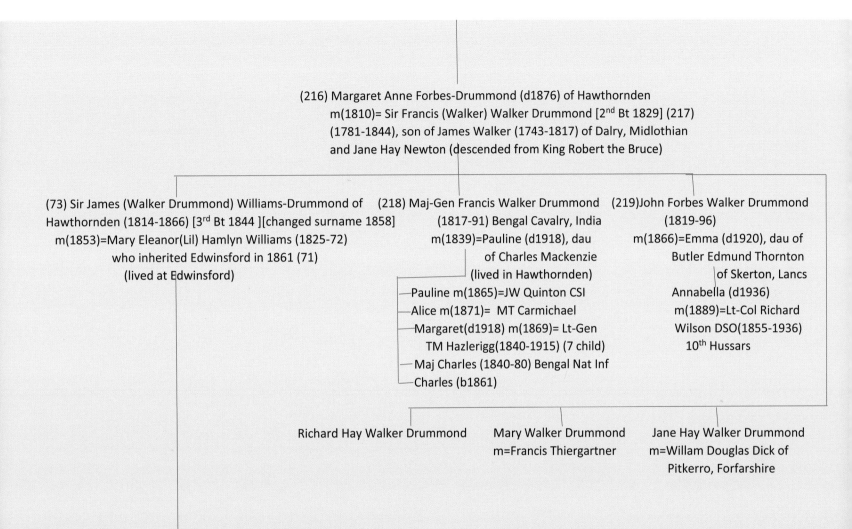

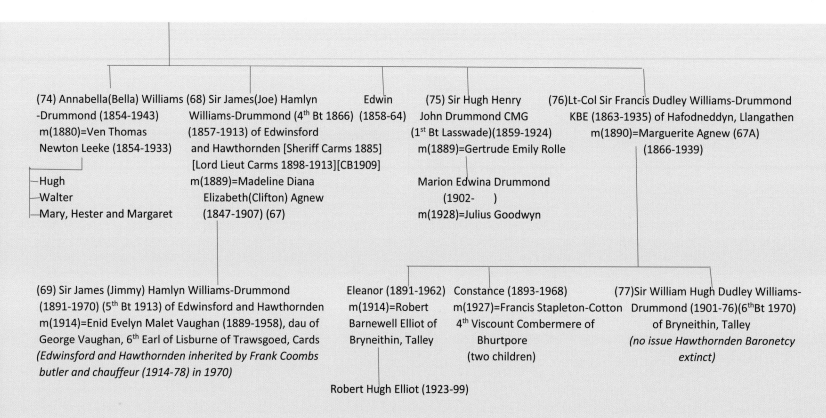

(74) Annabella(Bella) Williams -Drummond (1854-1943)
m(1880)=Ven Thomas Newton Leeke (1854-1933)

- Hugh
- Walter
- Mary, Hester and Margaret

(68) Sir James(Joe) Hamlyn Williams-Drummond (4th Bt 1866) (1857-1913) of Edwinsford and Hawthornden [Sheriff Carms 1885] [Lord Lieut Carms 1898-1913][CB1909]
m(1889)=Madeline Diana Elizabeth(Clifton) Agnew (1847-1907) (67)

Edwin (1858-64)

(75) Sir Hugh Henry John Drummond CMG (1st Bt Lasswade)(1859-1924)
m(1889)=Gertrude Emily Rolle

Marion Edwina Drummond (1902-)
m(1928)=Julius Goodwyn

(76)Lt-Col Sir Francis Dudley Williams-Drummond KBE (1863-1935) of Hafodneddyn, Llangathen
m(1890)=Marguerite Agnew (67A) (1866-1939)

(69) Sir James (Jimmy) Hamlyn Williams-Drummond (1891-1970) (5th Bt 1913) of Edwinsford and Hawthornden
m(1914)=Enid Evelyn Malet Vaughan (1889-1958), dau of George Vaughan, 6th Earl of Lisburne of Trawsgoed, Cards
(Edwinsford and Hawthornden inherited by Frank Coombs butler and chauffeur (1914-78) in 1970)

Eleanor (1891-1962)
m(1914)=Robert Barnewell Elliot of Bryneithin, Talley

Robert Hugh Elliot (1923-99)

Constance (1893-1968)
m(1927)=Francis Stapleton-Cotton 4th Viscount Combermere of Bhurtpore
(two children)

(77)Sir William Hugh Dudley Williams-Drummond (1901-76)(6thBt 1970) of Bryneithin, Talley
(no issue Hawthornden Baronetcy extinct)

Hawthornden
Edwinsford
Clovelly

The Edwinsford Families

1. Origins

1.1 The Heir to the Edwinsford Estate attains his majority

The years 1877-8 were eventful. In 1877 Queen Victoria had been proclaimed Queen Empress of India, Russia had declared war on the Ottoman Empire, Rodin had caused outrage in Paris by exhibiting a lifelike sculpture of a young male, the Washington Post newspaper had been founded, and Alexander Graham Bell had started the Bell Telephone Company. Early the next year Britain sent a fleet to Istanbul in support of the Turks and in July Tory Prime Minister Benjamin Disraeli brought back "peace with honour" from the Congress of Berlin under which the Balkans were divided, the Ottoman Empire which had started in the 13th century was further reduced, and Britain gained Cyprus; Disraeli's flamboyance in speech and dress made him a favourite of the Queen, unlike Gladstone, but already an earl he declined a Dukedom.

In Carmarthenshire rural life continued much as it had for generations. On Sunday 13 January 1878 Sir James (Joe) Hamlyn Williams-Drummond 4th Baronet (1857-1913) (68) reached the age of 21 and formally inherited the Edwinsford Estate in the Cothi Valley in Carmarthenshire and Hawthornden Castle in Midlothian near Edinburgh.

Joe's grandfather, Sir James Hamlyn Williams Bt MP (1790-1861) (61), had owned the Edwinsford Estate and the Derllys Estate in Wales as well as the Clovelly Estate in Devon totalling over 14,000 acres, but had died without male issue so his Hamlyn Williams baronetcy had expired on his death in 1861. He and his wife Mary Fortescue (1792-1874), who was descended from King Edward III and King Robert the Bruce, had three daughters: (1) Susan, who married into the Fane family of Avon Tyrrell in Hampshire, to whom they left their Clovelly Estate, (2) Edwina Augusta (Gussie), who married into the Ferguson Davie family, to whom they left their Derllys Estate, and (3) Mary Eleanor (Lil) (1825-72) (71), who married into the Walker Drummond family of Hawthornden, to whom they left their Edwinsford Estate. Joe was the eldest son of Sir James (Walker) Williams-Drummond 3rd Baronet of Hawthornden (1814-66) (73) and Lady Eleanor. Very sadly his father had died at the young age of 51 in 1866 and his mother had also died in 1872 at an equally young age while he was still at school so his uncle Sir John Ferguson Davie MP 2nd Baronet of Creedy Park in Devon (1830-1907) and his aunt Gussie (1834-89) (72) acted as his principal guardians until the attainment of his majority on 13 January 1878 when he formally inherited the Edwinsford Estate and Hawthornden Castle.

The attainment of his majority by an heir to an important estate particularly where such heir thereby also became the new landlord was an event which the county gentry, friends of the family, tenants and neighbours all gladly enjoyed. It was an opportunity for the tenants to show respect and support for their landlord and likewise an opportunity for the heir to confirm his continuing commitment to the estate and his tenants. Joe's attainment of his majority involved four days of uninterrupted enjoyment at Edwinsford which was described in detail[1] in the local press.

The press (perhaps with some understandable exaggeration) reported that the social and political influence of the family of Edwinsford had been second to no other house in the county, that Joe's grandfather and great grandfather had represented the county in Parliament for several years in the Liberal interest, and that following the serious loss of their mother Lady Drummond some six years ago Joe and his siblings had been brought up very well by their uncle and aunt as guardians while the Edwinsford Estate had been well managed by Mr David Long Price (of Talley House) the family agent and solicitor.

---

1 The Welshman; Llanelly Guardian

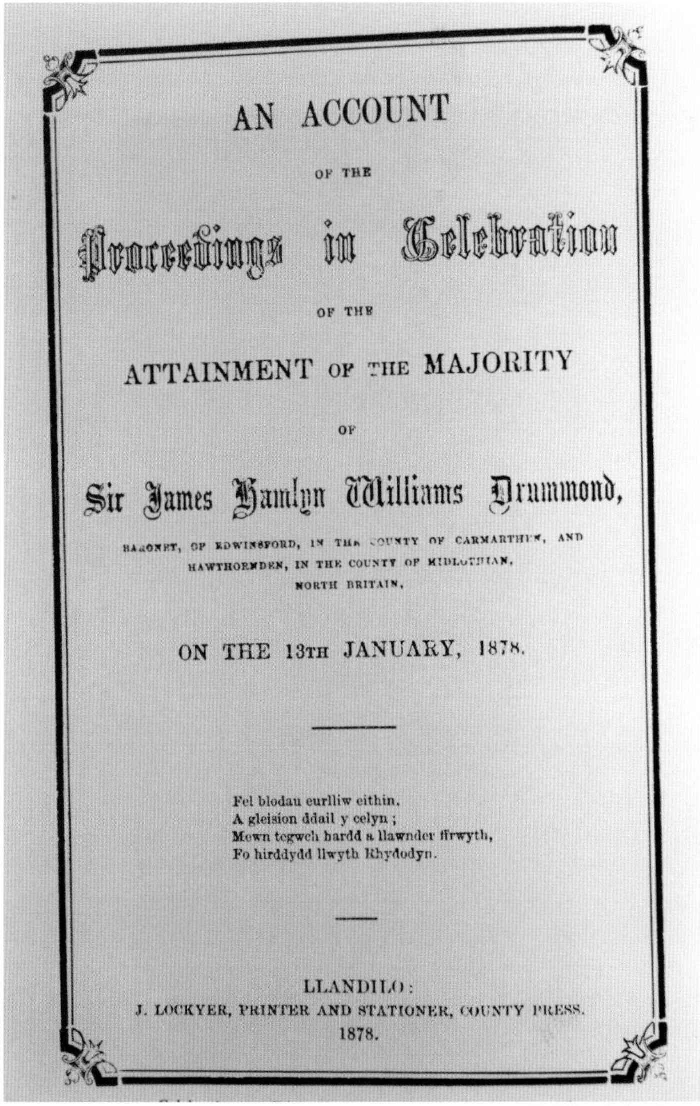
AN ACCOUNT

OF THE

Proceedings in Celebration

OF THE

ATTAINMENT OF THE MAJORITY

OF

Sir James Hamlyn Williams Drummond,

BARONET, OF EDWINSFORD, IN THE COUNTY OF CARMARTHEN, AND
HAWTHORNDEN, IN THE COUNTY OF MIDLOTHIAN,
NORTH BRITAIN,

ON THE 13TH JANUARY, 1878.

Fel blodau eurlliw eithin,
A gleision ddail y celyn ;
Mewn tegwch hardd a llawnder ffrwyth,
Fo hirddydd llwyth Rhydodyn.

LLANDILO:
J. LOCKYER, PRINTER AND STATIONER, COUNTY PRESS.
1878.

© Hon John Rous

© Hon John Rous
Sir Joe Williams-Drummond 1876

The vicars from the three local parishes in which the Edwinsford Estate was located namely Talley (Rev Rees), Llansawel (Rev JA Williams) and Conwil Gaeo (Rev C Chidlow) had been appointed as Chairmen of their respective parish committees to prepare for and carry out the proceedings, described by the press as "within living memory there has been nothing like it in North Carmarthenshire."

The proceedings started with a large procession of tenantry, friends and townspeople dressed in their Sunday best marching with the band of the Carmarthenshire militia from the Edwinsford Arms in Talley to Edwinsford Mansion. A grand arch had been erected in the centre of Talley with bunting galore and the usual banners of good fortune and the procession passed under another such arch at the entrance to

Edwinsford carriage drive. When they arrived at Edwinsford Mansion they were welcomed by Sir James with his aunt, Lady Gussie Ferguson Davie (her husband was unwell), together with numerous local gentry and family staying at Edwinsford including Lord and Lady Cawdor, Lady Evelyn Campbell, and Lord and Lady Dynevor. A presentation to Sir James was then made by the deputation from Llandeilo and a silvermounted claret jug with a lovely illuminated printed Address was delivered.

Thomas Phillips of Ffoeslas in Talley being the oldest tenant on the estate then had the honour of presenting a silver tray on behalf of all the tenants and said: "You are the fifth Sir James of Edwinsford whom

© Hon John Rous

© *Hon John Rous*
Sir John Ferguson Davie 1870

© *Hon John Rous*
Lady Gussie Ferguson Davie

I remember and all of them have enjoyed our confidence and respect." Sir James replied in kind. Following refreshments for all, the procession continued to Llansawel along the other carriage drive and arrived by 2.30pm at the Town Hall where lunch was provided at the Black Lion Inn by the publican Henry Rumbold for 100 people. Sir James presided and Mr Long Price occupied the vice-chairman's seat. Numerous toasts followed the meal including the loyal toast; a toast for the Bishop and clergy following which Rev C Chidlow spoke; a toast for the army, navy and reserve forces following which Joe's brother in law, Capt Leeke, spoke; and a toast for Joe's uncle and aunt.

Mr Long Price then proposed a toast to Sir James and reminded everyone that his own family had served the Edwinsford family for nearly 100 years and that while it was very sad that Sir James's parents were not present his guardian uncle and aunt did "guide him up to all good things". Sir James replied by saying that: "I hope that the respect and affection which has heretofore been shewn by all classes towards the old house at Rhydodyn will not fail in my hands.". He added that already serving in the army and about to join the Grenadier Guards (in which his father had served as a Captain) he had not been able to live at Edwinsford as long as he would have wished but in the future he intended to spend more time there.

Lady Ferguson Davie, his aunt, then spoke and said that she was very sorry that her husband was unwell and unable to attend, that they had always tried to spend two or three months each year in the old home at Edwinsford, and that "although my nephew is on his father's side a Drummond and a Scotsman, I hope and feel sure he will never forget that on his mother's side he is a Williams of old Rhydodyn and a Welshman."

Since the Black Lion Inn and the Town Hall were not large enough to seat all the guests for lunch, the remaining guests were seated and fed in the Angel Inn in Llansawel, the Bridgend Inn in Conwil Gaeo, and the Edwinsford Arms in Talley. At dusk bonfires were lit on the summit of local hills including Talley Beacon, Edwinsford Warren, and Caio Hill at Bronfin.

On the Tuesday a fat ox was given to the poor of the parishes. This was followed by rustic and athletic sports in the meadows near Edwinsford including prizes for 100 yards, three-legged race, one mile, sack race, blindfolded wheel barrow race, high jump, and tug of war, 200 yards for over 60s, 300 yards hurdles, donkey race, and of course lots of children's races all with prizes. On Thursday there were several coursing events with prizes awarded.

So ended the celebrations at Edwinsford. It would be another 11 years before Sir James then aged 32 and a most eligible bachelor married a widow with seven children aged 41; their story comes later. Sadly by 1939 Edwinsford Mansion was abandoned by the family who went to live in Hawthornden and today it is mostly rubble.

This book tells the tale of the origins of the various families who have owned Edwinsford in Carmarthenshire, Clovelly in Devon, and Hawthornden in Midlothian and of the social, political, military and economic times in which they lived. As with many old gentry families there are examples of success and failure, of wealth and poverty, and of philanthropy and greed. As can be seen from this book and from their public service described in Chapter 22, during the past several centuries these families have produced statesmen, Members of Parliament, Lord Lieutenants, High Sheriffs, Justices of the Peace, Crown servants, clerics, scholars, farmers, craftsmen, squires and a few black sheep amongst others. Outline pedigrees of the families are set out at the front of this book and in the relevant Chapters.

But before we can start the tale of these families we must first consider the origins of Sir Gâr (Carmarthenshire) and of the parishes in which the Edwinsford Estate was located.

1.2 The Origins of Carmarthenshire

Those who specialise in archaeogenetics[2] think that 80 per cent of the genetic characteristics of the average white British person can be traced back to a few hundred nomads who arrived in Britain about 14,000 years ago (12,000 BC) as Britain was thawing from the last Ice Age. They came from parts of what is now Western Germany, the Netherlands and Denmark and they followed herds of animals they were hunting eventually moving across a land bridge to what is now Eastern England. These original hunter-gatherers were relatively tall with very little body fat, athletic, fair-skinned and with red hair.

The other 20 per cent of our traits are thought to derive from "the Celts" who were a Semitic race of farmers from what is now Syria and Israel who arrived about 6,500 BC when the hunter-gatherers in Britain would have numbered about 5,000. It is thought that the Celts were the first farmers to move very gradually across Europe from their homeland in the Middle East and they brought crops and the first farm animals including sheep with them. They also brought the Celtic language dialects and a religion based around farming and the seasons, movement of the heavens and the concept of resurrection. They were slightly fatter, shorter and lived an average life span of 23 years compared with the average 30 years for the hunter-gatherers. The two waves of people expanded into a population of millions before further significant arrivals of immigrants, such as the Romans (AD 43-410) and then the Anglo-Saxons (from mid 400s) and the Vikings (8th century). But these immigrants had very little genetic impact and their impact was largely cultural and linguistic.

There is much doubt as to whether the Celts ever existed as a distinct genetic race on the Continent, or in Britain at all; many historians[3] consider "the Celts" had several different meanings over the past 2,500 years and that the idea of one Celtic identity is a 18th century invention.

---

2 See also Colin Renfrew and Katherine Boyle: *Archaeogenetics DNA and the Population Prehistory of Europe (2000)*

3 Simon James: *Exploring the World of the Celts (1993) p7-31*; TW Rolleston: *Myths and Legends of the Celtic Race (2004) p17-45*

Early Greek historians such as Hecataeus (500BC), Herodotus (450BC), Aristotle (350BC), and Plato (340BC) refer to *"the Keltoi"* or *"Gelatae"* who were many different tribes living in what is now North Germany and whose culture has been identified from the archaeological site at La Tene in Switzerland. They spread and conquered Gaul and Spain and parts of Turkey and went on to sack Rome in 390BC and Delphi in 279BC. Roman historians such as Virgil (40BC) and Julius Caesar (40BC) refer to them as *"Galli"*; Caesar conquered Gaul in 50BC which stopped their further spread or influence. Even if they were not one homogeneous race, these tribes constituted a body of people who spoke a tongue now termed Common Celtic, a language which divided into two main groups, Goidelic and Brythonic. The Welsh language was eventually to descend from the Brythonic group. Goidelic speakers occupied the north of Scotland, the Isle of Man and Ireland, while the Brythonic took root in Wales, England and the South of Scotland (it survives today principally in Wales, Cornwall and Brittany).

Welsh is the oldest language in Britain with a history of 15 centuries and as we have seen is derived from Brythonic (Brittonic) which was spoken over much of mainland Britain up to the time the Romans left in AD 410 although Latin was the language of government and administration. What is now Welsh evolved from the Brythonic after the Romans left and has been spoken in Wales since the 7th century. It became the language of everyday use and the language of administration and law (Hywel Dda's Laws in the 10th century were written in Welsh) until the Act of Union in 1536 when English was made the sole language of government and law ("...no person that use the Welsh speech or language shall have or enjoy any manner, office or fees within this realm of England, Wales or other of the King's dominions upon pain of forfeiting the same offices or fees...."). However most rural communities remained monoglot Welsh in practice and the fact that Bishop Morgan had translated the Bible into Welsh in 1588 guaranteed that the population continued to use the language.

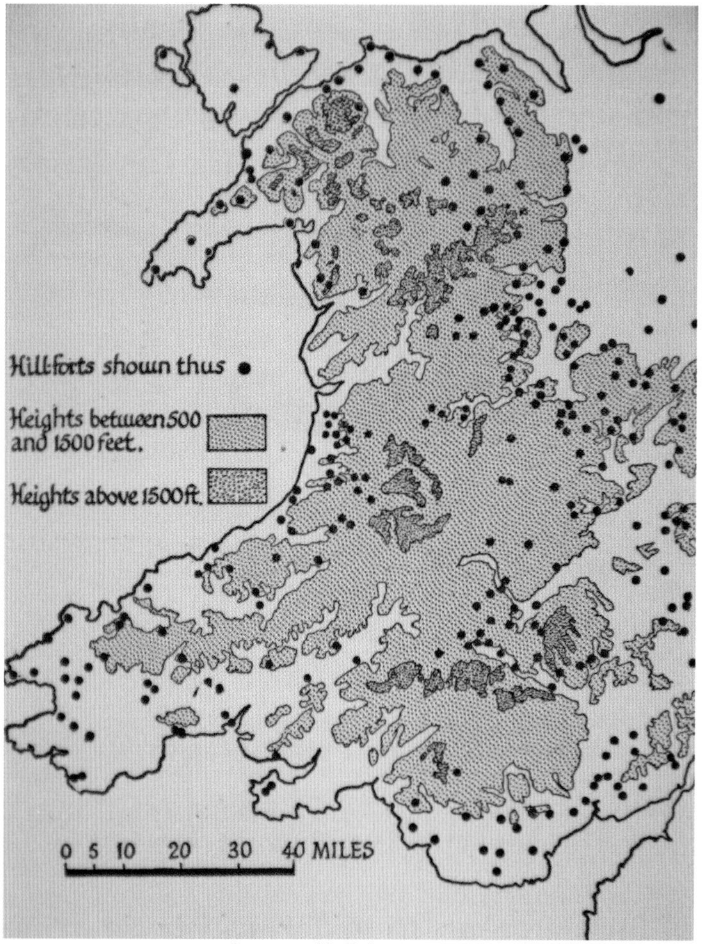

Distribution of hill forts in Wales (Prof Sir John Lloyd)

The Roman invasion of Britain[4] was ordered by the Emperor Claudius in AD 43 and penetration into Wales was initiated by Ostorius Scapula late in AD 47. By the late 70s there may well have been an occupation of some 30,000 Roman troops in Wales, such occupation being maintained by garrisoned forts, good administration and a network of

[4] I have sourced from Prys-Jones: *The Story of Carmarthenshire* in many of the sections relating to the history of Carmarthenshire. Arthur Glyn Prys-Jones OBE (1888-1987) was educated at Llandovery College and Jesus College Oxford where his history tutorial partner was TE Lawrence of Arabia. He then taught history before becoming Inspector of Secondary Education in Wales. See Don Dale-Jones: *AG Prys-Jones (1992)*

metalled surfaced and usually straight roads (like Sarn Helen[5]). The Romans established Moridunum (sea fort), a walled town at Carmarthen, as the civitas capital as recorded by Ptolemy and in the Antonine Itinerary. They crushed the local Demetae Celtic tribe and set up marching camps and forts at Llandovery, in Dinefwr at Llandeilo and at Llanio in c75 AD. The Romans were attracted by the lead, silver and gold in the area and they started mining gold at the Dolaucothi (Ogofau) mines at Pumsaint shortly afterwards with slaves and criminals as workers and with a Roman garrisoned fort to protect the area. Moridunum's Roman amphitheatre still survives (one of seven in the UK and, with Caerleon, the only two in Wales) and Carmarthen is probably the oldest town in Wales. The presence of the Romans did not materially affect the native way of life with the local people continuing to live in small settlements around their hill-forts[6] farming for the most part and speaking Welsh rather than Latin; they were principally pastoralists with stocks of oxen, sheep and goats. Some continued to worship their old Celtic gods and some were influenced by the Christian religion which the Romans first brought to Wales; by AD 378 Christianity had become the official state religion of the whole Roman Empire. By this time much of the land in Britain had been cleared of forests which now represented some 11 per cent of the land mass and the population had grown to about 5 million people.

After the Romans left Britain in around 410 the next 3 centuries of the Dark Ages began with invasions by the Picts and Scots in the north of Britain, the Angles, Saxons and Jutes in the east and south, and the Irish (Goidelic Celts) into Wales (Brythonic Celts) from the west. By c700 the whole of Southern Britain with the exception of Wales and Cornwall (which lasted as a Brythonic kingdom until the late 9th century) had become Anglo-Saxon/English kingdoms[7]; the Brythonic Welsh language[8], once the vernacular of Southern Britain, had disappeared in favour of early English. Identity of the Welsh of the region, now known as Wales, became clear, the word *"Cymry"* (people of the same region) being used to denote the people who belonged as opposed to the Saxon name of Wallas (Welsh) or waelisc meaning foreigners/strangers.

In Wales this was also the Age of the Saints with Christianity being spread between the 5th and 7th centuries by monks and missionaries[9] such as St David (c520-588) and St Teilo well before St Augustine was sent by Rome to Southern England in 597; the Book of St Teilo is one of the most important illustrated books of the period written c 740 well after his death and a facsimile copy of the Litchfield original is in Llandeilo Church. The places in Carmarthenshire beginning with "llan" meaning a sacred enclosure and later a church indicate the county's long religious tradition.

During the 7th and 8th centuries Wales was split into a number of small kingdoms which fought each other frequently, the loyalty of tribes being to their local rulers. The two largest kingdoms in the north were Gwynedd and Powys, and in the south were Dyfed (mostly Pembrokeshire), Ceredigion (mostly Cardiganshire) and Ystrad Tywi (Carmarthenshire). In the 8th century Ceredigion and Ystrad Tywi joined to become Seisyllwg later to become Deheubarth. Offa's Dyke built in around 790 by the King of Mercia was a defensive barrier and became a symbol of separation between Wales and England. The raids on Britain by the Danish, Norse and Swedish Vikings continued during the 8th to the 10th centuries; the first on Wales being in about 850.

1.3 The Origins of Talley, Llansawel and Cynwyl Gaeo

But what of the origins of the three Carmarthenshire parishes in which the Edwinsford Estate would be principally located?

The Celtic tribes ruled over small kingdoms in which areas of land were divided into hundreds or cantrefs (*cantrefi*) made up of about one hundred families or townships (*trefi*). The cantrefs were subdivided into smaller commotes (*cwmwdau*); the boundaries were often forested river valleys and lowlands between one territory and another and of course rivers formed natural boundaries which survived for centuries and indeed even today form the natural boundaries for several parishes. The commote was used by Hywel Dda for local administration purposes when he codified Welsh laws and customs in the 920s and

---

5 It is thought that the roads were built on the orders of Helen Luyddoc, a Celtic Princess who married Magnus Maximus the leader of the Roman army in Britain and later proclaimed Emperor in AD 383

6 EG Bowen: *Wales a Study in Geography and History (1941) p48*

7 The race character of the modern day British people can more accurately be described as Anglo-Celtic with its blend of Germanic and Celtic elements

8 Patrick Sims-Williams: *Studies on Celtic Languages before the Year 1000 (2007)*

9 Robert Bartlett: *Why Can the Dead Do Such Great Things (2013);* Janina Ramirez: *The Private Lives of the Saints (2015)*

this system continued with some modifications until the Act of Union of 1536. Each commote was ruled by a local lord who kept his court in his special township known as the *maerdref.* The members of the lord's tribe were either free tribesmen or bondmen. The bondmen gave service to the lord for a number of days each year and also tilled the soil and tended the cattle on his estate. So they did not live in villages or towns but in scattered homesteads with a cluster of bondmen's cottages and mud huts around the lord's court. In the summer months from about 1 May the tribesmen migrated from their homesteads on the lower valley slopes to pasture their flocks and herds on the hill pastures and lived in summer huts (*hafoty*); in the autumn they returned to their old settlements in the lower valley (*pentre* or *hendre*). These early farmers were pastoralists not agriculturalists[10].

According to Professor Sir John Lloyd[11] in early medieval times what is now Carmarthenshire included Ystrad Tywi (the Vale of Towy)(without Gower), Emlyn Uch Cuch (ie above the River Cuch) and Y Cantref Gwarthaf (ie the uppermost cantref of Dyfed); it also included Gower which was closely associated with Kidwelly in the early middle ages and was not finally divorced from it until the Act of Union in 1536. At some point before the Norman Conquest Ystrad Tywi itself was divided into Cantref Mawr (great) and Cantref Bychan (little) with the course of the River Tywi from Ystradffin to Abergwili being the dividing line. Then about the time of the Norman Conquest Cantref Mawr was itself divided into seven commotes: Mallaen, Caeo, Maenor Deilo, Cetheiniog, Widigada, Mabelfyw, and Mabudrud (see sketch map). Cantref Bychan consisted of the three commotes of Hirfryn, Perfedd and Is Cennen.

Mallaen corresponded to the modern parishes of Cilycwm and Llanwrda. Caeo included the modern parishes of Llansawel and Cynwyl Gaeo and the township of Mynachty (a grange of Talley Abbey) being part of Llanycrwys. Maenor Deilo comprised the modern parishes of Llansadwrn, Talley and Llandyfeisant (including Dinefwr) with some of Llandeilo parish to the north of the River Towy.

Gruffydd ap Rhys, son of Rhys ap Tewdwr, King of Deheubarth killed by the Normans in 1093, was allowed to retain the commote of Caeo by Henry I; it is thought that Caeo formed the core of the patrimony

Carmarthenshire map in Britannia by William Camden 1607

[10] EG Bowen: *Wales a Study in Geography and History (1941) p59*
[11] Prof Sir JE Lloyd: *History of Carmarthenshire Vol1 p6-9,14*

of the Princes of Deheubarth. Gerald of Wales (Giraldus Cambrensis 1145-1223) in his *Journey through Wales*[12] undertaken in 1188 with Baldwin, Archbishop of Canterbury, to gain support for the Third Crusade mentions that in the days of Henry I, Gruffydd, son of Rhys ap Tewdwr, was lord of a commote (equivalent to a quarter of a cantref or hundred hamlets) called Caeo which he held in tenure from the King. Caeo remained an independent Welsh lordship until 1284 and the local traditional system of land tenure survived for most of the Middle Ages.

By the time of the Act of Union in 1536 what is now Carmarthenshire was divided into the hundreds of Caeo, Perfedd, Cathinog (Cetheiniog), Elfed and Derllys plus the three commotes of Carnwyllion, Iscennen and Cydweli (Kidwelly). The former Caeo, Mallaen and Maenor Deilo were combined to form the hundred of Caeo. These hundreds remained the effective divisions of the county until superseded in the 19th century and each hundred contained several parishes.

Talyllychau "is widely but unacceptably known as Talley (admittedly a name first recorded in 1382)" according to the Encyclopaedia of Wales[13] although no explanation is given. Fred Price[14] says the word signifies the "head of the lakes" from *llwch (llychau)* referring to the two lovely lakes in front of the Abbey, which is the most popular derivation. He adds that in older documents the name is given as Tallach, Tallaghan, Tallesch, and Tally. But confusingly a Dictionary of Place Names in Wales[15] suggests that the Welsh word derives from *tâl y llech (llechau* plural) meaning "slate, rock or stone slab" or "end of stone slabs" possibly referring to the old wall near the lower lake or to an old chapel near the village called Capel Crist (Mynwent Capel Crist 1891). Alternatively it suggests the word refers to a causeway between the two lakes accessing the Abbey. It adds that "Talley" is probably a mistaken abbreviation or colloquial contraction by non-Welsh speaking clerks of previously used names including Thalelech in 1222, Telechu in 1239, Tal y Llecheu in 1271, Talcheulau 1284-7, Taleleze in 1291, Tilachlargy in 1307, Tal y Lleeche in 1566, Tal y Llechau in 1710 and Talau in 1740. In any event as we have seen Talley used to be in the hundred of Maenor Deilo before it combined with Caeo. It is most famous for its Abbey (see Chapter 29.1).

Llansawel was in the lower division of the hundred of Caeo comprising the hamlets of Edwin's with Glynn, and Wen with Ganol[16]. The name Llansawel or Llansawyl is probably derived from the 6th century St Sawl or Sawyl, an early form of Samuel. Sawyl Benuchel, the brother of Dunawd or Dunod Fyr and Cerwydd, was the son of Pabo Post Prydyn and a Welsh chieftain. He and his brothers are said to have been Saints of Bangor Dunawd. He married Gwenasedd, daughter of Rhain Rhieinwg, by whom he became the father of the famous St Asaph (d596); St Deiniol was also a grandson of Pabo Post Prydyn. In the old Welsh pedigrees[17] his name appears as Samuil Pennissel, being credited with having a low instead of a high head. He is celebrated in the Triads as one of the three Trahawg "overbearing ones of the Isle of Britain" and his Feast day is 15 January. St Sawyl is the Patron Saint of Llansawel. He may have died in the monastery of Bangor Iscoed in Flintshire. The Parish Church of Llansawel, St Sawyls, seems always to have been ecclesiastically attached to St Cynwyl's Church in Caio village in Cynwyl Gaeo.

The parish called Cynwyl Gaeo or Conwil Gaio is one of the largest in Sir Gâr. Cynwyl was a brother of Deiniol and in the Age of the Saints lived under the protection of St David, our Patron Saint. Cynwyl is the Patron Saint of the parish and of the parish church in Caio; St Sawyl the Patron Saint of Llansawel was the uncle of Deiniol. St Cynwyl's Church also has links with the 5th century Saint Paulinus, the teacher of St David, who is thought to have founded a community in the area. In his *History of Caio* Fred Price suggests that the word Caio or Cayo (land of Caeo) could derive from a Roman called Caius or Cai, and that the area may have been occupied by the advanced guard of Caius. Several bricks have been dug up in Caio with Roman initials and names on them and tradition suggests that the Welsh and the

[12] Gerald of Wales: *The Journey through Wales p94*

[13] Welsh Academy: *Encyclopaedia of Wales (2008) p853*

[14] Fred Price: *History of Talley and Talley Abbey (1934) p5*

[15] HW Owen and R Morgan: *Dictionary of Place Names in Wales (2007)*

[16] S Lewis: *A Topographical Dictionary of Wales (1844);* Fred Price: *History of Llansawel p15-18;* Sabine Baring-Gould*: Lives of British Saints*

[17] Harleian MS3859

Saxons fought a battle at "the red town of the south built of thin red bricks" meaning Roman bricks and that the Red Hill and the Hill of Corpses are nearby. The *Black Book of Carmarthen* in Jesus College Library says that the traditional graves of ancient warriors are located *"ig gwestedin caeau"* meaning perhaps "in the Plain of Caio". The spelling of the parish has changed over the centuries[18] including Kemmoto de kaeoe in 1191, Cayo in 1257, Kenwell Cayo in 1291, Kunwillgaeo in 1396, Caio in 1439, Kynwyl gayo in 1566 as well as Gaer-Gaio, Kenwell-Gayo, Cynwyl-Gaeo, Cynwil-Gaio, Counwellgaio, Comville Gayo, Conwil-Caio and Caeo or Gaio. Maes-Neuadd near Caio village may suggest that it could have been the site of a Roman Governor's palace with an open space (maes) nearby. Since the Act of Union the Lordship of the Manor of Caio has remained vested in the Crown. The Church of St Cynwyl with lands was granted to the Premonstratensian monks at Talley Abbey in about 1185 (see Chapter 29.1); they were the White Canons whose way of life was based on the Cistercians but whose beliefs were more Augustinian.

[18] Fred Price: *History of* Caio *(1904) p7*

2. Edwinsford Family Pedigree

As Professor Sir RR Davies[19] has shown the old Welsh families were inordinately proud of their past. Hence they especially emphasized the supposed unbroken link between the Old North (*Yr Hen Ogledd*), the kingdoms of North Britain of the 5th century, and the contemporary political order in Wales of their respective times. It was from the Old North that the major Welsh dynasties traced their origins and from its poetry that they drew their heroes and poetic exemplars. But their pride was balanced by a profound sense of loss and shame—the loss of sovereignty of the old Britons or Celts in Britain and the shame of the oppressions suffered at the hands of the Saxons and those who had helped them. Hence the constant hope for deliverance with prophecies about King Arthur and Merlin recovering the sovereignty of the old Britons in one country with the foreign invaders gone. Gerald of Wales comments[20] as late as 1193 that the Welsh "most confidently predict that they will soon reoccupy the whole island of Britain. It is remarkable how everyone in Wales entertains this illusion."

Status and kinship were at the centre of native Welsh society with all families proud of their descent and sensitive to the ties of kinship. Gerald of Wales[21] commented that: "The Welsh value distinguished and noble descent more than anything else in the world. They would rather marry into a noble family than a rich one. Even the common people know their family tree by heart and can readily recite from memory the list of their ancestors....back to the sixth or seventh generation." The Welsh families traced their lineage from an ancestor and the descent-group from that ancestor led to the kin-group of many descendants protecting their kinsmen in society and even standing surety for their behaviour. According to Gerald: "As they have this intense interest in their family descent, they avenge with great ferocity any wrong or insult done to their relations." The validity of a genealogy in such a society rested on its social acceptability and usefulness, not on its historicity and chronological accuracy.

During the last decade of the 16th century and in the early part of the 17th century most of the major families of Wales attempted to formalise their pedigrees and lineage, in some cases more successfully than others. In this endeavour to illustrate that their ancestors and tribal patriarchs were descended from the great Princes of Wales and even from King Arthur and his Knights of the Round Table they were ably assisted by heralds, bards and genealogists. Probably the most famous genealogist of his day was Lewys Dwnn (c1550-c1616) whose *Heraldic Visitations of Wales between 1586 and 1613* was a monumental and impressive work of truth and fiction to this end. Dwnn was a Deputy Herald to Robert Cooke, Clarenceux King of Arms to Queen Elizabeth I and also a prolific poet. Many of the families of Wales used his work and Dwnn's position to present petitions to the College of Arms in London to approve their pedigrees, which once granted assumed the status of fact irrespective of the truth. Modern day genealogists such as Dr Peter Bartrum[22] and others have tried to correct many of Dwnn's mistakes but it seems clear that most of such family pedigrees cannot safely be described as complete and accurate particularly prior to 1400. For example, in 1605 Sir Walter Rice of Dinefwr asked Thomas Jones (alias Twm Siôn Cati) another well-known genealogist to draw up his family tree on a ten feet long roll seeking to prove that Sir Walter was descended from seven Kings, five Dukes and twelve Barons![23]

In some pedigrees which have not shown accurate dates of birth, marriage and death there are obviously many opportunities for error.

---

19 Prof Sir RR Davies: *The Age of Conquest p78,122-3.* Rees Davies's prodigious and profound works on Welsh medieval history make him the leading authority on the subject. He was the Chichele Professor of Medieval History at All Souls College, Oxford and died in 2005 aged 66

20 Gerald of Wales: *The Description of Wales p265*

21 Gerald of Wales: *The Description of Wales p251*

22 Dr Peter Bartrum, a meteorologist by profession, died in 2008 aged 100 having published extensive research on Welsh lineages; he left to the Aberystwyth Welsh Department numerous research papers

23 Gerald Morgan: *Dinefwr p65*

Some pedigrees confuse men and women with similar or the same patronymic names who are in fact not the same person; in some cases the timing of births and marriage matches is impossible.

It is against this background that we should consider the pedigrees of the Edwinsford/ Rhydodyn families. I have prepared the pedigrees printed in this book based on a number of sources[24] in an attempt to give the most up to date reliable version, but the preparation of pedigrees is not an exact science.

Many of the persons mentioned in the text of this book are numbered in the family pedigrees to avoid confusion given the similarity of names and the problems which arise from the common use of patronyms by Welsh families. The dominance of a small number of family surnames, many of which derive from Biblical names, often leads to confusion. Even today by tradition the eldest son in a Welsh family often takes the first name of his father or grandfather, the eldest daughter often takes the first name of her mother or grandmother.

---

24 Lewys Dwnn p224-6; Peniarth MS156 (Francis Green p66); Golden Grove Book; Dale Castle MS (Francis Green p10); Alcwyn Evans p16-17 NLW MS 12359; Thomas Nicholas Vol 2 p306; Fred Price -Llansawel p53-60; Sir John Lloyd Vol 2 p477; Sir Francis Dudley Williams-Drummond; Francis Jones- THSC (1986-7); Peter Bartrum (1974) Vol 4 p847, Vol 2 p294 and (1983) p572-3; DL Baker-Jones CH (1968) p17-42; Michael Siddons (2017); Darell Wolcott: *ancientwalesstudies.org*; Burke; Debrett; NLW Edwinsford archives; thePeerage.com; HP; JL Vivian; Charles Worthy; Scottish Clan archives; ODNB; and family manuscripts.

3. Early Roots of the Williams Family

"Williams" is a patronymic form of the name "William" which originated in medieval Wales and England; its meaning is derived from "son or descendant of William" being the Northern French form which also gave the English name "William". It is derived from an Old French given name with Germanic elements, "will" meaning "desire" and "helm" meaning "helmet or protection".

The Williams family of Rhydodyn / Edwinsford as one of the ancient Welsh *uchelwyr* noble families has traditionally claimed ancestral descent from royal blood. Writing in 1924 Lt Col Sir Francis Dudley Williams-Drummond (76)[25] says: "A distinguished Welsh historian[26] has written: The Williamses of Rhydedwin have descended from Princely and Royal blood, and have never, through all the changes of time, fallen into an obscurity which threw into shadow any portion of their genealogy. Through Rhys ap Tewdwr (8) they descend directly from Howell Dda (7) and Rhodri Mawr (6), Kings of Wales, and through Ellen, wife of Llewellyn ap Philip (24), from Henry I of England". We must begin our journey by analysing this claim from the available sources and start by looking at the claimed female line of descent through Princess Nest (c1085-c1136)(11) who it is said was the mistress of Sutrick Centrick or Wygen (12) in the male Williams line.

Research suggests that Coel (Colius) Hen (the Old) Godebog (Hawk-beak)(c350-c420) (1) was High-King of North Britain and that he married Ystradwel ap Coel, Queen of Rheged or Dumnonia. Most of the old Celtic British monarchies and major families claimed descent from him and of course he is known to us via the famous nursery rhyme: "Old King Cole was a merry old soul….." He appears to have lived at the time when the Roman officials were returning to Rome and leaving the tribes in Britain to look after themselves. He may have been the last of the Roman Duces Britanniarum with his headquarters in York and so was probably the first King of Northern Britain in the area of Hadrian's Wall. He should not be confused with Coel Hen Godhebog (the Magnificent) King of Britain who legend suggests founded the City of Colchester (Cole's Castle) and whose daughter Helena married the Emperor Constantius Chlorus two centuries earlier. Coel Hen of North Britain was supposedly 18th in descent from the mythical King Beli Mawr[27], who married Anna, a cousin of the Virgin Mary, and whose son Aballach and successors were said in Celtic mythology to be the keepers of the Holy Grail from the time of St Joseph of Arimathea.[28]

It is thought[29] that North Britain, which later became Northumbria, was divided after the death of Coel Hen into a number of smaller kingdoms including Rheged (Lancashire and Cumbria), York, Elmet (south-west Yorkshire), Brynwaich (Northumberland and parts of Lothian), and Lothian and Din Eidyn (Edinburgh). This area was larger than modern Wales in size and had to be split because of the numerous male descendants in the Coel dynasty.

Coel's lineage continues with his son Cynan (or Cenau) ap Coel Hen St Cenue, King of North Britain (c382-c425); his grandson Gwrast Lledlwm (the Ragged) King of Rheged (c422); followed by Meirchion

25 FDWD: *Annals of Edwinsford, Clovelly and Hawthornden (1924) p5*

26 Thomas Nicholas: *Annals and Antiquities (1872) p306*

27 Beli Mawr supposedly reigned in the period before the Roman invasion

28 Joseph took the body of Christ from the cross at Golgotha and wrapped it in a linen shroud and then took the body to Joseph's own tomb in a garden of his house nearby: St John's Gospel 19:38-40

29 Timothy Venning: *The Kings and Queens of Wales (2012) p183-5.*

Edwinsford Williams Family Claimed Pedigree

(1) Coel Hen (the Old) Godebog (Hawk-beak), High-King of North Britain (c350-c420)
m= Ystradwel ap Coel, Queen of Rheged (c360-) (18th in descent from Beli Mawr)

Cynan ap Coel Hen St Ceneu, King of North Britain (c382-c425)

Gwrast Lledlwm (the Ragged), King of Rheged (c422-)

Meirchion Gul (the Lean), King of Rheged (c438-535)

(2) Elidyr Llydanwyn (the Stout and Handsome) (c462-), King of South Rheged

(3) Llywarch Hen (the Old) (c534-), the last King of South Rheged

Dwywg ap Llywarch (c560-)

Caid ap Dwywg (c595-)

Tegid ap Caid (c630-)

Alcun ap Tegid (c660-)

(4) Sanddle ap Alcun (c690-), King of Ynys Manaw — Cunedda Wledig (c440) King of Gwynedd

Elidyr ap Sanddle (c720-), King of Ynys Manaw

Gwriad (c750-), King of Ynys Manaw

(5) Merfyn Frych (Freckled) (c844-), King of Ynys Manaw and Gwynedd
m= Essylit, 13th in descent from Cunedda Wledig, King of Gwynedd

(6) Rhodri Mawr (the Great) (c820-c878), King of Gwynedd
m=Angharad, dau of Meurig ap Dyfnwal

Gul (the Lean) King of Rheged (c438-535). The pedigree continues through Elidyr Llydanwyn (2) (the Stout and Handsome), King of South Rheged (c462) (80). He married Gwawr, the daughter of Brychan King of Garth Madryn (Breconshire)(c467); Elidyr's brother, Cynfarch Oer, King of North Rheged, had married her sister. Their son and heir was Llywarch Hen (the Old)(3), the last King of South Rheged (c534)(3) who apparently had 42 children. The lineage then continues with Dwywg ap Llywarch (c560), Caid ap Dwywg (c595), Tegid ap Caid (c630), Alcun ap Tegid (c660), and Sanddle ap Alcun (c690)(4), King of Ynys Manaw and Prince of South Rheged. Manaw was probably the Isle of Man so he would have been King of Man. He is thought to have died in Wales and been buried in the Isle of Man. His son and heir was Elidyr ap Sanddle (c720) who was also King of Ynys Manaw and he was followed by his son Gwriad (c750), and then by Merfyn Frych (the Freckled) (c844)(5); he was King of Ynys Manaw but more importantly also of Gwynedd between c825 and 844 having claimed Gwynedd on the extinction of Cunedda's male line (Cunedda Wledig being the first King of Gwynedd from about 440 to 460).

Rhodri Mawr (6), the son of Merfyn Frych, became King of Gwynedd and earned the honour of being called "the Great". We now turn to his background.

4. Invasion, Conquest, Settlement and Revolt 850-1416

4.1 Rhodri Mawr (c820-878)

The first Viking raids on Wales took place in about 850 during the reign of Rhodri Mawr (Rhodri the Great) (6) as King of Gwynedd[30] between c844 and 878. He married Angharad, daughter of Meurig ap Dyfnwal. Rhodri fought the Danish Vikings (the "black pagans") in Anglesey and won a battle against them in 856. Other victories by him are recorded in the Chronicle of the Princes[31] in 872. He is thought to have died in battle either against the Vikings or possibly the Saxons since his son Anarawd's victory over the Mercians in the battle of Conwy in 881 was called "God's vengeance for Rhodri". He left four sons of whom Anarawd succeeded him as King of Gwynedd. The youngest, Tudwal Gloff (the Lame), is believed to have been wounded in the 881 battle, which left him lame and thus unqualified under Welsh customary law for any kingship. The history of one of Rhodri's other sons, Cadell ap Rhodri (c850-909), is uncertain. He certainly inherited Seisyllwg (Ceredigion and Ystrad Tywi) but there seems to be very little source evidence to validate the claims of some historians that he also acquired Ceredigion and Powys.

4.2 Hywel Dda (c880-950)

Cadell's son, Hywel ap Cadell known as Hywel Dda (Hywel the Good)(7), is very well known in Welsh history and is remembered as one of the most successful native Welsh rulers. Hywel and his brother Clydog succeeded their father Cadell. Hywel inherited part of Seisyllwg. He also ruled Dyfed as a result of marrying Elen the daughter of Llywarch the last Prince of Dyfed who died without sons, and on his brother's death in 920 Hywel merged Dyfed and Seisyllwg. His new kingdom was named Deheubarth. He also acquired the principality of Gwynedd on the death of his cousin Idwal Foel in 942 and may have acquired Powys as well. He thus ruled the greater part of Wales.

The lineage of the Royal House of Dyfed is unbroken from the 5th century down to Hywel Dda. Hywel is perhaps best known for convening the first Welsh Assembly at Whitland between 942 and his death in 950 and is venerated because he codified the customs and laws of Wales rather like King Alfred had done in England to enable one system of law to apply. Three copies of his Laws were prepared on the advice of twelve wise laymen and a number of scholarly clerics of which one copy was kept at Dinefwr, possibly the capital of the Princes of Deheubarth. This great code[32] or collection of unified laws and customs developed over time a feeling of national pride. No other ruler in Welsh history has been called "the Good".

Hywel is also well known because he visited Rome on a pilgrimage in 928. He made peace with King Edward the Elder and King Athelstan in Wessex to whom he paid tributes of gold, silver, cattle, hunting dogs and hawks, visited their courts and also attended the Witan which was the assembly who advised them. His peaceful approach also enabled him to mint his own coinage across the border in Chester. On his death his kingdom was split into three; the sons of Idwal Foel reclaimed Gwynedd, and Deheubarth was divided between Hywel's sons including Owain ap Hywel Dda (d987) in accordance with the Welsh customary law under which: "Brothers are to share the land of their father equally between them. The youngest is to divide, and the eldest is to have the first choice. If the brothers die without sons, the first cousins are to share the land equally. The second cousins also may further divide the land amongst themselves in equal parts. After that

---

30 Darrell Wolcott argues that he was too young in 844 aged 24 to have inherited the kingship and that there must have been some interim King of Gwynedd: *ancientwalesstudies.org/id165.* Darrell Wolcott runs the Center for the Study of Ancient Wales based in Jefferson, Texas.

31 Peniarth MS 20

32 Peniarth MS 28

Hywel Dda

there is to be no division." This rule of inheritance known as "gavelkind" was the principal reason why Wales was never fully united under one King and why there were so many feuds and so much bloodshed within families. Across the border the Norman rule of primogeniture had been followed ever since their invasion.

4.3 Tewdwr Mawr (bc977) and Rhys ap Tewdwr (c1040-1093)

Tewdwr ap Cadell was born in about 977 in Llandyfeisant, Dinefwr and was a great great grandson of Hywel Dda (7). He married Gwenllian daughter of Gwyn and became known as "Mawr" being the effective King of South Wales (Deheubarth). His children included Rhys ap Tewdwr (8) through whom the Tudor dynasty and King Henry VII descended. He also had a daughter Nest (8A), who may also have been born in Llandyfeissant; we shall discuss her in the context of the male Edwinsford pedigree below.

By 1039 Gruffydd ap Llywelyn, the ruler of Gwynedd and Powys, was trying to annex Deheubarth and succeeded in 1055 thereby uniting most of Wales. But his enemies including Earl Harold of Wessex plotted his downfall and he was killed by one of his own followers in 1063. Harold who gained the throne of England in 1066 was then killed at the Battle of Hastings by William the Conqueror of Normandy.

Following the Conquest the Normans had quite enough on their plate in England so William I (ruler 1066-87) encouraged his barons to seize much of lowland Wales while making grants to them of land along the Welsh borders or Marches. Rhys ap Tewdwr (8), a son of Tewdwr Mawr and a direct descendant of Hywel Dda took control of Deheubarth in 1075 on the death of his cousin. In 1081 William I made a pilgrimage to St Davids and Rhys ap Tewdwr paid homage to him and was allowed to keep his lands in Deheubarth without interference on payment of an annual tribute of £40. Rhys was killed in the reign of William II (ruler 1087-1100) in 1093 fighting invading Norman French in Breconshire[33].

The Norman invaders[34] arrived in what is now Carmarthenshire in 1093 and built a castle near Carmarthen at Rhydygors, and then a new one in Carmarthen in about 1106-9. Outside their castle they established a new market town called New Carmarthen to distinguish it from the old Roman town and Celtic monastery. It grew quickly under Royal protection, stone walls were built in the 1230s and it became an important port trading with Europe. During the Black Death of 1347-9 the plague came to Carmarthen via the river trade

33 Chronicle of the Princes (*Brut y Tywysogion*) Peniarth MS 20

34 Few Welshmen took part in the First Crusade (1096-99) which was planned by Pope Urban II, William II of England and Robert II of Normandy in the crypt chapel of the Knights of St John at St John's Gate near Smithfield in the City of London. It was a great success and Jerusalem was captured in 1099.

and emptied many villages; there was a mass burial pit in the town. The town was destroyed during the Owain Glyndŵr revolt in 1403 and 1405 and new walls were built in c1415-20. Carmarthen became the county town in 1282 and continued to be so after Greater Carmarthenshire came into existence in 1536 after the Acts of Union. It was the largest town in Wales with a population of 2,000, twice as large as Cardiff. Carmarthen also became the judicial headquarters of the Court of Great Sessions for South West Wales.

By 1135 at the end of the reign of Henry I (ruler 1100-35) the Normans were in control of Deheubarth although parts of the uplands were still enemy country for them. The Normans held the lowlands by building castles which were garrisoned; some were temporary castles consisting of mounds 30 or 40 ft high crowned with a wooden palisade enclosing wooden buildings within, while some were stone built often with a walled town outside. It should be noted however that Dryslwyn, Dinefwr and Carreg Cennen were castles built or rebuilt in stone by the Welsh, whereas Kidwelly, Llandovery, Laugharne, Llansteffan and Newcastle Emlyn were Norman. The lowlands were administered by the Normans, while the uplands including Caeo and Maenor Deilo in Cantref Mawr continued under the former Welsh tribal and pastoral system. Under the Norman feudal system the Norman Baron ruled from his castle over his lordship lands; in his castle lived his Constable who was in charge of his garrison, his Seneschal who was in charge of his courts, and his Receiver who ran the Exchequer and received all the dues and services formerly paid to the Welsh Prince of the area. Smaller lordships divided into manors were granted by the Baron to Knights who had to give forty days' military service annually. Most of the workers on the manors were serfs or bondmen under a bailiff. There were also some native freemen who paid dues for the use of their land and paid tributes in kind. Outside each castle there would usually be a borough or small township in which resided English and Norman soldiers, farmers, craftsmen and traders as in Carmarthen and in parts of Pembrokeshire which also had Flemish communities.

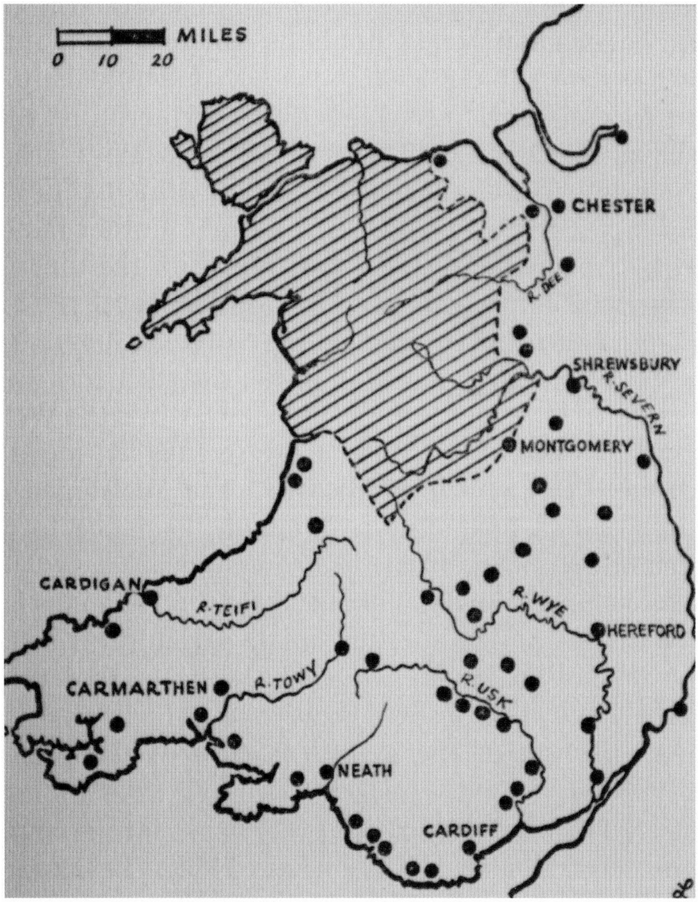

Norman Castles in Wales in 1135 (Prof Sir John Lloyd)

Following the death of Rhys ap Tewdwr in 1093 his son Gruffydd ap Rhys (c1081-1137) (10) fled to Ireland while his son Hywel was badly treated in captivity and became an invalid. Gruffydd returned to the Tywi valley and led revolts against Norman rule. In 1116 he destroyed Narbeth castle and damaged Llandovery and Swansea castles. He then attacked Carmarthen and set the town on fire. But his revolt failed and he had to pay homage to Henry I and was left in 1135 with only the lordship or single commote of Caeo in Cantref Mawr where he lived with his wife Gwenllian, daughter of Gruffydd ap Cynan, Prince of Gwynedd. On the death of Henry I the weak and ineffectual King Stephen (ruler 1135-54) succeeded and Gruffydd led another revolt while his wife Gwenllian and the men of Ystrad Tywi bravely attacked Kidwelly castle and were captured; she was put to death with one of her sons. Gruffydd died in 1137 and in the following year Carmarthen castle was taken.

Rhys ap Tewdwr (8) and his wife Gwladys had four sons and a daughter Nest. It is through this daughter, Princess Nest (c1085-c1136) (11), that the Williams family claimed descent from Hywel Dda and through him from Coel Hen. This brings us to the difficult Irish connections in the claimed pedigree of the Williams family through the male line.

4.4 Williams Claimed Male Pedigree

Irish connection

Lewys Dwnn[35] writing in about 1596 following his visit to Rhydodyn at the request of the family shows a family pedigree starting with Aelured Brennin Kirian (9) described as King of Kirian in Ireland. The Golden Grove Book, Peniarth MS 156, and the Dale Castle MS pedigrees[36] all show the same origin as Dwnn although Peniarth adds that Aelured lived at the time of Hywel Dda, which seems unlikely. Alcwyn Evans[37] also gives the same origin.

Parts of this lineage are however quite problematic. Afloed Brenin Kirian is a Welsh form of the Irish "Amblaib Cuaran" (Kirian being taken for Cuaran) which occurs in the Latin and Welsh manuscript versions of the Life of Gruffudd ap Cynan[38]. Welsh *cuaran* or *curan* means a shoe made with untanned hide so there has probably been a misinterpretation of the Irish word. Alured's coat of arms[39] was "a lion's head argent". Afloed's son (or grandson), Sutrick, has a name similar to the Irish and Old English forms of the Norse name *Sigtryggr* (Irish *Sitriuc*, OE *Sihtric*) as in the Anglo-Saxon Chronicle. Sutrick is described as King of Dublin and Desmont (a form of the anglicized Desmond for South Munster) but Sitriuc son of Olaf Cuaran never succeeded to this title and died as late as 1042. The lineage shows that Sutrick's son, Glynfawr or Alured, married Eva, daughter of Dermont Macmurg, King of Leinster. This might be the 12th century Diarmait Mac Murchada, King of Leinster, who invited the English to Ireland, but it could also be Diarmait mac Mail na mBo (d1072). The famous Eva (Irish Aife) who was the daughter of Diarmait Mac Murchada married Strongbow (Richard Fitz Gilbert). So there is much confusion with this lineage.

Bartrum[40] researching some 400 years after Dwnn and, more recently, Darrell Wolcott[41] provide different suggested connections with the Irish royal line.

So there can be no certainty that the Irish male pedigree is correct. It is said in the pedigree that "Eidio Wyllt Earl of Desmont came to Wales to the assistance of Rhys ap Tewdwr against Bernard Newmarch and for his good service had been given the Lordship of Lluwel"[42] (Llywel) in Breconshire. We know that Rhys ap Tewdwr found refuge in Ireland in 1088 and that he then regained his Welsh kingdom with the help of Irish troops, and that after his death in battle in Breconshire in 1093 his young son Gruffydd (10) was taken to Ireland for safety. It is claimed that Eidio's father had a relationship with Nest which resulted in the birth of Eidio Wyllt. Dwnn and others assume that this was the famous Princess Nest (11), daughter of Rhys ap Tewdwr (8), while Nicholas[43], Bartrum and Wolcott assume she was Nest (8A), sister of Tewdwr Mawr ap Cadell and thus an aunt to Princess Nest. Who is correct?

Princess Nest (c1085-c1136)

Nest or Nesta was born in about 1085 probably in Llandyfeisant or Dinefwr Castle, the daughter of Rhys ap Tewdwr (8) and his wife Gwladys, daughter of Rhiwallon ap Cynfyn of Powys. When her father was killed in battle in 1093 Prince Henry later King Henry I (ruler 1100-35)(youngest son of William the Conqueror) appointed himself as her protector. She became his mistress and she bore him a son, Henry FitzRoy (1103-58). The King then married her off to Gerald

---

35 Dwnn p224-6

36 NLW

37 NLW MS 12359; which is also adopted by Francis Jones: *Williams of Edwinsford—THSC (1986) p72-4* and by DL Baker-Jones*: Edwinsford: A Country House and its Families: CH (1968) p17-8.* DL Baker-Jones PhD of Felindre, Llandysul was educated at St David's College Lampeter and Jesus College Oxford and has written extensively on Welsh society and gentry families in Cardiganshire in particular; he is currently aged 94

38 I am very grateful to Emeritus Professor Thomas Charles-Edwards, former Jesus Professor of Celtic at Jesus College Oxford, for his help on the early Irish Edwinsford pedigree

39 Dwnn

40 Bartrum (1974) Vol 4 p847, Vol 2 p294 and (1983) p572-3

41 *ancientwalesstudies.org— Eidio Wyllt: What was his birthname?*

42 Dwnn p224-6; Peniarth MS 156

43 Thomas Nicholas: *Annals p306*

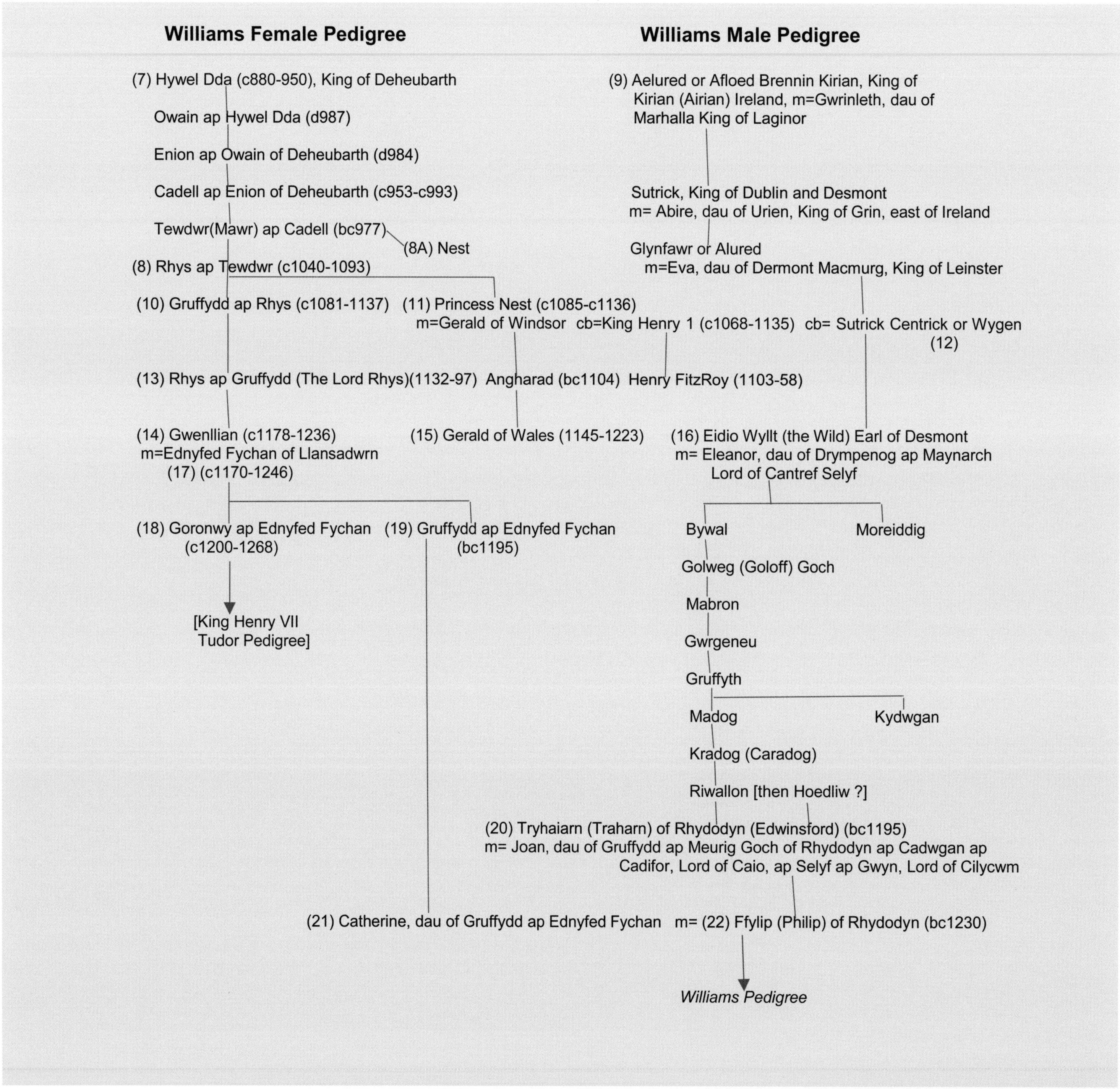
Williams Female Pedigree
Williams Male Pedigree
(7) Hywel Dda (c880-950), King of Deheubarth
Owain ap Hywel Dda (d987)
Enion ap Owain of Deheubarth (d984)
Cadell ap Enion of Deheubarth (c953-c993)
Tewdwr(Mawr) ap Cadell (bc977)
(8A) Nest
(8) Rhys ap Tewdwr (c1040-1093)
(10) Gruffydd ap Rhys (c1081-1137)
(11) Princess Nest (c1085-c1136)
m=Gerald of Windsor
cb=King Henry 1 (c1068-1135)
cb= Sutrick Centrick or Wygen (12)
(13) Rhys ap Gruffydd (The Lord Rhys)(1132-97)
Angharad (bc1104)
Henry FitzRoy (1103-58)
(14) Gwenllian (c1178-1236)
m=Ednyfed Fychan of Llansadwrn
(17) (c1170-1246)
(15) Gerald of Wales (1145-1223)
(18) Goronwy ap Ednyfed Fychan (c1200-1268)
(19) Gruffydd ap Ednyfed Fychan (bc1195)
[King Henry VII Tudor Pedigree]
(9) Aelured or Afloed Brennin Kirian, King of Kirian (Airian) Ireland, m=Gwrinleth, dau of Marhalla King of Laginor
Sutrick, King of Dublin and Desmont
m= Abire, dau of Urien, King of Grin, east of Ireland
Glynfawr or Alured
m=Eva, dau of Dermont Macmurg, King of Leinster
(16) Eidio Wyllt (the Wild) Earl of Desmont
m= Eleanor, dau of Drympenog ap Maynarch Lord of Cantref Selyf
Bywal
Moreiddig
Golweg (Goloff) Goch
Mabron
Gwrgeneu
Gruffyth
Madog
Kydwgan
Kradog (Caradog)
Riwallon [then Hoedliw ?]
(20) Tryhaiarn (Traharn) of Rhydodyn (Edwinsford) (bc1195)
m= Joan, dau of Gruffydd ap Meurig Goch of Rhydodyn ap Cadwgan ap Cadifor, Lord of Caio, ap Selyf ap Gwyn, Lord of Cilycwm
(21) Catherine, dau of Gruffydd ap Ednyfed Fychan
m= (22) Ffylip (Philip) of Rhydodyn (bc1230)
Williams Pedigree

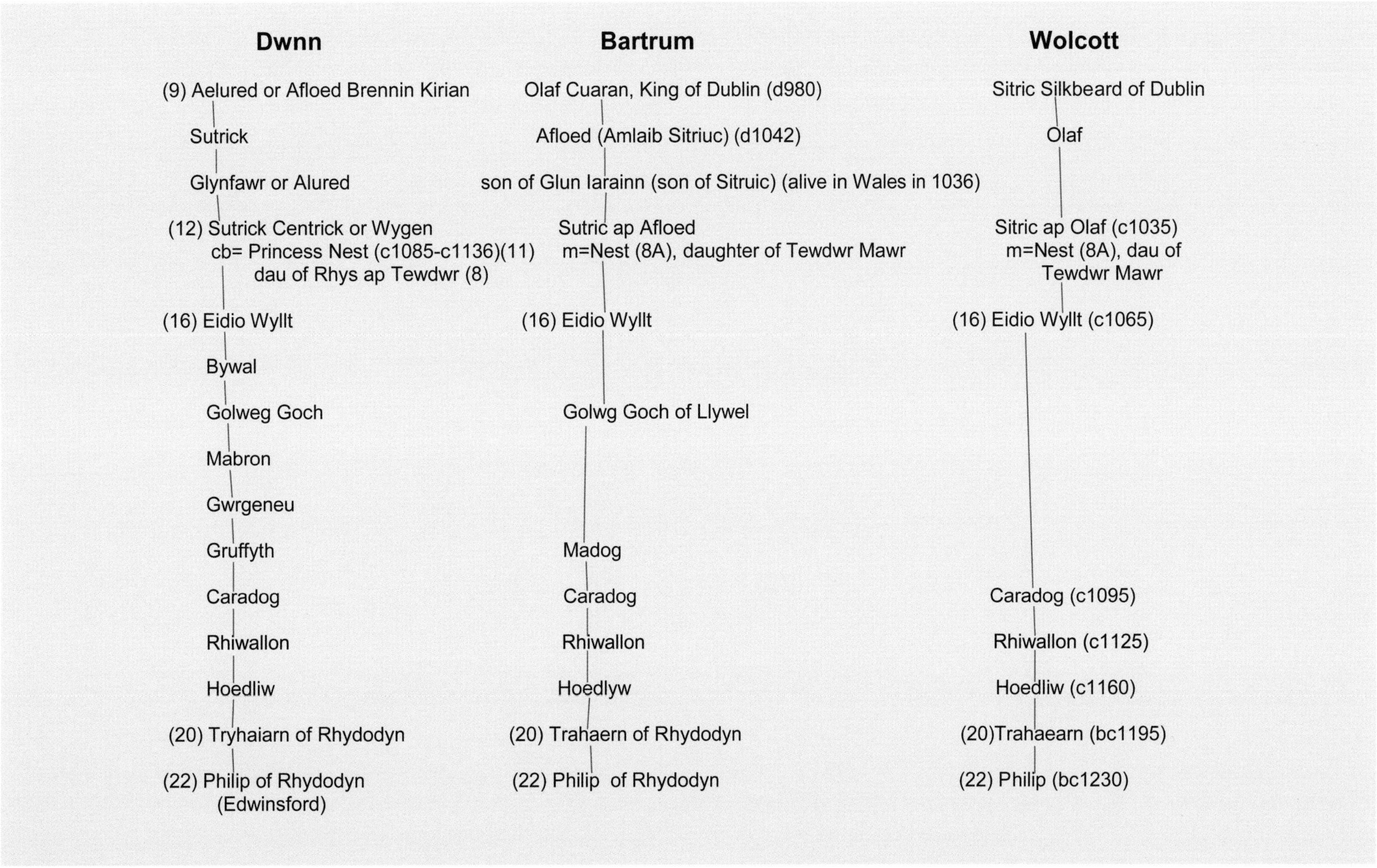

FitzWalter of Windsor, Constable of Pembroke Castle in about 1105. Nest was given Carew Castle as a dowry and she bore Gerald five children which was the start of the famous FitzGerald dynasty of Ireland; her daughter Angharad was the mother of Gerald of Wales (15).

In about 1109 her cousin, Owain ap Cadwgan of Powys, visited her and was so attracted to her that he is said to have attacked her home at Cenarth Bychan (which was probably Cilgerran Castle) during which Nest persuaded her husband Gerald to escape down a garderobe lavatory chute while she was abducted by Owain with her young children. Owain then raped her. Later she persuaded Owain to return her children to her husband Gerald and then to release her. There is much doubt as to whether she bore Owain any children. In about 1112 Owain and his supporters met Gerald by chance and Gerald took revenge by killing Owain.The account of this rape and abduction[44] is much doubted by several historians[45].

After her husband's death Nest married her husband's Constable of Cardigan, Stephen de Marisco, by whom she had further children thereby starting the Carew (Carey) dynasty.

---

44 Chronicle of the Princes

45 Darrell Wolcott: *Owain ap Cadwgan and Nest ferch Rhys—An Historic Fiction? ancientwalesstudies.org/id160*

Nest was obviously very attractive and during her lifetime she is said to have had numerous lovers thereby later earning herself the nickname of Helen of Wales. However there seems to be little evidence that she took Sutrick Centrick or Wygen (12) as a lover and bore him a son, Eidio Wyllt (16), as is suggested by the pedigrees produced by Dwnn and followed by some later genealogists. If Nest was the mother of Eidio Wyllt it seems much more likely that she was the Nest (8A) who was the sister of Tewdwr Mawr.

Eidio Wyllt

We have seen that the pedigree of Eidio Wyllt is uncertain with genealogists and historians taking different views of the few available sources about this Irish adventurer[46].

Francis Jones[47] concludes "that the Edwinsford family descended from a man named Eidio Wyllt is quite possible, but not in the manner recorded by Dwnn and his fellows, for the test of chronological stability, that is, comparisons with historical data and computations of three generations to a century from acceptable dates—-by which all early pedigrees should be tested—reveals serious discrepancy." He thinks that extra names must have been added to the accepted pedigree and lineages confused and suggests that the lineage prior to Tryhaiarn (20) needs to be taken with a large pinch of salt.

Wolcott suggests that a number of names in the Dwnn lineage were not real people at all. So "Bywal" was not a son of Eidio Wyllt but a corrupt rendition of "Llywel", that "Golwg Goch" meaning "red eyes" was just a nickname for Edio, and that "Wyllt" meaning "wild" was also a nickname. He concludes finally by arguing that there are no other occurences of a male name "Eidio" in either Irish or Welsh genealogies, that "Eidio" was probably nicknamed "the wild" in his youth and "red eyes" when older being a hard drinker and that Eidio's real birthname was probably Madog so his original name would have been "Madog eidio wyllt y golwg goch o Llywel".

I think we can safely assume that Tryhaiarn (20) is a valid ancestor of the Williams family. Before that there must be doubts but Wolcott has explained a more likely version of the real pedigree which works from the timing point of view. Tryhaiarn (Traharn) married Joan, daughter and co-heiress of Gruffydd ap Meurig Goch of Rhydodyn (Edwinsford) and thereby the Williams Edwinsford pedigree was founded.

Whether or not the Williams family can validly claim descent from Rhodri Mawr (6) and Hywel Dda (7) (and through them originally from Coel Hen) as a result of the Williams male line intermarrying with Nest (8A) or Princess Nest (11) is uncertain. However as we shall see they can probably do so through the marriage of Catherine (21) with Philip of Rhydodyn (22). This makes the pedigree of The Lord Rhys (13) a vital link.

4.5 Rhys ap Gruffydd (The Lord Rhys) (1132-97)

As we have seen in Chapter 4.3 Gruffydd ap Rhys ap Tewdwr (10) died in 1137 holding only the single commote of Caeo in Ystrad Tywi in the eastern part of Cantref Mawr. His wife Gwenllian had been executed by the Normans in 1136 so their surviving young children were left as orphans. The sons slowly set out to recover the lands which their grandfather Rhys ap Tewdwr (8) had once ruled. The eldest Anarawd was killed in 1143.

Gruffydd's son, Rhys, had been born in the winter of 1132 in Caeo. He was brought up under the guidance of his elder brother Cadell. At the age of only 14 in 1146 he helped his brother to successfully attack and take Llansteffan Castle[48] followed by the capture of Carmarthen in 1150. In 1152 Cadell was ambushed and badly injured out hunting in Dyfed; he never fully recovered and entrusted his lands to his younger brothers, Maredudd and Rhys, after going on a pilgrimage to Rome. Maredudd then died in 1155 aged only 25 so Rhys was left to recover his family's honour. Between 1155 and his death in 1197 Rhys recovered nearly all the original lands of Deheubarth by his brilliant tactics and cunning diplomacy. During his lifetime he was known as Prince of Deheubarth or Prince of South Wales, although in the 1184 Charter of Strata Florida Abbey he is called *Walliarum princeps* meaning Prince of Wales.

---

46 DL Baker-Jones: *Edwinsford CH (1968) p17; Dictionary of Welsh Biography (1959)*

47 Francis Jones: *THSC (1986-7) p72-4*

48 Peniarth MS 20

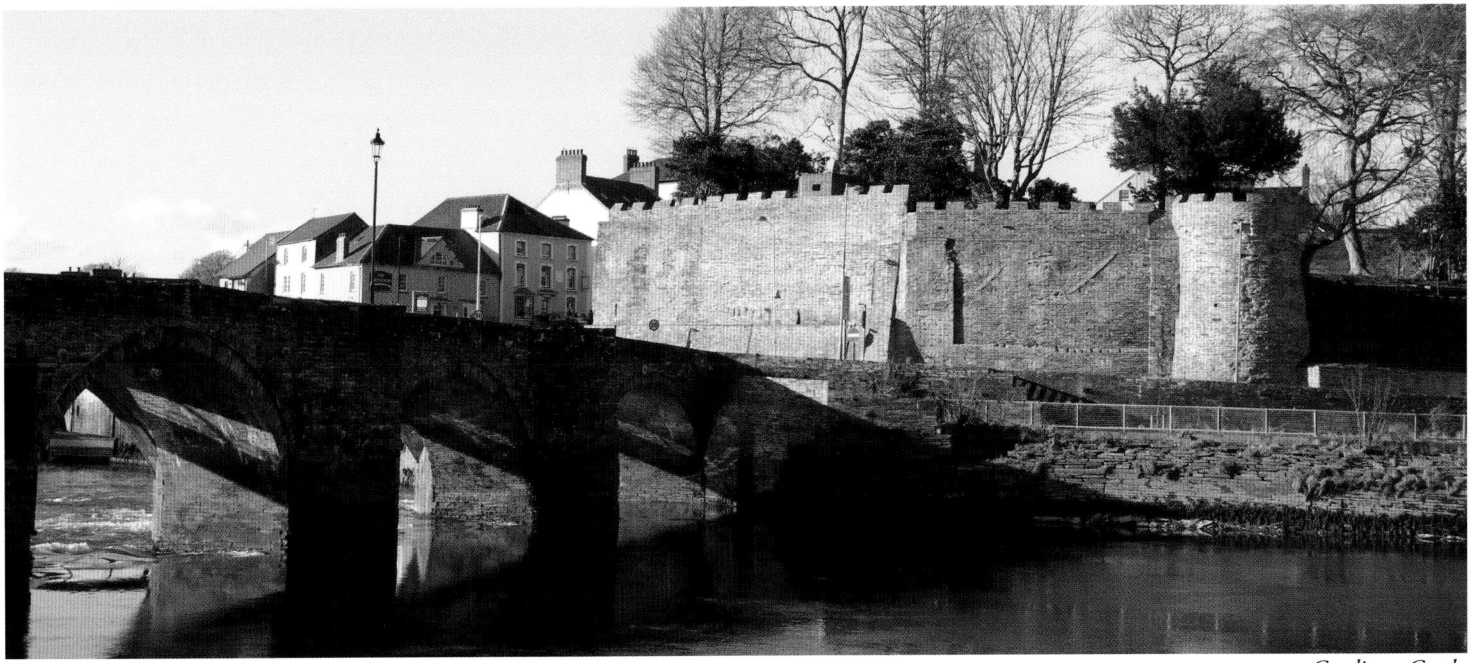

Cardigan Castle

So Rhys became sole ruler of Deheubarth in 1155 shortly after the death of King Stephen (ruler 1135-54). The new King Henry II (ruler 1154-89) was the first Plantagenet King of England, who married Eleanor of Aquitaine (d1205); she had been the Queen of France married to Louis VII who had divorced her. Henry was a powerful ruler unlike Stephen and spent much of his reign fighting the French to keep and expand his Angevin empire in France. In Wales Henry needed to keep Rhys and other rulers in check. He invaded Deheubarth in 1158 and again in 1163 in between his soldiering in France and on each occasion Rhys was obliged to do homage to Henry. In 1165 there was a Welsh uprising and Henry invaded Gwynedd first but had to retreat and cruelly had one of Rhys's sons blinded by his blacksmith. In retaliation Rhys attacked Cardigan Castle and burned the town which was a momentous achievement in the recovery of Deheubarth. In 1171 Rhys returned to Cardigan (Aberteifi) and rebuilt the castle in stone as well as the town.

Rhys became the leading Prince in Wales in 1170 on the death of Owain Gwynedd in North Wales. Henry was distracted by his battles in France, his serious quarrel with Archbishop Thomas Becket who four of his French Knights murdered in 1170 in Canterbury Cathedral, and by the need to invade Ireland in 1171. He wanted to make peace with Rhys and did so in 1172 by receiving tribute from him and by appointing Rhys as Royal Justiciar over South Wales, which meant he acted as the King's deputy in all matters relating to the Welsh affairs of that area. Rhys honoured their agreement until Henry's death in 1189.

Rhys had two principal homes, Cardigan Castle which he had rebuilt in 1171, and Dinefwr[49]. It is thought that he also rebuilt Carreg Cennen Castle. In 1176 he held an early type of eisteddfod in Cardigan Castle with competitors from all over Wales for two main competitions for poetry and music. His support for the arts, bards and musicians

[49] Gerald Morgan: *Dinefwr p17-20* comments that it is reasonable to suggest that Rhys built Dinefwr Castle although the Red Book of Hergest only says "1163: Rhys ap Gruffydd took Cantref Mawr, which was a large district, along with land that was at Dinefwr." Some historians think that the idea of Dinefwr as an ancient centre of power is probably a myth and that it was The Lord Rhys who used the myth as propaganda to give himself more status in Deheubarth. See also *Eurig Davies: The Dinefwr Family as Patrons of the Bards CA (2013) p16-20* and Roger Turvey: *King, Prince or Lord? CA (1994) p5-18*

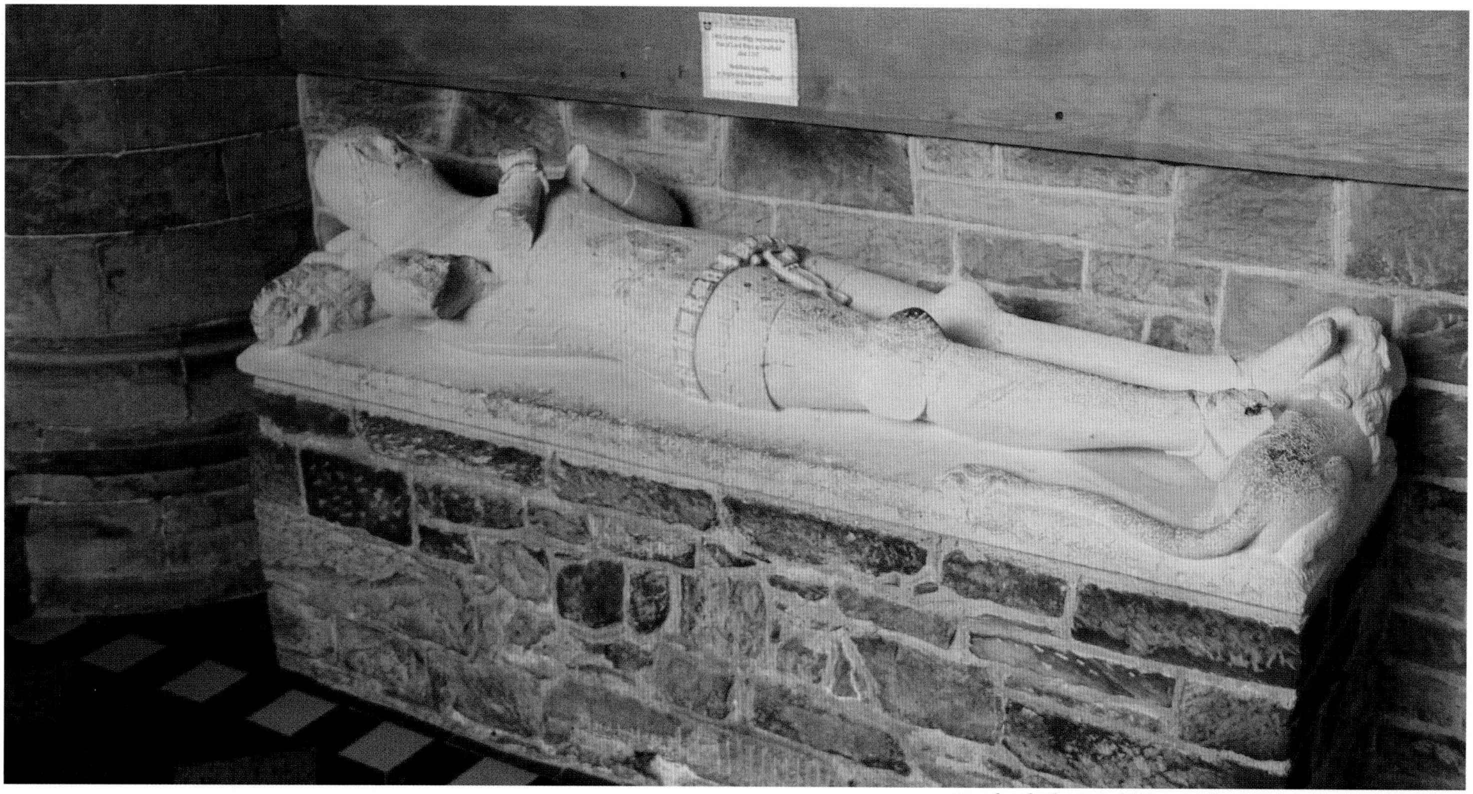

Tomb of The Lord Rhys in St Davids Cathedral 2016

also extended to clerics. He founded Talley Abbey (*Talyllychau*)[50] the first Premonstratensian abbey in Wales (see Chapter 29.1) and he also founded a Cistercian nunnery at Llanllyr in 1180 which came into the ownership of the Lloyd family[51]. He was the patron of abbeys in Whitland (*Alba Domus*) and Strata Florida (*Ystrad-Flur*) where the Chronicle of the Princes was compiled. In 1188 Rhys entertained his cousin Gerald of Wales with Archbishop Baldwin on their journey around Wales to raise support for the Third Crusade.

When King Richard I (ruler 1189-99) came to the throne Rhys considered he was no longer bound by his agreement with King Henry II and he attacked a number of neighbouring Norman lordships and in 1196 captured a number of castles including Carmarthen. Sadly Rhys and his sons fought each other during the last 10 years of his life, internecine warfare being a common problem in Welsh families. Rhys died in the south tower in Cardigan Castle in 1197 and "...a great pestilence ...killed innumerable people and many of the nobility and many princes, and spared none. That year, four days before May Day, died Rhys ap Gruffydd, Prince of Deheubarth and unconquered head of all Wales."[52] Rhys died having been excommunicated some years previously by the Bishop of St Davids over the alleged theft of some horses. Before he could be buried in St Davids Cathedral his corpse had to be scourged in posthumous penance.

---

50 He transferred to Talley Abbey the former lands and economic power of the religious community of St Teilo at Llandeilo—see William Strange: *The Early Medieval Community at Llandeilo Fawr CA (2012) p9*

51 David Lewis: *Dolaucothi and Brunant p470-472*

52 Peniarth MS 20

Having succeeded in recovering and reconstituting the kingdom of Deheubarth during 50 years of strife, sadly Rhys's lands were to be the subject of inter-family feuds between his sons and grandsons; the kingdom of Deheubarth was never again to be united under one Welsh native ruler. His daughter, Catrin, married Cydifor ap Dinawal, Lord of Castell Hywel, who was a valiant supporter of Rhys in battle. Both Cydifor and Catrin were direct descendants of the great Rhodri Mawr (6) and through them the famous Lloyd family pedigree emerged.

Another daughter, Gwenllian (c1178-1236)(14), married Ednyfed Fychan ap Cynwrig of Llansadwrn, Anglesey (c1170-1246) (17), Seneschal (Chief Minister) of Gwynedd under Llywelyn the Great. Ednyfed was described as "Fychan" meaning small or younger (and the word from which the later surname Vaughan is derived). It seems that Ednyfed was a fierce warrior and in one battle he decapitated three English lords and brought the heads to Llywelyn who told him to change his family coat of arms to show three heads. Gwenllian was his second wife and bore him several children including:

(a) Goronwy ap Ednyfed Fychan (c1200-1268)(18) who took over as Seneschal of Gwynedd and through whom the Royal Tudor dynasty was founded; this was one of the factors which enabled Henry VII to gain Welsh support at the Battle of Bosworth Field in 1485, and

(b) Gruffydd ap Ednyfed Fychan (19). The latter was born in Henglawdd, Cilcain in modern Denbighshire in about 1195 and married Gwenllian, daughter of Hywel. One of their children was Catherine (Catrin)(c1238-c1259)(21) who married Philip of Rhydodyn (22) and it was through them that the Williams family pedigree continued[53].

4.6 Gerald of Wales (1145-1223)

Gerald of Wales (15) (*Giraldus Cambrensis*) was the grandson of Princess Nest (11), the daughter of Rhys ap Tewdwr (8). He was three quarters Norman and one quarter Welsh. His life's ambition was to be appointed Bishop of St Davids and to be consecrated by the Pope as Archbishop of Wales with the St Davids see being independent of Canterbury. He was offered and refused four bishoprics in Wales and Ireland and preferred to remain Archdeacon of Brecon instead. He was a prolific author in Latin and is one of the best original sources for 12th century information and background detail on Welsh society. In his "*Journey through Wales*" undertaken in 1188 with Baldwin, Archbishop of Canterbury, to gain support for the Third Crusade[54] he gives a wonderful description of Wales and its social and economic condition during the reign of Henry II. In 1193 he finished his work "*The Description of Wales*" in which he describes the lives and the good and bad points of the Welsh themselves from his own mainly Norman viewpoint.

Hence he says[55] that: "The Welsh people are light and agile. They are fierce rather than strong and totally dedicated to the practice of arms... The whole population lives almost entirely on oats and the produce of their herds, milk, cheese and butter. They eat plenty of meat, but little bread. They pay no attention to commerce, shipping or industry... They are passionately devoted to their freedom and to the defence of their country...Their sole interest in life consists of caring for their horses and keeping their weapons in good order...Everyone's home is open to all, for the Welsh generosity and hospitality are the greatest of all virtues...Both men and women cut their hair short...Both sexes take great care of their teeth...The men shave their beards leaving only their moustaches...The Welsh are very sharp and intelligent...They are quicker-witted and more shrewd than any other Western people... Nature has endowed the Welsh with great boldness in speaking and great confidence in answering no matter what the circumstances may be...They do not live in towns, villages or castles, but lead a solitary existence deep in the woods. They content themselves with wattled huts on the edges of the forest...Most of the land is used for pasture... They cultivate very little of it, growing a few flowers and sowing a plot here and there. They use oxen to pull their ploughs and carts, sometimes in pairs but more often four at a time...When they marry

---

53 Darell Wolcott suggests that Philip (22)(bc1230) had a son called Philip Fychan ap Philip (bc1260) but none of the other pedigrees show this link: *ancientwalesstudies.org/id125*

54 King Richard the Lionheart raised huge sums of money in 1189 and sold castles, lands and sinecures to finance the Third Crusade (1189-92) which succeeded in recapturing Acre and Jaffa from Saladin but not Jerusalem.See Christopher Tyerman: *How to plan a Crusade (2015)* explaining the crusaders' motivation of knightly chivalry and killing infidels in the name of Christ with Papal blessing

55 Gerald of Wales: *The Description of Wales p233 et seq*

Tomb of Gerald of Wales in St Davids Cathedral 2016

or go on a pilgrimage or on the advice of the clergy make a special effort to amend their ways, they give a donation of one tenth of all their worldly goods, cattle, sheep and other livestock…called the Great Tithe…two thirds of it to the church in which they were baptised and the remaining third to the bishop of their diocese….You may never find anyone worse than a bad Welshman, but you will certainly never find anyone better than a good one.."

The less good points included: "The Welsh people rarely keep their promises…they are particularly stubborn…it is the habit of the Welsh to steal anything they can lay their hands on and to live on plunder, theft and robbery…their sole idea of tactics is either to pursue their opponents or else to run away from them…The Welsh people are more keen to own land and extend their holdings than any other I know. To achieve this they are prepared to dig up boundary ditches, to move stones showing the edges of fields…Quarrels and lawsuits result, murders and arson, not to mention frequent fratricides. Things are made worse by the ancient Welsh custom of brothers dividing between them the property which they have….The Welsh have gradually learnt from the English and the Normans how to manage their weapons and to use horses in battle…There are three things which are causing the ruin of the Welsh people and preventing them, generation after generation, from ever enjoying prosperity. The first is that all their sons, both legitimate and illegitimate, insist upon taking equal shares in their patrimony. One result of this…is that they not infrequently kill each other. The second is that they entrust the upbringing of their sons to important people of good family in the neighbourhood…Thirdly through their natural pride and obstinacy they will not order themselves as other nations do so successfully, but refuse to accept the rule and dominion of one single king….The English are striving for power, the Welsh for freedom; the English are fighting for material gain, the Welsh to avoid a disaster; the English soldiers are hired mercenaries, the Welsh are defending their homeland."

4.7 Welsh feudal system in Caeo and Maenor Deilo

Society was divided by status[56] which was determined by birth and lineage as Gerald of Wales noted. The difference between being free and unfree was enormous. Freemen (*uchelwyr*) were superior and regarded themselves as nobles despite in reality often being no more than peasant proprietors. While they still owed their lord military service often for six weeks annually, they owned their land by lineage, their status was the source of their judicial standing and their kinsmen were the guarantors of this status in practice. They owed fealty or homage to lords or the King but they themselves were lords of men with under-tenants and villeins owing duties to them. The unfree villeins (*bilain*) could be sold or left by will of their lord and were often dependent tenants who did not own their land but were tied to it and were bound to work for their lord. Slaves were still bought and sold in Wales whether native born or foreign. The servile peasantry included both slaves (*caeth)* and bondmen (*taeog, bilain, mab aillt*). In the Domesday Book for example some 17 per cent of the population of north-east Wales were classified as slaves or oxmen while two thirds of the rest were villeins, and this status distinction continued throughout most of the Middle Ages.

In the 11th century Caeo and Maenor Deilo would have been a backward and economically poor society. During the early Middle Ages it would have been an upland with forests and thick woods, part of the Caeo and Glyncothi forest. The local lords or the monks at Talley Abbey would have defended their hunting rights since the grant of tithes of hunting and honey were important income for them; on the other hand the local peasants would want freedom of access to the forests and nearby pastures so communal disagreements were common. By 1300 the population of Wales[57] had grown to some 300,000 compared with 4.6 million for England; this led to land shortage and land hunger. The Black Death and several epidemics of the plague changed society very substantially during the next century.

As we have seen in Chapter 1.3, at about the time of the Norman Conquest the hundred of Cantref Mawr was divided into seven commotes (*cwmwd*): Mallaen, Caeo, Maenor Deilo, Cetheiniog, Widigada, Mabelfyw, and Mabudrud. Caeo included the modern parishes of Llansawel and Cynwyl Gaeo. Maenor Deilo comprised the modern parishes of Llansadwrn, Talley and Llandyfeisant (including Dinefwr).

Cwmwd Caeo[58] was subdivided into *maenorau* (multiple estates) which included the lands which would later become the Edwinsford Estate called *Y Faenor Isaf* (the Lowest Maenor). A lesser administrative subdivision was the *"gwestfa"* meaning literally the place (*ma*) whose nobility had a duty to provide the sovereign and his court when they were travelling on circuit around his kingdom with food and lodging (*gwest*)[59]; the dictionary defines *gwestfa* as "a periodical obligation upon a vassal to contribute to the reception of the Prince on his own circuit". Later when holdings were too small to provide gwest this duty was converted into a food render which was to be delivered to the king's court (*llys*). Later this was commuted to a cash payment (*gwestfa)* and this term was also used to apply to the particular area whose responsibility it was to pay such sum to the king.

In Caeo there were nine gwestfa areas of different sizes. Each of the nine was responsible for cash payments of 53s 4d per annum, which was based on one mark payable on the four quarter days. Each gwestfa district was in turn subdivided into five *rhandiroedd* (sharelands) and from each of these 10s 8d was payable[60]. This equal cash burden of ancient origin on all gwestfa districts of different sizes was probably the result of a reassessment by The Lord Rhys in the 12th century following the depopulation of parts of the area devastated by former attacks from the Normans and more recent Welsh attacks by the men of Gwynedd and Powys. It is unclear whether this change resulted in a more equitable burden on the individual gwestfa areas. Originally the payments within each gwestfa area were raised from the freemen, bond tenants and villeins living in such areas. The latter paid for every 4d of the Lent quarterly payment of gwestfa the value of one bushel of oats each worth 1d. According to the Welsh law books *dofraeth* was the ancient render for the billeting of the king's retainers on the unfree

---

56 RR Davies p115-138

57 RR Davies p147

58 I have sourced from Glanville RJ Jones: *Studia Celtica XXVIII (1994) Tir Telych, the Gwestfâu of Cynwyl Gaeo and Cwmwd Caeo p81-95*

59 Prof TM Charles-Edwards: *Early Irish and Welsh Kingship (1993) p376-8*

60 W Rees: *South Wales and the Marches 1284-1415 (1924) p222-7*

communities of the commote, but in Cwmwd Caeo before its commutation it had become the provision of horses for the king and his officials. The imposition of a render of 40 bushels of oats or 40d on each gwestfa district suggests that every one of these areas was occupied by at least one bond community and two of the largest such communities were in the gwestfâu of *Y Faenor Isaf* and *Tre Cynwyl Gaeo.*

This system of taxing the local tenants continued for centuries in practice and by the 19th century none of the local tenants could understand what the gwestfa was or why they were paying it, so they rebelled because they thought that the local collector was putting the cash in his own pocket.[61]

4.8 Llywelyn the Great (c1172-1240)

We have seen that on the death of The Lord Rhys in 1197 Deheubarth was torn apart by strife between his sons Gruffydd, Maelgwn, Rhys Gryg and Maredudd, and his grandsons who King John (ruler 1199-1216) played off against each other to prevent any one of them gaining full control over their father's lands.

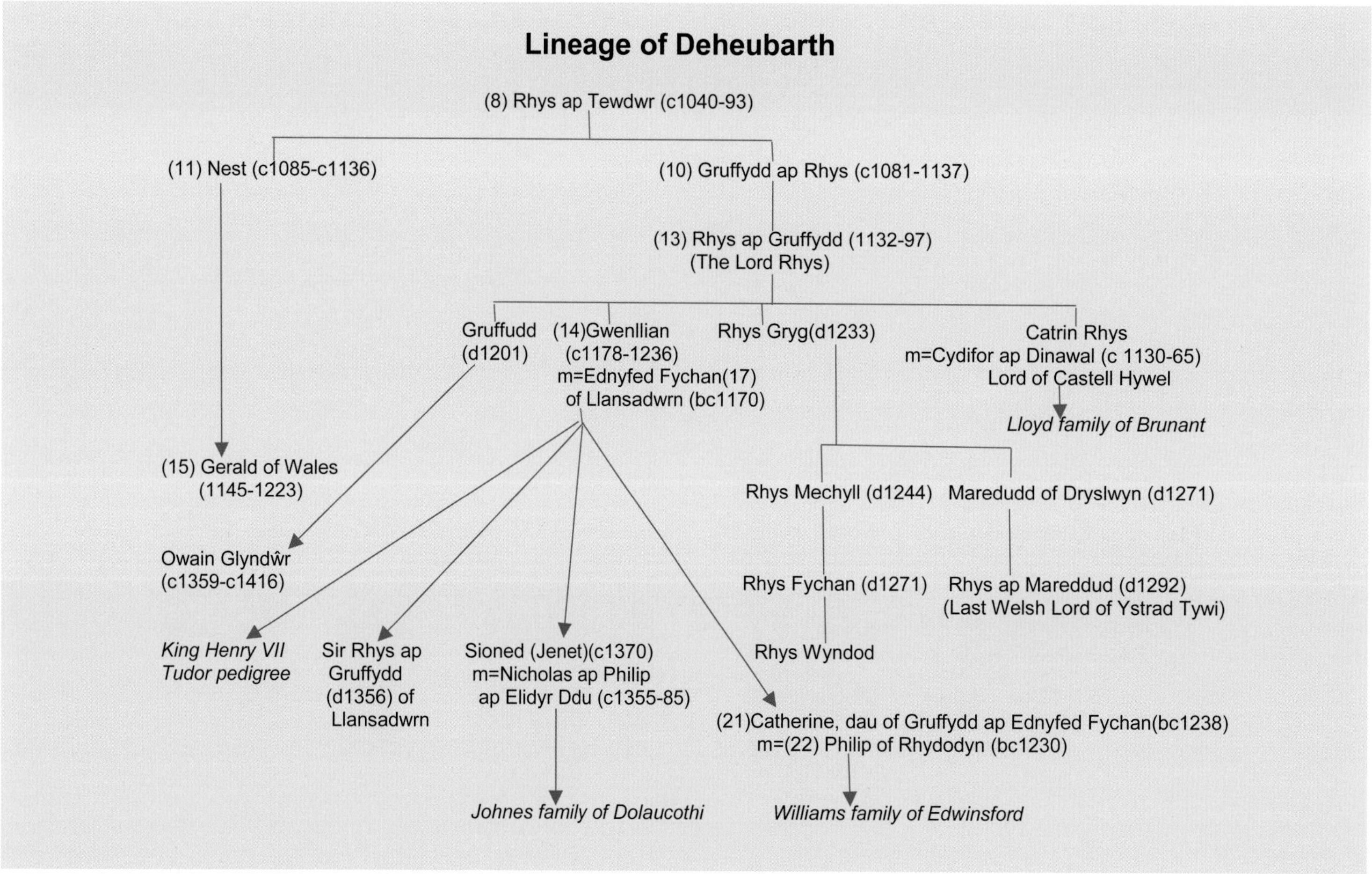

61 David Lewis: *Dolaucothi and Brunant p419-421*

Meantime Llywelyn ap Iorwerth, Prince of Gwynedd and descended from the senior line of Rhodri Mawr (6) was slowly becoming the de facto ruler over most of Wales. He dominated Wales for more than 40 years and was one of only two Welsh rulers to be called "the Great" albeit after his death. In 1205 he married Joan, the daughter of King John, but by 1210 his good relations with John had deteriorated and John invaded Gwynedd; Llywelyn was forced to come to terms and pay a large tribute to him. John who was King of England and Lord of Ireland was also Duke of Aquitaine having inherited the Angevin Empire (including Normandy, Anjou, Maine and Touraine from his father Henry II and Aquitaine from his mother) but he managed to lose most of it within five years to his arch enemy Philip II, King of France.

King John's poor relations with Pope Innocent III has resulted in him placing the whole country under a Papal Interdict in 1208 and excommunicating John in 1209; John retaliated by confiscating more and more Church property. With plenty of funds in his Exchequer he was intent on imposing his brutal discipline on the errant Welsh and Irish. His Barons who had estates both in England and in France were badly affected by the loss of French lands and became rebellious as did the Welsh rulers including the descendants of the Lord Rhys in Deheubarth.

Magna Carta

On 9 May 1215 in an attempt to keep the City of London as allies, John issued a Mayoral Charter granting "our barons of our city of London" permission to elect all future mayors and confirming all the City's other privileges and liberties. But the City decided to support the rebels.

On Sunday 17 May 2015 the Barons led by Robert Fitzwalter (Lord of Castle Baynard, the City of London's procurator and hereditary standard bearer and leader of the City militia) and assisted by the Mayor of London, William Hardell, were welcomed through the open gates of the City of London. John caved in and on 10 June he came to Runnymede.

As David Starkey[62] has shown, the Magna Carta which was agreed at Runnymede on 15 June 1215 and later sealed with the Great Seal only lasted until 24 August 1215 when a Papal Bull by Pope Innocent III declared it "null and void of all validity for ever" and in addition excommunicated many of the Barons. The Barons started a civil war against the King and continued to retain control of the City of London. They then went further and offered the throne to Prince Louis the eldest son of Philip II of France and invited Louis to invade with an army. He did so in May 1216 and was welcomed into the City of London, a shameful act of treason[63]. Fortunately for the country on 18 October 1216 John died. He was succeeded by his nine year old son Henry III (ruler 1216-72) who was very well advised by William Marshal, Earl of Pembroke, who saved the House of Anjou and the Magna Carta. On his advice Magna Carta was reissued by Henry III on 12 November 1216 with some changes and later the same year Louis was defeated by Marshall and renounced the Englist throne. The Magna Carta was reissued again on 11 February 1225 by Henry III with a number of additional changes, and again in 1237 and 1253. Edward I (ruler 1272-1307) also reissued it in 1297.

From the Welsh perspective Magna Carta[64] was particularly important at the time because Chapter 56 in the 1215 and 1216 Charters provided that: "If we have disseised or kept out Welshmen from lands or liberties or other things without the legal judgment of their peers in England or in Wales, they shall be immediately restored to them; and if a dispute arises over this, then let it be decided in the March by the judgment of their peers….for holdings in Wales according to the law of Wales….Welshmen shall do the same to us and ours." Chapter 58 in both Charters stated that: "We shall give back at once the son of Llywelyn and all the hostages from Wales and the charters that were handed over to us as security for peace." Hence the support given to the Barons by Llywelyn and his Welsh supporters paid off.

---

[62] David Starkey: *Magna Carta (2015) p164, 182, 206, 226-230*

[63] Dominic Reid: *Lord Mayor's Show 800 Years 1215-2015 (2015) p22*

[64] Only four provisions of the Magna Carta survive today as law: Chapter 1(A)—the Church of England is free with undiminished rights and liberties; Chapter 13— the City of London shall have all its ancient liberties and free customs (the Mayor of London signed the Charter); Chapter 39 (habeas corpus) "no free man shall be arrested or imprisoned…except by lawful judgment of his peers or by the law of the land"; and Chapter 40 (due process) "to no one will we …refuse or delay right or justice".

In 1216, after years of wrangling amongst the heirs of The Lord Rhys, the lands of Deheubarth were partitioned at an assembly at Aberdyfi convoked by Llywelyn along the traditional Welsh custom of partibility. The youngest claimant divided the land; and the eldest was then given the first choice of the divisions so made. Dinefwr including Ystrad Tywi went to Rhys Gryg (d1233) but the lands of Caeo and Llandovery went to Maelgwn. Deheubarth had become[65] a collection of petty principalities living by grace, or under the thumb, of either the King of England or the Prince of Gwynedd, its rulers being no more than "puny chiefs".

In 1218 Henry III concluded the Treaty of Worcester with Llywelyn who paid homage to Henry and was permitted to retain all his lands but on condition that Cardigan and Carmarthen castles were held for Henry until he came of age; they were returned to the Crown in 1226. In 1230 Llywelyn arranged a marriage between his heir Dafydd ap Llywelyn and Isabella, daughter of William de Braose, Lord of Abergavenny and Builth. However, William de Braose was found in Llywelyn's bedchamber with his wife Joan (daughter of King John). Unsurprisingly Llywelyn had him hanged[66] but the marriage went ahead. By 1234 another truce had been signed between Llywelyn and Henry III, the Peace of Middle, which lasted until Llywelyn died. In 1238 he held a council in the Abbey at Strata Florida to force the Welsh princes including the descendants of The Lord Rhys in the former Deheubarth to swear fealty to his son Dafydd (c1212-46). It is thought that Llywelyn suffered a stroke in 1237 and he spent the last two years of his life in the Cistercian Abbey of Aberconwy which he had founded; he died in 1240[67].

Dafydd, who was the nephew of Henry III, paid homage to him in 1240 and was invested with the hereditary lands of his father Llywelyn and the title Prince of Gwynedd, but his rights to other lands were not granted so the descendants of The Lord Rhys in Deheubarth tried again to recover their former lands. Dafydd retaliated by invading the south and besieged Carmarthen and burnt the town; he died without heirs in 1246. In 1254 Henry III bestowed all his royal lands in Wales including Carmarthen to his son Edward.

4.9 Llywelyn the Last (c1223-82) and the Edwardian Settlement

Llywelyn ap Gruffudd was the grandson of Llywelyn the Great and the son of his eldest illegitimate son, Gruffudd, who had died in 1244 escaping from the Tower of London by falling from its walls. In 1247 he made peace with Henry III by the Treaty of Woodstock. He then defeated his rival brothers Owain and Dafydd and became sole ruler of Gwynedd. In 1256 Llywelyn invaded the south to secure the allegiance of the Welsh rulers including Rhys Fychan of Ystrad Tywi, grandson of Rhys Gryg, who sided with King Henry in the hope of retaining Dinefwr and surrounding lands. In 1257 the King's army was in Llandeilo when Rhys Fychan suddenly changed sides and supported the Welsh who heavily defeated the English in a skirmish sited at Coed Llathen and Cymerau thought to be near Broad Oak between Llandeilo and Carmarthen; it was the greatest defeat of an English force in Wales for very many years. Llywelyn forgave Rhys Fychan.

In 1258 Llywelyn proclaimed himself Prince of Wales (*Princeps Wallie*) and the other Welsh princes and rulers swore fealty to him including Rhys Fychan and the other descendants of The Lord Rhys in Deheubarth. In the same year Henry III was forced by his barons under the leadership of his brother in law, Simon de Montfort (1208-65), to agree to the harsh terms of the Provisions of Oxford under which he effectively surrendered control of his realm to the council of barons. This led to civil war and eventually de Montfort, who is remembered as a champion of liberties, was defeated and killed at the battle of Evesham in 1265 owing to the military prowess of Prince Edward (the future King Edward I, ruler 1272-1307). Llywelyn had supported de Montfort who recognised him as Prince of Wales and Llywelyn was engaged to Simon's daughter, Eleanor (first cousin of Edward and a princess of the House of Plantagenet). By 1267 Henry had agreed to recognise Llywelyn as Prince of Wales by the Treaty of Montgomery and in return Llywelyn paid tribute to the King of 25,000 marks in annual instalments of 3,000 marks. Llywelyn was now the undisputed predominant ruler in native Wales. Since the Norman Conquest no Welsh ruler including his grandfather had achieved such authority.

---

65 RR Davies p227; David Thorne: *The Cwmwd Physicians of Cantref Mawr CA 2015 p39-47*

66 Peniarth MS 20

67 The wonderful tale of Llywelyn killing his dog Gelert by mistake is almost certainly a myth

Edward I

Edward I was away on the last Crusade when his father died and he became King of England in 1272. By this time Rhys Wyndod was the ruler of Dinefwr, Carreg Cennen and Llandovery. Llywelyn refused to attend the coronation of Edward I or do homage to him and his bride to be, Eleanor, was imprisoned at Windsor Castle. This was an act of disloyalty Edward could not overlook. He declared Llywelyn a rebel in 1276 and invaded North Wales in 1277. Rhys Wyndod surrendered quickly and lost Dinefwr to the King while being allowed to retain two small commotes of Mallaen and Caeo. His cousin Rhys ap Maredudd switched sides to support the King and was allowed to keep Dryslwyn and Newcastle Emlyn. In 1277 Llywelyn had to submit to the inevitable under the Treaty of Aberconwy under which he was allowed to keep part of Gwynedd and his title Prince of Wales but had to give up all other lands. Edward I and his Queen did however attend Llywelyn's wedding to Eleanor in Worcester Cathedral and the King was magnanimous enough to meet the costs of the wedding feast[68]. The Treaty was however a humiliation and Llywelyn had made a gross political misjudgement and lost his former position. Revolt was inevitable.

By 1282 the Welsh rulers had had enough of Edward I's taxes and high handed treatment. The rebellion started in March and was quickly joined by many as a massive protest against English rule. Rhys ap Maredudd of Ystrad Tywi decided to support Edward who was determined to suppress the rebellion and no expense was spared. It was not a revolt the Welsh could ever win against such odds and military power. Llywelyn was killed in an ambush on 11 December 1282 near Cilmeri close to Builth. His severed head was sent to London and was said to be still on display at the Tower of London some 15 years later. It is thought that his body was buried at Abaty Cwmhir. Dafydd who was Llywelyn's heir carried on the struggle but was captured in 1283 and hung, drawn and quartered. Rhys Wyndod died in prison while Rhys ap Mareddud was rewarded for his loyalty by being able to retain the commotes of Caeo and Mallaen and Dryslwyn castle but had to give up Dinefwr to the Crown. Subsequently the royal justiciar of south Wales provoked Rhys by bringing charges against him and he revolted in 1286 and captured Llandovery, Dinefwr and Carreg Cennen castles. This led to him being declared a rebel and he was captured in 1292 and hung, drawn and quartered as a traitor. So ended native Welsh rule in Deheubarth.

Monument at Cilmeri, Builth near the site where Llywelyn the Last was killed

68 RR Davies p341

Carreg Cennen Castle c1740 print

Edward I's "settlement" in 1284 was the final act in the conquest of Wales. Edward appropriated the houses of the Gwynedd dynasty, removed all their insignia and regalia, and melted down their seals and treasures. Hostages were taken, castles garrisoned to secure peace, and new castles built in stone. Under the Statute of Wales (or the Statute of Rhuddlan) in 1284 royal lands in north Wales were amalgamated into the new counties of Flint and Gwynedd with English governance introduced under a justiciar to govern the areas on behalf of the Crown, the Marcher lordship lands being left alone. Later the counties of Anglesey, Caernarfon and Merioneth were established. In the south a similar system of administration was introduced with new counties (shires) for Carmarthen and Cardigan, each having a Sheriff, twice annual sheriff's tourns, two coroners per shire, and monthly county courts. The Welsh commotes were retained for local administration purposes such as collection of dues etc. Wisely Edward retained much of Welsh law and local customs in civil matters including the custom of partibility on inheritance, but he insisted on English criminal law applying. Although the Statute applied only to the royal lands in north Wales it was also imposed in part on those parts of native Wales in the south acquired by the Crown. In 1284 the native monks of Talyllychau (Talley) were expelled[69] to make room for "others of the English tongue who are able and willing to observe the religious life" and Edward made sure that the Welsh church and its lands and finances were brought much more under royal and clerical control from Canterbury.

---

69 HM Colvin: *The White Canons in England (1951) p237-8*

Carmarthen Castle

The building of Carmarthen Castle[70] was probably started in c1106. During the ensuing armed conflicts between the English Crown and the Welsh Princes of Cantref Mawr over the next three centuries it changed hands on several occasions and was partially burnt down with the town of Carmarthen more than once. The castle was destroyed by Llywelyn the Great in 1215 and rebuilt. In 1405 the town was taken by and the castle destroyed again by Owain Glyndŵr. Under the 1284 Statute of Rhuddlan the Crown forfeited the captured lands and Cantref Mawr was merged with the Lordship of Carmarthen to form the new county of Carmarthenshire. Carmarthen Castle became the centre of administrative government[71] for Carmarthenshire and Cardiganshire as well as for the Marcher Lordships overseen by the Justiciar of South Wales. The Crown's civil service and its officials were based in the Castle which also served as a gaol and had a courthouse.

The "Englishry" included the Castle itself plus its own demesne lands and Carmarthen borough. The "Welshry" included the commotes of Widigada, Elfed and Derllys (*comitatus Wallensium*) where native Welsh law and custom was applied. In Carmarthenshire two systems applied side by side. In the "Welshry" where the residents were almost entirely natives, the Welsh county court sat in Carmarthen monthly to deal with minor crimes.

The officials of the court included the beadle (*rhingyll*), *maer* (mayor), serjeants of the peace (*ceisiaid*) and master serjeant (*pencais*). Into this court were paid fines and dues of cattle, for transporting timber and stone, for quarrying for castles, and pannage for the right to feed swine in the woodlands of the commote. In the "English county" or "Englishry" of Carmarthen the new administration rules applied. The chief royal officer for both parts of Carmarthenshire was the Justiciar whose headquarters were in Carmarthen castle. The court of great sessions was held in Carmarthen in addition to the Welsh and English county courts, the court of obligations for petty debt and petty sessions for minor crime.Over time a Constable of the Castle was appointed who reported to the Justiciar. The Chamberlain who was responsible for financial issues and the exchequer also reported to the Justiciar. The Justiciar's Mansion was within the Castle. Later the Justiciar was often an absentee aristocrat who relied on his Deputy who was usually a trusted Welshman. So for example Gruffydd ap Nicholas of Dinefwr (c1385-c1460) acted as the Deputy of Henry V's brother, Humphrey Duke of Gloucester, and ruled Carmarthenshire almost like a despotic king, and Sir Rhys ap Thomas KG (1449-1525) held all three offices of Justiciar, Chamberlain and Constable and rebuilt the Justiciar's Mansion in grand style.

The Black Death plague came to Carmarthen by river boats in 1347 and caused enormous devastation and the plague pit for mass burials is near the town centre. In the Middle Ages Carmarthen town was known as Llanteulyddog (after St Teulyddog) and was one of the seven main religious sees in Dyfed; in about 1110 the Benedictine Priory of St Peter was formed later to be replaced with the Augustinian Priory of St John and St Teulyddog near the river. By 1284 the Franciscan friars had built their Grey Friars friary as well which was eventually dissolved in 1538 by Henry VIII.

After the Acts of Union of 1536 and 1543 and the removal of many judicial cases to the Council for the Marches of Wales in Ludlow, Carmarthen Castle became much less important as an administrative centre of government. During the 1620s the Crown leased the Castle and its lands to the Phillips family of Cwmgwili who later sold the lease to the Vaughans of Golden Grove in 1639. During the Civil War the Castle served as the headquarters of the Royalists under Richard Vaughan, Earl of Carbery, but in October 1645 the Castle was surrendered to the Parliamentary forces. By 1660 the Castle had been mostly demolished. Thereafter it served as a gaol and then in 1789-92 John Nash the architect built a new gaol on the site, which was rebuilt again in 1868-72. In 1955 the new County Hall was finished and parts of the old Castle walls survive.

---

70 Neil Ludlow: *Carmarthen Castle (2014)*

71 Ralph Griffiths: *The Principality of Wales in the Later Middle Ages-The Structure and Personnel of Government 1 South Wales 1277-1536 (1972);* Ralph Griffiths: *The Making of Medieval Carmarthen CA (1973) p83-101;* Prys-Jones Vol I p147-150

Carmarthen Castle Great Gatehouse 2016

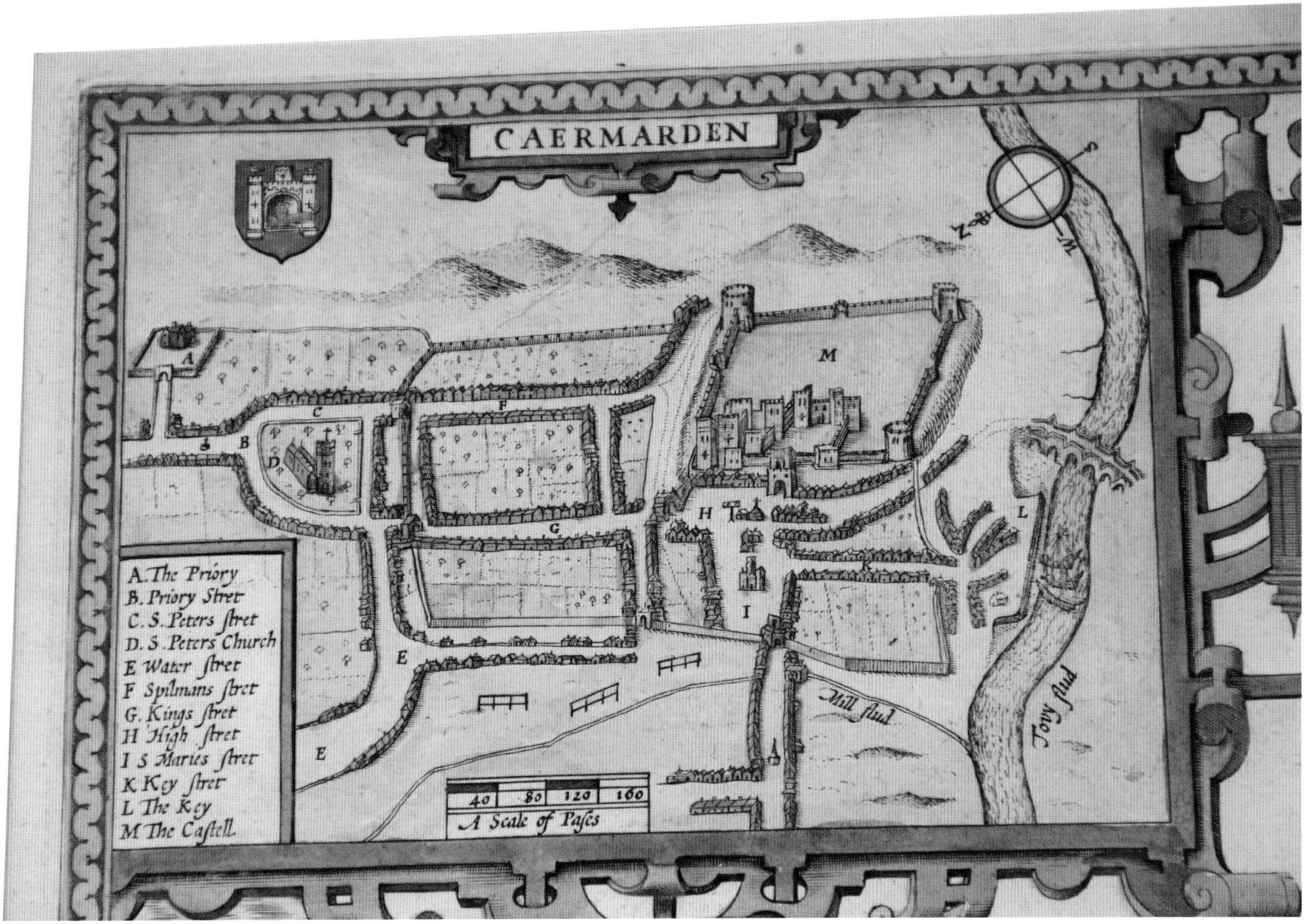

John Speed map of Carmarthen Castle 1610

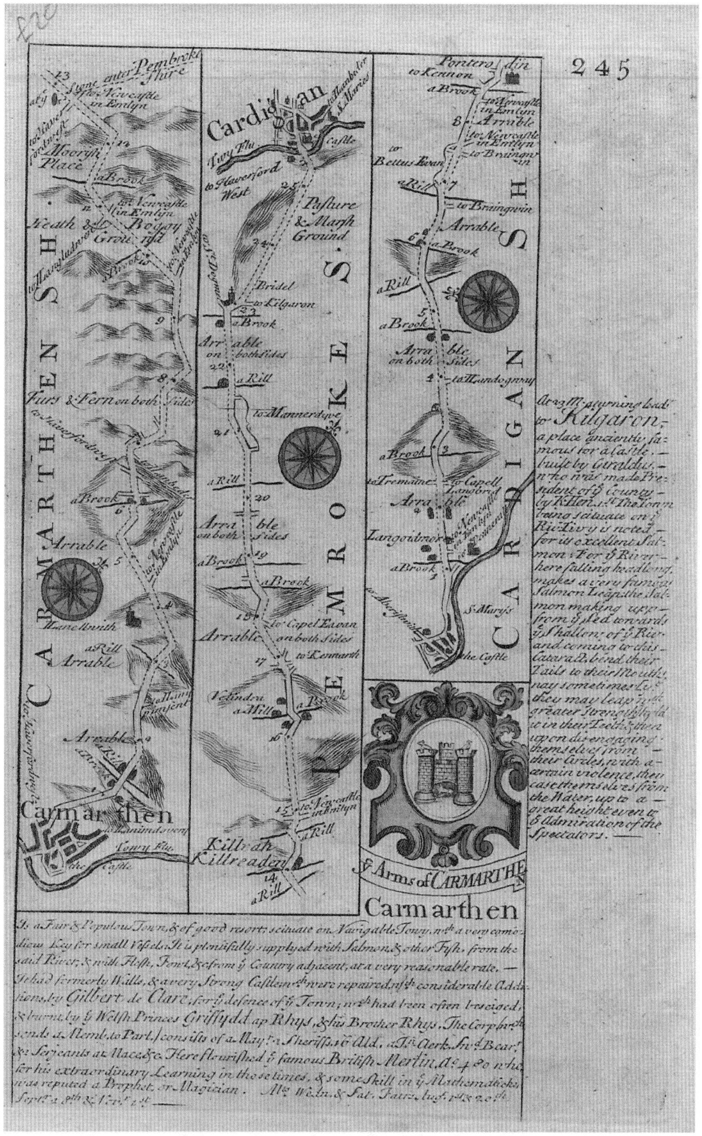

Emmanuel Bowen's roadmap for John Owen's Britannia Depicta c1720

In 1298 both Dryslwyn and Dinefwr (with the name Newtown) were granted borough status and Edward tried to colonise parts of Wales with English, Flemish and others to create "plantation boroughs".

Edward I took large swathes of lands to make royal hunting forests; Glyncothi royal forest[72] was one of them used by the Crown and its officials for leisure. The extermination of wild wolves[73] became necessary to protect the hunting and in Caeo wolf pits (*bleiddbwll*) were used to catch them. Cefn y Ffeiddiast (SN 668398) is close to the back road from Pumsaint to Caio and Cae'r Fleiddiast (SN 684456) is on the lands of Fronfelen[74] in Cwrt-y-Cadno; both names suggest that wolves were caught there.

In Scotland Sir William Wallace (c1270-1305) led the revolt against English rule in 1297 and defeated an English army at Stirling Bridge; he was later captured in 1305 and hung, drawn and quartered at Smithfield in the City of London. Some historians believe that although he was born in Scotland his family had Welsh origins and that his ancestors had fled to Scotland from the Welsh Marches. Unlike the Welsh who captured English castles and built their own, the Scots tended strategically to capture English castles and then destroy them which made it more difficult for the English to return. Robert the Bruce (1274-1329) was crowned King of Scotland in 1306 and led the Scots in their guerrilla war against Edward II, winning at Bannockburn near Stirling in 1314; as we shall see the Edwinsford, Clovelly and Hawthornden families were descended from his royal line (see Chapters 9.3, 9.4 and 18.3).

---

72 D Rees: *The Forest of Glyncothi CA (1995) p45-55*

73 Cledwyn Fychan: *The Wolf in Carmarthenshire CA (2009) p29-38;* David Lewis*: Dolaucothi Chp 41*

74 David Lewis: *Family Histories p323*

King Robert the Bruce

Stirling Castle near Bannockburn

4.10 Rhydodyn (Edwinsford)

As we have seen Cantref Mawr was divided into seven commotes (cwmwd) including Caeo and Maenor Deilo. Cwmwd Caeo was subdivided into *maenorau* (multiple estates) which included the lands which were called *Y Faenor Isaf* (the Lowest Maenor). This is the lovely scenic area of the Cothi valley of Lewis Glyn Cothi, bardic fame through which ran the Cothi river and its tributaries. Within this area encompassed by the modern parishes of Llansawel, Talley and Cynwyl Gaeo lay the Abbey of Talyllychau (Talley), the Crown manor of Talley with its seven granges and copyhold lands inheritable by the youngst son of the copyholder, the Forest of Glyn Cothi managed by the Royal foresters, and the lands of Rhydodyn; such lands were held at the beginning of the 13th century by Gruffydd ap Meurig Goch ap Cadwgan ap Cadifor, Lord of Caeo, ap Selyf ap Gwyn, Lord of Cilycwm.

The Williams family claim[75] that the original name of their ancestral home was "Rhyd Edwin" of which Edwinsford (the ford of Edwin) is a literal rendering and that this name was probably derived from Edwin (dc956), one of the three sons of Hywel Dda (7), who lost his life in battle at the ford across the Cothi. This is a lovely story but sadly there is no evidence to back it up. The name "Rhydodyn"[76] has been spelt in numerous ways over the centuries: "Ridodyn" in 1393 in a family document, "Rydodyn" in a 1526 mortgage, "Rhŷd Odyn" (Edwin's

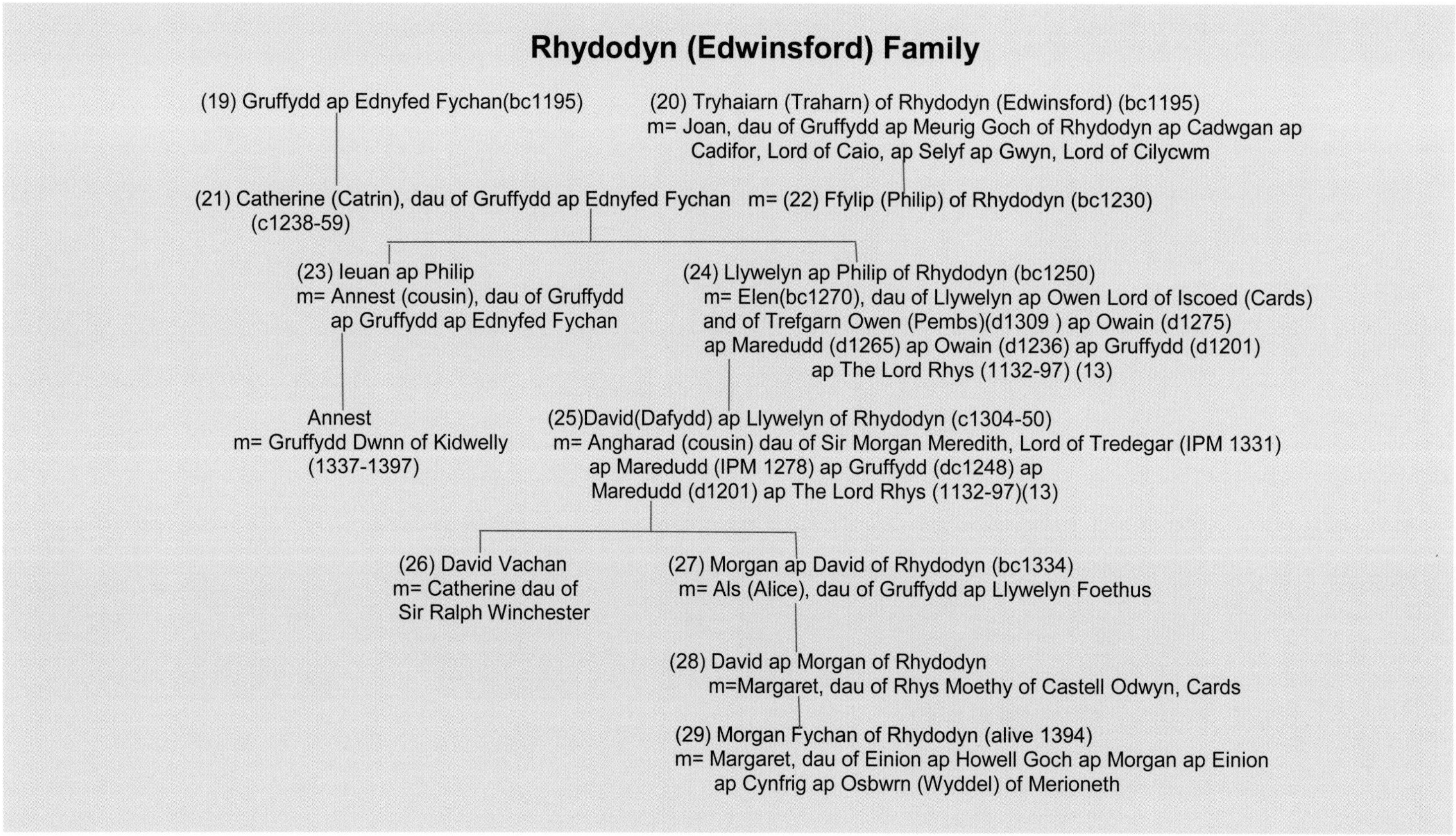

75 FDWD: *Annals p5;* Thomas Nicholas*: Annals p306*

76 Francis Jones: *THSC (1986) p62-65.* I have drawn heavily from this excellent and well researched paper relying on the family muniments deposited in 1946 in the NLW Edwinsford archives which I have also reviewed

Ford) in 1542, "Rhydodin" in 1648, and then "Rhyd Odwyn" in 1649, "Rhyd Odwynn" in 1651, "Rhyd Odwin" in 1659, "Rhydodwynne" in 1694, "Rhydodwynn" in 1701, and "Rhydodwin" in 1707. Then in 1710 the name "Edwinsford" first appeared in a document being a translation of Rhyd Odwin. "Edwins-foord" was possibly used to refer to the manor house (*plas*) while "Rhydodwyn issa" referred to the nearby home farm. A 1712 deed refers to "the capital messuage of Edwinsford formerly Rhydodwyn." The manor house is described in Chapters 5.4, 6.2 and 11.

Francis Jones has no doubt that the correct meaning of "Rhydodyn" is the "ford by the kiln" and certainly near the manor house there was a ford across the Cothi. But what of the reference to a kiln, and what type of kiln? The Welsh name "odyn" means a kiln or limekiln and the term "odyn" is used in other place names such as Pantyrodyn and Llwynyrodyn. I suspect we will never know the true origin.

Francis Jones describes the family well by saying: "the history of the Williamses illustrates the survival of an ancient family of *uchelwyr* throughout the uncertain middle ages, and its progression from the ranks of rural freeholders to the vanguard of Carmarthenshire's county families in post Tudor days. Throughout its earlier period it was an inward-looking family, content with acquiring properties in Llansawel and neighbouring parishes, stay-at-home squires, rarely venturing beyond those confines, and slowly but constantly increasing wealth and status, each generation being a re-enactment of its predecessor. Not until the 17th century did they become committed to affairs and concerns beyond the Cantref Mawr that had nurtured them."

Tryhaiarn (bc1195) and Llywelyn ap Philip (bc1250)

Tryhaiarn (Traharn)(20) married Joan, daughter and heiress of Gruffydd ap Meurig Goch of Rhydodyn (Edwinsford)[77] and thereby the Williams Edwinsford pedigree was founded in the early part of the 13th century. Joan inherited the Rhydodyn lands from her father and on her marriage Tryhaiarn settled at Rhydodyn (*y kynta a ddauth i Rydodyn*). It is stated[78] that Meurig Goch of Rhydodyn claimed descent from Selyf, King of Dyfed and that nineteen generations of the same family retained possession of Rhydodyn upto 1970. I can find no evidence for the validity of the claim of Joan's descent from a King of Dyfed.

Their son, Ffylip (Philip)(bc1230) (22) was born at Rhydodyn and married Catherine (Catrin)(c1238-59) (21), daughter of Gruffydd ap Ednyfed Fychan(bc1195)(19) who was Senescal to Llywelyn the Great of Gwynedd, and Lord of the manor of Llansadwrn close to Caeo.

Philip and Catherine had two sons: (1) Ieuan ap Philip, who married his cousin Annest, daughter of Gruffydd ap Gruffydd ap Ednyfed Fychan; their daughter married Gruffydd Dwnn of Kidwelly (1337-97) who was a royal officer, and (2) Llywelyn ap Philip of Rhydodyn (bc1250) (24). Llywelyn married Elen (bc1270), daughter of Llywelyn Lord of Iscoed in Cardiganshire and of Trefgarn in Pembrokeshire. Following the 1282 conquest of Wales by Edward I the Crown required trusted local Welsh speaking officials. Llywelyn ap Philip was appointed by the Crown to act as a minor local administrative official in Caeo reporting to his English absentee lord who was responsible to the King for the proper administration of the area.

The Ministers' Accounts show that Llywelyn acted as reeve (*prepositus*) of the commote of Caeo in 1286-9, reeve of the beadle of the commote of Maenor Deilo in 1304, and was responsible for the collection of yearly rents of *gwestfa, hildovraeth* and other dues, was constable of the commote of Maenor Deilo in 1306 as well as reeve of Llansawel in the commote of Caeo. So he had a minor trusted role in the locality.

His wife Elen was born in about 1270 in the Iscoed commote in what is now Cardiganshire. It is claimed by the Williams family[79] that the family descends "through Ellen, wife of Llewellyn ap Philip, from Henry I of England." I can find no evidence for this claim and indeed it seems clear that Elen's family descended from The Lord Rhys (13), Rhys ap Tewdwr (8), Hywel Dda (7) and Rhodri Mawr (6), which is probably how the Williams family also descended through the female line as we have seen.

77 Golden Grove MS

78 Eurig Davies: *Bardic Patronage by Some Carmarthenshire Families in the Middle Ages CA (2015) p16-18;* Francis Jones*: Historic Carmarthenshire Homes p61*

79 FDWD: *Annals p5* and repeated by DL Baker-Jones in *CH (1968) p17*

David ap Llewelyn (c1304-50)

Llewelyn and Elen had a son, Dafydd (David) ap Llewelyn of Rhydodyn (25), who took over his father's role and became a local magnate of some importance. He swore the required oath of fealty to the Prince of Wales in 1343 being described as a "Welsh baron by tenure", he served as *ringyll* (a Crown official) of the commote of Caeo in 1331-35, and in 1342-43 he led 819 Welsh archers to France to fight in Brittany for the Crown. So he was a trusted and loyal official.

Over the centuries the Edwinsford family prospered both financially and socially by marrying into some famous Welsh gentry families. David married into the Morgan family of Tredegar by taking as his spouse Angharad (bc1304)[80], his fourth cousin and the daughter and heiress of Sir Morgan ap Maredudd, who also descended in lineage from The Lord Rhys (13). So David followed his father and grandfather in marrying descendants of the royal house of Deheubarth. The Edwinsford family were making a name for themselves and gradually increasing their wealth but keeping their heads down and not becoming too involved in national politics or events at Court.

David had two sons: (1) David Vachan (Fychan)(26) who married Catherine, daughter of Sir Ralph Winchester, and (2) Morgan ap David ap Llywelyn of Rhydodyn.

Morgan ap David (bc1334), David ap Morgan, Morgan Fychan

Morgan (27) inherited Rhydodyn from his father. He married Als (Alice), daughter of Gruffydd ap Llywelyn Foethus, whose family descended from the 11th century Welsh Prince Elystan Glodrudd. Her brother, Rhys ap Gruffydd, served as Sheriff of Carmarthenshire in c1400 to c1409.

Morgan was a generous benefactor in his patronage of the bards[81] emulating his parents and their support for the renowned strict-metre bards of Caeo. In an ode of praise to Morgan, poet Madog Dwygraig says that Morgan's mead cellar is perpetually full, that he revels in feeding a veritable army of poets, that Rhydodyn is a destination for bards, and that his court is well-appointed and impressive, offering comfort and succour not found anywhere else. Lewis Glyn Cothi (c1420-90)[82] was a very well known Welsh poet who was one of the itinerant Welsh bards of his era and one of the important members of the *Beirdd yr Uchelwyr* (poets of the nobility) or *Cywyddwyr* (cywydd men). He was a frequent visitor to Rhydodyn and composed a few poems in the family's honour[83] including one to the four sons of Morgan ap David Fychan: Rhys (a squire over Caeo), Dafydd (well-known and highly respected in Cynwyl Gaeo), Llywelyn (very hospitable), and Thomas (one of the kindest and mild-mannered noblemen imaginable who lived in Cilycwm and was a poet of some repute). He also wrote an ode to Thomas's son, Dafydd of Rhydodyn, saying that crowning the tranquil landscape of Cynwyl Gaeo is Rhydodyn, the proverbial home of gentility and cordiality, that Dafydd maintains a comprehensive larder and cellar full of the best foods and wines, that his estate lands are very productive and that he is a highly respected leader. Rhydodyn is also quoted[84] as a national benchmark for gracious hospitality and exceptional patronage.

Sometime between 1383 and 1387 it seems that "the chief justice of Carmarthen was slain on the bench at Carmarthen by Morgan Dafydd Llewelyn son of Philip Trahearn of Rhydodyn in Conwil Gaio and brother maternally to Ifor Hael". Morgan was tried for murder by Sir David Hanmer[85] "and this was done in ye time of Rychard the second, then King of England, and the above named Sir davyd hanmer was chief Jestys in the countye of Karmarthinshire, when this Morgan was rayned for the killing of the said judge". Morgan is the subject of an

80 Some sources including Thomas Nicholas suggest her first husband was Lord Llywelyn ap Ivor, Lord of St Clear, with whom she had three sons and that she married David as a widow

81 Eurig Davies CA (2015) p 17

82 Lewis Glyn Cothi (Llywelyn y Glyn) was born in Rhydycymerau in the parish of Llanybydder near Llansawel and Cynwyl Gaeo. His bardic name comes from the nearby forest of Glyn Cothi. Some 230 of his poems survive. He compiled much of the White Book of Hergest and many of his poems are also in the Red Book of Hergest. He supported the Lancastrian cause in the War of the Roses

83 Dafydd Johnston: *Gwaith Lewys Glyn Cothi p35-37*

84 J Llywelyn Williams: *Gwaith Guto'r Glyn, Cardiff (1939) CVIII p47-8*

85 William Spurrell: *Carmarthen and its Neighbourhood (1879) p112*

Ode of Inquest[86] (*Cywydd y Cwest*) by poet Gruffudd Llwyd concerning this murder of Deputy Justice John Lawrence in 1385, which confirms Morgan's patronage in the bardic tradition. We do not know the verdict or what happened.

Dwnn and other historians record that Morgan and Als had a son, David ap Morgan (28) of Rhydodyn, who married Margaret, daughter of Rhys Moethy of Castell Odwyn in Cardiganshire and that they had a son, Morgan Fychan (29). Thomas Nicholas[87] however suggests (wrongly I think) that David ap Morgan married Margaret, daughter of Einion ap Howell Goch (who in fact married David's son, Morgan Fychan) and does not include Morgan Fychan in his pedigree; it seems he confused the two Margarets.

Morgan ap David ap Morgan (29) was often called Morgan Fychan to distinguish him from his grandfather. He married Margaret, daughter of Einion ap Howell Goch ap Morgan ap Einion ap Cynfrig ap Osbwrn (Wyddel) of Merioneth. All we know about Morgan is that he continued the family tradition of holding local minor Crown offices. The Ministers' Accounts for 1393-4 show him living in "Ridodyn" and refer to the mills of Ridodyn and Llansawel as well as the court of Maenordeilo. Morgan and Margaret had three sons who will meet in Chapter 5.4.

4.11 The 14th Century and the Great Revolt

Peace reigned in Wales for most of the 14th century but the seeds of revolt were planted in the minds of the Welsh people who continued to feel oppressed and humiliated.

The wealthiest and most influential native Welshman during the first half of the 14th century was Sir Rhys ap Gruffydd ap Hywel ap Gruffydd ap Ednyfed Fychan (d1356) who prospered greatly by supporting the Crown. He inherited the Lordship of Llansadwrn, became Steward of Cardigan in 1309, and in 1312 Forester[88] of Glyncothi and Pennant in the Caeo uplands, which were used for hunting and covered by strict laws dealing with timber, deer, boars, sparrow-hawks and wild honey. Special forest courts were held quarterly and dues paid for the feeding of swine on acorns and beech-mast in the woods. Edward II (ruler 1307-27) was a weak monarch bedevilled by his barons, the Lord Ordainers, who led by the Earl of Lancaster in effect took over the government. Edward supported the Marcher lords Hugh le Despenser and his son. Sir Rhys supported Edward and was rewarded with more lands in Cantref Mawr, and being appointed deputy justiciar in South Wales and custodian of the royal castle of Carmarthen.

In 1327 Edward's wife, Isabella, and her lover Roger Mortimer with French military assistance invaded England and forced Edward to abdicate in favour of his son Edward III (ruler 1327-77). Isabella and Mortimer then tried to starve Edward to death in Berkeley castle, but this failed so they had him murdered by the insertion of a red-hot poker into his rectum. Edward III was only 14 when he became King but within three years he had Mortimer arrested and executed, and his mother was made to spend the rest of her life out of harm's way.

Sir Rhys, who had fled to Scotland on the forced abdication of Edward II, returned to support his son Edward III and his eldest son, the Black Prince, who was very popular with the Welsh archers and spearmen. Welsh troops fought for the King in many campaigns during the 14th century; most famously at Crecy in 1346, at Poitiers in 1356 and then of course at Agincourt[89] in 1415. The Black Prince, Edward, fought on many occasions in France with Welsh troops including archers from the Tywi and Cothi valleys. The Hundred Years War[90] against France which started in 1337 dragged on and Edward III had much success. Rhys ap Gruffydd, who led some 1,000 Welsh troops from Carmarthenshire, fought at Crecy and was knighted after the victory;

86 Henry Lewis: *Cywyddau Iolo Goch ac Eraill, Cardiff (1972) XXXIX*
87 Thomas Nicholas Vol 2 p306
88 Prys-Jones Vol I p159
89 The City of London helped to finance many of the wars in which the monarch was involved. Following Agincourt Henry V gave a priceless gold and crystal sceptre to the City as a gift which to this day forms part of the Lord Mayor's regalia. Muster records suggest that of the 5,000 or so archers in the English army some 500 were Welsh longbowmen
90 The definitive work is *The Hundred Years War* (4 of 5 Vols published to date) by Lord Jonathan Sumption, a Justice of the Supreme Court and a former history don at Oxford

legend tells that the Welsh helped to save the life of the Black Prince at one point in the battle. Some even claim that the national emblem of Wales, the leek, originates from the battle when Welsh archers were told to pick the leeks growing under their feet and put them in their caps. Sir Rhys died in Carmarthen in May 1356 just prior to the victory at Poitiers and is buried in St Peter's Church. Rhys married Joan de Somerville, a wealthy heiress with much land. These lands passed down to his heirs and eventually to Elizabeth, daughter of Sir John Gruffydd of Abermarlais and Lord of Llansadwrn, who married Thomas ap Gruffydd (1415-73) of Dinefwr part of the Jones/Johnes and Rice/Dynevor family. His son was the famous Sir Rhys ap Thomas KG (1449-1525).

Following the great famine of 1315-17 the plague arrived in Europe in 1348 and within two years a third of the population of Europe was dead. It reached Wales in 1349 and devastated society returning on more than one occasion during the rest of the century. The Great Plague (*Y Farwolaeth Fawr*) resulted in a huge reduction in income for landlords, wage inflation, land becoming abundant with labourers travelling to seek work outside their home localities, unfree bondmen becoming enfranchised, and generally a redistribution of rural wealth. The grievances of the rural Welsh increased; resentment against dues and taxes for using forests and mills and local toll taxes worsened.

Richard II

The Black Prince died in 1376 and his 10 year old son Richard II became King in 1377 on the death of Edward III who died lonely and embittered having failed to recover his Angevin French lands. An early form of poll tax in England introduced by the power behind the throne, John of Gaunt, resulted in the Peasants Revolt in 1381; Richard then only 14 years of age met the leaders of the 10,000 peasants, Wat Tyler and the turbulent priest John Ball, in Smithfield. The Lord Mayor of London, William Walworth[91], in protecting the young King killed Wat Tyler with a dagger and the rebellion was halted. Throughout his reign Richard had serious disputes with his barons and on the death of John of Gaunt in 1399 he seized his estates. His son, Henry Bolingbroke, then rebelled and later the same year Richard II was deposed and Henry Bolingbroke (the Duke of Lancaster) was crowned Henry IV (ruler 1399-1413) the first Lancastrian monarch. Richard II was murdered and his corpse, which showed he had been starved to death, was displayed in London.

Stainless steel statue of Llywelyn ap Gruffydd Fychan at Llandovery Castle 2016

[91] William Walworth was knighted by Richard II and his dagger can be seen in Fishmongers' Hall in the City of London. He was the first Lord Mayor of London to be knighted and thought to be the first civilian to receive that honour. See Lord Melvyn Bragg: *Now is the time (2015)* and Dominic Reid*: Lord Mayor's Show 800 Years 1215-2015 (2015) p 80-83*

Owain Glyndŵr

The grievances of the Welsh, who had been relatively peaceful throughout the 14th century, came to the surface and in September 1400 the Great Revolt started when Owain Glyndŵr (c1359-c1416) was proclaimed as the Prince of Wales in a fight for Welsh independence. Owain was descended from the princes of Gwynedd and Powys as well as from Rhys ap Tewdwr (8) and The Lord Rhys of Deheubarth (13). In the past he had fought for the Crown and had retired to live quietly in late middle age to his estates at Sycharth in north-east Wales but had been provoked by a neighbour Lord Grey who wrongly accused him of being a traitor. A decade of guerrilla warfare followed. The English Parliament unwisely passed penal laws against Welshmen which merely encouraged more to rebel. In 1401 Henry IV came to Llandovery where he ordered and witnessed the hanging, drawing and quartering of a Caeo landowner, Llywelyn ap Gruffydd Fychan[92] (c1341-1401), before the gates of Llandovery castle on 9 October after being found guilty of deliberately leading the English forces who were chasing Glyndŵr in the wrong direction. Adam of Usk says that Llywelyn "willingly preferred death to treachery".[93] Llywelyn's father is thought to have been Gruffydd Fychan, Lord of Caeo and Cilycwm and the constable of Caeo in 1359, who is said to have married Jenet the daughter of Gruffydd ap Llewelyn Foethus of Dryslwyn castle and Lord of Llangathen.

In 1403 Glyndŵr was in Llandovery when Carmarthenshire rose to support him including Rhys ap Gruffydd of Dryslwyn. Llandeilo was burned, Carmarthen Castle surrounded and the town set on fire. Henry soon recovered his castles in Carmarthenshire but the rural areas remained under Glyndŵr's control. In 1404 Glyndŵr entered into an alliance with France; his plan was that the Welsh Church would become separate from the see of Canterbury, that Wales would have two universities, and he held a Parliament (*Cynulliad*) in Machynlleth where he was crowned Prince of Wales. The following year he came to an agreement with the Mortimers and the Percies against Henry to split up England and Wales between them. In 1405 a French force invaded to help Glyndŵr and captured Carmarthen, but the French alliance collapsed by the next year and slowly Henry gained the upper hand. The English army and its financial clout were simply too strong. Owain's wife Margaret Hanmer and two of her children were captured and later died in the Tower of London. Glyndŵr himself was last seen alive in 1412 but was never captured[94], ignored the offer of royal pardons by Henry V (ruler 1413-22), and is thought to have died about 1416. The Great Revolt had failed and his son Maredudd was offered a royal pardon in 1417 which he accepted in 1421.[95]

The consequences of the defeat for Carmarthenshire and the rest of Wales were dire. Fines were imposed on those who had supported Glyndŵr, lands were confiscated, and new penal laws forbid Welshmen from holding office or becoming burgesses or houseowners in towns such as Carmarthen. During the decade of war much of the lands and property in Carmarthenshire had been destroyed and lands in Ystrad Tywi were said to have suffered "very great damage and destruction at the hands of the rebels."[96] The rebels had destroyed two-thirds of Llandovery in 1409 and the town of Carmarthen had also been burnt. Monasteries including Talley Abbey had been almost destroyed. Many serfs and free tenants had fled their homes.

---

92 A 16ft tall stainless steel statue of an empty helmet, cloak and armour representing Llywelyn (the Welsh Braveheart) stands outside the ruins of Llandovery Castle in his honour

93 Sir Edward Thompson: *Chronicon Adae de Usk— J Murray (1876) p192*

94 *Annals of Owen Glyndŵr* in Peniarth MS 135; Sir JE Lloyd: *Owain Glendower (1931 reprinted 1966) p144*

95 RR Davies p456

96 Prys-Jones Vol I p206

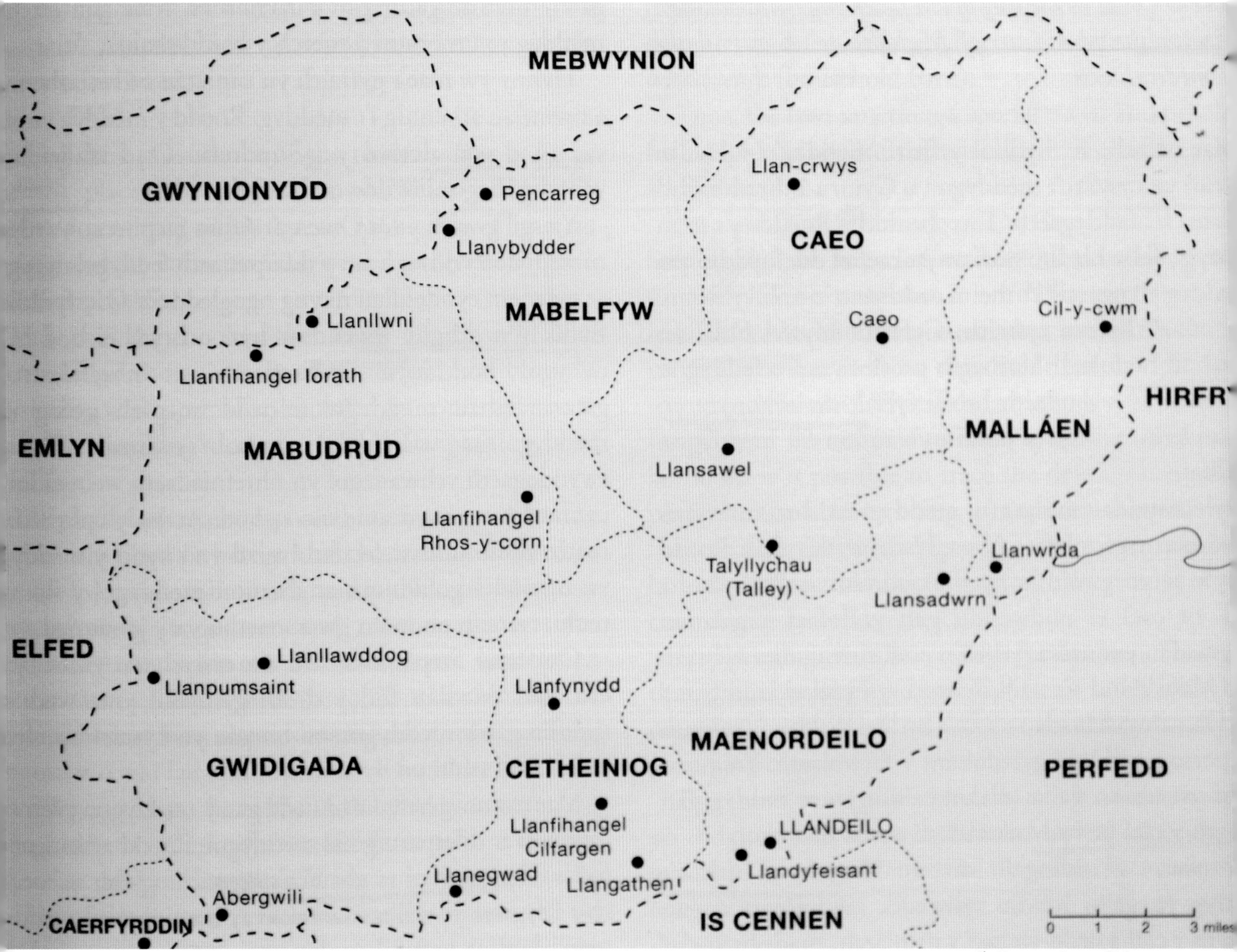

14th Century Cantref Mawr

5. The Pre-Tudor Period and War of the Roses 1416-1485

5.1 Carmarthenshire

Life in Carmarthenshire during the 15th century[97] was one of an underdeveloped pre-industrial economy based on peasant farming and numerous crafts. During the Middle Ages the subjugated native Welsh peasants lived on the higher valley grounds maintaining their own agricultural practices which were mainly pastoral. The Norman lords on the lower richer ground had peasants and bondmen who cultivated their arable land. Sheep were far less important than cattle in both economies within the lordships; indeed it was the great Cistercian abbeys who owned the largest flocks of sheep at this time and encouraged the export of wool. The Ordinance of the Staple[98] in 1353 appointed Carmarthen as the only staple town allowed to export wool to England. After the Black Death there were insufficient workers available so sheepfarming became more popular and cattle and sheep replaced the former dominance of arable farming in the manors in the lower valleys.

Carmarthen's weekly market had a wholesale trade in bread, ale, fish, meat, cheese and eggs which traders then sold outside the town walls. In the countryside the army of landless cottagers and tenants increased as a result of the Great Revolt and its consequences. Thousands of Welshmen recruited to fight in the French wars had died of disease rather than battle. It is estimated that the population of Wales in 1544 was about 250,000 which was still less than the population in 1300 prior to the plague and the wars and revolts. Mortality rates continued to be high and some 90 per cent of the population were under 14 years of age. Society was changing slowly. By 1530 a gentleman able to bear a coat of arms had to have a freehold income of at least £10 per annum in land. The distinction between freemen and bondmen was eroding.

After the Dissolution of the Monasteries in 1536 and of the priories thereafter their large estates were broken up and sold or let by the Crown giving many the opportunity to acquire lands and so there grew up wealthy landed families. One such family was the Rhydodyn / Edwinsford family but it would take them over two centuries of consistent growth and land acquisitions before they had really become a leading family in Carmarthenshire.

While the Rhydodyn family continued to act as trusted Crown minor officials in Caeo and Maenor Deilo, other families had much more power and influence in Carmarthenshire at this time. One such family, the Rhys / Rice family of Dinefwr, was also descended from The Lord Rhys (13) through his daughter Gwenllian (14) and was thus distantly related to the Rhydodyn family, who would undoubtedly have prospered under their local influence.

One of the leading authorities for this period of Welsh history is Professor Ralph Griffiths whose momentous book[99] *Sir Rhys ap Thomas and His Family* is the leading work; in Part II of his book he has also incorporated and edited *The Life of Sir Rhys ap Thomas* written by Henry Rice of Dinefwr (c1590-1651) in his quest to restore his family's reputation after the execution for treason of his forbear Rhys ap Gruffydd (306) in 1531; it was only published in 1796 in the first edition of The Cambrian Register[100].

---

97 Prof Sir Glanmor Williams: *Renewal and Reformation Wales 1415-1642 p55 et seq.* Glanmor Williams FBA (1920-2005) was one of Wales's most eminent historians and had a 37 years' academic career at Swansea University

98 EG Bowen: *Wales a Study in Geography and History (1941) p 76*

99 Prof Ralph Griffiths: *Sir Rhys ap Thomas and His Family (1993)* and article *Gruffydd ap Nicholas and the Rise of the House of Dinefwr (1964) NLWJ p256-268.* Ralph Griffiths OBE is now an Emeritus Professor at Swansea University

100 The Cambrian Register only had three editions in 1796, 1797 and 1818. The 1796 edition containing Henry Rice's work was later transcribed with notes by Richard Fenton (1747-1821) the Welsh antiquary

Edwinsford Family's Deheubarth and Tudor Connections

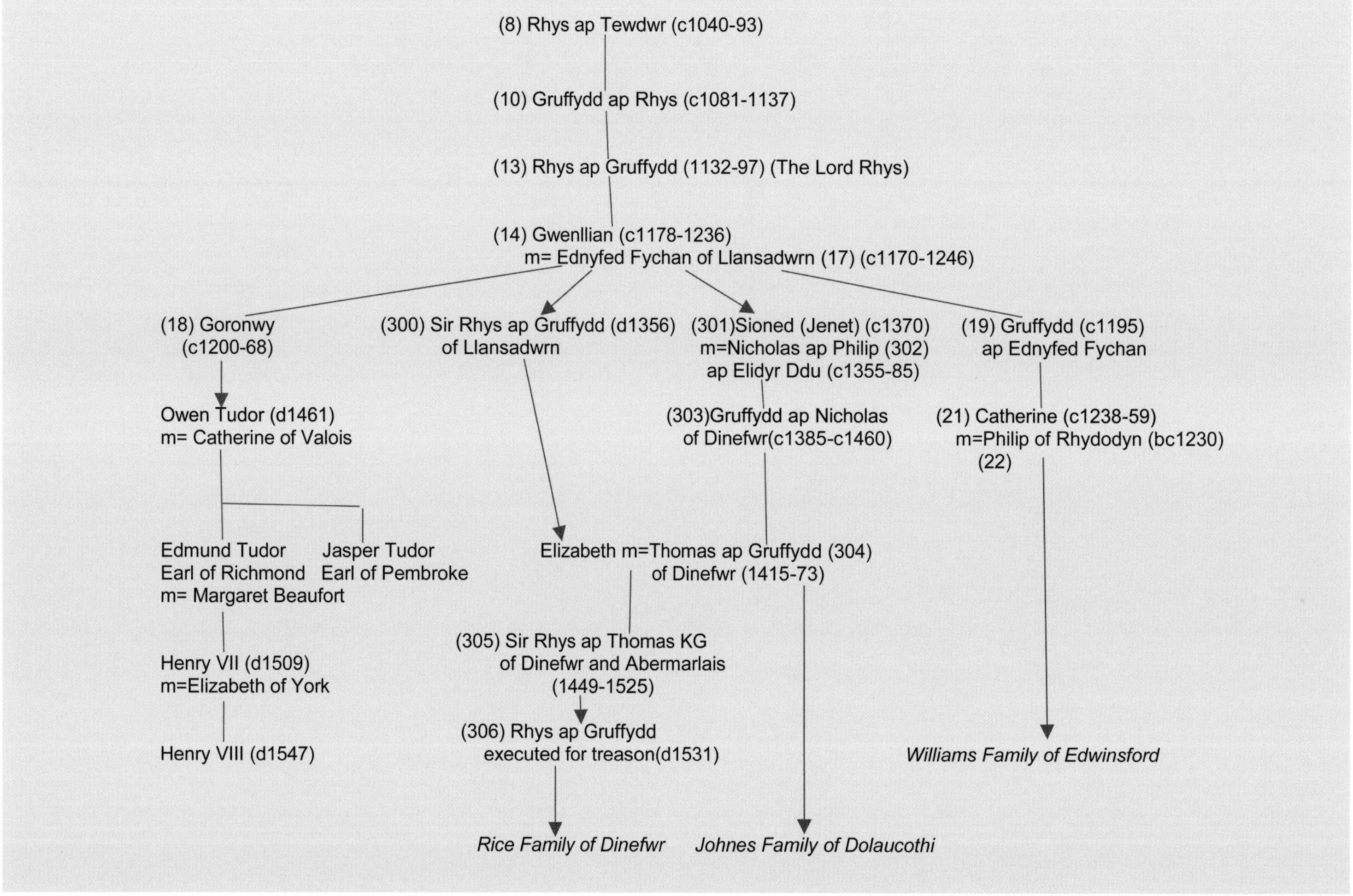

5.2 Nicholas ap Philip and Gruffydd ap Nicholas

Nicholas ap Philip (c1355-85)(302) married Sioned (or Jenet) (c1370)(301) the daughter of Gruffudd ap Llewelyn Foethus, the constable in the commote of Maenordeilo in 1355-6 and beadle there in 1382-3. They lived in Crûg in Llandeilo not far north of Dinefwr Park. Jenet was descended from Ednyfed Fychan (17), seneschal of Gwynedd under Llywelyn the Great, and his wife Gwenllian (14) daughter of The Lord Rhys and was thus a distant ancestor of the Tudor dynasty as well as the Rhydodyn family.

Nicholas and Jenet's son, Gruffydd ap Nicholas (c1385-c1460) (303) was born in very unusual circumstances. According to one story Nicholas had been wounded on his wedding day and was advised by his physician to abstain from sexual intercourse for a few days to enable him to recover from his wounds. But he decided to fulfil his marital duties with Jenet on his wedding night and then died, but his only son Gruffydd was conceived that night. An alternative version suggests that they had been married for several years before he was wounded and Gruffydd was conceived. Henry Rice[101] describes it thus:

"Nowe for Griffith ap Nicholas…I find that in his conception, and before he was borne, he was unwittinglie accessarie both to his father's and his mother's death. His father (Nicholas ap Philipp) being long married, and without issue, to a veretuouse gentlewoman…it happened he was embroiled in some quarrell, wherein he received a dangerous wound, of which despairing (though his surgeons sawe noe such cause), he adventured to lye with his wiefe (soe much did his thoughts worke upon the upholding of his name, that he forgot his owne safetie), and of her he begatt this sonne, which act of his suddenlie hastened him to his end….His noble mother…dreamt… .she was to dye of the birth…falling into a painfull and desperate labour, and being told that eyther she or her child must perish… said she….if that must be soe, let me perish…where upon her bellie, by the advise of surgeons, was cutt open, and soe the child was preserved; whoe indeed …grewe in time to be a man of greate power and authoritie in his countrie."

Ralph Griffiths suggests that he may in fact have had some siblings[102] with similar patronymic names while Darrell Wolcott thinks these people were the children of another earlier Nicholas ap Philip (born c1330)[103] and that Gruffydd was an only child. He was named after his maternal grandfather Gruffudd ap Llewelyn Foethus.The family lived at that time at Crûg outside Dinefwr.

Gruffydd was described by Henry Rice[104] as "a man for power, riches, and parentage, beyond all the greate men in thos parts" but also "a man of a hot, firie and cholerrick spirit…verie wise he was, and infinitlie subtile and craftie, ambitious beyond a measure, of a busie stirring braine". He was certainly successful, serving as bailiff of Kidwelly in 1424, as the King's approver for the lordship and new town of Dinefwr in 1425, Sheriff of Carmarthenshire in 1426, escheator of the county in 1429 as well as deputy constable of Dinefwr Castle, and deputy steward of Kidwelly in 1433. In 1437 his petition for denizenship[105] was approved following payment of a fee and the giving of an oath of allegiance thus proving his local importance and influence. In 1440 he and his family achieved the granting of a 60 year lease of Dinefwr castle and the old and new towns for an annual rent of £5. He had long abandoned his original home at Crûg just outside Llandeilo, built a new fortified manor house in Newton on the site of the present Newton House, and now made full use of the castle. So by the 1440s he and his sons had achieved much local administrative power in Carmarthenshire and Cardiganshire and the opportunity to exploit local revenues and oppress their enemies. He also became a burgess of Dinefwr and Carmarthen.

Gruffydd's first wife was Mabel (Mabli)(b1400)[106], the daughter of Maredudd ap Henry Dwnn of Kidwelly, and she bore him most of his twelve daughters and four sons[107] including Thomas ap Gruffydd

---

101 Griffiths p160
102 Griffiths: NLWJ (1964) p256-7
103 ancientwalesstudies.org/id163
104 Griffiths p160-1
105 It was unusual for Welshmen to be granted denizenship rights. Those who had it were exempt from many restrictions and had the rights of Englishmen
106 Mabli's grandfather, Henry Dwnn, was a strong supporter of Owain Glyndŵr and led the attacks on Dinefwr and Kidwelly castles in 1403, was outlawed and fined, but recovered his lands by 1413
107 Bartrum; NLWBO

Dinefwr Castle sketch c1740

Dinefwr Castle ruins 2016

(1415-73) (304), who was born in Maenordeilo. Gruffydd ensured wise marriages for his daughters while his son Thomas succeeded in marrying Elizabeth, daughter of Sir John Gruffydd of Abermarlais, Lord of Llansadwrn and a former constable of Aberystwyth Castle.

Gruffydd (303) was politically very adept and acted as deputy for Humphrey Duke of Gloucester, his patron, and for other well connected aristocracy including Edmund Beaufort and without falling foul of the intrigues in the Lancastrian / Yorkist feuds. In 1439 he and his sons were summoned to Westminster to answer charges of maladministration; he declined because of illness so a judicial enquiry in Carmarthen was set up by Henry VI which resulted in no action and the continuation by the family of their oppressive and sometimes violent administration to build up a large estate of lands in Carmarthenshire and Cardiganshire. Henry Rice[108] tells the story of Sir Robert Whitney and other commissioners in 1441 travelling to Carmarthen to review abuses by Gruffydd and his sons, placing the Royal warrant of arrest in his sleave for safe keeping, and then being entertained in the evening by Gruffydd during which "the commissioners were soe well liquor'd that for the night they forgot quite what the errand they came for" during which Owain removed the warrant. The next day Gruffydd asked the commissioners to read the warrant which of course was missing so no action could be taken. Other attempts to reduce his power resulted in pardons and he nearly always avoided his just desserts. But in 1456 Gruffydd was forced to relinquish his lease of Dinefwr Castle and of the old and new towns and to give up his possession of Carmarthen Castle where in 1453 he had presided over an eisteddfod; he was later described by Lewys Glyn Cothi as "the eagle of Carmarthen" and his men as wearing his livery of the three ravens of Dinefwr.

His power was curbed after the Yorkist victory at St Albans in 1455 but he remained a strong supporter of the Lancastrians in south Wales. It is thought he died in about 1460; but not, as Henry Rice[109] suggests, fighting in the battle of Mortimer's Cross in 1461, the first great battle in the War of the Roses. He was buried in Greys Friars' Church in Carmarthen but since the dissolution of the monasteries the tomb cannot be found. He died having achieved much and being the most powerful of the Welsh gentry of his time.

5.3 Thomas ap Gruffydd (1415-73)

Thomas (304), son of Gruffydd ap Nicholas (303), was escheator for Cardiganshire between 1438 and 1450 and he succeeded his father as deputy chamberlain in 1454. He and his brother Owain fought at the battle of Mortimer's Cross with the Lancastrian army in 1461 supported by many Welshmen led by Jasper Tudor, Earl of Pembroke, and brother to Edmund Tudor (d1456) and half brother to Henry VI. The Yorkist army won and Thomas and Owain returned to Carmarthenshire where the next year they defended Carreg Cennen castle against the Yorkist forces led by Lord Herbert of Raglan but had to surrender in May 1462; the castle was then partially pulled down to prevent any repetition. Lord Herbert took control of Carmarthenshire as Chief Justice and Chamberlain of South Wales while Jasper Tudor and his Lancastrian supporters stayed abroad in Ireland and then Brittany. In fact he stayed in Brittany with his young nephew, Henry Tudor (born in 1457 in Pembroke castle and later to become King Henry VII), for some 14 years.

Thomas married first (1) Elizabeth, the daughter and heiress of Sir John Gruffydd of Abermarlais and Lord of Llansadwrn (d1471), by whom he had several children including his heir Sir Rhys ap Thomas KG (305), and then secondly after Elizabeth's death (2) Jenet Malefant, the daughter of Henry Malefant (dc1460s) of Upton castle another of whose daughters, Alison, married Thomas's brother, Owain.

At some stage during the 1460s Thomas and his young son Rhys (305) went to Burgundy while Thomas's elder sons, Morgan and Henry, continued to be involved in local conflicts against the Yorkists at home who dominated Wales from 1461 to 1483. In 1470 Henry VI was briefly restored to the throne and he pardoned the family for their activities. When Henry VI was overthrown again by Edward IV and murdered in 1471 in the Tower the family helped Jasper Tudor and others to escape abroad via Tenby.

In about 1471 Thomas and his son Rhys returned to Wales from Burgundy and settled in Abermarlais near Llansadwrn, which became Thomas's home after the death of his father in law, Sir John Gruffydd that year. In 1474 the Yorkist Earl of Pembroke sent forces to capture Thomas at Abermarlais but he had been warned and fled northwards.

---

[108] Griffiths p164-6
[109] Griffiths p169

It seems that Thomas was killed at Pennal in Merionethshire by some of Pembroke's forces; Henry Rice[110] suggests that he was wounded in a fight with a David Gough and he lay down on his stomach to recover and was then run through by "some base fellow a servant noe doubt." It is said that he was then buried in the Augustinian abbey of Bardsey, which is the famous burial place of 20,000 legendary saints and martyrs. Shortly thereafter his sons Morgan and Dafydd died without issue leaving his very able son Rhys (305) to continue the family's fight for power in which he proved to be most successful. His outstanding career is described in Chapter 6.1.

5.4 Rhydodyn (Edwinsford) Family and Plas

There is some doubt[111] as to whether the later Edwinsford mansion (now derelict) stands on the original site of the earlier residence or manor house (*plas*) known as Rhydodyn. Originally there were two farms, Rhydodyn Ucha and Rhydodyn Issa, which were later combined to form one property. Rhydodyn Ucha and Rhydodyn Issa were both occupied by the family whose pedigree is shown in this book from early in the Middle Ages.

Rhydodyn Ucha was held by the family as tenants in common and the estate[112] consisted of: Rhydodyn Ucha; seven unnamed messuages; messuages called Llechwedd Llywelyn otherwise Bwlch y Dinas, Tir Bron Talwilkin, Tir y Llywele Mawr, Tir y Pant Gwyn, and Tir y Bryn Llwyd, all in Llansawel parish; messuages called Garth y Brichiad and Cwm Twrch, in Caeo parish; messuages called Tir Howel Guto and Tir Rhys ap Howel Jenkin, in Talley parish; and a messuage called Tir Ievan David Ychan in Llanycwrys parish.

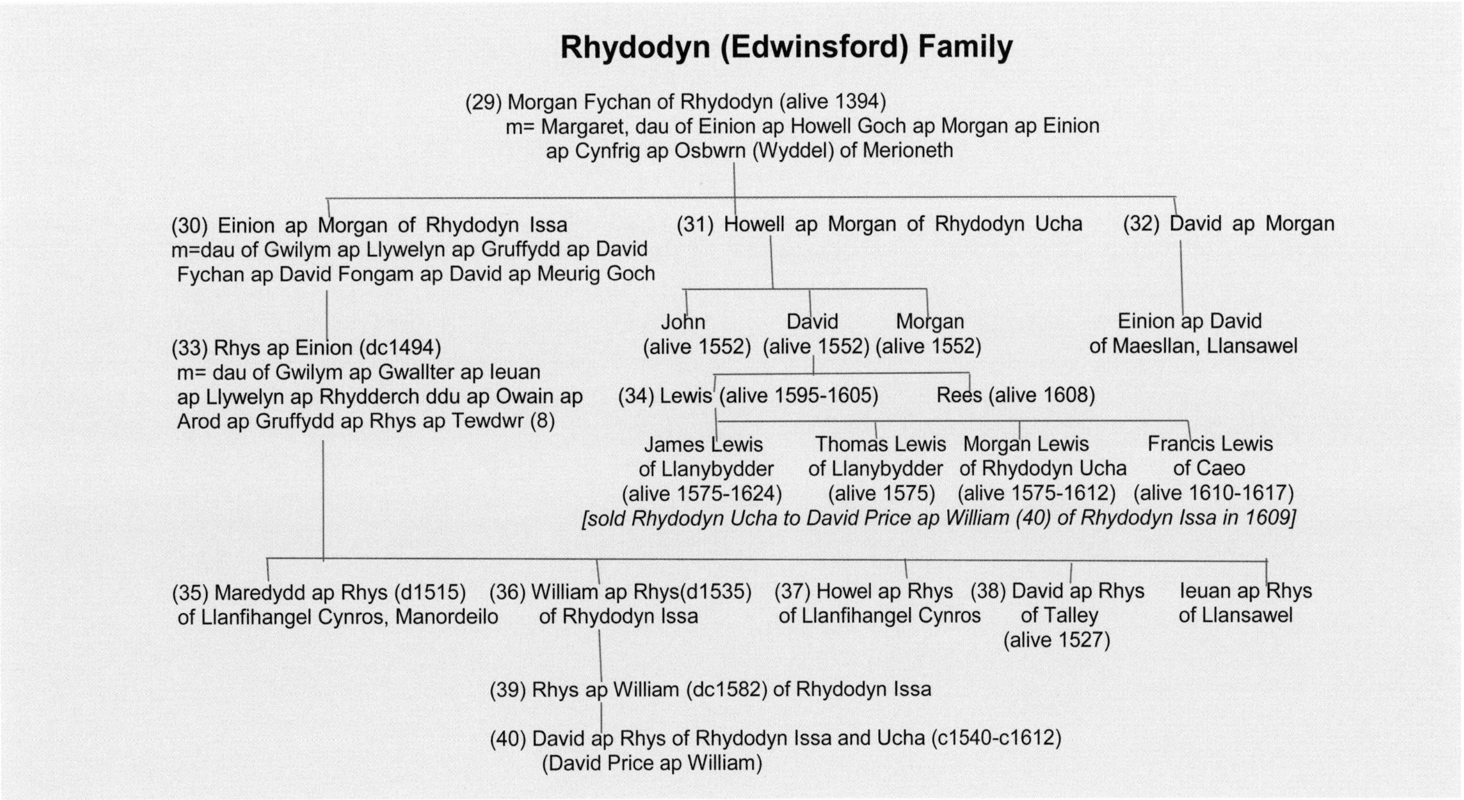

110 Griffiths p177-8

111 Francis Jones: *THSC (1986) p65-72*

112 NLW Edwinsford archives

As we saw in Chapter 4.11, the family were now trusted local Crown officials with an increasing status in the community, although not yet as influential and important as they would later become.

Morgan Fychan

Morgan Fychan (29), who was alive in 1394, and his wife Margaret had three sons:

(1) Einion ap Morgan (30) who inherited Rhydodyn Issa and married an unnamed daughter of Gwilym ap Llywelyn ap Gruffydd, so she was a distant relation of her husband; their son was Rhys ap Einion (dc1494)(33) who continued the family pedigree as we shall see although they probably had other children too;

(2) Howell ap Morgan (31) who owned Rhydodyn Ucha nearby. We do not know who he married but he had three sons, John, David and Morgan, who were all alive in 1552. It was David's son, Lewis (alive 1595-1605), who lost the family owned property at Rhydodyn Ucha. It seems that on 16 October 1605 Lewis David ap Howell Morgan (34) and his son, James Lewis David ap Howell, both of Llanybydder, described as "gentlemen", mortgaged Rhydodyn Ucha and Bwlch y Dinas to Francis Jones of Llanybydder, esquire, for £240. The mortgage was never redeemed and on 20 August 1609 Mathew Jones of Llanybydder (gentleman) who was the son of Francis Jones, his wife Margaret, Lewis David ap Howell Morgan (gentleman), together with three of his sons, James Lewis, Thomas Lewis and Morgan Lewis released Rhydodyn Ucha and the other mortgaged land totalling some 1,920 acres to their cousin David Price ap William (David ap Rhys)(40) gentleman of Rhydodyn Issa next door (whose patronymic surname became "Williams" in the next generation). So the Williams branch of the family who originally lived in Rhydodyn Issa acquired Rhydodyn Ucha and its lands as well at the beginning of the 17th century.

It it not clear whether or not Rhydodyn Issa is the site of the later Edwinsford Home Farm and Rhydodyn Ucha is the site of the Edwinsford Mansion which was built across the river in the early 17th century. Further details of the history of the plas and mansion are contained in Chapter 11; and

(3) David ap Morgan (32) who had a son Einion ap David of Maesllan in Llansawel.

Rhys ap Einion (dc1494)

Rhys ap Einion (33), the son of Einion ap Morgan (30), married an unnamed daughter of Gwilym ap Gwallter, a descendant of Rhys ap Tewdwr (8), who thus had a similar lineage to that of her husband. Rhys' draft will dated 26 January 1493-4[113] appoints his unnamed wife as his executor, lists a number of debts owing by and to Rhys, a list of mortgaged properties, and several bequests including 2s.6d to the Franciscan friars of "Kermerdyn", 10s to Llansawel Church, 26s.8d to the abbot of Talley, and 10d to the cathedral church of St Davids. He was buried in St Mary's Church in Talley. Rhys and his wife had five sons:

(1)Maredydd ap Rhys (d1515)(35) who lived nearby in Llanfihangel Cynros, Maenordeilo. He married Avys and they had five children who all died without issue except for the youngest daughter, Margaret; she married David ap Morgan and their son was Alderman John Morris of Carmarthen (d1604) a mercer. Maredydd is described as a gentleman;

(2) Howel ap Rhys (37), who is also described as a gentleman, lived in the commote of Manordeilo too. He married an unnamed daughter of Llywelyn Goch and they had a son, Philip (d1576) of Llandeilo Fawr. Philip married Tanglwst and they had six children;

(3) David ap Rhys (alive in 1527)(38), who lived in Talley parish, married an unnamed wife and they had an only child, Nest. Nest married twice and had at least three sons;

(4) Ieuan ap Rhys, who lived in Llansawel parish; and

(5) William ap Rhys (d1535) (36), who inherited the family property at Rhydodyn Issa and who is described in Chapter 6.2. It was his grandson, David ap Rhys (40), who acquired Rhydodyn Ucha as well for his side of the Williams family.

So by the end of the 15th century the family had become "gentlemen" and freeholders with property and farming assets including mortgages over other lands. As we have seen in Chapter 4.11 they were also important patrons of the bards. Their story continues in Chapter 6.2.

113 NLW Edwinsford archives

The War of the Roses (1455-85)

Throughout his reign Richard II (ruler 1377-99) had serious disputes with his barons and on the death of John of Gaunt in 1399 he seized his estates. His son, Henry Bolingbroke, then rebelled and later the same year Richard II was deposed and Henry Bolingbroke (the Duke of Lancaster) seized the throne and was crowned Henry IV (ruler 1399-1413) the first Lancastrian monarch. Richard II was murdered. Henry's son, Henry V (ruler 1413-22), was a success particularly in France where he won the battle of Agincourt in 1415 and forced the French to accept him as heir to the French throne. He married Catherine of Valois but died young of dysentery leaving Henry VI (ruler 1422-61 and 1470-1) a very young boy to rule under a Council headed by his uncle the Duke of Gloucester. Catherine later remarried Owen Tudor (d1461) grandfather of Henry VII.

Henry VI married Margaret of Anjou in 1444 while the French won back all their lands (except Calais) as the Hundred Years War entered its final phase ending in 1453. Henry was a very weak ruler and suffered from bouts of madness. This together with his loss of the French lands triggered a civil war between the Dukes of York and Somerset. In 1455 they clashed at the battle of St Albans where Somerset was killed. After the battle of Mortimer's Cross in 1461 the new Duke of York was proclaimed King Edward IV (ruler 1461-70 and 1471-83) with the help of Richard Neville 16th Earl of Warwick (the kingmaker) (1428-71) whose daughters married George Duke of Clarence and Richard III. In 1465 Henry VI was captured and imprisoned but in 1470 he was briefly restored to the throne after a dispute between Edward IV and Warwick. By May 1471 Edward IV had returned from abroad and Warwick was killed at the battle of Barnet and Henry VI was once more a prisoner of Edward who had been restored to the throne; Henry was stabbed to death in the Tower of London on 21 May 1471. Edward IV died unexpectedly in April 1483 aged only 41.

Edward V (aged only 12 and ruler for only two months in 1483) was arrested by Richard Duke of Gloucester (brother of Edward IV) who seized the throne as Richard III (ruler 1483-5); he was almost certainly responsible for the deaths of his nephews Edward V and his brother Richard in the Tower who are believed to have been killed by Sir James Tyrell (who was subsequently beheaded for treason in 1502). The bodies of the two Princes were not discovered until 1674. The Duke of Buckingham, a strong supporter of Richard III, became Justiciar and Chamberlain of Carmarthen with other powers in Wales but then decided to switch sides to help the Lancastrian cause. He raised an army against the King; wisely and partly because of the long standing feud between the two families Rhys ap Thomas (305) and his Carmarthenshire men did not support Buckingham and the revolt failed resulting in his execution. As a reward Richard III gave Rhys an annuity of 40 marks and Rhys swore loyalty to him.

Owen Tudor (d1461) was descended from the old Anglesey family of Penmynydd who had supported the Owain Glyndŵr revolt and Owen's father was executed as a traitor. However Owen fought for the Crown at Agincourt and then following the early death of Henry V in 1422 he married the King's widow, Catherine of Valois, who was the mother of Henry VI. Their two sons, Edmund and Jasper, were brought up under the protection of their half brother, Henry VI, and were created the Earls of Richmond and Pembroke. The family and most of Carmarthenshire including Gruffydd ap Nicholas (303) were strong supporters on the Lancastrian side. At the battle of Mortimer's Cross in 1461 won by the Yorkists, Owen Tudor was captured and executed at Hereford; his son, Jasper Tudor, and the sons of Gruffydd ap Nicholas, Thomas (304) and Owain, escaped. In fact by lineage Henry Tudor (1457-1509) did not have a particularly strong claim to the Crown and was only a quarter Welsh but he was the only surviving Lancastrian male heir being the son of Lady Margaret Beaufort (who was only 13 years old when she gave birth) and Edmund Tudor (who died of the plague in 1456); Henry had been born in Pembroke castle and lived as a boy in Wales in Pembroke and Raglan (1457-71) before his exile to France (1471-85).

On 7 August 1485 having spent most of his life in exile Henry Tudor landed at Mill Bay in Milford Haven[114] with a small force with the odds stacked against him of taking the English Crown. But with the assistance of his uncle Jasper Tudor and Welsh troops led by Rhys ap Thomas (305) he defeated Richard III at the battle of Bosworth on 22 August in which Richard became the last King of England to die in battle. Henry was proclaimed King Henry VII (ruler 1485-1509) on the battlefield.

So the House of York (descendants of Edmund, Duke of York, the fourth son of Edward III Plantagenet King of England) during the course of the War of the Roses had overthrown the Lancastrian and more senior line of the Plantagenets (descendants of John of Gaunt, Duke of Lancaster and son of Edward III) in 1461. But they were finally displaced themselves by the last Lancastrian descendant, Henry Tudor, Earl of Richmond, who seized the throne by conquest. In 1486 he married Elizabeth of York, the heiress of the cadet branch, whom he had promised to marry in 1483; Elizabeth of York[115] claimed, through her Mortimer family, descent from Llywelyn the Great via his daughter Gwladus Ddu. Their first son, Arthur (d1502 and named after King Arthur) and their second son and heir, Henry VIII (ruler 1509-47), united both branches of the Plantagenets. Thus was founded the famous House of Tudor.

Elizabeth of York was only 17 when her father, Edward IV, died in April 1483. After the murder of her two brothers she had a better claim to the throne than Richard III or Henry VII so her life was fraught with danger. Her mother, Queen Elizabeth Woodville (Wydeville), had to take sanctuary in Westminister Abbey with her young children for fear of attack by Richard III; there was talk of her being married off abroad and even a suggestion that Richard III, her uncle, would marry her himself. Margaret Beaufort, Henry VII's mother, was scheming for her to marry her son. This marriage took place on 18 January 1486 once Henry VII had won his throne by conquest; he was 29 and Elizabeth was 20. After giving birth to Prince Arthur she had her coronation on 25 November 1487 following a state entry into London and a procession by barge along the Thames to Westminster Abbey accompanied by "the Mayor, sheriffs, aldermen and many out of every craft guild in a flotilla of boats freshly furnished with banners and streamers of silk richly beseen with the arms and badges of their crafts and rowed by liveried oarsmen….and a model of a great dragon, the red dragon of Cadwaladr, from whom she claimed descent."

---

[114] Chris Skidmore: *Bosworth The Birth of the Tudors (2014) p231-262*

[115] Alison Weir: *Elizabeth of York The First Tudor Queen (2013)*

The Tudor Dynasty and Edwinsford Pedigree

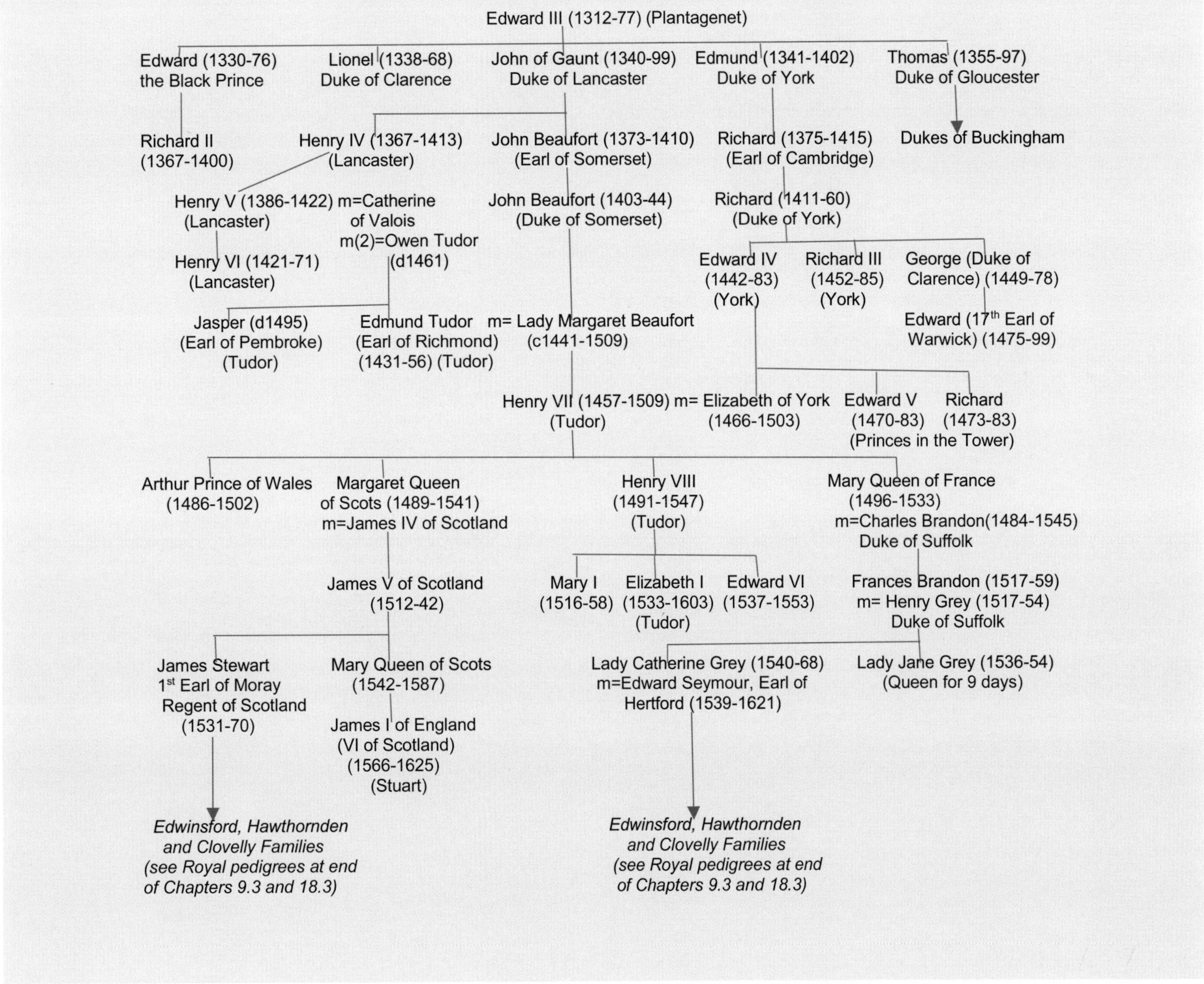

6. The Tudor Period 1485-1603

6.1 Sir Rhys ap Thomas KG (1449-1525)

Before the Battle of Bosworth on 22 August 1485 Rhys (305) had raised an army of some 2,000 men including 500 cavalry in Carmarthenshire and Cardiganshire under his family banner of the three black ravens before meeting Henry Tudor near Welshpool whose own forces were mainly French and Scots. In addition Henry's step-father Lord Stanley and his brother Sir William Stanley had some 8,000 troops, but Richard III's army was larger. Henry Rice[116] writing in the early 17th century states that during the battle Rhys persuaded the Stanleys to join the battle at a crucial moment and together their forces won the day and King Richard was killed either by Rhys himself in hand to hand combat (which seems unlikely given no official corroboration at the time) or by others. During his lifetime Welsh bards including Rhys Nanmor, Tudur Aled and Guto'r Glyn wrote praise poems in his honour some of which hint at his involvement in the death of Richard III at Bosworth.[117]

At the end of the battle Sir William Stanley "set the crowne upon the Earle his head" meaning that Henry Tudor, Earl of Richmond, was proclaimed King Henry VII. On 3 September Henry went to St Paul's Cathedral[118] to give thanks bearing the Red Dragon of Cadwaladr and his coronation took place on 30 October. Shortly thereafter Henry enacted a Statute confirming that he had begun his reign the day before the Battle of Bosworth, thereby making all those who had fought against him guilty of treason. Henry cleverly invented the double Tudor rose combining the white rose of York with the red rose of Lancaster and in 1486 he married Elizabeth of York, daughter of Edward IV, thereby unifying the two factions. He also issued gold "sovereign" crown coins with the new Tudor rose imprinted on them for all to witness. His chapel in Westminster Abbey is perhaps his greatest legacy; the ceiling is peppered with Tudor roses and the portcullis badge of the Beaufort family.

On 25 August 1485, three days after the victory at Bosworth, Rhys was knighted by a grateful King. Honours galore followed with Rhys being appointed the royal lieutenant and steward of Brecon for life, chamberlain of South Wales including Carmarthenshire and Cardiganshire for life, steward of Builth for life, mayor of Carmarthen four times, a Knight Banneret for his bravery in 1497, and Chief Justice of South Wales in 1495 on the death of Jasper Tudor thus becoming virtual ruler of South Wales. Rhys loyally supported his King in dealing with Yorkist rebels including imposters such as Lambert Simnel and Perkin Warbeck who claimed the throne, and he fought in France in 1492. He reached the zenith of his career when in 1505 he was appointed a Knight of the Garter and a Privy Councillor, the first Welshman to be given that personal honour. Sir Rhys was also granted Lord Audley's lands after his execution including the lordship of Llandovery[119] but this was lost in 1531 when the lands of his grandson Rhys ap Gruffydd (306) were forfeited to the Crown on his execution.

In 1507 Rhys celebrated the anniversary of his elevation to a KG by holding a tournament and jousting competition at Carew Castle, his principal residence in Pembrokeshire over which he had been granted a lease. Henry Rice[120] says the preparations for this event "were both sumptuose and magnificent well fitted to the occasion", that it was attended by many eminent families and hundreds of troops, "this festival and time of jollitie continued the space of five dayes" during which Rhys's son Sir Gruffydd ap Rhys played a prominent role in the jousts with the competitor guests and then "having performed their devoirs, both with sword and speare, they mutuallie embraced each other, and soe hand in hand they went to the judge [Rhys] to receave a definitive sentence of their activities". Rhys as judge "commended them for their heroicall deedes" and then they heard divine service before going to dinner. After dinner Sir Rhys "leads his noble guests into the parke a hunting, where they killed divers bucks".

---

116 Griffiths p229

117 Dafydd Johnston: *Sir Rhys ap Thomas and the Battle of Bosworth CA (2014) p21-7*

118 Glanmor Williams p227; Glanmor Williams: *Henry Tudor CA (1985) p3-9*; Thomas Penn: *Winter King The Dawn of Tudor England (2011)*

119 AT Arber-Cooke: *Pages from the History of Llandovery Vol 1 (1975) p165*

120 Griffiths p245-258

In April 1509 Henry VII died of tuberculosis at his Palace at Richmond. His eldest son, Arthur (b1486), had died aged 15 in 1502 the year after his unconsummated dynastic marriage to Catherine of Aragon. Shortly thereafter Henry's loving wife Elizabeth of York had died in 1503 in childbirth. But Henry had successfully claimed the English Crown by conquest, dealt with all the Yorkist attempts to unseat him and had left an heir, Henry VIII, aged only 17 to cement his legacy. Rhys, who was then about 60, had been a great and loyal supporter of Henry VII and had received every honour save that of a Peerage. He was the most powerful person in Wales and a very rich man. He married Efa, daughter of Henry ap Gwilym of Cwrt Henry near Dryslwyn, and his only legitimate heir was her son, Sir Gruffydd ap Rhys, who was created a Knight of the Bath when Prince Arthur, married Catherine of Aragon in 1501. Rhys's second wife was Jenet, daughter of Thomas Mathew of Radyr who was the widow of Thomas Stradling of St Donat's; in addition he had numerous mistresses and several illegitimate children.

Sir Gruffydd ap Rhys had been a member of Prince Arthur's household and was a personal friend so Arthur's early death was a blow; indeed Sir Gruffydd was the chief mourner at Arthur's funeral[121] on St George's Day 1502 (in accordance with tradition neither of his parents attended). The second son Henry VIII (ruler 1509-47) took the throne. Sir Gruffydd followed in his father's footsteps and gained influence at Court and looked as if he would gradually succeed to his father's many large Welsh offices. In about 1507 he married Catherine St John, whose great grandmother was Margaret Beauchamp, the grandmother of Henry VII, which indicates the growing influence of the family with the House of Tudor. His son and heir Rhys ap Gruffydd (306) was born the following year. In 1514 the family struck gold socially when a commercially motivated marriage agreement was made between Sir Rhys, Sir Gruffydd and Thomas Howard, Duke of Norfolk (1443-1524), for young Rhys to marry his daughter Catherine Howard by the time he was 14 years old.

In 1513 Sir Rhys aged 64 raised 3,000 infantry and cavalry to accompany King Henry VIII to France; Sir Gruffydd who was not such an accomplished soldier as his father accompanied them. The French were defeated and Rhys and Gruffydd returned to Wales where Gruffydd became mayor of Carmarthen for the third time in 1513-4. Both of them accompanied King Henry and Cardinal Wolsey to the Field of the Cloth of Gold in France in 1520 to meet with King Francis I of France to negotiate peace. Sadly Sir Gruffydd died young, intestate and in debt[122] in 1521 possibly as a result of a tournament accident; he was buried in Worcester Cathedral near the tomb of his close friend Prince Arthur who had died of consumption aged only 15 without having consummated his marriage to Katherine of Aragon.The death of his son and heir was a great blow to Sir Rhys and to his family succession plans. He set about planning for his grandson Rhys to succeed to his lands and offices and in 1522 Rhys married Catherine Howard as agreed. Yet within three years Sir Rhys had also died at the Franciscan Carmarthen Grey Friars Friary and the young Rhys aged only 17 was too young and inexperienced to assume his responsibilities effectively. Sir Rhys's tomb is now in St Peter's Church in Carmarthen to which it was moved after the dissolution in 1538; the tomb was restored by his descendant Lord Dynevor in 1866 and moved to between the chancel and the Consistory Court. The inscription around the base of the tomb says: *"Here rests the remains of Sir Rhys ap Thomas KG, who fought at Bosworth Field and of Dame Eva his wife, they were originally buried at the Monastery of White Friars in this town; removed into this Church when that Monastery was supressed and placed within the altar rails. Finally they were reinterred in this place when their monument was restored by the care of their descendant George Rice, 4th Baron Dynevor, 1866."* Historians differ as to whether the second effigy is in fact of his wife given the destruction at the time of the dissolution.

The tomb of Edmund Tudor, Earl of Richmond, father of Henry VII, was also moved from the Friary to St Davids Cathedral in a very prominent position in front of the High Altar even upstaging the shrine of St David. The cult of St David, who had flourished in the 6th century, became very popular in Deheubarth and he was accepted as the Patron Saint of Wales by the 10th century; he was the only Welsh Saint to be canonised by the Pope (in the 1120s). Henry VII was perceived by the Welsh as being the saviour who had fulfilled the old prophesy of a Welsh Prince who would defeat the English and rule Britain again. Henry VII did much to support the Welsh and their culture and traditions and many Welshmen attended his Court. However for sensible political reasons the clerics at St Davids thought

121 Alison Weir: *Elizabeth of York The First Tudor Queen (2013) p379*
122 Griffiths p76

Tomb-effigies of Sir Rhys ap Thomas KG and (possibly) his first wife Efa in St Peter's Church, Carmarthen 2016

it wise to give prominence to the father of the Tudor dynasty and hence having his tomb positioned strategically in the Cathedral was a strong defence to possible actions during the Reformation and later religious purges.

Sir Rhys was the most outstanding and powerful Welshman of his age, "a man noted for strength of will and military experience", a man referred to as "Father Rice" by Henry VII, and his motto "*Secret et Hardy*" is on his Garter plate in St George's Chapel in Windsor. He was also a rich man having acquired numerous lands, leases and mortgages with his many offices as well as having inherited other lands from his father and grandfather or acquired them by marriage. His properties included Carew Castle, Abermarlais, Dinefwr Castle and his house at Newton[123], Newcastle Emlyn, Pembroke Castle, Weobly Castle in the Gower, and Narberth Castle. In addition his will and the survey of his estates carried out in 1532[124] suggest that he held gold

[123] Described in Gerald Morgan: *Dinefwr (2014)*
[124] Griffiths p60

and silver of some £10,000 and that his annual income from estates was some £638 with additional annual income of some £400 from offices and annuities. His reputation for acquiring lands and wealth, sometimes ruthlessly, was great; one example is his lease of the Slebech estates of the Knights of the Hospital of St John of Jerusalem where in 1520[125] the local commander, Sir Clement West, presented a Bill of Complaint to the Court of Requests accusing Sir Rhys, Sir Gruffydd and others of cutting down and destroying 2,000 oaks, overtaxing the tenants on the estates, of forcible entry with weapons, and of seizure of goods and chattels without rights.

6.2 Rhydodyn (Edwinsford) Family

William ap Rhys (d1535)

As we have seen in Chapter 5.4, William ap Rhys (d1535) (36) inherited Rhydodyn Issa although he was the second son while his brothers inherited other properties possibly pursuant to some family settlement. William like his father was successful in acquiring additional lands as well as mortgages over third party properties which usually resulted in his acquiring those too in due course. The family muniments[126] disclose a number of property transactions during the early 16th century which resulted in his property estate increasing and those lands remained part of what was to become the Edwinsford Estate.

He became a man of influence locally as well as a landowner of substance. On 12 March 1520 his distant relation[127], Sir Rhys ap Thomas KG (305), appointed William as his deputy as seneschal of the Lordship of Talley. In late 1531 we see him submitting his yearly account as Bailiff of Caeo.

William died in late 1535 or early 1536 having made his will on 9 July 1535. He asked to be buried within Talley monastery (which of course was soon to suffer greatly under the dissolution of the monasteries), and left 2s to St Davids Cathedral (a very traditional legacy for men of substance), 3s.4d to Talley monastery, 10s towards the fabric of St Sawyl's Parish Church, half his goods and chattels, sheep and corn, three horses and lands at "Redodyn" to his wife Eva for her life, and the rest of his estate to his two sons, Rhys and Howel, who were his executors.

William married Eva (dc1539), daughter of Gruffydd ap Rhys ap Gruffydd ap Rhys ap Gruffydd Fychan ap David Fongam ap David ap Meurig Goch; she was therefore a distant relation of her husband. She died in about 1539 having made her will on 26 February 1537. She too was buried at Talley monastery and left legacies to St Davids Cathedral and Llansawel Parish Church. She left only cloth and clothing to her daughters, Margaret, Maud and Dienis, which suggests that they were already married. Her two sons had inherited much of their father's estate on his death and now also received her share on her death.

William and Eva had five legitimate children including the three daughters mentioned. Their second son, Howel ap William (who was alive in 1552), married a daughter of Lewis Fychan, and they had a daughter, Mary, who had children.[128] Their eldest son was Rhys ap William (39). William also had two "base sons", Morgan and Ieuan, mentioned in his will to whom he left legacies (the mothers are unknown).

Rhys ap William (dc1582)

Rhys ap William (39) (described as a gentleman) inherited Rhydodyn Issa and continued his father's policy of acquiring more and more lands and mortgages over third party lands. Between 1541 and 1580 he entered into no fewer than 35 different property transactions including seven mortgages in the parishes of Llansawel, Talley and Cynwyl Gaeo. He bought from freeholders and Francis Jones describes these transactions as illustrating the process whereby successful landowners bought out their lesser neighbours to build up substantial estates. This process of great changes in the ownership of land was accelerated by the dissolution of the monasteries which gave such acquirors the opportunity to buy former Church lands offered for sale or lease by the Crown; it was also helped by the Acts of Union which led to the abolition of the old Welsh custom of gavelkind and the substitution

125 Francis Jones: *CA (1951) p 70-4*
126 NLW Edwinsford archives; Francis Jones: *THSC (1986) p81 et seq*
127 See the pedigree in Chapter 5.1
128 Dwnn

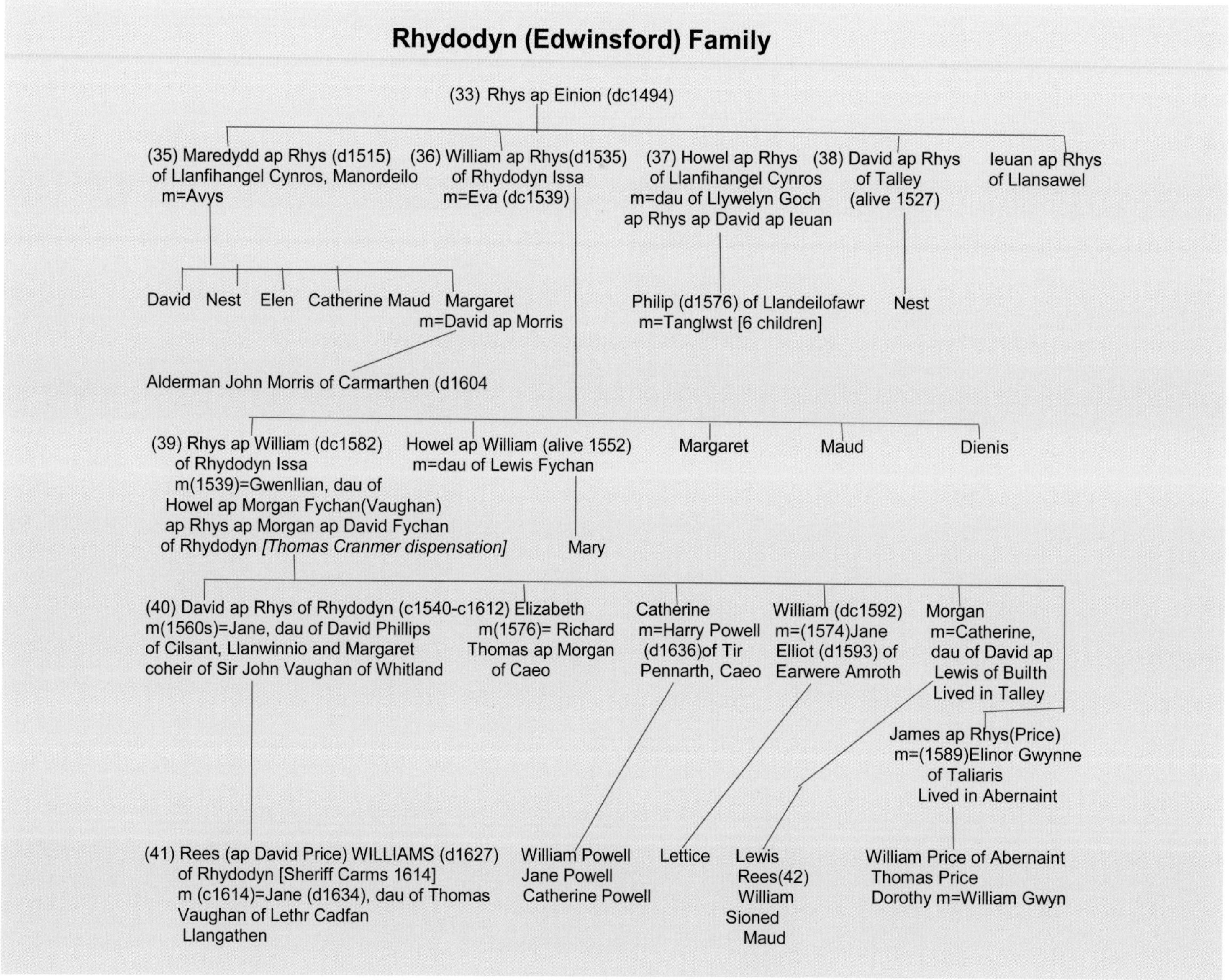
Rhydodyn (Edwinsford) Family
(33) Rhys ap Einion (dc1494)
(35) Maredydd ap Rhys (d1515) of Llanfihangel Cynros, Manordeilo m=Avys
(36) William ap Rhys(d1535) of Rhydodyn Issa m=Eva (dc1539)
(37) Howel ap Rhys of Llanfihangel Cynros m=dau of Llywelyn Goch ap Rhys ap David ap Ieuan
(38) David ap Rhys of Talley (alive 1527)
Ieuan ap Rhys of Llansawel
David
Nest
Elen
Catherine
Maud
Margaret m=David ap Morris
Philip (d1576) of Llandeilofawr m=Tanglwst [6 children]
Nest
Alderman John Morris of Carmarthen (d1604
(39) Rhys ap William (dc1582) of Rhydodyn Issa m(1539)=Gwenllian, dau of Howel ap Morgan Fychan(Vaughan) ap Rhys ap Morgan ap David Fychan of Rhydodyn *[Thomas Cranmer dispensation]*
Howel ap William (alive 1552) m=dau of Lewis Fychan
Margaret
Maud
Dienis
Mary
(40) David ap Rhys of Rhydodyn (c1540-c1612) m(1560s)=Jane, dau of David Phillips of Cilsant, Llanwinnio and Margaret coheir of Sir John Vaughan of Whitland
Elizabeth m(1576)= Richard Thomas ap Morgan of Caeo
Catherine m=Harry Powell (d1636)of Tir Pennarth, Caeo
William (dc1592) m=(1574)Jane Elliot (d1593) of Earwere Amroth
Morgan m=Catherine, dau of David ap Lewis of Builth Lived in Talley
James ap Rhys(Price) m=(1589)Elinor Gwynne of Taliaris Lived in Abernaint
(41) Rees (ap David Price) WILLIAMS (d1627) of Rhydodyn [Sheriff Carms 1614] m (c1614)=Jane (d1634), dau of Thomas Vaughan of Lethr Cadfan Llangathen
William Powell
Jane Powell
Catherine Powell
Lettice
Lewis
Rees(42)
William
Sioned
Maud
William Price of Abernaint
Thomas Price
Dorothy m=William Gwyn

of primogeniture under which the eldest son inherited and was able to build up the family estate more easily to pass on to the next generation.

During the dissolution of the monasteries in the 1530s Talley Abbey and its lands were acquired by the Crown and converted into a crown manor[129] under which some of its valuable lands were held by copyhold and thereafter usually descended to the youngest son of the copyholder. Some of the Abbey's other former lands were held direct by the Crown as of the royal manor of East Greenwich. Some of these were acquired by Rhys ap William including a grist corn mill called "Melyn y Weyn vaure" in Talley manor (which might be Felin Waun; see Chapter 14.9). Rhys also farmed some Church lands and there is evidence that he acquired an interest in part of the lands of Llansawel Parish Church.

Rhys married Gwenllian, daughter of Howel ap Morgan Fychan (Vaughan) ap Rhys ap Morgan ap David Fychan of Rhydodyn. Since they were closely related (in the fourth degree) a dispensation to marry had to be sought from Archbishop Thomas Cranmer. The dispensation was granted on 24 October 1539 and they were married. The actual date of the marriage is unknown but later for some unkown reason there was some doubt as to the legitimacy of the children. When Lewys Dwnn visited Rhydodyn much later in 1596 to prepare the family pedigree he was asked by David ap Rhys (40) the eldest son to include the following note[130] in Welsh on it: "Be it known to all Christians that this Gwenllian is wedded wife to Rys ap Wiliam of Rydodyn, and that she had all her children after marriage, and before her marriage had none. This is attested by witnesses, Lord Prestens (President) Sir Henry Sidney, Thomas Archbishop of Canterbury, and many others—Anno 1539".

Rhys died in about 1582 having made his will on 16 January of that year. He was buried in Talley, gave the normal legacies to St Davids Cathedral and Llansawel Church, and divided up his sizeable estate amongst his sons with a few gifts of cattle to friends. His inventory of goods shows that he died owning 100 oxen (worth £100), 120 kine (£80), 100 bullocks and heifers (£33), a gelding (£5), a horse (£3), 18 mares (£13), 300 sheep (£30), and household goods (£10). His total moveable estate was valued at £314. In addition most of his 39 properties were inherited under a family settlement by his eldest son, David ap Rhys (40), whilst his other three sons also inherited some lands.

Rhys and Gwenllian had six children:

(1)Elizabeth, who married in 1576 Richard Thomas ap Morgan ap Ieuan ap Owen of Caeo. They were living without issue in 1596;

(2) Catherine, who married Harry Powell (Harry ap Sion ap Howel ap Sion) (d1636) of Tir Pennarth in Caeo. Their children included William (whose own children were William, Morris and Dorothy), Jane and Catherine Powell;

(3) William ap Rhys (dc1592), the second son who married Jane Elliot (d1593) of Earwere, Amroth in Pembrokeshire. They lived in Talley parish and he inherited from his father Tyr Rhydygwin and Tyr Penbont in that parish. Their only child was Lettice;

(4) Morgan ap Rhys, the third son who married Catherine, daughter of David ap Lewis ap Rhys ap Philip of Builth. They lived in Talley parish and he inherited Tyr Bryngwyn from his father. They had five children, Lewis, William, Sioned (Jenet), Maud and Rees (42), whose son, David Rhys Williams (c1660-1714), is probably the member of the family who emigrated as Quakers in 1693 to Philadelphia County in Pennsylvania (see Chapter 29.7 for details of their successors);

(5) James ap Rhys (Price), the fourth son who lived in Talley parish and in 1589 married Elinor Gwynne, eldest daughter of Rhydderch Gwynne David Rees of Taliaris near Talley on the way to Llandeilo. James had inherited Abernaint (see Chapter 28.1) from his father and he brought up his family there. James and Elinor had three children: William Price of Abernaint, Thomas Price, and Dorothy who married William Gwyn of Piodau near Llandybie. It seems that James and Elinor were listed[131] on the Recusant Rolls for 1606 meaning that they had refused to attend the established church as required by law so could face financial penalties as papists; and

(6) David ap Rhys (40), the eldest son and heir who inherited Rhydodyn and who was alive in 1612.

---

[129] See Chapter 29.1
[130] Dwnn pedigree
[131] Alan Randall: *Recusancy in Carmarthenshire CA (1997) p72*

David ap Rhys (c1540-c1612)

Francis Jones describes[132] David ap Rhys (40) (sometimes known as David Price) of Rhydodyn Issa and his father, Rhys ap William, as the two "squirrel-squires" of the family because they methodically extended their estate and the wealth of the family by large numbers of property acquisitions including mortgages with a view to later purchase of the relevant lands. Between 1568 and 1612 David entered into no fewer than 48 transactions including 23 purchases in the three parishes of Llansawel, Talley and Cynwyl Gaeo thereby increasing the estate very considerably. He took advantage of his neighbouring yeomen and gentlemen as well as the misfortunes of his distant cousins, the Dynevor family[133], many of whose lands had been appropriated by Henry VIII following the execution for treason of Rhys ap Gruffydd (1508-31). David acquired freeholds or leases from the Crown of some of such lands. As we have seen, in 1609 he acquired Rhydodyn Ucha from his cousins so that he owned all the properties within the Edwinsford demesne both sides of the River Cothi. He also invested in tithes and acquired from the Crown a moiety (half) of the rectory of Caeo and the chapel of Llansawel and their tithes formerly owned by the dissolved Talley monastery for which he paid the Crown a rent.

In 1583 David served as beadle of Caeo and was responsible for the collection of Crown rents; in 1602 he was raglor of that commote. We do not know what other official local public offices he held.

Like so many other squire and gentry families of the time David was keen to promote his family's credentials by creating a family pedigree and acquiring a coat of arms. He commissioned Lewys Dwnn to do so and Dwnn visited Rhydodyn in 1596. Lewys Dwnn (c1550-c1616) was probably the most famous genealogist of his day whose *Heraldic Visitations of Wales between 1586 and 1613* was a monumental and impressive work of truth and fiction. Dwnn was a Deputy Herald to Robert Cooke, Clarenceux King of Arms to Queen Elizabeth I and was also a prolific poet. Many of the families of Wales used his work and Dwnn's position to present petitions to the College of Arms in London to approve their pedigrees, which once granted assumed the status of fact irrespective of the truth. I have already commented in Chapter 2 that some of the Edwinsford early pedigree produced by Dwnn must be taken with a pinch of salt since there is very little hard evidence for some of his assertions. The coat of arms recorded at the College of Arms at the time was *argent a lion rampant sable, the head, paws, and tuft of tail argent* (for Eidio Wyllt (16)), quartering the arms of Meurig, King of Dyfed, Sawl Felyn, Rhys ap Tewdwr, Rhiwallon ap Cynfryn, and others, derived through marriages. The crest was a lion as in the arms, and the motto was "Kowir I Dduw a Prins (Faithful to God and my Prince)[134]. Whether the quartering as described was correct is somewhat doubtful given later research reflected in the pedigree shown in this book.

David appears to have died intestate in about 1612 suffering badly from toothache in later years. There is no evidence of the size of his estate which must have been much larger than his father's but we do know that he had 36 tenants. He died a rich man despite a few court appearances in litigation with neighbouring landowners. In 1600 he even took on the powerful Sir Thomas Johnes MP DL of Abermarlais[135] and Haroldston (1554-1604) who owned some of the former Talley monastery lands and whose tenants were complaining about his behaviour. David took out a Bill of Complaint in the Court of Chancery against Sir Thomas on the basis that Sir Thomas was defrauding the county of monies raised for the administration of the militia, a very serious charge for an MP and Deputy Lieutenant of the county. The Court held that Sir Thomas was innocent but that his deputies were guilty of taking bribes and they were sent to the Fleet prison and had to repay all missing militia monies.

The Crown did not renew the lease of the lordship of Llandovery in favour of Sir Thomas Johnes notwithstanding that his father and grandfather had held it. This led to disagreements with the new owner, Lord Audley, who sued Sir Thomas in the Court of Exchequer in 1592. In 1602 Sir Thomas was summoned before the Court of Star Chamber charged with violence and entry to a corn mill in the county. He was also accused of various breaches of his duties as Deputy Lieutenant. He seems to have been a litigious man like some of his forbears with a penchant for grabbing land when the opportunity arose. He increased

---

132 Francis Jones: *THSC (1986) p91 et seq*

133 Gerald Morgan: *Dinefwr*; David Lewis: *Dolaucothi p82-87*

134 Dwnn

135 David Lewis: *Dolaucothi p107-8*

his properties in Carmarthenshire including leases of parts of the Talley estate[136].

Research by Dr Roger Turvey[137] has shown that during the 16th century Tudor period there were some 320 gentry in Carmarthenshire of whom only eight were Knights, being the most powerful political elite including Sir Thomas Johnes and his family of Abermarlais and Haroldston. Of such 320 gentry approximately one third served unpaid as JPs on the commission for life. The chief magistrate was the Custos Rotulorum, an office almost owned by the Johnes family under the Tudors (although Sir Thomas was removed from the commission between 1592 and 1595 for reasons unknown). The Johnes family also held the influential position of Sheriff many times and served as MPs for the county. Justice in the Courts of Quarter Sessions, Great Sessions and at the Council of Wales and the Marches was thus effectively controlled by a few powerful families including the Johnes family. It seems these families took every opportunity to abuse[138] their powers by acquiring lands from lower gentry and yeomen including by extortion, forgery, and buying under duress at an under value. The Court of Star Chamber in London was the only independent court available to those victims who tried to oppose this abuse of power and seek justice. Dr Turvey has shown that in addition to the 1602 case referred to above there were several trials in which the Attorney-General brought cases for such abuse against Sir Thomas and his friends; sadly the verdicts of such cases do not survive but it would seem that Sir Thomas retained his position, except during 1592 and 1595, so we must presume that such cases were dismissed. He and his family were members of the "tafia" who did well for themselves under the Tudors. The Rhydodyn family were not yet in that league but during the next century would become one of the leading families in the county.

In the 1560s David married Jane, daughter of David Philipps of Cilsant in Llanwinnio and his wife Margaret who was the daughter and coheiress of Sir John Vaughan of Whitland, a most influential family. Their only child was Rees ap David Price (41), who as we shall see in Chapter 7.2 abandoned his Welsh patronymic name and adopted the surname of "Williams" from about 1604 and was thereafter known as Rees Williams.

The Reformation and Acts of Union 1536 and 1543

Henry VIII was a most selfish man who concentrated on his own pleasures and pursuits. In his early reign he relied on Cardinal Wolsey to control and govern the Welsh which he did with the help of loyal subjects like Sir Rhys ap Thomas (305). By 1529 Henry's marital problems had led to the Reformation Parliament, the downfall of Wolsey and the rise to power of Thomas Cromwell. Then came the 1534 Act of Supremacy with the establishment of the Church of England having the King as its Supreme Head, a strategy supported by Cromwell and the new Archbishop of Canterbury, Thomas Cranmer. The few who disagreed were executed including Sir Thomas More[139]. This was followed by the annulment or divorce of his first marriage to Catherine of Aragon (his "great matter") and his second marriage to Anne Boleyn, who was executed for adultery in 1536.

The logic of the Act of Supremacy led to the dissolution of the monasteries and all Church lands from 1536 with much of them being sold and huge amounts of money going to the Crown needed for military campaigns; this dissolution resulted in the largest change in land ownership since the Norman Invasion in 1066 and the

---

136 Dwnn; Bartrum; Golden Grove book of pedigrees (NLW); Thomas Nicholas; Rowland; EG Jones: *Univ of Wales Board of Celtic Studies history and law service*; HP

137 Dr Turvey's lecture on Gentry Abuse of Power in Carmarthenshire at the Carmarthenshire Antiquarian Society meeting held on 13 February 2016; *CA (2016) p24-32*

138 DJ Williams: *Hen Dŷ Ffarm (1953) p92-6.* DJ Williams (1885-1970) was brought up in Abernant, Llansawel, was educated late at Jesus College Oxford (1916-8), became a teacher and one of the best-known writers of Welsh literature. His book "The Old Farmhouse" was translated in 1961 by Waldo Williams and gives an excellent description of country life in the Talley and Llansawel area around 1890. He suggests that his Williams family of Llywele and the Williams family of Rhydodyn were closely related and that his family were deprived of Llywele and their lands by David ap Rhys (40)

139 Sir Thomas More (1478-1535), Lord High Chancellor and personal adviser to Henry VIII, was executed for refusing to take the oath of supremacy and acting in breach of the new Treason Act 1534 on untrue evidence provided by Sir Richard Rich. He was executed on 6 July 1535 in the Tower of London and is buried there in the chapel of St Peter ad Vincula. He is a Saint. Tradition says that one of his priceless gold Collars of Esses was sold by Henry VIII to the Lord Mayor of London, Sir John Aleyn, who bequeathed it to the City in 1545. It has been worn by every Lord Mayor ever since although a more recent copy is used for every day use (see Dominic Reid: *Lord Mayor's Show 800 Years 1215-2015 (2015) p 70-71)*

Domesday Book survey in 1086. The consequences for Carmarthenshire were grave with the destruction of many religious houses, unemployment for former clerics and their employees, and the despoiling of libraries, scholarship, books and relics. To prevent their destruction some relics from Talley Abbey[140] were given by the Abbot to the Johnes family of Dolaucothi including the altar piece of the Abbey and a silver backed case containing a filigree and coloured crucifix, possibly a "Tawdrey" from a shrine of pilgrimage, and a monk's spoon; some are now in the Carmarthen Museum at Abergwili and the Elijah painting (an ikon of a religious painting on wood of the Orthodox Church) is in St Davids Cathedral; they were inherited by Thomas Johnes of Hafod whose estate sold some of them to the Duke of Newcastle and they were later bought back at auction by Herbert Lloyd-Johnes who donated them to the Bishop. Some others including the altar piece[141] were acquired by the Johnes family and kept at Dolaucothi.

Henry remained a Catholic (he had been named by the Pope as the "Defender of the Faith") and opposed the new Protestant movement on the continent. St Davids Cathedral was neglected while its Bishop's residence was transferred to Abergwili near Carmarthen where it has remained. One of the lasting changes saw the former Church tithes being sold by the Crown to lay impropriators, usually wealthy local families, who thereafter collected the tithes formerly paid to the clerics and parish churches; most of the local tithes in the parish of Cynwyl Gaeo ended up in the ownership of the Williams-Drummond family of Edwinsford.

Carmarthenshire was divided between those parts including Talley, Llansawel and Cynwyl Gaeo which were ruled by the Crown through the Prince of Wales and those parts which were Marcher lordships ruled by independent wealthy families; some of these lordships had been forfeited by the Crown (for example the Dinefwr estates following the execution of Rhys ap Gruffydd in 1531) or bought by the Crown and held by the Duchy of Lancaster. Cromwell and some Welsh gentry considered that Welshmen should have the same rights and privileges as Englishmen in terms of justice and land and inheritance rights. This resulted in the 1536 Act of Union (An Act for Laws and Justice to be ministered in Wales in Like Form as it is in this Realm) which with other legislation[142] was probably a genuine attempt by Cromwell to improve the governorship of Wales and to improve the lot of Welshmen.

The Acts of 1536 and 1543 :(a) created a single united State by incorporating the whole of Wales into the Realm of England; (b) abolished the former Marcher lordships and their powers by dividing Wales into shires (and hundreds) with Carmarthenshire being enlarged by incorporating some former Marcher lordships; (c) gave the same civil rights and privileges to Welshmen as were enjoyed by Englishmen including the same laws and Parliamentary representation; hence each Welsh shire was represented by one Knight and each shire town by one burgess (the freemen who were electors) so shire towns such as Llandovery and Llandeilo voted in the Carmarthen election with Carmarthenshire (on the basis of all 40 shilling freeholders having the vote) thereby having two MPs until the Reform Act 1832; (d) English laws replaced Welsh law and practice so the Welsh tradition of gavelkind (dividing land between sons on death) was abolished and replaced by primogeniture; (e) the border between Wales and England was fixed (although Monmouthshire was made part of England probably because it was attached to the Oxford judicial circuit) and all parts of Wales were subject to taxation after 1 November 1536; and (f) for judicial purposes the 12 shires in Wales were divided into four circuits so the Justices of Carmarthenshire, Cardiganshire and Pembrokeshire in their own one circuit sat as the Court of Great Sessions for six days twice each year in the shire towns of their circuit. Justices of the Peace were appointed with eight JPs in each shire usually being wealthy gentry sitting at Quarter Sessions for more serious cases and also acting as the administrative body within each shire while each local hundred had their Petty Sessions for less serious cases. There were also monthly freeholders' courts in each shire chaired by the Sheriff, hundred courts every fortnight or so chaired by the Deputy Sheriff while manorial courts leet and courts baron also continued to be summoned as in the past.[143]

140 See Chapter 29.1

141 South Wales Daily News 8 July 1911

142 Glanmor Williams p264 et seq; Prys-Jones p33-45

143 See Chapter 35 for a description of manorial courts

The abolition of the Marcher lordships brought to an end some 470 years of an attempt by William I and his successors to keep the unruly Welsh at bay by delegating this task to powerful nobility. However at times this led to internecine warfare between such nobles with rival territorial claims, feuding loyalties and blood ties, and consequent risk to the Crown itself. Henry VII was perceived as Welsh by the Welsh and succeeded in bringing the feud between the red and white roses to an end. Henry VIII decided that central rule from London was overdue so the abolition of the Marcher lordships and the imposition of the Council for Wales and the Marches with a new more powerful and centralised government dependent on the King himself was a much more effective method of controlling the Welsh in future.

The most controversial aspect of the Acts of Union was the requirement that the Welsh language be banished from all court proceedings and that "no person that use the Welsh speech or language shall have or enjoy any manner of office or fees within this Realm of England, Wales or other of the King's dominion upon pain of forfeiting the same office or fees unless he or they use and exercise the English speech or language". While this provision was probably not intended to destroy the Welsh language (no law could achieve that) it led in practice to the division of society into anglicised gentry and town burgesses sitting as Sheriffs and JPs while rural communities often became monoglot Welsh speaking.

When Henry VIII came to the throne there were 37 shires, 12 urban counties and 98 towns and boroughs which sent representatives to the House of Commons. By 1559 when Elizabeth I had taken the throne (and after Welsh constituencies had been added after the Acts of Union) there were 402 elected Members of the House of Commons, 78 sitting for the 39 English counties, 12 for the 12 Welsh counties, 12 for the Welsh boroughs, and the remaining 300 sitting for English boroughs. By 1601 the number elected for boroughs alone had grown to 372 Members covering the newly enfranchised boroughs in England.

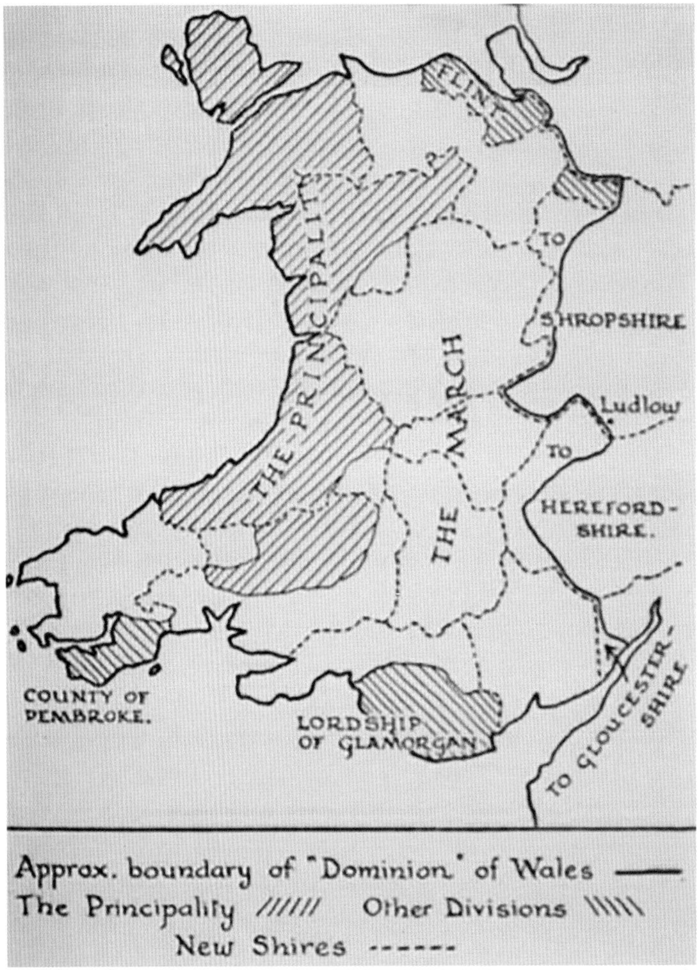

Wales in the 16th century prior to the Acts of Union (Prof Sir John Lloyd)

6.3 Patronyms and Surnames

In England fixed surnames were adopted during the Middle Ages whereas in Wales a patronymic naming system was used based on the person's baptismal name being linked by *"ap"* or *"ab"* (son of) or *"ferch"* or *"uch"* (daughter of) to the father's baptismal name; women kept their patronymic names even after marriage. This system arose[144] because of the Welsh Laws of Hywel Dda which made it essential for inheritance and landowning reasons that people could prove their lineage up to seven generations if necessary; these laws survived until the Acts of Union of 1536 and 1543 which abolished the native laws and customs[145] including the custom of partible inheritance or gavelkind (under which land was divided on death) which made it redundant to know the lineage line. While the English living in Wales adopted fixed surnames early on, the Welsh did so only gradually during a transitional period with the gentry adopting the new system in the 16th and 17th centuries while the yeomanry and peasantry did so later. The keeping of parish registers also encouraged the use of fixed surnames; the coming of Protestantism resulted in the use of a very small number of Biblical names such as John, David, Thomas and William which resulted in the surnames Jones, Davies, Thomas and Williams, the "s" at the end of the fixed surname denoting "son of". Roberts from Robert and Edwards from Edward have become more common since. Powell from ap Hywel, Upjohn from ap John, and Bowen from ap Owen have also flourished. Vaughan was the anglicised version of Fychan.

As we shall see the first member of the Williams family of Rhydodyn to adopt the surname of "Williams" was Rees (ap David Price) Williams (d1627)(41) of Rhydodyn who served as Sheriff of Carmarthenshire in 1614, being the first member of the family to hold such high office. Those gentry families who aspired to be High Sheriffs of Welsh counties after the Acts of Union or wished to seek Crown appointments probably had to adopt fixed surnames in practice.

During the past five centuries in Wales a number of fixed surnames[146] have become popular including Jones (5.75 per cent of all surnames in modern day Wales), Williams, Davies, Evans, Thomas, Roberts, Lewis, Hughes, Morgan and Griffiths with some 35 per cent of today's population in Wales having a family surname of Welsh origin.

6.4 Synopsis of Carmarthenshire under the later Tudor Monarchs

Edward VI's six year reign (1547-53) was dominated by religious controversy with the very young King, who was only nine when he took the throne, ruling under a Council of Regency under the influence of his uncle, the Protestant Earl of Hertford and Duke of Somerset[147]. Carmarthenshire under Henry VIII was still very much Catholic in religion albeit within the new Anglican Church. Under Edward Protestantism flourished with the abolishing of Latin services, pilgrimages, holy days, candles, frescoes, roods and pictures, stained glass windows, sculptures and even bell ringing under an Act of Uniformity. Clerics were allowed to marry, treasures of churches in Carmarthenshire and elsewhere were looted and even in St Davids Cathedral the shrine and plate disappeared as did the famous Book of St Teilo from Llandaff Cathedral. This type of Protestantism was encouraged by Thomas Cranmer, Archbishop of Canterbury, who published a new Anglican Book of Common Prayer in 1549. Much of this new religious approach was resented in Wales although the gentry did little about it in practice. Edward was a sickly child and died in 1553 aged only 15. Despite an attempt by the Earl of Warwick (and Duke of Northumberland) who controlled the Council of Regency to have the 15 year old Protestant, Lady Jane Grey, proclaimed Queen on 10 July 1553, within a few days she was deposed and the Catholic, Mary, daughter of Henry VIII and Catherine of Aragon, was proclaimed Queen. Northumberland and Lady Jane Grey were executed.

Mary I, who had previously been declared illegitimate by an Act of Parliament, had grown up as an ardent Catholic. Initially she was welcomed in Wales where Protestantism had not been popular. She

---

144 *The Welsh Academy Encyclopaedia of Wales (2008) p838.* See also *Welsh Surnames (1985)* by Prof TJ Morgan and his son Prof Prys Morgan who is an Emeritus Professor at Swansea University

145 Prof Prys Morgan: *The Rise of Welsh Surnames in Carmarthenshire CA (2010) p73-9*

146 UCL research data

147 Somerset House in London was his residence

ruled for only five years (1553-8) and reversed her brother Edward's Protestant reforms and laws, restored Papal supremacy and will forever be remembered as "Bloody Mary" for her burning[148] at the stake for heresy of 287 Protestants including Bishops Latimer and Ridley in Broad Street in Oxford[149]; Thomas Cranmer was to follow soon thereafter. Only three Protestants were burnt in Wales one of whom was Bishop Robert Ferrar[150], Bishop of St Davids, who was imprisoned under Edward VI for not being enough of a Protestant reformer, and then under Mary I was deposed for heresy and for marrying and after refusing to recant and renounce Protestantism was burnt at the stake in the market place in Carmarthen on 30 March 1555. Mary's disastrous marriage in 1554 to King Philip of Spain was childless and she died in 1558 having lost the last English possession in France and knowing that her attempt to reintroduce Catholicism to England had failed.

Elizabeth I, the daughter of Henry VIII and Anne Boleyn, was very well educated and, despite inheriting a difficult foreign war, an empty treasury and political and religious divisions, her long reign (1558-1603) is remembered as one of the most successful in English history. In matters of religion she sensibly adopted a middle course of returning to the monarch being the Supreme Governor of the Anglican Church, Protestant doctrine being brought back but Catholic ritual also being retained; in Carmarthenshire worship continued in much the same way as before in practice[151] but the local clergy were very poor. The Pope excommunicated Elizabeth for heresy in 1570 but it was only during the last 20 years of her reign that over 200 clerics were executed for treason including several Welshmen. There were many plots against the Crown including the Ridolfi Plot of 1572, the Throckmorton Plot of 1583 and the Babington Plot of 1586; Mary Queen of Scots was executed in 1587; and the Spanish Armada was defeated in 1588 at a time when the risk of foreign Catholic invasion by Spain and France was very real. In Wales Elizabeth appointed 16 Bishops during her

Tablet in St Peter's Church, Carmarthen commemorating Bishop Ferrar

reign of whom 13 were Welshmen[152] and she encouraged by law the translation into Welsh of the Bible and the Book of Common Prayer. The new Welsh Bible produced by Bishop Morgan in 1588, which the

[148] Virginia Rounding: *The Burning Time-The Story of the Smithfield Martyrs (2017)* shows the zeal of the Tudors for burning hundreds of people for heresy between 1531 and 1558. Sir Thomas More was also a self declared persecutor of heretics

[149] The Oxford martyrs are commemorated by the stone monument called the Martyrs' Memorial opposite Balliol College Oxford containing statues of Latimer, Ridley and Cranmer erected in 1843 to oppose the Anglo-Catholic tractarian movement led by John Keble and Cardinal John Henry Newman. They are also commemorated in *Foxe's Book of Martyrs* published in 1563 with details of the sufferings and burnings of Protestant martyrs under Queen Mary I

[150] Prys-Jones p72

[151] In Cynwyl Gaeo the Ffynnon Gweno healing well (named after one of the five saints of Pumsaint) was a pagan tradition which became popular with the masses

[152] Glanmor Williams p307. Bishop Richard Davies rebuilt the diocese of St Davids accepting the Elizabethan settlement. Bishop Barlow had earlier tried and failed to have the see transferred to Grey Friars in Carmarthen

Privy Council instructed all Welsh Bishops to use in church, was a huge success and helped to save the Welsh language. Whilst the Authorised Version of the Bible in English appeared in 1611, the first Welsh Bible for people to use at home did not appear until 1630 at a price of five shillings and was nicknamed the Little Bible (*Y Beibl Bach*); it was published at the expense of a Welsh Aldermen of the City of London, Sir Thomas Myddleton of Denbigh (1550-1631) who was Lord Mayor of London in 1613-4[153], and his colleague Rowland Heylyn.

Following the Acts of Union 1536 and 1543 described in Chapter 6.2, Carmarthenshire, Cardiganshire and Pembrokeshire like other counties gradually changed socially and politically. Rural society consisted of knights, esquires (usually the younger sons of the principal families), gentlemen, yeoman (freeholders worth 40 shillings per annum), husbandmen, craftsmen, cottagers, labourers and the poor; urban communities in the towns consisted of gentry, merchants, shopkeepers, artisans, labourers and paupers with the professions such as physicians, lawyers, clerics and scholars as well. A handful of families effectively controlled the most prestigious offices[154] such as Deputy Lieutenants of which most counties had two, Members of Parliament of which most counties had one for the county and one for the county boroughs, Sheriff (one for each county, and then being the head of the administration for each county and the returning officer in elections) and Justices of the Peace (usually eight but often more in practice for each county). Below them came the local parish gentry of freeholders and yeomen who held the offices of coroners, escheators, high and petty constables, and jurors. Each Sheriff had an Under-Sheriff with gaolers and bailiffs in each parish or hundred reporting to them. JPs had the Custos Rotulorum in charge of them who was usually the pre-eminent landowner in the county with the Clerk doing the administration. Each of the major county families such as the Vaughans of Golden Grove and the Jones/ Johnes families in Carmarthenshire and the Pryse of Gogerddan and the Lloyd families in Cardiganshire had junior or cadet braches whose members would also occasionally be drafted in to hold some of the county offices, although the most important such as MP was usually held by the head of the pre-eminent family or his son and heir; the MP for the county boroughs might also be from one of the major families or sometimes from a wealthy burgess family.

An interesting analysis[155] of the marriages between Welsh knighted gentry reveals that of the wives of Welsh knights of Henry VII's reign some 16 were Welsh and 11 were English; in Henry VIII's reign some 19 were Welsh and 16 were English; and in the reigns of Edward and Mary some 15 were Welsh and 11 English.In Carmarthenshire Sir Rhys ap Thomas (d1525) married two Welsh wives; Sir Gruffydd ap Rhys of Dinefwr (d1521) married an English wife; Sir Thomas Philipps of Picton Castle (d1520) married a Welsh wife; Sir William Thomas of Aberglasney (d1543) married a Welsh wife; Sir Thomas Jones MP of Abermarlais (d1558) married a Welsh wife and then an English wife; Sir John Vaughan of Whitland (d1564) married a Welsh wife; Sir James Williams of Betws (d1582) married a Welsh wife; and Sir Henry Johnes MP of Abermarlais (d1586) married two Welsh wives and an English wife.

Bribes, corruption, illegal electioneering, abuses and violence were rampant in most counties including Carmarthenshire and some Sheriffs showed little attempt to follow the rules of democracy in contested elections. Hence the proliferation of litigation and civil suits in the Star Chamber and Council of the Marches and frequent convictions in the criminal courts.

In the countryside life was very difficult for most of the population who were monoglot Welsh speaking. Very bad harvests and famine during parts of the last half of the 16th century, rising inflation, enclosure of common land and woodland, rising rents without increases in wages, and a gradual increase in the population made life more and more tough for all but the gentry; the latter prospered and were keen to promote their old or supposedly old pedigrees. Hence the activities of Lewys Dwnn who between 1586 and 1614 visited all the Welsh nobility and gentry to record their pedigrees and family seats, which were mostly located in the valley bottoms which had long been cleared of their former heavy forest cover. Gentry bought or built large houses or mansions and created deer-parks, pheasantries, dovecotes,

---

153 City of London Corporation archives; AB Beaven: *The Aldermen of the City of London (1908)*

154 Glanmor Williams p342 et seq

155 WRB Robinson: *The Marriages of Knighted Welsh Landowners 1485-1558 NLWJ XXV p387-398*

fishponds, lakes and gardens while many of the poor lived in one roomed mud hovels with earth floors. During the occasional famine many died. The labourer of 1326[156] who was paid one and a half pennies each day could buy much more with his wages than his counterpart of 1615 who was paid six pennies per day.

In addition there was for most of Elizabeth's reign a continuing risk of foreign invasion by the French and Spanish quite apart from the revolt in Ireland. The Welsh gentry had to muster local troops in preparation for defence and many Welshmen were forced to go into the army and serve in Ireland. Sir John Perrot (1530-92) was the Custos Rotulorum and in charge for the three south-western counties. He was presented by Queen Mary with the castles and lordships of Carew and Laugharne and under Elizabeth he became the most powerful man in South Wales as well as Lord Deputy in Ireland, but eventually was tried for treason on a trumped-up charge and died before execution in the Tower of London.

[156] Glanmor Williams p394

7. The Stuart Period 1603-1714

7.1 Synopsis of Carmarthenshire under the Stuarts

James I

James I (ruler of Scotland 1567-1625 and ruler of England 1603-25) was the son of Mary Queen of Scots and Lord Darnley who was murdered. So he had already been King James VI of Scotland for 36 years when he succeeded to the English throne on the death of Elizabeth I. He was a descendant of Henry Tudor and was enthusiastically welcomed in Wales.

The Established Anglican Church with its Calvinistic approach was here to stay and with Welsh translations of the King James Authorised Version of the Bible and a new Prayer Book the Welsh were content. The famous Vicar Rhys Prichard (1579-1644) of Llandovery was an ardent Calvinist Puritan believing in predestination and the salvation of the elect; he wrote popular moralist verses and songs for his flock to memorise (*Canwyll y Cymry*) and became chancellor of St Davids Cathedral. Despite being a Calvinist he was a strong Royalist and died before the Civil War had ended.

James was an intellectual ("the wisest fool in Christendom" according to the French) and keen to unite England and Scotland using the Welsh precedent for well intentioned reasons, a project in which he failed so both countries remained separate with their own laws and administration. Sadly he replaced the Welsh dragon with the Scottish unicorn in his coat of arms. He achieved peace during his reign despite the risk of Catholic invasion and the Thirty Years War on the continent which started in 1618.

However Catholic plots such as the failed Gunpowder Plot of 1605 to blow up Parliament resulted in more anti-Catholic feeling and this encouraged James to effect the Plantation of Ulster. Elizabeth I had quashed an Irish rebellion in 1593; by 1607 the landowning Irish Earls had submitted to James I and their lands were forfeited to the Crown. James decided that in order to avoid any future Catholic rebellion or risk of invasion by the French or Spanish via Ireland it was necessary to colonise Ulster with Scots and English who were loyal. Lacking funds for the purpose James forced 55 of the Livery companies in the City of London to finance the settlement having first gaoled in the Tower of London those of their Masters who proved reluctant to pay up. In 1613 the City of London formed by Royal Charter "The Honourable The Irish Society" which developed County Londonderry and thereby became reluctant landlords having built the City of Londonderry and the town of Coleraine[157]. James also continued with the Tudor tradition of forcing Livery companies in the City of London to enter into compulsory long term loans to the Crown which nearly bankrupted some of them; it is not surprising that the City supported Parliament in the Civil War.

James promoted his bisexual Court favourites such as Robert Carr who became the Earl of Somerset and George Villiers who became the Duke of Buckingham. In Carmarthenshire he promoted the Vaughan family of Golden Grove of whom six supported Charles I in the Civil War, five were knighted and the sixth, John Vaughan (1573-1634), became the Ist Earl of Carbery in the peerage of Ireland having served the Crown on the Privy Council of Ireland. He served as Sheriff, as MP for the county, and as a member of the Council of Wales.

George Owen in his *Brief Account of Wales (1602)* says that "Carmarthen, the largest town in Wales, fair and in good state, yet many unruly and quarellous people there". In Carmarthenshire the rest of the towns were poor and the people "tall and personable, many recusants lately sprung up, theft much nourished, often brawls and other disorders".

---

[157] James Curl: *The Honourable The Irish Society and the Plantation of Ulster 1608-2000 (2000);* Rev George Hill: *The Conquest of Ireland Book 3 (1846).* By tradition a former Lord Mayor of London acts as the Governor (Chairman) of the Society which is controlled by the City of London Corporation. The Society still owns the walls of Londonderry and is now a charity which is responsible for some of the rivers and uses its fishing and other income to help local Ulster charities

John Speed's Carmarthenshire

John Speed (1552-1629) was born in Cheshire and followed his father by becoming a tailor. At the age of 18 he became an apprentice and freeman of the Merchant Taylors' Company of the City of London (which shares every alternate year with the Skinners' Company the No 6 or 7 place in the order of seniority of the Livery Companies, hence the phrase "at sixes or sevens"). At 20 he married and he and his wife produced 12 sons and 6 daughters. In 1598 at the age of 46 under the patronage of Lord Brooke, a man of influence in the Elizabethan Court, he started writing and researching county maps and principal towns. In 1611-12 he published his first editions of 67 maps in an atlas called The Theatre of the Empire of Great Britain, most of which were engraved by Jodocus Hondius in Amsterdam. Numerous further editions in English followed including in 1616 the only edition in Latin on the reverse of each map. The publishers included John Sudbury and George Humble; the printers included William Hall, John Beale, Thomas Snodham, John Dawson and Samuel Simmons. John Speed died at St Giles, Cripplegate in the City of London on 28 July 1629.

The English text accompanying and on the reverse of the county map of Carmarthenshire (some of which comes from Camden's Britannia) includes the following:

"Caermarden-shire, so called from the chief town Caermarden... this shire is not altogether so pestered with hills as her bordering neighbours are...and therefore is better for corn and pasturage, yea and in woods also, so that for victuals this country is very well stored, which the stomach doth as well digest, the air being wholsom, temperate and pleasing. Anciently these parts were possessed by the *Dimatre* (Demetae tribe) as *Ptolemy, Gildas* and *Ninius* do name them, though *Pliny* holds opinion that they were part of the *Silures*, with whom no doubt they were subdued to the Romans yoke by Julius Frontius... The commodities of this shire chiefly consist in cattle, pitcoal, fowl, and sea fish, whereof salmon is common among them...the shire town Caermarden which town by *Ptolemy* is called *Maridunum*, by Antonine the Emperor *Muridunum*, by the Britains *Caer-fridhin*, and by us *Caermarden*. It is pleasantly seated upon the south-west side of the River Towy that runneth through the midst of this shire....At the entrance of the Normans this town was brought under their obedience, and for a long time was distressed with the calamites of war, yet afterwards was made by the English Princes the Chancery and Exchequer for all South Wales, and at this day is yearly governed by a Mayor, who ever after is an Alderman and Justice of the Peace, two Sheriffs elected out of fifteen Burgesses, all in scarlet, a Sword-bearer, a Town Clerk, and two Sergeants with Maces". His list of the memorable places in the shire includes "*Talley*", "*Llansawil*" and "*Conwillgaio*" all in the Hundred of *Cayo* (the other Hundreds being *Cathinok, Perueth, Kidwelly, Elluet and Derllys)*.

One of John Speed's sons, Samuel, was later involved in a plot against Cromwell and fled to the West Indies where he became a sea chaplain.

7

John Speed Map 1610

Charles I

James's elder son, Henry Prince of Wales, had died in 1612 so on James's death in 1625 his younger son, Charles I (ruler 1625-49), succeeded to the throne aged 25. He was only 5ft 4ins tall, had a bad stutter and was so certain of his divinely ordained absolute right to rule that he failed to appreciate the changing times in which he ruled resulting eventually in his execution. His marriage to the Catholic, Henrietta Maria of France, in 1625 added petrol to the fire as did his appointment of Archbishop Laud in 1633 who looked as if he would reintroduce Catholicism. In 1629 he alienated the political class by ruling alone and dispensing with Parliament altogether for 11 years and when short of funds (for which the summoning of Parliament was necessary) he instead imposed an artificial ship money tax on every town. In Wales despite the unpopularity of ship money the fears of a Catholic invasion resulted in support for Charles. In 1639 the Scots rebelled and this was followed in 1640 by Charles summoning his first "Short" Parliament since 1629 but then he dismissed it in less than a month. By November 1640 he had to summon another Parliament (the Long Parliament) but by now many of the Lords and Commons were against his style of governing. In 1641 a Catholic uprising in Ireland started. By 1642 following an embarrassing failure by Charles to arrest some ringleaders in the House of Commons relations had become so bad that civil war seemed almost certain. In South Wales the House of Commons appointed Richard Vaughan, 2nd Earl of Carbery (son of John Vaughan), as the Lord Lieutenant of the Carmarthenshire and Cardiganshire militia; when however the Civil War started in August 1642 he supported the King and was appointed the commander of the Royalist Forces in south Wales; Charles made him Baron Vaughan of Emlyn in the English peerage. The first inconclusive Battle at Edgehill in October 1642 resulted in both sides realising that the war would last much longer than one battle and that their forces needed to be more professional.

In general[158] the Royalists in the Civil War tended to be the aristocracy, gentry (who saw the threat to the Crown as a threat to their own local power), clergy, country squires and many of the peasantry. To devout gentlemen and clergymen, rebellion against the Crown was a heinous sin[159]. The Parliamentarians consisted of the majority of MPs, many commercial and trading classes, lesser gentry and prosperous farmers. In South Wales the strong tradition of loyalty to the Tudor Crown and their successors resulted in strong Royalist support. In the House of Commons some 175 moderates sided with the King while 30 Peers in the Lords fought against him; of the 24 Welsh MPs only two supported Parliament. The City of London and East Anglia strongly supported the Parliamentary cause and their cause had superior resources of manpower and wealth as well as control of the Navy.[160]

While most of the gentry of Carmarthenshire and Cardiganshire supported the Royalist cause, families and communities were split including the various branches of the Lloyd family. Sir Francis Lloyd MP (d1669) of Maesyfelin (son of another Royalist, Sir Marmaduke Lloyd (1558-c1651)), sat in the House of Commons for Carmarthen for the very Short Parliament in 1640 and then in the Long Parliament from 1640 to 1644. He was Comptroller of the Household for Charles I and was knighted in Oxford (where Charles had resited his Court) on 24 March 1643. Having been disbarred from sitting in the Commons in 1644 as a punishment for supporting the King he served as the commander in chief of the horse for Charles I in Pembrokeshire. Sir Walter Lloyd MP for Cardiganshire (1580-c1662) of Llanfair Clydogau was also a strong Royalist who was knighted in 1643 and lived to see the Restoration.

In South Pembrokeshire the Roundhead Parliamentarians had much Welsh support from Pembroke, Tenby and Haverfordwest which had Puritan sympathies; John Wogan MP for Pembroke and his two sons fought in the Parliamentary army. The Royalist troops under the Earl of Carbery initially had some success in Pembrokeshire but then had to withdraw to Carmarthen, which was taken by Rowland Laugharne and his Parliamentary forces later that year. Carbery stepped down and retired to his estates in Carmarthenshire while Sir Charles Gerard took control of the Royalist forces and had some success in retaking Carmarthen, Cardigan, Newcastle Emlyn and Haverfordwest; only Tenby and Pembroke still flew the Parliamentary banner. In North Wales Sir Thomas Myddleton (son of a former Lord Mayor of London)

---

158 Prys-Jones Vol 2 p171

159 Prof Geraint Jenkins: *The Foundations of Modern Wales 1642-1780 p5*

160 Prof Blair Worden: *The English Civil Wars 1640-60 p62*

led the successful Parliamentary forces at the victorious battle of Montgomery in 1644, the biggest battle on Welsh soil. Oliver Cromwell led the Parliamentary forces and his "ironsides" to a decisive victory at Marston Moor in July 1644 defeating Prince Rupert. Cromwell followed this with a brilliant victory at Naseby in June 1645 by his new Model Army, long remembered in Wales because some 100 Welsh women accompanying the defeated Royalist forces were brutually slaughtered and the rest had their noses and faces slashed.[161] Fortunately for Welsh women the witchfinding activities of Matthew Hopkins (c1620-47) the so called "Witchfinder General" never seem to have reached Wales; he was responsible for hanging over 300 women in three years (1644-47) mostly in Eastern England. So ended the First Civil War with Major General Rowland Laugharne as commander in chief of the Parliamentary forces in South Wales being in almost total control and Carmarthen surrendered to his forces; he was rewarded in March 1645 by both Houses of Parliament settling on him the Slebech estates.

Instead of capitulating, agreeing to Parliament's demands, and suing for a peaceful return to his throne the King prevaricated and exploited the continuing divisions between Parliament and its successful army led by Cromwell. The wish of the Puritans in Parliament, with the strong support of the City of London, was to establish Presbyterianism as the national religion but this was not the wish of Cromwell who favoured toleration of all religions (except Catholicism) as Independents. The Scots rebelled again in 1648 starting the Second Civil War in support of the King and invaded England. In South Wales the Royalists strengthened their resources and three important Parliamentary commanders changed sides and supported the King, namely General Rowland Laugharne of St Bride's, Colonel Rice Powell (whose forces comprised some 8,000 cavaliers, Parliamentarians and disbanded troops) and Colonel John Poyer (Mayor of Pembroke). They assembled their forces at Carmarthen and then advanced to St Fagans near Cardiff on 8 May 1648 where they were heavily defeated with 3,000 prisoners taken by a smaller more professional Parliamentary army led by Colonel Horton.

Cromwell quickly marched to South Wales to restore order, besieged Pembroke and ordered the demolition of a number of castles including Carmarthen Castle. Pembroke surrendered to Cromwell on 11 July 1648 on terms that: (a) Laugharne, Poyer and others surrender to the mercy of Parliament; (b) other senior commanders "do within six weeks next following depart the kingdom and not return within two years"; (c) "all other officers and gentlemen shall have free liberty to go to their several habitations and there live quietly submitting to the authority of Parliament"; (d) "all private soldiers shall have passes to go to their several houses without being stripped or having any violence done to them"; (e) "the townsmen shall be free from plunder and violence and enjoy their liberties as heretofore they have done" and (f) "the town of Pembroke with all arms, ammunitions and ordnance together with the victuals and provisions for the garrison be forthwith delivered unto Lt-General Cromwell or such as he shall appoint for the use of Parliament". Laugharne, Powell and Poyer were sent to the Tower and then Windsor Castle and their trial took place in 1649; they were all found guilty and sentenced to death. The three were made to cast lots for their lives with one lot being blank and the other two saying "Life given of God". Poyer drew the blank and was shot in the Piazza at Covent Garden on 21 April 1649. Laugharne returned home and later went to fight in Ireland against Cromwell and was captured in 1650 and shot. Powell sensibly went home.

South Wales suffered greatly from the Civil War with towns, castles, houses, churches and buildings looted or destroyed and the general population suffered from misery, famine and much hardship. Roads and bridges were in a very poor state; there were several harvest failures which led to inflation and more poverty. Parliament fined Carmarthenshire £4,000 for supporting the King. Fines were also imposed on a number of gentry and other "delinquents" including Sir Francis Lloyd (£1,050). The Earl of Carbery was very lucky not to be fined at all; he was to keep a very low profile until the Restoration in 1660 when his loyalty to the Crown resulted in him being appointed President of the Council of Wales. Fines were also raised for general expenses of the Commonwealth; for example in 1657 Cromwell as Lord Protector fined Cardiganshire £366 towards the expenses of the Spanish War with Thomas Lloyd of Llanfair Clydogau as Sheriff in 1656-7 instructed to raise such amount.

161 Jenkins p17

Regicide

The Army had decided that Charles had to be executed in order to establish peace. On 6 December 1648[162] the Army purged Parliament by Colonel Thomas Pride (Pride's Purge) effectively removing the great majority of Presbyterian members. The rest, commonly called "the Rump", set up a High Court of Justice to try King Charles I. Some 80 MPs attended the trial with Charles charged with (1) having pursued "a wicked design to erect and uphold in himself an unlimited and tyrannical power to rule according to his will, and to overthrow the rights and liberties of the people" and (2) having "traitorously and maliciously declared war" on his subjects. The trial took place in Westminster Hall and Charles conducted himself with much dignity refusing to accept the legality of the proceedings. He was found guilty by a small majority and on 30 January 1649 he was publicly executed by beheading on a scaffold outside the Banqueting Hall in Whitehall. Only 57 MPs signed the death warrant including two Welshmen, Colonel John Jones of Maesygarnedd (husband of Cromwell's sister) and Colonel Thomas Wogan MP for Pembroke. After the Restoration in 1660 nine of the 55 signatories to the regicide were themselves killed and many were imprisoned; Wogan was fortunate to escape from the Tower in 1664 and died abroad while Jones was hanged at the gallows at Charing Cross in October 1660.

The Rump Parliament continued to govern through committees. In May 1649 it established "the Commonwealth", declared that Parliament was supreme, and abolished the monarchy and the House of Lords as well as the Anglican Church and its bishops. Cromwell was busy ruthlessly pacifying Ireland and Scotland. By April 1653 he had grown weary of the MPs in the Rump and abolished it in a rage in breach of the principles for which he had fought the Civil War. He replaced it with a nominated unelected Barebones Parliament which lasted a few months before it dissolved itself. By December 1653 Cromwell had been made Lord Protector and considered himself as a constitutional ruler with popular support. In Wales[163] each county had two seats in the new Protectorate Parliament with the traditional 40 shilling freeholder voter being replaced by a landed qualification of £200 real or personal property; it only lasted five months. In July 1655 Cromwell divided the country into 12 regions each governed by a Major-General; Wales was governed by Major-General Berry. The majority of Welshmen had been appalled by the regicide of Charles I and did not approve of Cromwell's form of new government; his close friends, Colonel John Jones and Philip Jones of Llangyfelach, assumed great powers and estates which made them very unpopular. Cromwell may have been the monarch in all but name, but the populance did not approve of the republic and the gentry in Wales certainly disapproved of the social upstarts who were in positions of power locally.

After Cromwell's death in September 1658 Cromwell's son, Richard, became Lord Protector but he only lasted eight months. It was clear that people wanted the monarchy to be restored when the Rump was dissolved in 1659. George Monck, commander of the Parliamentary army in Scotland, marched his men to London, restored the Convention Parliament and the MPs who had been purged in 1648 were restored.

The Restoration

In May 1660 King Charles II landed in England at the request of Parliament to take the throne. He was to become the most successful Stuart King. In Wales the news was greeted with much rejoicing. In London his triumphant procession of 20,000 horse and foot with crowds throwing flowers and the church bells ringing led John Evelyn[164] to describe it: "I stood in the Strand, and beheld it, and blessed God. And all this without a drop of blood, and by that very army which rebelled against him." Samuel Pepys[165] records in his diary: "I in very good health. And all the world in a merry mood because of the King's coming….the Parliament had ordered the 29 of May, the King's birthday, to be for ever kept as a day of thanksgiving for our redemption from tyranny and the King's return to his Government, he entering London that day." 29 May was thereafter called "Oak Apple Day" after the oak tree in which Charles hid during his escape from Cromwell.

---

162 Worden p99

163 Jenkins p33

164 John Evelyn (1620-1706*): Memoirs illustrative of the Life and Writings of John Evelyn comprising his Diary from 1641 to 1705/6 (1818 William Bray)*

165 Samuel Pepys (1633-1703): *The Shorter Pepys (1985 Robert Latham) p53*

Charles II, the son of Charles I and Henrietta Maria the sister of Louis XIII, had acceded to the throne of Scotland in 1650 and been crowned in 1651 but had been deposed shortly afterwards and sent back into exile when Cromwell had defeated the Scots at Dunbar and Worcester. He acceded to the throne of England and was restored to the throne of Scotland on 29 May 1660. After the failed experiment of republican rule under Cromwell (whose statue stands outside the Houses of Parliament[166]) the relaxed kingship of Charles II helped slowly to heal the enormous divisions in society despite the problems caused by the Great Plague in 1665 which killed nearly 20 per cent of the population of London followed the next year by the Great Fire of London which destroyed 13,200 homes, 88 churches and St Paul's Cathedral.

Charles was by nature indolent, had an interest in the arts and Restoration comedy and literature, and had numerous mistresses including Nell Gwyn. His attempts to permit religious toleration were not always successful because of the views of Parliament. The Anglican clergy were reinstated in their livings and many Welsh royalists and clergy were returned to Parliament but the Clarendon Code against nonconformists made life difficult for both Catholics and Protestants; the Five Mile Act forbid nonconformist ministers from living within five miles of a town or to run schools. Many were imprisoned or went abroad. The Declaration of Indulgence in 1672 encouraged religious freedom but the next year was withdrawn and replaced with a Test Act under which Catholics could not hold public office. The attempt by Titus Oates in 1678 to panic the public with rumours of Popish plots led to a census[167] of dissenters and Catholics. In Carmarthenshire it showed that nonconformists numbered only 179. The fear that Catholicism might reappear was never far away and this was not helped by rumours of the secret Treaty of Dover in 1670 by Charles II with Louis XIV of France who paid Charles £160,000 per annum. Attempts to pass legislation in 1681 to prevent the King's brother, the Catholic James Duke of York, from succeeding to the throne were thwarted by Charles dissolving Parliament and ruling without one for the last four years of his reign; this Exclusion Crisis led to the terms "Whigs" (a derogatory Scottish name for the exclusionists) and "Tories" (a derogotary Irish word for Royalists) being adopted.The Rye House Plot in 1683 to assassinate Charles and the Duke of York in favour of Charles's illegitimate son, the Protestant Duke of Monmouth, failed but added to the fears of the population. In 1685 Louis XIV revoked the Edict of Nantes and some 200,000 Protestant Hugenots fled overseas, many to Wales, with stories of Popish cruelty.

Charles died aged 54 in February 1685 being received into the Catholic faith on his deathbed and leaving no legitimate heir. His eldest illegitimate son, the Duke of Monmouth, led a rebellion aginst James II but was defeated at Sedgemoor in July and executed; the infamous Judge Jeffreys dealt very harshly with the defeated rebels.

James II

James II, Duke of York, acceded to the throne (ruler 1685-88) despite being an ardent Catholic and a strong believer in absolute monarchy; he deluded himself into believing that he could reconvert his kingdom into a Catholic country once again. His Indulgences of 1687 and 1688 suspended penal laws against Catholics and dissenters and led to opposition even in Wales which had been a traditional royalist stronghold, although the beginnings of nonconformism in Carmarthenshire can be seen from this time. He then arrested seven Bishops who opposed him and they were acquitted of seditious libel to the delight of the public (see Chapter 7.2).

James's first marriage to Anne Hyde (d1671) in 1660 produced two daughters, Mary who married the Protestant William of Orange, and Anne who married the Protestant son of the King of Denmark. However, James's second marriage to the Catholic Mary of Modena in 1673 caused opposition; their first 10 children died so the risk of a Catholic Stuart succession seemed remote. Then she unexpectedly produced a son in June 1688 with rumours that the baby had been smuggled into the royal bedchamber in a warming pan. This caused great consternation amongst nearly all politicians who feared another civil war. A coalition amonst Whigs and Tories led to an invitation to Mary (James's daughter) and her husband William of Orange, both Protestants, to save English Protestantism and the constitution. They landed with an army in Devon in November 1688 and James fled to France on Christmas Day.

---

166 Cromwell famously referred to the Magna Carta as the Magna Farta which must put in some doubt his views on liberty

167 Prys-Jones Vol 2 p229

William III and Mary II

William III (ruler 1689-1702) and Mary II (ruler 1689-94) were proclaimed joint monarchs in February 1689; the Glorious Revolution had confirmed that absolute monarchy was dead and that a constitutional monarchy would survive with a Protestant Parliament being supreme and the guarantor of the liberties and freedoms of the citizen as originally enshrined in the Magna Carta of 1215. The Bill of Rights excluded James II and his descendants from the English throne as well as any Catholic or person married to a Catholic, and the monarchs swore that Protestantism would remain the established religion of the country. The Toleration Act 1689 allowed freedom of worship to nonconformists who had pledged oaths of allegiance (including Baptists and Congregationalists) but not Catholics, provided their meeting houses were licensed, but they were still debarred from public office; in Carmarthenshire some nonconformists avoided this by attending their local Parish churches only at Christmas and Easter. In 1697 Sir Humphrey Edwin[168], the Lord Mayor of London and the son of a Carmarthenshire feltmaker, thought nothing of attending Anglican communion in full mayoral dress in the morning and then a Welsh dissenting service in the afternoon.

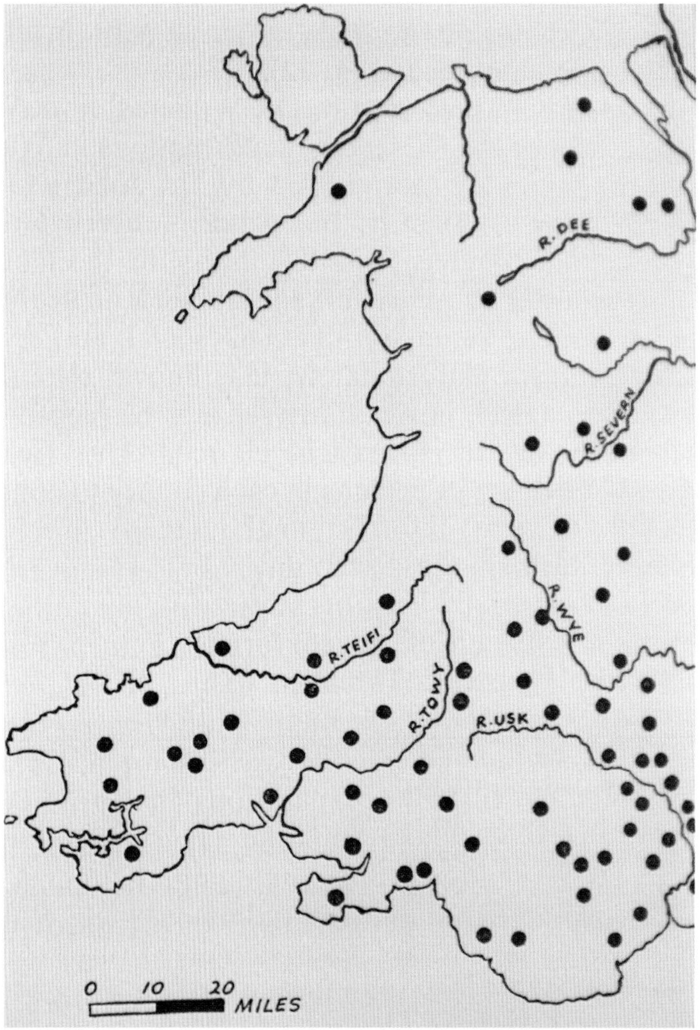

Distribution of Puritan congregations in Wales c 1715
(Prof Sir John Lloyd)

In Wales the great majority of the country greeted the prospect of peace without civil war with pleasure even if some of the gentry Tory families were privately of the Jacobite persuasion because of their belief that the choice of monarch should be in accordance with the royal hereditary succession principle irrespective of religion (legitimism) rather than a gift by Parliament. However, William was faced with a Catholic Jacobite rebellion in Scotland in 1689 which collapsed and led to the Glencoe massacre in 1692 when the Macdonald clan refused to take the oath of loyalty. In Ireland James II arrived with Catholic forces in 1689 and was supported by the Irish Parliament; William and his Protestant forces defeated James at the Battle of the Boyne in 1690 while the siege of Londonderry[169] lasted some 105 days before the Protestant residents were relieved, resulting in religious troubles which have lasted ever since. In 1694 Mary II sadly died of smallpox while William continued with his Protestant war against the Catholic Louis XIV of France which he had started in 1689 with his Dutch and other allies. In the same year the Bank of England was founded to finance

[168] Jenkins p139

[169] BG Scott: *The Great Guns like Thunder (2008)* describes the cannons used in the siege on the City walls of Londonderry provided by the Livery Companies of the City of London and by The Honourable The Irish Society (see footnote 157)

the war; its first Governor was Sir John Houblon, who also served as Lord Mayor of London and was Master of the Grocers' Company in whose Hall the Bank was a tenant for its first 40 years until the current building was erected in the Grocers' former garden in Threadneedle Street.

Queen Anne

William III died in 1702 and was succeeded by Queen Anne (ruler 1702-14), the younger Protestant daughter of James II; the Act of Settlement 1701 had provided for the throne on Anne's death to go to the Protestant Princess Sophia, Electress of Hanover, thereby cutting out all Stuart hereditary claims.

Anne's reign saw England participating in the War of Spanish Succession from 1702, victories for John Churchill (to become the Duke of Marlborough) at Blenhein, Ramillies, Oudenarde and Malplaquet, the acquisition of Gibraltar, and the Act of Union with Scotland in 1707 resulting in her being the first monarch of Great Britain. By 1710 the expensive continental war supported by the Whig controlled Parliament had led to the country returning a Tory administration which negotiated the Treaty of Utrecht in 1713. Anne and her husband, George Prince of Denmark, produced numerous pregnancies but only one son survived until he died in 1710 thereby ending the Stuart monarchy.

Parliamentary Sovereignty

There has been a battle between Royal authority and Parliamentary authority for much of our history. In 1539 Henry VIII had acquired royal prerogative executive powers under the Statute of Proclamations which gave him the ability to make laws as well as sign treaties and appoint friends to important offices and remove them at will. This Statute was repealed in 1547 but the Crown carried on "by divine right" in practice much as before. James I was then met with the Case of Proclamations in 1610 when the famous Lord Chief Justice Edward Coke ruled that: "The King by his proclamation or other ways cannot change any part of the common law, or statute law, or the customs of the realm....the King hath no prerogative power but what the law of the land allows him." This of course was at the core of the dispute which resulted in the Civil War and the regicide which followed it. The final constitutional settlement contained in the Bill of Rights of 1689 provided that: "The execution of laws by regall authority without consent of Parlyament is illegall." Today four centuries later the Prime Minister (as the Executive) essentially holds prerogative power on loan from the Crown and cannot claim any divine right or sovereignty to change laws without the consent of Parliament (as the Legislature), whose powers are defended under our mainly unwritten constitution and the rule of law by our independent Judiciary[170]. The Supreme Court judgment[171] concerning the UK's exit from the European Union confirmed that the Executive does not have power under the royal prerogative to change statute law or common law unless so authorised by an Act of Parliament.

7.2 Edwinsford Family

Rees Williams (d1627)

As we saw in Chapter 6.2, David ap Rees (40) and his wife Jane had only one child and heir, Rees (41), who in about 1604 adopted the family surname of "Williams", which the later Edwinsford family used thereafter abandoning the former Welsh patronymic tradition. Rees successfully continued with the family strategy[172] of acquiring additional lands and mortgages. Between 1605 and 1623 he entered into 19 property transactions, 11 being purchases of land and the rest being mortgage acquisitions which would lead later to acquisitions of the properties themselves. Some of the properties were formerly owned by his distant cousin, Rhys ap Gruffydd (1508-31), of the Dynevor family who had been executed for treason in 1531 when his lands were expropriated by Henry VIII.

Rees was the first member of the family to serve as Sheriff of Carmarthenshire, in 1614, and be described as an "esquire" rather then just as a "gentleman". His son and grandson were also to follow him in this office of importance and influence, and his great grandson was to promote the family to one of the foremost in the county by being its first member to be elected as a Member of Parliament as well as serving as the Lord Lieutenant of the county (see Chapter 22.2) and becoming a Baronet.

---

170 By comparison under the US Constitution of 1789 the nine Supreme Court Justices, who are appointed by the President and Congress, often in practice decide matters on partisan political lines

171 R (Miller) v Sec of State for Exiting the European Union-Times Law Report (25 Jan 2017)

172 NLW Edwinsford archives; Francis Jones: THSC *(1987) p9 et seq*

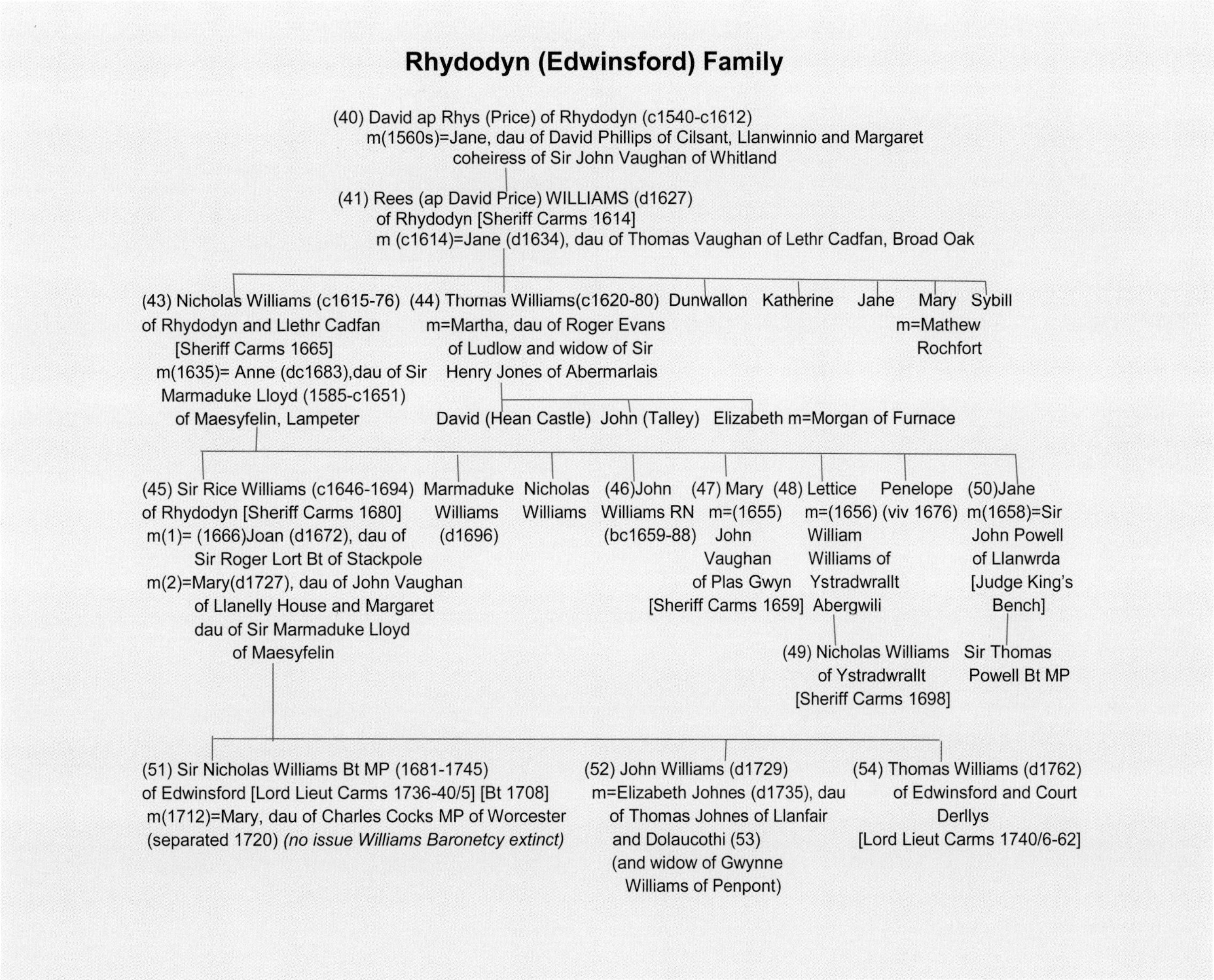

Also in 1614 Rees entered into a most advantageous marriage with Jane, the eldest daughter of Thomas Vaughan of Llethr Cadfan in Broad Oak near Llangathen and Catherine from a wealthy Anglesey family. All Jane's eight brothers and sisters died young and unmarried save one sister, so Jane and that sister became co-heiresses of Llethr Cadfan. For much of their marriage Rees and Jane lived in Llethr Cadfan rather than in Rhydodyn. The house is a large Grade 2 listed cross-passage house (see below).

Rees seems to have inherited some of the litigious nature of his forbears since we know he was sued in 1615 only a year after his marriage in the Court of Great Sessions by his mother in law and widow, Catherine

Llethr Cadfan 2016

Vaughan. He was also sued for cutting down 40 oak trees valued at £40 each. It also seems that Rees and Jane were listed[173] on the Recusant Rolls for 1624-6 meaning that they had refused to attend the established church as required by law so could face financial penalties as papists.

He made his will on 13 July 1627 and he probably died shortly afterwards. His estate was large and included Llethr Cadfan, Rhydodyn, and numerous other properties plus 922 sheep, 399 lambs, various bee-hives, mares and colts, swine, geese and poultry as well as cattle including three bulls each valued at 26s.8d. Under his will he left money to the cathedral and to a pauper of the parish, 2s to repair the highways, £40 per annum for life to his second son Thomas (44), £30 per annum for life to his third son Dunwallon, £100 per annum for life to his wife Jane provided she remained a widow, £500 to his eldest daughter Katherine when she married, and he provided that his four daughters were to be maintained and educated and lodged until they married. He left a yearling beast to each of his seven manservants and four maidservants. The rest of his estate went to his wife and eldest son Nicholas who were the executors, but his son was a minor so unable to act and his wife Jane renounced the role. As a result his mother in law Catherine Vaughan and his kinsman John Morgan were appointed as executors when the will was proved on 22 December 1632.

His widow Jane continued to live in Lethr Cadfan and she is thought to have died in about 1634. Rees and Jane had three sons and four daughters:

(1)Thomas Williams (c1620-1680)(44) who was educated at Gray's Inn in 1639 and served as steward of the manor of Talley for the years 1654-59. He also served as Captain of a company of foot in the Carmarthenshire militia. It is thought that he lived on the site of what is now Talley House in the village of Talley (see Chapter 24.1). Since

[173] Alan Randall: *Recusancy in Carmarthenshire CA (1997) p70.* The Vaughans of Llethr Cadfan were also a recusant family

the Acts of Union and the dissolution of the monasteries Talley had been a Crown Manor where the old tradition of gavelkind had been abolished and "Borough English" tenure applied meaning that instead of the eldest son inheriting the youngset son did so. It is thought that Dunwallon, the third and youngest son, died young, so Thomas inherited many of his father's properties including Ffynongrech (see Chapter 26.1). He married Martha, daughter of a wealthy lawyer, Roger Evans of Ludlow; she was the widow of the powerful Sir Henry Jones Bt of Abermarlais (d1644) of the Dolaucothi family who had died without a male heir so his baronetcy became extinct. Thomas and Martha had three children: (a) David who lived at Hean Castle in Pembrokeshire, (b) John who as the youngest son succeeded his father in Talley, and (c) Elizabeth who married a Mr Morgan of Furnace in Llangyndeyrn;

(2) Dunwallon who died young and so did not inherit;

(3)-(5) Katherine, Jane and Sybill about whom we know very little;

(6) Mary who married Mathew Rochfort; and

(7) Nicholas Williams, the eldest son.

Llethr Cadfan

By tradition Llethr Cadfan[174] (the slope of the field of battle) at Broad Oak near Llangathen is believed to be the site of the famous battle of Coed Llathen (or Llangathen) at Whitsun in 1257. As mentioned in Chapter 4.10, the Welsh troops of Llywelyn the Last (c1223-82) fought the army of Henry III led by Stephen Bauzan; he was killed and the English army completely routed with some 3000 dead. The names of the local fields reflect this defeat: *cae dial* (field of vengeance), *cae yr ochain* (field of groaning), *cae tranc* (field of death), *llain dwng* (field of oaths) and *congl y waedd* (corner of shouting). An iron cannon ball, presumably of later date, was dug up in nearby fields and is still preserved.

The house is located about half a mile on the left north of the Broad Oak (Dderwen Fawr) crossroads and is a large Grade 2 listed cross-passage house consisting of an original 16th century part still used as a farmhouse, and a 17th century part which is now partly derelict with lovely original rooftiles and three impressive round chimneys preserved but showing some signs of decay. It was a tall house with a lateral chimney, storeyed porch, and an impressive parlour block. The parlour on the first floor used to have an ornate plaster ceiling which has collapsed. There used to be an old baronial hall which until 1840 was panelled with oak. Sadly the interior doors, fireplaces and panelling were removed to Edwinsford Mansion and fitted into that house; they were sold off in the late 20th century when Edwinsford became derelict. A dovecote outside is still visible. The current owner Gwyn Morgan bought the farm in the 1970s.

The house was owned first by the Vaughan family descended from the aristocratic family of Elystan Glodrudd whose coat of arms used to be seen above the entrance. The north chapel in Llangathen Church is called the Cadfan Chapel because it was once owned by the Vaughan family. Thomas ap Thomas Fychan (Vaughan) of Llethr Cadfan was the father of Gwilym ap Thomas, who married Gwenllian, daughter of Llewelyn ap Gwilym of Bryn Hafod nearby. Their son, David, inherited and his son, Thomas Vaughan, invited Lewys Dwnn in 1597 to record and certify the family pedigree. Thomas died leaving two daughters who were co-heiresses and the eldest, Jane, who married Rees Williams (41) of Rhydodyn (Edwinsford), inherited Llethr Cadfan. In 1670 the house was assessed at 5 hearths so it was a large but not enormous house at the time. The house and its lands continued to be part of the Edwinsford Estate until the late 19th century but was occupied by tenant farmers from about the mid 17th century.

Jane's surviving sister, Joyce, married David Lloyd of Ynys y Borde and their son was Isaac Lloyd MP (c1628-75) who was a successful lawyer and served as MP for Haverfordwest in 1661-3.

[174] Francis Jones: *Carmarthenshire Homes p109*; DL Baker-Jones: *Edwinsford a Country House and its Families CH (1968) p18;* Thomas Lloyd*: Carmarthenshire and Ceredigion p311;* Peter Smith*: Houses of the Welsh Countryside (1975) p187*; Francis Jones*: The Vaughans of Golden Grove THSC (1963);* John Lloyd*: Henry ap Gwilym CA (1998) p11*

Nicholas Williams (c1615-c1676)
Nicholas (43) was a minor when his father died and he was brought up by his mother in Llethr Cadfan until her death in 1634. His appointed guardian and tutor was the formidable Sir Marmaduke Lloyd (1585-1651)[175] of Maesyfelin in Lampeter.

Sir Marmaduke was the son and heir of Rev Thomas Lloyd (1544-1612) the precentor and treasurer of St Davids Cathedral from the Llanllyr Lloyd family. Marmaduke matriculated (entered) at Oriel College Oxford on 19 October 1599 aged 14 and received his BA degree on 28 June 1603. He then entered the Middle Temple in March 1604 qualifying as a barrister in November 1609. He had a most successful career[176] serving as the King's attorney in Wales and the Marches (1614-22), as a member of the Council of the Marches from 1614, Recorder of Brecon (1617-36), Puisne Justice of Chester (1622-36), and Chief Justice of Brecon and Radnor (1636-45). He was knighted on 7 April 1622. He inherited Maesyfelin and the Lordship of Lampeter.

Marmaduke was a stout Royalist and was taken prisoner with his son Francis when Hereford was captured by the Parliamentary forces on 18 December 1645. He was imprisoned and then released in 1647 after compounding and paying a fine. But he then took up arms again, fought as a General for Wales at the battle of St Fagans on 8 May 1648 and with his son Francis was taken prisoner again. He died some time in 1651. His estate included Maestroyddin just outside Pumsaint in Cynwyl Gaeo.

One of his closest friends was the famous Vicar Rhys Prichard (1579-1644)[177] of Llandovery, the author of numerous religious books and songs including *Canwyll y Cymry* (The Welshman's Candle) published in parts in 1659-60 and completely in 1681. It is said that he laid a curse on the Lloyd family. Apparently his son Samuel, an undergraduate at Jesus College Oxford, who frequently visited Maesyfelin made advances to one of the daughters of Marmaduke and was lured one evening into a bedroom by his sons where he was smothered with a feather mattress, his body was placed on a horse and he was then allowed to fall off as the horse was made to cross the River Tywi to simulate an accidental drowning. The Vicar is then said to have put his curse[178] in writing in a Welsh poem with alternative translations:

"May God with heavy curses chase
All Maesyfelin's villain race
For they have drowned in Tywi's tide
Llandovery's flower, Cymru's pride.

May God's curse be upon Maesyfelin
On every stone and every root
For casting the flower of Llandovery town
Headlong into the Tywi to drown."

This curse is almost certainly a much later invention[179] to explain the numerous later misfortunes of the family at Maesyfelin and Peterwell; in fact Samuel was already married when he was at Oxford and later became his father's curate.

It appears that in 1632 Sir Marmaduke disagreed with Nicholas Williams's mother and grandmother about his minor's upbringing and finally the matter had to be adjudicated by Richard Earl of Carberry and enforced by the Court in Chancery. Nicholas was a most eligible bachelor and the heir to the Rhydodyn and Llethr Cadfan estates. After his mother's death in 1634 his guardian, Sir Marmaduke, cleverly arranged in 1635 for Nicholas to marry one of his own daughters, Anne (dc1683). The usual prenuptial settlement resulted in part of Nicholas's estate being settled to protect Anne and their future children. Family muniments[180] show that in the 1630s the Rhydodyn Estate consisted of 69 messuages, 3 mills, and 4000 acres in Talley, Llansawel, Caeo, Llangathen and Llandeilo; the Llethr Cadfan Estate consisted

175 David Lewis: *Dolaucothi p172-5*
176 Herbert Lloyd-Johnes NLWBO
177 Nesta Lloyd: *Rhys Prichard CA (1998) p25-37*
178 AT Arber-Cooke: *Pages from the History of Llandovery Vol 1 (1975) p206*
179 Bethan Phillips: *Peterwell The History of a Mansion and its Infamous Squire (1983) p4-13;* Thomas Nicholas: *Annals and Antiquities of the Counties and County Families of Wales p173*
180 NLW Edwinsford archives

of 9 messuages and lands and 1000 acres in Llangathen, Llanfynydd and Llanfihangel Cilfargen.

Nicholas successfully continued with the family tradition of acquiring more properties and mortgages. Between 1627 (his father's death) and 1663 he made 12 land purchases and another 12 properties were mortgaged to him so he increased the family estates quite considerably. He also seems to have sold Rhydodyn Issa to Walter Lloyd and his family from Llansawel for a period of years and then bought it back, suggesting that he used Rhydodyn Ucha to live in after Llethr Cadfan had been let following his mother's death in 1634.

Nicholas seems not to have played any serious role in the Civil War, unlike his guardian Sir Marmaduke, although he was almost certainly a Royalist like so many other Welsh squire and gentry families. In June 1647 under the "Ordinance for the raising of Moneys to be imployed towards the maintenance of Forces within this Kingdome, under the Command of Sir Thomas Fairfax, Knight, and for the speedy transporting of, and paying the Forces for the carrying on the Warre of Ireland" he was appointed one of the commissioners in Carmarthenshire to enforce the payment of funds, in the case of Carmarthenshire being £1001.15s.6d per month, to be used for the above purpose between 25 March 1647 and 25 March 1648. In 1660 he was nominated as a knight of the proposed Order of the Royal Oak, a new order of knighthood which was intended to be a reward for those who had supported Charles II during his exile in France before the Restoration. The idea was abandoned out of concern that it would perpetuate dissension so Nicholas never received his silver medal with ribbon depicting the King in the royal oak tree in which he hid to escape the Roundheads after the Battle of Worcester in 1651. A total of 687 people[181] were nominated each with a valuation of their estates of whom eight were in Carmarthenshire including Nicholas Williams (£1000 annual estate income), three Vaughans and three Gwynns.

After the Restoration in 1665 Nicholas followed in his father's footsteps by serving as Sheriff of Carmarthenshire.

Nicholas and Anne were liberal and tolerant supporters of religious nonconformity. They helped the first group of non-conformist worshipers in Cynwyl Gaeo who met at Crugybar[182]. The exact date that the Chapel was established is not known although there was a chapel there in 1662. During the reigns of Charles II and James II the worshipers (a mixed group of Independents and Baptists) were cruelly persecuted. They therefore moved to Bwlchyrhiw and like the Independents at Cefnarthen used the caves in the area to worship in secret. There is an area at Bwlchyrhiw that is called Craig yr Eglwys. The Independents and some Baptists returned to worship at Crugybar in 1688 when William III and Mary came to the throne. Many of the Baptists stayed at Bwlchyrhiw or Glynyrefail as it was then called. Stephen Hughes (1622-88) is generally thought to be the preacher that motivated the establishing of Crugybar Chapel. As we shall see Nicholas and Anne taught their children to be tolerant in religious matters while remaining Protestant themselves; this was to lead to their son, Sir Rice Williams (45), being dismissed as Mayor of Carmarthen in 1688 before the arrival of William and Mary.

Nicholas made two wills in 1666 and 1674 plus codicils but they do not all survive. He died sometime during 1676 and his wife Anne, his eldest son Sir Rice Williams (45), and youngest daughter Penelope were appointed executors. His wife Anne made her will on 15 July 1683 and it is thought she died later that year.

Nicholas's seal shows a shield quartered with a lion rampant (in quarters 1 and 4) and a lion rampant regardant (in quarters 2 and 3) with a lion rampant for a crest.

Nicholas and Anne had eight children:

(1) Marmaduke Williams (d1696), the second son who spent his life in London as a barrister at Gray's Inn and never married. His will was dated 7 January 1696 and he died shortly thereafter. He generously left his lands in Talley, Cayo, Llanfynydd, Llansadwrn and Llandylae (Llandeilo) to his cousin, John Williams of Talley, who was a son of his Uncle Thomas (44), on condition that John paid an annuity of £10 for life to his nephew, Luke Williams (son of his sister Lettice). All his other lands were left to his nephew, Thomas Powell of Broadway (son

---

181 William Dugdale (1605-86) Garter King of Arms recorded the names

182 David Lewis: *Family Histories p32-33*; Ben Davies: *Crugybar (1927)*

of his sister Jane), again on condition that Thomas paid an annuity for life to Luke (who presumably needed some income). The executors were John Williams and Thomas Powell;

(2) Nicholas Williams, the third son. All we know about him is that he was educated at Jesus College Oxford;

(3) John Williams RN (c1659-1688)(46), the fourth son and much younger than his siblings. He was about 17 when his father died and seems to have enlisted at a young age in the Royal Navy as a "reformade" (volunteer). His tomb and a wall tablet in St Peter's Church, Carmarthen state that he served "with resolution worthy of a gentleman" under Captain Morgan Kempthorne[183] of HMS Kingfisher against seven enemy Algerine pirate ships. The Kingfisher was 663 tons with 46 cannon built in 1675 and of a type[184] which was the largest of the frigates just below the smallest of the ships of the line. Capt Kempthorne took command in 1679 and in 1681 was ordered to the Mediterranean to deal with pirates (known as Barbary corsairs) who were attacking English shipping and selling men as slaves; between 1677 and 1680 some 160 English ships had been captured by these pirates. In 1681 England was at war with Algiers and the Kingfisher[185] was off Messina in Sicily on 22 May when she was attacked by eight Algerian ships. Despite being outnumbered the Kingfisher attacked and the battle went on for many hours finishing at 1am the next morning. Captain Kempthorne was shot in the hand and hit by a cannon ball in the stomach and died of his wounds. The Kingfisher lost seven crew with 38 wounded and sailed to Naples for repairs where the Captain was buried; the crew including John Williams were discharged in Livorno on 25 June 1681. Peace was made and John Williams returned to Carmarthenshire and died aged only 29 on 28 February 1688. He was unmarried and was buried in Carmarthen at St Peter's rather than at Talley in the family vault;

(4) Mary Williams (47), the eldest daughter who married in 1655 John Vaughan of Plas Gwyn in Llandyfaelog, home of a cadet branch of the influential Vaughan family of Golden Grove. Henry Vaughan was the younger son of John Vaughan of Golden Grove and settled at Plas

Sir John Powell

Gwyn in 1560; seven generations followed him there. John Vaughan served as Sheriff of Carmarthenshire in 1659; his father had served as Sheriff in 1643 and was a Royalist who was fined for his activities during the Civil War. Mary's portion under the prenuptial settlement was £700 and it is clear from the family muniments that her husband's family were wealthy. Their children included their son and heir, John Vaughan of Plas Gwyn;

(5) Lettice Williams (48), the second daughter who married in 1656 William Williams of Ystradwrallt, Abergwili. They had two sons: (a)

183 Alfred H Miles: *Fifty-two Stories of the British Navy (1896);* GA Kempthorne*: Sir John Kempthorne and his sons-Mariners' Mirror 12 (1926) p301.* Morgan was the son of Vice Admiral Sir John Kempthorne (1620-79) who had been knighted by Charles II in 1670 for capturing several pirate ships

184 William Strange: *John Williams of Edwinsford-Carmarthenshire Squire and the Barbary Corsairs CA (2006) p125-9*

185 JD Davies: *Gentlemen and Tarpaulins-The Officers and Men of the Restoration Navy (1991)*

Nicholas Williams (49) who served as Sheriff of Carmarthenshire in 1698 and who later sold his estate, and (b) Luke Williams, who as we have seen received annuities under the will of his Uncle Marmaduke;

(6) Jane Williams (50), the third daughter who married in 1658 Sir John Powell (1632-96)[186], son of John Powell of Pentre Meurig in Llanwrda. Sir John was educated at Jesus College Oxford (BA in 1653), King's College Cambridge (MA in 1654), and Gray's Inn (called to the Bar in 1657). His legal career was rapid and in 1686 he was appointed a serjeant at arms and then a judge of the Court of Common Pleas and knighted. In April 1687 he became a Judge in the Court of King's Bench. In 1688 he was one of the Judges at the famous trial of the Seven Bishops for seditious libel which held against King James II; he thereby made himself unpopular in Royal circles and was dismissed from office the next month. After the Glorious Revolution the Prince of Orange, William III, offered him the post of Lord Keeper of the Great Seal but he declined. In May 1689 he was reappointed as a Judge in the Court of Common Pleas. He died on 7 September 1696 in Exeter and is buried near Laugharne. He and Jane had several children one of whom, Sir Thomas Powell (1665-1720) of Broadway near Laugharne and Coldbrook Park in Monmouthshire, was created a Baronet in 1698, and served as MP for Monmouth Boroughs from 1705 to 1708 and for Carmarthenshire from 1710 to 1715;

Trial of the Seven Bishops 1688

In 1685 James II succeded to the throne (ruler 1685-88) despite being an ardent Catholic and a strong believer in absolute monarchy; he deluded himself into believing that he could reconvert his kingdom into a Catholic country once again. In April 1687 he issued the First Declaration of Indulgence which suspended the restrictions on Catholics and nonconformists or dissenters holding public office. In April 1688 he went further in his Second Declaration of Indulgence by ordering that the Anglican clergy read it out in full in their churches. On 13 May seven bishops signed a Petition to James II requesting that they be excused since they did not believe that the King had the legal right to grant exemptions or exclusions from statutes enacted by Parliament. The seven bishops, William Sancroft (Archbishop of Canterbury), Francis Turner (Ely), Thomas White (Peterborough), Thomas Ken (Bath and Wells), John Lake (Chichester), William Lloyd (St Asaph) and Jonathan Trelawny (Bristol) delivered their Petition on 18 May which led to the King dismissing them and saying that he had the power to dispense individuals from the provisions of a statute; indeed the recent case of *Godden v Hales* [187] had confirmed this prerogative right after James II had dismissed judges he disliked or who opposed his view. On Friday 8 June (Black Friday) the seven appeared before the Council. Later the King had them arrested and put in the Tower of London for a week and then put on trial for seditious libel. Lord Jeffreys the Lord Chancellor advised the King to drop the charges but was ignored.

The Trial[188] was held on 29-30 June 1688 before the Court of King's Bench. The Judges hearing the case were: Sir Robert Wright (d1689) the Chief Justice who later in December 1688 was accused by William III of high treason and imprisoned in Newgate where he died of fever; Sir John Powell (1632-96) of Pentre Meurig, Llanwrda who had been appointed to the King's Bench in April 1687 and after the trial was dismissed from office by James II; Sir Richard Allibond (1636-88) a Catholic who died later that year; and Sir Richard Holloway (d1695) who was also dismissed from office after the trial by James II and lived in retirement until his death. Counsel for the King included Sir Thomas Powys (1649-1719) the Attorney General; William Williams the Solicitor General; and Sir Robert Baldock (d1691). Counsel for the bishops in their defence included Sir Francis Pemberton a former Chief Justice; Sir Robert Sawyer (1633-92) a former Attorney General;

[186] ODNB

[187] State Trials Vol IX p196

[188] Thomas Basset: *The Proceedings and Tryal in the Case of the Most Reverend Father in God, William Lord Archbishop of Canterbury (1689);* Thomas Macaulay*: The History of England Vol II Chp VIII (1890);* William Gibson*: James II and the Trial of the Seven Bishops (2009)*

 Edwinsford by Paul Sandby c1774

Heneage Finch (1647-1719) who later became Earl of Aylesford and a Privy Councillor; Sir Henry Pollexfen (1632-91) who later became Chief Justice under William III; Sir Creswell Levinz (1627-1701) a former Attorney General; and John Somers (1651-1716) who was later the principal author of the "Declaration of Rights" and became Lord Chancellor. The bishops argued that everyone had the right to petition the King under Clause 61 of the Magna Carta of 1215 and to do so could not amount to the very serious offence of sedition.

At the end of the Trial[189] the four judges divided equally in their guidance to the jury. The jury deliberated all night and in the morning gave their verdict of Not Guilty, a verdict received with enormous acclaim by the population worried by the prospect of a Catholic heir.

James's second marriage to the Catholic Mary of Modena in 1673 had caused opposition; their first 10 children died so the risk of a Catholic Stuart succession seemed remote. Then she unexpectedly produced a son in June 1688 with rumours that the baby had been smuggled into the royal bedchamber in a warming pan. This caused great consternation amongst nearly all politicians who feared another civil war. A coalition amonst Whigs and Tories led to an invitation to Mary (James's daughter) and her husband William of Orange, both Protestants, to save English Protestantism and the constitution. They landed with an army in Devon in November 1688 and James fled to France.

The Trial and its verdict were important in preserving the rights of the ordinary citizen and in encouraging the opposition to James II; within six months he had fled. The Bill of Rights of 1689 preserved the rights of subjects to petition the King; the First Amendment to the US Constitution also contains the same right to petition for redress of grievances and of religion and conscience.

(7) Penelope Williams, the youngest daughter who was appointed as one of her father's executors. All we know from the family muniments is that she was alive in 1676 and unmarried; and

(8) Sir Rice Williams, the eldest son and heir.

Sir Rice Williams (c1646-94)
Rice (Rees) Williams (45) was brought up in Rhydodyn and Llethr Cadfan as the Civil War came to an end and the Restoration was effected. The little evidence available in the family muniments suggests that he was educated at Gray's Inn in London starting in about 1664-5 and then went on the Grand Tour of Europe for two years like so many gentry sons. Rather later in 1673 while still reading law he was the object of a writ[190] issued to the High Sheriff of Carmarthenshire requiring him to "take an inquisition of the estate of Rees Williams of Gray's Inn who had been sentenced to outlawry". The inquisition stated that Rice was the owner of Llethr Cadfan (240 acres) but since the Sheriff could not find him he was unable to arrest him; it must have been a fairly minor offence since Rice's career was unaffected.

Rice took a much more active part in public life than his father had, but he seems not to have expanded the family estate to any great extent unlike his forbears and not to have entered into many property transactions; at one point he needed money so in 1693 he mortgaged Llethr Cadfan to his unmarried brother Marmaduke Williams of Gray's Inn but soon redeemed the mortgage and recovered the property.

By Letters Patent dated 25 July 1688 (in Latin) James II granted Sir Rice Williams the right to hold a market in Llansawel "every Friday in every week through the year forever" plus two Fairs or Holydays on 15 July and 12 October annually. The fees and dues payable would have been received by the Rhydodyn Estate.

189 12 Howell's State Trials 183 (1688)
190 Francis Jones: *THSC (1987) p26 et seq*

In the summer of 1676 aged about 30 he became the first member of the Williams family to be knighted thereby making the family one of the foremost families in the county; he recorded that the fees and other dues paid to the Attorney General's Office, the Solicitor General's Office, the Signet Office, the Petty Bag Office, the Clerk of the Patents, the Privy Seal, the Lord Chancellor and the Hamper Office totalled some £80.0s.8d, a large sum. He was also appointed a magistrate for the county and on 3 May 1676 was commissioned as a Deputy Lieutenant. In 1680 he served as Sheriff of Carmarthenshire following in his father's and grandfather's footsteps; he appointed his kinsman John Morgan of Furnace (a grandson of Rice's uncle Thomas Williams (44)) to be his Under-Sheriff. In 1686 Rice was named as one of the Common Councilmen appointed when a new charter was granted to Carmarthen Town. He also served in the local Carmarthenshire Militia and in August 1681 was commissioned as a Captain of a company of foot commanded by Colonel Altham Vaughan of Golden Grove.

We have seen from the Trial of the Seven Bishops in 1688 how King James II's First Declaration of Indulgence of 1687 had divided the nation by suspending the restrictions on Catholics and nonconformists or dissenters holding public office and risking the return of Catholicism. When Deputy Lieutenants and magistrates around the country were asked whether they would support the King's policy the great majority of Carmarthensire squires refused. Rice however being a liberal and tolerant supporter of religious nonconformity like his parents gave a qualified assent by stating that in his opinion the penal laws against dissenters were contrary to the principles of Christianity and he would agree to the declaration only if the "preservation of ye Protestant religion" was guaranteed. This was too lukewarm for the majority of the county elite who strongly opposed the King's policy and as a result Rice, who had been elected Mayor of Carmarthen in October 1688, was dismissed only three weeks after taking that office.

Rice married twice:

(1)on 11 September 1666 at Kidwelly Church when he was about 20 he married Joan, the daughter of Sir Roger Lort Bt (c1608-1663) of Stackpole Court in Pembrokeshire; Joan's mother was Anne Wyndham of Dunraven Castle in Glamorgan who had remarried after Sir Roger's death and lived at Muddlescomb with her second husband, Sir Edward Mansel Bt. Sadly Joan died without children after only six years and was buried in St Bride's Church, Glamorgan on 22 November 1672. After her death there was a family disagreement concerning her prenuptial settlement and Rice had to bring an action against the Lort family in the Court of Chancery.

The Lort family owned the Stackpole Estate from 1611 when they bought it from the Stanleys to whom they were agents. The Lorts were Royalists during the Civil War and Stackpole was besieged by the Parliamentarians. Sir Roger Lort (1st Bt) had to hide in a cave near Barafundle Bay to avoid being captured but after a short siege he surrendered. Sir Roger's son and heir, Sir John Lort (2nd Bt) (c1637-73), left Stackpole to his daughter Elizabeth Lort (1666-1714) and she married Sir Alexander Campbell of Cawdor in 1689; the Cawdors built a new Georgian mansion on the site of the earlier fortified house in the 1730s. Sadly the estate was requisitioned by the Ministry of Defence in 1938 to form the Castlemartin Range and the house was demolished in 1963. The National Trust acquired Stackpole in 1976; and

(2) Mary (d1727) the daughter of John Vaughan of Llanelly House (a cadet branch of the Golden Grove family) and a great niece of the first Earl of Carberry. Her mother was Margaret, daughter of Sir Marmaduke Lloyd of Maesyfelin (another of whose daughters, Anne, had married Nicholas Williams (43) of Rhydodyn, her husband's father). Mary became, with her three sisters, one of the coheiresses of her unmarried brother, Walter Lloyd (d1683); the Llanelly Estate was then partitioned following Walter's death and Mary thereby brought part of it to her husband's Rhydodyn Estate.

Rice died on 27 February 1694 aged 47 and was buried on 5 October at Talley in the family vault and his memorial is affixed over the family pew; it states "Here LYETH Body of Sir Rice Williams Kt, who departed this Life the 27th Day of February AD 1694 aged 47, leavin behind him his Lady Mary ye daughter of John Vane of Llanelly Esq, by whom he had V sons, Nicholas, John, Walter, Charles and Thomas."

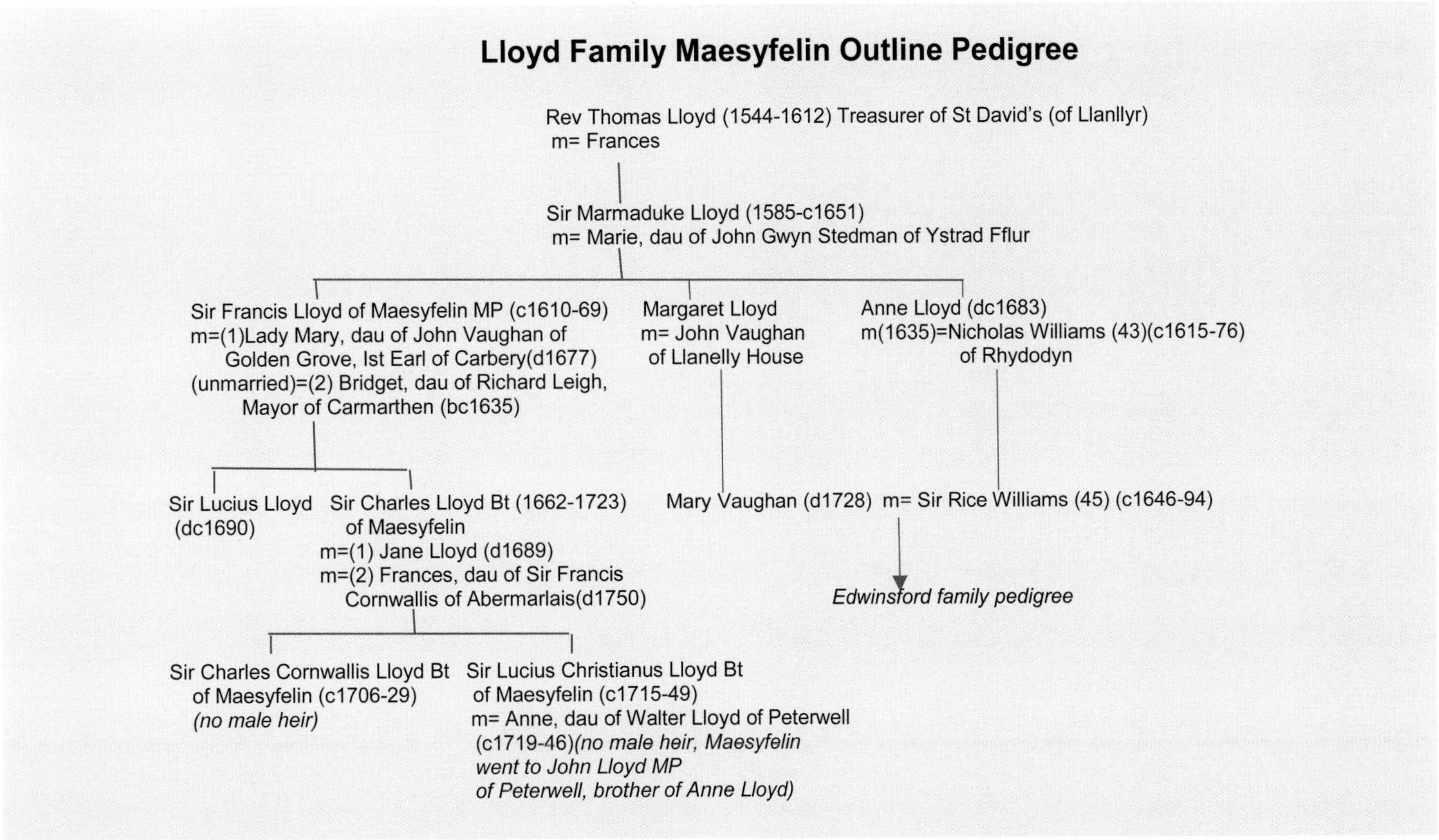

His will dated 3 June 1690 and two codicils were proved on 18 March 1695. He appointed his wife Lady Mary as sole executrix and left his estate as follows: (a) to his wife in lieu of dower a number of properties for her life with remainder to his eldest son Nicholas, (b) to his wife, the rents and profits of the estate for her life plus a legacy of £4000 "being given her as further testimony of my love and conjugal affection for her", (c) to his wife, Lethr Cadfan, Rhydodyn Issa, lands called Rhydodyn Fawr and other lands for 11 years on trust to pay his debts and maintain his children, (d) to his son John, various lands pending payment to him by his eldest son and heir Nicholas of £1200 after which such lands would pass to Nicholas, (e) to his son Walter, the sum of £800, (f) to his son Charles, the sum of £500,(g) to his son Thomas, the sum of £500, (g) to his heir Nicholas, all the plate brass pewter books furniture etc at Rhydodyn when he comes to keep house there, (h) to St Davids Cathedral 20 groats and (i) to the poor of Talley and Llansawel the sum of £20.

Lady Mary lived for another 34 years in widowhood dying in 1727 by which time only three of her five sons were still living; she was buried in her husband's grave in Talley. By 1726 she had moved to live in London in St Giles in the Fields where she made her will on 5 July 1726. In her will, which was proved on 2 March 1728, she left 40sh to the poor of Talley and Llansawel; mourning rings to her Stepney sister and cousins; all her china to her daughter in law Arabella

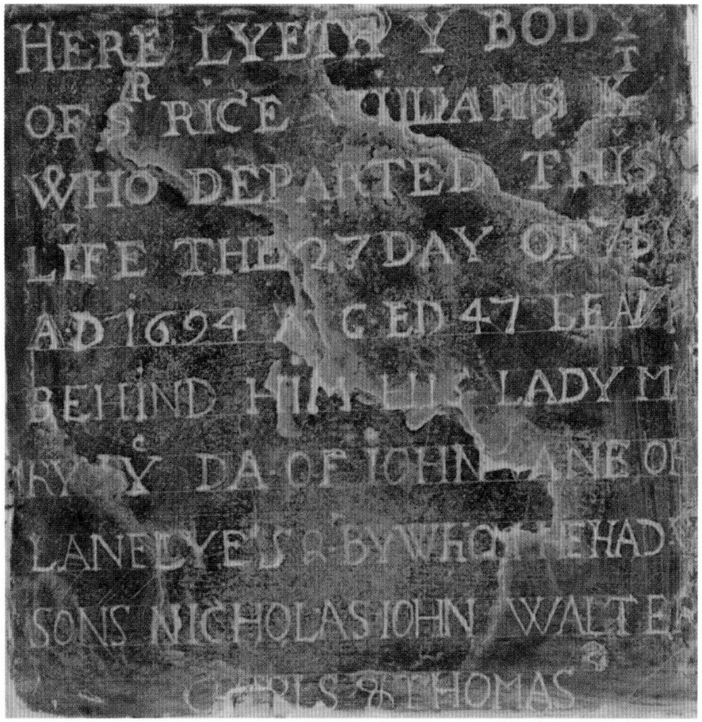

Sir Rice Williams tablet in Talley Church

Williams (who died the next year); clothes and other articles to various maids and friends; the sum of £5 per annum for six years to her servant Thomas Gething; and the residue to her eldest son Sir Nicholas Williams (51) whom she appointed her sole executor.

Sir Rice and Lady Mary had five sons:

(1) John Williams (d1729)(52), the second son, is the subject of some interesting allegations. Carmarthenshire Notes published by Arthur Mee between 1889 and 1891 was "an anthology of antiquarian, topographical and curious" information about the county. It contains a fascinating attack[191] on the validity of the pedigree of the Johnes family of Dolaucothi by William Gwynne Stedman Thomas (a well-known genealogist and descendant of the Stedman family being distant relations of the Jones family) with his own axe to grind.

In summary his allegations state that:

(a) the old patrician Jones family of Haroldston, Abermarlais, Emlyn Castle, Dolaucothi and Abermâd has no relationship with the "pretentious and usurping family of Johnes of Penybont in Caron, Tregaron, and later of Dolaucothi and Llanfair Clydogau who were merely successors in the two latter places by grant or purchase (as well as of Hafod) of the old Jones family, and most assuredly not descended, as they wish us to believe, from that old patrician stock in the male line of the Urien Rheged lineage";

(b) Thomas Jones MP of Llanfair Clydogau who died in 1734 was the last in the male line of the old Dolaucothi line of Jones, and certainly not Johnes a different family who came from Penybont, Tregaron;

(c) Col Thomas Johnes MP of Hafod (1748-1816), the grandson of Thomas Jones MP "not altogether approving of his own paternal lineage, and thus aspiring to something higher, assumed that of the old Joneses of the Urien Rheged lineage" and thereby created a second and subsequent family and line of Johnes there;

(d) John Williams of Talley (who was the second husband of Bridget Johnes, the widow of Thomas Lloyd of Bronwydd, Cardiganshire) acquired Dolaucothi through his marriage to Bridget and both were living in Dolaucothi from at least 1711 up to his death in 1729 following which under his will his servant Elizabeth Williams was permitted to live there until her death in 1735;

(e) Dolaucothi and Llanfair Clydogau were then "probably sold" to Thomas Johnes in about 1746 or after his death in 1749 to his wife Mary Anne Powell by the executors of Sir Nicholas Williams of Edwinsford Bt (51) to whom the demesne of Dolaucothi had been bequeathed by his brother John Williams (52); and

(f) that the correct lineage of the old Jones family is that recorded in the College of Arms in 1599 and that the "second and totally distinct as well as then very unimportant family resident at Penybont in Caron were not themselves at that date even possessed of a surname" and are "derived in direct male line from a very mediocre branch of the tribe of Gwaethvoed Prince or Lord of Cardigan who died about 1057."

[191] Mcc: Vol 1 pp 36-38, 44-45, 61-63,78-79, 103-104, 135-137, 170-17; Vol 2 pp1-3, 30-33, 75-78, 116-127; David Lewis: *Dolaucothi p125-127*

Dolaucothi Mansion c1920s

This series of very rude and provocative articles was met with a firm letter in reply printed in Carmarthenshire Notes in 1891 from Sir James Hills-Johnes VC KCB of Dolaucothi (1833-1919), who was married to Elizabeth (Betha) Johnes (1834-1927) co-owner of Dolaucothi, defending the lineage of his wife's Johnes family as follows:

"Sir
My attention has been called to the following passage in the April issue of the Carmarthenshire Notes page 45: "The present and former family of Johnes of Hafod are quite distinct from the old houses of "Jones" of Abermarlais, Glansowthy and Dolaucothy and Abermad and Llanfairclydogau, all of whom were "Jones"."

I have already corrected this and other mis-statements concerning the family of Johnes of Abermarlais, Hafod, Dolaucothy etc in the Red Dragon of December 1886 made by the writer of this "Note"……I request that you will be good enough to read pages 560-562. I shall be obliged by your giving my unqualified contradiction to the statement above quoted, and to that which follows concerning John Williams Esq of Edwinsford……………
…The pedigree of the family of Johnes of Abermarlais, Dolaucothy, Llanfairclydogau, Hafod etc is officially recorded in the Herald's College from ancient time up to this date—a proof sufficient of its authenticity.
I am, sir, yours faithfully,

J. Hills-Johnes, Lt Gen, KCB etc"

In his Red Dragon article[192] Sir James makes a number of very valid points:

(a) Col Johnes of Hafod did not assume a fictitious pedigree. The family patronymic name was spelt both as "Johnes" as well as "Jones" with both surnames being used up to 1700. This is evident in the will of Sir Thomas Johnes MP of Abermarlais in 1603 which refers to himself and his wife and children as Johnes while also referring to his father as Sir Henry Jones thus showing that both spellings of the surname were then in use;

(b) the younger male branches of the old Jones family did not become extinct (as suggested by Stedman Thomas) in 1734 on the death of Thomas Johnes/Jones as evidenced by the Johnes families in Abermâd and Dolaucothi;

(c) Stedman Thomas has confused two persons with the name of "John Williams". One "John Williams" (d1729) (52), the second son of Sir Rice Williams of Edwinsford (45), married in about 1707 the widow Elizabeth Williams (nee Johnes) (53) who was the younger sister of Thomas Johnes MP (d1734) of Llanfair Clydogau and Dolaucothi and the widow of Gwynne Williams (d1707) of the Inner Temple and son of Daniel Williams of Penpont, Brecon. They lived in Dolaucothi from their marriage until 1727 paying rent to the owner Thomas Johnes as shown by the account books. In March 1727 they separated under a deed of separation. Elizabeth then left Dolaucothi but returned in 1729 on the death of her estranged husband John Williams and lived there until her own death in 1735 and by her will dated 18 February 1735 she asked "to be buried privately with torches at night in the chancel of Conwilgaio church". On the death of Thomas Johnes in 1734 he left by his will dated 1733 a life interest in Dolaucothi to his sister Elizabeth Williams now a widow. His will also provided that on her death as life tenant Dolaucothi should revert to his cousin and legal heir, Thomas Johnes of Penybont (d1749/51), and then to his eldest son and heir, Thomas Johnes MP (1721-80) of Croft Castle.

The other "John Williams" of Talley was the second husband of Bridget Johnes who was the youngest daughter of James Johnes (d1680) of Dolaucothi and Abermâd. So Stedman Thomas mixed up two different people, and the Williams family of Edwinsford never had any legal ownership interest in Dolaucothi; and

(d) hence the claims by Stedman Thomas are baseless.

It seems that during his occupation of Dolaucothi as a tenant, John kept 13 servants and farmed on a large scale including at Blaencothi and Blaentwrch up the valley near Ffarmers. He also acquired lands elsewhere.

On 26 August 1719 John Williams (52) entered into articles of partnership with five others to dig and search for lead and other ore upon the Cardiganshire lands of Thomas Johnes (d1734) of Llanfair Clydogau then living in Bristol who had granted them a 21 year licence; John was to receive a quarter of the profits. It is not known to what extent this venture was successful.

John and his wife Elizabeth had no children. John died on 29 April 1729 and under his will made in 1728 he left (a) all his freeholds and copyholds in Carmarthenshire and Cardiganshire to his eldest brother and sole executor, Sir Nicholas Williams (51) of Edwinsford (as we have seen these did not include Dolaucothi which had merely been leased to him); (b) small legacies to his servants and cousins; (c) £10 to the poor of Conwil Gaeo and £5 each to the poor of Talley and Llansawel; and (d) personal goods plus £100 and an annuity of £20 to his servant maid "Elizabeth Williams spinster daughter of Thomas Williams of Pencarreg mercer". It seems clear that his relationship with his servant maid (who had the same name as his wife, hence perhaps the misunderstanding by Stedman Thomas) probably led to the separation with his wife in 1727;

(2) Walter Williams, the third son, was alive when his father died in 1694 but not when his mother died in 1727. It seems he died young and unmarried;

(3) Charles Williams, the fourth son, was born in about 1691 and also seems to have died young and unmarried;

(4) Thomas Williams (1693-1762) (54) of Edwinsford and Court Derllys is described in Chapter 8.3; and

(5) Sir Nicholas Williams Bt MP (1681-1745)(51) of Edwinsford the eldest son and heir.

[192] Red Dragon (December 1886) p560-2

Sir Nicholas Williams Bt MP (1681-1745)
Nicholas Williams (51), the eldest son and heir to the family estates including Edwinsford (first described as "Edwins foord" rather than Rhydodyn in a deed of 1711), was born in 1681. He was educated at Eton College and then Queen's College Cambridge (1698) followed by the Inner Temple (1699) and was called to the bar in 1705.

His father, Sir Rice Williams, died in 1694 before Nicholas had come of age. Like his father Nicholas took an active part in public life but was not particularly active in running the estates or in property acquisitions unlike his forbears who had built up the estates; indeed he relied on his land agent, Thomas Thomas, who was a tenant in Llethr Cadfan to deal with such matters. Some short leases were granted and timber on the Lethr Cadfan estate was sold for charcoal but the family muniments reveal few other property transactions. Generally leases of 21 years[193] for tenants were dominant on the Edwinsford Estate at this time.

Nicholas hit the jackpot when on 30 July 1707[194] aged 26 he was created a Baronet (Sir Nicholas Williams of Edwinsford in the county of Carmarthen). On 11 October in the same year he paid the sum of £1095 for the maintenance of 30 foot soldiers for three years for the defence of the province of Ulster, which was probably the effective cost of the Baronetcy. Following his father's knighthood he had now firmly cemented the family's influential position in the county's gentry hierarchy. Sadly he was to have no legitimate children so this Williams Baronetcy expired on his death in 1745.

In 1722 Sir Nicholas stood as a Whig for election as the MP for Carmarthenshire against Edward Rice of Newton House of the Dynevor family, the sitting MP. Rice had powerful supporters including the Duke of Bolton, who also spoke for the Vaughans of Golden Grove, and who wrote to Sir Nicholas asking him to stand down in return for his support at the following election. The poll book showed that Rice had received 593 votes and Sir Nicholas 588. Sir Nicholas then petitioned the House of Commons as was usual in close elections alleging malpractice and fraud by the High Sheriff and his Under-Sheriff who had conducted the election. On 18 December 1724 the Committee of Privileges and Elections held that Sir Nicholas was the valid holder of the seat and he became the MP for the next 21 years until his death on 19 July 1745 when the Vaughan faction recovered the seat; the Under-Sheriff was fined £500 for foul play. Sir Nicholas retained his seat in 1727 against Richard Gwynne of Taliaris and again in 1734 "after sham opposition from Sir Edward Mansel" and was unopposed in 1741, so the Whig faction prevailed against the Tory faction[195]. These Parliamentary elections, as we shall see in Chapter 8.2, were essentially contests between the powerful gentry Whig and Tory factions in the county. Nicholas was a strong supporter of Robert Walpole from whom he received some legal offices carrying a salary of £500 each for himself and his youngest brother, Thomas (54). After Walpole's fall he voted with the new administration.

Sir Nicholas served as a magistrate and Deputy Lieutenant for the county. On 16 April 1734 Sir Nicholas was appointed as Chamberlain[196] of the town and borough of Brecon and of the counties of Brecknock, Radnor and Glamorgan; Steward and keeper of the Courts Leet of several lordships including Caeo, Manordeilo and Mallaen and of the forests of Glyncothi and Pennant; Steward and Bailiff of the manors, granges and lands of the dissolved monastery of Talley (see Chapter 35.1); and Steward of the lordship and manor of Brecon for an annual fee of £100 (confirmed by a warrant[197] dated 9 July 1734 authorising the Receiver of Wales). On 11 June 1736[198] he was appointed Lord Lieutenant and Custos Rotulorum[199] of Carmarthenshire (see Chapter 22) and thereby responsible for organising the militia and the administration of local justice through the appointment of magistrates. Reaching the heights of the office of

---

193 Joan Thirsk, Christopher Clay: *Chapters from the Agrarian History of England and Wales-Rural Society 1500-1750 (1990) Vol 2 p406*
194 Letters Patent were dated 6 July 1708 according to FDWD: *Annals p37*
195 FDWD: *Annals p8*
196 FDWD: *Annals p37*
197 FDWD: *Annals p37*
198 FDWD: *Annals p37*
199 DL Baker-Jones *CH (1968) p 20* states incorrectly that he served as Sheriff of Carmarthenshire; he confuses him with his cousin Nicholas Williams (49) who was Sheriff in 1698

Lord Lieutenant, the first member of the Edwinsford family to do so, was a major coup and achievement. He held the office of Lord Lieutenant until 1740.

Sir Nicholas also served as one of the trustees of a new school for poor boys opened in Carmarthen in a property formerly called the Angel Inn which had been bought and rebuilt by Sir Thomas Powell Bt MP (Nicholas's cousin who was a senior Judge and the son of his aunt, Jane Williams (50)).

Nicholas married on 19 June 1712 at St Mildred's, Poultry in the City of London. His bride was Jane Mary Cocks, one of the daughters of Charles Cocks of Worcester (MP for Worcester 1694-5 and then for Droitwich) by Mary, daughter of an attorney, John Somers of Clifton, Bristol, and sister of John Somers (d1716), 1st Baron Somers of Evesham, Lord Chancellor. His wife Mary had a fortune of £5000 and in the prenuptial settlement dated 12 June 1712 Sir Nicholas settled Edwinsford and several other properties on trust in the usual way; the trustees included John Somers the Lord Chancellor, Sir Thomas Powell Bt and his own brother John Williams (52). Sadly the marriage did not last and on 25 June 1720 articles of separation was executed by which he allowed her £100 per annum and she was to take with her "her cloaths, Towells and also her horse and furniture thereunto belonging, which she usually rides upon, and also her Dressing Glass, Comb Box, Powder Box and Patch Box, and her Books etc". The marriage however was never annulled. There were no children and no heir.

The family muniments[200] contain some interesting accounts of the Edwinsford Estate at this time including the tithe accounts (which are shown in Chapter 16.2) and the weekly wine accounts of Sir Nicholas, by then living alone, for the three months before his death from 18 April to 21 July 1745:

Purchase Dates	Wines	Cost
18 April 1745	12 pints of Port	£0.10s.0d
	12 pints of White	£0.10s.6d
25 April	6 pints of Lisbon	£0.5s.3d
28 April	1 pint of Lisbon	£0.0s.10d
1 May	3 pints of White	£0.4s.4d
7 May	6 pints of Lisbon	£0.5s.3d
15 May	ditto	£0.5s.3d
23 May	ditto	£0.5s.3d
29 May	ditto	£0.5s.3d
5 June	ditto	£0.5s.3d
10 June	ditto	£0.5s.3d
17 June	ditto	£0.5s.3d
23 June	ditto	£0.5s.3d
29 June	ditto	£0.5s.3d
5 July	ditto	£0.5s.3d
12 July	ditto	£0.5s.3d
21 July	6 pints of Port	£0.5s.0d
Total		£4.13s.9d

Sir Nicholas died aged 64 on 19 July 1745 and was buried in the family vault in Talley where his memorial[201] in the church says: *"Near this Place lie the remains of Sir Nicholas Williams Bart, who represented this County 23 years in Parliament, where his zeal for the great cause of Truth and Liberty, his unshaken virture and Integrity in an age of Falsehood and corruption will be remembered to after ages. He was Humane, Charitable, Benevolent, and seemed born to retrieve the antient British Hospitality, To compose animosities, To spread Friendships, To make all men to one another what He Himself was to all men was the uniform and perpetual endeavour*

[200] NLW Edwinsford archives
[201] FDWD: *Annals p31*

of a life spent in promoting the happiness of his fellow creatures. The poor man whom living he never forgot, Dying he had in remembrance, all these social and Christian virtues made him Beloved by his Friends, his Neighbours, His Relatives By whom whilst they have love and gratitude He will be universally lamented." He was clearly a great personality and was also known to be a great sportsman and his silver hunting horn was preserved at Edwinsford for decades.

He made a will leaving much to his wife Mary but this was replaced after their separation by a new will dated 14 March 1745 proved on 27 July 1745. He left all his estate to his youngest and only surviving brother, Thomas Williams (54) of Court Derllys, plus a few legacies to servants and to the poor of Llansawel, Talley and Caeo.

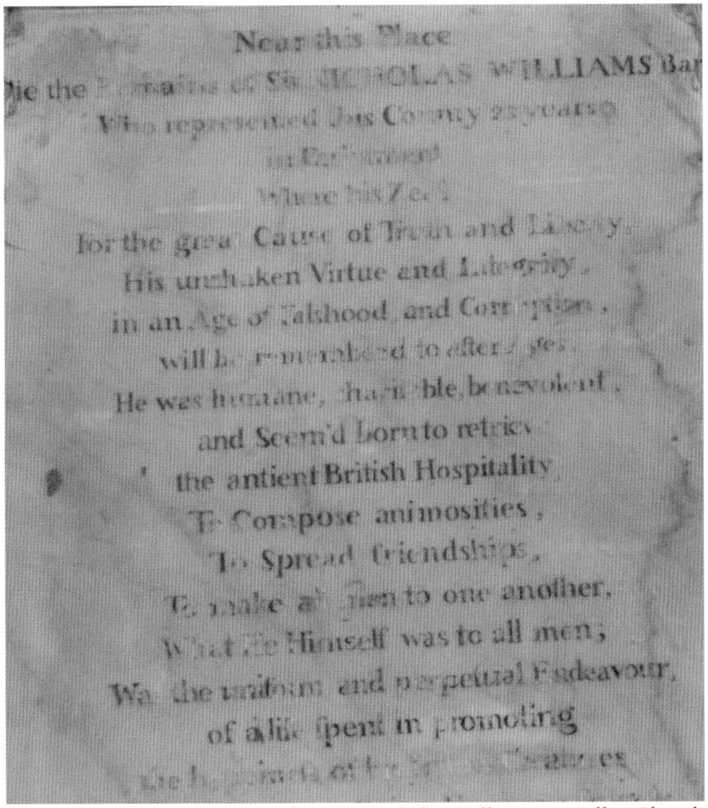

Memorial to Sir Nicholas Williams in Talley Church

Sir Nicholas was indeed one of the "stars" of the Edwinsford family[202] who added both wealth and prestige to it. During the early part of the 17th century the old Welsh house of Rhydodyn mentioned by the bards including Lewis Glyn Cothi was replaced with a much grander mansion. During the time of Sir Nicholas he enlarged and rebuilt parts of the mansion[203], he improved and enlarged the gardens and parkland, he built a bridge over the river described below, he added an apartment which became known as Sir Nicholas's Room with its rib and panel plaster ceiling, and he added some early dormer windows with leaden quarries showing the taste of the early 18th century. He also added some unique life-size leaden figures[204] in the grounds locally cast and dating from about 1720 including one of his Gamekeeper (of whom there used to be an oil painting in the upper corridor of the house[205]) with his gun to his shoulder and his spaniel dog at his heel; another one of his Dairy Maid which stood opposite and was blown down and damaged beyond repair in the 18th century; two beautiful leaden figures of "The Mercury with Caduceus" on the roof of the house; and a leaden figure of a Boar which formerly occupied a site in the farmyard. As late as 1913 a large leaden escutcheon hung in the hall of the mansion bearing the lion rampant and the legend "S'r Nicholas Williams of Edwyns Ford Bar AD 1708."

He built a stone bridge over the River Cothi which had two spans and can be seen in the 1776 copper plate engraving of "Edwinsford, the Seat of R Banks Hodgkinson Esqr" by the artist Paul Sandby and engraved by William Watts (see also Chapter 8.3). It shows the mansion in all its magnificence with what looks like a side chapel with a bell and cross on the roof, two men approaching the front gate, a man riding a horse in front, the gardens in front running down to the River Cothi and the park behind, the bridge which had two spans (the new bridge built by Robert Banks Hodgkinson in 1783 had one span), and on the right a farmhouse and other farm buildings across the river. The accompanying text of the description includes:

---

202 Francis Jones: *THSC (1987) p36*
203 Richard Fenton and Samuel Lewis also referred to this rebuilding. See Chapter 11
204 FDWD: *Annals p7*
205 See Chapter 15

Edwinsford by Paul Sandby 1776

Mercury with Caduceus

"A bridge near the house, for the use of the family, was built by Sir Nicholas Williams, Bart, which is of great use to the country, who, by permission, (upon floods, which frequently happen here) have leave to pass it.
About the distance of three miles upon the point of the hill, in view of the house, the same gentleman built a banquetting room, with a large spire over it, an useful land mark from all the neighbouring hills. This whole building was entirely demolished by a severe storm of lightning Feb .6.1772."

The Gamekeeper

The banqueting room built by Sir Nicholas Williams, who died in 1745, referred to by Sandby[206] in 1776 as having been destroyed by lightening in 1772 is thought to refer by Richard Llwyd in 1832[207] to "a singular conical structure called Pigyn Nicholas, ie "Nicholas's Peak" upon the summit of one of the most elevated hills, which was conspicuous at an immense distance; it had several extensive rooms, and might probably have been used as a fortress; but latterly it was only a place of amusement, and through the inattention of the proprietors was suffered to fall into decay, and is now in ruins". On Colby's map of 1831 there is a peak some two and a third miles north-east of the mansion rising to some 1,000ft with a magnificent view overlooking the area with the current Pantyffynon and Cwmyryn farms far below it on former Edwinsford Estate lands; it is marked as Pigoden St Nicholas (Pigyn Shon Nicholas) now at map reference SN668357. No

---

206 Also referred to by Joseph Gulston: *Bibliotheca Elegans et Curiosa (1783-4)* who says that "Sir Nicholas built a banqueting house on the point of a hill about three miles distant which was destroyed by lightening 8 February 1772. NB it had a spire". References to the structure (Pigyn Syr Nicholas) were also made by Richard Fenton (1804 -13 Tours in Wales) and Samuel Lewis (1833). This is exceptionally early for a landscape folly in Wales.

207 Richard Llwyd: *Topographical Notices on the History of Wales by Caradog of Llancarvan (1832) p175*

The Boar

ruins[208] remain of the former building and I suspect that its stones were used to build new farmhouses and outhouses nearby in the 1830s and thereafter when we know that the Edwinsford Estate invested in new buildings.

One of his additions to the ornamental gardens was a sundial[209] which stood in front of the mansion and which dates from 1710 and was made by the Royal Clockmaker, Daniel Delander[210]. It has the inscription "Sir Nicholas Williams Baronet AD 1710" with the Williams crest, the lion rampant, beneath and the motto *"Mea Virtute me involvo."*

It is now in two pieces; the elaborate brass upper part and gnomon is in the Carmarthen museum at Abergwili, and the stone column on which it stood is probably incorporated into the Edwinsford bridge over the Cothi at the southern end of the parapet where the carved and moulded stone can still be seen.

One of the interesting parts of researching families is that sometimes one discovers unexplained relations. In his Memoirs[211] of the Williams-Roper family a Williams descendant chronicles the fact that in 1737 Robert Williams (d1776) of Edwinsford and his first wife Margaret with their two children, Mary (b1726) and Robert Jr (1732- 1808), emigrated to America and settled in St Helena's parish, Beaufort County in South Carolina. Robert bought 1300 acres of land so he must have been a man of means. Both father and son were enrolled as magistrates there in 1756. Robert Sn died in 1776 and was buried in St Philip's churchyard in Charlestown. Robert Jr was born in Edwinsford in 1732, married Elizabeth Hext in 1755 and had five children before she died in 1769. He then returned to England and in 1771 went back to Carolina where he remarried Ann Roper (d1809) with whom he had four children. In 1777 he left for Holland (presumably because he was a Royalist) leaving his family behind and returned to Charlestown in 1778 under a flag of truce. He took the oath of allegiance to the local US government to avoid his lands being confiscated but was finally banished in 1782 and then left with his family for England. His large landed estates were confiscated and he also lost all his loans of £20,000 which he had made to local residents. His son, also Robert Williams (d1833), was educated at Westminster School when the family returned to England in 1770 and entered Lincoln's Inn where he studied until 1778; his father (d1808) could no longer support him so he went back to South Carolina and qualified as a Public Notary. He lived at 18 Tradd Street, Charlestown.

Who was Robert Williams Sr (d1776) of Edwinsford? It seems likely that he was born between 1700 and 1706 at a time when Sir Nicholas Williams Bt was in occupation of Edwinsford but not yet married. Was Robert an illegitimate son who took his father's name? When he emigrated in 1737 he had the means to buy lands in South Carolina; did this financial support originate from Sir Nicholas?

---

208 Elizabeth Whittle: *The Historic Parks and Gardens of Carmarthenshire CA (2000) p97* and C Stephen Briggs: *The Fabric of Parklands and Gardens in the Tywi Valley and beyond CA (1997) p96* both suggest (wrongly I think) that this was the same building as the gazebo situated on Pen Dinas near the Llansawel quarry nearby overlooking the park which RCAHMW (*Carmarthenshire Inventory p190*) found in ruins in 1917

209 FDWD: *Annals p7*

210 Daniel Delander (c1678-1733) was apprenticed to Thomas Tompion and became a member of the Clockmakers' Company. He invented the lock spring for clock cases as well as the first independent seconds stopwatch. He practised from the Dial in Devereux Court, Two Temple Gardens, and then in Fleet Street

211 JW Soady: *Memoirs of a Nonagenarian (1940)*

Peak of Pigyn Syr Nicholas 2017

Baronetcies

A Baronetcy is an hereditary title below the level of the five classes of British nobility, namely Dukes, Marquesses, Earls, Viscounts and Barons (all commonly called Lords). Since the Life Peerages Act 1958 permitted non-hereditary peerages very few hereditary peerages have been created. Originally all peers had the right to sit in the House of Lords; today only 92 hereditary peers are permitted to do so, but all non-hereditary life peers and baronesses can do so.

Baronetcies were first created in the 14th century by Edward III but those have since all become extinct. The current Order of Baronets first dates from 22 May 1611 when James I granted Letters Patent to 200 gentlemen of good birth with an income of at least £1,000 per annum. His purpose was to raise cash to help maintain his army and the obligation of the baronet was to upkeep 30 soldiers for three years at 8d per day, initially probably to fight in Ireland during the Plantation of Ulster with Protestants. He also wanted to create a sixth divison of the aristocracy between the nobility and the knighthood. In 1625 Charles I continued with this policy by creating the Baronetcy of Scotland and Novia Scotia for the plantation of Novia Scotia and such baronets were obliged to pay 2,000 marks and to support six settlers for two years; 100 such Scottish baronetcies survive to this day.

After the Union of England and Scotland in 1707 all future baronetcies were styled as baronets of Great Britain. Some 1,262 baronetcies survive. Originally the eldest son of a baronet became a knight on his 21st birthday but this was stopped by George IV in 1827. Baronetcies are usually hereditary and on the death of the holder the title passes to the eldest in the male line subject to the Garter King of Arms or (in Scotland) the Lord Lyon King of Arms confirming the pedigree and evidence of succession. The grant of a new baronetcy is now very rare indeed; the last was in 1990 to the husband of Baroness Thatcher (whose own title was not hereditary) to enable her son to inherit an hereditary baronetcy from her husband which he did on his death. A baronetcy and a knighthood are not peerages so the holder is a commoner not a nobleman. There have only ever been four female holders of baronetcies, called baronetesses, all of whose male lines have inherited their titles.

8. The Early Hanoverian Period 1714-1837

8.1 Early Hanoverian Synopsis

George I and II

On the death of Queen Anne, George, the son of Princess Sophia Electress of Hanover (who was the heir to the throne but had died before Anne), took the throne as King George I (ruler 1714-27); he did not speak English, was not popular, had a fierce temper and spent a lot of time in Hanover but, as required by Parliament, he was a Protestant monarch and prevented the Catholic Jacobite dynasty from returning to the English throne and causing another civil war. He did not get on with his son and heir, George Prince of Wales, and he favoured the anti-Catholic Whigs rather than the Tories, the traditional pro-Royalist party.

The Jacobite rebellions of 1715 and 1745 caused serious problems for George I and his son George II (ruler 1727-60). The Catholic James II had been ousted and fled to France in 1688. He died in 1701 and his supporters then looked to his son, James (the Old Pretender), aided by Louis XIV (d1715) and Louis XV in France and by the Spanish monarchy who were all strongly in favour of Catholic absolute monarchy rather than the constitutional monarchy and Parliamentary supremacy of the English type. Catholics in the Highlands of Scotland and in Ireland supported a return to Jacobite rule in England. In Wales there were some gentry who also did not favour the Hanoverian succession but in practice very few were going to take up arms to support the Catholic Stuart cause. The rebellion of 1715 was very much a Scottish event with the Old Pretender (half brother of Queen Anne and called James III by his supporters) landing in Scotland and staying for only six weeks before fleeing. By 1745 the Young Pretender (Charles Stuart, Bonnie Prince Charlie, son of James the Old Pretender) was much more of a real threat when he landed in Scotland and attracted some clan support, but had to flee into hiding; his supporters were roundly defeated in 1746 at the Battle of Culloden following which he fled back abroad to the Stuart exiled court in Rome supported there by the Pope.

In Wales[212] legitimism (the traditional loyalty and support of the Welsh for the monarch and for hereditary succession), which had been seen during the Civil War with many gentry families supporting the Royalists, gradually declined after James II fled to France in 1688. The growth of nonconformity especially in Carmarthenshire and the lack of any substantial Catholic community encouraged this trend. Few Welshmen fled to the exiled Stuart court in France, although David Lloyd (d1722) of the Ffosybleiddiaid branch of the Lloyd family did so with his son. There were however some Jacobite sympathisers in North Wales; a tradition in Radnorshire was to plant groves of Scottish firs near the homes of Jacobite supporters to attract Jacobite emissaries from the continent and such firs were known as "Charlie" or "Prince Charlie." The Society of the Cycle of the White Rose formed in 1723 in North Wales whose festival was held on 10 June (White Rose Day the birthday of James Stuart) and the Society of Sea Serjeants formed in 1725 in South Wales were both Jacobite supporters of gentry families and in their meetings toasts were made to the exiled Stuarts and Jacobite ballads were sung. So some Tory Welsh gentry families had Jacobite sympathies but took very little action in practice while the mass of the population were indifferent and the nonconformists certainly opposed any return to Popish monarchy.

In about 1717 George I fell out with Robert Walpole and his Whigs who then schemed against the Tories with the rival heir in waiting the Prince of Wales. In 1720-1 the South Sea Bubble triggered a crisis when many investors lost fortunes in buying shares in a company set up to

[212] Herbert Vaughan: *Welsh Jacobitism: THSC (1920-1) NLWJ p11-35* based on "Rhosyn Gwyn" which won the prize at the National Eisteddfod in London in 1909

take over the national debt. Walpole restored calm and in 1721 was appointed First Lord of the Treasury, thereby becoming the first Prime Minister in all but name and the Whigs were restored to power. George I died in Hanover and was succeeded by his son, George II, who also chose not to get on with his son, Frederick Prince of Wales (d1751). George II's reign saw Britain expand its influence globally and becomer a world power. In addition to the Jacobite rebellion of 1745 the country was involved in conflict with France, with Spain in the War of Jenkins Ear, in the War of Austrian Succession (1740-48), and in the Seven Years War (1756-63). George II was the last British monarch to lead his troops into battle which he did with success in 1743 at the Battle of Dettingen when France was defeated. By the time of his death Britain had expanded its growing empire in India and North America. Walpole had been in power since 1720 controlling major domestic and foreign policy but resigned from office in 1742 and William Pitt the Elder, later to be Earl of Chatham (1708-78), became the effective Prime Minister in 1746; the Tories stayed out of power until 1783.

George III

George III (ruler 1760-1820) was the grandson of George II and the son of Frederick Prince of Wales, who had died in 1751, and Princess Augusta of Saxe-Gotha. He was born in Britain and spoke English fluently as would all his successors and he never visited Hanover. He succeeded to the throne aged only 22 and his reign was one of the longest in British history. He married Princess Charlotte of Mecklenburg-Strelitz and they had 15 children. During his long reign Britain defeated France in the Seven Years War becoming the dominant European power, increased its power in India, defeated the French by sea at the Battle of Trafalgar (1805), finally defeated Emperor Nalopeon at the Battle of Waterloo (1815) thereby saving itself and the rest of Europe, and acquired additional lands in Canada, New South Wales, South Africa and India as well as numerous island colonies. However, his reign will always be remembered for the loss of the American colonies as a result of the War of American Independence revealing the risks to Britain of being overstretched and under-funded in foreign wars. Given that George was in reality a constitutional monarch and Parliament was supreme in matters of finance and foreign policy it is perhaps fairer to blame Prime Minister Lord North's Tory administration for this calamity rather than the monarch alone. Lord North's administration collapsed in 1782 and by 1783 William Pitt the Younger (1759-1806) at the age of only 24 was Prime Minister calling himself an Independent Whig; his administration lasted 17 years. His opponent, also a Whig, was Charles James Fox (d1806) who tried to undermine the monarchy by supporting the Prince of Wales's rival court in his attempts to be appointed Regent especially during George III's bouts of "madness", thought to be caused by the genetic disease porphyria. Recently available papers from the Royal Archives suggest that, despite his reputation, George was dedicated to his oath of office and to his family, had an inquiring intellect, a voracious appetite for science and a direct involvement in the operation of a constitutional government, was methodical, never allowed himself a moment of idleness, and was cultured in the era of a new Britain.

When the French Revolution started in 1789 and the French monarchy had been overthrown and Louis XVI executed there was a real risk of invasion. France declared war on Britain in 1793 and in February 1797 a French force[213] with Irish and American soldiers landed at Fishguard on the Pembrokeshire coast. It was quickly defeated and surrendered. France only ceased to be a threat after the defeat of Napoleon in 1815. Ireland became part of the United Kingdon in 1801 despite the King blocking the attempt by Pitt to emancipate Catholics. By 1811 George III was very ill and his son, the Prince of Wales, acted as Regent for the rest of his reign.

George IV and William IV

George III was succeeded by two of his sons, George IV (ruler 1820-30) and William IV (ruler 1830-37). George IV, the former Prince Regent, was recklessly extravagant, and not interested in the administration of government. He caused his father much stress by his rival court at Carlton House supported by Charles James Fox, but was a patron of the arts and of grandiose architectural schemes such as the Brighton Pavilion (designed by John Nash who was also did work at Dolaucothi Mansion), Regent Street, Regent's Park, Buckingham Palace and Windsor Castle. He had numerous mistresses, unwisely illegally married a Catholic widow, Maria Fitzherbert, and then married the German Caroline of Brunswick which was a huge mistake for both of them. They left no surviving heir. However during his reign the British Empire continued to expand particularly in the Far East including Australia.

213 JE Thomas: *Britain's Last Invasion (2007)*

William IV only became King because of the deaths of his elder brothers who left no heirs. He too produced no legitimate heirs. He acted for his short seven year reign very much as a constitutional monarch and following the electoral defeat of the Duke of Wellington as Prime Minister in 1830, he did not oppose Parliamentary reform which led to the passing of the very controversial Reform Act 1832, the start of real democracy in Britain. William lived long enough for his niece and heir, Victoria, to become Queen in 1837 without the need for another Regency at the very young age of 18; her very successful 64 year reign would see the British Empire grow to one fifth of the globe in size.

8.2 Whig and Tory Politics in Carmarthenshire

As we have seen in Chapter 6.4, following the Acts of Union 1536 and 1543 Carmarthenshire, Cardiganshire and Pembrokeshire like other counties gradually changed socially and politically. During most of the period from the late Tudors to after the Reform Act 1832 a handful of families effectively controlled the most prestigious offices[214] such as Deputy Lieutenant, Member of Parliament, Sheriff and Justice of the Peace. Each of the major county families such as the Vaughans of Golden Grove, the Williamses of Edwinsford, and the Jones/ Johnes families in Carmarthenshire and the Pryses of Gogerddan and the Lloyd families in Cardiganshire had junior or cadet branches whose members would also occasionally hold some of the county offices, although the most important such as MP was usually held by the head of the pre-eminent family or his son and heir; the MP for the county boroughs might also be from one of the major families or sometimes from a wealthy burgess family.

There were no political parties as we would recognise them today and politics was the preserve of the wealthy large landowning families of the county. A county seat in Parliament carried more prestige than a county borough seat and because of the sometimes crippling cost of contested elections, more often than not the ruling families agreed amongst themselves which family member or ally would be elected; seats were almost family heirlooms to be passed from father to son. Only about 4 per cent of the population in Wales were entitled to vote; each voter required a property qualification of 40s value per annum. After 1711 MPs needed to have lands of £600 value per annum to qualify to stand for the county seat and £300 for the county borough seat. Most of the very small electorate were politically apathetic and merely followed the lead of their landlords either out of loyalty or fear. Bribery and corruption[215] were common; landlords would increase their electorate by creating artificial leases to be surrendered after the election and creating new burgesses such as their employees and tenants who thereby had the right to vote, Sheriffs would change the dates and venues for voting at the last moment, and bribing voters was standard practice.

In Tudor Carmarthenshire the Jones/Johnes family of Abermarlais was the leading family followed by the Vaughans of Golden Grove. Under the Stuarts the Vaughans/ Carberys family faction (including the Rices at Dinefwr) dominated local politics under the Whig brand. So Carmarthenshire became largely Whig in a generally Tory Wales. In Cardiganshire the Jones/Johnes and Lloyd families held the county seat several times, but the Pryse family of Gogerddan and the Vaughans of Trawsgoed were the two principal families. No Hanoverian monarch visited Wales at all during the 18th century so perhaps it is unsurprising that most gentry were keener on drinking smuggled alcohol, gambling, fox hunting, shooting, cock fighting, Hunt balls, archery competitions, croquet parties and other rural pursuits; certainly local issues seemed more important than Westminster politics. Meantime the poverty of the poor was extreme and life was made harder by tolls, famines, poor harvests, disease, and JPs failing in their duty to raise poor relief and distribute it to the numerous needy paupers.

The term "Whig" originated from an insulting Scots word for cattle driver whilst the term "Tory" came from an equally insulting Irish word for outlaw. Both terms were first used during the Whig supported Exclusion Bill crisis of 1678-81 in relation to the succesion of James II to the throne and the prospect of a return to a Catholic monarchy. In general the Tories were the conservative Royalist supporters (the old cavaliers) who wanted a strong monarchy (some were Jacobites) and a strong Church of England and later adopted free trade principles; the Whigs (the old roundheads) supported a supreme Parliament with a constitutional monarchy without prerogative powers, toleration of

214 Glanmor Williams p342 et seq
215 Jenkins p158, 303 seq

Protestant dissenters, opposed a Catholic monarch and later adopted protectionist anti-continental economic policies. Tory and Whig factions fought for power during the reigns of William and Mary and Queen Anne, but on the succession of George I the Whigs began 45 years of power under Robert Walpole and Henry Pelham. Tory squires were prevented from favouring their families in public offices, Tory JPs were removed from office, and Tory clergy could not become bishops; anti-Tory discrimination was rife and in part led to some Tories becoming Jacobites. In 1715 Wales returned 15 Tory and 12 Whig MPs, but this changed and in Carmarthenshire the Whigs under the Vaughan/Carbery faction gained supremacy, although in elections loyalty to the principal county families continued to count for much more in practice than their party badge. By 1747 there were 18 Whigs and only 9 Tory MPs in Wales. The few pro-Jacobite Tories, viewed as traitors, and the failure of the Jacobite rebellions led to the virtual demise of their political faction. The old Tory party ceased to exist as an organised political party and a new Tory party did not really reinvent itself until 1783 when William Pitt the Younger took power.

Leaders of the Whigs included Robert Walpole, William Pitt the Elder, Charles James Fox and Charles Grey. In 1760 George III took the throne and the Whig party began to split into different factions. Prime Ministers Lord Bute in 1762-3 and Lord North in 1770-82 were described as Tory but were really Old Whigs. William Pitt the Younger during his leadership periods in 1783-1801 and in 1804-6 could be described as a new Tory although he considered himself to be an Independent Whig and his followers were called the Friends of Mr Pitt. His opposition led by Charles James Fox and Lord North and their followers were called (new) Whigs and it is at this time that a genuine two party system can be said to have started. The emerging new Whigs supported a constitutional monarchy with as little patronage as possible, some limited electoral reform, the abolition of slavery and emancipation for Catholics. In these policies they largely succeeded with the Reform Act 1832 led by Lord Grey, which expanded the franchise and ended the system of rotten and pocket boroughs, the Slavery Abolition Act 1833 and the Catholic Relief Act 1829. In 1859 a new Liberal Party supported by Lord Palmerston (1784-1865) emerged as a result of a coalition of some Whigs with the free trade supporters of Robert Peel. William Gladstone (1809-98) who served as Prime Minister four times in 1868-74, 1880-85, 1886, and 1892-94 started as a Tory, then joined the Peelites to merge with the Whigs to form the new Liberal Party.

The new Tories espoused new "conservative" policies. Their leader was Sir Robert Peel (1788-1850) who served as a Tory Prime Minister from 1834 to 1835 and again from 1841 to 1846. The party split over the issue of free trade in 1846 with the protectionists joining the new Liberal Party and the rest under the Earl of Derby and then Benjamin Disraeli calling their party "Conservatives".

In Carmarthenshire the Vaughan/Carbery domination of the county seat under the Whig banner continued from 1601 to 1710. John Vaughan, the third Earl of Carbery died in 1713 without a male heir and his sole daughter and heiress Anne inherited the Golden Grove estate. The Tories gained the seat briefly then lost it in 1715 to Anne's new husband, the Marquess of Winchester; his Whig ally, Edward Rice of Dinefwr, took over a few years later. There then followed some contested elections within the divided Whig faction between the Vaughans (the Reds), the Rices (who moved between being Reds and Blues when it suited them), and Sir Nicholas Williams Bt of Edwinsford (1681-1745)(51) who held the seat for 23 years until his death. John Vaughan was then elected in 1745. George Rice took the seat in 1754 and held it until his death in 1779 when the Vaughans returned to power. Sir James Hamlyn (1st Bt) of Clovelly and Edwinsford (1735-1811)(57) was then elected in 1793 and held the seat until the infamous 1802 election when he stood down in favour of his son.

The election of 1802 between Sir James Hamlyn Williams (2nd Bt)(60) supported by the Dinefwr faction for the Reds and Sir William Paxton[216] of Middleton Hall supported by the Golden Grove faction for the Blues resulted in 15 days of lavish bribery, personal abuse and rioting. It is probably the most notorious and bitter election in the annals of Carmarthenshire and is described in Chapter 8.4. It was won at great expense by Sir James Hamlyn Williams of Edwinsford who held the seat until 1806 when Paxton eventually won it.

---

[216] ODNB; Edna Dale-Jones: *Sir William Paxton, his Family and his Monument CA (2009) p64-73*

In 1804 John Vaughan of Golden Grove, the Lord Lieutenant and leading Whig, died without an heir and left his large 50,000 acre estate to his friend Lord Cawdor[217] of the Scottish Campbell family of Stackpole Court in Pembrokeshire (see the Vaughan Family Pedigree below). The Cawdors (Whigs) and the Rice/Dynevor family (Tories) continued to compete for local power while George Rice, Lord Dynevor, served as Lord Lieutenant from 1804 to 1852 following which two Earl Cawdors held that position from 1852 until 1898. The Cawdor faction controlled the county borough seat while from 1820 to 1831 George Rice of Dinefwr held the county seat. Local and national political issues came to the fore including whether the Welsh Courts of Great Sessions should be abolished (the Blues in favour and the Reds against but in favour of reform), the repeal of the usury laws, the repeal of the window tax, Catholic emancipation, corn law reform, the abolition of slavery (strongly supported by nonconformists), the improvement of the Llanwrda Llandovery and Lampeter roads, and the Llanelli railway and docks legislation. John Johnes of Dolaucothi an able lawyer unsuccessfully helped the Reds' opposition to the latter legislation which affected landowners' rights.

The Reform Act 1832 brought local political feuds to a head. Lord Grey had a large Whig majority in favour of electoral reform in the Commons but the House of Lords controlled by Tory peers opposed it and only the threat of appointing hundreds of new peers persuaded the Tory Duke of Wellington to accept the inevitable and abstain. The Bill was enacted in June 1832. George Rice who opposed the Bill had sensibly stepped down in 1831 and been replaced unopposed by Sir James Hamlyn Williams (3rd Bt) of Edwinsford (1790-1861)(61) supported by the Cawdor faction who were in favour of reform. Under the Act Carmarthenshire gained an extra county seat and Wales had 32 MPs in total. Votes were extended to copyholders and long leaseholders of land worth £10 per annum and to tenants who paid annual rent of £50. This resulted in 3,887 voters in Carmarthenshire; in Carmarthen borough however the electorate actually fell[218] because of the disenfranchisement of so many non resident burgesses. In practice the landed gentry families continued to have the political power in Carmarthenshire and the two county seats in 1833 were won by Tories and this dominance lasted until 1868. Full electoral reform and enfranchisement would take another century.

In the countryside great changes took place with subsistence farming being replaced with more efficient agricultural methods and surplus wool and other products being exported. But the urban towns were growing fast and the population of Britain in 1850 had grown to some 18 million people of whom about half now lived in towns.

The less wealthy landlords in Carmarthenshire were a very different breed from the generally benevolent Williams family at Edwinsford and life for the poor must have been very difficult indeed.

217 It was Lord Cawdor who in February 1797 commanded the Welsh troops which captured the French, Irish and American force which had landed at Fishguard on the Pembrokeshire coast. It was quickly defeated and surrendered.

218 Rees p95

8.3 Edwinsford Family

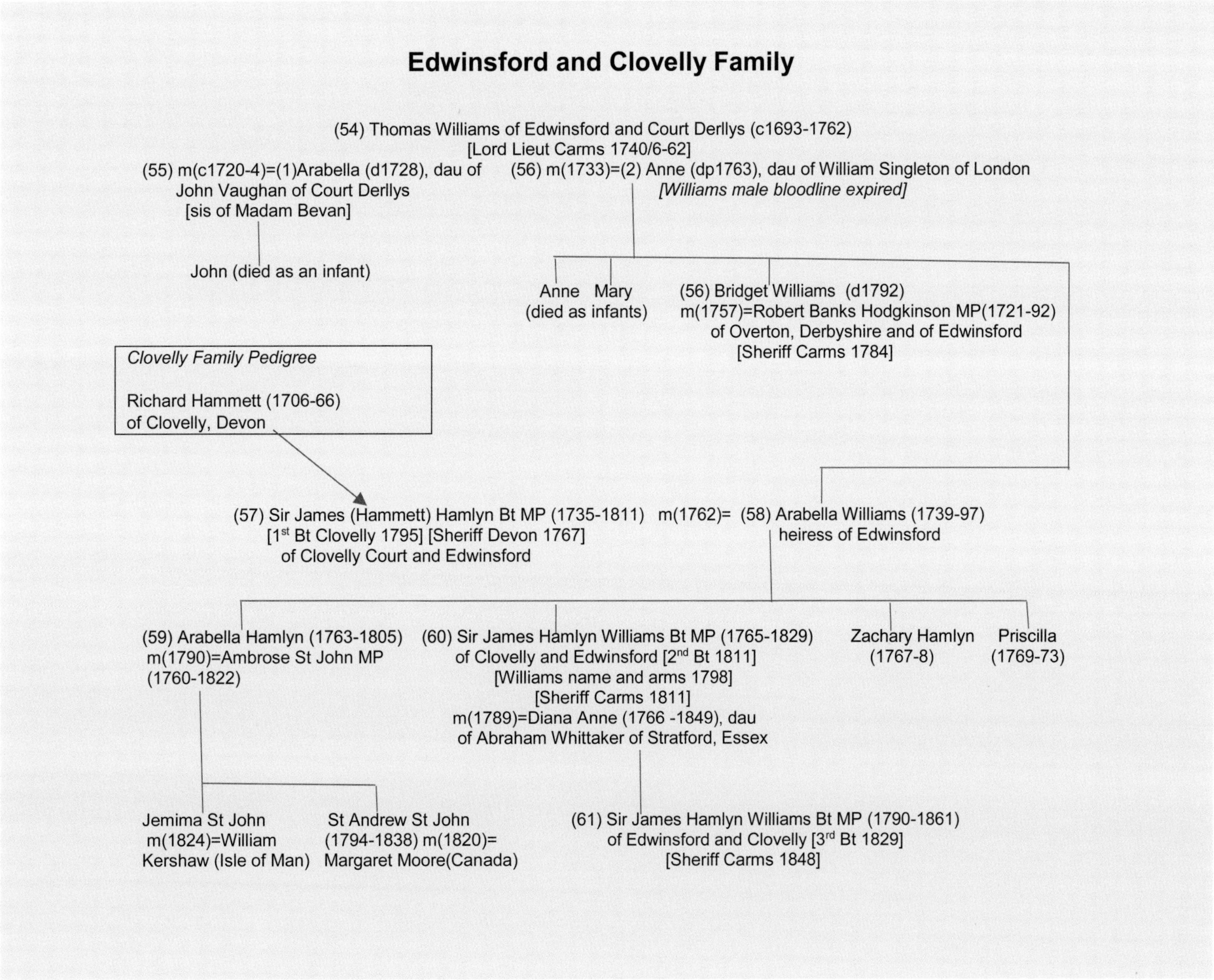

Thomas Williams (c1693-1762)

As we saw in Chapter 7.2, Thomas Williams (54) was the youngest son of Sir Rice Williams (45). In his father's codicil dated 22 December 1693 Thomas was left £500 to be paid when he reached the age of 18 with the interest in the meantime being used for his maintenance and education. As the youngest son he was entitled under the Borough English custom to some copyhold lands in Talley manor; in 1706 his mother had to present a Bill of Complaint[219] in the High Court of Chancery to protect his rights against the claims of a cousin, Thomas Williams of Talley House who was the son of John Williams and grandson of Thomas Williams (44).

Thomas spent some of his younger years at Edwinsford and later was educated at Gray's Inn; he became a barrister and lived in Great Russell Street. Helped by the influence of his eldest brother, Sir Nicholas Williams MP (51), he was appointed on 21 June 1731 to the offices of Chamberlain and Chancellor in the counties of Carmarthen, Pembroke and Cardigan as well as the towns and boroughs of Carmarthen and Haverfordwest.

Between 1720 and 1724 Thomas married Arabella (d1728), the daughter of John Vaughan (1663-1722) of Court Derllys in Merthyr parish just west of Carmarthen, by his wife Elizabeth Thomas (d1721) of Meidrim near to Merthyr (the sole heiress of her own mother's Protheroe estate at Hawksbrook in Llangynog). Arabella and her two sisters were the co-heiresses to the Derllys and Hawksbrook estates and also inherited the Derwydd estate on the death of their uncle Richard Vaughan MP in 1724. Arabella's inheritance share was the mansion at Derllys and 51 other properties. At the height of its prosperity the Derllys Estate comprised 215 properties producing an annual income of £1,237 in 1725. Arabella and her husband Thomas spent their short married life at Derllys Court; he was not to inherit Edwinsford until his elder brother's death many years later in 1745. Arabella died on 26 January 1728 and was buried in the Church of St Martin and St Enfael in Merthyr parish (possibly in the former Derllys Chapel) where there is a marble memorial in her memory; her only child John died in infancy. Under her will all her estate including the Derllys estate and her share of the Hawksbrook estate passed to Thomas.

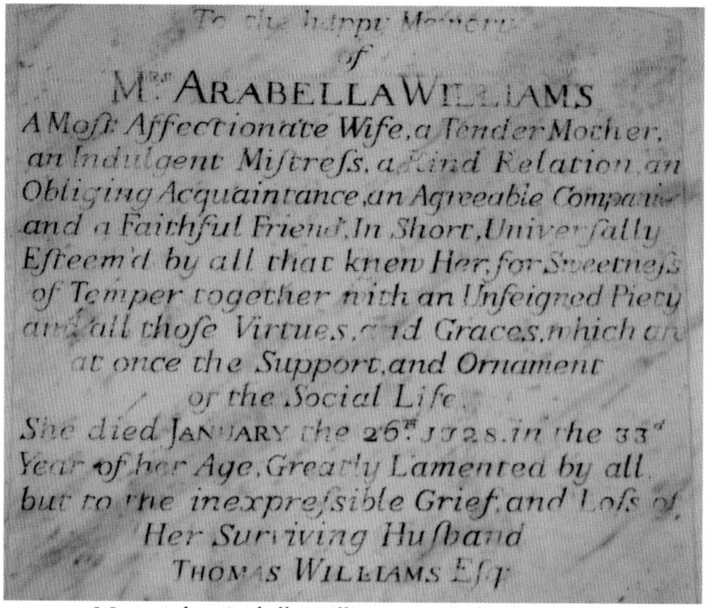

Memorial to Arabella Williams in Merthyr Parish Church near Carmarthen 2017

Arabella had two surviving sisters one of whom was the famous educationalist, Madam Bevan (1698-1779), the patron of Rev Griffith Jones and the SPCK charity school movement which is described in Chapter 30.1. Derllys continued as part of the Edwinsford Estate and Thomas leased out the Hawksbrook and Derllys properties; in 1758 he granted a 99 year lease of Court Derllys to John Davies a farmer. Derllys was retained by the Edwinsford family until 1915.

[219] Francis Jones: *THSC (1987) p37 et seq*

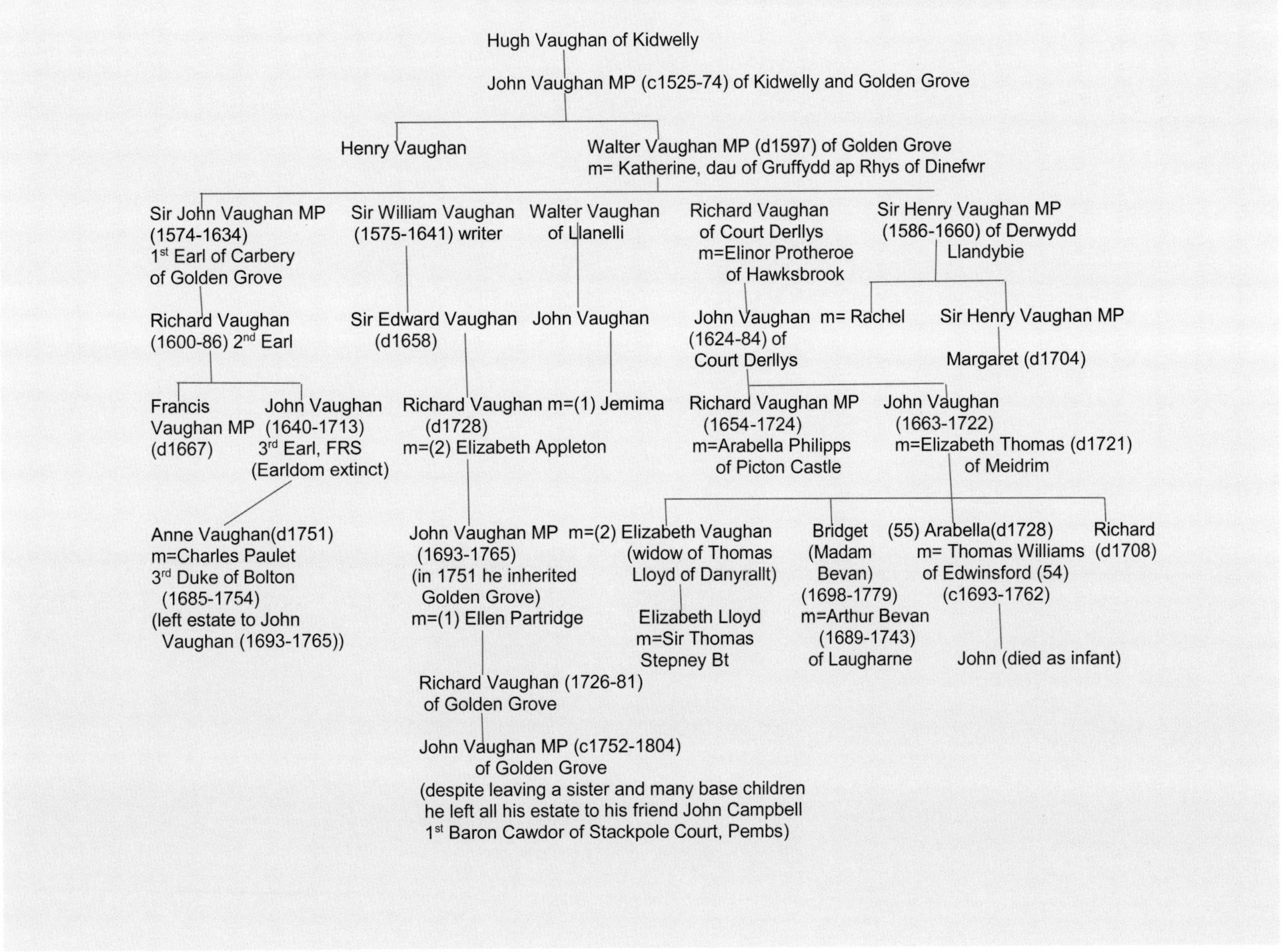

Vaughan Family of Golden Grove and Court Derllys

Cawdor Family of Golden Grove

John Campbell, 1st Baron Cawdor MP (c1753-1821) (inherited Golden Grove)

John Frederick Campbell, 1st Earl Cawdor MP (1790-1860)

John Frederick Vaughan Campbell, 2nd Earl Cawdor (1817-98)

Frederick Campbell, 3rd Earl Cawdor (1847-1911)

Hugh Campbell, 4th Earl Cawdor (1870-1914)

John Campbell, 5th Earl Cawdor (1900-70)
(Golden Grove leased to Carms CC in 1952 and sold in 1972)

Hugh Campbell, 6th Earl Cawdor (1932-93)

Court Derllys

The Vaughan family were one of the preeminent families in South Wales for nearly five centuries. Golden Grove (Gelli Aur) [SN597198] was their principal seat and there have been three successive mansions[220] there. The first was built in 1560-5 by John Vaughan MP and assessed at 30 hearths in 1670 but was destroyed by fire in 1729. The second was built in 1754-7 alongside the old mansion but was pulled down in 1862. The third was built in 1826-34 by 1st Earl Cawdor (whose father had inherited Golden Grove from his friend John Vaughan in 1804) higher up the slope and about 700 yards from the previous mansion. At the height of their affluence the Golden Grove estate comprised over 50,000 acres, 27 extensive manors and lordships, and five castles, and when these are added to the lands of the many branches of the Vaughan family it is probable that nearly half of Carmarthenshire had a Vaughan as a landlord. Their successors, the Campbells[221], in 1883 owned over 100,000 acres in the UK but have since lost most of it.

Derllys or Derllys Court or Cwrt Derllys [SN356202] stands half a mile south of Merthyr Parish Church and about two miles west of Carmarthen. In pre-Norman days the area formed the commote of Derllys lying within the cantref of Gwarthaf. It later became a Welshry as part of the royal county of Carmarthen and then after the Acts of Union 1536-43 it became the Hundred of Derllys. The first Vaughan[222] of the cadet branch of the family to own the house[223] and its lands was Richard Vaughan, a younger son of Walter Vaughan MP (d1597) of Golden Grove and grandson of John Vaughan MP (c1525-74). Richard, who served as Sheriff of Carmarthenshire in 1631, bought it from Lewis Philip Hugh. He married Elinor, daughter of James Protheroe of Hawksbrook (Nantyrhebog)[224] and their son, John Vaughan (1624-84), inherited Derllys and he improved and extended the mansion; a stone inscribed "JV 1660" used to be seen on an old barn once forming part of the original house. The mansion contained six hearths in 1670. John married his first cousin, Rachel (d1713), daughter and heiress of Sir Henry Vaughan MP of Derwydd. John and Rachel had two sons:

220 Francis Jones: *Historic Carmarthenshire Homes p84;* Eurig Davies*:CA (2015) p22-24*
221 Liza Campbell: *Title Deeds: A Work of Friction (2006)*
222 Francis Jones: *THSC-Cadets of Golden Grove (1977) p77-92;* Francis Jones*: Carmarthenshire Homes p54-5*
223 Lewis Glyn Cothi praised the princely mansion in one of his bardic poems
224 Francis Jones: *THSC-The Squires of Hawksbrook (1937) p339-56*

(1) Richard Vaughan MP (1654-1724) who was a successful lawyer inherited Derylls from his father and also the Derwydd estate from his uncle Sir Henry Vaughan on his death in 1676. He lived at Derwydd with his wife Arabella (d1729), daughter of Sir Erasmus Philipps of Picton Castle in Pembrokeshire who had a dowry of £4000; they had no children and Richard died intestate in 1724, and

(2) John Vaughan (1663-1722) a social and religious reformer who with his friend, Sir John Philipps of Picton Castle, founded charity schools (SPCK) in Carmarthenshire and Pembrokeshire. John married Elizabeth, daughter of Thomas and Elizabeth Thomas (nee Protheroe) of Meidrim; they had three surviving daughters, who were co-heiresses to the Derllys and Hawksbrook estates and also inherited the Derwydd estate on the death of their uncle Richard Vaughan. Their son Richard (1697-1708) died young.

The three daughters amongst whom the various estates were partitioned were:

(1) Arabella Vaughan (d1728) who married between 1720 and 1724 Thomas Williams of Edwinsford (c1693-1762) (54) who later became the Lord Lieutenant of Carmarthenshire. Arabella's inheritance share was the mansion at Derllys and 51 other properties. Arabella died young in 1728 and was buried at the Church of St Martin and St Enfael in Merthyr Parish, Carmarthen;

(2) Elizabeth Vaughan (d1754) who married (a) Captain Thomas Lloyd (d1734) of Trehir a younger son of Danyrallt and they had a surviving daughter, Elizabeth Lloyd (b1725) who married Sir Thomas Stepney Bt of Llanelli and inherited Derwydd, and (b) secondly in 1740 her cousin John Vaughan MP who inherited Golden Grove in 1751. Elizabeth's share of her inheritance was 71 properties; and

(3) Bridget (Madam Bevan) (1698-1779) who received 92 properties as her inheritance. On 30 December 1721 she married Arthur Bevan of Laugharne (1689-1743) in Merthyr Parish Church. She later became famous for her educational and religious zeal following in the footsteps of her father (see Chapter 30.1).

Thomas Williams (later of Edwinsford) leased out the Derllys estate after Arabella's early death in 1728 and in 1758 he granted a 99 year lease on Court Derllys to a farmer, John Davies. Later the mansion became ruinous and in 1809 Fenton described it as disappointing "expecting to have found it larger and retaining marks of more consequence". The house was rebuilt in the early 19th century and part of the old mansion is thought to have been made into a barn. In 1814 the Edwinsford land agent, Daniel Price, asked David Davies a carpenter to draw up plans for a new house using old materials from the timbers and beams. The 1838 tithe map shows the current buildings and a holding of 273 acres occupied by David Phillips as tenant with the owner being Lady Diana Anne Hamlyn Williams (1766-1849), wife of Sir James Hamlyn Williams Bt MP (1765-1829)(60) of Edwinsford and Clovelly. At that time following her husband's death she owned 10 farms in the Merthyr area of Derllys totalling some 752 acres. The barn being part of the old mansion had datestones of 1660 and 1850 but was burnt down in the 1970s.The new 19th century house is a Grade 2 listed late Georgian style country house with three stories. In 1914 the Derllys estate was put up for sale but did not reach its expected price. It was sold by the executors of Sir James Hamlyn Williams-Drummond (1857-1913)(68) on 24 March 1915 for £8,250 to John Thomas on a mortgage of £5,500 provided by the executors and subject to a yearly tenancy in favour of the sitting tenant, Percy Thomas, at an annual rent of £550. John Thomas died in 1916 and his widow Elizabeth Thomas married TR Benjamin in 1921. Elizabeth Benjamin died in 1949 and her executors sold Derllys Court with 277.55 acres to Mrs Violet David for £125,000. She leased it to Robert Walters[225] in 1973 and then sold him the freehold in 1978 for £81,500. In 1993 Robert converted part of his farm into the Derllys Court Golf Club and later built a clubhouse.

[225] I am grateful to Robert Walters for this background

Newer 19th century Court Derllys 2017

On 11 April 1733 Thomas Williams (54) married for a second time some five years after Arabella's early death in 1728. His new wife was Anne (dc1763)(56), the daughter of William Singleton of London. They lived in Gray's Inn where he continued with his legal career, at his London home in Great Russell Street, and at Court Derllys. Thomas and Anne had four daughters, two of whom, Anne and Mary, died as infants and were later reburied in the family vault at Talley on 31 October 1762. The surviving two were:(1) Bridget Williams (d1792) and (2) Arabella Williams (1739-97) both of whom would marry and live with their husbands at Edwinsford as we shall see.

Following his eldest brother's death in 1745 Thomas inherited a large property portfolio including the Edwinsford and Lethr Cadfan Estates. However his brother left debts and Thomas had paid off some £9,069 by 1748. He acquired some additional properties and granted several short term leases including one for 21 years in 1750 to John James the innkeeper at the Black Lion in Llansawel, and another in 1762 to Francis and John Morgan of the mill and great house at Abergorlech.

By Letters Patent dated 10 March 1740 he was appointed Lord Lieutenant and Keeper of the Rolls (Custos Rotulorum) of Carmarthenshire[226] following in his eldest brother's footsteps and being

[226] FDWD: *Annals p37.* It is possible that he was only appointed to these offices in 1746 after his eldest brother's death since the family muniments and other records are inconsistent as to the dates. Another appointment of Thomas as Custos Rotulorum is dated 10 March 1746

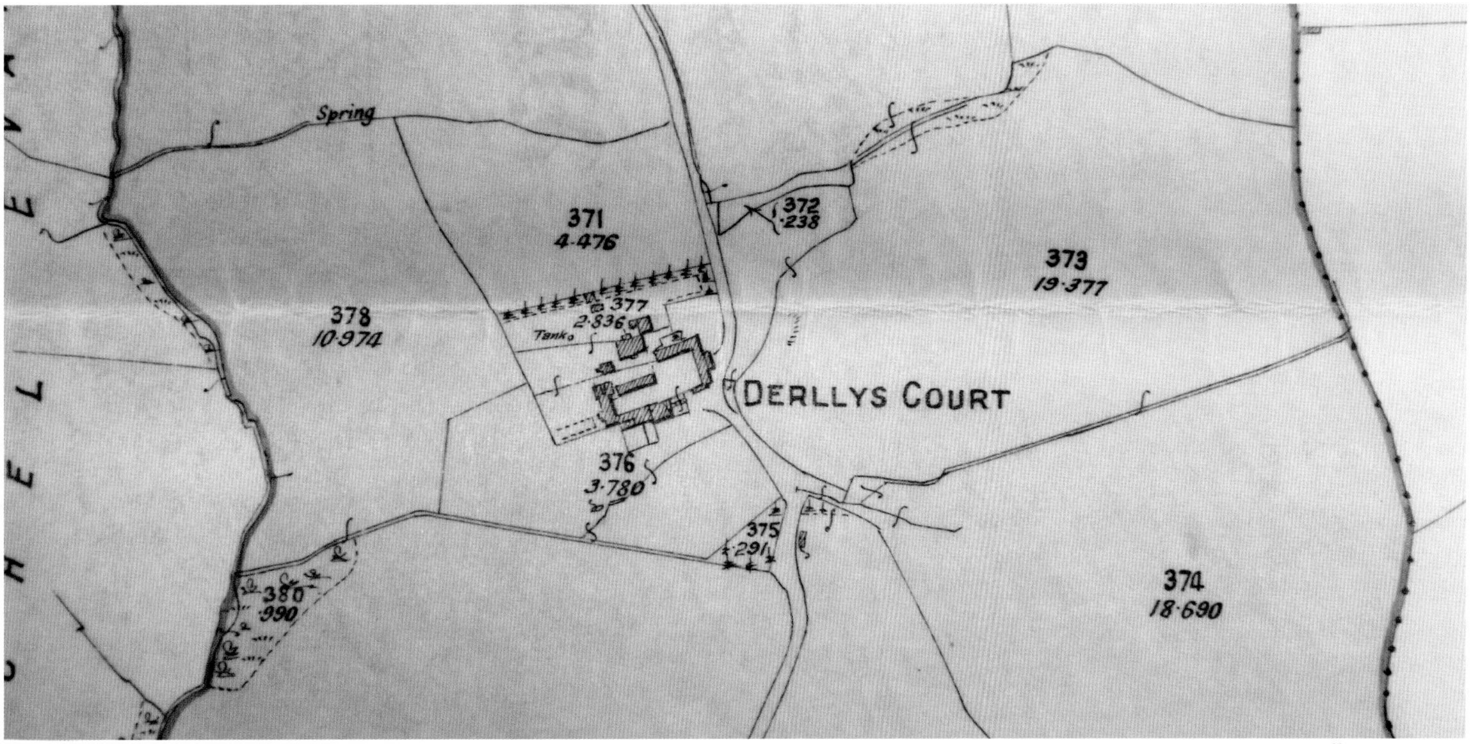

Court Derllys map 1915

only the second of the three members of the family to hold that prestigious office.

In 1760 aged about 67 Thomas divided his share of the Hawksbrook estate and the Court Derllys estate, being 1180 acres in Carmarthenshire and 190 acres in the county borough, between his two daughters, Bridget and Arabella. He made his will on 21 July 1762, died in London and his body was then brought down to Talley where he was interred in the family vault on 31 October 1762[227] with his two daughters who had died in infancy. In his will trust expressed to last for 600 years he left: (a) to his second wife Anne the sum of £100 guineas plus the use of his house in Great Russell Street and his furniture there but not the plate and books for her life unless she remarried with remainder to his daughter Bridget (Anne would of course have had the benefit of her marriage settlement income); (b) the rectory rights of Caeo and Llansawel and all tithes he held to trustees for his daughter Bridget (to whom he had paid £6,000 on her marriage in 1757); (c) to his first wife's sister, Madam Bevan, £100; (d) small legacies to his trustees, his land agents and maid servant; and (e) all his property and residuary estate first to his sons (there were none) and then to his surviving daughters, Bridget and Arabella in turn, subject to the beneficiary taking the surname "Williams" failing which the property would pass under the trust to the next son or daughter in age. His will was sealed with his eldest brother's lovely armorial seal showing a shield of a lion rampant and a crest being the same with supporters being two wolves salient.

Although Thomas was the last male bloodline heir to the original Williams pedigree, the family surname "Williams" continued as provided under Thomas's will trust, either alone or coupled with another surname, sometimes hyphenated and sometimes not, up until the death of the last estate heir in 1970.

[227] FDWD: *Annals p36*

Bridget Williams (d1792) and Robert Banks Hodgkinson MP (1721-92)

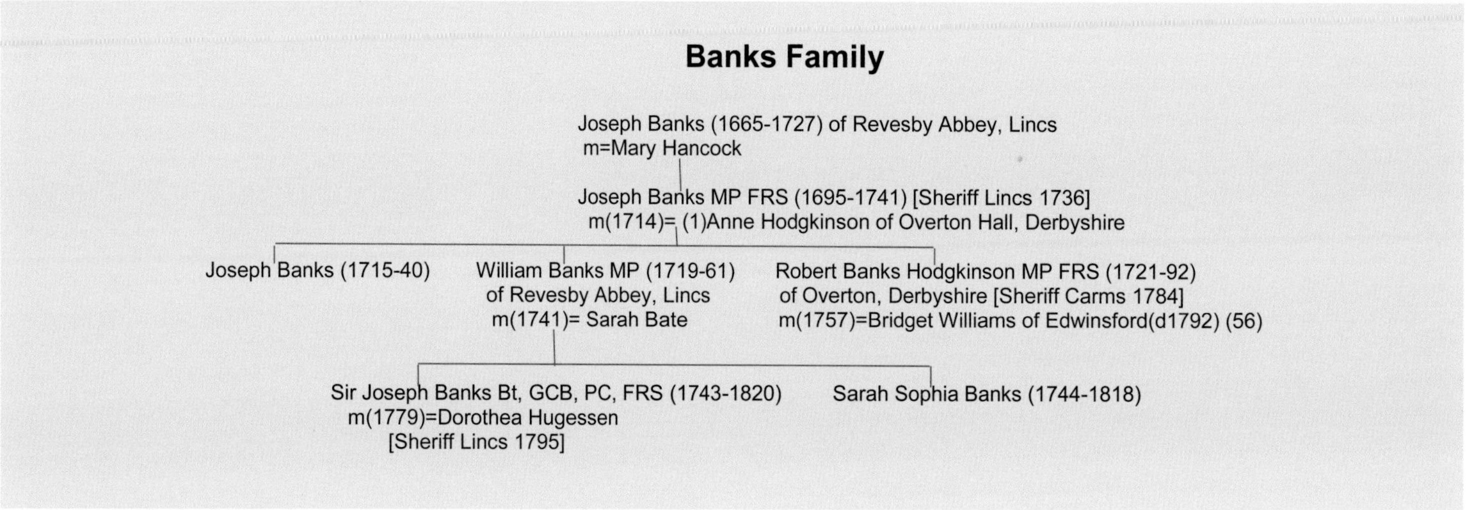

The Banks family were high achievers[228]. Joseph Banks (1665-1727) was a successful Sheffield lawyer who also made a fortune in property investment and in 1714 acquired Revesby Abbey in Lincolnshire. His son, Joseph Banks MP (1695-1741), was educated at the Middle Temple in 1711, served in the Nottingham militia, and inherited Revesby Abbey in 1727 on the death of his father giving him an annual income of some £3,000, although he did not live there very much preferring his house in Lincoln. On 11 April 1714 he married Anne (d1730), the daughter and heiress of William Hodgkinson of Overton Hall, Ashover in Derbyshire. He served as MP for Peterborough from 1728 to 1734 initially supporting the Government but then applied to be the Custos Rotulorum and failed to obtain the post following which he then voted for the opposition; he did not stand in 1734. He was a Fellow of the Royal Society and a Fellow of the Society of Antiquaries who collected art as did his successors. He remarried Catherine Collingwood in 1731 after the death of Anne and had two sons by her. He served as Sheriff of Lincolnshire in 1736 dying in 1741. He was a man of ability but overshadowed by his father, and a devoted husband and father.

Joseph and Anne had three daughters and the following three sons:

(1) Joseph Banks (1715-40) the eldest son and heir who died before his father;

(2) William Banks MP (1719-61) who was educated at Westminster from 1730 to 1733, and then at the Middle Temple. He assumed the surname of Hodgkinson in 1733 (from his maternal grandfather) in preparation for inheriting Overton Hall but when his elder brother died in 1740 he relinquished it since his younger brother Robert thereby became the heir to that estate. William became the heir to Revesby Abbey which he inherited in 1741 on the death of his father where he fashionably created a menagerie. In 1741 he married Sarah Bate, niece of Hannah Chambers wife of the 8th Earl of Exeter at Burleigh House, Stamford. They had a famous son, Sir Joseph Banks, and a daughter, Sarah, described below. William died in 1861 before his children came of age so his younger brother Robert and his widow assumed their guardianship. William served as MP for Grampound in Cornwall from 1741 to 1747 consistently voting for the Opposition. In 1745 he contracted a fever which deprived him of the use of his legs and he did not stand for his seat again.

228 Letters and papers of the Banks Family: Lincoln Record Society (1952); HP

Their son, Sir Joseph Banks (1743-1820), was born in London and educated at Harrow (1752-56), Eton (1756-60) and then studied botany at Christ Church Oxford but left without a degree owing to the reluctance of the Professor of Botany to teach him. He divided his time between Oxford and London where he spent hours in the British Museum. He travelled to Labrador and Newfoundland in 1766 and then made his name by taking part in Captain James Cook's first great circumnavigation of the world in HMS Endeavour in 1768-71; he brought with him four servants and a secretary, two artists to sketch the plants and fauna, another botanist and his two dogs. His two negro servants died of the cold at Tierra del Fuego, one of the artists died of fever in Tahiti, he discovered over 1000 botanical species previously unknown, sketched numerous animals in Australasia including the kangaroo, discovered Botany Bay, and nearly died himself. On his return he became very famous and popular without any political aspirations. In 1772 he travelled to Iceland. He was a close confidant of George III and in 1773 he was put in charge of the Royal Botanical Gardens at Kew which he transformed into a major scientific centre devoted to botanical exchanges round the world. He was elected a Fellow of the Royal Society in 1766 and served as its President for a record 42 years from the age of only 35 (1778-1820). He was also a Fellow of the Society of Antiquaries and for a time a Fellow[229] of the new Society of Arts. He was made a Baronet in July 1781, a Privy Councillor in 1797 and his KB (1795) was elevated to a GCB in 1815. He served as Sheriff of Lincolnshire in 1795. He was a very close friend[230] of Charles Francis Greville PC MP FRS (1749-1809) who famously introduced his uncle Sir William Hamilton (d1803) aged 61 to his second wife Emma Hamilton aged 26, who became the mistress of Admiral Lord Nelson (d1805); the three of them formed a ménage à trois in Palermo in Sicily in 1798 before they returned to London where Lady Hamilton gave birth to Nelson's daughter Horatia. Nelson was killed on HMS Victory in 1805. Sir Joseph Banks married in 1779 Dorothea Hugessen and their London home was at 32 Soho Square where they lived with his unmarried sister, Sarah. He died in 1820 without issue so his baronetcy expired. His correspondence was enormous and his papers voluminous.

William's daughter, Sarah Banks (1744-1818), has been described[231] as "the most noteworthy female collector of coins and tokens this country has known." At the height of the Enlightenment in England when new discoveries were stimulating an excited fascination with the physical world, Sarah was one of those who observed, collected and recorded with meticulous dedication. From about 1780 she lived with her famous brother and his wife in Soho Square rather than in the country. She collected, books, objects of natural history, ephemera, and coins tokens and medals. All her books were left to the British Museum and her collection of coins etc are now at the Royal Mint Museum in Llantrisant. Sadly she died in 1818 as a result of a drunken driver causing the coach in which she was travelling with her brother to overturn. She was buried at Revesby Abbey; and

(3) Robert Banks Hodgkinson MP (1721-92) who was born in 1721 in Lincoln where his parents had a house and baptised there that year. He enrolled at Merchants' Hall in Bristol in October 1739 having been indentured there to a Bristol merchant, Mr Jeffries. He was educated at Christ Church Oxford and matriculated on 8 June 1741 aged 19. In 1743 the second brother, William Banks MP conveyed to Robert the Overton Estate under a decree of the Court of Chancery since following the death of his eldest brother Robert had become the second surviving son under entail and heir to that estate of his maternal grandfather, William Hodgkinson. Robert assumed the surname and arms of Hodgkinson in the same year in which he inherited Overton Hall and its estate. In 1748 he was elected MP for Wareham in Dorset, although he was a stranger there, probably as a government supporter and he remained in this seat until 1754 when he retired and did not stand again. He was elected[232] a Fellow of the Royal Society and a Fellow of the Royal Society of Antiquaries, and was also a Fellow of the Society of Arts for a time like his nephew, Sir Joseph Banks.

Bridget Williams (56), heiress to the Edwinsford Estate, lived with her father and stepmother in Edwinsford, Court Derllys and their London home until her marriage on 1 October 1757 to Robert Banks Hodgkinson MP whom she probably met in London society. As we have seen he was the third son of Joseph Banks MP (1695-1741) of

[229] DGC Allan: *Joseph Banks and the Society-RSA Journal Vol 141 (1993);* NA Chambers: *The Society of Arts and Joseph Banks (2007)*

[230] Both were members of the Society of Dilettanti of noblemen and scholars who sponsored the study of ancient Greek and Roman art

[231] RJ Eaglen: *Sarah Sophia Banks and her English Hammered Coins-British Numismatics Society (2009)*

[232] Alumni Oxoniensis (1715-1886) Vol 2

Revesby Abbey in Lincolnshire by his first wife, Anne, daughter and heiress of William Hodgkinson of Overton Hall, Ashover in Derbyshire. Under the prenuptial settlement[233] dated 29 September in which Robert is described as "of New Burlington Street London" properties in 13 Derbyshire parishes were settled to the use of the marriage. Bridget inherited the Edwinsford Estate in 1762 on the death of her father, Thomas Williams (54), and Robert and Bridget lived in Edwinsford and Overton Hall during their married life. Edwinsford tithe books and estate accounts[234] show that Robert took a keen interest in the management of the estate and that he received tolls (see Chapter 16.3) for the holding of the Llansawel Market and Fair. In 1784 he followed in the family tradition by serving as Sheriff of Carmarthenshire as well as taking part in public affairs. He also exchanged numerous interesting letters with his close neighbour, John Johnes (1724-81) at Dolaucothi.

Robert took a keen interest in the management of the Overton Estate. In addition he and his nephew, Sir Joseph Banks, who inherited that estate after Robert's death, were closely involved in the use of steam power[235] to pump out the water in the Gregory and Overton Lead Mines on their land in Ashover close to Overton Hall. The lead mines had been active since about 1695 but had suffered from water problems; between about 1768 and 1807 three different types of new steam engine were used to extract the surplus water.

During their 30 year tenure at Edwinsford, Robert and Bridget made a number of improvements to the mansion and the gardens. Robert rebuilt the bridge over the Cothi and transformed it into a wide single span bridge (instead of the former two span bridge built by Sir Nicholas Williams Bt much earlier in the 18th century); the new bridge was of stone laid in fine diminishing courses having an elliptical arch with dressed stone voussoirs and a low parapet wall rising to a central point. On the bridge there can still be seen a stone which reads *"This Bridge is the sole Property of the Family of Edwinsford. Rebuilt by Robert Banks Hodgkinson, Esq, 1783".* The builder[236] was David Edwards of Pontypridd, son of the celebrated bridge builder Rev William Edwards of Eglwysilan (1719-89) famous for the Pontypridd bridge (1755) and the bridge at Llandeilo-yr-ynys (1787) whose extortionate tolls helped fuel the Rebecca Riots. The Edwinsford bridge is now grade 2 listed.

The 1776 copper plate engraving of "Edwinsford, the Seat of R Banks Hodgkinson Esqr" by the artist Paul Sandby[237] and engraved by William Watts (on the front cover of this book) shows the mansion in all its magnificence with what looks like a side chapel with a bell and cross on the roof, two men approaching the front gate, a man riding a horse in front, the gardens in front running down to the River Cothi and the park behind, the old bridge which had two spans, and on the right a farmhouse and other farm buildings across the river. The accompanying text of the description says:

"Edwinsford, the seat of Robert Banks Hodgkinson Esq; in Carmarthenshire, is situated about six miles north-west of the great turnpike road. The family of Williams have possessed this house many ages. It stands upon the banks of the river Cothy, which runs through the middle of the demesne. The house is an ancient building, but rendered very convenient by the present possessor for a large family. Behind the house is a large lawn containing above eighty acres, surrounded by rising hills, woods, and walks; at the bottom of which the hills draw together, and the river runs a narrow channel, through rocks, covered with woods, for many miles, affording many most delightful and romantic scenes.
A bridge near the house, for the use of the family, was built by Sir Nicholas Williams, Bart, which is of great use to the country, who, by permission, (upon floods, which frequently happen here) have leave to pass it.
About the distance of three miles upon the point of the hill, in view of the house, the same gentleman built a banquetting room, with a large spire over it, an useful land mark from all the neighbouring hills. This whole building[238] *was entirely demolished by a severe storm of lightning Feb .6.1772"*

233 FDWD: *Annals p38*
234 NLW Edwinsford archives
235 SR Band: *The Steam Engines of Gregory Mine Ashover-Bulletin Peak District Mines Historical Society Vol 8 No 5 (1983)*
236 FDWD: *Annals p8*
237 Paul Sandby RA (1731-1809) was an English map-maker and landscape painter in watercolours and one of the founding members of the Royal Academy in 1768. Many of his drawings and paintings were bought by Sir Joseph Banks (whose uncle was then living in Edwinsford) with whom he toured South Wales in 1773 resulting in his publication of Views in South Wales in 1775 and their later copper engravings
238 See reference to Pigyn Sir Nicholas in Chapter 7.2 under Sir Nicholas Williams

1783 bridge stone

Robert Banks Hodgkinson

Robert and Bridget did not have any children. Bridget died on 14 July 1792 probably in London. Following her death Robert is said[239] to have "declared it his solemn wish that he might as soon as possible follow her". Later that autumn Robert died of pleurisy and kidney failure on 11 November 1792 and was buried with Bridget in St Mary's Church, Battersea where there is a rather cold monument in their memory. On his death the Overton estate passed to his nephew, Sir Joseph Banks, who was very close to his uncle and guardian Robert especially after the death of his own father, William Banks MP, in 1761. Under the will trust of Thomas Williams (54) the Edwinsford Estate passed next to his second surviving daughter, Arabella Williams (58), who had married Sir James Hamlyn Bt MP of Clovelly in 1762. The Williams family thereby became joined with the Hammett / Hamlyn family of Devon and the Edwinsford and Clovelly Estates united; if Bridget and Robert had had a son a very different pedigree and ownership of Edwinsford would have resulted. A new and important chapter in the family saga had begun.

Arms

[239] Neil Chambers: *The Letters of Sir Joseph Banks A Selection 1768-1820 (2000)* and a letter from him to a friend dated 12 November 1792 confirming the death and the circumstances. It would thus seem clear that the notion that he committed suicide suggested by *Gentlemen's Magazine 1792 p1060* is wrong

8.4 Clovelly and Edwinsford Families united

Arabella Williams (1739-97) and Sir James (Hammett) Hamlyn 1st Bt MP (1735-1811)

As we have seen in 1760 Thomas Williams (54) of Edwinsford divided his share of the Hawksbrook estate and the Court Derllys estate, being 1180 acres in Carmarthenshire and 190 acres in the county borough, between his two daughters, Bridget and Arabella. He made his will on 21 July 1762 and died in London that autumn. Bridget then inherited the Edwinsford Estate. His other daughter, Arabella Williams (58), lived with her father and stepmother in Edwinsford, Court Derllys and their London home until her marriage on 11 June 1762, just before her father's death, to James Hamlyn (57) of Clovelly Court in Devon whom she will have met in London society.

Clovelly was described[240] a century later: *"Clovelly, or Clovelleigh, is a pleasant village and fishing station, occupying a singular and picturesque situation, on the side of a steep rock, adjoining Bideford Bay, about 4 miles E of Hartland and 11 miles WSW of Bideford. It is one of the most romantic places in Devon, and the houses being built on the precipitous side of the sea cliff, one above the other; the main street ascends in terraces and flights of steps from the beach and pier. Clovelly is celebrated for its herring fishery, besides which large quantities of conger, whiting, hake, pollock, and cod fish are caught in the winter; and turbot, sole, plaice, gurnet and mackerel in summer. Its parish had 950 inhabitants in July 1841, besides 40 seamen who were then absent; and contains about 4,200 acres of land, mostly the property of Sir James Hamlyn Williams Bart, who is lord of the manor, and has a large and handsome seat, called Clovelly Court, erected about 1780, on the site of the ancient mansion which was destroyed by fire* [241]*. The views from the house and grounds are extremely grand; and above the cliffs, to the south-east of the village, are the remains of an entrenchment, called Clovelly Dykes, of a square form, and unknown origin."*

The history of the Cary and Hamlyn families who owned Clovelly for centuries is given in Chapters 17 and 18. Zachary Hamlyn (1677-1759) (116) a lawyer of Lincoln's Inn bought Clovelly from the Cary family in 1738 and lived there. When he died without issue he left it under his will dated 17 May 1758 to his great nephew, James Hammett (57). In accordance with the terms of the settlement made by his great uncle Zachary Hamlyn, James had changed his surname from "Hammett" to "Hamlyn" by Act of Parliament in 1760 and adopted the arms of the Hamlyn family: *Gules, a lion rampant ermine crowned or.*

James Hamlyn was educated at Lincoln's Inn in 1750 and married Arabella Williams in 1762. They lived in Clovelly and London. A pair of portraits[242] show James wearing a double-breasted brown coat, white waistcoat, chemise, stock, tied cravat, and with powdered hair, and Arabella wearing a white dress with strands of pearls to her frilled collar and sleeve, coral and pearl pendant necklace, pearl pendant earing, and with powdered hair. There is another full-length portrait[243] of them by the same artist, Richard Cosway, portraying the couple walking arm in arm wearing Van Dyck costume; by choosing to be portrayed in this playful attire the couple were associating themselves with contemporary London society.

Sir James Hamlyn Bt

[240] White's Devonshire Directory 1850

[241] In 1789 when most of the estate records were destroyed

[242] Richard Cosway RA (1742-1821)

[243] Victoria & Albert Museum

Clovelly Court 1831 by GB Campion

In 1767 James served as Sheriff of Devon. On 27 January 1789 Clovelly Court was destroyed by fire along with most of the estate records and family muniments and deeds; James rebuilt it in the then fashionable Georgian Gothic style.

In 1792 Arabella's sister, Bridget, died and under her father's will trust the Edwinsford Estate passed to Arabella. Bridget had owned and lived at Edwinsford with her husband for some 30 years; Arabella was only to do so for five years before her death in 1797 in her 58th year. John Swete[244] wrote in 1797 in his journal about James Hamlyn: "This gentleman was originally in the law and marrying a Miss Williams of vast fortune in Carmarthenshire, he has lately taken up the chief part of his residence at his seat in that county." Together with Clovelly Court and its lands James and Arabella had some 14,000 acres. James had of course been born and brought up in Devon and managed the Clovelly Estate but he now took much interest in their 10,000 acre Carmarthenshire estate. He carried out much rebuilding and built a new stable block in 1802; a tablet[245] over the archway used to record this fact.

In April 1793 James stood for election as the Tory MP for Carmarthenshire when George Talbot Rice of Dynevor was elevated to the House of Lords. It had been some 50 years since Edwinsford had provided the county MP (Sir Nicholas Williams) but with the support of the Vaughans of Golden Grove he was elected unopposed. In 1796 he was reelected with only token opposition from Lord Dynevor's brother in law, Magens Dorien Magens, a wealthy London banker. In 1802 he retired from Parliament in favour of his son since his health was not up to the infamous contest which is described below against William Paxton of Middleton Hall. James made no mark in Parliament and there is no record of his making any speech, although he did on one occasion vote in the minority against the land tax in 1798. He was described as "a plain downright country gentleman totally devoid of all pride and affectation."

On 7 July 1795 James was appointed a Baronet (the Hamlyn, later Hamlyn Williams, Baronetcy of Clovelly in the County of Devon)[246]. The Patent was recorded in the College of Arms on 25 July and announced in the London Gazette on 20 June that year.

On 22 May 1797 Arabella died aged only 57 and was buried in the Williams family vault in Talley[247]. Her husband James (57) continued to live principally at Clovelly and sometimes at Edwinsford (with it seems a resident harpist[248]) while their son and heir, Sir James Hamlyn Williams Bt MP (1765-1829)(60), lived principally in Berkeley Square while occasionally visiting Clovelly and Edwinsford. On 14 March 1798 Garter King of Arms granted James Hamlyn of Edwinsford (60), Captain East Devon Militia, "only son and heir apparent the right to take the surname and arms of Williams" so that under his grandfather's will trust he was able to inherit the Edwinsford Estate. Thereafter the family surname became "Hamlyn Williams" as recorded at the College of Arms although not all members of the family always used both names as the surname.

Family letters[249] written between 1799 and 1807 evidence that there was much travelling by family members between Clovelly Court and Edwinsford often by sea and that the family complained obsessively about the state of the roads in Wales and Devon. Money was spent by the family on repairing the roads to make coach journeys more comfortable. The family would travel by horse and carriage from Edwinsford to Swansea (or sometimes Llanelli) and then take a boat to Bideford or Ilfracombe, and another horse and carriage the other end to Clovelly. This method avoided the long and arduous road journey all the way round the coast via Bristol.

---

244 John Swete: *The Illustrated Journals of the Rev John Swete 1789-1800*
245 FDWD: *Annals p12*
246 DL Baker-Jones and others suggest he also served as Lord Lieutenant which is incorrect, that office being held by the Rice, Johnes and Vaughan families during his lifetime
247 In Clovelly Church there is a mural monument in her memory to which her husband was added on his death in 1811
248 Probably Mr Williams the same harpist (salary £17.15s.0d pa) who performed at Golden Grove-see Francis Jones: *Ceredigion Vol 4 (1960-3) p266*
249 NLW Edwinsford archives; FDWD: *Annals p39-54*

"Letter from Sir James Hamlyn (57) to David Thomas, bailiff at Edwinsford:

Clovelly Court
Sunday 5th December, 1802

Dear Mr ThomasYou'll be surprised to receive this at the hand of my Coachman. He is sent for my Chariot and the Curricle with the pair of Coach Horses, and the Black Mare and Morgan, with the proper apparatus of Harness etc……Two four horse whips and the white, one pair of horse whip, to be packed in the long box that is in the Sportsman's Hall. The Harper and Harp will travel in my chaise……I expect Mrs Williams (*his daughter in law, Diana*) here on Tuesday next, and hope all things turning out well, that the importation from Wales will arrive on Friday next.

Yours very truly,
JAS. HAMLYN"

***

"Letter from B Foard, bailiff at Clovelly to David Thomas, bailiff at Edwinsford:

Clovelly,
Dec 12, 1802

Dear Sir
I received your letter this day—all is safe arrived—they were not three hours a coming from Swansey to Illfordcoomb. Mr Williams (60) arrived here last Tuesday in grate spirits…Mrs Williams (*Diana*) is at Tunbridge Wells…I am afraid Sir James (57) will not go to London this year, but Mr Williams family come here as soon as they leave London so I may not expect to see Wales again for some time…

Your humble servant,
B. Foard"

"Letter from James Hamlyn Williams (60) to David Thomas:

Clovelly Court,
Dec 30, 1802

Dear Sir
The boys have desired me to send you the enclosed letters, they are highly delighted with your present. James (61) will return to School very soon, Charles' (62) holidays will not expire these three weeks. They have much indulged in too much eating and drinking by their grandfather.We all unite in wishing you a Merry Xmas and many Happy New Years, and I am

Yours truly
JH Williams

PS. Be so good as to make up my account…..I hope that every attention is paid to the Roads, otherwise I shall never persuade Mrs Williams (*Diana*) to return to Wales."

***

"Letter from James Hamlyn Williams (60) to David Thomas:

Clovelly Court
April 22nd, 1804

Dear Sir
You will be glad to hear of our safe arrival here, after having been detained in Herefordshire some days by Mrs Williams's illness. We found Sir James and the children in high health, but notwithstanding all you have heard my father say of Devonshire, I can assure you that Edwinsford is full forward as Clovelly, and the farm, I think, looks much better at Edwinsford than here…..I may visit you again this Summer, I hope the road through the Meadows will be finished in good manner, and the gates hung, as well as the roads kept in order both from Maes and Talley…..if you wish me to reside in Wales the roads must be kept good. They are bad here, and have put me out of humour with Devonshire. My residence must be where the roads are best….

Yours truly
JAS. H. Williams"

Sir James had bad health in the last few years before he died in London on 28 May 1811 aged 76; his body was then brought down to Clovelly where he was buried in the family vault. In Clovelly Church there is a memorial[250] to him which includes: "To the strictest Integrity, Honesty, Justice and exemplary Piety was added a Disposition mild, placid, benign; Inferior to none in Virtue and peculiarly happy in the sweetness and urbanity of his Manners and in the exercise of a liberal Hospitality. This Monument was erected by his affectionate Son, who, having had the happiness of enjoying his Friendship, was enabled to admire and appreciate his many Virtues, and who will never cease to lament his loss."

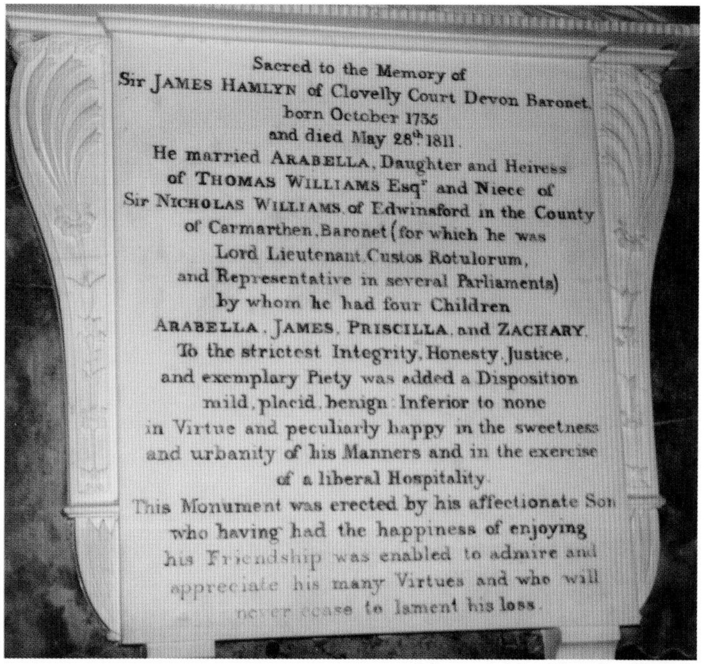

Memorial in Clovelly Church

Arms of Sir James Hamlyn Bt

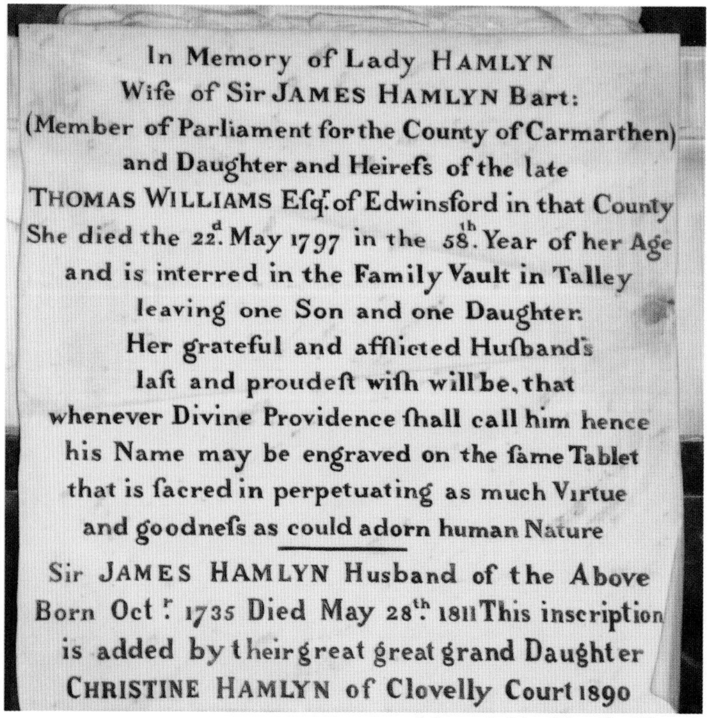

Memorial in Clovelly Church

250 William Grigs: *A Guide to All Saints' Church Clovelly (rev 2010) p9*

Sir James and his wife Arabella had four children:

(1) Arabella Hamlyn (1763-1805)(59) who was baptised in Clovelly Church on 13 November 1763. She was brought up in Clovelly Court and would have been introduced to London society when her father was an MP and a baronet. On 22 February 1790 at Bletsoe in Bedfordshire she married Ambrose St John MP (1760-1822), eldest son of the Very Rev The Hon St Andrew St John DD, Dean of Worcester, second son of John, the 10th Baron St John of Bletsoe of Melchbourne Park, Bedford, by Sarah Chase. Ambrose was educated at Christ Church Oxford in 1777 and at the Inner Temple where he was called to the bar in 1784 although he never practised. Ambrose and Arabella are thought to have lived at Prior Park in Berkshire and the Close in Winchester. In 1793 he served as Captain in the Worcestershire Militia and in 1795 he inherited his father's estate.

He was a trustee of his kinsman Lord Clinton, patron of Callington in Cornwall, and when there was a vacancy there for the seat as MP in May 1803 he stood and was elected; he supported the Pitt administration. Sadly his wife Arabella died in June 1805 and he wrote to William Pitt asking for an office with an emolument referring to his "domestic calamities" (his wife had died leaving him with a young family to bring up). He held on to his seat until Parliament was dissolved in 1806 and did not stand again. He later went to live in the Isle of Man and died in Douglas on 29 November 1822 aged 63. There is some evidence that he had two sons and five daughters in total and it is possible that he remarried after Arabella's early death.

In August 1824 their daughter, Jemima St John, married William Kershaw of the Isle of Man. In 1820 their son, St Andrew St John (1794-1838), who was a Captain in the service of the 9th Foot, married Margaret Moore (d1875) of the Isle of Man and they had three daughters, Jane (d1886), Sarah (d1882) and Arabella. St Andrew died in Ontario in Canada in 1838 aged 43. Little is known of the other children;

(2) Zachary Hamlyn (1767-8) was baptised in Clovelly Church on 23 June 1767 and buried on 25 February 1768;

(3) Priscilla Hamlyn (1769-73) was baptised in Clovelly Church on 26 November 1769 and buried on 25 November 1773; and

(4) James Hamlyn (1765-1829) (60) the eldest surviving son and heir who was baptised in Clovelly Church on 25 October 1765.

Sir James Hamlyn Williams 2nd Bt MP (1765-1829)
James Hamlyn (60) was born, baptised and brought up in Clovelly. He was educated at Westminster School (1773-81) and then Emmanuel College Cambridge in 1782-5. He served as a Captain in the East Devon Militia in 1787, was promoted to Major in 1798 and continued with his regiment at Kingsbridge in Devon for some years. On 22 June 1789 at St Mary's Church in Marylebone he married Diana Anne (1766-1849), daughter of Abraham Whittaker, a merchant of Stratford in Essex and Lyston House in Herefordshire. Diana had been christened in Eastcheap on 7 March 1766. She was later to be scurrilously described by a political opponent of her husband as "foolish, fond of drink and a tradesman's daughter". Diana's sister, Charlotte (1769-1856), was the second wife of John Rous, Ist Earl of Stradbroke (1750-1827) whose descendant, Hon John Rous, is the current owner of the Clovelly estate in Devon.

As we have seen, on 14 March 1798 Garter King of Arms granted James Hamlyn of Edwinsford (60) by Royal licence "only son and heir apparent the right to take the surname and arms of Williams" so that under his grandfather's will trust he was able to inherit the Edwinsford Estate on the death of his mother, Arabella Williams (58), in 1797. The family lived principally in London in Berkeley Square and later at 21 Upper Grosvenor Street as well as visiting Clovelly and Edwinsford. They also seem to have spent time at 11 Hertford Street in Mayfair since there is a letter dated 1 March 1805[251] from Diana at that address to David Thomas at Edwinsford requesting that he send hams, bacon, cheese, eggs and meats to her in London where she complained about the cost of food. She adds that James is busy arguing in the Commons against the duty on agricultural horses, that her son James (61) is doing well at Winchester and her other very young son Charles in the Navy "is expecting to attack two Spanish Frigates from the Havannah with a Hundred sail under their Convoy". She added finally that her husband James "continues tolerably well but a London life does not agree with him like the country".

[251] NLW Edwinsford archives; FDWD: *Annals p51*

Paxton's or Nelson's Tower 2016

Sir James Hamlyn (57) had held the county seat in Parliament since 1793 but he retired in 1802 in favour of his son at the 1802 election. The 1802 Carmarthenshire election[252] between Sir James Hamlyn Williams (2nd Bt)(60) supported by the Dinefwr faction for the Reds (Tories) and Sir William Paxton[253] of Middleton Hall supported by the Golden Grove faction for the Blues (Whigs) resulted in 15 days of lavish bribery by Paxton, personal abuse and rioting with fights between the two factions. Paxton (1745-1824) had made a fortune in India, returned to buy Middleton Hall and was ambitious to gain political power and win respectability. Paxton is estimated to have spent £15,690. 4s. 2d on 11,070 breakfasts, 36,901 dinners, 684 suppers, 25,275 gallons of ale, 11,068 bottles of spirits, 8,879 bottlers of porter,

[252] FDWD: *Annals p9*; DL Baker-Jones *CH (1968) p24 et seq*

[253] ODNB; Edna Dale-Jones: *Sir William Paxton, his Family and his Monument CA (2009) p64-73;* Conrad Davies*: Nelson's Tower in Image and Word CA (1998) p 44-53*

460 bottles of sherry, 509 bottles of cider etc. Sir James probably spent a similar sum and was constantly complaining about the expense in his family correspondence and was fearful of visiting Edwinsford because of more bills. Paxton was nicknamed the "Nabob" by the Edwinsford family presumably because he had made his money in India.

Paxton had promised the electorate to build a bridge over the River Tywi but lost the election and then petitioned Parliament accusing his opponents of bribery and corruption of which of course he had been guilty himself. Over 1,000 witneses were brought from Carmarthen to London but Sir James was declared the winner. Paxton lost against the power of the local families and perhaps because his opponent started an untrue rumour that he was insolvent. Local tradition suggests that Paxton decided to gain revenge[254] by refusing to build the bridge and instead building a 500 ft tall Gothic style folly on a hill dominating the landscape and overlooking Middleton Hall, now called Paxton's Tower or Nelson's Tower, near Dinefwr in honour of Nelson's victory in 1805. Paxton gained the county borough seat from 1803 to 1806 and then the more prestigious county seat in 1806 for only six months; he was the last Whig to hold that seat for many years. He died aged 80 and his estate was sold.

The election victory was perhaps a Pyrrhic one since it cost Sir James heavily. He wished to ensure that all expenses were paid so that his honour might be preserved. He wrote to his Edwinsford bailiff David Thomas: "I fear I must soon sell myself to satisfy the rapacity of the Carmarthenshire Hell Devils…I am sick of spending all my money on paying ale-house men and lawyers. You must never expect to see me in good humour again". Some of the Edwinsford rental income was used and much timber was sold to pay his election debts and it was some years before they had been paid in full. In Parliament James (60) gave independent support to the government like his father had done, but he does not seem to have given any speeches. He voted against additional taxation on horses in husbandry, and against the iron tax and the salt tax. In the 1806 election he could not afford to stand but criticised Paxton for his pro-Catholic Whig views. He did not stand again.

His father, Sir James (57), died in 1811 and James (60) then inherited the Clovelly Estate too as well as the title of 2nd Baronet. James served as Sheriff of Carmarthenshire in 1811-12. While remaining based in London, unlike his father James and Diana lived in later years for more of the year at Edwinsford than at Clovelly although they improved all their estates at Edwinsford, Court Derllys and Clovelly. In December 1828 they bought the Plas Demesne and the two Talley Lakes and built a canal connecting the two Lakes on the flat ground below Rhiw Paderau (Hill of Prayer); this hill was so named by the pilgrims[255] on their journey from the Abbey of Strata Florida to Talley Abbey as they caught their first glimpse of Talley from the hill overlooking the lakes. The canal enabled the family to take a boat from the boat shed on the edge of Edwinsford to Talley Abbey. At Clovelly they built the celebrated Hobby Drive (being their great hobby)[256] along to the London Lodge, extended the pier in the harbour, laid out the paths in Clovelly Park, built the summer house in the "wilderness" and the cabin in the Park, and erected the Angel's Wings with carvings by their butler (from which they could see their daughter Lady Chichester's home at Youlston).

Chapter 16 contains details of some of the Edwinsford Estate accounts and the rental income of the 88 farms there in this period. While all the Carmarthenshire estates totalled some 10,000 acres on which rental income was received, this figure included the Home Farm at Edwinsford of about 569 acres in size which was profitable on its own particularly as it could sell its livestock and produce without having to feed and cater for the family who were rarely in residence.During the years before the defeat of Napoleon in 1815[257] the profitability of the estate gradually increased aided by the sales of timber and bark, rent received for summer grazing, and tithes from Llansawel of which Sir James was the lay impropriator. Capital expenditutre on the estate increased on road building, new farmhouses and outhouses, a new ice house (built with the expertise of Lord Dynevor's servants) and the

[254] In fact it was built in c1808 long after the election as a landscape ornament
[255] FDWD: *Annals p14*
[256] Some claim that Napoleonic French prisoners of war were used as labourers but there is no hard evidence of this
[257] RJ Collyer: *The Edwinsford Estate in the Early Nineteenth Century-Bulletin of the Board of Celtic Studies (1975) p200-217*

planting of thousands of trees (over 100,000 during 1818-22). In 1808 there was an outbreak of typhus around Edwinsford caused by lack of personal hygiene among the poor so money had to be spent on improving the cottages. Post 1815 there was a severe depression for about 20 years resulting in Edwinsford tenants' rents having to be materially reduced by 20 per cent and for a while some farms became untenanted including some large ones such as Lethr Cadfan (250 acres). By the 1830s the accounts reveal a worrying financial position on all the Edwinsford, Court Derllys and Clovelly Estates but the postion improved slowly during the decades thereafter.

Sir James died in Clovelly after a long illness on 3 December 1829 aged 64 and was buried in the family vault in Clovelly. A monument was also erected in his memory in St Peter's Church in Carmarthen which refers to him as being "of Cwrt Derllys, Rhydodwyn and Clovelly Court" and that "he was beloved and respected by all who had witnessed his pious resignation during a long period of bodily suffering, and may his virtuous and amicable character prove an example for his children's imitation".

After his husband's death Diana went to live in Ferryside and bought Parc Portes Cliff (Portiscliff) where she arranged a picturesque landscape garden; we are told her landscape sketchbook[258] showed real artistic ability. On 9 October 1833 she gave this home to her second son, Rear Admiral Hamlyn Williams (62), following his marriage; her letter to him dated 5 September 1833[259] states: "In consequence of your marriage with Miss H Rycroft (that you may have a home to take her to) and out of the love and affection I bear you, I hereby present for your acceptance a gift of my houses and premises called by me Parc Ports Cliff, as now held by me on Lease......to be yours absolutely." She died at Norwood aged 84 on 7 September 1849 and was buried[260] in West Norwood cemetery (Grave No 1518).

SIR JAMES HAMLYN WILLIAMS 2ND BART
DIED AT CLOVELLY 1829
DAME DIANA ANNE HIS WIFE
DAUGHTER OF ABRAHAM WHITTAKER
DIED AT NORWOOD 1849
TO THE HONOURED MEMORY OF THESE HER ANCESTORS
WHO PLANNED THE HOBBY DRIVE
AND LAID OUT THE PATHS ON HIS DEMESNE
THIS TABLET IS DEDICATED BY THEIR GREAT GRANDDAUGHTER
CHRISTINE HAMLYN
IN GRATITUDE FOR THE HERITAGE OF BEAUTY
BEQUEATHED THROUGH THEIR CARE TO CLOVELLY
FOR THE GREATER GLORY OF GOD
AND THE FULLER DELIGHT OF MAN IN HIS WORKS
UNTO ALL GENERATIONS THAT SERVE HIM
1899

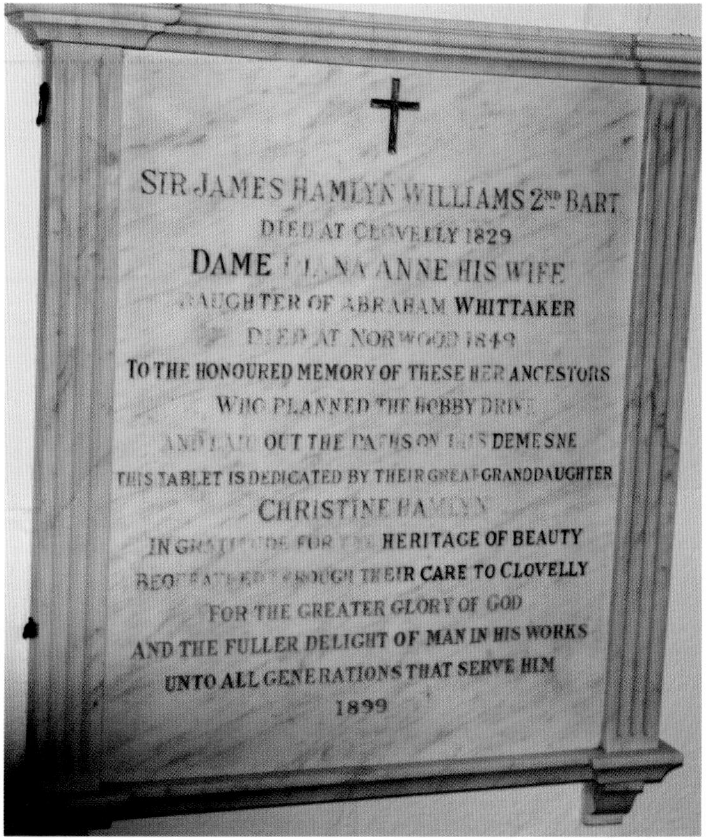

Memorial in Clovelly Church

258 FDWD: *Annals p15*
259 FDWD: *Annals p55*
260 In Clovelly Church there is a mural monument erected by Christine Hamlyn in memory of Sir James and Lady Diana "in gratitude for the heritage of beauty bequeathed through their care to Clovelly"

Children of Sir James Hamlyn Williams 2nd Bt MP (1765-1829)

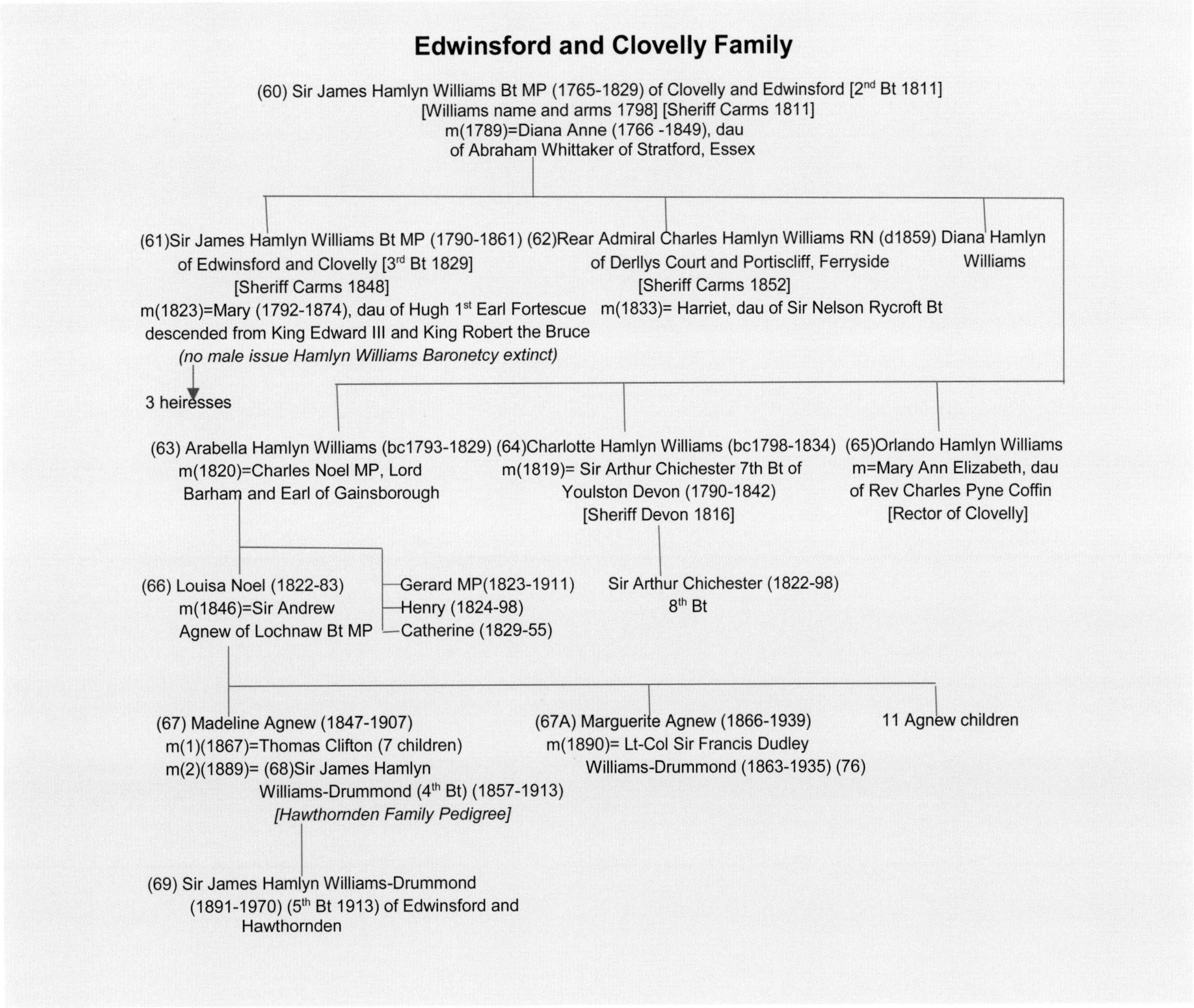

Sir James and Lady Diana had six children:

(1) Charles Hamlyn Williams (d1859) (62) the second son who entered the Royal Navy[261] in August 1803 when he must have been very young. He obtained his first commission as a Lieutenant on 24 April 1811, served some time under the flag of Sir William Sidney Smith, was promoted to the rank of Commander on 27 August 1814, was appointed on 21 September 1830 to HMS Racecourse and then on 31 January 1832 to HMS Champion both on the West Indian station. He left HMS Champion on 23 June 1832 and "as a reward for the important services he had rendered at Jamaica during the insurrection of the slaves, particularly for the manner in which he had succeeded by his advice and judicious measures in restoring confidence in the town of Montego Bay, and in saving it from the rebels, who intended fully to burn it, was promoted" to the rank of Captain on 4 July 1832. His last appointment was on 24 May 1838 to HMS Tribune; this was a sailing frigate (5th rate frigate class) built in 1803 by Parsons, Burlesdon[262] and had 36 cannons. Sadly this ship ran aground and was wrecked and lost under his command off Tarragona in Spain on 28 November 1839. He returned to England with his officers and crew on board HMS Minden and was court-martialled but was honourably acquitted of all blame for this disaster. He retired from the Navy on 19 May 1855 with the rank of Rear Admiral.

Charles lived for some time during his early spells on land at Derllys Court which was owned by his father. In 1852 he served as Sheriff of Carmarthenshire being described as "of Derllys Court".

On 15 August 1833 Charles married Harriet (d1882), daughter of the late Sir Nelson Rycroft 2nd Bt (1761-1827) of Calton in Yorkshire and Charlotte Read.They had no children and lived in Portiscliff in Ferryside, which his mother had given to him on his marriage. In 1842 he was elected as a member of the Royal Yacht Squadron and in 1846 he won the Prince Consort's Cup at Cowes in his 45 ton cutter "Will o' the Wisp"; there is an oil painting by Stewartson and two watercolour sketches of him winning the cup. He bought other cutters and remained a member of the RYS until his death in 1859;

(2) Diana Hamlyn Williams, who died unmarried and about whom we know very little;

(3) Arabella Hamlyn Williams (bc1793-1829)(63), who was born at Clovelly Court and on 29 June 1820 at St George's, Hanover Square married Charles Noel MP born as Charles Edwardes (1781-1866). He married four times and Arabella was his third wife following the deaths of his first two wives in 1811 and 1818. He succeeded his father as MP for Rutland in 1808 and held the seat until 1814. In 1823 he succeeded his mother, Baroness Barham, in the barony of Barham and thereby became Lord Barham and entered the House of Lords; his maternal grandfather was the great Lord Barham, First Lord of the Admiralty and Admiral of the Red in 1805, and very unusually the title was passed down through the female line. In 1838 he also succeeded his father, Sir Gerald Noel Bt, in the baronetcy. In 1841 he was created Earl of Gainsborough, a title which had become extinct in his family and was revived for his benefit.

Arabella sadly died at Barham Court in Kent on 4 October 1829 following the birth of her last child; she was buried at Teston in Kent. She bore Charles four children:

(a) Louisa Noel (1822-83)(66) who married on 20 August 1846 Sir Andrew Agnew MP 8th Bt (of Nova Scotia 1629) (1818-92) of Lochnaw Castle, Wigtownshire. He was born in Edinburgh, educated at Harrow and served as a Captain in the 4th Light Dragoons[263]. He served as MP for Wigtownshire[264] from 1856 to 1868. They had 13 children, eight daughters and five sons: (1) Madeline (1847-1907)(67) who married Thomas Henry Clifton of Lytham and following his death then married Sir James Williams-Drummond of Edwinsford and

[261] Naval Biographical Dictionary p1295; FDWD: *Annals p15*

[262] Colledge and Warlow: *Ships of the Royal Navy*

[263] On 27 June 1743 at the Battle of Dettingen his kinsman, Lt Col Sir Andrew Agnew the 5th Bt (1687-1771), famously coined the phrase "Don't shoot until you see the whites of their eyes" when instructing his troops in the 21st Foot Scots Fusiliers to fire on the French cavalry. This was the last time a reigning English monarch, George II, personally led the army into battle

[264] Sir Andrew Agnew: *The Agnews of Lochnaw (1864)*

Hawthornden (68) described in Chapter 9.6; (2) Arabella (1848-1910) unmarried; (3) Caroline (1848-1934) unmarried; (4) Sir Andrew Noel Agnew MP 9th Bt (1850-1928) who was Liberal MP for the University of Edinburgh from 1900-1906; (5) Henry (1851-1910) who had two daughters; (6) Louisa (1852-1913) who married Duncan MacNeill; (7) Mary (Alma) (1854-1923) who married Arthur 11th Baron Kinnaird and had seven children; (8) Catherine (1855-58); (9) Major Charles (1859-1928) who fought in the 4th Hussars in the Third Burma War (1885-7) and in Rhodesia in 1896, and his son Fulque became the 10th Baronet; (10) Colonel Quentin (1861-1937) who fought in the Royal Scots Fusiliers in the Third Burma War, in the Tirah campaign (1897-8), in the Boer War (1899-1902), and in the Great War in France and Gallipoli, and won a DSO in 1902. He had four children; (11) Gerald (1862-1919) who served as Lieutenant in the Buffs; (12) Rosina Constance (1863-1920) who married Rev James Davidson whose son, Neville Davidson, became the Moderator of the General Assembly of the Church of Scotland; and (13) Marguerite (1866-1939)(67A) who married Lt-Col Francis Dudley Williams-Drummond (76),brother of Sir James Williams-Drummond of Edwinsford (68) who married the eldest sister Madeline (67);

(b) Gerard Noel MP PC (1823-1911) who was MP for Rutland (1847-1883) and served as a Tory Minister under Lord Derby and Benjamin Disraeli. He was a Captain in the 11th Hussars. On 30 June 1863 he married Augusta Mary Lowther (d1916) and their country home was at Catmose in Oakham where they developed a fine arboretum requiring 15 gardeners. They had two children, Gerard (1864-1925) and Henry (1868-1931);

(c) Henry Noel (1824-98) who served as Captain in the 68th Foot and as Sheriff of Rutland in 1963. He married twice and had six children; and

(d) Catherine Noel (1829-55) who married on 19 June 1849 James Carnegie, 9th Earl of Southesk, at Exton Park in Rutland. She had four children but sadly died aged 25 on 9 March 1855 at Cavendish Square in London. Her grandson, Lord Carnegie (1893-1992), married on 13 November 1923 at the Royal Military Chapel at Wellington Barracks, Princess Maud (1893-1945) a grand daughter of Edward VII;

(4) Charlotte Hamlyn Williams (bc1798-1834)(64), who on 8 September 1819 at Clovelly married Sir Arthur Chichester 7th Bt of Raleigh (1790-1842) of Youlston Park, Shirwell in Devon, north of Clovelly. The manor of Shirwell was the seat ot two leading families in North Devon, the Beaumonts to the end of the 15th century and then their heirs the Chichesters of Raleigh, Pilton, both of which lived on the estate of Youlston. Youlston Park is now largely Georgian but retains some fine 17th century interiors. The 6th Baronet died unmarried in 1808 so he was succeeded by his first cousin once removed, Arthur, who was the grandson of Rev William Chichester, younger son of the 4th Baronet. Arthur served as Sheriff of Devon in 1816-7. Arthur and Charlotte had several children including Sir Arthur Chichester (1822-98) 8th Bt. This baronetcy is still extant and the 12th Baronet, Sir James, was born in 1951. Sir Francis Chichester, the famous circumnavigator of the world, was the son of Rev Charles Chichester, seventh son of the 8th Baronet.

Charlotte died on 18 August 1834 and was buried at Shirwell, Devon. Arthur died on 6 June 1842 and was also buried at Shirwell;

(5) Rev Orlando Hamlyn Williams (1801-31)(65), who married Mary Anne Elizabeth Coffin, daughter of Rev Charles Pyne Coffin. Orlando served as the rector of Clovelly (1826-31) (see Chapter 21.1). The father of the famous author, Charles Kingsley, was his curate there and succeeded him as rector. They had a daughter. Orlando died very young on 30 November 1831 and was buried in Clovelly; and

(6) Sir James Hamlyn Williams 3rd Bt MP (1790-1861)(61) the eldest son and heir described in Chapter 9.3.

9. The Later Hanoverian Period 1837-1917

9.1 Later Hanoverian Synopsis

Queen Victoria

Victoria (ruler 1837-1901), niece and heir to William IV, was born in Kensington Palace in 1819 and become Queen in 1837 without the need for another Regency at the very young age of 18. She was the first monarch to live in Buckingham Palace. During her long 63 year reign, second in length only to that of our current British monarch Queen Elizabeth II, Britain underwent enormous economic, industrial and political change; as a result of the industrial revolution the country became a major world power.

In 1840 she married her first cousin, Prince Albert, Duke of Saxe-Coburg and Gotha, who realised the importance of a constitutional monarchy at a time when politics was becoming more and more run by political parties rather than the previous factions. The monarchy became increasingly popular and removed from day to day politics, and therefore not subject to political attack as it had been in the past. Albert gained the trust of the administration and one of his greatest achievements was the organising in 1851 of the Great Exhibition in the Crystal Palace built entirely of glass within a steel frame, a wonderful showcase of Britain's growing industrial and technological advances. Tragically he died of typhoid aged only 42 in 1861; of their nine children, eight married into European royalty and nobility and their 42 grandchildren included Tsar Nicholas II of Russia and Kaiser Wilhelm II of Germany. After Albert's death Victoria carried on with her private duties of State but went into mourning for some 15 years, wearing black for the rest of her life, and neglected her public duties to the consternation of her administrations and the general public.

During her reign Britain became the world's largest colonial power and the British Empire grew to one fifth of the globe in size. Her reign witnessed the Irish potato famine of 1845 with one million dying and another million emigrating, the disaster of the Crimean War in 1855-6, the Indian Mutiny of 1857, Canada being given Dominion status in 1867, the Anglo-Zulu War, the Anglo-Afghan Wars, and Victoria being appointed Empress of India in 1876 and attending the Delhi Durbar on 1 January 1877. In 1887 her Golden Jubilee was attended by 50 Kings and Princes and her Diamond Jubilee 10 years later witnessed large numbers of British Empire troops from all over the world marching through London. Victoria was by now immensely popular having come out of public mourning. The Boer Wars in South Africa (1899-1902) were a great worry to her and caused much political unpopularity for the administration.

During her reign no fewer than 20 Prime Ministers held office including Sir Robert Peel (Tory) in 1841, Lord Palmerston (Liberal) in 1855 and 1859, Benjamin Disraeli (Tory) in 1868 and 1874, William Gladstone (Liberal) in 1868, 1880, 1886 and 1892, and the Marquess of Salisbury (Tory) in 1885, 1886, and 1895.

The Victorian era saw the success of our constitutional monarchy system of government with the sovereign having the right to be consulted by her Prime Minister but not to appoint administrations or to manage domestic and foreign policy. With reforms to the voting system and revised Reform Acts the power of the electorate and of their representatives in the House of Commons gradually increased while the power of the monarch and of the House of Lords diminished. Parliamentary democracy was supreme.

During the Victoria era the population of the country doubled to 35 million people while the proportion of the workforce in agriculture dropped to only 20 per cent as the industrial revolution changed the face of Britain; today it is about 0.5 per cent out of a total population of some 60 million.

Edward VII

Queen Victoria died in January 1901 aged 81. Her heir was her eldest son, Edward (ruler 1901-1910), who was present at her bedside together with her grandson, Kaiser Wilhelm II of Germany.

Edward (1841-1910) known as Bertie had a strict upbringing which may have encouraged his later playboy lifestyle. Despite attending Edinburgh, Oxford and Cambridge he was not an academic but he then acted as a roving royal ambassador visiting Canada, the US, France, India, Russia and several other countries where his charm and sociability made him popular. His father seems to have had a low opinion of him and his mother would not permit him to be involved in matters of State; he spent much time in pleasure including gambling, shooting, horse racing in which he won the Derby three times and the Grand National, sailing, womanising, smoking 12 cigars and 20 cigarettes daily, and eating very large meals. He was married off aged 21 to the long suffering Princess Alexandra of Denmark aged 18 in 1863; this did little to stop his womanising and he had several mistresses (some say as many as 55) including Lillie Langtry, Lady Randolph Churchill mother of Winston, and Alice Keppel one of whose great granddaughters is the current Duchess of Cornwall.

Bertie was 59 when he became King and following his successful visit to France in 1903 he helped to broker the Anglo-French Entente Cordiale signed in 1904. Bertie was related to almost every ruler in Europe and made it his business to foster good relations with them with the sole exception of his cousin Kaiser Wilhelm II of Germany. In 1908 he helped broker the Triple Entente between Britain, France and Russia to counter the threat from Germany and Austria.

In general terms Bertie was liberal in views and, unlike his mother, supported Gladstone. In the last year of his reign he became involved in a major constitutional crisis when the Liberal Prime Minister, Herbert Asquith, proposed a People's Budget which was vetoed by the Tory majority in the House of Lords led by Arthur Balfour and Lord Lansdowne. The Liberals then proposed a new Parliament Act under which the power of the House of Lords to veto money Bills would be removed, their power to vote down other Bills would be reduced to delaying them for 12 months only, and the term of a Parliament would be reduced from seven to five years. They also stated that their Ministerial advice to the sovereign, which he was bound to follow constitutionally, would be that the House of Lords should be filled with a majority of new peers to ensure that this Act would be enacted. Before the crisis was over Bertie died in April 1910 at Buckingham Palace from heart failure following bronchitis and was buried at Windsor on 20 May; the Parliament Act was later enacted in 1911. The lying in State of his coffin took place at Westminster Hall from 17 to 19 May and over 400,000 members of the public were allowed to pass it and pay their respects[265] including my father and grandparents.

George V

Some argue that Edward VII was not a true Hanoverian because his father's family was Saxe-Coburg and Gotha. George V (1865-1936) (ruler 1910-36) was undoubtedly German in background. He was the second son of Edward VII and became the heir when his elder brother, Albert, died in 1892. In 1893 he married his elder brother's fiancée, Princess Mary of Teck.

George may have been German by origin but he made it clear even before the outbreak of war in 1914 that the Hanoverians were British now. On 17 July 1917 in the midst of war he changed the family's name to the House of Windsor and dropped all the numerous Germanic titles. His patriotism, sense of duty and his actions and those of his wife ensured the future of the British monarchy during a reign which saw many European rulers removed or murdered. The Windsors have survived two World Wars, an abdication by Edward VIII in 1936, numerous divorces, an annus horribilis, and newspaper sensations; yet today the monarchy has never been so popular and the British Empire has successfully converted itself into the Commonwealth.

9.2 Carmarthenshire politics

Under the Reform Act 1832 Carmarthenshire gained an extra county seat and Wales had 32 MPs in total in the House of Commons. Votes were extended to copyholders and long leaseholders of land worth £10 per annum and to tenants who paid annual rent of £50. In practice the landed gentry families continued to have the political power in Carmarthenshire and the two county seats in 1833 were won by Tories

[265] The diary of my grandfather, Detective Inspector David Lewis of Scotland Yard

and this dominance lasted until 1868. Following the 1832 Act there was much disillusionment amongst the masses who were still disenfranchised; after the passing of the Poor Law Amendment Act 1834 which deprived poor people of outdoor relief, many paupers were driven into the workhouse which split up families and caused more hardship. This led to the Chartist working class movement for political reform; in Wales it started in 1836 with the founding of the Carmarthen Working Men's Association. Between 1838 and 1858 there was growing radical unrest, strikes and petitions in South Wales. In Carmarthenshire and South Wales the Rebecca Riots (see Chapter 37) started in 1839 and continued until 1844 causing further unrest.

The Second Reform Act 1867 widened the franchise to include male householders in towns and tenants of small farms and some of the skilled working class in the countryside. In the 1868 Election 21 Liberal MPs were elected from Wales. Meantime the non-conformist denominations in Wales were growing in numbers and protest with a great religious revival encouraging dissent in a period of rising rents, bad harvests and evictions. The Ballot Act 1872 forced all elections to be conducted with secret ballots to avoid duress by landlords seeking to make their tenants vote as they directed, but bribery continued for some years despite it becoming illegal.

The Third Reform Act 1884 gave the vote to tenant farmers and labourers in the countryside as well as miners and industrial unskilled workers if they were paying annual rent of £10 or held land valued at £10. This increased the British electorate to 5.5 million and the electorate in Carmarthenshire to over 18,500, but all women and 40 per cent of adult men were still without the vote. In Carmarthenshire the Liberal and non-conformist vote was still strong and up to 1906 the great majority of MPs in Wales were Liberal.

The religious, educational, local justice and local administration changes in Llansawel and Talley during the 19th and early 20th centuries are described in Chapters 29,30,35 and 36.

9.3 Edwinsford, Clovelly and Hawthornden

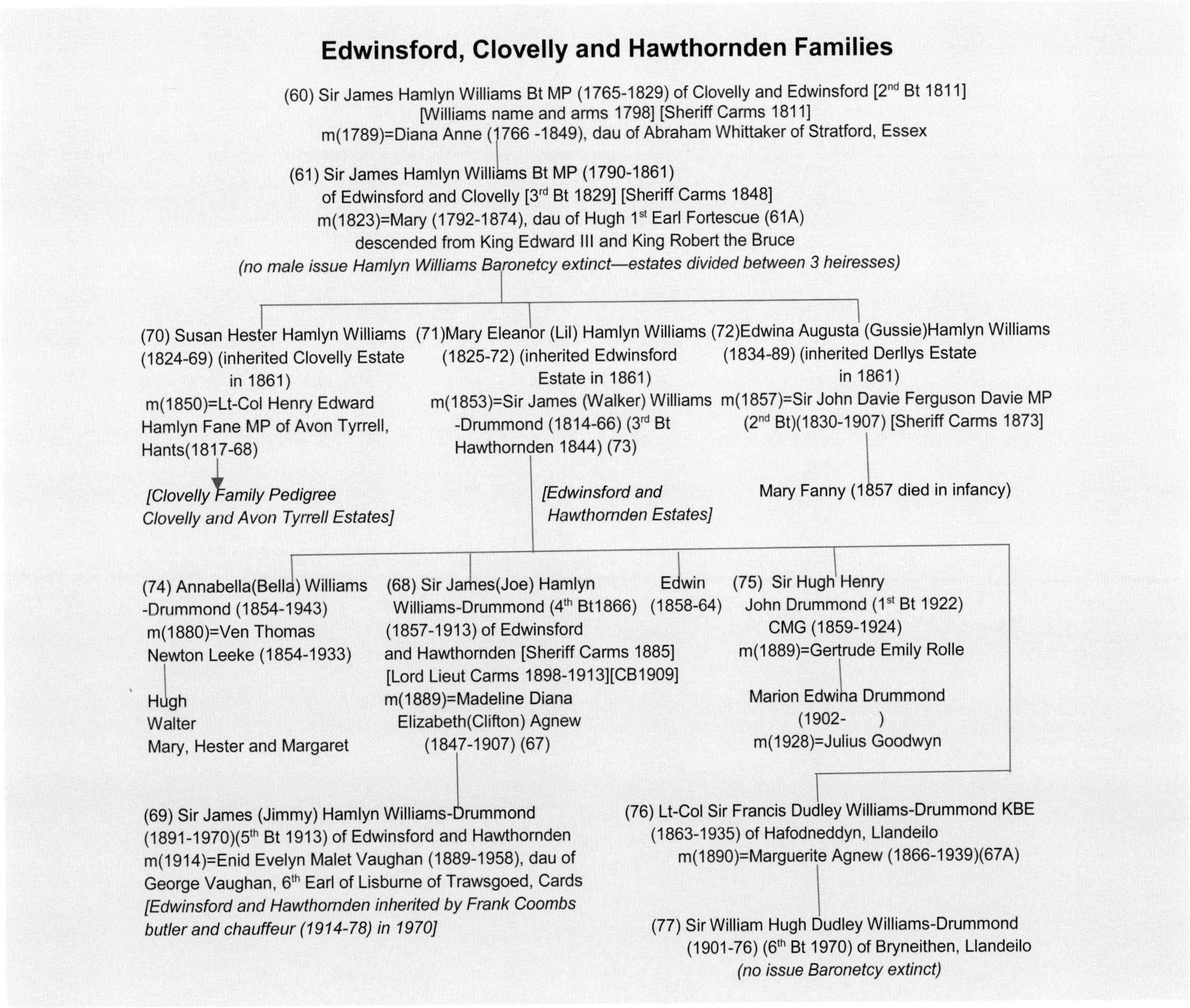
Edwinsford, Clovelly and Hawthornden Families
(60) Sir James Hamlyn Williams Bt MP (1765-1829) of Clovelly and Edwinsford [2nd Bt 1811]
[Williams name and arms 1798] [Sheriff Carms 1811]
m(1789)=Diana Anne (1766 -1849), dau of Abraham Whittaker of Stratford, Essex
(61) Sir James Hamlyn Williams Bt MP (1790-1861)
of Edwinsford and Clovelly [3rd Bt 1829] [Sheriff Carms 1848]
m(1823)=Mary (1792-1874), dau of Hugh 1st Earl Fortescue (61A)
descended from King Edward III and King Robert the Bruce
(no male issue Hamlyn Williams Baronetcy extinct—estates divided between 3 heiresses)
(70) Susan Hester Hamlyn Williams (1824-69) (inherited Clovelly Estate in 1861)
m(1850)=Lt-Col Henry Edward Hamlyn Fane MP of Avon Tyrrell, Hants(1817-68)
[Clovelly Family Pedigree Clovelly and Avon Tyrrell Estates]
(71)Mary Eleanor (Lil) Hamlyn Williams (1825-72) (inherited Edwinsford Estate in 1861)
m(1853)=Sir James (Walker) Williams -Drummond (1814-66) (3rd Bt Hawthornden 1844) (73)
[Edwinsford and Hawthornden Estates]
(72)Edwina Augusta (Gussie)Hamlyn Williams (1834-89) (inherited Derllys Estate in 1861)
m(1857)=Sir John Davie Ferguson Davie MP (2nd Bt)(1830-1907) [Sheriff Carms 1873]
Mary Fanny (1857 died in infancy)
(74) Annabella(Bella) Williams -Drummond (1854-1943)
m(1880)=Ven Thomas Newton Leeke (1854-1933)
Hugh
Walter
Mary, Hester and Margaret
(68) Sir James(Joe) Hamlyn Williams-Drummond (4th Bt1866) (1857-1913) of Edwinsford and Hawthornden [Sheriff Carms 1885] [Lord Lieut Carms 1898-1913][CB1909]
m(1889)=Madeline Diana Elizabeth(Clifton) Agnew (1847-1907) (67)
Edwin (1858-64)
(75) Sir Hugh Henry John Drummond (1st Bt 1922) CMG (1859-1924)
m(1889)=Gertrude Emily Rolle
Marion Edwina Drummond (1902-)
m(1928)=Julius Goodwyn
(69) Sir James (Jimmy) Hamlyn Williams-Drummond (1891-1970)(5th Bt 1913) of Edwinsford and Hawthornden
m(1914)=Enid Evelyn Malet Vaughan (1889-1958), dau of George Vaughan, 6th Earl of Lisburne of Trawsgoed, Cards
[Edwinsford and Hawthornden inherited by Frank Coombs butler and chauffeur (1914-78) in 1970]
(76) Lt-Col Sir Francis Dudley Williams-Drummond KBE (1863-1935) of Hafodneddyn, Llandeilo
m(1890)=Marguerite Agnew (1866-1939)(67A)
(77) Sir William Hugh Dudley Williams-Drummond (1901-76) (6th Bt 1970) of Bryneithen, Llandeilo
(no issue Baronetcy extinct)

Sir James Hamlyn Williams 3rd Bt MP (1790-1861)

As we saw from the end of Chapter 8.4, James Hamlyn Williams (61) was the eldest son and heir of his parents. He was born in Marylebone, London on 25 November 1790 and was brought up in London and Clovelly with holidays in Edwinsford. He was educated at Winchester College (1802-6) where on 5 March 1805 he wrote to David Thomas (bailiff at Edwinsford and living at Blaenug) asking[266] for "a ham and a fowl or two in a little parcel to me directed to me at Dr Goddard's, Winchester, and any other thing in your power...... PS Be so good as to send the parcel immediately". His father forbade it saying "he has everything that he ought to have and he is very apt to send to shops and all other places to get things in my name....we must look sharp after him. He is a wag".

After leaving school aged 16 he was privately tutored before joining the Army and obtaining a commission as a Lieutenant in the 7th Hussars in 1810. He served with distinction in the Napoleonic Peninsula Wars as an aide-de-camp to General Sir William Henry Clinton (1769-1846) who commanded the 1st Division during the Duke of Wellington's Spanish Campaign of 1812-3. James was promoted to Captain in 1813 and received medals[267] for bravery at the battles of Orthez (1814) and Toulouse (1814) where the French armies were defeated after which Napoleon abdicated. The family used to have a brass inlaid rosewood despatch box[268] engraved "Captain Hamlyn, 7th Hussars". He was promoted to Major in 1821 and retired from the Army in 1823 following his marriage.

On 15 February 1823 he married Lady Mary Fortescue (1792-1874)(61A), fourth daughter of Hugh Fortescue, 1st Earl Fortescue (1763-1841) and Hester Grenville; Mary had been born at Castle Hill mansion in Filleigh, Devon one of the the seats of the Fortescues. Mary had English and Scottish royal blood and, as can be seen from the pedigrees, her family could claim direct descent[269] both paternally and maternally from William the Conqueror (1028-87) and King Malcolm 1 of Scotland (895-954). The Fortescue family originated from Sir Richard le Forte a soldier in the invading army of William the Conqueror who protected his royal master at the battle of Hastings by

© Hon John Rous *Sir James Hamlyn Williams 3rd Bt c1810*

bearing a strong shield before him from which event the word *escue* (a shield) was added to his surname of Forte. The family received a grant of land in Devon. Their motto was *Forte scutum salus ducum* (a strong shield proves the safety of the leaders).

266 NLW Edwinsford archives; FDWD: *Annals p53*

267 In 1911 these medals were on show in Edwinsford Mansion-*South Wales Daily News (29 July 1911)*

268 FDWD: *Annals p16*

269 FDWD: *Annals p58*

Lady Mary was also the sister of Viscount Ebrington (1783-1861) son of the Earl, a Reformist Whig politician who played an important role in the passing of the Reform Act in 1832, and a grand-daughter of the Whig Prime Minister George Grenville (1712-70). James therefore had strong ties with Whig politicians of influence at Westminster.

James and Mary lived principally in London at this time but visited Clovelly and Edwinsford frequently. James's sister, Arabella (63), was of course married to Lord Barham so relations with other influential families including the Gainsboroughs, Noels, Carnegies and Agnews were close.

James enjoyed hunting at Edwinsford and on neighbouring sporting estates; he protected his own partridges and pheasants avidly and was warned against being too over zealous in prosecuting poachers in case it adversely affected his reputation and his future chances of getting elected to public office. His father and grandfather had both represented Carmarthenshire in Parliament so in late 1825 he asked Lord Cawdor, the leading Whig / Blue in the county, for advice on standing in the 1826 election. In the end he did not stand against the incumbent, George Rice-Trevor of Dynevor. In 1827 with his own father quite ill he took over the running of the Edwinsford Estate which with Court Derllys was worth some £7,000 per annum in income. In December 1829 his father died and James inherited the estates and the Hamlyn-Williams Baronetcy of Clovelly.

By 1831 he had decided to stand and as foreman of the Carmarthenshire grand jury he supported a petition for reform including the repeal of assessed taxes and the duty on malt tax as well as the abolishing of all sinecures. In the 1831 election he was returned unopposed at a cost of £817. 17s as a supporter of reform including the Great Reform Bill "unshackled and unconnected to any party". There was much discontent in Carmarthenshire with the radicals and independents agitating for the removal of tithes and church rates, against inequality in education and the poverty of the peasants, while the church and many landlords opposed reform. The Reform Act became law in June 1832 and gave Carmarthenshire an extra member. Another election was called in late 1832. In one of his Election Addresses dated 24 August 1832 James stated that: "My principles are

© Hon John Rous *Sir James Hamlyn Williams*

well known to you—I have advocated Reform and Retrenchment in every department of the State. I have proved myself to be the Enemy of Slavery…" and spoke strongly in favour of reform of the church, a commutation of tithes, and abolishing all monopolies, sinecures and slavery. His political views were almost unique amongst Carmarthenshire landowners and he said in Quarter Sessions that "the magistrates of the county have completely lost the confidence of the people". Sir James lost this election in December 1832 having lost the support of the major landowners including the families of Dynevor and Golden Grove.

By the 1835 election Sir James had mellowed and stood as a Whig rather than an independent and was elected with the support of Lord Cawdor of Golden Grove. He remained a radical at heart and voted for the expulsion of Bishops from the House of Lords. By the 1837 election he had lost the support of Cawdor who was now supporting the Tories so he was not elected and did not stand again. The Tories held on to the county seats until 1868. Despite local opposition[270] from his political opponents Sir James was presented with a gold snuff box inscribed "This tribute of respect was presented to Sir James Williams Baronet MP purchased with the penny pieces of upwards of 6,000 of his friends and constituents in the County of Carmarthen, April 1836".

In his retirement Sir James spent more time at Edwinsford and served as Sheriff of Carmarthenshire in 1848 some four years before his brother, Admiral Charles (62). He continued to protest against the misuse of public funds in Carmarthenshire and opposed the formation of a local police force at local expense when there was serious rioting in the winter of 1842-3. He was appointed to the honorary office of Gamekeeper for the manors of Caio and Talley in 1845. At Clovelly he completed the Hobby drive started by his parents and at Edwinsford the circular drive round the demesne.

In 1833 Edwinsford was described[271] by a visitor: "The lands are for the greater part enclosed and in a state of good cultivation. The surrounding scenery is pleasingly diversified with wood and water, and from some of the higher grounds are fine prospects extending over a tract of well cultivated country….The mansion appears to have been formerly of greater magnitude; the grounds, which are extensive and judiciously disposed, comprehend much beautiful scenery". At Edwinsford Sir James made a number of alterations[272] and improvements including the building of a new dining room in 1840 furnished with oak panelling and sideboards from the old hall at Lethr Cadfan; the Peacock (Best) Rooms were above this room. In 1861 a new drawing room, the north wing and two corridors were added. New lodges were built at Iron Gate and Moelfre, and the old fishpond (*Pysgodlyn*) opposite the stables (rebuilt in 1802) was drained. The attractive bell roof wing and the main part of the old house remained

© Hon John Rous *Lady Mary Hamlyn Williams*

untouched as did the exquisite ceilings in Sir Nicholas' Room, the boudoir and the library, which were supposed to be the work of English plasterers in about 1660 in the time of Nicholas Williams (43) who served as Sheriff in 1665.

Sir James was a great character[273] and numerous are the anecdotes of his generosity, quick temper and geniality. As can be seen from the Clovelly census returns for 1851 and 1861 in Chapter 19.3 he had a large household. He died at Clovelly on 10 October 1861 aged 70 and was buried in the family vault there. It was erroneously reported[274] that his brother, Admiral Charles, had succeeded to the baronetcy; in fact

270 DL Baker-Jones CH (1968) p35
271 Samuel Lewis: *A Topographical Dictionary of Wales (1833)*
272 FDWD: *Annals p25*
273 FDWD: *Annals p16*
274 Gentleman magazine (1861) p577; Carmarthen Journal 18, 25 October 1861

brother Charles had died in 1859 and brother Orlando in 1831 so, there being no male heirs, the Hamlyn Williams baronetcy became extinct. Sir James appointed his nephew, John William Fortescue, and his nephew, Gerard James Noel MP PC (son of his sister Arabella and described in Chapter 8.4), as the executors under his will dated 21 December 1858[275] drawn up by David Long Price his lawyer in Talley. He left his estates and all his chattels and mineral rights to each of his three daughters described below. He made bequests to his orphaned godson, James George Glyn Shaw of Blackheath, of £10,000 and to his widow Lady Mary of £500 (who was well catered for under her marriage settlement) plus all personal effects and a life interest in the Upper Grosvenor Street house which he had inherited from his father and which was to pass on her death to his nephew Gerard Noel. His advowsons in Clovelly and tithes in Llansawel and Cynwyl Gaeo were left to his wife for life and then to his daughters. There being no male heir the estates were divided so the Edwinsford and Clovelly Estates which had been united since 1792 were split and the families' futures changed.

Lady Mary died at 39 Portland Place in London on 12 August 1874 and was buried in the family vault at Talley at her special request among the surroundings which she loved so much rather than at Clovelly.

Sir James and Lady Mary had three daughters through whom the English and Scottish royal blood line continued:

(1) Susan Hester Hamlyn Williams (1824-69)(70) who inherited the Clovelly Estate in 1861 on the death of her father. Like her mother she was born (on 1 January 1824) at Castle Hill mansion in Filleigh, Devon, a seat of the Fortescues; she married on 9 April 1850 Lt-Col Henry Edward Fane MP (1817-68) of Avon Tyrrell in Hampshire. He added his wife's surname when his wife inherited in 1861 so their surname changed to "Hamlyn Fane". Susan died at Clovelly Court on 19 May 1869 and was buried at Clovelly Church. She and her family are described in Chapter 18.2 and it is a descendant of that family, John Rous (127), who now owns and manages the Clovelly Estate;

(2) Edwina Augusta (Gussie) Hamlyn Williams (1834-89)(72) who inherited the Derllys Estate in 1861 on the death of her father. She was born at Clovelly Court and married on 17 March 1857 Sir John Ferguson Davie MP (2nd Bt)(1830-1907) of Bittescombe Manor, Upton, Taunton in Somerset and of Creedy Park, Sandford in Devon. He was the second son of Sir Henry Ferguson Davie Bt (1797-1885). He served as a Captain in the Grenadier Guards, as a Liberal MP for Barnstaple (1859-65) and as Sheriff of Carmarthenshire in 1873. Gussie and John lived in Derllys Court as well as at Bittescombe Manor and later at Creedy Park (after he succeeded to the baronetcy in 1885). They also visited and stayed at Edwinsford frequently following the death of Gussie's sister, Lil, in 1872.

As we saw in Chapter 1.1, on Sunday 13 January 1878 Sir James (Joe) Hamlyn Williams-Drummond 4th Baronet (1857-1913) (68) reached the age of 21 and formally inherited the Edwinsford Estate in the Cothi Valley in Carmarthenshire and Hawthornden Castle in Midlothian near Edinburgh. Until his majority his uncle and aunt, Sir James and Lady Gussie Ferguson Davie, acted as his guardian and mentors (his mother Lady Eleanor having died in 1872 and his father in 1866). They were a big influence on his upbringing.

Sir John and Lady Gussie had a daughter, Mary Fanny, who was born at Abbotshall, Fife and died in infancy in 1857. Lady Gussie died at Dropmore Park on 15 August 1889; she was visiting relations of the Grenville family; her mother had been the grand daughter of Prime Minister George Grenville who had built Dropmore Park near Cliveden, Maidenhead in Berkshire in 1795. Under her father's will her interest in the Derllys Estate then reverted to the children of her two sisters, Susan and Lil. A memorial stained glass window exists in Sandford Church near Creedy Park to Lady Gussie and there is also a brass tablet in memory of Sir John who died in 1907; and

(3) Mary Eleanor (Lil) Hamlyn Williams (1825-72)(71) who inherited the Edwinsford Estate on the death of her father and is described in Chapter 9.5. She married into the Scottish Drummond family of Hawthornden Castle near Edinburgh and started a whole new chapter in the history of the Welsh Williams family of Edwinsford, which would remain close to but no longer part of the Clovelly branch of the family.

We now turn to the background of the Drummond family of Hawthornden.

[275] NLW Edwinsford Estate archives

English Royal Pedigree of Edwinsford, Clovelly and Hawthornden Families

King William I The Conqueror (1028-87)

King Edward III (1312-77)

John of Gaunt Duke of Lancaster (1340-99)

John Beaufort Earl of Somerset (1373-1410)

John Beaufort Duke of Somerset (1403-44)

Edmund Tudor (1431-56) m= Margaret Beaufort (1443-1509)

Edmund Duke of York (1341-1402)

Richard Earl of Cambridge (1375-1415)

Richard Duke of York (1411-30)

King Edward IV (1442-83)

King Henry VII (1457-1509) m=Elizabeth of York (1466-1503)

Mary Tudor, Queen of France (1496-1533) m= Charles Brandon Duke of Suffolk (1484-1545)

Lady Frances Grey, Duchess of Suffolk (1517-59) m=Henry Grey Duke of Suffolk (1517-54)

Lady Catherine Grey (1540-68) m=Edward Seymour Earl of Hertford (1539-1621)
(sister of Lady Jane Grey)

Edward Seymour, Lord Beauchamp (1561-1612)

Francis Seymour 1st Baron Seymour of Trowbridge (1590-1664)

Charles Seymour 2nd Baron Seymour (1621-65)

Charles Seymour 6th Duke of Somerset (1662-1748) of Petworth House

Lady Catherine Seymour (1693-1731) m=Sir William Wyndham Bt (1688-1740)

Elizabeth Wyndham (c1731-69) m= George Grenville PC (1712-70)(Prime Minister)

Hester Grenville (c1767-1847) m= Hugh Fortescue 1st Earl Fortescue (1753-1841)

(61A) Lady Mary Fortescue (1792-1874) m= (61) Sir James Hamlyn Williams Bt MP (1790-1861)
of Edwinsford and Clovelly (3rd Bt Clovelly)

(70) Susan Hester Hamlyn Williams (1824-69)
(inherited Clovelly Estate in 1861)
m=Lt Col Henry Edward Hamlyn Fane MP
of Avon Tyrrell, Hants (1817-68)

(122) Constance Hamlyn Williams (1861-1920)
m= John 3rd Baron Manners (1852-1927)

(123) Betty Manners (1889-1962) of Clovelly
m= Brig Gen Arthur Asquith DSO (1883-1939)

(126) Mary Asquith (1919-2002) of Clovelly
m=Keith Rous, 5th Earl of Stradbroke (1907-83)

(127) Hon John Rous (b1950) of Clovelly
m= Zeenat Hameed

(71) Mary Eleanor Hamlyn Williams (1825-72)
(inherited Edwinsford Estate in 1861)
m= (73) Sir James (Walker) Williams-Drummond Bt (1814-66)
of Edwinsford (73) (3rd Bt Hawthornden)

(68) Sir James (Joe) Hamlyn Williams-Drummond Bt (1857-1913)
(4th Bt Hawthornden) of Edwinsford and Hawthornden

(69) Sir James (Jimmy) Hamlyn Williams-Drummond Bt (1891-1970)
(5th Bt Hawthornden) of Edwinsford and Hawthornden

Scottish Royal Pedigree of Edwinsford, Clovelly and Hawthornden Families

King Malcolm I of Scotland (895-954)

King Robert I (The Bruce) of Scotland (1274-1329)

Princess Marjorie Bruce (1296-1316) m=Walter 6th High Stewart of Scotland (1296-1327)

King Robert II (1316-90)

King Robert III (1337-1406) m= Annabella Drummond (1350-1401) dau of Sir John Drummond of Stobhall
(lived at Hawthornden)

King James I of Scotland (1394-1437) m= Lady Joan Beaufort (1404-45) grand-dau of John of Gaunt

King James II of Scotland (1430-60)

King James III (1451-88)

King James IV (1473-1513) m= Princess Margaret
(1489-1541) dau of Henry VII

King James V (1512-42)

James Stewart 1st Earl of Moray (1531-70)
Regent of Scotland

Elizabeth Stuart (1565-91) m=James Stewart
2nd Earl of Moray(1565-91)

James Stuart 3rd Earl of Moray (1581-1638)

James Stuart 4th Earl of Moray (1611-53)

Lady Henrietta Stuart (1640-1704)m=Sir Hugh Campbell
15th Thane of Cawdor (1635-1716)

Sir Alexander Campbell of Cawdor (d1697)

John Campbell of Cawdor MP (1695-1777)
of Cawdor, Nairn and Stackpole Court, Pembs

Anne Campbell (d1812) m=Mathew 2nd Lord Fortescue
(1719-85)

Hugh 1st Earl Fortescue (1753-1841)

(61A) Lady Mary Fortescue (1792-1874)
m= Sir James Hamlyn Williams Bt MP (1790-1861)
of Edwinsford and Clovelly (3rd Bt Clovelly)(61)

Princess Mary Stewart (1453-88) m= James 1st Lord Hamilton (1415-79)

James Hamilton1st Earl of Arran (1475-1529)

James Hamilton 2nd Earl of Arran (1516-75) Regent for Mary Queen of Scots

Lady Barbara Hamilton m= James 4th Lord Fleming(1534-58)

Jean Fleming (1553-1609) m=John 1st Lord Maitland (1537-95)
Lord Chancellor of Scotland

John Maitland 1st Earl of Lauderdale (d1645)

John Maitland 1st Duke of Lauderdale (1616-82)

Lady Mary Maitland m=John Hay 2nd Marquess of Tweeddale
(d1702) (1645-1713) Lord Chancellor Scotland

Brig Gen Lord William Hay of Newhall (d1723)

Richard Hay-Newton (d1776) m=Anne Stuart

Jane (Jean) Hay-Newton m=James Walker of Dalry, Midlothian
(1743-1817)

Sir Francis (Walker) Walker Drummond (1781-1844)
(2nd Bt Hawthornden)(216)
m=Margaret Anne Forbes-Drummond (d1876)
of Hawthornden

(70) Susan Hester Hamlyn Williams (1824-69)
(inherited Clovelly Estate in 1861)
m=Lt Col Henry Edward Hamlyn Fane MP
of Avon Tyrrell, Hants (1817-68)

(122) Constance Hamlyn Williams (1861-1920)
m= John 3rd Baron Manners (1852-1927)

(123) Betty Manners (1889-1962) of Clovelly
m= Brig Gen Arthur Asquith DSO (1883-1939)

(126) Mary Asquith (1919-2002) of Clovelly
m=Keith Rous, 5th Earl of Stradbroke (1907-83)

(127) Hon John Rous (b1950) of Clovelly
m= Zeenat Hameed

(71) Mary Eleanor Hamlyn Williams (1825-72)
(inherited Edwinsford Estate in 1861)
m= (73) Sir James (Walker) Williams-Drummond Bt (1814-66)
of Edwinsford (73) (3rd Bt Hawthornden)

(68) Sir James (Joe) Hamlyn Williams-Drummond Bt (1857-1913)
(4th Bt Hawthornden) of Edwinsford and Hawthornden

(69) Sir James (Jimmy) Hamlyn Williams-Drummond Bt (1891-1970)
(5th Bt Hawthornden) of Edwinsford and Hawthornden

9.4 The Drummond Family of Hawthornden

Midlothian was the name of an historic county formed in the Middle Ages which included Edinburgh and was formerly known as Edinburghshire. One of its parishes south of the City of Edinburgh is Lasswade (*laes* meaning meadow and *waed* meaning ford) within which is located Hawthornden Castle, Rosslyn Chapel[276] in Roslin village, and Melville Castle which are all close to each other. Hawthornden Castle [NT287637] stands on a cliff above the River North Esk and is downstream from Rosslyn Castle. Today it consists of a 15th century ruin with a 17th century house attached.

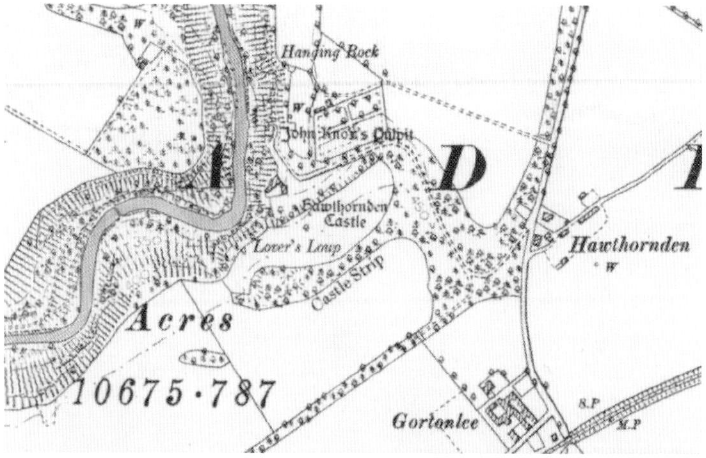

Map of Hawthornden c1893

Hawthornden Castle 2017

---

[276] Associated with the Knights Templar, the Holy Grail legend and the Priory of Sion the subject of the book by Dan Brown: *The Da Vinci Code (2003);* see also JJ Robinson: *Born in Blood-The Lost Secrets of Freemasonry (1989).* The Chapel was built by the St Clair (Sinclair) family in 1446-see Earl of Rosslyn: *Rosslyn Chapel (2012).* See also Andrew Sinclair: *The Secret Scroll (2001) p15, 23*

Rosslyn Castle by Paul Sandby c 1780

Rosslyn Chapel 2017

Hawthornden Castle c1789

Abernethy and Douglas Clans

Hawthornden was owned by the Abernethy family[277] of Salton from the 12th century. That family was the hereditary holder of the church and lands of the Scottish monastery at Abernethy from the 12th to the 14th centuries, the lay abbots of Abernethy being descendants of Gille Micheil, Earl of Fife. Lord Abernethy still retains the honour with the Duke of Hamilton of presenting the Sovereign following the coronation with the Crown of Scotland.

Hawthornden then passed to the Douglas clan in about 1388 when Sir William Douglas of Strabrock (203) acquired it; it is unclear[278] whether this was by inheritance or purchase. It remained[279] in the Douglas clan for two centuries until in December 1597 James Douglas (204) sold Hawthornden to Sir John Drummond (c1553-1610)(206).

Drummond Clan

The clan of Drummond (*dromainn* meaning ridge or high ground) with its mottoes "Gang Warily" (proceed with caution) and "virtutem coronat honos" (honour crowns virtue) is said to originate from Maurice, son of George, a younger base son of King Andrew I of Hungary. According to the legend[280] (probably a myth) Maurice arrived in Scotland at St Margaret's Hope in a storm on a ship which carried Edgar Atheling ((c1051-c1126), being the last male member of the royal house of Cerdic of Wessex and the Saxon claimant to the English throne) and his sisters Margaret and Christian (grand daughters of Edmund Ironside) in 1068 after their exile to Hungary following the Battle of Hastings. Margaret married King Malcolm (Canmore) III of Scotland and with her support Maurice and the Drummond family acquired large possessions in Scotland including the lands of Drymen or Drummond. Maurice was also given his armorial bearing of *three bars wavy, or undy, gules* in memory of his having helped Margaret on her safe landing in Scotland. Maurice was the progenitor of the noble family of Drummond of Perth, of which Drummond of Hawthornden is a cadet. Also on Margaret's ship was William (the Sturdy) St Clair carrying a portion of the true cross (or "holy rood", hence Holyrood Palace) to Scotland. King Malcolm III granted him the barony of Roslin as a reward and the St Clair (Sinclair) family settled in Scotland and were later appointed by King Robert the Bruce as hereditary Grand Masters of the Knights Templars; they also had very close connections with the prime Masonic Lodge of Scotland, which predates the later Grand Lodge of Freemasons in London set up post the Jabobite rebellion of 1715.

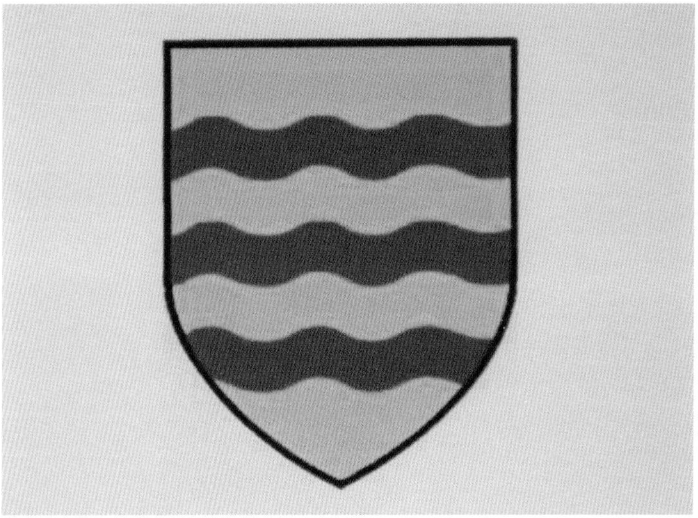

Arms of Clan Drummond

It is more likely that the Drummond clan derives its name from the lands of Drummond or Drymen in Stirlingshire, its progenitor probably being Malcolm Beg, Chamberlain of Lennox, who was the Laird or Clan Chief in 1225. He married Ada, the daughter of the Earl of Lennox. Their descendant Malcolm de Drummond fought at Bannockburn in 1314 supporting Scottish independence and after the battle was rewarded by King Robert I The Bruce (ancestor of the Edwinsford, Clovelly and Hawthornden families) with lands in Perthshire. In 1345 John Drummond married an heiress of the Montfichets and became Sir John Drummond of Stobhall, 11th Thane of Lennox, and Clan Chief. His daughter, Annabella Drummond (1350-1401), married John Stewart, Earl of Carrick, who later became

277 ODNB

278 The Douglas archives

279 Martin Coventry: *Castles of Scotland (2001)* and *Castles of the Clans (2008)*

280 FDWD: *Annals p18.* See Andrew Sinclair: *The Secret Scroll p15, 23,100,105, 108, 158, 172* for the connections between the Sinclair family, Rosslyn Chapel, the Knights Templar, the Cistercians, King Robert the Bruce, and the Freemasons

Drummond Family of Hawthornden

(200) Sir William de Abernethy of Salton, Lord of Hawthornden (viv 1314)

(201) Sir Lawrence de Abernethy, Lord of Hawthornden (dc 1338)

Hugh de Abernethy

(202) Elen de Abernethy (dc1388)
m(1)=Reginald le Cheyne of Duffus and Strabrock (dc1353)
m(2)= David de Graham

(dau)
m=Thomas Melville

Robert III King of Scotland
(1337-1406)
m(1367)= Annabella Drummond
(c1350-1401), dau of Sir John
Drummond, 11th Thane of Lennox

Mariota le Cheyne
m= John Douglas (dc 1369)

John Melville of Hawthornden

(203) Sir William Douglas of
Strabrock and Hawthornden
(bought/inherited Hawthornden c1388)

James I of Scotland (1394-1437)

(204) James Douglas of Hawthornden
(sold Hawthornden in Dec 1597)

Alexander Drummond of Carnock and Arnmore

(205) Sir Robert Drummond of Carnock, Stirling (d1592)
m(2)(c1542)=Marjorie, sis of Lord Elphinstone

Patrick Drummond of Carnock
(Royal master stabler)

(206) Sir John Drummond (c1553-1610) (bought Hawthornden Dec 1597)
m(1583)=Susannah Fowler, bro of William Fowler (1560-1612)

(207) William Drummond (1585-1649)
of Hawthornden (the poet)
m(1632)= Elizabeth Logan, granddau
of Sir Robert Logan of Restalrig Edinburgh

James

Alexander

John

Ann
m=Sir John Scot
of Scotstarvet

Jane

Rebecca

(208) Sir William Drummond (d1713)
of Hawthornden
m(2)=Barbara, dau of Sir William Scott
of Clerkington

Robert (d1687)

Elizabeth
m=Dr Henderson
of Edinburgh

3 sons

3 daus

(209) William Drummond (1664-c1735) of Hawthornden
m=Isabella, dau of Sir John Ramsay Bt of Whitehall

(210) William Drummond of Hawthornden (d1760)
m=Jean, dau of Sir Charles Milne Bt and Mary Drummond

Alexander Abernethy of Corskie, Banff

Dr William Drummond
(died in Jamaica)

(211)Mary Barbara Drummond (bc1721-1789)
of Hawthornden
m(1)= Robert Macgregor
of Glengarnock
m(2)(1760)= Dr William Abernethy-Drummond,
Bishop of Edinburgh (1720-1809)
(took Drummond surname
in 1760)(212)
(only dau died aged 13)

(213)Anne Abernethy
m=Robert Forbes
of Corskie, Banff

(214) Mary Ogilvie of Murkle, Angus
(heiress of Hawthornden,
cousin of Barbara Drummond)
m(1785)=(215) Capt Sir John Forbes-Drummond RN
(1746-1829)[1st Bt of Hawthornden 1828]

(216) Margaret Anne Forbes-Drummond (d1876) of Hawthornden m(1810)= Sir Francis (Walker) Walker Drummond
(1781-1844) [2nd Bt Hawthornden 1829] (217)

King Robert III (1337-1406) "the worst of kings and the most miserable of men", being Robert I's great-grandson. He was an invalid since a horse riding accident in 1384. Annabella was crowned as Queen Consort of Scotland at Scone Palace in 1390; she died at Scone Palace in 1401 and was buried at her birthplace in Dunfermline Abbey. They are thought to have lived in part at Hawthornden. Their youngest son born in Dumfermline Palace was King James I of Scotland (1394-1437), who in 1406 fled on a ship to France but was captured by pirates aged 12 and delivered to King Henry IV of England who detained him for 18 years at his Court in London. He was then ransomed and became King of Scotland in 1424; he was murdered in 1437 aged 42.

Queen Annabella's brother, William Drummond, married Elizabeth, daughter and coheiress of Sir William Airth of Airth and by this marriage acquired the barony of Carnock in Stirlingshire (the Clan Chief of the senior branch of the Drummonds of Stobhall in Perthshire became Lord Drummond of Stobhall in 1471). A direct descendant was Alexander Drummond of Carnock and Arnmore (near Kippen also in Stirlingshire). His son, Sir Robert Drummond of Carnock (d1592)(205), was Master of Work to the Crown of Scotland from 1579 to 1583 and as an architect did important repairs and alterations to a number of royal residences. The poet Alexander Montgomerie said *"All buildings brave bid Drummond now adieu; Whose life demonstrated he loved them more than any other; Where now shall we seek building and estate improvement?"* He married Marjorie Elphinstone and one of their six children and second son was Sir John Drummond (c1553-1610)(206), who in 1590 was appointed to the position of gentleman-usher in the Court of King James VI, knighted in 1603 when King James VI went to London to become King James I of England, died in 1610 and was buried at Holyrood. He bought the barony of Hawthornden (including Hawthornden, Slipperfield, Whitfields and Kingsfield) from James Douglas in December 1597 and founded the Drummond family of Hawthornden. In 1583 he married Susannah Fowler, sister of the poet and courtier William Fowler (1560-1612) who became Private Secretary to Queen Anne of Denmark (1574-1619, wife of King James VI). Their son was the famous poet William Drummond of Hawthornden (1585-1649)(207) described below. The senior branch of the family became Earls of Perth in 1605.

The main seats of the Drummond clan have included:

(1) Drummond Castle near Crieff in Perthshire which was built around 1491 by Sir John Drummond, 1st Lord Drummond. The castle was damaged during the Civil War in the 1650s by Oliver Cromwell and again in 1715 after the Jacobite rebellion. It was confiscated from the Drummond family senior branch after the 1745 Jacobite rebellion, but the family recovered the Earldom of Perth in 1853 and their forfeited lands and the Earls of Perth now live in Stobhall Castle;
(2) Stobhall Castle, near Perth which used to be the main seat of Clan Drummond from about 1360 until they moved to Drummond Castle and has now reverted to be their main seat;
(3) Balmoral Castle in Aberdeenshire which was built by Sir William Drummond in 1390 and then sold to the Gordons in the 15th century, to the Farquharsons of Invery in 1662, to the 2nd Earl of Fife in 1798, and eventually in 1852 to Prince Albert and Queen Victoria who had rented it initially. They enlarged it and it has been a royal residence ever since; and
(4) Hawthornden Castle

William Drummond of Hawthornden (1585-1649)

William Drummond (207) the poet[281] was the most famous Drummond of Hawthornden. He was the eldest son of the first Drummond Laird of Hawthornden and born in Hawthornden on 13 December 1585. His royal Scottish pedigree (and that of the Drummond Clan) deriving through Annabella Drummond, Queen Consort of Robert III, and subsequent Scottish monarchs became only more prestigious when James VI also became James I of England; indeed all the Scottish sovereigns had intermarried so much with other crowned Houses that there were numerous royal descendants of Annabella. William was educated at Edinburgh High School and Edinburgh University (founded in 1582) and was one of 24 students to graduate in 1605 (in the graduation book he called himself "Gulielmus Drummond"). He then studied law at Bourges and Paris for two years 1606-7 before returning to Scotland and being called to the Scottish Bar. In 1610 his father, the first Laird of Hawthornden, died aged 57 leaving William aged 24 as the third Laird. His father's estate was Scots £14,084 (Scots pounds which were only one twelfth of an English pound) and he inherited the house and one third of the

---

281 David Masson: *Drummond of Hawthornden The Story of His Life and Writings (1873);* John Sage: *The Works of William Drummond of Hawthornden (1711);* Poetry Foundation; Prof Oliver Elton: *The English Muse (1937)*

money, but his father also left debts of Scots £9,900. He had enough to rebuild and extend Hawthornden. His sister Ann married his good friend Sir John Scot of Knightspottie (later Scotstarvet).

He gave up any intention of practising law and studied literature and became fluent in numerous languages. His library at Hawthornden was enormous including books in Latin, Greek, Hebrew, Italian, Spanish and French. He also started writing poetry in the English style and not in Scots. The first of his prodigious writings was an *Elergy on the death of Prince Arthur*, Prince of Wales in 1612. In 1614 he fell in love with the daughter of Alexander Cunningham, Laird of Barns about 30 miles north of Hawthornden but she died in 1615 before the wedding (possibly on the actual wedding day). He was heart broken and published a book of poems in 1616 illustrating his sorrow. In 1618 the famous playwright, poet and critic, Ben Jonson (1572-1637), spent some months in Scotland having walked there from London probably researching his Scottish ancestry[282] and stayed at Hawthornden for two or three weeks; their correspondence[283] shows that young Drummond took much notice of their conversations and indeed recorded them in detail. In 1820 Drummond became ill but recovered. He published *Flowers of Sion* and the famous *A Cypress Grove* in 1623. He made great use of the sonnet and preserved it as a literary form. He bought avidly the works of contemporary poets and playwrights including those of Shakespeare (1564-1616), Camden (1551-1623), and Spenser (1552-99). In 1627 he donated a collection of 500 books to "the Toun's College" of Edinbuirgh, now Edinburgh University which was a huge addition to its then meagre library.

In 1627 he was granted 16 patents for military weapons, mathematics and mechanical science being another of his other loves (in addition to genealogy). These were for cavalry weapons, a new type of pike, a chariot, a large gun, a mortar, a battering machine, a telescope, burning glasses, and instruments for measuring wind, distances at sea and for converting salt water into sweet water. There is no evidence that any of these went into production.

In 1632 aged 46 he married Elizabeth Logan[284], grand daughter of Sir Robert Logan of Restalrig, which is near Arthur's Seat in Edinburgh. By 1638 William had decided to repair and rebuild part of Hawthornden and the family moved to live with his brother in law, Sir John Scot, while this was being done. When it was completed William had an inscription carved over the doorway: *"Divino munere Gulielmus Drummondus ab Hawthornden, Joannis, Equitis Aurati, Filius, ut honesto otio quiesceret, sibi et successoribus instauravit, 1638"* (By the divine favour, William Drummond of Hawthornden, son of Sir John Drummond, Knight, that he might rest in honourable ease, founded this house for himself and his successors).

During the political troubles in Scotland and in England from about 1640 and during the Civil War William kept his head down although his natural Royalist sympathies were apparent. He was fortunate that Hawthornden was not attacked. The regicide of Charles I in 1649 caused him much anguish and he died some months later aged 64 on 4 December at Hawthornden; he was buried in a vault in old Lasswade Kirk under the Drummond Aisle. His tomb was restored in the 1880s and a bronze relief added over the entrance in 1893 when the aisle was restored. His *History of Scotland under the Five Jameses* which he started in 1633 was not published until 1655. Many of his papers and works were presented to the Scottish Society of Antiquaries in 1782 by Dr Abernethy-Drummond described below.

William and Elizabeth had five sons and four daughters but he outlived all of them except for his wife and three of his children, William, Robert and Elizabeth. In his will[285] dated 1 September 1643 he left 500 marks and his moveables to his daughter Elizabeth as a portion, £1,000 each to his sons Robert and James (who was dead), and the rest to his son and heir William and requested to be buried within 24 hours of his death. His estate was valued at Scots £3,936. He is one of the 16 poets and writers whose heads appear on the Scott Monument on Princes Street in Edinburgh. On 27 October 1893 a bronze memorial was unveiled[286] in the poet's memory in Lasswade Kirkyard

282 David Masson p87. He was a descendant of the Johnstone family of Annandale

283 The Hawthornden Manuscripts (1619); RF Patterson: *Ben Jonson's Conversations with William Drummond of Hawthornden (1923)*

284 David Masson p194 refers to the suggestion that William married another Elizabeth Logan, being the daughter of the parish priest of Eddleston in Peebleshire. This is also referred to by John Sage in 1711, in Douglas's *Baronage of Scotland*, in David Laing's paper in *Archaeologia Scotica iv p66*, and by Mark Napier in *Life of Napier of Merchiston p220*

285 David Masson p458

286 Weekly Mail (28 Oct 1893)

Old Lasswade Kirk 2017

outside the Drummond mausoleum in the presence of Sir James (Joe) Williams-Drummond (68).

Robert died aged about 40 in 1687 without issue. Elizabeth married Dr Henderson a physician in Edinburgh and died before 1711. The eldest son and heir, William, inherited Hawthornden.

Bronze Memorial to William Drummond

Sir William Drummond of Hawthornden (d1713) and successors

William Drummond (208) became the third Laird of Hawthornden on the death of his father in 1649. He is said to have "inherited his father's principles and virtues, and even a portion of his genius, though he published nothing to the world." In his later years he seems to have been a very respectable old Scottish gentleman looking now and then over his father's papers and jotting down comments. He married twice, had three daughters by his first marriage, and three sons and six daughters by his second marriage to Barbara, daughter of Sir William Scott of Clerkington. He was knighted in the time of Charles II and lived to 1713.

He was succeeded as fourth Laird by his eldest son, William Drummond (1664-1735)(209), who married Isabella, daughter of Sir John Ramsay Bt of Whitehall. We are told[287] that "having improved himself by travelling abroad" he "became a well-bred, polite, and accomplished gentleman". However he then sustained a head injury after falling from his horse which affected him so much that "in a great measure he retired from the world during the remainder of his life." He had five daughters and one son, William.

William Drummond (d1760)(210), the fifth Laird of Hawthornden, married his cousin, Jean, the daughter of Sir Charles Milne (Mylne) Bt of Barnton and his wife Mary Drummond, the fifth daughter of the poet's son. So the Laird was the great grandson of the poet while his wife was the great granddaughter of the poet. They had two children: (a) Dr William Drummond who went to Jamaica as a physician and died there before his father's death, and (b) Mary Barbara Drummond (bc1721-89). Barbara married Robert Macgregor of Glengarnock, "a Highland gentleman of Jacobite distinction" but he died in 1758 without issue. She inherited Hawthornden on her father's death in 1760 and on 3 November 1760 she married William Abernethy (c1720-1809)(212). He changed his surname to Abernethy-Drummond on his marriage. He was descended from the family of Abernethy of Saltoun in Haddingtonshire (now East Lothian) which borders Midlothian and Edinburgh; that family of course had owned Hawthornden before the Drummonds. William Abernethy had taken a medical degree (MD) but was also a minister of an Episcopalian church in Edinburgh and initially had Jacobite sympathies. In 1787 he became Bishop of Brechin and and shortly afterwards was promoted to be Bishop of Edinburgh and held that office until 1805. William and Barbara lived at Hawthornden from 1760 and had one daughter, Jean Drummond, who died in 1777 aged 13.

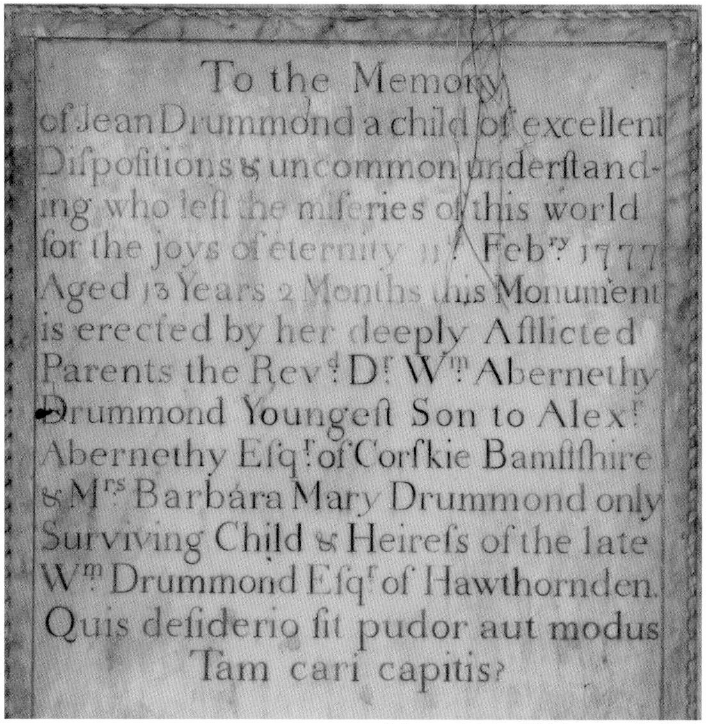

Memorial in Old Lasswade Kirk

Barbara died at Hawthornden on 11 December 1789. She settled Hawthornden on trustees on the basis that her husband could continue to live there during his life (he died at Hawthornden on 27 August 1809 aged 89) paying rent and on his death the estate would go to her cousin, Mary Ogilvie of Murkle in Angus (214), who had married her husband's nephew Captain John Forbes RN (1745-1829)(215) who changed his surname to Forbes-Drummond. So while the "Drummond" surname continued at Hawthornden, the direct Scottish royal blood line had been broken, although the Walker Drummonds who had an equally strong Scottish royal bloodline would soon restore that family honour in the form of Sir Francis (Walker) Walker Drummond (217).

[287] David Masson p460

A relation whom I have been unable to trace called James Drummond (1784-1863), son of Thomas Drummond, was born in Hawthornden and sailed to Western Australia on board the *Parmelia* in 1829. He was the first resident government naturalist/ botanist and his family established the property of Hawthornden[288] in the Toodyay valley.

Capt Sir John Forbes-Drummond RN 1st Bt Hawthornden (1746-1829)

Robert Forbes (son of John Forbes) of Corskie in Banff (a cadet of the Pitsligo family) married Anne Abernethy (213) the sister of Dr William Abernethy-Drummond (212) and daughter of Alexander John Abernethy of Corskie. They had two sons, Captain Robert Forbes RN who was killed in action, and Captain John Forbes RN (215). On 1 November 1785 John Forbes married Mary Ogilvie (b1758) (214) daughter of Dr Ogilvie of Forfar and of Murkle, Angus; she was a cousin to Barbara Drummond (211) and became the heiress of Hawthornden under Barbara Drummond's will settlement of 1789. In 1786 John's surname was legally changed to Forbes-Drummond. Mary and John moved to Hawthornden on the death of Dr William Abernethy-Drummond in 1809.

The landscape painter, Hugh Williams (1773-1829), painted several watercolours of Hawthornden in 1796-8 which were mounted in the Forbes-Drummond Album but sadly this album was broken up and sold in 1990.

On 27 February 1828 John Forbes-Drummond was granted[289] for distinguished naval service a Baronetage of Hawthornden (with a special remainder to his son in law, Francis Walker Drummond and the heirs male of his body). His motto was *Hos gloria reddit honores.* His quartered arms were *or three bars wavy within a bordure gules* (for Drummond) *and azure three bears's heads coupled close argent muzzled gules* (for Forbes). He died on 23 May 1829.

Sir Francis (Walker) Walker Drummond 2nd Bt Hawthornden (1781-1844)

John and Mary had one daughter, Margaret Anne Forbes-Drummond of Hawthornden (d1876)(216), who on 4 January 1810 married Francis Walker (1781-1844)(217) who was born on 9 June 1781. He had a maternal Scottish royal pedigree being the eldest son of James Walker (1743-1817) the Principal Clerk of Session of Dalry, Midlothian and Jane (Jean) Hay-Newton; they lived at East Fortoun in East Lothian. On his marriage Francis assumed the additional surname and arms of his wife, and on the death of his father in law in 1829 he succeeded to the baronetcy and became Sir Francis Walker Drummond 2nd Bt of Hawthornden. Francis and Margaret lived at Hawthornden. Francis died on 29 February 1844 aged 62 and Margaret continued to live there until her death on 14 May 1876 as can be seen from the census returns below. She lived there with her eldest son and heir, Sir James the 3rd Bt (73), until his marriage in 1853, and then with other sons.

Francis and Margaret had six children (see the pedigree in Chapter 9.5):

(1)Maj-General Francis Walker Drummond (1817-91)(218) who was born on 1 March 1817 and served with the Bengal Cavalry in India. He was born in Edinburgh and on 28 July 1839 he married Pauline (d1918), daughter of Charles Mackenzie a civil servant in Bengal. After he retired he lived in Hawthornden as can be seen from the census return for 1881 and by 1891 had moved to live in Hawthornden Lodge on the estate close-by where he died on 4 August that year aged 74; one assumes that his nephew, Sir James Williams-Drummond the 4th Bt (68), who would by then have been the owner of the estate used Hawthornden himself while he was not in London or Edwinsford. Pauline died on 24 April 1918. Francis and Pauline had five children: (a) Pauline who in 1865 married James Quinton the Chief Commissioner of Assam who gained a Companion, Order of the Star of India (CSI) and was murdered by natives during the Manipur Mutiny on 25 March 1891; (b) Alice who in 1871 married MT Carmichael (d1892) and lived at Eastend in Lanarkshire; (c) Margaret (d 1918) who in 1869 married Lt-Gen TM Hazlerigg (1840-1915) of the Royal Horse Artillery and the Royal Artillery who fought in the Afghan Wars. They had seven children; (d) Mayor Charles (1840-80) who served in the 7th Bengal Native Infantry and died unmarried in 1880 aged 39; and (e) Charles (b1861);

[288] Rica Erickson: *The Drummonds of* Hawthornden *(1969)(Perth)*

[289] Debrett's Baronetage of England 1832

(2) John Forbes Walker Drummond (1819-96)(219) was born in Edinburgh in January 1819 and on 11 September 1866 married Emma (d1920), the daughter of Butler Edmund Thornton of Skerton in Lancashire. John lived at Hawthornden with his widowed mother and is described as a wine merchant; he probably moved there when his eldest brother married in 1853. He was still living there with his mother and brother Richard after his marriage but his wife Emma must have been absent on census day. John died on 4 June 1896. John and Emma had a daughter Annabella (d1936) who on 17 January 1889 married Lt-Col Richard Wilson DSO (1855-1936) of the Royal Navy and then the 10th Hussars who served in the Ashanti War, in Afghanistan, Sudan, Suakin and the Boer War. They lived at Ednam House;

(3) Richard Hay Walker Drummond who died unmarried;

(4) Mary Walker Drummond who married Francis Thiergartner;

(5) Jane Hay Walker Drummond who on 14 July 1840 married William Douglas Dick of Pitkerro, Forfarshire; and

(6) Sir James Walker Drummond 3rd Bt of Hawthornden (1814-66)(73) the eldest son and heir who succeeded to the baronetcy in 1844 on the death of his father and who changed his surname to "Williams-Drummond" in 1858 as we will see in Chapter 9.5. He and his wife, who was the heiress of Edwinsford, lived at Edwinsford while his widowed mother continued to live at Hawthornden.

Hawthornden Castle

Who knows not Melville's beechy grove,
And Roslin's rocky glen,
Dalkeith, which all the virtues love,
And classic Hawthornden?
(Sir Walter Scott: The Grey Brother)

Midlothian was the name of an historic county formed in the Middle Ages which included Edinburgh and was formerly known as Edinburghshire. One of its parishes south of the City of Edinburgh is Lasswade (*laes* meaning meadow and *waed* meaning ford) within which is located Hawthornden Castle. Hawthornden Castle [NT287637] stands on a high cliff above the River North Esk on a triangular promontory and is downstream from Rosslyn Chapel and Castle. Today it consists of a 15th century ruin with a 17th century L-shaped house attached.

There are several caves under the Castle which probably date from the Bronze Age. The caves are also said to have been used by King Robert I The Bruce (1274-1329) and by Sir Alexander Ramsay of Dalhousie following battles against the English. The upper cave is known as the King's Chamber and used to be accessed by a flight of stone steps down the cliff face now covered with ivy. On a nearby step is the Wash Basin in which Queen Victoria washed her hands on her visit[290] with the Prince Consort in 1847; there used to be a large oil painting in the dining room at Edwinsford depicting this visit. This Chamber leads to a complex of other caves and long passageways under the Castle. The lower cave known as the King's Dining Room or King's Gallery can only be accessed via an entrance in the cliff face using a ladder; it is a single room lined with some 370 small square holes which were probably used as a dovecote. A third cave contains carved chairs and cupboards, a fireplace and windows. There are also other caves called The Temple, The Grotto where the poet is said to have sat to write, and Wallace's Cave where Sir William Wallace is thought to have hidden.

The first reference to the Castle is in records dated 1433 and the earliest part of the castle is a square tower measuring about 8 sq mts and being three storeys high with a vaulted prison pit below. The 15th century tower is now in ruins and was probably destroyed by Edward Seymour, Duke of Somerest and Earl of Hertford (1500-52), in 1544 when during the war of the Rough Wooing he burned Edinburgh and Rosslyn Castle, or when as Lord Protector he invaded Scotland in 1547.

290 FDWD: *Annals p22-4*

By 1638 William Drummond (207) the poet had decided to repair and rebuild part of Hawthornden and the family moved to live with his brother in law, Sir John Scot, while this was being done. When it was completed William had an inscription carved over the doorway: *"Divino munere Gulielmus Drummondus ab Hawthornden, Joannis, Equitis Aurati, Filius, ut honesto otio quiesceret, sibi et successoribus instauravit, 1638"*. The fine old knocker on the outer door bears the initials "SWD-DBS" (Sir William Drummond, the poet's son, and Dame Barbara Scott) dated 1650.Over the entrance door in the courtyard is a medallion on a square with cross and pastoral staff beneath bearing a shield showing a man of war in a storm (the Abernethy Arms) with the motto "Salvus per Christum", while the motto underneath is the Drummond one "Hos gloria reddit honores". Below are the initials "WA-BMD" (William Abernethy, the bishop, and Barbara Mary Drummond) dated 1795.

The L-shaped 17th century house is attached to the ruinous 15th century tower remains. In 1895 Sir Joe Hamlyn Williams-Drummond (4th Bt)(68) and his wife Lady Madeline carried out extensive alterations and improvements, particulary in the upper storey and gardens.The house has a 19th century attic and baronial stair tower and is of harled rubble, with three storeys and a garret in height. It has a 5 bay castle style L-plan tower with internal triangular courtyard with pink sandstone rubble and ashar dressings. It is listed as being of special architectural or historic interest.Heirlooms in the Castle used to include a beautiful black and white marble card table bearing the Royal Arms of Scotland and the initials R and A (King Robert III and Queen Annabella Drummond) dated 1396; a silk dress and pair of shoes belonging to Mary Queen of Scots; a tartan coat said to have been worn by Bonnie Prince Charlie in 1745; a magnificent two-handed sword of Robert The Bruce five feet long with a long ivory handle and quadrangle guards; and John Knox's desk.

In the grounds there is a seat cut in the rock near the house which is called the Cypress Grove where the poet is said to have sat when he composed his moral treatise of that title on the vanity of human life. There used to be a great sycamore tree in front of the house under which it is said the poet was sitting in 1618 when Ben Jonson first came to see him at Hawthornden; probably a myth. There is a 17th century drinking fountain in the grounds with a carved armorial shield in pediment and obelisk finial above. There is also a well with a circular wall surrounding it in the triangular courtyard facing the glen. The views from the Castle down the glen are spectacular. Indeed Sir Walter Scott remarked[291] that the narrow glen is one of those beautiful and sequestered valleys, which so often occur in Scotland, and generally where they are least to be expected.

Hawthornden remained in the ownership of the Williams-Drummond family until 1970 when Sir James Hamlyn Williams-Drummond (1891-1970)(5th Bt Hawthornden)(69) died without issue leaving his estate to his butler and chauffeur, Frank Coombs (1914-78). Hawthornden was put up for sale in 1977 and on 15 March 1978 was bought by Alexander and Diana Adamson. The Adamsons sold off some of the estate lands including the Garden Cottage (sold in 1978) and Hawthornden Lodge (sold in 1980). In 1982 the house and the remaining estate were sold to Mrs Drue Heinz DBE (born Doreen Mary English), the philanthropist and generous supporter of numerous literary and educational causes (now a centenarian) and widow of HJ Heinz II (1908-87), former Chairman of the American 57 varieties food company. Since 1982 part of the house has been used as a private retreat for writers, who also have a library in the grounds. Residences usually last for four weeks with six writers in residence. It is appropriate that some 400 years after the famous poet, modern authors and poets continue to contemplate and work in the peaceful and tranquil 120 acre surroundings of the former castle adopting a strict rule of silence during the working day with no visitors permitted.

The annual Hawthorden Prize is a British literary award established in 1919 by Alice Warrender (1857-1947) for a work of imaginative literature in poetry or prose by an author under the age of 41.

291 Adam and Charles Black: *Guide to Edinburgh and Environs-Hawthornden and Roslin (1868) p83-5*

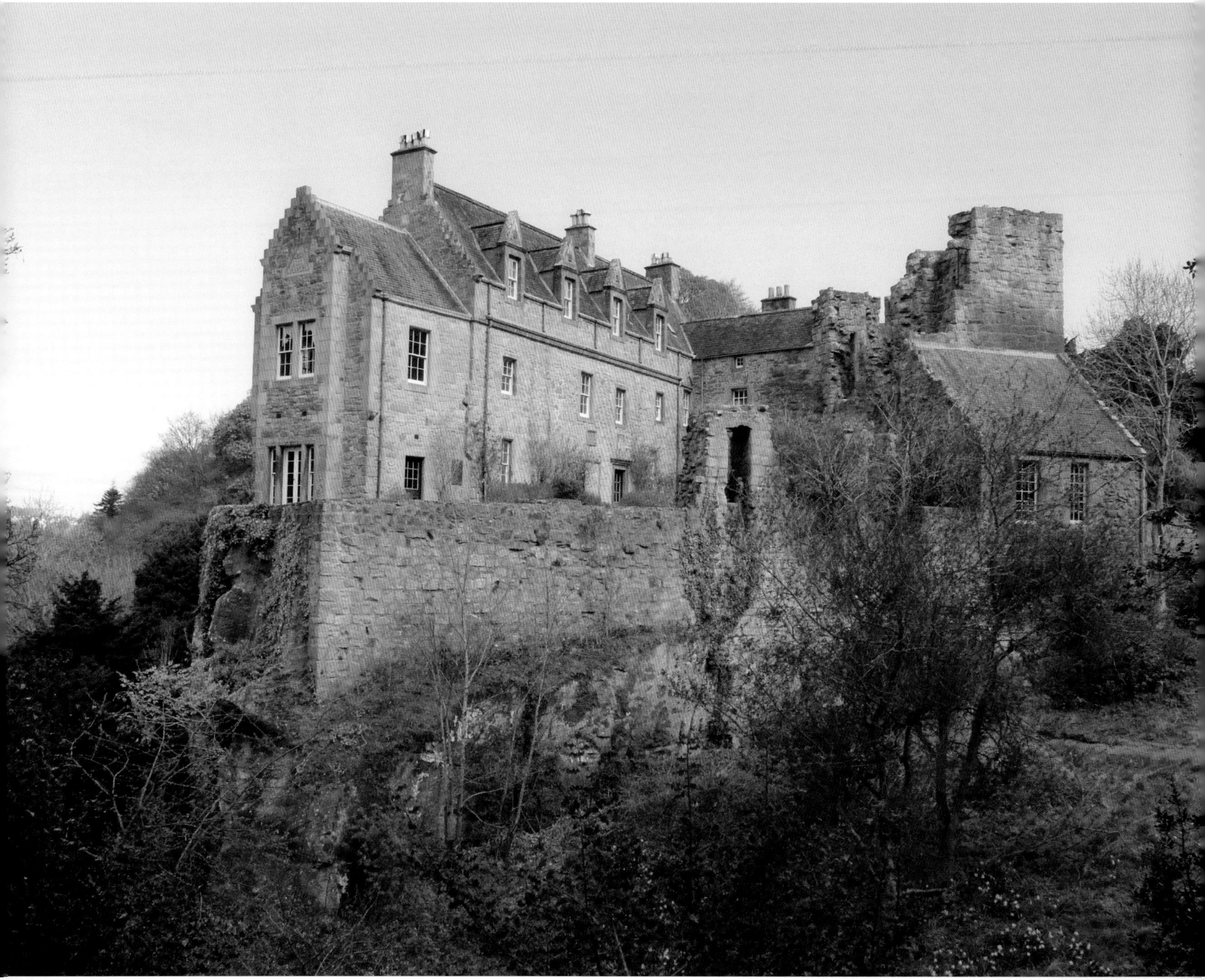

Hawthornden 2017

King's Gallery cave at Hawthornden

Rock seat

Medallion and square above entrance door

Entrance door knocker

17th century drinking fountainhead

Library

Hawthornden

Drive to Hawthornden

Hawthornden Lodge

The following table is an estimate from available records of the owners and residents of Hawthornden.

YEAR	OWNER	RESIDENTS
14th Cent	Abernethy and Douglas Families	
c1388	Sir William Douglas (203)	Sir William Douglas
	Douglas Family	
-1597	James Douglas (204)	
1597-1610	Sir John Drummond (206)	Sir John and Susannah
1610-1649	William Drummond (207)	William and Elizabeth
1649-1713	Sir William Drummond (208)	Sir William and Barbara
1713-1735	William Drummond (209)	William and Isabella
1735-1760	William Drummond (210)	William and Jean
1760-1809	Barbara Drummond (211)	Barbara and William Abernethy
1809-1829	Mary Ogilvie (214)	Sir John (215) and Mary Forbes -Drummond
1829-1876	Margaret Forbes- Drummond (216)	Sir Francis (217) and Margaret Walker Drummond
1876-1913	Sir James HW Williams -Drummond (68)	Sir James and Lady Madeline (67)
1876-1891		Gen Francis Walker Drummond (218) and Pauline
1913 70	Sir James HW Williams- Drummond (69)	Sir James and Lady Enid
1970-78	Frank A Coombs (d1978)	Frank Coombs
1978-1982	Alexander and Diana Adamson	Alexander and Diana Adamson
1982-	Drue Mary Heinz DBE	used as a writers' retreat

YEAR	HAWTHORNDEN CASTLE CENSUS RETURNS
1851	**DRUMMOND: James** (38) born Edinburgh, Laag Drummond (58) mother, Lilias Christison (39) cook, George Bullie (37) butler, Robert Rachard (28) lad man, Isabella Gilchrist (26) ladies maid, Ann McLarin (28) housemaid, Mary Sandilands (44) under cook
1861	**DRUMMOND: John** (41) wine merchant born Edinburgh, Margaret Drummond (66) mother, Richard Drummond (32) bro, Samuel Gebson (28), Margaret Baxter (31), Ms McBain (34), Gessie Clerk (38), Margaret Paterson (25), George Brown (17)
1871	**DRUMMOND: John F** (51) Baronet's son born Edinburgh, Margaret AC Drummond (76) Baronet's widow mother, Richard H Drummond (41) bro, Henry Earl (42), Joseph Patrick (20), Flora Fraser (54), Jane Reith (44), Janet Alexander (38), Catherine Smith (20)
1881	**DRUMMOND: Francis Walker** (64) Major Gen Indian Army Cavalry born Edinburgh, Pauline (60) wife, Charles (20) son, Isabella Sim (30), Agnes Mason (26), Jessie Alexander (32), Maggie Grant (18)
1891	[Family at Edwinsford]
1901	[Family at Edwinsford] Elizabeth Mcgowan (50) ser carstake, Margaret Leadbitter (16) housemaid
1911	[Family at Edwinsford]

YEAR	HAWTHORNDEN LODGE CENSUS RETURNS
1871	**BODGER: William** (36), Eliza (35) wife, William (11) son, Margaret Brown (6), Janet Drummond (5), Eliza Bodger (11 mon) dau, Janet Bell (65)
1881	No entry
1891	**DRUMMOND: Francis Walker** (74) retired military officer, Pauline (70) wife, Thomas Hattamore (25) ser, Barbara McLeod (28) ser, Maggie McKoy (23) ser
1901	**DONALDSON: Agnes** (46) lodge keeper

9.5 The Williams-Drummond Family of Hawthornden and Edwinsford

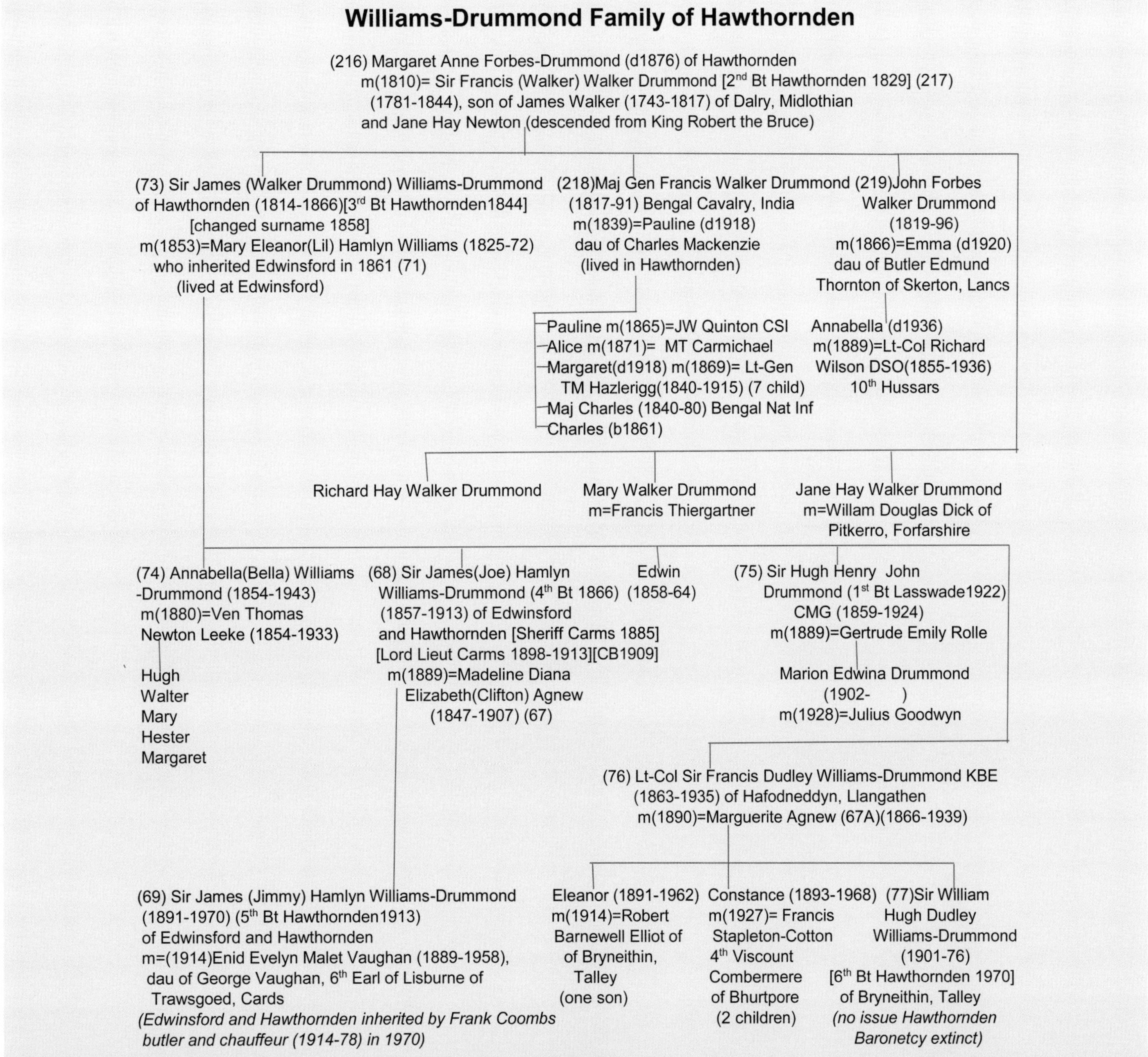

Mary Eleanor Hamlyn Williams (1825-72) and Sir James (Walker Drummond) Williams-Drummond 3rd Bt Hawthornden (1814-66)

As we saw at the end of Chapter 9.3, Mary Eleanor (Lil) Hamlyn Williams (71) was one of the three daughters and heiresses of Sir James and Mary Hamlyn Williams (61) of Edwinsford and Clovelly. She was born at Edwinsford on 19 July 1825 and christened in St Sawyl's Church in Llansawel in August of that year. On 14 July 1853 she married Sir James Walker Drummond (73), who was born on 11 August 1814 and had succeeded his father as 3rd Bt of Hawthornden on the latter's death on 29 February 1844. So Lady Eleanor married into a noble Scottish clan. On 20 December 1853 the tenants and residents of the Edwinsford Estate and area welcomed the couple back as they first arrived at Carmarthen from Capt Hamlyn Williams' home at Ferryside, with bells ringing out and arches of flowers as they arrived in Llandeilo at the Castle Hotel with banners and bunting, then the journey to Edwinsford with 21 cannons firing from local moutaintops and banners from Penbullan bridge as they entered the estate with 150 tenants on horseback waiting to greet them, a procession to the Edwinsford Arms in Talley where they were met by the Ancient and Independent Order of Odd Fellows wearing their insignia, the schoolchildren laden with flowers, an archway with the arms of Sir James and motto (*Hos gloria reddit honores)* and some 1,000 spectators. Then the presentation[292] was made to Sir James and Lady Eleanor which read:

"We have this day assembled together to evince our sincere and cordial delight at greeting your arrival amongst us, and to express our united hopes that henceforth Sir James Drummond may look upon the Land of the Cumry with the same affection as, we trust, your Ladyship feels for it, from the association of your childhood and youth, and that you may both bear testimony, from experience, to this warmth and devotion of Welsh hearts. It is our earnest prayer that many happy and prosperous years await you both, and that the auspicious day which in your persons united the Leek and the Thistle may be ever remembered with joy and thanksgivings as the first step in a path which we heartily hope may be crowned with every blessing, and that you may long live endeared to all around you by those benevolent and kindly graces for which the Family of Edwinsford have always been so highly distinguished and so deservedly beloved. Talley December 20th 1853".

Sir James and Lady Eleanor then embarked in their carriage which was pulled by relays of 10 men before they arrived at Edwinsford to be greeted by the guests, family and servants with more flowers and banners emblazoned with the family arms and inscribed with *Groesaw Adre* and *Ffrynd y Cymry.* That evening some 80 tenants and friends had dinner at the Edwinsford Arms with David Long Price in the chair with the usual toasts and speeches in honour of the couple; Lady Eleanor they all knew from birth but Sir James from Scotland was a man they did not yet know. They would not be disappointed.

Sir James served as a Captain in the Grenadier Guards and later as Lieutenant-Colonel commanding the Royal Carmarthen Artillery Militia, which he reorganised on his succession to and at the request of its former Colonel, Lord Dynevor, the then Lord Lieutenant of Carmarthenshire. He was also a member of the Dalkeith Masonic Lodge[293] which met near Hawthornden and on 30 September 1850 was presented with a gold masonic jewel in esteem of his being Master of the Lodge. He was appointed a Deputy Lieutenant of Midlothian on 16 December 1845 by the Lord Lieutenant, the Duke of Queensberry.

Sir James Walker Drummond of East-Fortoun, East Lothian, changed his surname to "Williams-Drummond" (adding "Williams" to and before that of "Drummond") in 1858 pursuant to the will of his father in law dated 21 December 1858 under which Eleanor was to inherit the Edwinsford Estate. On the death of her father in 1861 Eleanor duly inherited the Edwinsford Estate, while her two sisters inherited the Clovelly and Derllys Estates. Sir James and Lady Eleanor lived at Edwinsford while his widowed mother, Lady Margaret (216), continued to live at Hawthornden until her death in 1876. She outlived both Sir James and Eleanor, so Sir James and Eleanor only visited and never lived at Hawthornden during their married life.

On 13 January 1862 Sir James received a grant from the Lord Lyon of the arms of Williams quartered with those of Drummond. So his arms

[292] NLW Edwinsford Estate archives MS 22869F; Welshman (23 Dec 1853)

[293] NLW Edwinsford Estate archives

were quartered with the 1st and 4th grand quarters, quarterly; 1st and 4th being *or, three bars, wavy, within a bordure, gules* (for Drummond), and the 2nd and 3rd, *azure, three bears' heads, coupled close, argent, muzzled, gules* (for Forbes); 2nd and 3rd grand quarters, *paly, argent and gules, a saltier, also paly, counterchanged, on a chief, invected, azure, a crescent of the field, between two spur-rowels, gold.* The crest was a *demi-pegasus, argent, winged, or.* The supporters were two naked men wreathed about the loins, and over the exterior shoulder of each a club, all ppr. The motto was *Hos gloria reddit honores.*

Williams-Drummond crest

Sir James took an active part in the public affairs of Carmarthenshire and sat on numerous committees and presided over many events, including for example the Llansawel Eisteddfod on 23 September 1863. Lady Eleanor was also very active in her many and wide charitable pursuits locally. They continued with the upgrading of Edwinsford Mansion started by Sir James's father. They enjoyed an active social life and a typical week's wine consumption at Edwinsford during the time of Sir James and Lady Eleanor can be seen from the wine accounts[294] for the week of 8th to 15th June 1862; these reveal the consumption of 23 bottles namely 1 Old Port, 1 Hock, 2 Malaga, 2 Claret Laffitte, 3 Montilo, 3 Sherry, 2 Champagne, 1 Old Green Sherry, 1 Marsala, 4 Claret, 1 Chateau Margaux, and 2 Samper Sherry.

Sir James died on 10 May 1866 aged only 51 at 23 Portman Square in London. Under his will dated 5 July 1865 (and proved on 9 October 1866), witnessed by his lawyer David Long Price of Talley and his gamekeeper Henry Fulford, he appointed his wife as sole executrix. The Edwinsford Estate passed to trustees to hold for his eldest son and heir in accordance with the will settlement of Sir James Hamlyn Williams (61) dated 21 December 1858, while his Scottish estates were left to his wife. He appointed his cousin Gerard Noel MP (1823-1911) and his wife's cousin Hon Dudley Francis Fortescue MP to be the guardians of his children. His personal effects were valued at under £800.

After her husband's death Lady Eleanor went to live in London at their flat at 34 Great Cumberland Place with her young children and her widowed mother, Lady Mary Williams (1792-1874) (61A), as can be seen from the 1871 census return in Chapter 12. She died aged only 47 on 18 August 1872 at her London flat. Under her will dated 30 January 1872 (proved on 16 October 1872) in which interestingly she gives her name as "Dame Mary Eleanor Drummond of Edwinsford" she appointed Hon Dudley Francis Fortescue MP of 8 Hertford Street in Mayfair as sole executor. Her personal effects were valued at under £10,000. She exercised her right under her father's will and her own marriage settlement to settle £36,000 on trustees for her children in equal shares payable to sons on reaching the age of 21 and to daughters on marrying or reaching the age of 21 (except for her eldest son who of course inherited the Edwinsford Estate); interest and other income was to be used for the education and upbringing of the children in the meantime. She appointed her sister Lady Gussie and her husband Sir John Ferguson Davie as the guardians of her children (in addition to the guardians appointed under her husband's will) and she made "this

[294] NLW Edwinsford Estate archives

request which I have much at heart…that my dear sister will together with her husband do all they can to promote the welfare and happiness of my children….and that my children may be enabled to live at Edwinsford until my eldest son attains the age of 21". She left her Scottish estates (left to her by her husband) to her eldest son together with all her other assets except for some silver and jewellery which went to her younger sons and daughters and some pecuniary legacies to friends and her executor.

Lady Mary Williams-Drummond (71) and her son Hugh 1865

Sir James Williams-Drummond 3rd Bt c1862

© Hon John Rous Sir James Williams-Drummond 3rd Bt

© Hon John Rous Lady Mary

© Hon John Rous Annabella, Edwin and James 1860

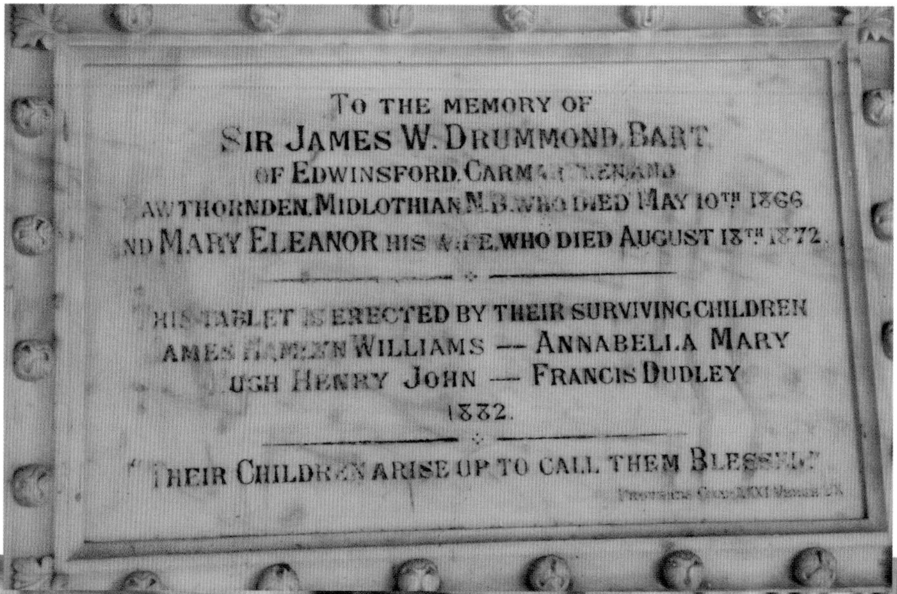

Memorial in Talley Church

© Hon John Rous

Outside Edwinsford c1868 L to R: Francis Dudley Williams-Drummond (76), Annabella Williams-Drummond (74), Madamoiselle Bourgoise, Lady Mary Williams (61A), Lizzie Gulston

Both Lady Eleanor and Sir James were buried at Talley and there is a monument in Talley Church to their memory.

Sir James and Lady Eleanor had five children:

(1) Annabella Mary (Bella) Williams-Drummond (1854-1943)(74) who was born at Edwinsford and on 21 April 1880 married at Talley Church Rev (later Ven) Thomas Newton Leeke (1854-1933) of Longford Hall in Shropshire; he was nicknamed Nutty. He served as Rector of Longford 1880-3, Vicar of Inkberrow 1883-96, Rector of Bideford in Devon1896-1921, Archdeacon of Totnes and Rural Dean of Hartland 1914-21, Prebendary of Exeter 1915-21 and Canon of Exeter 1921-33. Bella died on 3 June 1943 and Nutty on 26 October 1933. They had six children: Hugh who served in the African Rifles in the Great War and then worked for the Siamese State Forestry Department before farming in Uganda, Walter a Commander in the Royal Navy who was involved in several engagements in the China and North Seas, and three daughters Mary Eleanor, Hester and Margaret;

(2) Edwin Williams-Drummond (1858-64) who was born at Edwinsford and died aged 5;

(3) Sir Hugh Henry John Drummond Bt CMG (1859-1924)(75) who was born at Edwinsford on 29 November 1859 and on 15 May 1889 married Gertrude Emily Rolle (d1954), eldest daughter of Hon Mark George Kerr Rolle and Lady Gertrude Douglas. In 1889 he unsuccessfully stood as a Tory candidate for Parliament in the West Carmarthenshire Bye-election[295]. He hunted his father in law's North Devon Foxhounds for five seasons. He served as a Lieutenant in the

Hugh Drummond 1881 Rifle Brigade

Hugh Drummond 1918

[295] Carmarthen Journal (12 July 1889)

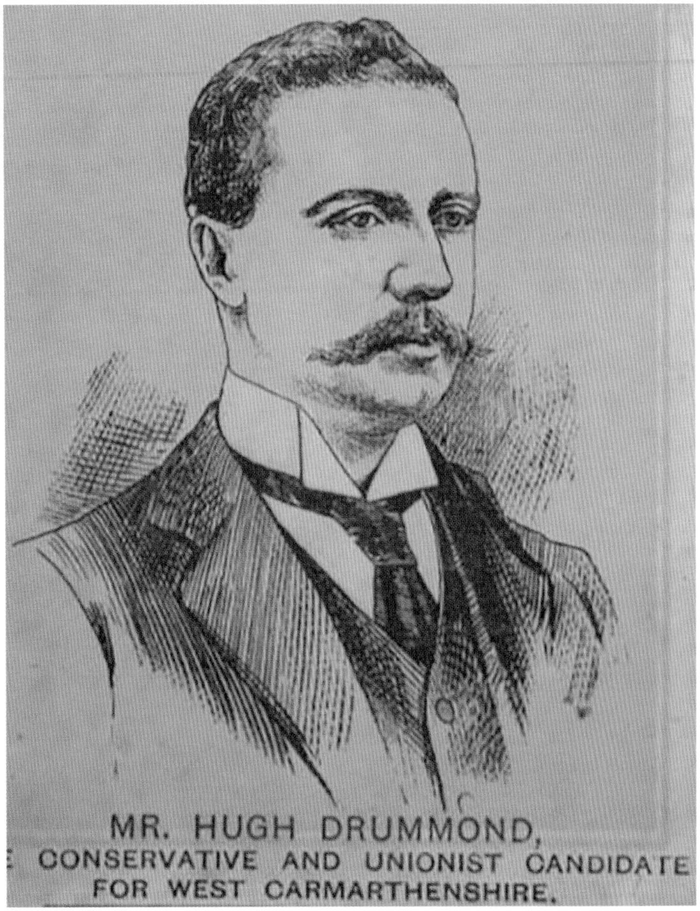

Rifle Brigade (Prince Consort's Own) and commanded the Royal North Devon Imperial Yeomanry (Hussars) until 1898. On the outbreak of war in 1914 he raised a Reserve Regiment and served as Lt-Col in the Territorial Force Reserve on the East Coast becoming an Honorary Brig-General in 1917. He later became a member of the Royal Company of Archers (the King's Bodyguard in Scotland).

He was a director of the National Provincial and Union Bank, Deputy Chairman of the Alliance Assurance Co, and in 1911 Chairman of the London and South Western Railway, which in 1923 became the principal partner of the Southern Railway Combine of which he was appointed Chairman.

He was awarded a CMG (Companion, Order of St Michael and St George). In the 1922 Birthday Honours he was appointed on 27 June 1922 a Baronet (1st Bt Drummond of Lasswade) having changed his surname by deed poll on 12 June in that year from "Williams-Drummond" to "Drummond". Lasswade of course was very close to Hawthornden Castle. Hugh and his family lived at The Chase, Churt in Surrey and their London home was at 88 St James's Street. Hugh died on 1 August 1924 aged 64 and the baronetcy became extinct since they had one daughter, Marion Edwina Drummond born on 1 March 1902. She married in 1928 Julius Goodwyn;

(4) Lt-Col Sir Francis (Dudley) Williams-Drummond KBE (1863-1935)(76) the youngest son who married a cousin in the Agnew family and is described below; and

(5) Sir James Hamlyn Williams-Drummond 4th Bt (1857-1913)(68) the eldest son and heir who also married a cousin in the Agnew family.

9.6 The Williams-Drummond, Agnew and Clifton Families

Sir James Hamlyn Williams-Drummond 4th Bt Hawthornden CB (1857-1913)

James (68) was born at Clovelly Court on 13 January 1857 and was educated privately and at Eton. As we have seen, his father (73) died aged only 51 on 11 May 1866 when James (known as Joe) was only 9 years old; so he then succeeded his father as the 4th Baronet of Hawthornden. His mother, Lady Eleanor (71), died aged only 47 on 18 August 1872 at her London flat (when Joe was 15 years old), and his grandmother, Lady Mary (61A), died two years later in 1874. The death of both his parents at such a young and formative age must have been a huge shock to Joe and to all his siblings.

As we have seen, under his mother's will his uncle and aunt, Sir John and Lady Gussie Ferguson Davie, were appointed his principal guardians. It is clear that his guardians were successful in supporting Joe at this young age and had a material influence on his upbringing. In Chapter 1.1, I have described the occasion of Joe's attainment of his majority on 13 January 1878 when he formally inherited the Edwinsford Estate and Hawthornden Castle. The attainment of his majority by an heir to an important estate particularly where such heir thereby also became the new landlord was an event which the county gentry, friends of the family, tenants and neighbours all gladly enjoyed.

It was an opportunity for the tenants to show respect and support for their landlord and likewise an opportunity for the heir to confirm his continuing commitment to the estate and his tenants. Joe's attainment of his majority involved four days of uninterrupted enjoyment at Edwinsford which was described in detail[296] in the local press.

Before continuing with Joe's life and career I must first refer to a mystery concerning the birth[297] of Elizabeth Davies (1874-1934). Her grandparents, Benjamin and Mary Davies, lived at Maesyrhaidd in Cwrt y Cadno in 1861 with their young family although their unmarried daughter, Mary Davies, was not then at home and was probably a maid elsewhere. On 17 February 1874 Mary Davies gave birth (probably aged in her mid 20s) to her daughter Elizabeth in the very cold and confined caretaker's room under the old schoolroom of the Vestry of Cwrt Methodist Chapel; the Elders of the Chapel acted compassionately given the circumstances of an unmarried mother and the mores of that time. Elizabeth (and her elder brother Thomas (b1867)) were brought up by her grandparents at Glanrhyd near Maesyrhaidd in Cwrt y Cadno. By 1891 Elizabeth was living with John Davies nearby in Pantglas described as his daughter and housemaid. She later married a Thomas Davies and raised a large family of 11 children. We know little of Mary herself although she might be the Mary Davies shown as living in Glanrhyd in 1901 aged 54. The mystery concerns Elizabeth's true father since I have been told by many sources (handed down through the generations) that her father was not John Davies (1823-97) who was born in Llwyndiriaid, who is named as her father on Elizabeth's 1894 marriage certificate and who left her £250 in his will. The strong suggestion is that she was the daughter of Sir James Drummond of Edwinsford or of one of the other sons of that family. Although possible it seems highly unlikely that Sir James was the father since in 1874 when Mary gave birth, Sir James (born in January 1857) was aged 17 and still at school, both his parents had died and he was being looked after by his uncle and aunt, Sir John and Lady Ferguson Davie, and he only visited Edwinsford for a couple of months each year during his holidays (as related in Chapter 1.1). As for other members of the Edwinsford family, Sir James's brothers were too young so I conclude that this rumour which has been passed down through a number of local families is very probably a myth; whilst Elizabeth's father may not have been John Davies, he was not a member of the Edwinsford family. So Elizabeth and her descendants do not have any English or Scottish royal blood in their veins.

Joe had already joined the army before attaining his majority and then joined the Grenadier Guards (1878-83) at Chelsea Barracks in which his father had served as a Captain. His London address was 4 Albert Mansions. He then joined the County Militia Artillery and later served as Lt-Col commanding and Honorary Colonel of the Carmarthen Royal Field Artillery (Reserve) as well as of the General Reserve of Officers, and President of the Carmarthen Territorial Force Association. He served as the Llansawel and Talley representative on the Carmarthenshire County Council after the Local Government Act came into force, as Sheriff of Carmarthenshire in 1885 and then as Lord Lieutenant and Custos Rotulorum of Carmarthenshire (the third member of the family to hold that office) from 7 July 1898 to his death on 15 June 1913. He served as a magistrate in Midlothian and in Carmarthenshire. He was a Unionist politically and served as President of the West Carmarthenshire Conservative Association. He was also a stauch Churchman. He chaired the Talley and Llansawel School Boards and the Cambrian Archaeological Association.

On 30 January 1889 at the Parish Church of St Mark in North Audley Street Joe aged 32 (described as of 20 North Audley Street) married his distant cousin Mrs Madeline Clifton (née Agnew)(1847-1907)(67) aged 41 of 35 Hill Street London, eldest daughter of Sir Andrew Agnew 8th Bt MP of Lochnaw (1818-92), and the widow of Thomas Henry Clifton (1845-80) with whom she had seven surviving children. The marriage certificate was witnessed by her father Sir Andrew Agnew Bt and by Arthur 11th Baron Kinnaird, who was the husband of her sister Mary and whose son would later marry her daughter Frances. The vicar was Joe's brother in law, Rev Thomas Newton Leeke (1854-1933) married to his sister Bella (74), who was then vicar of Inkberrow. The Agnew cousins are described at the end of Chapter 8.4 including the 13 children (of whom Lady Madeline was one) of Sir Andrew Agnew and Lady Louisa Noel (66).

[296] The Welshman; Llanelly Guardian

[297] David Lewis: *Family Histories (2012) p220-1,233,239,243,333*

On his wedding day[298] in accordance with custom Joe gave dinners at the Black Lion and Angel Inns in Llansawel to some 175 of his local tenants and friends; tea and cakes and other festivities were provided to about the same number of children at the Schoolroom. When Joe and Madeline returned to Edwinsford on 21 February after their honeymoon they were met with banners of welcome from tenants and friends, the horses were taken from their carriage and the tenants then pulled the carriage with ropes from the village to Edwinsford where Joe and Madeline were presented with a silver chandelier by Mr James James of Ynysau (see Chapter 28.6) on behalf of them all. Other gifts were made to them too. In the evening huge bonfires were lit on the Dinas, Caio, Talley, Pigyn Syr Nicholas, and Abergorlech peaks. The following day there were sports in the fields near Edwinsford including running, jumping, throwing, donkey and obstacle races, ladies races, and then horse races. The next day the cantata "John Bull" was performed by the Llansawel Schoolchildren under the leadership of the headmaster, DB Evans, accompanied by Miss Davies of Froodvale. Joe thanked them all in Welsh and was joined by his agent and adviser David Long Price of Talley House in thanking the organising committee.

© Hon John Rous *Sir James (Joe) in Grenadier Guards c1878*

Carmarthen Royal Field Artillery

[298] Carmarthen Journal (1 March 1889)

© Hon John Rous *Sir James (Joe)*

© Hon John Rous *Lady Madeline*

© Hon John Rous *Sir James (Joe)*

© Hon John Rous *Sir James (Joe)*

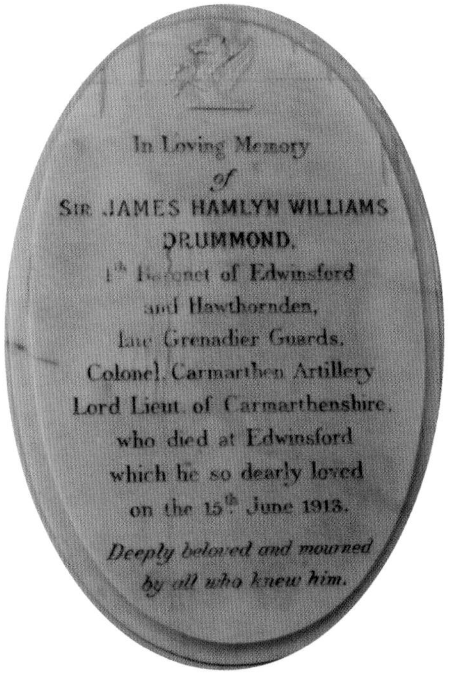

Memorial in Talley Church

Arms

Madeline and Joe were cousins because they had the same great grandfather, Sir James Hamlyn Williams Bt MP of Clovelly and Edwinsford (1765-1829)(60). Joe's younger brother, Francis (Dudley) Williams-Drummond (76), married Madeline's youngest sister Marguerite (67A) the following year in 1890. Joe and Madeline would have met in London where Madeline was living as a widow. What is perhaps perplexing is why Joe as a very eligible bachelor aged 32 would marry a widow nearly 10 years older than himself who already had seven children. Perhaps the answer lies in the love letters[299] which they exchanged some of which still survive in a damaged state and were found in a box in an outhouse at Edwinsford in about 1977.

Joe and Madeline resided mostly at Edwinsford or in London although for many years they spent the months of January to April at Hawthornden[300] where they carried out extensive alterations and improvements in 1895, particulary in the upper storey and gardens. When in London Joe made full use of his Clubs which included White's, the Guards and the Travellers. Joe was a keen yachtsman, the owner of the 63 ton yawl "Edwina" and a member of the Royal Yacht Squadron Club. His love for Edwinsford exceeded all other things and he devoted himself to its interests as well as to his many county interests and public duties particulary during the last 25 years of his life. As can be seen from the Edwinsford Estate accounts of 1903 and the list of Edwinsford Estate properties in Chapter 16 he and his land agent took an active and hands-on approach to estate management. His loyal tenants were a great comfort to Joe and when all his stock of hay was destroyed[301] by fire in 1906 he received a touching delegation of tenants expressing their sympathies to whom he replied in kind in English and Welsh.

The Penygareg (Pengarreg) silver and lead mines[302], which were a few hundred yards to the west of the Talley Lower Lake (as can be seen on the 1886 map) within the Edwinsford Estate were operated between 1863 and 1865 and again between 1885 and 1891. Joe would not permit the effluent from the mines to run into the lakes and kill his fish so he had a trench cut all the way from Penygareg along and below

299 Dane Garrod a philatelist has acquired some of these letters and has been researching their background for some years. They were found in about 1977 in an Edwinsford outhouse
300 FDWD: *Annals p27*
301 Evening Express (15 Sept 1906)
302 Alun Morgan's talk in the Edwinsford Arms 1992

the road down to Talley Church, quite an engineering achievement. By the lake there were two boathouses and the canal which had been built earlier linked both lakes. Joe and Madeline would continue his parents' tradition of travelling by boat down to Church on a Sunday morning. In the lakes there are signs of a pre-historic lake dwelling[303], possibly a crannog, discovered by Rev Charles Chidlow; it is a mound of about 100ft diameter with a height of some 10ft with a trench running round the base. When the level of the lakes, which long ago were probably one lake, was higher than that currently the mound with its platform would have stood out as an island.

On 22 August 1902 Joe and Madeline entertained[304] some 2,000 residents, tenants, schoolchildren, and friends at Edwinsford on the occasion of her birthday to rejoice in the recent coronation of Edward VII and the peace in South Africa. The Shrubbery Avenue running along the Cothi in the gardens was laid out with tables galore bearing food and drink and decorated by the head gardener, Thomas Evans. Coronation medals and mugs were distributed to all the children. This was followed with rustic games and then fireworks, all organised by Lewis Bowen (bailiff) and Charles Needs (butler) with the Llandeilo Brass Band playing to the delight of all.

Joe was created a Companion of the Order of the Bath (CB) in 1909.

Joe and Madeline had only one child, his first and her eighth, James (Jimmy) Hamlyn Williams-Drummond (1891-1970)(69) described in Chapter 10.2. He succeeded as 5th Bt Hawthornden on his father's death aged 56 on 15 June 1913 at Edwinsford from cardiac disease as certified by Dr John Thomas Price MD. His youngest brother, Sir Francis (Dudley) Williams-Drummond (76), was present at the death. He was buried at Talley on 18 June in the family plot and there is a monument in his memory ("deeply beloved and mourned by all who knew him"). His beloved wife Madeline had died before him aged 60 in 1907. At his funeral[305] the route from Edwinsford to Talley Church was lined by red uniformed Grenadier Guardsmen, the 4th Welsh Regiment, and the Territorials. Crowds of people attended and Talley was full of vehicles with residents, tenants and friends paying their respects. The coffin of estate oak made by the estate carpenter was drawn by the estate workers on a cart from the mansion to Talley and then buried in the family plot covered with the Union Jack. The chief mourners included Joe's good friend and neighbour, General Sir Jimmy Hills-Johnes VC of Dolaucothi, and the family members from London and Clovelly followed by county representatives including magistrates. The service was led by the Bishop of Swansea assisted by the local vicars. Numerous tributes followed his death and it is clear that he was admired for his affable disposition, integrity, sense of duty, and unfailing courtesy; a much missed Lord Lieutenant.

In his will dated 7 December 1904 (probate granted on 8 October 1913) Joe appointed his two brothers, Hugh (75) and Dudley (76), as well as his deceased wife Madeline as executors. His gross estate was valued at £157,495 and his net personal estate at £13,776. He made some pecuniary legacies and settled his estates including Edwinsford and Hawthornden on his trustees with the intent that they be inherited in the usual way by his sons by seniority in age in tail failing which to his brother Hugh's sons failing which to his brother Dudley's sons all by seniority in age. As stated Joe had one son so the estates were held by his trustees for James (Jimmy) Hamlyn Williams-Drummond (69) when he reached 21 (which he had on 25 May 1912). Brother Hugh had a daughter and brother Dudley had one son (who succeeded as the 6th Bt Hawthornden in 1970) and two daughters, but as we shall see the Edwinsford and Hawthornden estates did not pass in 1970 to the 6th Baronet as Joe would have wished.

Lady Madeline Williams-Drummond (1847-1907)

Madeline (67) was born on 22 August 1847 at Exton Hall in Oakham, Rutland, the family seat of her mother's family, the Noels. Her grandfather was Charles Noel MP, Lord Barham and 1st Earl of Gainsborough, while her grandmother was Arabella Hamlyn Williams (63), Lady Barham, hence the blood relationship with the Hamlyn Williams and Williams-Drummond family. Her parents were Lady Louisa Noel (1822-83), eldest Noel daughter, and Sir Andrew Agnew MP 8th Bt of Lochnaw Castle in Wigtownshire in Scotland (1818-92); he was commissioned as an Ensign in 1835, served in the 93rd Foot

303 Arthur Mee (1892); Lynn Hughes: *Carmarthenshire Anthology p199*
304 Carmarthen Journal (29 Aug 1902)
305 Carmarthen Journal (20 June 1913)

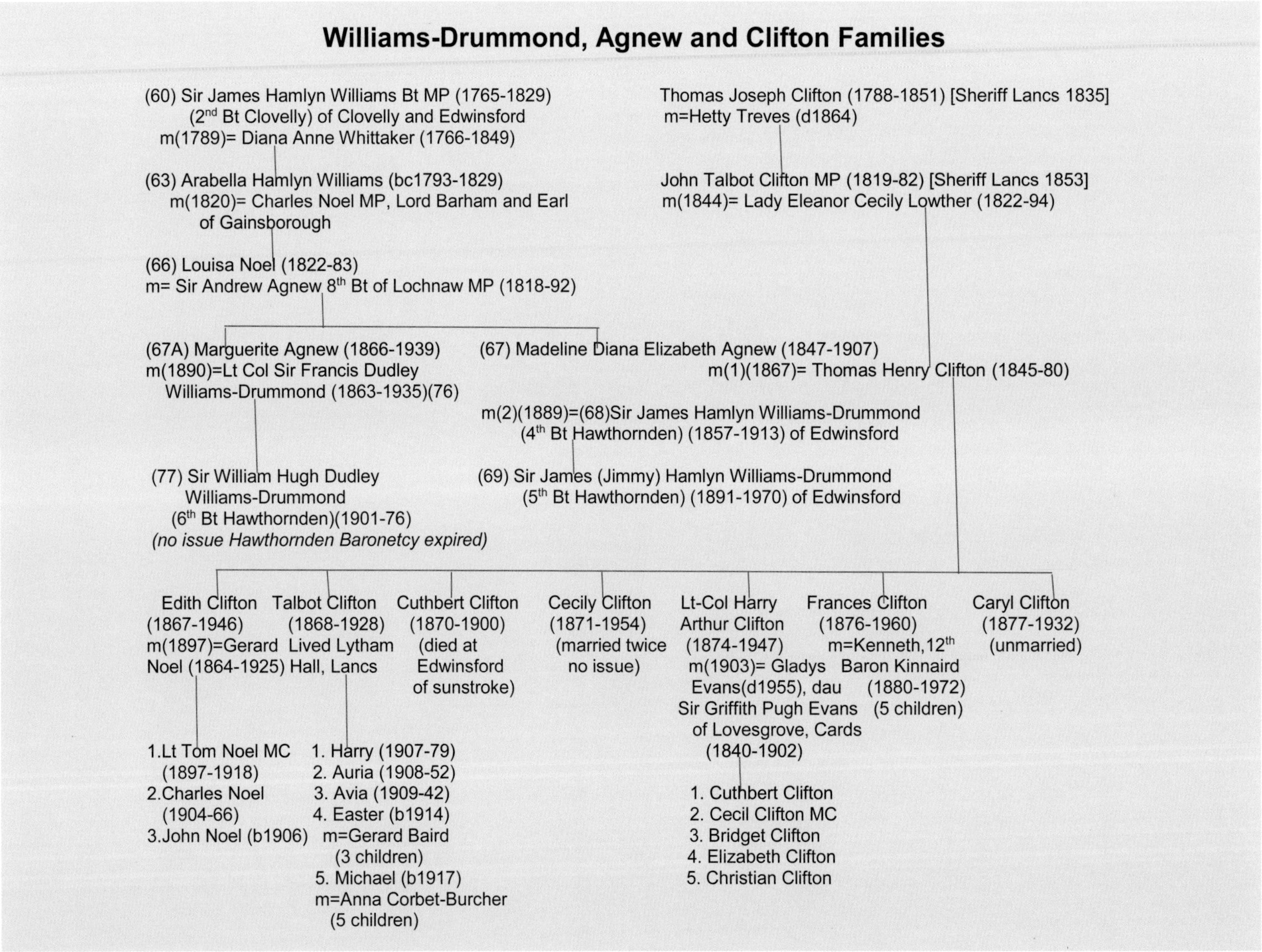

in Canada in 1838, was promoted to Captain in 1841 and then served in the 4th Light Dragoons. He married Lady Louisa in 1846 and succeeded to the baronetcy[306] in 1849. He served as MP for Wigtownshire 1856-68. He died after his wife aged 74 on 25 March 1892 at his home in Scotland.

Madeline and her 12 siblings were brought up in Scotland and London although it is unclear whether or not she was educated by a private tutor. On 7 February 1867 aged 19 she married Thomas Henry (Harry) Clifton (1845-80) at St George's Church, Hanover Square in London. Harry, who suffered from ill health, was the son of John Talbot Clifton MP (1819-82) of Lytham Hall, Lytham St Annes in

[306] Sir Andrew Agnew: *The Agnews of Lochnaw (1864)*

Lancashire, who served as MP for North Lancashire 1844-47 and as Sheriff of Lancashire in 1853. Lytham Hall is now a grade 1 listed fine Georgian Palladian style house one mile from the centre of Lytham and set in 78 acres of wooded parkland. It was built by Sir Thomas Clifton in 1752-64 to replace a previous house on the site, the seat of the Clifton family[307] (arms: *sable on a bend argent three mullets pierced gules*) since early in the 17th century. The Cliftons had been Roman Catholics and Royalists during the Civil War and had had their estates partially sequestrated and fined. Their baronectcy expired in 1694 and eventually the manors of Clifton and Westby which they owned descended to Thomas Joseph Clifton (1788-1851) who became a Protestant in 1831 and served as Sheriff of Lancashire in 1835. His son, Col John Talbot Clifton MP (1819-82), described above died in 1882 in Algiers having returned to the Roman Catholic faith. His son, Thomas Henry (Harry) Clifton (1845-80) who married Madeline died aged only 35 and before his father, so Lytham Hall was inherited by his and Madeline's eldest son, John Talbot Clifton (1868-1928) who was only 14. Since 1997 the Hall and estate have been owned by Lytham Town Trust which in 2000 leased it to the Heritage Trust to carry out a major restoration of the Hall and Jacobean courtyard.

Madeline and Harry had seven children, who would become half-brothers and sisters of her eighth child, Sir Jimmy Hamlyn Williams-Drummond (5th Bt Hawthornden)(69), by her second marriage to Joe (68) in 1889. The half siblings were often at Edwinsford after their mother's marriage to Joe in 1889 as can be seen from the census returns for 1891 in Chapter 12. They were:

(1) Madeline Edith (1867-1946) who in 1897 married Gerard Cecil Noel (1864-1925), a cousin and son of her great uncle Gerard Noel MP (1823-1911). They lived at Cottesmore, Oakham, Rutland and had three sons: (a) Lt Tom Noel MC and bar who fought in the Great War and served as a Lieutenant in the King's Own Scottish Borderers and then as a fighter ace with 24 kills in the Royal Air Force and was shot down on 22 August 1918 and is buried in the Perth cemetery in Belgium (his citation for conspicuous gallantry after his death says that in four days he and his pilot destroyed seven enemy machines and drove three out of control) ; (b) Charles Noel (1904-66) unmarried; and (c) John (b1906) who married Nancy Hood and served as a Captain in the Royal Artillery Territorials and as a Flying Officer in the RAF;

(2) Talbot Clifton (1868-1928) the heir who inherited Lytham Hall from his grandfather. He was educated at Eton and Magdalene College Cambridge, and served as a Lieutenant in 3rd Battalion, Loyal North Lancashire Regiment. Talbot was "an eccentric chap of many tastes, mostly expensive ones, and of considerable ability" but he was a reckless spender, bought a yacht, travelled widely and had an affair with the infamous Lillie Langtry[308]. He was an avid sailer and motorist, received several speeding summonses, and used to drive down to Edwinsford to see his mother. He travelled widely abroad seemingly without regard to expense. He met in Peru and then married Violet Beauclerk (1883-1961)[309] in 1907 and they lived at Lytham Hall (1908-22) and had five children. In 1917 he was commissioned as a lieutenant in the RNVR, went to Ireland, bought Kylemore House in Connemara and nearly got killed by Sinn Fein. In 1922 he had to flee Ireland and bought the Kildalton Estate of 16,000 acres with a castle on the southern end of the Isle of Islay in Scotland; he never returned to live at Lytham Hall. His heir, Harry Clifton (1907-79), was a film producer who spent some years in Hollywood during the 1930s. He disentailed the estate and was as extravagant as his forbears but with no control over his spending. During WW2 Lytham Hall was a hospital for soldiers. In the 1950s Harry sold Lytham Hall and its 8,000 acres estate. He had received some £3.5m in total from his land sales over the years and spent the family's entire wealth. He died[310] a nomadic white-bearded recluse, once one of the richest landowners in the country, aged 72 in 1979 in Brighton almost penniless;

(3) Cuthbert Clifton (1870-1900) also got into severe debt at a young age, had to resign his army commission and became the black sheep of the family. Despite the wishes of her land agent Madeline often supported Cuthbert financially and in 1896 even bought a sheep station for him in Queensland which was a disaster. In 1900 he went to fight in South Africa but became ill and had to return to Edwinsford

[307] John Kennedy: *The Clifton Chronicle (1990)* the definitive history of the Clifton family
[308] John Kennedy p111-4 for their love letters
[309] Violet Mary Clifton: *The Book of Talbot (1933)*. She was a writer who wrote this colourful biography of her husband
[310] John Kennedy p284

where on 14 October 1900 he died aged 30 from the effects of sunstroke received in South Africa. He is buried at Talley in the family plot;

(4) Constance Gertrude (Cecily) Clifton (1871-1954) who was born in London. She was married twice without issue: (a) in 1891 to Capt Hon James Cumming-Bruce (1867-99), son of 5th Baron Thurlow, who was killed serving with the Black Watch at Magersfontein during the Boer War in South Africa, and (b) in 1910 to Brig-Gen Edward Cuthbertson CMG, MVO (d1942). She served as a Woman of the Bedchamber[311] to HRH Princess Christian of Schleswig-Holstein. She lived at Jermyns in Romsey, Hampshire;

(5) Lt-Col Harry Arthur Clifton (1874-1947)[312] who fought in the Boer War 1899-1902 with Bethune's Mounted Infantry[313] and gained the rank of Captain in the 7th Dragoon Guards. He also fought at Gallipoli and in Egypt. Later he commanded the Scottish Horse. On 2 January 1903 he married Gladys Evans (d1955), the daughter of Sir Griffith (Gruffy) Pugh Evans (1840-1902) of Lovesgrove[314], near Aberystwyth in Cardiganshire, who had a fascinating career as a barrister in Calcutta and came from a very high achieving family who won three VCs and six DSOs. Harry and Gladys had five children;

(6) Frances Clifton (1876-1960) who in 1903 married Kenneth 12th Baron Kinnaird (1880-1972), the son of the husband of Madeline's sister, Mary Alma Agnew. They had five children; and

(7) Charles Caryl Clifton (1877-1932) who fought in the Mashonaland Campaign in 1897, in the Boer War in Natal where he gained the rank of Lieutenant in the Royal Scots Fusiliers, and in the Great War. On 15 November 1902 on his return to Edwinsford from South Africa he was presented[315] with an address from the local tenants and residents by a local committee including John Thomas of Blaenug Farm (the oldest tenant-see Chapter 24.14), Rev JH Lloyd of Talley, Rev J Phillips of Llansawel, and Dr TJ Evans of Llansawel. In the 1911 census return in Chapter 12 he can be seen staying at Edwinsford with his stepfather Joe who was by then a widower. He died unmarried aged 54 on 28 February 1932.

Following the death of her first husband at Lytham Hall in 1880, Madeline (as her husband's sole executrix) and her seven young children lived in London[316] at 35 Hill Street London (bought for her by the family trustees) at the insistence of her mother in law, Lady Cecily Clifton, rather than at Lytham Hall in Lancashire. Madeline received £2,000 pa, but her father in law had left debts and the Clifton Estate land agent, Thomas Fair, had to make economies to pay off the bank debt. In London Madeline had good aristocratic family and social connections and became friendly with many ladies in London society. She was also befriended by HRH Princess Helena (Princess Christian of Schleswig-Holstein) (1846-1923) who was the third daughter of Queen Victoria and married in 1866 the impoverished Prince Christian of Schleswig-Holstein; they lived at Cumberland Lodge in Windsor Park and Princess Helena was the most active member of the royal family in carrying out an extensive programme of royal engagements and attending charity events and was one of the founders of the Red Cross. Madeline's daughter, Cecily, became a Woman of the Bedchamber to the Princess.

By all accounts[317] Madeline was a very gracious lady who knew the names of every child on the Edwinsford Estate farms which she visited frequently armed with a basket of goodies to hand round. Following her death there were numerous press articles[318] with tributes to her good works, her universal charity of thought and action, her untiring labour in the interest of the poor, and her unselfish, generous and noble character. She showed no partisanship and helped all irrespective of their politics or religion. She was a keen attender at Talley Church.

---

311 Women of the Bedchamber are junior in rank to the Mistress of the Robes and Ladies of the Bedchamber. The latter two are normally only required for ceremonial events while the former are usually in regular attendance. They are all known as Ladies in Waiting

312 Hugh Clifton

313 He was welcomed back to Edwinsford after the Boer War by a mounted procession of tenants and a public presentation followed by fireworks, as was Major Quentin Agnew DSO, Madeline's brother— Weekly Mail (30 August 1902)

314 David Lewis: *Dolaucothi and Brunant p199, 217-9*

315 Carmarthen Journal (21 Nov 1902)

316 John Kennedy p104

317 W Barry Evans: *Y Llychau (November 2011); Weekly Mail (26 Oct 1907)*

318 Weekly Mail (9 Nov 1907); Evening Express (24 Oct 1907)

Madeline had been unwell for some time and had gone to Folkestone to recuperate and then went to London en route to Edwinsford. She died on 19 October 1907 aged 60 of septic pharyngitis at 13 Southwick Crescent, Hyde Park Square in London with Joe present at her side. Her body was taken down to her beloved Edwinsford[319] and she was buried on 24 October at Talley in the family plot. She was very much loved and admired locally at Edwinsford for her good works and charitable activities with the poor and others; she served on numerous local committees and for example founded the Girls' Friendly Society in Llansawel and Talley which had some 170 members. She will be particularly remembered for the enormous time and energy she put into the founding and building of the West Wales Alltymynydd Sanatorium[320] for tuberculosis (consumption) near Llanybyther which cost £8,000. The foundation stone was laid on 25 April 1905 by her friend HRH Princess Helena who in company with her daughter, Princess Victoria, paid a four day visit to Edwinsford[321]. An oak tree was planted on the lawn at Edwinsford to commemorate the occasion. The whole event was of course recorded at length in the press[322] recounting Princess Helena's leaving Cumberland Lodge and travelling to Llandeilo where she was warmly welcomed with an illuminated address by the Lord Lieutenant and many spectators; the journey to Edwinsford where the royal party stayed; the journey from Edwinsford to Alltymynydd with four carriages of royalty, ladies in waiting and the hosts; the laying of the foundation stone by Princess Helena in the presence of the three Lord Lieutenants of Carmarthenshire (Sir James), Cardiganshire (Col Davies Evans) and Pembrokeshire (Earl Cawdor); and the lunch at Highmead as guests of the Lord Lieutenant and then a concert there with a choir from Talley which had been practising for months led by Caradog Davies, the village grocer. Madeline had played a vital part in raising funds to finance the building of the sanatorium and was publicly thanked for all her efforts. Sadly she died before the building was opened on 20 July 1908 by Princess Helena who returned to Carmarthenshire for the event. The family continued for many years to donate large baskets of fruit and vegetables from the Edwinsford gardens and greenhouses to the hospital.

Funeral of Lady Madeline at Talley 1907

319 Welsh Gazette (24 Oct 1907); Carmarthen Journal (1 Nov 1907)

320 DH James: *Guide to Llanybyther and a short history of the foundation of Alltymynydd Sanatorium (1908)*

321 The Princess's room was redecorated with a pretty blue wallpaper covered with pictures of peacocks—Brenda James: *Fond Memories of Talley (1994) p38;* Thomas Lloyd: *Tearful Memories of a Royal Visit CH (1985)*

322 Cardiff Times and South Wales Weekly (29 April 1905)

Royal Visit to West Wales 1905

Under Madeline's will[323] dated 16 January 1900 and codicil dated 7 June 1902 she left her personal effects to her husband Joe; Lytham Hall to her son John Talbot after the expiry of her life interest together with the advowsons of Blackpool and St Anne's on the Sea; other property to her son Charles; and £10,000 to each of her children Madeline, Cecily, Frances, Harry, Cuthbert and Charles (her eighth child Sir Jimmy Williams-Drummond was of course the principal beneficiary under her husband Joe's will).

Lt-Col Sir Francis Dudley Williams-Drummond KBE (1863-1935)

Dudley (76) was the youngest brother of Sir Joe (68) and the youngest child of Sir James Williams-Drummond (73) and Lady Eleanor (71). He was born at Edwinsford on 27 June 1863 and educated at Eton in the family tradition. He then went on to Trinity College Cambridge (BA 1884). His father died when he was only three years old and his mother died in 1872 when he was only nine, so he was brought up like his older siblings in the care of his guardians, Sir John and Lady Ferguson Davie (72), his uncle and aunt.

On 23 July 1890 he married Marguerite Violet Maude Agnew (1866-1939)(67A) the youngest of the 13 Agnew children and cousins; he would have known her as a child and more recently because his eldest brother, Joe (68), had married her eldest sister Madeline (67) some 18 months earlier. They had two daughters and a son, William (77), later to become the 6th Bt Hawthornden as described in Chapter 10.2.

Sir Dudley Williams-Drummond

Dudley 1881

323 Carmarthen Weekly Reporter (20 March 1908)

Dudley was a land agent by profession and later became the agent for the Cawdor Estate; he was also the agent[324] who dealt with all the property dealings of the Edwinsford Estate including the sale of the Derllys Estate in 1915 and of some of the Edwinsford farms and small holdings in 1918 and 1919. He contributed greatly to public life in Carmarthenshire. Initially he served in the Carmarthen Artillery gaining the rank of Major at which time he lived at Portiscliff, Ferryside, where his great uncle, Rear Admiral Charles Hamlyn Williams (62), had lived after it was given to him on his wedding by his mother in 1833. He later moved to live until his death at Hafodneddyn, Llangathen near Llandeilo where he and Marguerite brought up their family. Hafodneddyn[325] was originally the seat of the ap Owen (Bowen) family in the 16th century who were descendants of David Fychan of Rhydodyn (28). The house was acquired by the Mansel family at the end of the 17th century who built a larger house on the site, and later sold it to Dr Charles Morgan in 1838 on whose death it was sold to the Philipps family of Aberglasney. By 1900 the house was a large building with two main storeys plus an attic storey, and a high tower with four Scottish type turrets with iron work on top. It must have looked a little like Hawthornden, which perhaps attracted Francis to buy it.

He later served as Lt-Col of the Carmarthen Field Artillery, as a member of the Royal Company of Archers being the King's Bodyguard of Scotland, as Chairman of the Court of Quarter and County Sessions, as a magistrate for many years, as a Deputy Lieutenant of the county, as Chairman of the Territorial Force Association of the county, and for many years as a member and then as an Alderman and Chairman (1924) of the Carmarthenshire County Council for which he received an OBE. During the Great War he served as Agricultural Commissioner for all Wales and then as Food Controller for the seven counties in South Wales; in 1919 he was awarded a CBE for his War duties. He was also a member of the Government's Advisory and Reconstruction Committee on Forestry. In 1927 his CBE was upgraded to a KBE.

He was a keen historian and wrote his Annals[326] in 1924, which he circulated privately and which have been most helpful to me in my research for this book. He was also keen on shooting, fishing, yachting and motoring; when he was in London he used the Travellers Club like his father. He had a large collection of land maps which on his death were deposited with his solicitors, DM Charles.[327]

He died on 26 September 1935 and was buried in the family plot at Talley. His wife Marguerite, who was born on 9 January 1866, died on 3 April 1939 and was also buried in Talley next to her husband.

---

324 The auditors of both the Edwinsford and Cawdor Estates in Carmarthenshire were Frank C Bevan & Co—see Stan Page: *An insight into the first 100 years of Bevan & Buckland accountants*

325 Francis Jones: *Historic Carmarthenshire Homes p90*

326 Copies are deposited in the British Library and the National Museum of Wales Library

327 David Charles bought Aberglasney from the Pugh Evans family, who were cousins of the Cliftons via Gladys Evans (d1955), daughter of Sir Gruffy Pugh Evans of Lovesgrove—David Lewis: *Dolaucothi and Brunant p219*

10. War and Decline

10.1 Wales and Carmarthenshire

Before the Great War at the turn of the century much of Wales remained depressed and impoverished notwithstanding the great achievements of the industrial revolution; those working outside the coal, slate, tin, copper, and rail industries did not share in their spoils. Life in farming continued to be difficult with increasing rents and low wages. Then came the First World War (1914-18) during which many men from Carmarthenshire served their country with distinction, many died in each parish as can be seen from the numerous war memorials, and many women did their duty in the factories or fields or in the medical or non-combative services. Many men who stayed at home worked on the farms (one male farmer was allowed to stay to run the farm to provide essential food) or in other reserved occupations. Some of the great houses were used as hospitals and Aberglasney was a German POW camp.

After 1918 life would never be the same again for the majority of the population. The Spanish flu reached the UK; world-wide it killed well over 50 million people including some 228,000 in the UK, more than the total number of people killed during the Great War.

Women suffragettes had become more and more vocal leading up to the war and in 1918 women over the age of 30 who were either a member or married to a member of the local government register were given the franchise for the first time and entitled to be elected as MPs. They would have to wait until 1928 to have the vote on the same terms as men.

David Lloyd George, who had served as Minister of Munitions in 1915 and then as Prime Minister in 1916 effectively split the Liberal Party and was re-elected in the 1918 Election leading a Tory dominated coalition government which lasted until 1922. Liberalism was on the wane, while socialism in the form of the Labour Party which had taken many years to get a foothold slowly achieved political success and in the 1922 Election gained some 40 per cent of the Welsh vote. The General Strike in 1926 may have lasted only a few days but its failure led to further unhappiness and strife. The Great Depression followed starting with the Wall Street Crash in 1929 and lasted 10 years during which the banking system collapsed and many families lost their homes and savings. Misfortune befell many of the gentry families and led to the decline, sale or insolvency of their estates as we shall now see.

10.2 Edwinsford—Decline and Fall

The Finance Act 1894 imposed for the first time a new controversial tax on death, estate duty. It is difficult to overestimate the effect this had on the gentry families of Britain over the following decades and how it developed not only as a source of revenue for the State but also how the State tried to make it an instrument for the redistribution of wealth. Initially the rate of tax was only 1 per cent on estates between £100 and £500 rising to 8 per cent for estates over £1 million. Eventually over a period of seven decades the rate would rise to 75 per cent on the slice of the estate above £500,000.

In addition, the economic consequences of the Great War for Britain and for the landed families in particular with many of them dead or badly wounded, heavy employment and other overheads and only modest rent rolls resulted in many such families having to sell their estates. The effect on many landed estates over time was devastating. It is estimated that between 1918 and 1922 a quarter of the landed gentry's property in Britain was sold. The traditional life style for the landed gentry of country pursuits such as hunting, weekend parties and balls with a large domestic service to enable this to continue changed dramatically and by 1939 had disappeared. By 1950 the National Trust had acquired 42 of the larger country houses usually because of estate duty liabilities which could be saved by gifting such houses to this charity. Today less than 1 per cent of employees work in agriculture and Britain has not been self sufficient for food for over a century.

In the upper Cothi valley the gentry[328] were faced with the same issues as elsewhere. George Lloyd (1866-1926) had put his Brunant Estate[329] up for sale in 1918 immediately after the War in the desire that his tenants should have the opportunity to buy their freeholds, and to a very great extent that desire had been fulfilled to the benefit of all. At neighbouring Dolaucothi Lady Betha Johnes (1834-1927) was faced with the dilemma of what to do given that she had no heir; eventually she left the Dolaucothi Estate to a clerical cousin, who was unable to manage the estate properly and donated it to the National Trust who oversaw the destruction of the derelict mansion in 1954-5. So what happened at Edwinsford and Hawthornden?

Sir James Hamlyn Williams-Drummond 5th Bt Hawthornden (1891-1970)

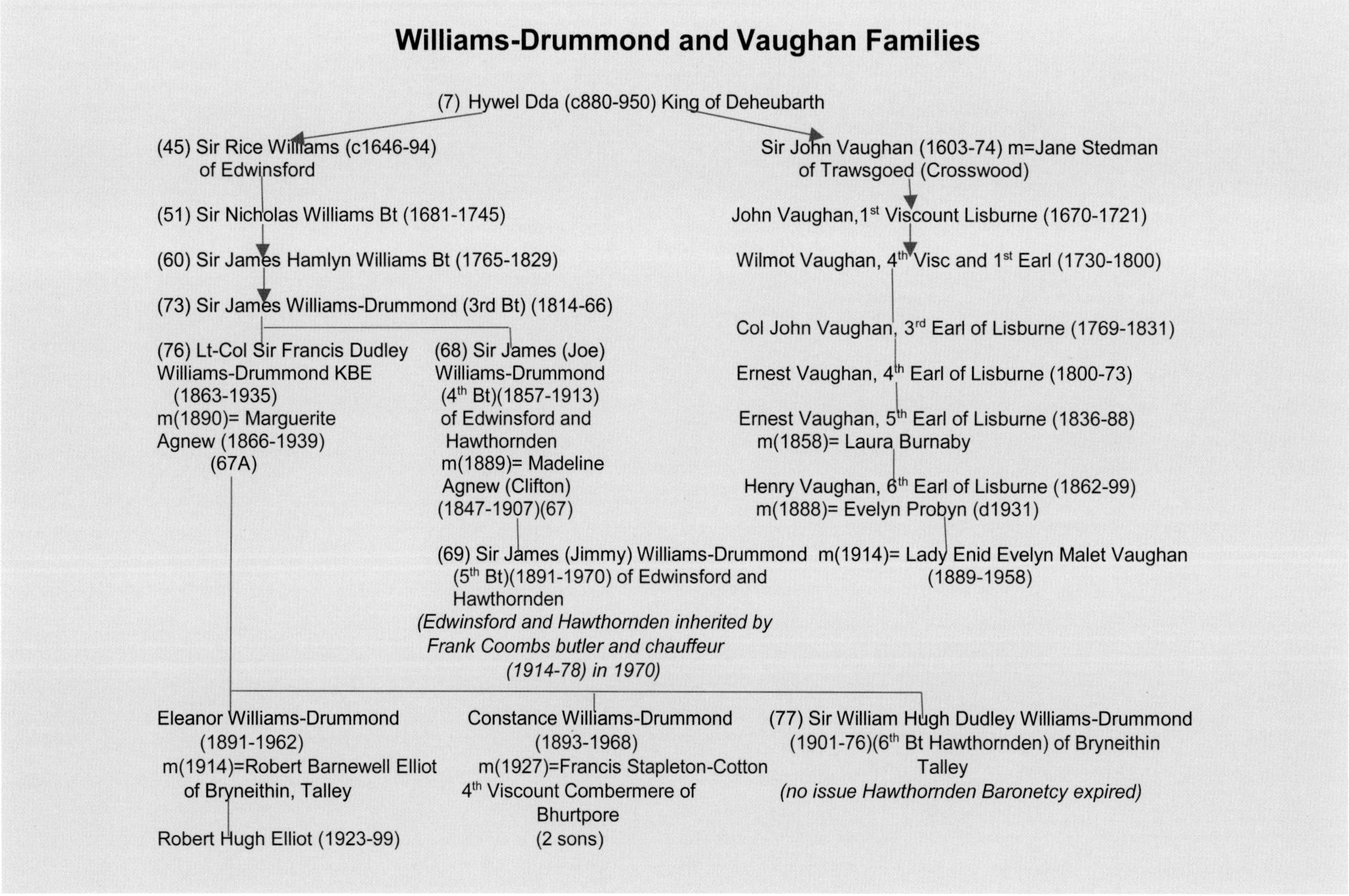

---

328 David Lewis: *Dolaucothi and Brunant (2016)*

329 Carmarthen Journal 17 October 1919

Sir James (Jimmy) Hamlyn Williams-Drummond (69) was the only child of Sir Joe (4th Bt) and Lady Madeline. He was born on 25 May 1891 at 7 Stratford Place in London and then educated at Wellington House Prep School in Westgate on Sea in Kent before going on to Eton. His mother Madeline died aged 60 on 19 October 1907 when he was only 15 years old and this was a great blow for him. Apparently[330] he absconded frequently from Eton and the butler at Edwinsford was given the job of taking him to Llandeilo Station to get the train back to Windsor, but he then used to leave the train at Llanwrda and walk home from there; he was obviously unhappy at school. His traditional coming of age celebrations[331] locally at Edwinsford on 25 May 1912, to which all estate workers and tenants were invited, were very similar to those experienced by his father in 1878 as described in Chapter 1.1 with dinners for the locals, blazing bonfires on the surrounding hilltops and sports events, although his father was still alive to support him together with his Clifton half brothers and sisters. The following year his father died of a heart attack aged only 56 and under his will appointed his two brothers, Hugh (75) and Dudley (76), as his executors and trustees. Jimmy lived in the shadow and memory of his high achieving father for the rest of his life.

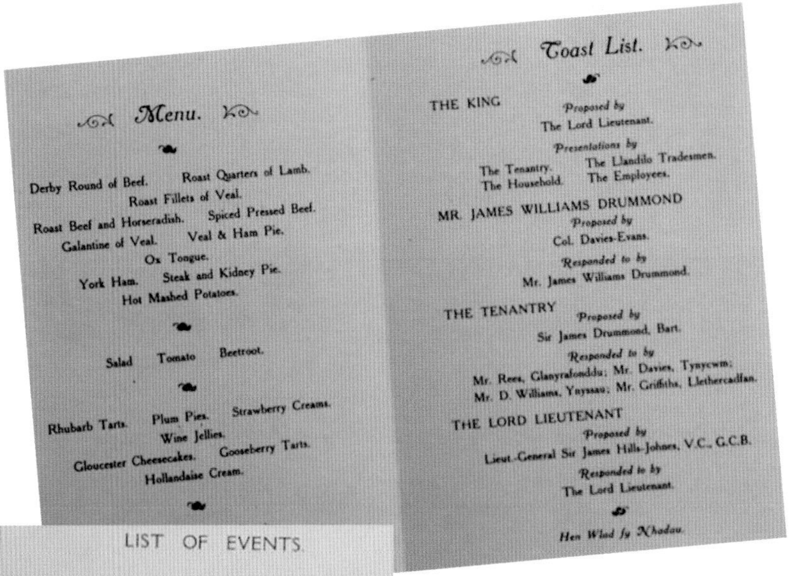
Menu.

Derby Round of Beef. Roast Quarters of Lamb.
Roast Fillets of Veal.
Roast Beef and Horseradish. Spiced Pressed Beef.
Galantine of Veal. Veal & Ham Pie.
Ox Tongue.
York Ham. Steak and Kidney Pie.
Hot Mashed Potatoes.

Salad Tomato Beetroot.

Rhubarb Tarts. Plum Pies. Strawberry Creams.
Wine Jellies.
Gloucester Cheesecakes. Gooseberry Tarts.
Hollandaise Cream.

Toast List.

THE KING
Proposed by
The Lord Lieutenant.
Presentations by
The Tenantry. The Llandilo Tradesmen.
The Household. The Employees.

MR. JAMES WILLIAMS DRUMMOND
Proposed by
Col. Davies-Evans.
Responded to by
Mr. James Williams Drummond.

THE TENANTRY
Proposed by
Sir James Drummond, Bart.
Responded to by
Mr. Rees, Glanyrafonddu; Mr. Davies, Tynycwm;
Mr. D. Williams, Ynysau; Mr. Griffiths, Llethercadfan.

THE LORD LIEUTENANT
Proposed by
Lieut.-General Sir James Hills-Johnes, V.C., G.C.B.
Responded to by
The Lord Lieutenant.

Hen Wlad fy Nhadau.

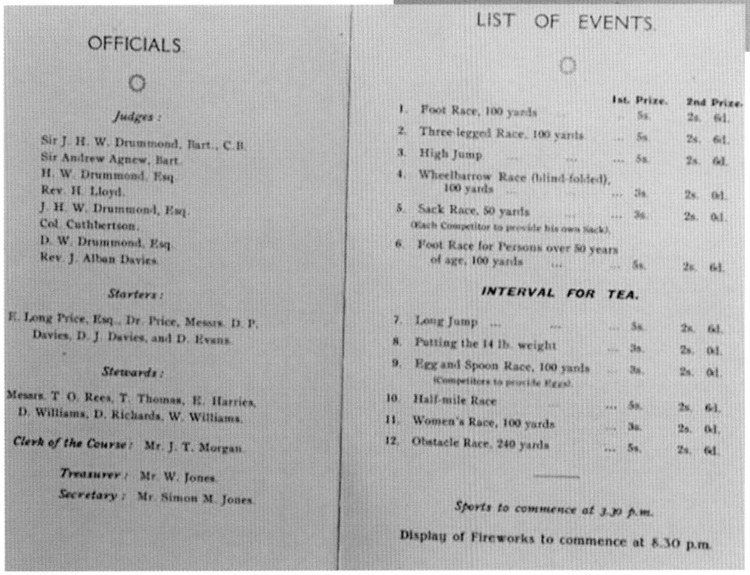
OFFICIALS

Judges:
Sir J. H. W. Drummond, Bart., C.B.
Sir Andrew Agnew, Bart.
H. W. Drummond, Esq.
Rev. H. Lloyd.
J. H. W. Drummond, Esq.
Col. Cuthbertson.
D. W. Drummond, Esq.
Rev. J. Alban Davies.

Starters:
E. Long Price, Esq., Dr. Price, Messrs. D. P. Davies, D. J. Davies, and D. Evans.

Stewards:
Messrs. T. O. Rees, T. Thomas, E. Harries, D. Williams, D. Richards, W. Williams.

Clerk of the Course: Mr. J. T. Morgan.
Treasurer: Mr. W. Jones.
Secretary: Mr. Simon M. Jones.

LIST OF EVENTS

	1st. Prize.	2nd Prize.
1. Foot Race, 100 yards	5s.	2s. 6d.
2. Three-legged Race, 100 yards	5s.	2s. 6d.
3. High Jump	5s.	2s. 6d.
4. Wheelbarrow Race (blind-folded), 100 yards	3s.	2s. 0d.
5. Sack Race, 50 yards (Each Competitor to provide his own Sack).	3s.	2s. 0d.
6. Foot Race for Persons over 50 years of age, 100 yards	5s.	2s. 6d.
INTERVAL FOR TEA.		
7. Long Jump	5s.	2s. 6d.
8. Putting the 14 lb. weight	3s.	2s. 0d.
9. Egg and Spoon Race, 100 yards (Competitors to provide Eggs).	3s.	2s. 0d.
10. Half-mile Race	5s.	2s. 6d.
11. Women's Race, 100 yards	3s.	2s. 0d.
12. Obstacle Race, 240 yards	5s.	2s. 6d.

Sports to commence at 3.30 p.m.
Display of Fireworks to commence at 8.30 p.m.

Sir Jimmy's coming of age 1912

---

330 Brenda James: *Fond Memories of Talley (1994) p41*

331 Brenda James p35; DJ Williams p282 describes similar rejoicings for Cyril Jones, son of John Morgan Davies DL of Frwdfâl

He served as a 2nd Lieutenant with the Pembrokeshire Yeomanry although it is unclear whether or not he saw action during the Great War. He also served as a magistrate locally in Carmarthenshire and was a member of Carmarthenshire County Council representing the Llansawel and Talley district.

On 18 November 1914 at the Church of St Peter and St Paul in Salle, Norfolk he married Lady Enid Evelyn Malet Vaughan (1889-1958), daughter of the 6th Earl and Countess of Lisburne (née Evelyn Probyn) of Trawsgoed in Cardiganshire. Given the recent outbreak of war it was no doubt a quieter wedding than the society wedding which would normally have taken place probably in London.

The Vaughan family[332] had owned the manor and mansion of Trawsgoed (Crosswood) some eight miles east of Aberystwyth since 1200. Sir John Vaughan (1603-74), Chief Justice of Common Pleas, married a Stedman heiress and also acquired the former monastic lands of Strata Florida Abbey. The family was granted an Irish title in the 17th century. Ernest (1836-88) the 5th Earl[333], a bon viveur and philanderer in his youth, often ran up debts and eventually the estate trustees refused to bail him out. He was briefly forced to take his son, Henry the 6th Earl (1862-99), out of Eton and have him educated by the local vicar. However by 1873[334] the estate was the second largest in Wales with 42,666 acres and an annual rental of £10,579. The 6th Earl benefitted from owning the second largest Welsh lead and zinc mine under his lands and became rich enough to build a 50 room wing onto the Georgian house which already had 20 rooms. He died young in 1899 leaving his wife, Evelyn Countess of Lisburne, living at Trawsgoed. Their son, Ernest the 7th Earl (1892-1965), the brother of Lady Enid, lived in a grand manner, and eventually got rid of the estate's entailment, selling land to cover costs. The mansion house and home farm were sold in 1946 to the Ministry of Agriculture although the 7th Earl retained some 12,000 acres. Fifty years later his grandson, the Hon John Vaughan (b1952), exercised a pre-emption right to buy back the mansion, upgraded it and then sold most of it while keeping one flat together with some 5,000 acres which today is managed by a family company. Over the past centuries the family produced several Members of Parliament and were very influential in local politics; indeed particularly during the 18th and early 19th centuries the Pryse family of Gogerddan and the Vaughans of Trawsgoed were the two principal families in Cardiganshire.

Initially Jimmy and Enid lived locally in Cawston near Salle in Norfolk after their marriage. In January 1915 Jimmy had an operation for appendicitis[335] and then went to join his wife at Edwinsford. Very sadly the couple's marital problems[336] started very early on. Jimmy said he wanted to leave and get rid of Edwinsford and suggested that they separate and that Lady Enid should go to live with her mother, which she declined. Jimmy then went to London and feeling ill spent some time in a nursing home presumably as a result of his operation but refused to see his wife. On 9 August 1915 Enid wrote to Jimmy:

"My darling Jimmy
I feel so terribly upset....I do it for your sake and for the sake of the whole family....it is most imperative that you should get rid of the Longs at once. You have her and her husband sleeping in the next room to you, and it would be a public insult to me if you allow it to continue. Now pull yourself together, and we may be as happy together again as we used to be, but as we never can be till you make this change."

It seems that Enid was expecting a child which was later still-born, although we do not know if Jimmy knew this at the time. There was clearly no medical reason why they should not have children together.

Jimmy replied the next day:

"I cannot comply with your request. I have found since our marriage that I do not love you, though I care for you very much. I love Mrs Long, and so it will be best for us to separate. You can have Edwinsford. When we married I thought I could care only for you, but I find I cannot. Try and forget, and forgive me the pain I have caused you. I am sorry I can never return to you.

Jimmy"

---

332 Gerald Morgan: *A Welsh Home and its Family The Vaughans of Trawsgoed (1997)* the definitive history of the Vaughan family; Francis Jones: *Ceredigion (1960) p16*
333 Hon John Vaughan; Telegraph (6 Aug 2005)
334 Return of Owners of Land 1873; Brian James NLWJ (1966) Vol XIV p301-320
335 Appendicitis caused many more medical problems at that time than it does today. Edward VII famously had to postpone his coronation to have a similar operation
336 Amman Valley Chronicle (20 Jan 1916)

On 21 September 1915 Enid, who by then was living at 36 Egerton Crescent in London one of her parents' homes, again wrote to Jimmy:

"I have not seen you since March. Of couse things cannot remain like this. People are already talking and will talk more. I am willing to take you back if you will return to me, and will do all I can to make you happy. Your affectionate Enid"

Lady Enid received no reply so she then commenced legal proceedings for restitution of conjugal rights in the Probate and Divorce Division of the High Court. The case was heard before Mr Justice Bargrave Deane in January 1916 and Enid gave evidence in person. Jimmy however did not attend and his barrister, Walter Frampton, said that he was absent in Madeira. Quite what he was doing in Madeira is very unclear; perhaps he was recuperating but one can only imagine how the above facts in the press were interpreted by London society and by the tenants and residents of the Edwinsford Estate particularly at a time when thousands of their countrymen were dying on the fields of Flanders. The Judge granted Lady Enid her petition with costs and ordered that it be complied with within one month after service. Jimmy complied with the court order and returned to live with Enid, albeit reluctantly. It is perhaps unsurprising that they had no children, although they lived together for the rest of their lives.

Sir Jimmy 1924

Lady Enid 1919

Sir Joe and Jimmy c1905

Sir Jimmy at Hawthornden c1960s

After the War he served from 1918 until 1922 as Hon Attaché in the Diplomatic Service to the Legation at Lisbon where his cousin, Sir Launcelot Carnegie GCVO KCMG PC (1861-1933), was the British ambassador, a man who was deaf from the age of 30 but who did not allow this affliction to dent his very successful career. Enid continued at Edwinsford. During the 1920s Enid's mother, Evelyn Countess of Lisburne (d1931)[337], who had been a widow since 1899 left her home at Trawsgoed to live with and support her daughter at Edwinsford.

As regards the management of the Edwinsford Estate it is clear that the Great War was leading to cashflow problems, increased overheads and reduced rents. In 1914 the Derllys Estate was put up for sale but did not reach its expected price. It was sold by the trustees and executors of Sir Joe Williams-Drummond (68) on 24 March 1915 for £8,250 to John Thomas on a mortgage of £5,500 provided by the executors and subject to a yearly tenancy in favour of the sitting tenant, Percy Thomas. As shown in Chapter 16, some of the Edwinsford Estate properties totalling some 821 acres were auctioned for sale in September 1918. The sale took place at the Cawdor Arms in Llandeilo and fortunately many of the lots were bought by the occupying tenants[338] in accordance with the wishes of Sir Jimmy. A further 18 Edwinsford Estate freehold farms and small holdings totalling some 1,871 acres were auctioned for sale on Saturday 30 August 1919 at the Drill Hall in Llandeilo; Sir Jimmy's uncle, Dudley (76), handled the sale being himself the Land Agent for the Cawdor Estate. But cashflow problems persisted during the post war years and the depression.

Lady Enid was much loved[339] by the Edwinsford estate workers and tenants, as her mother in law had been before her. She was often to be seen carrying her basket containing a jar of calf's foot jelly or other suitable nourishment on her way to visit a sick person. She entertained the Talley Church Sunday School pupils to tea, muffins and cakes; she also gave them suitable Christmas presents including a copy of "Black Beauty" to one boy whose family still treasures it. On Sunday afternoons she could be seen riding in her horse-drawn carriage on the circular route around the demesne and the lakes. Hannah Williams

337 Hon John Vaughan: *Cambria magazine (March/April 2009)*
338 Carmarthen Journal (27 Sept 1918)
339 Brenda James p39

from Penlan Farm overlooking Llansawel was Enid's dressmaker and travelled with her to stay at Hawthornden until later in life arthritis made her return home; her sister Nellie also worked in the mansion.

The domestic servants[340] had a long day. Meals were prepared by the cook and the kitchen maid while the footman served at table. One of the footmen served Jimmy's breakfast in his bedroom while Enid was served by Hannah. The cleaning of the mansion including the bedrooms, sportsman's hall, stone hall, dining room, library etc was done by the maids while the staff hallway was cleaned by the hallboy who would set the table for the staff in the kitchen. Lunches were light meals and grilled trout a popular dish. Dinner was more elaborate with popular dishes including chicken in sherry or cream sauce, chicken soufflé, and on Jimmy's birthday, his favourite dish of rabbit soufflé. Sunday dinner was sirloin of beef with all the trimmings and, when in season, pheasant, grouse, woodcock and partridge. Salads and vegetables were sourced from the gardens and greenhouses with numerous varieties of fruit desserts and strawberry ice-cream from Swansea. There were dogs as family pets as well as farm and hunting dogs, and a pet parrot lived in the china pantry which escaped one day but later returned for food.

Jimmy had a good sense of humour and would tease and play tricks on the staff. He loved his hunting, shooting and fishing; the cook would prepare lunch for the guests in large hampers which would be taken on horseback to Jerusalem, a site where a hunting lodge once stood. On one occasion during a Sunday service in Talley Church Jimmy fell asleep in the family pew during the sermon to be awakened by the vicar mentioning Jerusalem in a loud voice. He jumped to his feet thinking that he was at the Jerusalem hunting lodge and needed to continue with the day's shooting.

In his father's time the family had usually spent the grouse and pheasant shooting season in August and September at Hawthornden and the rest of the year at Edwinsford. However Jimmy and Enid soon tired of the mansion and found it more convenient and warmer to live in the Home Farmhouse across the Cothi. By the mid 1930s they had decided to spend most of their time at Hawthornden and by the outbreak of the Second World War Edwinsford mansion was effectively mothballed.

In 1931 Jimmy erected a tombstone in Talley Abbey over the entrance to the family vault saying: "In memory of the members of the Edwinsford (Rhyd Edwin) family buried in (or near) this vault from the twelfth century (or earlier) to the nineteenth century. This monument is inscribed by their descendant James Williams-Drummond 5th Baronet, 1931."

Shortly following the outbreak of war in 1939, the moveable contents of the mansion were put into storage (to reappear for auction after the war) and the mansion was requisitioned like so many gentry mansions. It was used to house Whittingehame (Whittingham) College[341], a private boarding school for Jewish boys from Brighton (most of whom were from Arab countries) who had been evacuated initially to Danyrallt Park in Llangadog but following a serious fire there in July 1940 had then been transferred to Edwinsford; the headmaster and founder was Jacob Halevy, an ardent Zionist and promoter of sometimes eccentric curriculums including dancing. The headmaster and staff arranged several events at Edwinsford to raise money for the Red Cross such as sports and horse races in the parkland behind the mansion. The day would end with a dance[342] in the ballroom, the length of which was equivalent to the depth of the building. On the walls were beautiful gilt-edged mirrors. They looked after the mansion well and several local girls[343] had cleaning and domestic jobs there.

Following the War the mansion was leased to three Polish refugee families; the male heads of the families had all fought against the Nazis. It seems that[344] they were finding it increasingly difficult to pay the rent to Jimmy's London lawyer, so one of them wrote to Jimmy at Hawthornden saying that they had problems paying the annual rent of £600. Jimmy wrote back saying he was mystified because the rent was only £300. The explanation was that his London lawyer had been

340 Brenda James p40
341 Leslie Brown: *jtrails.org.uk (2010)*
342 Jack Roberts of Ffaldybugail, now aged 90, well remembers attending a dance and witnessing the very strict way in which the servants were treated
343 Gwyneth Jones: *Y Llychau*—dances were held there as late as the early 1960s
344 Conversation by Neil Callan, the current owner, with one of the sons of the Polish families who lived at Edwinsford

creaming off the difference. In a fit of rage one of the Poles went to London with his pistol with the intention of killing the lawyer, but as he was crossing the street outside the lawyer's office he was knocked down and killed by a bus. The Polish families were making money by growing mushrooms[345] in long boxes full of soil row upon row in the darkness on the Edwinsford ballroom floors with pealing plaster on the once beautiful ceilings and walls with enormous mirrors facing each other; a room formerly used in its prime for happy couples in their gorgeous dresses dancing the minuet to the sound of the harpsichord and fiddles. The mansion was never again used as a home, although unsuccessful attempts were made to let it as an old peoples' home, hospital or school. Someone stole the lead on the roof and the rain started to damage the structure of the building.

Jimmy and Enid continued to live at Hawthornden; visits thereafter to Edwinsford were rare although Jimmy enjoyed fishing in the Cothi when he did visit. Enid died at Hawthornden on 14 April 1958 and was buried locally; she was later disinterred in 1970 when her husband died and both their bodies were then brought down and buried in the family plot at Talley. Their life together had initially been sad and unhappy but they seem to have patched things up later and lived together for many years thereafter in some harmony but without producing an heir.

In 1957 Jimmy once drove his blue Rolls-Royce[346] down from Scotland to Edwinsford to inspect its condition. He got as far as the bridge over the Cothi in front of the Home Farmhouse but was so upset by the state to which the mansion had obviously been reduced that he turned his car round and went back to Scotland without even stepping out of the car.

Jimmy continued living at Hawthornden being looked after by his trusted butler, chauffeur and companion, Frank Aubrey Coombs (1914-78), by the cook, Bessie Booth, who had worked for years for the family at Edwinsford, and a small number of other staff. When Brenda James[347] visited Hawthornden in 1963 she received a very warm welcome from Bessie and Frank Coombs as well as from Sir Jimmy, who took her inside the courtyard to show her the ruins of the old castle and then to look down the 250ft cliff to the river below in the glen. Inside the castle was the great hall with a large antique coffer on which rested the sword of King Robert the Bruce. Above the coffer was a painting of Queen Victoria standing on the balcony outside; she visited the castle twice to see the caves below. In the diningroom there was an enormous table on the centre of which was a massive silver salver. All around the walls hung paintings of the Stuart Kings and Queens, to which of course the family were related. In the kitchen there was a modern aga cooker but otherwise it looked as if it had not been changed for years.

During my research I have been told by numerous people that Jimmy and his companion and butler, Frank Coombs, had a sexual relationship. There is of course no surviving hard evidence one way or the other. Whatever view one takes of his initially unhappy marriage it is clear from his expressed love for Mrs Long in 1915 that Jimmy was not homesexual, but he might have been bisexual. It could be that Frank was merely a trusted and loyal companion. However local residents including some of the families of those who were servants of Jimmy and Enid seem to be convinced from what they were told by their relations that there is some truth in this notion. In addition when Jimmy died at Hawthornden on 7 January 1970 aged 78 by his will dated 29 March 1968 (as amended on 15 July 1969) he appointed Frank as his sole surviving executor and trustee and instead of leaving the Edwinsford and Lethr Cadfan Estates and his other lands to his cousin, William (77) who inherited the Baronetcy, in accordance with his father's stated wishes, he left them all to Frank instead; this was on condition that there should be no development or building near the Talley lakes, that the Talley lakes be made a bird sanctuary, and that none of the trees be cut down (as drafted I believe he meant on the estates rather than near the lakes since he did not limit this condition). This action can only be described as highly unusual to say the least; indeed I am not aware of any other gentry family leaving their estates to a butler. Jimmy's only legacy was the sum of £1,000 to the Church in Wales to upkeep in perpetuity the family plot "in good order and repair and the monuments restored when necessary", "the fence around my graveyard be painted with black anti-rust paint, that a padlock be put on the gate, that the grass be cut and that the grave be kept tidy in

345 Aneirin Talfan Davies: *Crwydro Sir Gâr*—Lynn Hughes p238-9; DJ Williams: *Hen Dŷ Ffarm p96*

346 Sunday Telegraph (30 Sept 1990)

347 Brenda James p37-8

perpetuity." His will continued by stating that in the event of Frank predeceasing Jimmy, all the estate was to go to the National Trust. Jimmy was buried at Talley in the family burial plot on 13 January 1970. We do not know why he left nothing to his relations although it seems there might have been some family disagreement. William (77) was already aged 69 and unmarried when Jimmy died, and died himself six years later in 1976; William's two elder sisters had already died but had sons who survived and could have inherited in accordance with the wishes of Sir Joe, their great uncle, as expressed in his will. Attempts were made by the family to claim the estate but these failed.

Following Jimmy's death in 1970 Frank the butler and Bessie the cook stayed at Hawthornden initially but then returned to Talley and lived together in Moelfryn Old Forge described in Chapter 14.11 until

SALES

EDWINSFORD ESTATE, TALLEY, LLANDEILO

Clear Out Sale of the Whole of the

LIVESTOCK, FARM MACHINERY, IMPLEMENTS, TOOLS AND PART OF THE EDWINSFORD ANTIQUE FURNITURE & EFFECTS

(Upon instructions of Mr and Mrs L. R. Moult who have sold the estate)

SALE THIS SATURDAY

145 Sheep — 65 Speckle Face and Cross Texel Ewe & Lamb Couples

3 Cattle — Pedigree Welsh Black Cow with Cross Hereford Heifer calf at heel, Welsh Black Steer, 12 months old

Farm Machinery — Land Rover Defender TDI (1990 H Reg) fitted with all extras, 1989 G Reg Zetor 7245 Tractor, 550 hours fitted with Trima 912 Loader. 4 Grey Ferguson Vintage Tractors (restored), Chilton Silage Grab, David Thomas Post Driver, Old Edwinsford Fire Engine, Saw Benches, Band Saw etc. etc.

Furniture — Unrestored 17th Century Welsh Oak Coffer, Victorian Mahogany Round Top Table on centre pedestal with claw feet, 19th Century Secretaire Bookcase, Carved Wooden Salmon, inscribed caught by "Herbert Peel of Taliaris" on River Cothi 9 May 1879, Original Edwinsford Royal Seals, Rare Heavily embossed book by Charles Smith Allen of Photographs of South Wales Stately Homes, various Prints and Watercolours together with numerous items of antique furniture and miscellaneous.

Illustrated catalogues and further information from the auctioneers 50 Rhosmaen Street, Llandeilo Tel. 0558 822468. R61131.

Sale 22 June 1991

Frank died in 1978; he was buried (uniquely for a servant) in the private Edwinsford family burial plot in Talley Churchyard; as the owner of the estate he could presumably ensure this in practice.

It is believed Frank left his estate to his sister; his executors put the estate up for sale at an auction in Lampeter in 1979 including many family heirlooms some of which were acquired by the Vaughan family. Items sold included fireplaces, oak panels, pictures and the like; the lifesize leaden figures originally on the Home Farmhouse gates and on the farm roofs went to London dealers, and an excellent collection of needlework furniture including an embroidered sofa was also sold some of which is now in the National Museum of Wales at St Fagans. Fortunately the lovely openwell staircase[348] of the 1660s with its big twisted balusters and broad handrail was saved and sold to the Llwynybrain Estate, whose large three storey house was being restored by Mrs Rosemary Rooney (née Pryse-Rice); this house lies between Llanwrda and Llandovery and has a lovely plaster ceiling of the 1620s salvaged from Vicar Prichard's house in Llandovery.

Sadly it was not long before many of the lovely oaks on the estate were cut down for profit contrary to the condition in Jimmy's will, although thankfully the wonderful oak-lined "Moelfre Walk" road from Moelfryn Forge to Moelfre Lodge remains so that we can still imagine the lovely entrance roads to the Estate before the other oak trees were cut down. Some of the grand oaks in the former park dated from the 16th century.

The mansion in very bad repair and some cottages and land were sold to Len Moult (1926-92) and his wife Irene (1919-99) who are buried in Talley Churchyard; he was a relation of the comedian Ted Moult. By this time the lead on the roof had been stolen and the rain was badly damaging the interior. He auctioned many remaining items at a sale under a marquee in the grounds held on 22 June 1991. Sadly there was little of value left. In 1991 Len Moult sold the remaining estate to Bernard Kettle, a haulage contractor and demolition and construction expert, who later onsold[349] much of the property to Jonathan and Nikki Heron as described in Chapter 14.1. Since 2001 the derelict mansion has been owned by Neil Callan, who has removed hundreds of tons of rubble from the site and cleaned the area up. The mansion, which is

---

348 Thomas Lloyd: *Carmarthenshire and Ceredigion p263*

349 Knight Frank sales particulars c1997 offered the Home Farmhouse with 8 acres for £180,000

grade 2 listed, is now wholly in ruins, most of the walls have fallen down and the little which remains of the structure is in a dangerous condition. It is a heritage disaster having been one of the finest houses in Carmarthenshire with a wonderful history. No one individual owner can be expected to rebuild such a house without a substantial heritage grant and full cooperation from the local authority and planning authorities; sadly this has not been forthcoming.

As explained in Chapter 9.4, Hawthornden remained in the ownership of the Williams-Drummond family until 1970 when Jimmy died without issue leaving his Scottish estate to Frank Coombs who died in 1978. Hawthornden was put up for sale in 1977 and on 15 March 1978 was bought by Alexander and Diana Adamson. In 1982 the house and the estate were sold to Mrs Drue Mary Heinz DBE, the philanthropist and widow of HJ Heinz (1908-87), former Chairman of the American 57 varieties food company. Since 1982 part of the house has been used as a private retreat for writers.

Children of Lt-Col Sir Francis Dudley Williams-Drummond KBE (1863-1935)

Dudley (76), the youngest brother of Sir Joe as described at the end of Chapter 9, and his wife Marguerite had three children:

(1)Eleanor Mary Williams-Drummond (1891-1962) was born on 16 June 1891 and on 5 November 1914 at the end of the Great War married at St George's in Hanover Square Robert (Robin) Barnewell Elliot of Clifton Park, Kelso, Roxburghshire, the son of Thomas Elliot (c1871-1949) the first person to own a motorcar in Scotland in 1895. Eleanor and Robin moved to Bryneithin [SN633255] near Salem between Taliaris and Llandeilo in 1950 where Eleanor died on 26 December 1962 aged 71. She and Robin had been living at Bryneithin with her brother William. Robin died on 13 February 1973. Robin and Eleanor had a son, Robert Hugh Elliot, born on 19 September 1923 who continued to lived with his wife Rosemary and children, Frances and Hugh, at Bryneithin. He sold Bryneithin in 1977 to Henri Lloyd Davies the current owner and moved to Manordeilo. After Robert's death in 1999 his widow Rosemary and their two sons moved back to Scotland;

(2) Constance Marie Katherine Williams-Drummond (1893-1968) was born on 3 June 1893 and on 1 January 1927 married Francis Stapleton-Cotton, 4th Viscount Combermere of Bhurtpore (1887-1969). Francis had first married Hazel Agnew in 1913 but they were divorced in 1926. He was educated at Harrow and served as a Lieutenant in the Royal Garrison Artillery (Special Reserve) in 1916 and fought in Flanders where he was wounded. Constance and Francis had two sons: (a) Michael 5th Viscount (1929-2000) who went on to have three children, and (b) David (b1932) who had four children. The title of Bhurtpore in the East Indies was created in 1827 for the prominent military commander, Field Marshal Stapleton Stapleton-Cotton MP (1773-1865), who also held a Barony created in 1814 and a Baronetcy created in 1677. Combermere Abbey, the family seat, is in Combermere Park between Nantwich and Whitchurch in Cheshire; and

(3) Sir William Hugh Dudley Williams-Drummond 6th Bt Hawthornden (1901-76) was born on 13 February 1901 and educated at Eton. After leaving home in his earlier years he lived at The Manor, Marston Maysey in Wiltshire, although in later years he lived at Bryneithin near Talley with his sister Eleanor and brother in law Robert Elliot. He succeeded to the Baronetcy of Hawthornden on the death of Jimmy without issue on 7 January 1970, but did not inherit any of the family estates. William died on 27 May 1976 unmarried and without an heir. Under his very short will made years before on 27 February 1945 (proved on 10 March 1977) he appointed his local solicitor as his executor and left all his estate to his sister Eleanor or if she should predecease him (as she did) then to her son, Robert Hugh Elliot (1923-99). His gross estate was valued at £8,830 and his net estate at £5,827. He was not buried in the family plot at Talley for reasons unknown (although his parents had been) but his name appears on a memorial in Talley Church adopting the surname "Drummond" which he preferred.

So ended the Baronetcy of Hawthornden which became extinct on his death and so ended the male line and pedigree of the Williams and Drummond families of Edwinsford and Hawthornden.

We shall now look at the Edwinsford demesne and estate before, in Chapters 17 to 21 completing the full family history by going back to consider the Clovelly pedigree of the family which split in 1861 from the Edwinsford pedigree following the death of Sir James Hamlyn Williams Bt MP (61) who left three daughters to inherit his three estates.

Memorial in Talley Church

Edwinsford by Paul Sandby 1776

Edwinsford by Paul Sandby c1776

c1870s

c1870s

c1885

©Hon John Vaughan

From the river c1926

Published by permission of The National Library of Wales

© Hugh Clifton c1912

© Hon John Rous

© Hon John Rous

© Hon John Vaughan

Drawing room ceiling c1926

© Hugh Clifton c1912

© Hugh Clifton

The park view c1912

© Hugh Clifton The river view c1912

© Hon John Vaughan Gardens c1926

© Hon John Vaughan Back of Edwinsford c1926

© Hon John Vaughan
Attic window c1926

© Hon John Vaughan *River with distant dovecote c1926*

1928

1980s

c2000

c2000

2016

Bridge 2016

Cothi valley 2017

Cothi valley with Edwinsford ruins 2017

Map of Edwinsford c1886

Map of Edwinsford c1930

The Edwinsford Estate

11. Edwinsford Plas and Mansion [SN 632346]

Edwinsford is located in a beautiful picturesque part of the Cothi valley. The two lovely Talley lakes are to the south and the Talley Abbey ruins and the village of Talley are beyond. The former demesne lands include rolling hills each side of the valley to a height of some 1,000ft with former parkland and meadows behind the now derelict mansion. The farm buildings are across the river which has a bridge over it described below. Trees abound on both sides of the valley. The owners and occupiers of Edwinsford over the centuries are listed in Chapter 12.

There is some doubt[350] as to whether the later Edwinsford mansion (now derelict) stands on the original site of the earlier residence or manor house (*plas*) known as Rhydodyn. Originally there were two farms, Rhydodyn Ucha and Rhydodyn Issa, which were later combined to form one property. Rhydodyn Ucha and Rhydodyn Issa were both occupied by the family whose pedigree is shown in this book. Rhydodyn Ucha was held by the family as tenants in common and the estate[351] consisted of: Rhydodyn Ucha; seven unnamed messuages; messuages called Llechwedd Llywelyn otherwise Bwlch y Dinas, Tir Bron Talwilkin, Tir y Llywele Mawr, Tir y Pant Gwyn, and Tir y Bryn Llwyd, all in Llansawel parish; messuages called Garth y Brichiad and Cwm Twrch, in Caeo parish; messuages called Tir Howel Guto and Tir Rhys ap Howel Jenkin, in Talley parish; and a messuage called Tir Ievan David Ychan in Llanycwrys parish.

On 16 October 1605 Lewis David ap Howell Morgan and James Lewis David ap Howell, both of Llanybydder, described as "gentlemen", mortgaged Rhydodyn Ucha and Bwlch y Dinas to Francis Jones of Llanybydder, esquire, for £240. The mortgage was never redeemed and on 20 August 1609 Mathew Jones of Llanybydder (gentleman) who was the son of Francis Jones, his wife Margaret, Lewis David ap Howell Morgan (gentleman), together with three of his sons, James Lewis, Thomas Lewis and Morgan Lewis released Rhydodyn Ucha and the other mortgaged land totalling some 1,920 acres to their cousin David Price ap William (40) gentleman of Rhydodyn Issa next door (whose patronymic surname became "Williams" in the next generation). So the Williams branch of the family who originally lived in Rhydodyn Issa acquired Rhydodyn Ucha and its lands at the beginning of the 17th century.

The James I (1603-25) Cayo and Llansawel rent roll[352] states that Walter Lloyd, gent, occupied one tenement called Tir Rhydodyn Issa for which he paid annual rent of 16 pence, and that Rees Williams (41)(who had several holdings) had one tenement called Tir Rhidodyn now in the tenure of (leased to) David Powell for which he paid annual rent of 4 shillings and 8 pence.

It is possible[353] that Rhydodyn Issa was the site of the later Edwinsford Home Farm described in Chapter 14.1, while Rhydodyn Ucha was the site of the Edwinsford Mansion which was built across the river.

---

350 Francis Jones: *Cymmrodorion (1986-7) p65-72*
351 NLW Edwinsford archives
352 Mee: *Carmarthenshire Notes 1891 p78*
353 Francis Jones: *Cymmrodorion p67*

Alternatively[354] both houses could have been on the same site and were later enclosed into one mansion. The earliest part of the subsequent mansion was built about 1635 on a square plan[355] with a large central chimney going up to a high pyramidal stone clad roof; the traditional Renaissance plan of the time presented practical problems where the chimney was sited opposite the entrance so instead the chimney could be made the focal point of the house, as here, where the rooms were sited around a single huge stack incorporating fireplaces facing each external wall. The additional central block[356] was built about 1660 probably for Nicholas Williams (c1615-76)(43) and consisted of two main rooms on each floor with two fine plaster ceilings. These fine Jacobean ceilings were probably the work of craftsmen who also decorated the ceilings of Newton House at Dinefwr, Derwydd, and Taliaris near Talley. In about 1710 the dormer windows were added.

Sir Nicholas Williams (1681-1745)(51) enlarged and rebuilt parts of the mansion[357], he improved and enlarged the gardens and parkland, he built a bridge over the river described below, he added an apartment which became known as Sir Nicholas's Room with its rib and panel plaster ceiling, and he added some early dormer windows with leaded quarries showing the taste of the early 18th century. He also added some unique life-size leaden figures[358] in the grounds dating from about 1720 including one of his gamekeeper (of whom there used to be an oil painting in the upper corridor of the house[359]) with his gun to his shoulder and his spaniel dog at his heel; another one of his dairy maid which stood opposite and was blown down and damaged beyond repair in the 18th century; two beautiful leaden figures of "The Mercury with Caduceus" on the roof of the house; and a leaden figure of "The Boar" which together with "The Gamekeeper" later stood on the gateposts to the farmyard; the leaden figures were later sketched by Private Joseph Milner of 7th Battalion, Manchester Regiment. As late as 1913 a large leaden escutcheon hung in the hall of the mansion bearing the lion rampant and the legend "S'r Nicholas Williams of Edwyns Ford Bar AD 1708."

In 1911 a visitor[360] described Edwinsford as having an imposing porch leading to the large entrance hall off which the passageway led to the drawing room, library, billiard room and a number of other rooms on the ground floor including the Sportsman's Hall. In the entrance hall there was a 4.75 lbs trout in a case caught from the Cothi and a plastercast of a 27 lbs salmon caught by William Peel of Taliaris. The library had an old 17th century panelled plastered ceiling similar to that in Taliaris and Derwydd. In the drawing room (formerly the library) there was a long sofa[361] covered with a tapestry made in 1842 by members of the family consisting of several different squares illustrating different subjects including the Rebecca riots and an officer of the 4th Light Dragoons. On the walls hung a (possible) Van Dyck and paintings by Vanderbank, Sir Godfey Kneller, Thomas Hudson, Gavin Hamilton, Guercino, Salvator Rosa, Francesco Mola, and Eddis. In the dining room there was a painting of Hawthornden by Sir William Allen, medals won in the Peninsula Wars, a 1836 gold snuffbox, Worcester china, and Crown Derby figures. The house contained much oak furniture as well as Dresden vases. The Sportsman's Hall had a wonderful carved oak ceiling.

Sir Nicholas built a stone bridge over the River Cothi which had two spans and can be seen in the 1776 copper plate engraving of "Edwinsford, the Seat of R Banks Hodgkinson Esqr" by the artist Paul Sandby[362] and engraved by William Watts (see Chapter 8.3). It shows the two early blocks forming an L-shaped mansion which faces east-

354 Peter Smith: *Houses of the Welsh Countryside (1988) p167, 232*
355 Other Welsh houses with the same plan were Cemais Bychan, Cemais, Monts; Ty-mawr, Llansilin, Denbs; and Trimley Hall, Llanfynydd, Flints (1653)
356 Thomas Lloyd: *Lost Houses of Wales (1989) p61*; Thomas Lloyd: *Carmarthenshire and Ceredigion (2006) p382;* Francis Jones*: Carmarthenshire Homes p61;* Cadw: *Register of Landscapes, Parks and Gardens of Special Historic Interest in Wales*; NLW Edwinsford archives; Dyfed Archaeological Trust; Western Mail (17 Dec 1841)
357 Samuel Lewis also referred to this rebuilding
358 FDWD: *Annals p7*
359 See Chapter 15
360 South Wales Daily News (29 July 1911)
361 Now in St Fagans Museum in Cardiff
362 Paul Sandby RA (1731-1809) was an English map-maker and landscape painter in watercolours and one of the founding members of the Royal Academy in 1768. Many of his drawings and paintings were bought by Sir Joseph Banks (whose uncle was then living in Edwinsford) with whom he toured South Wales in 1773 resulting in his publication of Views in South Wales in 1775 and their later copper engravings

north-east in all its magnificence, a rectangular side chapel with a bell (now on the Dairy House roof) and cross on the roof, two men approaching the wrought iron front gate in front of a bowling green, a man riding a horse in front, the lovely gardens in front running down to the River Cothi, the park behind, the bridge which had two spans (the new bridge built by Robert Banks Hodgkinson in 1783 had one span), to the north a farmhouse and other farm buildings across the river, groups of trees in the background, cattle drinking by the bridge and a family of ducks in the foreground of the picturesque sight. The accompanying text of the description includes:

"Edwinsford, the seat of Robert Banks Hodgkinson Esq; in Carmarthenshire, is situated about six miles north-west of the great turnpike road. The family of Williams have possessed this house many ages. It stands upon the banks of the river Cothy, which runs through the middle of the demesne. The house is an ancient building, but rendered very convenient by the present possessor for a large family. Behind the house is a large lawn containing above eighty acres, surrounded by rising hills, woods, and walks; at the bottom of which the hills draw together, and the river runs a narrow channel, through rocks, covered with woods, for many miles, affording many most delightful and romantic scenes.
A bridge near the house, for the use of the family, was built by Sir Nicholas Williams, Bart, which is of great use to the country, who, by permission, (upon floods [363]*, which frequently happen here) have leave to pass it."*

The highly influential Miller's Gardeners' Dictionary[364] encouraged the importance of a lawn (a great plain in the park) which for a large park such as that at Edwinsford, should be 30 to 40 acres in size and be situated to the south of the house front. The site of the mansion and the park which extended behind the mansion was therefore almost perfect with its lovely rolling parkland and meadows stretching out down the valley. The former park has been divided more recently into fields. The pleasure gardens including a lovely rose garden were laid out to the front and north-west side and, although not as formal as others and without numerous fountains, were close to the riverside walk; the gardens used to have rare plants from South America. In the 19th century creepers and climbers grew up the walls of the mansion. Some think that there was at one time a small ornamental lake by the drive but this is not shown on the 1886 map or thereafter. The creation of oak avenues[365] and the interest in trees for aesthetic value and for providing timber during the 18th and 19th centuries is marked.

During their 30 year tenure at Edwinsford, Robert Banks Hodgkinson (1721-92) and his wife Bridget Williams (d1792)(56) made a number of improvements to the mansion and the gardens. Robert rebuilt the bridge[366] over the Cothi and transformed it into a wide single span bridge (instead of the former two span bridge); the new bridge was of stone laid in fine diminishing courses having an elliptical arch with dressed stone voussoirs and a low parapet wall rising to a central point. On the bridge there can still be seen a stone which reads *"This Bridge is the sole Property of the Family of Edwinsford. Rebuilt by Robert Banks Hodgkinson, Esq, 1783".* The builder[367] was David Edwards of Pontypridd, son of the celebrated bridge builder Rev William Edwards of Eglwysilan (1719-89) famous for the Pontypridd bridge (1755) and the bridge at Llandeilo-yr-ynys (1787) whose extortionate tolls helped fuel the Rebecca Riots. The Edwinsford bridge is now grade 2 listed.

In about 1842 Sir James Hamlyn Williams (61) made substantial changes by adding a new dining room (with early 17th century panelling removed from Llethr Cadfan) and a service block probably designed by Edward Haycock. In about 1862 Sir James Williams-Drummond (73) added a tall block to the north end near the river and remodelled the front and parapeted entrance porch which also provided corridors behind; in 1863 he added the large ballroom to the east of the house on the site of the chapel. There were two main rooms on each floor and a central open-well oak staircase (which as we have seen is now at Llwynybrain) with heavy twisted balustrades and squared newels. On the ground floor there was a fine plaster ceiling[368] in four panels each with an oval and surrounding cherubs.

---

363 DJ Williams p30 describes how lime carts from the Llandybie kilns were allowed to use the bridge when the river was in heavy flood
364 Philip Miller: *Miller's Gardeners Dictionary 8th edition 1768*
365 Simon Butler: *Preliminary Investigation of the Pollen Record from Talley Lakes CA (1984) p3-13*
366 BH Malkin: *The Scenery, Antiquities and Biography of South Wales (1807) Vol 1 p196*
367 FDWD: *Annals p8*
368 The ceiling was very similar to that at Coalbrook, Pontyberem dated c1670 (demolished c1960)

Richard Fenton[369] wrote in his journals whilst touring Wales during the early 19th century: *"Hence to Llansawel, a small Village with 2 or 3 publick Houses. The Church has a tower, but is a poor miserable building without and within. No monument. Pass Edwinsford, and old Mansion, pretty large, lying low on the banks of the Cothy, which winds under the beautifully wooded Hills near it. There is a large walled Garden, a great part of which is of mud, said to be best for fruit. To characterize the different farm Officers, there occur several well executed figures in lead painted, such as a large Pig near the Piggery, Hay makers near the Haggard, and at the Stables or Kennel an admirable fowler. Near the House are shewn 13 large Trees planted the year Thos Williams Esq of this House was Sheriff* [370]*, by him and his 12 Javelin Men after their return from the Spring Assizes—a central tree with 12 others round it."*

In 1803 Benjamin Malkin[371] noted that the house was *"beautified above, below, around, with leaden mercuries, shepherdesses and sportsmen. (The gardens were) in the genuine style of King William's reign, with all its absurdities, more interesting, as shewing us a specimen of that time, than if it were patched up with modern improvements.... We rode through the long avenue of trees that extend from the house."*

The Tithe map and returns of 1838 (referred to in Chapter 16.6) show that the Edwinsford demesne lands (excluding tenants and the rest of the estate) was 569 acres in size. The Tithe map does not show the walled garden for unknown reasons, but does show the circular carriage drive around the perimeter of the demesne. The 1886 map shows the mansion with gardens[372] in front going down to the river, the carriage drive with both Iron Gate Lodge to the south-east and Moelfre Lodge to the south-west, the parkland to the west behind the mansion, outbuildings and the water tank which served the mansion on the slope of the hill to the south, the bridge across the Cothi, the farm buildings (including the Home Farmhouse, the Coach House complex and stables, Garden House, Waggoners House, the dovecote and other buildings) plus the walled garden. Interestingly it also shows a Tennis Ground in the field between the Coach House and the river. The 1886 and 1906 maps show the drives across the bridge to a forecourt in front of the mansion where there is a large circular bed probably containing yews. Some 1871 photographs[373] show the house to be well-kept, white painted with a weed free forecourt and creepers trained up the walls. Two large Scots pines are shown to the north of the mansion and a shrub border with yews and rhododendrons to the south.

The park which extended behind the mansion was the venue for the "Annual Treat" held between the 1880s and the 1950s. It was a tradition in Carmarthenshire and other parts of Wales that the local gentry[374] supported the schools in their parishes. The Edwinsford family did so in relation to the schools in Llansawel, Talley and Abergorlech; they served on their boards, attended events, granted prizes, and most importantly provided and hosted the annual sports day and tea on their demesnes attended by pupils, parents and tenants. These included marches by the children carrying flags and banners, running races and wheel barrow competitions, a men's tug of war, a ladies' race including the housemaids running in full uniform, and children's fun competitions. These were followed by a feast of cakes, sandwiches, and other refreshments, then the prize-giving, speeches by the hosts and schoolmasters, and always ended with the English and Welsh national anthems. All the children were given a small gift and some sweets to take home with them. A truly memorable day for all and much appreciated by all attendees.

As we have seen from Chapter 10.2, after the 1950s the mansion fell into decay. Despite being grade 2 listed it is now wholly in ruins, most of the walls have fallen down and the little which remains of the structure is in a dangerous condition. It is a heritage disaster having been one of the finest houses in Carmarthenshire with a wonderful history.

---

369 Richard Fenton (1746-1821) toured Wales and wrote several journals. John Fisher edited and published these journals in 1917 as *Tours in Wales (1804-1813)*

370 He must have meant either Sir Rice Williams who was Sheriff in 1680 or Thomas Williams who was Lord Lieutenant in 1740/6-62

371 BH Malkin: *The scenery, antiquities and bibliography of south Wales (1807).* JT Barber: *A Tour Throughout South Wales (1803)* made very similar comments in its description of Edwinsford

372 C Stephen Briggs: *The Fabric of Parklands and Gardens in the Tywi Valley and beyond CA (1997) p88-105.* The Carmarthenshire gentry were all interested in the development of formal gardens with woodlands, ponds, statues, dovecotes and icehouses coupled with kitchen gardens, glasshouses and sporting areas for archery, croquet and tennis

373 CS Allen: *Photographs in South Wales patronized by Her Majesty the Queen and dedicated to the Rt Hon Countess of Cawdor (1871)*

374 For a description and photos of the Annual Treat at Dolaucothi—see David Lewis: *Dolaucothi and Brunant p23-6*

Today across the bridge and outside the Home Farmhouse stands an old sundial in the form of a sandstone obelisk of about 1.5 m in height, which has been grade 2 listed since 1995, and was erected in 1889 for Sir Joe and Lady Madeline Williams- Drummond (68/67). Until the mid 1950s it formerly stood in the front garden of the mansion across the drive towards the Cothi. The sundial was made from two red sandstone blocks. The upper block is about 0.75 m tall, four sided with a pyramidal top. The lower base block also some 0.75 m in height is square with a triple stepped circular base, square pedestal with moulded base and cornice. All the brass as well as the gnomon has been removed. The inscriptions can still be read; one cartouche says "Watch and pray for ye knoweth neither the day nor the hour"; another says "Do today's work today"; and another "The night cometh when no man can work". An heraldic shield below the gnomon contains the initials JSD 1889 (for Sir James Drummond) and another the initials MLD (for Madeline Lady Drummond). The "X" on the side is probably intended to represent the 10th anniversary of their wedding in 1889.

1889 sundial

This sundial should not be confused with the other one which also used to stand in front of the mansion; it dates from 1710 and was made by the Royal Clockmaker, Daniel Delander[375]. It has the inscription "Sir Nicholas Williams Baronet AD 1710" with the Williams crest, the lion rampant, beneath and the motto *"Mea virtute me involvo."*
It is now in two pieces; the elaborate brass upper part and gnomon is in the Carmarthen museum at Abergwili, and the stone column on which it stood is probably incorporated into the Edwinsford bridge over the Cothi at the southern end of the parapet where the carved and moulded stone can still be seen. Thomas Jenkins[376] of Llandeilo in his diary entries for 25 -27 April 1844 recounts that he "set a sundial in the churchyard…went to Edwinsford to compare the dial there with the one I had set up and found it 4.5 inches after….to Golden Grove, found there 5 inches before Edwinsford dial lat.52 deg.6 mins. Golden Grove 51 deg.32 mins."

Thomas Jenkins notes in his diary that he purchased "timber for the Edwinsford new bridge for which I have drawn plans" (25 June 1847), then on 20 October he was at Edwinsford to mark out the timber for the bridge, on 26 October he "took Peter, Ben Jones and David Davies to Edwinsford to commence the timber work" and took lodgings at the Swan Inn in Talley, by 30 October he had laid all the beams on the piers, by 5 November he had finished planking the roadway, on 10 November having framed the hand-railing for the bridge he got them

375 Daniel Delander (c1678-1733) was apprenticed to Thomas Tompion and became a member of the Clockmakers' Company. He invented the lock spring for clock cases as well as the first independent seconds stopwatch. He practised from the Dial in Devereux Court, Two Temple Gardens, and then in Fleet Street.

376 *The Diary of Thomas Jenkins p44.* Thomas Jenkins (1813-71) started as a carpenter and cabinet maker. He helped to design and build the new bridge at Llandeilo. He also built pile drivers and pumps, boats, coracles, made violins, coffins, artificial legs, and apparently sundials. He was a quite remarkable self-taught man interested in science and engineering, astrology, mining and public utilities like gas and water, which he brought to Llandeilo. He walked for miles everywhere. He started his diary in 1826 and kept it throughout his life. See Chapter 15.5

taken by wagon to Edwinsford, on 18 November "fine moonlight, frosty night. Borrowed Mr Price's boat. Peter and self boating on the lake [at Talley] from 7 to 9pm". On 19 November he completed the bridge at 1pm and went with Peter to Llansawel Fair. On 2 May 1849 he "took Peter to paint Edwinsford bridge. Walked on from there over the hills to Aberdauddwr" (where his sweetheart lived). I assume that this bridge built in 1847 was a second wooden one in addition to the existing stone bridge and that it has not survived.

There is some confusion on the old maps as to whether Edwinsford was located in the parish of Llansawel or the parish of Talley. The River Cothi was the boundary traditionally so all the demesne north and east of the river was in the parish of Llansawel. However the family for unknown reasons (and despite their family vault being at Talley Abbey) wanted the mansion and part of the demesne south and west of the river to be in the parish of Llansawel so they simply used their influence to change the boundary accordingly; hence the maps and census returns showed the mansion in the parish of Llansawel.

12. Residents and Census Returns

The following table is an estimate from available records of the owners and residents of Edwinsford / Rhydodyn.

YEAR	OWNER	RESIDENTS
13th Cent	Gruffydd ap Meurig Goch	
13th C	Tryhaiarn ap Riwallon (20)	Tryhaiarn and Joan
	Philip (22)	Philip and Catherine
14th C	Llywelyn ap Philip (24)	Llywelyn and Elen
	David ap Llywelyn (25)	David and Angharad
15th C	Morgan ap David (27)	Morgan and Als
	David ap Morgan (28)	David and Margaret
	Morgan Fychan (29)	Morgan and Margaret
	Einion (30) issa; Howell (31) ucha	Enion and Howell
	Rhys (33) issa; John ucha	Rhys and John
16th C	William (36) issa; Lewis (34) ucha	William and Lewis families
	Rhys (39) issa; Lewis family ucha	Rhys and Lewis families
-1612	David (40) issa and ucha	David and Jane
-1627	Rees Williams (41)	Rees (ucha); Walter Lloyd (issa)
-1676	Nicholas Williams (43)	Nicholas (ucha); Lloyds (issa) until 1661
1676-94	Sir Rice Williams (45)	Sir Rice and Lady Mary Williams
1694-1745	Sir Nicholas Williams (51)	Sir Nicholas and Mary (to 1720)
1745-62	Thomas Williams (54)	Thomas and Anne Williams
1762-92	Bridget (56) and RB Hodgkinson	Bridget and Robert Hodgkinson
1792-1797	Arabella (58) and Sir James Hamlyn (57)	Sir James and Arabella Hamlyn
1797-1829	Sir James Hamlyn Williams (60)	Sir James and Lady Diana
1829-61	Sir James Hamlyn Williams (61)	Sir James and Lady Mary
1861-72	Mary Eleanor (71) and Sir James Williams-Drummond (73)	Sir James and Lady Eleanor
1872-1913	Sir James HW Williams- Drummond (68)	Sir James and Lady Madeline (67)
1913-70	Sir James HW Williams- Drummond (69)	Sir James and Lady Enid (to c1939)
1940-45		Jewish school from Brighton

YEAR	OWNER	RESIDENTS
1945-		3 Polish refugee families
1950s-60s		(becoming derelict)
1970-78	Frank A Coombs (d1978)	(derelict)
1980s-1991	Len and Irene Moult	(derelict)
c1991-97	Bernard Kettle	(derelict)
c1997-2001	Jonathan Heron	(derelict)
2001-	Neil Callan	(derelict)

The British Government took its first national census in 1801 and a census has been taken every 10 years since then except in 1941, although the 1841 census was the first to give details of names and addresses. One cannot wholly rely on the ages given in some of the early census returns since ages were rounded down to the nearest five years (children under the age of 15 were recorded with their exact age) and often women seem to have changed their ages for several reasons. The 1851 census (on 30 March), 1861 census (on 7 April), 1871 census (on 2 April), 1881 census (on 3 April), 1891 census (on 5 April), 1901 census (on 31 March) and 1911 census (on 2 April) do provide much information. However census returns are only released to the public after 100 years so we have no official information after 1911 and have to depend on local family knowledge and other sources. The 1911 census was interesting because it gives details of how long a present marriage had lasted, the number of children born alive and the number who had died. But because of the suffragette movement many thousands of women refused to participate either by not including their names or by staying away on the night of 2 April 1911; I do not believe that this has affected the local census returns which are relevant.

The Edwinsford Estate was managed by the Williams family for generations with the assistance of bailiffs, gamekeepers, farm labourers and other servants housed in the various farm buildings, the lodges and in other surrounding buildings; some details are given below in Chapter 14.

YEAR	EDWINSFORD MANSION (EDWINS HAMLET) LLANSAWEL CENSUS RETURNS
1841	[Family not at home] David Morgans (65) farm bailiff, Grace Morgans (45)
1851	[Family at Clovelly Court Devon] Grace Morgan (59) widow housekeeper
1861	[Family at Clovelly Court Devon] Grace Morgan (69) housekeeper,
1871	[Family at London home at 34 Great Cumberland Place] Mary Morgan (21) laundress, Kezia Devonald (22) housemaid
1881	[Family not at home] Amelia Pentoney (35) housekeeper, Margaret Edwards (30) laundry maid, Sarah Rees (23) housemaid, Rose Smith (19) housemaid, William Reynolds (19) groom
1891	**WILLIAMS DRUMMOND: James Hamlyn** (34) Baronet and magistrate born Clovelly Court Devon, Madeline (43) wife born Exton Rutland, Annabella Leeke (36) sis born Llansawel, Francis Drummond (27) bro land agent and magistrate born Llansawel, Marguerite Drummond (25) sis in law born Kensington, Frances Clifton (14) step-dau born Westminster, Charles Clifton (13) stepson, Eleanor Clifton (68) visitor widow, Elsie Inglis (20) governess born Scotland, Janet Gracie (38) housekeeper, Mary Maddison (38) lady's maid, Sarah Elford (22) cook, Kate Williams (26) laundry maid, Annie Whitmore (38) housemaid, Sarah Davies (23) laundry maid, Elizabeth Davies (18) housemaid, Catherine Morgan (16) scullery maid, Catherine Lowson (20) housemaid, Catherine Jamieson (23) lady's maid, Sarah Harries (38) lady's maid, Charles Needs (41) butler born Exeter, Edred Gray (19) footman
1901	**DRUMMOND: Sir JHW Bart** (44) Lord Lieutenant, MD Drummond (53) wife, JHW Drummond (9) son, Ethel Young (26) governess, Sarah Elford (33) cook, Elizabeth Weatherly (32) lady's maid, Kate Davies (24) nurserymaid, Elizabeth Price (23) housemaid, Eleanor Leigh (17) housemaid, Sarah Robinson (21) laundrymaid, Catherine Jones (17) housemaid, Elizabeth Leigh (19) scullerymaid, Mary Hayward (27) kitchenmaid, Kate Williams (35) laundrymaid, William Knight (20) footman, David Jones (14) boy serv

YEAR	EDWINSFORD MANSION (EDWINS HAMLET) LLANSAWEL CENSUS RETURNS
1911	**WILLIAMS DRUMMOND: James** (54) widower born Clovelly Court, James Hamlyn Williams Drummond (19) son born Stratford Place London, Charles Clifton (34) stepson Capt Army Ret born Richmond Terrace London, William Wright (30) footman, Eliza Price (33) housemaid, Emily Prickett (19) housemaid, Jane Pratt (38) cook, Ellen Barber (20) kitchen maid, Rose Williams (44) laundry maid, John Trace (24) footman, Elizabeth Weatherley (42) housekeeper, Charles Needs (62) butler born Exeter

YEAR	34 GREAT CUMBERLAND PLACE LONDON CENSUS RETURNS
1871	**WILLIAMS: Lady Mary** (78) born Castle Hill Devon, Lady Eleanor Drummond (45) dau born Edwinsford, Annabella Drummond (16) granddau born Edwinsford, Sir James HW Drummond (14) grandson born Clovelly, Hugh Drummond (11) grandson born Clovelly, Francis Drummond (7) grandson born Edwinsford, Annie Fairbrother (30) governess, Eliza Morgan (65) housekeeper, Annie Jones (34) lady's maid, Mary Smith (43) cook, Susan Addicott (24) kitchenmaid, Maria Short (21) maid, Mary Nathan (20) maid, John Micklewright (64) butler, Henry Rumbold (30) coachman

13. Major Carmarthenshire Landowners

In 1837 the major landlord landowners in the parishes of Llansawel, Talley and Cynwil Gaeo were Sir James Hamlyn Williams (61) of Edwinsford, the Earl of Cawdor, Judge John Johnes of Dolaucothi, and George Lloyd of Brunant. By 1873 the Williams- Drummond family were in the most senior ranks of the county gentry while their close neighbours, the Johnes of Dolaucothi and the Lloyds of Brunant, were not if we assess their rank by acreage, although the public service and philanthropy of all three families to the local community was undoubtedly impressive.

The Great Landowners of Wales in 1873[377] were defined as those landowners with both estates exceeding 3,000 acres and having rentals of at least £3,000 per annum; the best agricultural estates yielded about £1 per acre. The Return of Owners was compiled by the Local Government Board from material received from the clerks to guardians of the poor for their respective districts obtained from valuation lists used for rating purposes. Many of the landowners had estates in more then one county of course. In Carmarthenshire the total acreage held by the great landowners was 157,807 acres being 30.9 per cent of the total acreage, and their total rentals were £112,752 being 26.8 per cent of the total rentals for the county. The results for Carmarthenshire were as follows:

Owner	Address	Size of Estate	Gross Rental pa
Lord Ashburnham	Sussex	5,685	£3,548
Lord Cawdor[378]	Golden Grove	33,782	£20,780
AH Saunders Davies	Pentre, Pembs	3,702	£3,118
Sir JH Williams-Drummond	Edwinsford	10,281	£6,357
Lord Dynevor	Llandeilo	7,208	£7,253
AJ Gulston	Derwydd	6,744	£10,976
JWM Gwynne Hughes	Tre-gib	6,797	£3,990
ACH Jones	Carmarthen	7,662	£4,610
Morgan Jones	Llanmilo	11,031	£5,867
CW Mansel-Lewis	Stradey	3,139	£4,265
David Pugh	Llandeilo	6,198	£3,569
HL Puxley	Llethr Llesti	6,522	£4,969
Sir JS Cowell-Stepney	Llanelli	9,841	£7,047
WDH Campbell-Davys	Neuadd Fawr	4,000	£1,992
John Johnes	Dolaucothi	3,172	£1,615

377 Return of Owners of Land 1873; Francis Jones: *Ceredigion (1960) p12-3*; Brian James NLWJ (1966) Vol XIV p301-320; Gerald Morgan: *Trawsgoed p224*; Dylan Rees p84

378 Lord Cawdor had 70,000 acres in three counties

William Peel of Taliaris were noted as a major landowner in Carmarthenshire without satisfying both of the above conditions.

Of those other landowners with estates in more than one county it is worth noting that John Davies-Lloyd of Alltyrodyn was listed as having a total of 6,877 acres and £3,231 annual rental split between Cardiganshire and Carmarthenshire; and Sir Thomas Davies Lloyd Bt of Bronwydd Cards had 7,913 acres and £5,361 annual rental split between Pembrokeshire, Cardiganshire and Carmarthenshire.

In 1904 Fred Price listed the major local landowners as being Sir James Williams- Drummond Bt (68), Sir James Hills-Johnes VC GCB of Dolaucothi, Lt Col Methuen, JM Davies JP of Froodvale, C Froodvale Davies JP, Meuric Lloyd JP, and Capt GWDB Lloyd of Brunant.

By comparison in Cardiganshire in 1873 the major landowners included the Vaughan/Lisburne family of Trawsgoed (42,666 acres and £10,579 income pa); the Pryse family of Gogerddan (28,684 acres and £10,623 pa); the Powell family of Nanteos (21,933 acres and £9,024 pa); and the Waddingham family of Hafod (10,963 acres and £1,638 pa).

14. Edwinsford Demesne

In the feudal system the demesne (derived from the French, demeine, and the Latin, dominus) was all the lands retained by a Lord of the Manor for his own use and support which were farmed by villeins and serfs for him; these did not include his other lands leased to tenants and others. There were several houses and other buildings on the Edwinsford demesne within the so called Edwins Hamlet in which the estate workers and their families lived; governesses, cooks, maids, footmen and other house servants lived in the mansion itself as we have seen from its census returns. The demesne also contained the locations for the gamekeeping, hunting, fishing and other sporting and leisure activities described in Chapter 15. When the last ox[379] to plough at Edwinsford died its hoof was preserved by the Williams-Drummond family as a symbol of the decline of traditional farming and a way of life which had lasted for generations.

Today much of the area including the remaining buildings across the Cothi opposite the derelict mansion are grade 2 listed.

Home Farmhouse 2016

[379] Mark Baker: *Y Plas-The Story of the Welsh Country House (2013)*

14.1 Edwinsford Home Farmhouse [SN 633347]

YEAR	EDWINSFORD HOME FARM HOUSE CENSUS RETURNS
1841	**JONES: Sarah** (25) agric lab, Ann Pritchard (20) agric lab, Jane Jones (14) ser
1851	**DANIEL: David** (68) agric serv born Conwil Gaeo, Mary Rees (52) dairymaid, Margaret (25) dairymaid, Thomas Peters (19) under waggoner
1861	**BROCTICE: James** (35) farm manager, Elizabeth (33) wife with 4 children and 2 dairymaids
1871	**REES: Morgan** (57) waggoner, Margaret (53) wife dairymaid, Mary (14) dau
1881	**TROTTER: Alexander** (56) farm bailiff of 500 acres employing 12 labourers, Margaret (52) wife, Margaret (21) dau governess, Mary (16) dau, Lily (13) dau, Alice (10) dau
1891	Emma Needs (38) wife of Charles Needs, Hercules (8) son
1901	**NEEDS: Charles** (53) butler, Emma (50) wife
1911	Emma Needs (61) wife of Charles Needs, Sarah Trace (31) visitor

The Home Farmhouse is across the River Cothi over the bridge opposite the mansion and was occupied by various farm bailiffs, some labourers and then the butler Charles Needs and his family. Employees occupied it, although for a short time during the 1930s Sir Jimmy and Lady Enid lived there instead of in the mansion before they left to live full-time at Hawthornden.

The 1841 Tithe Apportionment Agreement states that the mansion and demesne totalled some 569 acres and the farm bailiff would have been responsible for farming it and for the employees on the farming land, but not for the estate lands which were tenanted and managed by the estate's land agent.

The estate accounts for 1903 (see Chapter 16.7) show that the land agent for Sir Joe Williams-Drummond (68) paid the sum of £67.17s.4d in total for annual outgoings for the demesne (which included stables, gardens, ironmongery, grain, straw and saddlers) and another £104.17s.9d for the expenses of the Home Farm out of a total expenditure of some £7,266; the largest outgoings were £2,817.13s.8d being interest on loans, £500 for the Mortgage Sinking Fund and £1,115 to Sir Joe personally for payment of private bills. The total annual rental and other receipts were £6,380.11s.0d so the estate was then running at a loss.

After the deaths of Sir Jimmy Williams-Drummond (69) and of Frank Coombs his butler, the various farm buildings opposite the mansion were sold in the late 1970s and there have been a number of owners since that time. Frank Coombs's executors sold off the lovely staircase, fire places and wooden panels in the mansion itself which by then had become uninhabitable together with numerous family heirlooms (including Lady Madeline's photo album which was bought by her relative Hon John Vaughan of Trawsgoed) at a sale in Lampeter in 1979. Len Moult the new owner then had another sale at Edwinsford on 22 June 1991 of livestock, farm machinery, tools and antique furniture. He sold the remaining estate to Bernard Kettle in 1991 who later onsold[380] to Jonathan and Nikki Heron, who lived in the Farmhouse for some time. By all accounts the Herons were difficult neighbours who split the estate up and sold parts of it off. The Herons sold the Home Farmhouse and moved to live down the valley in Slatehill Farmhouse on the estate, which they built and from where they continued to manage the sporting rights and timber. In 2011 they sold the farming and sporting estate to Jamie Philipps (see Chapter 15); Jonathan Heron moved to Pembrokeshire leaving his wife resident in Slatehill Farmhouse, which she left when it was sold in late 2016 to Jamie Philipps.

[380] Knight Frank sales particulars c1997 offered the Farmhouse with 8 acres for £180,000

The Herons had sold the Home Farmhouse to Richard and Fiananda Curtis from Brecon; he had worked in RAF Intelligence. Fiananda and her friend Diana Millbery then turned the house into the Self Realization Meditation Healing Centre (SRMHC); this was run as a charitable trust "bringing uplifting and spiritual renewal to all who visit" and offering a retreat for meditation. It was part of a worldwide meditation movement founded by Mata Yogananda Mahasaya Dharma. It also provided a residential "animal healing" course involving horses. They marketed[381] themselves as members of UK Healers, British Wheel of Yoga, International Yoga Network, Register of Exercise Professionals and National Federation of Spiritual Healers. It was not a great success and relations between husband and wife were soured when she donated the house to the charity without her husband's consent and left to live with her lover. The husband sued her for his share in the property and eventually won his case. After being empty for some time following the court case the property was bought in 2014 and then renovated by the current owners, Jonathan and Marlene Davies, who have three children. Jonathan is a director of the Cambrian Pet Foods business based in Pencader and Llangadog while Marlene had recently opened a furniture shop, Davies & Co, in Llandovery.

Originally there was an early mid 18th century cowhouse[382] on the site. An engraving by Sandby c1776[383] shows an 8-bay cowhouse which was remodelled when a new farmhouse was built on the east side forming an L shape. The 1882 estate accounts record expenditure on repairing "some inconsiderable part of the farmhouse at Edwinsford and building a new and residue of the same". The farmhouse which was rebuilt in 1822 was thus a remodelling of the earlier building built onto the east end of the cowhouse or byre. To the west of the old cowhouse is a long barn range with a projecting loading bay and a cartshed and granary. The farmyards lie behind. The old cowhouse was a one and a half storey, random rubble construction with a stone tiled roof which was hipped to the two-storey farmhouse. Its south-facing frontage was accessed via eight equally spaced openings headed with cambered stone voussoirs. Five of these were retained when the farmhouse was built to the east; the windows are sashes under stone voussoir heads. The remainder were modified to form a central door and windows to either side and became incorporated into the farmhouse. During the 19th century two hipped dormer windows with slated sides were added above this converted part of the cowhouse. An old arched cart entrance at the western end has been blocked off while a door at the eastern end incorporated into the latter farmhouse is now accessed via a 20th century porch.

© *Hugh Clifton*

Home Farm gates with the Gamekeeper and the Boar c1912

Today the picturesque Edwinsford Farmhouse[384], which has been grade 2 listed since 1995, has some lovely old flagstones and is oakbeamed with an inglenook fireplace. It has five double bedrooms, a dining room, hall, drawing room with oakbeamed fireplace, kitchen, utility room and two bathrooms with an attached barn, walled garden with an old small pond, and a kitchen garden. It also has studio accommodation in an old building which may have been used as a smithy, some outbuildings which could have been livestock sheds or cowsheds for the dairy, and has a total area of some 7.5 acres.

---

381 Y Llychau

382 Cadw: *Register of Landscapes, Parks and Gardens of Special Historic Interest in Wales*; NLW Edwinsford archives; Dyfed Archaeological Trust

383 P Sandby: *Views in Wales in Aquatinta from drawings taken on the spot (1776)*

384 Strutt & Parker sales particulars c2013

© Hon John Vaughan
Home Farm gates with the Gamekeeper and the Boar c1926

© Hugh Clifton
Gamekeeper and family c1912

© Hugh Clifton
The Butler c1912

© Hugh Clifton
Coachman c1912

© Hugh Clifton
Charcoal burning c1912

© Tom Lloyd
Charles Needs, butler c1921

14.2 Edwinsford Coach House [SN 633347]

YEAR	EDWINSFORD COACH HOUSE CENSUS RETURNS
1841	**COLEGATE: Catherine** (35) with 5 children
1851	**COLEGATE: Catherine** (49) coachman's wife and laundress with 3 children
1861	**COLEGATE: Catherine** (59) wife of coachman born Ireland, Elizabeth (18) dau and 1 lodger
1871	**GWYNNE: Isaac** (57) coachman, Elizabeth (52) wife
1881	**LABAN: George** (34) coachman, Ellen (34) wife, Ethel (1) dau, George (2 mon) son
1891	**HOARE: William** (38) coachman, Mary (40) wife, Gladys (2) dau, Richard Powell (19) groom
1901	**COOK: William Thomas** (28) groom
1911	**HALL: Charles** (46) widower coachman

Coach House 2017

The Coach House is a good late Georgian estate building and was occupied by the coachman and his family for generations; it was a large complex of stables and coach houses around an enclosed square courtyard and is shown on the 1838 Tithe Map. It is next to the Home Farmhouse nearest to the main road (B4337) through the iron gates entrance. It is a rubble stone building with hipped slate roofs and attic gables. It was remodelled after a fire at the beginning of the 19th century. Sir James Hamlyn (57) built a new stable block in 1802; a tablet[385] over the archway used to record this fact. The front stands on two storeys with a central carriage arch and there is a single storey extension. The 1886 map shows the stable yard having four sides behind the front. The central round entrance arch which used to lead to the courtyard has since been infilled and there remains an open yard in front of the building. The wings formed a range of courtyard buildings originally with round arched doorways.

© Hon John Vaughan
Gates to Coach House c1926

385 FDWD: *Annals p12*

The coachman and groom from 1823 was James Colegate who had several children with his wife Catherine. Their children included: Mary Anne (b1822) who married William Jones (d1871) in 1853 and emigrated to New York in 1878 with her son Edwin; James (1823-4); John (b1825), a postboy at Llansawel who later lived at the Black Lion, married Mary Moore (d1856) and their daughter was Mary (d1857); Thomas (b1827); James (b1829); William (b1831); Henry (b1833); and George (b1835). The family was living at 2 George Terrace in Llansawel from the 1870s until about 1883.

In the early 20th century the building was left empty for many years and became derelict until in 1984 Brian and Linda Giles bought it from Len Moult (then the owner of the mansion) and converted it into a private residence. They have lived there ever since and run a domiciliary care agency which provides packages of care to the needs of local people with complex needs.

4.3 Edwinsford Dairy [SN 633347]

The dairy house (now Dairy Cottage) is near to the Home Farmhouse across the lane and on the other side to the Waggoners House. Its garden runs down to the Cothi. It is probably early 18th century[386] rubble built and was formerly whitewashed. It was repaired in 1822 probably when the current panelled window shutters were installed. It had a stone tiled roof with an early 19th century timber consoled

Dairy Cottage with bell tower 2016

[386] Cadw

cornice, slated barges, and on the roof has a dressed stone belicot with rounded head containing an impressive bell dated 1743 which came from the former chapel attached to the mansion; presumably the bell was used to summon the estate workers. Its two-storey rear wing contains evidence of the former dairy. It has been grade 2 listed since 1966 and is now a delightful residence with three bedrooms, and a lovely garden of about 0.6 acres.

Ron Thomas used to live there in the 1980s. When the property was put on the market in c1997[387] the asking price was only £20,000 since it was subject to occupation for life by a Mrs Philips. The current owner is an absentee landlord who lets the property as a holiday cottage.

14.4 Cothi View and Cothi Lodge [SN 633347]

In the 1886 map there is shown a long building next to the Home Farmhouse which, being close to the dairy, was probably used as a cowbarn, cowshed and outbuildings. Part of this building was later demolished and today the rest is divided into two residences, Cothi View and Cothi Lodge. Cothi Lodge was bought by Peter and Lorna Jones from Bernard Kettle, who owned the mansion before the Herons. Sadly Peter, who was keen on the local estate shoot, has recently died and Lorna who is in her eighties now lives there with her daughter.

2016

[387] Knight Frank sales particulars

14.5 Edwinsford Stables, Barns and Waggoners House [SN 633347]

© Hugh Clifton
Sir Joe with Cecil and Cuthbert Clifton at the Stables c1912

© Hon John Vaughan
Barns and stables c1926

©Hon John Vaughan
c1926

Modernised Stables 2016

YEAR	EDWINSFORD STABLES CENSUS RETURNS
1841	**Daniel: David** (55) serv, John Davies (35) ser, David Edwards (25) ser, James Bowen (14) ser
1851	No entry
1861	**REES: Morgan** (48) labourer, Margaret (45) wife, Mary (5) dau, James Gorley (39) boarder painter
1871	No entry
1881	**REES: Morgan** (68) waggoner, Margaret (64) wife dairymaid
1891	**REES: Margaret** (75) widow dairymaid
1901	**REES: William** (27) gamekeeper
1911	**LLOYD: Samuel** (37) waggoner, Mary (39) wife, David (6) son

The stables and barns (referred to in some census returns as the Waggoners House) were occupied by farm workers and from the late 1840s by the Rees family. Morgan Rees worked on the estate as a labourer and later as a waggoner with his wife Margaret working as a dairymaid. William Rees was probably their grandson who is stated in 1901 to be a gamekeeper. The other senior gamekeeper, Daniel Lewis, was living in Cwm Cottage (see Chapter 15).

The building was later reduced in size and when the estate was divided up and sold in lots the property was divided into two mews. The Mews (as they are now called) are owned by Bernard Kettle, the former owner of the mansion. The Upper Mews on the first floor is currently empty, while the Lower Mews on the ground floor is let to tenants for disabled people who are in need of care; they are supported by Brian and Linda Giles who live nearby in the Coach House.

14.6 Edwinsford Garden Cottage [SN 633347]

© Hugh Clifton *Garden gate and gardener c1912*

Garden Cottage 2016

Dai and Elais Evans (gardeners) c1920

YEAR	EDWINSFORD GARDEN COTTAGE CENSUS RETURNS
1841	**FULFORD: William** (55) gamekeeper, Susanna (45) wife with 2 children
1851	No entry
1861	No entry
1871	**BOWEN: Lewis** (30) gardener born Llandeilo, Rosa (31) wife, Rosa (11 mon) dau, Jessie (30) cousin
1881	**NEEDS: Charles** (53) butler born Devon, Emma (31) wife, Mary Cottrell (25) sis in law, Charles Cottrell (1) nephew
1891	No entry
1901	**WILLIAMS: John** (50) agric labourer
1911	**WILLIAMS: John** (60) labourer, Hannah (61) wife dairymaid

The Garden Cottage was built about 1811 and was occupied by estate gardeners, the butler and other estate labourers during the 19th century. In 1841 the gamekeeper, William Fulford, lived there with his family before the gamekeeper was moved to Cwm Cottage nearer the pheasants.

In 1871 Lewis Bowen, a gardener looking after the gardens both sides of the river, was living there; by 1881 he and his family had moved to Iron Gate Lodge and they stayed there until his retirement even though he was later to become the farm bailiff.

In 1881 Charles Needs, the butler from Devon who was known by the family in Clovelly, was living there with his family, but by 1891 he had moved up-market to live in the Home Farmhouse which had traditionally been occupied by the farm bailiff. By 1911 he was living in the mansion itself while his wife continued to live in the Farmhouse.

Behind and adjacent to the cottage there is a most impressive gateway over 3m tall which leads to a lovely walled garden. The doorway used to be arched and to either side there were two stone pillars topped with stone balls on plinths. The space between the pillars was infilled with stone and the whole was capped with stone slabs. The walled garden dates from about 1811 and its 3m high rubble walls enclosed the irregular shaped garden of some 2.2 hectares. Other entrance doorways to the garden were sited behind Garden Cottage, to the right of the Coach House, and in the north-east corner. The 1886 and 1906 maps also show some glasshouses. Fruit and vegetables were grown in abundance for use in the mansion and also given to the poor.

Following the break up of the estate in the 1970s the property was sold. In 1997 the property was put on the market[388]. It was later bought by Jonathan Heron who sold it in 2011. The current owners are Catherine and Alan Griffiths who bought it in 2013.

© Hugh Clifton *Adjacent to Garden Cottage c1912*

388 Knight Frank sales particulars

14.7 The Barn [SN 633347]

The 1886 map shows the Barn as a long single storey building next to Garden Cottage and opposite Tŷ Peggi across the lane. I can find no census returns for it which suggests that it was indeed used merely as a barn and outbuildings for farming. It has since been wholly renovated and is now a three bedroom house with a long and large living room with exposed beams and a stone fireplace.

Andrew Roberts, who owns the Plough Inn at Rhosmaen, bought it from Jonathan Heron and lived there for some years. The current owners are Derrick and Georgina Pounder who bought it for retirement. Derrick Pounder used to be a forensic pathologist and Professor of Forensic Medicine at Dundee University and the Director of its Centre for Forensic and Legal Medicine with an impressive record of serving on international investigations including in Kosovo, Bosnia, the Middle East and South Africa.

The Barn 2016

14.8 Tŷ Peggi [Peggy's house] [SN 633347] and Dovecote

This is a picturesque late 19th century cottage near the Garden Cottage and has been grade 2 listed[389] since 1995. It is unclear why it is so named but presumably Peggi was a former occupant; some believe she might have been a seamstress. The cottage is approached by a private track which continues past the Barn to the Garden Cottage. The house consists of a main one and a half storey range with a single storey parallel range at the rear. The walls are of stone rubble and the main range has a gabled roof. It has been extended by one bay and has a four-bay façade. There are three slate-hung gabled dormers on the roof and three groundfloor windows with pointed brick heads. This façade has much latticed detail. A more modern extension was added later. Today the house has three bedrooms, kitchen, two reception rooms, two bathrooms, exposed oak beams, an inglenook fireplace, oak floors, period oak surround lattice glazed windows, and a lovely garden of about one acre with two outbuildings.

Dovecote 2016

[389] Cadw; BJP sales particulars

In the garden there is an old 18th century dovecote which is a small square pyramidal stone-tiled roof structure; the birds gained access through a small square stone-roofed wooden tower in the centre of the main roof. On the other side is a door for collecting birds or eggs. It is a rare and well preserved feature of the demesne which reminds us of its history. On the 1886 map there is shown a "stone" in what is now the garden; sadly it is no longer there.

The ownership history of the house is unclear since the estate was broken up. Barry David bought the property in 2002 and he sold it to the current owners, Peter and Brenda Christman, in 2005. Peter is a delightful man and retired mechanical engineer from near Birmingham. They have put the house on the market with a view to retiring to the West Country to be near their grandchildren.

Tŷ Peggi 2016

14.9 Edwinsford Mill and Old Lodge [Felin Waun] [SN 634345]

YEAR	EDWINSFORD (MILL) OLD LODGE CENSUS RETURNS
1841	**MURRY: Peter** (60) agric lab, Elizabeth (55) wife, Thomas (20) son
1851	**MURRY: Elizabeth** (70) agric lab
1861	**RICHARDS: Rachel** (44) stocking knitter born Talley
1871	**THOMAS: William** (62) carpenter, Margaret (60) wife
1881	**EVANS: David** (83) labourer, Mary (8) granddau
1891	**DAVIES: William** (28) agr labourer, Mary (27) wife, David (11) son, Thomas (2) son, William (7 mon) son
1901	No entry
1911	**DAVIES: Lettice** (71) widow

Old Lodge 2016

As shown on the 1886 map there were originally two buildings at this entrance (one of seven) to the Estate, which was planted with lovely oak trees. Very sadly most of these oaks were felled when the estate was broken up in the 1970s.

The corn mill itself used to be just off the main road and this medieval mill is mentioned in the Talley parish registers of 1685-1808[390].The mill was a whitewashed masonry building close to the River Cothi and there was a leat taking water from the river to power the internal overshot waterwheel which had a large oak shaft with six timber arms and an iron rim. Sadly this has all gone although some residents can still remember it in situ. Residents and others used to take their wheat to the mill[391] to be ground and from this they made their bread.

The estate accounts for 1903 (see Chapter 16.7) show that the land agent for Sir Joe Williams-Drummond (68) paid the sum of £86.14s.9d to Mary Williams of Felinwaun for grain and meal for game and another £5.3s.0d to Mary Williams for the kennels; this suggests that she was the miller who produced feed for the pheasants and other game as well as for the farm dogs and hounds in the kennels used for foxhunting and coursing. It is unclear where the kennels were but there is some evidence to suggest that they were close to the mill or closeby between the mill and Moelfre Lodge.

On the other side of the river over a small bridge is the Old Lodge which is now a cottage and used to be occupied by estate workers as shown by the census returns; the road was once one of the seven entrances to the estate. Former owners of the Old Lodge built a new house called Barnsdale on the mill's side of the river where they still live.

[390] Dyfed Archaeological Trust historic environment record

[391] Brenda James p35

14.10 Edwinsford Iron Gate Lodge [SN 634344]

YEAR	EDWINSFORD LODGE CENSUS RETURNS
1841	**Margaret Goan** (70) ser, Mary David (60) ser, Sarah Jones (30) ser
1851	No entry
1861	uninhabited
1871	**EVANS: David** (70) gardener, Mary (70) wife
1881	**BOWEN: Lewis** (39) head gardener, Rosa (41) wife, Rosa (10) dau, Caroline (1) dau
1891	**BOWEN: Rosa** (20), Caroline Bowen (11)
1901	**BOWEN: Lewis** (58) farm bailiff, Caroline (21) dau housekeeper, Lewis (8) son
1911	**BOWEN: Lewis** (69) widower farm bailiff, Caroline (31) dau widow housekeeper, Ethel (4) granddau, William (2) grandson

There used to be two houses opposite the entrance to the estate on the corner across the B4302 main road; one was called Iron Gate and the other Vendale. The houses were originally built as a curious smaller model of the original Edwinsford Mansion and were later merged; the current house is called Vendale and is owned by Anthony Rees. The census return for 1841 shows some estate servants living there.

In 1861 Sir James Williams-Drummond (73) built the Edwinsford Iron Gate Lodge on the other side of the road within some new iron gates; his initials are marked on the front east side of the building (JWD 1861)[392]. I believe it is this building in which those estate employees shown in the later census returns lived. The original building has been extended into a two storey L-shaped house with dressed stone quoins. The windows are also of dressed stone.

The main estate entrance retains its appearance but used to be much more impressive, set back slightly from the main road and flanked by six dressed stone pillars about 2.5m tall with three pillars on each side. The middle pillars are topped with stone balls and those which hold the iron gates up are topped with two majestic stone lions sitting on their haunches and holding the Edwinsford coat of arms between their paws. The pillars are of rusticated sandstone and the central pair used to have pineapple finials which were later replaced with the lions. The wrought iron gates are simple in design with spear headed finials.

There used to be a circular drive around the demesne which had seven separate entrances in the early 19th century. By midway through that century the circular drive remained for carriage drives and walking but there were only two main entrances still in daily use; one of them was from the new Iron Gates to the mansion along the rhododendron lined drive.

As we have seen, in 1871 Lewis Bowen, a gardener who tended the gardens both sides of the river near the mansion, was living at that time in Garden Cottage; by 1881 he and his family had moved to Iron Gate Lodge and they stayed there until his retirement even though he was later to become the farm bailiff. He was obviously a loyal and trusted servant. Indeed Sir Joe (68) advertised Edwinsford as a Hydropathic Centre for people to recover their health and Lewis Bowen was the manager of this unsuccessful attempt to make money.

It is unclear who the occupiers of the property were thereafter until in 1974 Douglas and Helen Thomas took a 20 year lease of the house which had been left empty for six years. They bought the freehold in 1981 when the estate was broken up and tenants were given the opportunity to buy the freehold of their tenanted properties. They have lived there since 1974.

[392] Cadw

Iron Gate Lodge 2016

14.11 Moelfryn Edwinsford Forge (forge on a hilltop)(Tŷ Newydd) [SN 634344]

YEAR	EDWINSFORD FORGE CENSUS RETURNS
1841	**THOMAS: John** (25) blacksmith, Georgina (20) wife, Thomas (15) son
1851	**THOMAS: John** (38) blacksmith born Llandeilo, Georgianna (30) wife with 6 children, David Griffiths (21) blacksmith journeyman, Elizabeth Williams (13) nursemaid
1861	**THOMAS: John** (49) blacksmith, Georgianna (40) wife, David (20) son blacksmith, Sarah (18) dau, Anne (15) dau, William (11) son, Mary (9) dau, John (7) son, Thomas (5) son, Priscilla (2) dau, Anne Jones (73) lodger mother in law
1871	**THOMAS: John** (58) master blacksmith, Georgina (50) wife, Mary (18) dau, John (16) son, Thomas (14) son, Priscilla (12) dau
1881	**THOMAS: John** (69) blacksmith born Llangathen, Mary (28) dau, Sarah (7) granddau
1891	**THOMAS: John** (35) blacksmith and farmer born Llansawel, Elizabeth (38) wife born Haverfordwest, William (10) son, Annie (6) dau, John (4) son, Robert (1) son, Hugh Callum (52) servant and blacksmith
1901	**THOMAS: JOHN** (46) blacksmith, Elizabeth (45) wife, William (20) blacksmith, Harry (11) son, Albert (9) son, May (8) dau
1911	**THOMAS: John** (56) blacksmith, Elizabeth (54) wife, William (30) son blacksmith, Mary (58) sister

Blacksmiths were essential contributors to the rural economy. They made the essential handtools which all farmers needed before the tractor and mechanisation arrived. They made scythes, sickles, billhooks, spades, shovels and hand shears as well as much larger implements such as ploughs, harrows, carts and gamboes. They shod the working horses (and the oxen and cattle who used to do the ploughing before them) and they shod for the drovers on their way to the marts in England. Many did the work of farriers, coopers, saddlers and wheelwrights. They worked closely with the carpenters and wheelwrights in making wheels for the carts and putting iron tyres on them. They made horseshoes, nails, axes, pitchforks, hammers, hog's rings, hay knives, chains, gate hinges, as well as making parts of boots and shoes for the cobbler. Many blacksmiths apprenticed their own sons to carry on their trade and some took on other apprentices usually for only board and lodging. Every village used to have its own blacksmith with the noise of the anvil hammering and the forge but most blacksmiths were unable to compete with mechanisation and disappeared after the First World War. Some still survive and only trained farriers are now permitted to shoe horses.

The Moelfryn Edwinsford Forge was located across the road from Iron Gate / Vendale on the corner of the B4302 road and the lane to Moelfre Lodge. It provided the smithy services to the employees and tenants of the estate for many decades. We know from the estate accounts that it was flourishing in the early 18th century. We also know[393] that the famous blacksmith and hymn writer, Thomas (Tomos) Lewis (1759-1842), served his apprenticeship there before starting his own smithy in Talley itself at Blaenug Issa (see Chapter 24.13). As can be seen from the census returns, the Thomas family were blacksmiths there for at least a century and until after WW1.

Sir Jimmy Williams-Drummond (69) died in 1970 and left his estate to his butler and companion, Frank Coombs (1914-78), who had been living with him in Hawthornden Castle in Midlothian. Frank and the housekeeper and cook, Bessie Booth, then moved down to live in the Forge. Bessie has been born and brought up round the corner in the Old Lodge next to Felin Waun; she married a Mr Booth and they later divorced. She was a longtime and loyal servant who had been employed for many years at Edwinsford and Hawthornden. Frank and Bessie lived at the Forge until he died in 1978 and was buried (uniquely for a servant) in the private Edwinsford family burial plot in Talley Churchyard. The Forge was left to Bessie who continued to live there until the 1980s when she died of complications following her need for dialysis.

The Forge was then inherited by John and David Price, who were nephews of Bessie (her sister was their mother). It was left empty for some time before John Price and his wife Rhiannon moved in some 24 years ago (1992). They rebuilt and completely renovated the

[393] DG Griffiths: *Centenary of Thomas Lewis CA (1949) Vol 1 p15-9*; T Griffiths and Alun Morgan: *Y Llychau*

building and renamed it Tŷ Newydd after one of their previous homes. Rhiannon is a lovely lady with a fine memory and over the years has converted the plot behind the house into a fine garden. She remembers visiting and staying at Hawthornden Castle in the 1960s; she remembers in particular that the servants had to close the window shutters every evening which took a long time because there were so many of them on all the floors.

Tŷ Newydd 2016

14.12 Moelfre Lodge (lodge on a hill)[SN 626338]

YEAR	MOELFRE LODGE CENSUS RETURNS
1841	**JONES: Evan** (75) Ann (45), Mary Williams (15), Thomas Williams (6),John Thomas (25) blacksmith
1851	**JONES: Evan** (90) under keeper, Anne (59) wife, Thomas Williams (16) nephew
1861	uninhabited
1871	No entry
1881	**BLACKER: Arthur** (36) head gamekeeper, Anne (39) wife, Frank (12) son, Arthur (9) son, John (5) son
1891	**THOMAS: John** (42) labourer born Llanwenog, Hannah (42) wife, Mary (12) dau
1901	**DAVIES: Benjamin** (36) gardener, Mary (38) wife, Lizzie (9) dau
1911	**EVANS: David** (54) labourer, Mary (55) wife, Eleanor (28) dau cook in private house, Daniel (27) son working on farm, David (22) groom, Annie (19) dau, John (18) cowman, Tom (16) son, Sarah (13) dau, Hannah (12) dau, Kate (10) dau, Edith (7) dau

Moelfre Lodge stands south-east of the mansion and to the west of Iron Gate Lodge and the Moelfryn Forge. In 1838 there were seven entrances to the demesne with the main entrance then being from the west. A circular route went from the Talley road to the east, turning north and then running east across the parkland at the back of the mansion. A circular perimeter drive[394] met the first drive at Moelfre Lodge. Very fortunately the old oak-lined "Moelfre Walk" road from Moelfryn Forge to Moelfre Lodge remains so that we can still imagine the other lovely entrance roads to the Estate before the oak trees were cut down. Some of the grand oaks in the former park dated from the 16th century and are English oak (Quercus robur) rather than the native Welsh species (Quercus petraea).

Moelfre Lodge is in the same style as Iron Gate Lodge and thought to have been constructed shortly afterwards in 1864; it has not been materially altered. The old drive which used to run to the entrance can still be seen and a small earthwork in the field behind shows the course of the old perimeter drive.

There must have been some other building on or near the site where the Jones family (shown in the 1841 and 1851 census returns) lived before the new Lodge was built. Thereafter a number of estate families lived there up to the mid 20th century before the estate was broken up and many of the trees cut down.

Moelfre Lodge 2016

394 Cadw

During the 1920s Tom Evans[395] was a gardener at Edwinsford and lived in Warren Cottage opposite the Llwyncelyn cottages by Penlan overlooking Llansawel. His wife Jane was the cook at Edwinsford and their daughter Claudia was a pantrymaid. Their son Johnny was apprenticed as a cabinet-maker by his uncle Rees Jones in Ammanford and on his death Johnny, who had a rich baritone voice in the choir, took over the shop and also became the local undertaker which he did with great dignity and compassion. He fought in the Middle East during the Great War. His daughter Ness graduated from Aberystwyth University, became a teacher and married a consultant psychiatrist, Dr Gaius Davies of King's College Hospital in London.

It is thought that a Williams family who were tenants of Moelfre Lodge took the opportunity to buy the freehold. Mrs Williams retired to Llandeilo in 1995 and sold the property to a delightful Irishman, Francis O'Dempsey, who has lived there ever since.

Moelfre Walk 2016

Moelfre Walk c1910

395 Brenda James p35-6

15. Sporting and Leisure

The Edwinsford Estate enjoys a spectacular rural location in the glorious Cothi Valley bounded by wooded hillsides which run from Edwins Hamlet (described in Chapters 11 and 14) to Abergorlech. The rural estate within the demesne traditionally had an area of over 500 acres within the total of over 10,000 acres (including tenanted farms and village houses); since the breakup of the estate the sporting and leisure area now totals some 540 acres plus an additional 318 acres of sporting rights. The countryside remains unspoilt and timeless with an abundance of wild life, flora and fauna next to the beautiful River Cothi, which flows down the valley from the meadows of the former Dolaucothi and Brunant Estates not far away upstream near Pumsaint; an ideal landscape and contours for a fine sporting estate.

During the 18th and 19th centuries most Welsh gentry, like their English cousins, had a passion for field sports of all varieties. Country life and local town amusements and pursuits[396] for many residents of all classes in society involved aggression and cruelty whether it was cock fighting, bear baiting, bull baiting, hare coursing, foxhunting, shooting of game birds, or otter hunting; in the cities even watching executions in public following trials for murder or similar grave offences was a popular event. The population in local Carmarthenshire certainly did not agree with the sentiments of Sir Thomas More[397] that *"Thou shouldst rather be moved with pity to see a silly innocent hare murdered of a dog, the weak of the stronger, the fearful of the fierce, the innocent of the cruel and unmerciful. Therefore, all this exercise of hunting is a thing unworthy to be used of free men."*

The gentry considered that field sports, keeping hounds and horses, holding country house sporting weekend parties, hunt balls and hunt dinners were all an essential part of the annual social calendar. The Edwinsford families and their guests participated in these pursuits with enthusiasm, as evidenced by their game books[398] and accounts, along with their gentry neighbours in the county; indeed they considered it to be their duty to do so. Providing sporting pursuits and hospitality on one's own estate and visiting neighbouring estates for the same entertainment was very much part of the social intercourse of the day.

In Wales generally the gentry were tenacious to protect their exclusive right to hunt game and to fish. The Game Laws[399] since the end of the 17th century gave them such rights and these were enforced often very cruelly by the gentry sitting locally as magistrates with fines and imprisonment being imposed; even transportation of poachers to Australia was not unknown. Ordinary people[400] could not keep dogs, nets or guns which might be used for poaching and most could not shoot even on their own land. Sheep stealing[401] was fairly common and often seasonal reflecting changes in economic activity and the employment opportunities of the working class; records of the Gaol Fines of the Court of Great Sessions in Carmarthen show that food stealing and poaching during the 18th and early 19th centuries was affected by harvest patterns as well as hardship. The 1741 Act which made sheep stealing a capital offence led to a growing reluctance of Welsh juries to convict; indeed only about 37 per cent of defendants were found guilty in the mid 18th century.

Whilst many rural residents were suffering poverty, tolls, tithes, disease, unemployment, harvest failures, rising inflation in food prices and often religious discrimination, the Game Laws caused increasing social conflict. After 1784 only those granted game licences were allowed to kill game and of course the gentry and their gamekeepers all registered their names whereas tenants and others had no such licences. In the

---

396 Leslie Baker-Jones: *Princelings p184-195*; Herbert Vaughan: *South Wales Squires p223-232*
397 Sir Thomas More: *Utopia (1516)*
398 NLW Edwinsford archives; Colin Matheson: *Gamebook Records of Pheasants and Partridges in Wales NLWJ ix p287-294*
399 The 1671 Act gave the right to hunt game only to landowners worth £100 pa, 99 year leaseholders worth £150 pa, eldest sons of Esquires or with higher rank, and holders of licences
400 Leslie Baker-Jones: *Princelings p293 et seq*
401 N Woodward: *Seasonality and Sheep-stealing in Wales 1730-1830 Agricultural History Review 56 p25-47*

mid 19th century there were more gamekeepers[402] than policemen in the country. In 1880 the Ground Game Act gave tenants (but not employees on the estates) the right to destroy rabbits and hares on their holdings. But pheasants continued to destroy crops with no compensation for tenants so poaching[403] increased. Many gentry employed water bailiffs with police powers to enforce fishing and other rights and only the gentry riparian owners could grant permission to fish. It would not be until after the Rebecca riots and the tithe wars (see Chapter 37) that relations improved in the early 20th century. Whilst I have found no evidence of major social discontent on the Edwinsford Estate (or the Dolaucothi or Brunant Estates closeby) it must be assumed that there were such cases in the area; poaching was rife and magistrates enforced the law but often with leniency.

There is some dispute as to the validity of a painting by an unknown artist of a gamekeeper who some believe may be the gamekeeper to Sir Nicholas Williams Bt MP (1681-1745)(51); he is shown in working dress carrying a flintlock musket with his spaniel next to what is perhaps a dovecote and part of the house in the background across the river is supposed to be Edwinsford. We know that Sir James Hamlyn-Williams 3rd Bt MP (1790-1861)(61) enjoyed hunting at Edwinsford and on neighbouring sporting estates; he protected his own partridges and pheasants avidly and was warned against being too over zealous in prosecuting poachers in case it adversely affected his reputation and his future chances of getting elected to public office. Sir Joe (68) and his son Sir Jimmy Williams-Drummond (69) were also avid supporters of shooting and fishing.

Game keeper c1725

[402] Gerald Morgan: *Trawsgoed p231*

[403] DJ Williams p14, 202-220 recounts that many locals were conscientious poachers since gun licences cost £3.10sh, the value of a year old heifer in 1890. It was almost a dishonour for a local resident to take out a gun or rod licence so poaching was rife with everyone trying to avoid the bailiffs of the Edwinsford and Frwdfâl estates

15.1 Shooting

On the Edwinsford Estate we have seen that the head gamekeeper or under gamekeeper and their families were housed in the Garden Cottage in 1841, in Moelfre Lodge in 1851 and 1881, and in the Waggoners House in 1901. However the principal home for the senior gamekeeper was at Cwm Cottage [SN 613341] which is located along the north part of the valley from Edwinsford towards Abergorlech and where the game birds were reared nearby. The building has not been inhabited for several decades.

Cwm Cottage 2016

As can be seen from the census returns, the gamekeepers were William Fulford in 1841, John Jones in 1861, David Evans in 1871, and Arthur Blacker and Daniel Lewis in 1881, with Daniel Lewis continuing in that position until the early 20th century.

Keepers Cottage and the Bothy 2016

YEAR	CWM COTTAGE CENSUS RETURNS
1851	**JONES: Benoni** (49) farm lab, Anne (48) wife with 3 children
1861	**JONES: John** (30) under gamekeeper born Llansawel, Rachel (30) wife with 5 children, John Morgans (36) labourer
1871	**EVANS: David** (41) gamekeeper born Llanybyther, Anne (39) wife and 6 children
1881	**LEWIS: Daniel** (27) under gamekeeper, Gwen (24) wife, David (20 son, Thomas (4 mon) son
1891	**LEWIS: Daniel** (35) under gamekeeper, Gwen (34) wife, David (12) son, Thomas (10) son, John (4) son, Catherine (2) dau
1901	**LEWIS: Daniel** (45) gamekeeper, Gwen (44) wife, Jane (10) dau, Daniel (8) son, Blodwen (5) dau
1911	**LEWIS: Daniel** (55) gamekeeper, Jane (19) dau housekeeper, Daniel (17) son gamekeeper

Historically the Edwinsford Estate was one of the finest sporting estates in South Wales and in its prime offered pheasant, partridge, duck, woodcock, snipe and even grouse shooting. The birds were reared locally and bags of pheasant in particular were plentiful for the needs at that time. It was never a top grouse shooting estate and in the Edwardian years before the Great War guests of Sir Joe Williams-Drummond (68) would expect to bag only three or four brace of grouse[404] on a good day. When there was a grouse shoot[405] at Edwinsford on Mynydd Cynros Sir James used to invite all the lads of Talley and Llansawel to act as beaters and they of course readily took the day off school to attend. The Head Gamekeeper was in command who set the guns and planned the whole occasion. A cold lunch was brought up to the hunting lodge (nicknamed Jerusalem) by horseback after which the shoot continued. In the evening a splendid meal would be served in the mansion for the guns and other invited guests, while the beaters and the many helpers were entertained by the Head Gamekeeper in an outbuilding at Edwinsford with piles of cold beef, hams, pies etc all washed down with copious supplies of beer.

Sir Joe's near neighbour, Sir James (Jimmy) Hills-Johnes VC of Dolaucothi (1833-1919)[406],was also keen on field sports. He supported the need to grant farmers exemptions from the Dogs Act 1906 for sheepdogs. Jimmy also rode and shot game[407], went hunting for foxes and otters, and sometimes fished; the Cothi was renowned for its trout[408] and for its sewin and salmon. The press[409] recounted that "the big houses of Carmarthenshire are shortly likely to be full of guests, as shooting parties have been arranged at Pantglas, Edwinsford, Golden Grove, Dynevor, Dolaucothi and Tregybe during the ensuing month."

As we have seen in Chapter 14.9, Mary Williams of Felinwaun provided the grain and meal for the game birds on the Edwinsford Estate being reared by the gamekeepers living in Cwm Cottage. During the 1930s the housekeeper and cook, Bessie Booth[410] (see Chapter 14.11), would prepare wonderful lunches for the family's shooting guests which were held on the top of the Llether-Llwyd mountain (913ft) above Cwm Cottage with its wonderful vista over the valley below. Today the ancient and mature woodland and the steep valley sides continue to provide a good terrain for a high pheasant shoot with a variety of different drives. There is also some rough shooting for snipe, woodcock, mallard, teal, and wigeon.

In recent years up until 2011 the shooting was owned and managed by Jonathan Heron who lived close to Cwm Cottage in Slatehill Farmhouse which he built after selling the Home Farmhouse. In 2011 Jonathan Heron sold the farming and sporting estate of over 500 acres with an additional 318 acres of sporting rights to James AH Philipps (b1961), a descendant of Baron Milford of Llanstephan from the Philipps family of Picton Castle in Pembrokeshire. Jonathan Heron moved to near Newport in Pembrokeshire leaving his wife resident in

404 David SD Jones: *A Brief History of Welsh Grouse Shooting*
405 W Barry Evans: *Y Llychau (November 2011)*
406 David Lewis: *Dolaucothi p201-215*
407 Evening Express 10 September 1898 refers to a shoot of 29 brace of partridge at Dolaucothi
408 Carmarthen Journal 13 November 1891
409 Carmarthen Journal 24 October 1902
410 Bessie would continue to do the same when she moved to work at Hawthornden before WW2

Slatehill Farmhouse, which she left when it too was sold in October 2016 to Jamie Philipps. He has owned and managed the shooting and fishing activities since 2011 and is proposing to build up the shooting days from the current number of about 12 per annum without overshooting. The birds traditionally come from gamefarms in Worcestershire and the season lasts from October to January. Next to Slatehill Farmhouse is the Keepers Cottage and the Bothy [SN 614342]. The current keeper and ghillie, Neil Robbins, who is an employee of the estate lives in the Keepers Cottage; the Bothy which is attached may be used in the future as a holiday cottage or for overnight guests or customers to stay. The 380 acres of woodland is managed commercially and the farmland is let for sheep grazing to neighbouring farmers.

15.2 Fishing

Fishing has always been a popular pastime for gentry and poachers on the Rivers Tywi and Cothi including at Edwinsford which of couse also owned the additional Talley lakes for generations; indeed the family and their guests would often fish in the lakes from boats kept in the two boathouses which have not survived except for the remains of a jetty. In 1911[411] in the entrance hall at Edwinsford there was a 4.75 lbs trout in a case caught in the Cothi and also a carved wooden replica of the 27 lbs salmon caught by William Peel of Taliaris on 9 May 1879 (later auctioned on 22 June 1991 in the sale by Len Moult). The record for a pike caught in the Talley lakes was 22 lbs by Mr Long Price, the estate's agent and solicitor.

Many gentry employed water bailiffs with police powers to enforce fishing and other rights and only the gentry riparian owners could grant permission to fish. There was widespread poaching often at night. Thomas Jenkins[412] for example records in his diary that on 24 November 1830 he "went to the River Teifi to see fishing for salmon with dried straw set on fire", on 11 June 1835 he "went with father to fish for pike to the pools above Abergwili, took one of 4.5 lbs", and on 1 January 1834 he "went out shooting with Lewis Jones. Killed 1 hare and 2 rabbits."

Today the Edwinsford Estate continues to offer over five miles of private double banked fishing in the River Cothi for salmon, sea trout (known as sewin) and brown trout. It is a varied fishery with the upper beat running through meadows with few restrictions to casting and ideal for fly fishing; the lower beat runs through a wooded gorge giving anglers a variety of different waters to fish and where spinning is allowed. There are over 60 named pools and glides some of them man-made and others natural. The River Cothi is the main tributary of the River Tywi which is renowned for its sewin and it is thought that some 40 per cent of these sea trout migrate up the Cothi. Over the past 30 years pollution has been a problem further up the Cothi in the Pumsaint area (where the Dolaucothi Arms used to be an anglers' paradise) but the fish have been slowly returning in recent years. Catch and release is much encouraged these days.

© Hugh Clifton *Gamekeeper c1911*

411 South Wales Daily News (29 July 1911)
412 DC Jenkins: *The Diary of Thomas Jenkins of Llandeilo 1826-1870 (2010 Historia Wales)*

Salmon have been seen at Edwinsford as early as March but the first salmon are not usually caught until May. Salmon and grilse (a salmon which has returned to fresh water after a single winter at sea) run the river during the summer with a good autumn run from September to the season's end. In the 2007 season some 44 salmon were caught with the largest being 22 lbs; in recent years the river has been underfished and the numbers caught have been fewer. In 2016 the largest trout was 15 lbs.

Sewin are present throughout the season with good runs in April and May. Most sea trout are caught in the evening or at night with both spinner and fly. In the 2009 season some 94 sewin were caught with the largest being 14 lbs; in 2016 the largest was 8 lbs. There are also good numbers of brown trout.

15.3 Foxhunting

Hunting in Britain has of course been undertaken for centuries and there is evidence that the Celtic tribes hunted in the forests with dogs before the Romans invaded. The Laws of Hywel Dda (c880-950) make mention of the Welsh hounds and the bards wrote odes praising individual hounds. Fox hunting[413] with hounds has been prevalent in rural areas of Wales for a very long time. In Carmarthenshire some gentry families owned their own private foxhunting packs in the late 17th and early 18th centuries (some of which also hunted hares and otters); in addition some farmers owned trencher fed packs where the hounds were kept on various farms and met together on hunting days. The Tivyside Hunt[414] is probably the county's oldest Hunt which can trace its activities as far back as the 1700s. Walter Powell MP, who was Master of the Maesgwynne Hunt 1839-89 achieved a great bloodline in breeding his pack of 50 couple of hounds with some 60 horses who were good steeplechasers. The Carmarthenshire Hunt founded in 1889 prospered under various Masters including WJ Buckley and the infamous[415] Lord Kylsant MP (Owen Philipps of the Picton Castle family). The Hunt also had otterhounds to hunt otters during the summer.

Unlike shooting game and fishing which were exclusively gentry and landowning class pursuits, horse racing and fox hunting have been popular with all classes of society; indeed they required the participation of rural communities with the presentation of prizes and other social intercourse being encouraged. It has been part of the rural social culture for generations and useful for conservation and pest control in areas where lambs and other farm animals need to be protected.

At Edwinsford the hounds and other dogs used by the family were probably kennelled near Moelfre Lodge while the horses were stabled at the Coachman's Stables in Edwins Hamlet itself. Coachmen and grooms had the responsibility of keeping sufficient horses in good condition as were required by the family not only for hunting but also for pulling the carriages and traps to take the family out of the estate when required to visit neighbours, go to town or to church; stronger horses were used to pull the carts and gamboes used on the farm by the farm manager or bailiff. We know that Sir Nicholas Williams Bt (1681-1745)(51) was a great sportsman and keen on hunting; his silver hunting horn[416] was preserved at Edwinsford for many decades.

Since the post war period the two Hunts which have operated in the Edwinsford area around Talley and Llansawel have been the Cwrtycadno Farmers Hunt and the Llandeilo Farmers Hunt.

The Rhandirmwyn Hunt[417] dates back to 1914 when Mr Jones of Penrhyn Farm and Mr Alfred Jones of Rhandirmwyn were given a draft of Welsh cross hounds from Mrs Hughes of Neuaddfawr in Lampeter. The hounds were housed in a carthouse at Galltybere and then moved to a kennel at Broncwrt and were initially known as the Rhandirmwyn Hunt. Hunt meetings were held at the Miners Arms, the first Huntsman being Tom Jones of Troedrhiwcymer and the first Master being Mr AW Jones. Subsequent Masters were B Williams, GN Lloyd, Mrs Blandy and DE Thomas. Then in 1954 DE Thomas resigned as Master and formed a new pack of Welsh foxhounds called the

413 EW Price: *Horn and Hound in Wales (1890);* E Atkinson: *The Carmarthenshire Hunt (2014)*

414 Herbert Vaughan: *South Wales Squires p40-52;* Leslie Baker-Jones: *Princelings p185*

415 Lord Kylsant (1863-1937) was a businessman and MP who was found guilty at the Old Bailey in 1931 of issuing a false prospectus with intent to deceive and gaoled for 12 months [R v Kylsant 1932 1 KB 442]

416 FDWD: *Annals p7*

417 Glyn Price: *LCTA Llandovery and its Environs p457*

Cwrtycadno Hunt, and the Rhandirmwyn Hunt was then renamed the Towy and Cothi Hunt. Subsequent Masters of the Towy and Cothi Hunt have included J Davies, WE Price, Arwyn Clemens, DJ Lewis and RM Powell. The Towy and Cothi are today kennelled at Cilycwm.

The Masters of the Cwrtycadno Farmers Hunt[418] have been DE Thomas, T Jones, C Evans, Ronald Jones, Dewi Jones, Albert Williams, Huw Williams and Anthony Frost; the current Master is Goronwy Jones. The Huntsmen have been Dennis Davies, Ronald Jones, Benny Jones, Elgan Evans, Dylan Davies, Donald Jones, Hywel Herbert and Eirian Evans; the current Huntsman is Cliff Williams of Fronhaul (see Chapter 24.16). The kennels of the Cwrtycadno Hunt are next to the River Fanagoed behind Abermangoed Mill having moved there from the other side of the bridge several years ago. Many of the local farmers take one of the foxhound puppies every year to bring up with their own farmdogs until lambing time when they are old enough to return to the kennels. The Hunt meets on Tuesdays and Thursdays on foot and on Saturdays mounted. The Hunt shares some of the countryside in the north and Llandeilo to the south, and it hunts from Bwlchyrhiw across Mynydd Mallaen to Porthyrhyd, across to Llansadwrn, down to Talley across to Llanfynydd, up to Abergorlech, Llansawel, Esgairdawe and across to north of Ffarmers and via Nantyrast to the north of Bwlchyrhiw. So it hunts on the traditional former Edwinsford Estate lands to the west of Edwinsford towards Llansawel and Abergorlech.

The Llandeilo Farmers Hunt has traditionally hunted in and to the south of Talley and often started the day in front of the Edwinsford Arms in Talley. It was formed in 1948 and its Masters[419] have been: TH Jones (1948-56), Capt PG Francis (55-61), WD John (61-6), Major RS Gardner (64-74), Major JW Buckley (67-75), TMO Jenkins (74-6), CH Evans (73-7), CR Birt (74-7), WA Johnstone (76-7), P Treharne (77-8), M David (77-8), DTE Evans (77-9), J Philpin (79-85), R James (79-85), G Davies (82-7), E Bell (85-6), DE John (85-6), J Roberts (85-7), E Bell (87-9), K Mason (88-8), R Nicholson (89-90), PG Murrel (89-95), J Reed-Boulton (89-95), E Bell (95-2007), DJW Griffiths (99-2002), DE John (96-2006), P Hancock (02-04), J Barton (04-08), Mrs K Barton (04-07), C Roberts (07-09), G Guntrip (08-10), DE John (10-11), K Floyd (10-12), C Evans (10-17), M Griffiths (11-12), J Strong (13-15) and K Lawson (16-17). The Huntsmen have been: TH Jones (1948-56), T Swain (51-8), Capt PG Francis (56-61), DJ Thomas (58-65), M Morgan (65-73), P Shillam (73-5), C Shillam (75-7), I Williams (77-8), J Davies (78-9), J Roberts (79-87), D Evans (87-90), J Barton (90-3), P Murrel (93-5), E Bell (95 -2004), J Barton (04-07), E Bell (07-08), and C Evans (08-17).

Llandeilo Hunt outside Edwinsford Arms in Talley c1987. John Roberts, the Master in red coat

Since February 2005 "hunting wild mammals with a dog" has been unlawful in England and Wales under the Hunting Act 2004 except in limited circumstances although shooting foxes with a gun is lawful; hunting with dogs was banned in Scotland in 2002 but remains lawful in Northern Ireland and in the Republic of Ireland. Since the ban Hunts have continued to operate along limited lines, either by trail or drag hunting or by using the exemptions, and the numbers of participants in such hunting do not seem to have fallen. There have been a number of convictions for breach of the legislation but very few have been in Wales. In practice in the Edwinsford area the killing of foxes as pests to prevent the deaths of lambs has continued much as before whether on foot or horseback albeit in a different way in order to comply with the new regime.

418 I am grateful to Anthony Price for this information
419 I am grateful to Colin Evans for this information

15.4 Hare Coursing

Whether for sporting or hunting purposes hare coursing (the pursuit of hares with greyhounds chasing and killing hares by sight rather than by scent) has been popular since the time of the Ancient Greeks. It is mentioned by Xenophon in his work "Kynegetikos" (On Hunting) and then by Arrian in c180 AD. In England the first rules were drawn up by Thomas Howard 4th Duke of Norfolk in the reign of Elizabeth I providing for a pursuit of no more than two hounds and giving the hare a headstart (a fair law). By the mid 1850s coursing, which had originally been the preserve of the gentry, became popular with all clases and there were more than 150 coursing clubs in Britain attracting many thousands of people. The season usually ran from October to February.

At Edwinsford there were frequent coursing matches. For example[420] in February 1863 the third annual meeting of the Edwinsford Coursing Club met under the stewardship of JL Price of Talley. 29 dogs were entered for the All Aged Stakes while only 9 were entered for the Puppy Stakes. Lady Eleanor Drummond (71) was in attendance with several other ladies and gentlemen and both winning dogs were owned by David Long Price of Talley House, the family solicitor.

As we saw in Chapter 1.1, at Edwinsford in 1878 there were several coursing events attended by the residents of Llansawel and Talley and Estate tenants and employees with prizes to celebrate the coming of age of the heir to the Edwinsford Estate, Sir James (Joe) Williams-Drummond (68) the 4th Baronet.

During the 20th century coursing declined in popularity due to the development of greyhound track racing with more professional betting; by 2005 when the Hunting Act made the sport illegal there were only 30 coursing clubs left. Since 1993 in the Republic of Ireland where the practice remains lawful the hounds have been muzzled while they chase the hare. They have some 70 coursing clubs holding about 80 meets per annum in total. The dog which first causes the hare to turn wins the points.

15.5 Other Pursuits

By the 19th century well mannered and sophisticated gentry and their ladies, particularly those with London residences like the Edwinsford family who as Lord Lieutenants also had an important position in local county society, ceased to support the worst type of cruel sports like cockfighting. They participated in other activities with their families and guests including: house parties, home theatrical shows and piano recitals after dinner (some houses even had their own harpist); backgammon, snooker, bridge and other card games; concerts and garden fêtes; poetry and reading events; charity events to support and be seen to attend; croquet and tennis; even swimming at the sea side on holidays in Tenby or taking the waters at the spas in Llandrindod Wells or at the Lake Hotel in Llangammarch Wells.

Horse racing, steeplechasing, and point to pointing (often an integral part of hunting life) became very popular with all classes from about 1800 although betting sometimes caused social tensions. Indeed the Carmarthen Steeplechases became the premier meet in Wales during the mid 19th century. Horseracing and point to points continue to be well attended today despite the popularity of other forms of dog and pony racing and trotting.

Tenants and other local residents had fun with ratcatching parties and with the influence of non-conformism attended concerts, poetry recitals, singing and choral competitions, eisteddfods etc which have remained popular ever since. Many attended local travelling fairs as well as their own village fairs, horticultural shows etc (see Chapter 34).

Thomas Jenkins of Llandeilo (a hardworking undertaker and carpenter of modest means) recounts[421] that on 12 August 1835 he "went to the fair [Llandeilo], several shows. Saw a Giantess, a Hottentott woman, a flaxen-haired negro, 2 serpents, crocodile, alligator, porcupine, lemon-crested cockatoo, sand sloth, jackal, Muscovey cat, American sea-serpent, boa constrictor etc., saw a woman raise 200 lbs by her hair"; he visited many sights including Carreg Cennen Castle, Dynevor Castle, Middleton Hall, Tregib House gardens, Golden Grove gardens, St David's Column at Derry Ormond, Paxton's (Nelson's) Tower, the Dolaucothi Golds Mines[422], the Cilrychen and Llygad Llwchwr caves,

420 Welshman (13 Feb 1863)

421 Diary of Thomas Jenkins

422 David Lewis: *Dolaucothi p297-307*

© Hon John Rous and Hon John Vaughan

House party at Edwinsford November 1911 L to R: HH Prince Maurice of Battenburg (1891-1914), Major Cuthbertson, Mrs Cuthbertson, Earl of Lisburne (Trawsgoed), Miss Romily, Miss Foster, Mr Drummond, Miss Hazel Agnew, Sir Joe Williams-Drummond (68), Delme Davies Evans, HH Prince Leopold Mountbatten of Battenburg (1889-1922), Edmond Long Price

© Hon John Rous

House party at Edwinsford c1900 L to R (back): Hugh Drummond (75), Marguerite Drummond (67A), Dudley Drummond (76), anon, anon, anon, anon, Howard Meurig Lloyd (Glanyrannell)L to R (front): Lt-Gen Sir James Hills-Johnes VC (Dolaucothi), Lady Betha Hills-Johnes, Sir Joe Williams-Drummond (68), Lady Madeline (67), Viscount Emlyn (4th Earl Cawdor), anon, anon

Devil's Bridge, Hafod, and the ruins of Strata Florida Abbey; in the summer he went further afield and travelled from Swansea to Bristol by steamer to see the Clifton suspension bridge and the iron steamship SS Great Britain being built; he travelled to Pembroke Dock to see the warships and dockyard; he saw the SS Great Eastern the largest ship afloat at 24,000 tons as well as the Channel Fleet lying off Milford Haven; he visited coal mines and iron foundries; he saw the new telegraph cable which was being laid across the Atlantic; he marvelled at eclipses of the sun (15 May 1836 and 15 March 1858); he went to Swansea to bathe in the sea; he enumerated the Rhosmaen and New Inn districts of Llandeilo for the 1841 and 1851 censuses; he saw 200 families boarding a ship to emigrate to New York (23 April 1842); he went to the theatre with his family; he witnessed the Rebecca riots in 1843 and saw the Dragoons quartered in the Cawdor Arms; he helped design and build the new bridge in Llandeilo; he served on Court Leet juries and as a local constable; he served as a juror at Quarter Sessions and at the County Court; he witnessed a general fast day "ordered owing to the famine in Ireland and Scotland" (24 March 1847); he saw lightning destroy an oak and split it to the roots; he visited the famous astrologer Henry Harris[423] on 6 April 1849 just before his death; he made a tricycle (homomotive carriage with three wheels) and velocipede; he attended a "steeplechase over Dr Rees's fields, being the first exhibition of the kind at Llandeilo" (18 April 1850); he attended the Great Exhibition in London and also saw the Zoological Gardens (14 October 1851); he witnessed the first train from Swansea to Carmarthen (17 September 1852) and the opening of the Llandeilo railway (20 January 1857); in December 1858 he helped organise the welcoming reception of bands and fireworks etc for the arrival of Lord Dynevor and family at Newton House when there was a fire which he helped to extinguish; he made rifle stands for the Carmarthenshire Volunteer Rifle Corps and attended the armoury and rifle range as well as witnessing the Rifle Corps review at Dinefwr Park; he made and set up the tables at the Shire Hall for a dinner to be given to the poor and tea for the school children in commemoration of the Prince of Wales's marriage to Princess Alexandra of Denmark (10 March 1863); he noted the murder of President Abraham Lincoln at Ford's Theatre in Washington on 14 April 1865; he fitted up the market place to dine 500 people for the Choral Union and the Hall for a concert (3 October 1866); he helped set up the celebrations for Viscount Emlyn attaining his majority with bonfires, cannon and fireworks etc (13 February 1868); he witnessed an earthquake at 10.30 pm on 30 October 1868 which was felt all over the district; and he valued the personal effects of the late Lord Dynevor for probate purposes in November 1869 at £3,996.

Thomas Jenkins (1813-71) aged 33

[423] Henry Harris (1821-49) of Pantcoy in Cwrt y Cadno was the son of the infamous Dr John Harries (1785-1839)—see David Lewis: *Family Histories p228-230*

15.6 Ploughing Competitions

In the late 19th century ploughing competitions[424] for adults and boys became very popular for obvious reasons. Often these competitions would be part of a larger Show of horses, cattle, sheep, poultry etc and sometimes with a hedging and digging/ditching competition too. The annual Caio and Llanycrwys Ploughing and Hedging Match and Horse Show was famous and was held for many decades. There were similar matches in the Llansawel and Talley areas and it was a treasured family memory for anyone who won first prize.

My grandfather, David Lewis (1867-1912), who was brought up in Brynteg Farm at Cwrt y Cadno before he left to join the Metropolitan Police in London, says in his diary that in 1882 aged 14 he won 5 shillings for 1st prize in the boys class in the ploughing match at Llwynceiliog, did the same again in 1884 at Frongoch, and then he won the 1st prize of 10 shillings in the adult second class in the winter of 1886-7 at Brynteg. As with most shows there were often three or four different classes. With the advent of the tractor the art of ploughing with a horse or pair gradually died out but competitions continued for many years. I remember attending a ploughing competition on Brynteg fields in the 1960s and marvelling at the straightness of the furrows.

In 1958 the Welsh Ploughing Association was formed to encourage the art and skill of ploughing, hedging and other rural crafts including wirefencing, stonewalling, sheepdog trials etc. Horse ploughing still provides the star attraction at the shows but with the new farm machinery available today which can do reversible ploughing and seedbed cultivation there is healthy competition in that area too at the local shows. The All Wales Ploughing and Hedging Championships are held annually with over 100 competitors performing on a 100 acre site in September each year. The local South and West Wales Association was formed in 1989.

Ploughing competition at Gellicefnrhos Talley 3rd May 2010 with Ford 5000 (left), Fergie T20 and two Ford 4000

424 Elfyn Scourfield: *Y Preimin Aredig yn Sir Gaerfyrddin CA (1993) p51-60*

15.7 Tug of War Competitions

Before and after the Second World War there were several tug of war competitions in the area in which local teams participated. The competition was treated by all very seriously with great pulling battles involved; winning was a much valued feather in the cap of any local team. Teams consisted of eight men pulling the rope and one team captain who used his acumen and experience to instruct his team on tactics and when to pull and just as importantly when not to pull but hold fast.

The most prestigious local competition was held each year in Llandovery and the annual winners were crowned the South Wales Champions. On 24 September 1921 the Llandovery Licensed Victuallers Association, who had an obvious interest in the sport, donated a silver cup on terms that it could be retained by any team which won the annual competition three times. The first team to achieve this feat was the Cwrt-y-Cadno team between 1942 and 1946.

This winning team in 1946 consisted of three of the sons of Howell Jones (1869-1957) namely Seth Jones (1909-1980), Ben Jones (b1905) and Howell (known as Howell Bach)(1913-92) all very strong men from Glanmeddyg, Cynwil Jones (of Cwmdâr), Tommy James (of Esgairddâr), Emrys Jones (of Tyllwyd), Sam Jones (of Llwyndiriaid) and Ieuan Williams (then of Brynteg) with Dai Williams (1915-2005 of Brynteg) as the team captain. The reserves were Elwyn Williams (of Pentwyn) and Myrddin Davies (of Blaenrhisglog). In the final in 1946 this team beat the Llanwrda team with some pulls lasting up to 45 minutes according to Ieuan Williams.

In previous years the Cwrt team had been drawn against the Monmouthshire Police team (Gwm Wysg) which is mentioned in the autobiography of the artist Aneurin Jones.

Tug of war competitions were also common at the local Shows but sadly are rare today.

Men's Tug of War at Dolaucothi School Sports c1900

15.8 Sheepdog Trials

Sheepdog trials first started in New Zealand in 1868. The first dog trials in Wales were held in Bala on 9 October 1873 with 10 dogs and 300 spectators, and trials quickly spread to England and Scotland. Today there are local trials, area trials, county trials, national trials which are televised to great acclaim, and also World Championships. The layout of the trial field differs from country to country although the competition will normally include tests on driving, cross driving, shedding, penning and singling. Enormous prices are often given for pedigree border collies.

For most elements the judge focuses on the behaviour of the sheep not the dog or handler. Dogs are judged on the efficiency of their work and on qualities of good stockmanship. A dog which needlessly harasses or hurries sheep is penalised and a dog which bites a sheep may be disqualified. The South Wales Sheepdog Association is the local association. The International Sheep Dog Society organises national and international championships. Some of the local Shows still have classes for sheepdog trials which are very competitive.

There were local annual sheepdog trials held in the Llansawel and Talley area as well as at Pumsaint, Caio and Cwrt-y-Cadno for many years but sadly these ceased some years ago.

15.9 Shearing Matches

In the 19th century sheep were often washed in the river before shearing but it was found that washing the wool in hot water was more effective so the custom became obsolete. Until relatively recently in Carmarthenshire shearing day on each farm was a major event as well as a social event for the farmer and his family and for the visiting neighbours who helped; no money changed hands and each farmer would help his neighbour. Shearing in the early days was done with hand shears consisting of two blades arranged like scissors with a hinge at one end. When diesel machine power and, later on, electricity arrived it became much more common and quicker to use machine shears which operate like human hair clippers.

Today some farmers still shear themselves with the paid help of some friends but generally it is quite common to hire professional shearing teams to do the annual job. They are very fit indeed. They also perform at sheep shearing and wool handling competitions locally, nationally and internationally. It used to be common to have sheep shearing competitions at the local shows with competitive local farmers determined to win the annual prizes, although this has become less prevalent in recent years.

The principal event in Wales takes place at the Royal Welsh Show in Builth Wells each July. World Championships are hosted by different countries every 2 to 3 years; the first was held in Bath in 1977. Huw Davies of Llandre Farm, Pumsaint hosted the annual local Dyffryn Cothi Young Farmers Club's shearing match at his farm for many years before the Builth Show; the standard was always very high with the winners of the Builth Show usually attending including the famous Sir David Fagan, the New Zealander from Te Kuiti, who was World Shearing Champion many times. I have watched him perform, always so professional and timing himself usually to win just at the last moment; his fellow town resident, Sir Colin Meads, was voted the best All Black of the last century.

16. Edwinsford Estate, Tenants and Accounts

16.1 Estate Landlords

In 1837 the major local landlord landowners in the Llansawel, Talley and Caio districts were Earl Cawdor, Sir James Hamlyn Williams Bt (61) of Edwinsford, John Johnes of Dolaucothi, and George Lloyd of Brunant. By 1873 their family landholdings were as shown in Chapter 13. Rent was paid by all tenants on the rentdays in March and September in cash or in kind; usually the tenants all met with the relevant land agent (in the case of the Edwinsford Estate at the Edwinsford Arms or at one of their inns in Llansawel) and were entertained by him to a good rent dinner afterwards.

These gentry landlords generally supported their tenants and were eager to promote good husbandry and new agricultural techniques. The less wealthy landlords were a very different breed however and life for the poor must have been very difficult indeed.The Royal Commission on Land in Wales and Monmouthshire which met at

Published by permission of The National Library of Wales

Rent Day at Edwinsford 1906

Llansawel in April 1894 heard evidence for example from Timothy Pugh of Penlan in Pumsaint (who had been selected to speak by the farmers in Cynwyl Gaeo) that "rents had increased on 30 farms in the area between 1853 and 1894 by over 40%; that a wood called Allt Goch had been enclosed some 50 years previously so the poor could not go there to cut wood; dwellings were generally in poor condition and some were exceptionally bad; many of the poor farmers live meanly; bread is made of wheat grown on the farm, bara clatsh, cheese made of skim milk; for dinner broth with turnips or potatoes, sometimes plain broth cawl dwr; for supper the broth is warmed which was left after dinner".

Mr JM Davies the landowner from Froodvale gave rebutting evidence. At other hearings in the area Lord Cawdor was accused of increasing his rents by 30% over the previous 25 years resulting in depopulation. One witness said that he did not think the differences in language, creed and politics between landlords and tenants made any difference to their relations, and denied that he had been asked to give evidence by his landlord but admitted that he had been brought to the hearing in a carriage belonging to his landlord's agent.

A local tenant David Edwards of Groesfach did not have his annual farm tenancy renewed by his landlord apparently for not voting for the landlord's chosen political party. This sort of action was more common in other areas and there is no evidence that it happened on the Edwinsford, Dolaucothi or Brunant Estates.

The 20th century had a marked effect on the gentry landlords. Death duties on their estates were imposed in 1894, many of them and their employees were killed in the First World War, the 1920s depression resulted in their cost base increasing and in the Edwinsford, Dolaucothi and Brunant Estates selling farms to raise cash, and then after the Second World War the welfare state and the whole structure of society changed materially. It is unsurprising that the Edwinsford Estate (some of which was sold in 1918-9 and the rest in the 1970s), the Dolaucothi Estate (donated to the National Trust), the Brunant Estate (largely sold in 1918-9), and the Cawdor Estate are no longer privately owned or that their families are no longer the pillars of local society.

16.2 Tithe Books for Edwinsford Estate 1745 and 1761

The following shows the amounts of total tithes[425] for the estate:

PARISH	1745 TITHES	1761 TITHES
Llansawel	£68.15s.6d	£65.4s.6d
Cayo	£24.13s.6d	£28.3s.3d
Cwmcothy	£21.16s.6d	£30.3s.3d
Maestroyddyn	£45.11s.9d	£53.3s.6d
Lower Hamlet of Cayo	£42.16s.3d	£51.11s.6d
Total	£ 203.13s.6d	**£228.6s.0d

The tithe books state that Thomas Williams (54) "pays three parts in four of Land Tax for his share of tithes in Cayo and two parts in three for Llansawel. He should not pay any part of the Church rate because he repairs the Chancel and he ought not to pay but ye tenth of ye Poor rate betwixt him and ye Vicar." Tithes became profitable assets like mortgages and many gentry bought and sold them.

** In 1761 the total tithes also included the following:

87 lambs at 2/6d	£10.17s.6d
Small tithes	£4.11s.4d
81 wool at 6d	£2.0s.6d
Labourers carter offerings	£0. 11s.1d
11 geese at 7d	£0.6s.5d
4 pigs at 18d	£0.6s.0d
1761 Total Tithes	£246.18s.10d

425 NLW Edwinsford archives

16.3 Llansawel Fair / Market Tolls 1764-5

On 25 July 1688 by Letters Patent[426] King James II granted Sir Rice Williams (45) the right to hold a Market in Llansawel "every Friday in every week through the year for ever" and two Fairs or Holydays in Llansawel on 15 July and 12 October annually.

Tolls paid by attendees to Robert Banks Hodgkinson of Edwinsford (56) via his agent, Nicholas Davies, for permitting such Fairs and Markets totalled 14s.5d (including 4s.3d paid to the watchmen) for the Fair held on 18 May 1764; 12s.9d for the Market held on 20 September 1765; and £1.9s.5d (less 8s.6d for "ale and dinner") for the Fair held on 23 October 1765.

16.4 Edwinsford Estate Accounts 1804-1832

The accounts prepared by the land agent (David Thomas up to his death in 1808 and then Daniel Price) for Sir James Hamlyn Williams (60) reveal[427] that total estate rentals were 1804: £3,108; 1808: £4,111; 1810: £4,655; 1814: £5,059; 1820: £4,307; 1822: £3,623; 1829: £4,795; and 1833: £5,210. In addition to rents most tenants also had to pay for or provide lime, coal, fowls, and reaping and shearing services which were in effect payments in lieu of additional rent.

The individual Edwinsford Estate accounts for 1809 show the following annual rentals due by the tenants of properties in the relevant parishes:

PARISH	ANNUAL RENTALS
Llansawel	£711.9s.0d
Talley	£1947.11s
Conwil Gaeo	£1027.9s.0d
Llansadwrn	£130.0s.0d
Pencarreg	£109.15s.0d
Llanybyther	£25.10s.0d
Llanfynyth	£114.0s.0d
Llangathen	£272.0s.0d
Llanfihangelfach gilfergan	£50.5s.0d
Llandeilo fawr	£53.10s.0d
Cilycwm	£48.0s.0d
Llanegwrd (Quit rents)	3s.8d
TOTAL	£4,489.12s.8d

An analysis of the accounts[428] shows that (a) total gross income (including home farm sales, sales of timber and bark, and Llansawel Fair tolls) and (b) total net income (after expenditure on the Home Farm, wages of tradesmen and labourers etc) from the Edwinsford Estate were 1804: £3,965 and £1,476; 1808: £5,538 and £3,464; 1810: £6,212 and £4,300; 1814: £6,835 and £4,387; 1819/20: £7,282 and £4,645; 1822/3: £4,405 and £1,513; and 1831/2: £7,444 and £761. These accounts illustrate the long depression which followed the end of the Napoleonic Wars in 1815.

An analysis[429] of the percentage distribution of output from the Edwinsford Home Demesne Farm shows:

426 NLW Edwinsford Estate archives
427 NLW Edwinsford archives
428 See the excellent article by RJ Collyer: *The Edwinsford Estate in the Early Nineteenth Century-Bulletin of the Board of Celtic Studies (1975) p200-21*
429 RJ Collyer

	Cattle	Sheep	Pigs	Wool	Butter	Cheese	Wheat	Barley	Oats	Misc
1804	30	11	8	8	5	11	17	6	6	0
1810	29	14	6	10	11	5	6	13	6	1
1814	35	23	4	9	11	4	0	4	2	5
1820/1	24	8	7	12	11	6	15	13	0	3
1822/3	23	11	4	11	9	6	18	4	9	7

The profitability of the Home Farm declined markedly following the 1815 victory at Waterloo.

Weekly accounts were kept showing the amounts for "corn put in granary, corn given out, corn sold, wool put in storehouse, wool given out, wool sold, butter made and used, butter sold, cheese made, cheese used, cheese sold, sundries sold, bark sold, hay and straw sold".

In 1826 there were 54 workmen hired during that year with an average of 24 per day. In addition on Sundays for example Thomas Peter was hired to work in the stables at 12d per day while William Peter was hired to work in the gardens at 6d per day.

The weekly estate workmen's accounts show that their jobs included cleaning, washing, gardens, stables, timber, mending, roads, quarrying, coalhouse, brewing, labouring at mill, taking tithes, fencing, drains, mountain shepherding, hedging, graveling, digging stumps of trees, mending the warren, mill grinding, making candles, melting tallow, drawing potatoes, pheasants, felling timber, painting, and collecting bark.

Separate accounts dealt with estate purchases such as buying baskets, bowls, woodcocks, hares, carding, spinning, birch brooms, and selling animals such as sheep and calves. Also separate were the housekeeping accounts for food, dairy maids, cow maids, shepherds, and ploughmen.

16.5 Edwinsford Estate 1813

The Edwinsford Estate accounts[430] for 1813 show the following tenants and properties (with their original spellings as shown in the accounts):

PROPERTY	TENANT
LLANSAWEL PARISH	
Penpontbren	David William
Bwlchydinas	David Henry
Brynau	John Griffith
Cwmcwtta	Thomas Davies
Treglog	Levy Job
Bank	Anne Morgan
Cil-llyn fawr	David Morgan
Lletherllwyd Cwmyglawissa	William John
Fosgotta	Lewis Lewis
Cwmglaw ganol	Thomas Jones
Nantygroes	David Davies
Abercrymlyn Dolegleison	Evan Jones
Pantyoie	Lewis Lewis
Rhydymeirch	Jane Richard
Penrhiw	Thomas Thomas
Bank	Mary Lloyd

430 NLW Edwinsford archives

PROPERTY	TENANT
Bwlchyrhyd	John Jones
Broken	John David Jenkin
TALLEY PARISH	
Cwmywrch	David Williams
Cwmcochied	Thomas David
Abernaint	David Williams
Cwmcerrig	Benjamin Griffiths
Foelas	Rev Henry Phillips
Penyrhose ucha and issa	John Williams
Llwyncelyn	Benjamin Thomas
Cwmyryn	David Rees
Foesywhied	Thomas Thomas
Penrhiw Crernien	Thomas Thomas
Tynycwm	David Thomas
Gwynion Lethy	Thomas Edwards
Glanyrafonddu ucha	David Evan
Glanyrafonddu	Lewis Harries
Park	John Thomas
Penlanfawr	John Thomas
Gellygoedog	John Evans
Cilwr (Blaenywayn)	Rees Griffiths
Bolahaul	William Edwards
Bank Eskernant	Mrs Williams
Bank Llanvihangel	Thomas Williams
Cil-llynfach	Morgan Thomas
Trewern	William Griffiths
Cwmcawlwd (part in Llandeilo)	Simon Thomas
Coedhirion	Rees Thomas
Ty Howell	Rees Williams

PROPERTY	TENANT
Cilhoil	David Evan
Fynongrech	John Parry
Cwmllethy	Peter John
Garreglwyd	David Lewis
Fuarele	James William
Hafodwen	James William
Melynywayn	William Richard
Blaenug	Thomas Williams
CONWIL GAIO PARISH	
Penarth	Thomas Williams
Pantyfynon	Joseph Davis
Tynyrhos	Joseph Davis
Tynygwndwn	William Davy Esq
Bwlchycwney	Thomas Williams
Goligoed issa	William David
Goligoed	Nathaniel John
Llathuge	Daniel Evan
Tynywaya	Rees David
TiryCaeGwyn	Rees David
Tynycoed	Harry Jones
Penrhiw	Mary Evan
Cilygawadd	Rees David
Coedygofe	William Rees
New Mill	John Daniel
Nir Fran	Rev Richard Davies
Bronyfin	William Thomas
Blaendulas	Rees
Cwmpriddfa	Thomas Evan
Penarth	John William

PROPERTY	TENANT
Garreg	Joseph David
Nasfrau	William Williams
Lelly Cadwgan	James Williams
Nysau	Evan Jones
Nysau (Fynonlas)	John Edwards
Dufadfa	John Thomas
Pencilmaren	David Edwards
Bwllfa	David Harry
Bwllfa (part)	James Evans
Gwaryfena	John Thomas
Part of Crugybar	David Daniel
LLANSADWRN PARISH	
Gellydeg	Timothy Thomas
Foeswhied	David Price
Cwmynidd	Gradock Evans
LLANDEILO PARISH	
Tyddynyberthlwyd	John Harries
LLANFYNYDD PARISH	
Cathilas (Llwyncelyn)	James David
Whitlera	Thomas Williams
Llangrogan	Mary Evan
PENCARREG PARISH	
Gwarycoed	Thomas Davies
Fredomen	David Thomas
Maeslile	Thomas Morgan

PROPERTY	TENANT
LLANYBYTHER PARISH	
Abergorlech Mill	Margaret Griffiths
LLANFYHANGEL FACH PARISH	
Tyrytile	John Rees
Cwmcrwth	David Thomas
LLANGATHEN PARISH	
Llether Cadfan	William Jones
Tyllwyd	Lewis Jones
Cilywern	Mary Williams
Parke	Henry Tacharias

16.6 Tithe Apportionment Agreements 1838-41

Tithes, which had been payable in many countries since Biblical times, were originally paid in kind as one tenth of the produce of the land (crops, eggs, cattle, sheep, timber, fishing etc) to the local rector for payment for his services. The tithes were often stored in a tithe barn attached to the Parish. After the dissolution of the monasteries in 1536 some of the land in question, having passed out of church ownership, had tithes paid to private landlords called Lay Impropriators. Over time some tithes were paid in cash instead of in kind whether or not the payer went to church, and by the 1830s this caused much local resentment generally in the country (there was a tithe war of civil disobedience in some parts of the UK) but particularly in areas of non-conformism such as Carmarthenshire. The Tithe Commutation Act 1836 set up a Tithe Commission charged with creating a Tithe Map of each tithe district (usually the parish), fixing a global assessment for that district then apportioning the tithe rent charge on the individual properties in that district, which was then recorded in a written agreement (some land was free of tithe due to custom or prior agreement).

In the parish of Talley there was one Tithe Apportionment Agreement[431] dated 28 September 1838 (prepared by William Morgan of Llansawel the valuer and land surveyor) and made between the relevant landowners and Rev William Thomas Nicholls of Glandulas, the Lay Impropriator and sole owner of all the parish tithes; the agreement provided for a new annual district payment of a total of £300 by way of rentcharge by the landowners in substitution for the payment of all previous tithes.

Unusually in the parish of Llansawel there were two Tithe Apportionment Agreements[432] which gave details of landowners, tenants and the acreage of properties, dated 17 February and 12 July 1838. Both were prepared by John Bowen and William Morgan the valuers and land surveyors. The first gave details of the agreement made following a meeting in the Black Lion in Llansawel on 24 May 1837 between the vicar William Morgan (owner of the Church's portion of the tithes and glebe lands) and the relevant landowners in the hamlet of Wen; the agreement provided for a new annual district payment of a total of £102.5s.0d by way of rentcharge by the landowners in substitution for the payment of all previous tithes to the vicar. The second gave details of the agreement made between Sir James Hamlyn Williams Bt (61) of Edwinsford as the Lay Impropriator and owner of the other tithes in the parish and provided for an annual rentcharge of £232 in lieu of all former tithes due to him.

Also unusually there were two Tithe Apportionment Agreements[433] for the parish of Cynwyl Gaeo, which gave details of landowners, tenants and the acreage of properties, both dated 18 May 1841. Both were approved by Thomas Hoskins, assistant tithe commissioner. The first gave details of the agreement made following a meeting in the Dolaucothi Arms on 22 May 1837 between the vicar William Morgan (owner of the Church's portion of the tithes) and the relevant landowners in the hamlets of Cwmtwrch and Cwmcothy; the agreement provided for a new annual district payment of a total of £142.10s.0d by way of rentcharge by the landowners in substitution for the payment of all previous tithes to the vicar. The second gave details of the agreement made between Sir James Hamlyn Williams Bt of Edwinsford (61) as the Lay Impropriator and owner of the other tithes in the parish and provided for an annual rentcharge of £400 in lieu of all former tithes due to him.

The respective valuers and land surveyors surveyed all the properties in the parishes and their tithe payment apportionments were calculated based on the areas of arable, meadow, woodland, and common land set out in the Tithe Map of 1837. The total areas of land the subject of tithes in the parish of Talley relevant to the Lay Impropriator were estimated to be some 7,167 acres; in the parish of Llansawel the areas relevant to the vicar and to Sir James were estimated to be some 2,850 acres and 7,167 acres respectively. The individual quantities of land in each property were expressed in ARP measurements: acres, roods (4 roods to one acre) and perches (40 perches to one rood).

The Edwinsford Estate of Sir James Williams totalled some 8,570 acres. By way of comparison the Dolaucothi Estate properties in the parishes of Cynwyl Gaeo, Llanycrwys and Talley totalled in area some 2,891 acres, 1 rood and 13 perches; the Brunant Estate totalled some 2,279 acres and 15 perches; and the Cawdor Estate totalled some 1,371 acres,1 rood and 17 perches in such parishes. The Brunant and Cawdor Estates also owned properties elsewhere.

The Edwinsford Estate properties and occupying tenants stated in the Tithe Apportionment Agreements 1838-41 included the following (with original spellings):

431 CRO and NLW
432 CRO and NLW
433 CRO and NLW

OCCUPIER	PROPERTY	ACRES
LLANSAWEL PARISH		
Sir James Williams Bt (61)	Edwinsford house and land	569
Evan Jones	Abercrymlyn house and land	7
David Thomas	Danyddinas house and land	69
Joseph Davies	Lletherllwyd	42
Thomas Davies	Bank house	9
John Bowen	House and garden	1 rood
John Thomas	House and garden	6 perches
Thomas Peter	Blaenypound house and land	8
John Jones	Molfryn	9
William Peter and Tim Isaac	House and garden	37 perches
John Davies	Molfryn meadow and land	5
David Morgan	Gil-llyn fawr	140
Mary Williams	Bwlchyrfiyd	65
Thomas Jones	Cwmglawissa	82
Thomas Jones	Cwmglawucha	86
John Jones	Cwmglawganol	83
John Thomas	Nantygroes	46
Hugh Williams	Bank house and land	113
Thomas Roberts	Cwmcwtta	110
David Davies	Ffoesgothi	305
Timothy Evan	Ffoesgothi, part of house and land	15
William Thomas	Achethganol	64
John Williams[434]	Llewele	452
Mary Evans	Bryngwynbach	26
William Joshua	Rhyudymeirch	45
David Lewis	Treglog	63
James Davies	Treglog (part)	10

434 John Williams was the grandfather of DJ Williams and the 16th generation of his family to be born in Llywele. He left in 1838 after a quarrel with the Edwinsford Estate's agent and moved to Clun March and again in 1840 to Penrhiw. See DJ Williams p72-80

OCCUPIER	PROPERTY	ACRES
Annie Lewis	Pantyoie	130
John Joshua	Pantywincen	14
John Davies	Black Lion house and garden	1 rood
Rees Thomas / Mary Morgan	house	3 perches
William Morgan	Brynneucha	120
John Evans	Bwlchyddinas	7
Thomas Jones	Penyrhiw	59
James Evans	Penpontpren	33
David Davies	garden	26 perches
Llansawel Parish Total		3,024 acres
TALLEY PARISH		
William Griffiths	Trewern land (part)	1
Simon Thomas	Cwmcawrllwyd	41
Thomas Thomas	Glanyrafonddduganol	252
John Jones	House and land	3 roods
David Jones	Bankycelwydd	3 roods
Thomas Lewis	Smith's shop and land	6 roods
John Jones	Talley demesne and Pengarreg house	224
David Davies	Cross Inn	8
William Price	Quarrel house and land	33
William Price	Hafodwen land	17
James Hunt	Langwm	5
Daniel Price	land	14
David Davies	Dablenaur	3 roods
Thomas Thomas	Gil-llynfach	60
James Thomas	House and garden	21 perches
William Williams/John Jones	House and garden	2 roods
David Davies	Parkbach	24
David Beynon	Penybont house and garden	30 perches

OCCUPIER	PROPERTY	ACRES
Thomas Jones	land	25 perches
MorganJones/John Mainwaring/Mary Rees	Cross Inn cottages and gardens	1 rood
John Davies	land	5
William Richard	Gwnbyr	69
Sir James Williams Bt (61)	Plantations	34
Sir James Williams Bt (61)	House and land	108
Rees David	Hafodwen house and land (part)	2
David Thomas	Llwyncelyn	82
David Evans	Cilhaul house and land	66
Thomas Griffiths	Blaenwaun	79
Mary Rees	Cwmyrynn	81
Benjamin Griffiths	Cwmcerrigucha	49
John Evans	Gellygoedog	133
Benjamin Griffiths	Cwmcerrigissa	43
David and Williams Williams	Abernaint	128
John Williams	Dolegleison	115
David Thomas	Tynycwm	65
Evan Jones	Dolegleisonissa	30
Evan Jones	Part of Abercrymlyn land	2 roods
Sir James Williams Bt (61)	Part of Edwinsford land	3
Sir James Williams Bt (61)	Parkland	16
John Parry	Ffynongrech	79
Margaret Evans	Penrhiw	6
Peter Murray	gardens	3 roods
William Richard	Waunfawr	4
Lettice William	House and garden	34 perches
John Timothy	House and garden	10 perches
Mary Jones	Parkydilfa	55
William Lewis	Park and Penlanfawr house	186
William Lloyd	Gwnwniethry	71

OCCUPIER	PROPERTY	ACRES
William Williams	Cwmllethry	80
David Levy	Garreglwyd	53
Rees Thomas	Coediwrwn	128
Thomas Jones	Penlanfach	85
James Thomas	Part of Blaenug land	4
David Evans	Blaenug house and land	73
William Griffiths	Trewern house and land	49
John Edwards	Bolahoyl house and land	147
Evan Thomas	Bank house and land	40
David Davies	Glanyrafondduucha	87
David Phillips	Cwmcochied	59
Thomas Williams	Bankllanfihangel house and land	80
Rees Williams	Tir Howell	48
Thomas Thomas	Penrhiwpopinpen	47
Thomas Griffiths	Ffoesywhied	29
Thomas Phillips	Ffoeslas	56
	Upper Lake	14
	Lower Lake	26
Talley Parish Total		3,419 acres
CONWIL GAEO PARISH		
Lettice Jones	Dyfadfa house and land	92
Lewis Lewis	Llain Nicholas land	26
Thomas Lewis	Pencilmaren	132
William Lloyd	Cilgawad	91
David Edwards	Bronfinfach,Cwmgerwnganol, Nantygigfrane, Pantnoyddfa	360
David Edwards	Llain Cilgawad land	92
William Evans	Tynywaun	105
Benjamin Lewis	Cwmclynyn	83
Conwil Gaeo Parish Total		984 acres

OCCUPIER	PROPERTY	ACRES
LLANGATHEN PARISH		
Timothy Griffiths	Lether Cadfan	72
David Evans		76
John Griffiths		16
David Jones		14
Llangathen Parish Total		130 acres
LLANFYNYDD PARISH		
Hannah Davies	Llwyncelin	133
Thomas Williams	Whitlera	112
Henry Jones	Llangrogan	42
William Gwynne		14
	Churchyard, School House, Chapel yard	1
Llanfynydd Parish Total		302 acres
LLANSTEPHAN PARISH		
Ann Finnion	Trewaun	27
Ann Finnion	Black Anchor	2
James Phillips	Penlanfach	31
Jeremiah Meyck	Llainucha	13
Llanstephan Parish Total		73 acres
LLANSADWRN PARISH		
Mary Thomas	Gellideg Farm	63
William Price	Ffoshwgaid	27
David Williams	House and garden	1 rood
William Price	Part of Ffoshwgaid	51
David Williams	Cwmynydd	50
Jane Rees	Graig	104
Llansadwrn Parish Total		295 acres

OCCUPIER	PROPERTY	ACRES
CILYCWM PARISH		
David Thomas	Gellyhernin	219
John Davies	Blaendulas	124
Cilycwm Parish Total		343 acres
ESTATE TOTAL		8,570 acres
The Edwinsford Estate also held lands elsewhere.		

16.7 Edwinsford Estate Accounts 1903

The annual estate accounts[435] for the year ended 31 December 1903 show the following:

RECEIPTS

Parish	Arrears 1/1/1903	Annual rent	Property tax	Received	Arrears 31/12/1903
Llansawel	£174.1s.6d	£1972.11s.0d		£1961.11s.0d	£183.6s.6d
Talley	£109.17s.6d	£2883.9s.6d		£2890.2s.0d	£104.10s.0d
Llanfynydd		£50.0s.0d	£2.14s.8d	£50.0s.0d	
Conwil Gaio	£9.5s.8d	£1105.6s.7d		£1101.17s.9d	£9.6s.6d
Llanstephan	£0.5s.1d	£45.5s.1d	£2.8s.5d	£45.10s.0d	£0.0s.2d
Fields at Edwin		£123.0s.0d		£123.0s.0d	
Totals	£293.9s.9d	£6,176.11s.8d	£5.3s.1d	£6,172.0s.9d	£297.3s.2d

Rents less allowances	£6,172.0s.9d
Tithes refunded by tenants	£114.14s.10d
Llansawel tithe rentcharges	£91.0s.8d
Miscellaneous	£2.4s.9d
Total receipts	£6,380.11s.0d

435 NLW Edwinsford archives

PAYMENTS	
Balance brought forward from 1902	£488.17s.11d
Allowances to tenants	nil
Buildings and repairs	£629.2s.11d
Demesne (incl stables, gardens, ironmongery, grain, straw, saddlers)	£67.17s.4d
Home Farm	£104.17s.9d
Game (meal, grain—Mary Williams, Melinwaun)	£86.14s.9d
Interest on loans	£2817.13s.8d
Mortgage Sinking Fund	£500.0s.0d
Kennel (Mary Williams, Melinwaun)	£5.3s.0d
Misc (incl distress allowance, insurance, trap hire, Post Office Talley deficiency)	£178.0s.4d
Rates and taxes	£27.11s.5d
Roads, rivers and draining (labouring)	£14.15s.3d
Sir James HW Drummond (68)—bills	£1115.0s.2d
Salaries (incl Agent's salary)	£250.0s.0d
Tithes	£104.11s.6d
Workmen's wages	£310.4s.3d
Total payments	£7,266.12s.10d

Under pre-decimal currency 12 pence (d) equalled one shilling (s) and 20 shillings equalled one pound (£) sterling.

16.8 Edwinsford Estate 1903

The Edwinsford Estate accounts[436] for the year ended 31 December 1903 prepared by the land agent for Sir Joe Williams-Drummond (68) show the following properties (with original spellings):

PROPERTY	OCCUPIER	ANNUAL RENT
LLANSAWEL PARISH		
Abercrymlin	Anne Jones	
Achethganol	Henry Williams	
Angel Inn	Margaret and William Griffiths	
Bank	William Williams	
Bankbach	John Jones	
Blaenyresgair	Daniel Davies	
Black Lion	Henry Rumbold	
Penrhiw	Henry Rumbold	
Black Lion (part shed)	Parish Council	
Black Lion Hearse house	Parish Council	
Baileytew	John Richards	
Blaenypound (J Peters)	Lady Drummond (67)	
Blaenypound	Alice Micklewright	
Brochin	David Jenkins	
Bryngwynbach	David Davies	
Bwlchyrhyd	David Davies	
Bwlchyddinas	Lettuce Davies	
Cilyllynfawr	Evan Morgan	
Cwmcwtta, Abergorlech	John Jones	
Cwm cottage (rent free) fields	Daniel Lewis	
Cwmglawucha	Evan Evans	
Cwmglawganol	Thomas Evans reps	
Cwmglawissa	John Thomas	
Esgair (Pantywhimben)	William Davies	

436 NLW Edwinsford archives

PROPERTY	OCCUPIER	ANNUAL RENT
Ffosgotta, Abergorlech	William Jones	
Lletherllwyd	David Williams	
Llywelemawr, Abergorlech	David Jones	
Market House cottage	John Jones	
Market House cottage	Margaret Evans	
Moelfre Lodge	Benjamin Davies	
New Lodge	Lewis Bowen	
Nantygroes	John Williams	
Old Lodge	William Davies	
Penpontbren	David Davies	
Penpontbren	Hannah Evans	
Pantiauau	James Davies	
Penypound (E Jones)	Lady Drummond	
Penlan	John Davies	
Penlan part of Garnwen	Esther Williams	
Penlan Garnwen cottage	Mary Thomas	
Penlan Llwyncelin	Elias Evans	
Penlan Llwyncelin cottage	Thomas Williams	
Penlan Smithy and land	Margaret/William Griffiths	
Rhyglin	John Morgan	
Rhyglin (part) and factory	Joseph Jones	
Smith Forge House and garden	John Thomas	
Treglog and part Rhydymeirch	David Davies	
Rhydymeirch (part) and Waun Pugh	James Evans	
Town Hall (holding of Petty Sessions)	County Council	
Warren cottage	Thomas Evans	
Weion	David Davies	
Edwinsford	Sir James Williams-Drummond (68)	
Llwynblyfyn	David Jones reps	
Pengelly	Thomas Humphreys	

PROPERTY	OCCUPIER	ANNUAL RENT
Drefach (part)	John Morgans	
Drefach (part)	D Price Lewis	
Llainau	Sarah Davies	
Cilwenne ucha	Evan Davies	
Cilwenne issa	James Davies	
Bank Rhosgotta	David Richards	
	Parish Total Annual Rentals	£1,970. 17s.0d
TALLEY PARISH		
Abernaint, Crugybar	Thomas Evans	
Abernaint fach	David Williams	
Abernaint (part) Warnrhos	J Williams reps	
Abbey View	D Evans reps	
Banke or Penrhiw	Evan Evans	
Bank Esgairnant	Thomas Thomas	
Bank Llanfihangel	Elizabeth Griffiths	
Bank Llanfihangel	D Thomas reps	
Bank Celwydd	Thomas Price	
Blaenug	John Thomas	
Blaenugissa	Morgan Griffiths	
Blaenywaun	William Davies	
Blaenycwmrefail	William Thomas	
Bolahaul	Margaret Thomas reps	
Belle Vue (Rhoslyn)	Mary Rees	
Cilyllynfach	John Morgan	
Coedhirion	John Thomas	
Cwmbyr	Joshua Davies	
Cwmcerrig	Henry Thomas	
Cwmcochied	Evan Jones	

PROPERTY	OCCUPIER	ANNUAL RENT
Cwmllethri	John Evans	
Cwmyryn	Hannah Griffiths	
Cilwr and Nantygroes	Thomas Evans reps	
Cross Inn cottage	Daniel Evans	
Old Cross Inn	AD Townsend	
Danygraig House and field	Lady Drummond and Rev JH Lloyd	
Dolaugleision and Penpontbren	Thomas Thomas	
Disgwilfa	David Davies	
Dablenaur	Thomas Davies	
Dark Gate Lodge (Porth Tywyli)	JA and DA Price	
Edwinsford Arms house, stable, garden, Caerbrynerach, Mynwent Capel Crist	E Griffiths reps	
Foeslas	William Phillips	
Ffynongrech	Eleanor Davies	
Garreglwyd	John Williams	
Gellygoedog	Elizabeth Davies	
Glanrafondduganol	Thomas Rees	
Glanrafondduucha	D Davies reps	
Gwinionllethri	William Rogers	
Handirlan	T Griffiths and J Isaac	
Llangwn	Thomas Williams	
Llwyncelin and part of Cilhaul	David Thomas	
Melinwaun	Mary Williams	
Mynydd Cefnrhos (part)	Sir James Williams Drummond (68)	
Mynydd Cefnrhos (part)	DD Rees	
Malakoff House and garden	AD Townsend	
Parkmawr	Elizabeth and Thomas Morgan	
Penrhiwgeingen	Henry Davies	
Penlanfach	David Thomas	
Penlanfawr	David Evans	
Pencarreg cottage, Waunllin Llansawel, Pencarreg Minefield	William Williams	

PROPERTY	OCCUPIER	ANNUAL RENT
Waunmorfa	Sir James Williams-Drummond (68)	
Pencarreg Mines	Sir James Williams-Drummond (68)	
Parcbach field	David Lewis	
Parcydilfa	David Evans	
Porthselly	Elizabeth Thomas	
Rose cottage (Rhos)	John Morgan	
Talley demesne and Pengarreg field	Anne Jones	
Talley demesne allotment on mountainTalley mountain allotment	Evan JonesD Davies reps	
Ty Howell and Rhadodwen	M Williams reps	
Trewern	Margaret and William Griffiths	
Tynycwm and Tanyddinas	Thomas Davies	
Talley Village cottage	Hannah Evans	
Talley Village schoolroom	Anne Beynon	
	Parish Total Annual Rentals	£2,884.14s.6d
LLANFYNYDD PARISH		
Esgaircarn	Thomas Thomas	£50.0s.0d
CONWIL GAEO PARISH		
Brigend Inn	William Jones	
Bronfin and Blaendulais	Samuel James	
Bronfin right of water	Cayo School Board	
Bwllfa	Mary Williams	
Castell	John Harries	
No 1 Church Lane, Caio	Mary Evans	
No 2 Church Lane, Caio	James Jones	
No 3 Church Lane, Caio	J Griffiths reps	
No 4 Church Lane - Sextons Arms, Caio	Lewis James	
No 5 Church Lane, Caio	James Morgan	

PROPERTY	OCCUPIER	ANNUAL RENT
No 5A Church Lane, Caio	Thomas Simons	
No 6 Church Lane, Caio	Anne Davies	
Gwarfrena cottage	Morgan Jenkins	
Cayo Inn	Lewis James	
Cilgawad	John Davies	
Ddolas cottage	JR James	
Gwarfrena field	James Morgan	
Garth	Thomas Davies	
Gilfachwen	Thomas Jones	
Garreg	David George reps	
Frena Lodge	David Williams	
Goleugoeducha	David Lewis	
Goleugoedganol	David Williams	
Goleugoedissa	John Jones	
Lethy Cadwgan	Rees Davies	
New Mill	Daniel Davies reps	
Penrhoe cottage and part New Mill	William Rees	
Troedyrhiw	Joseph Williams	
Tynywaun	Thomas Thomas	
Tir Crugybar Glanrhyd	John Evans	
Tir Crugybar shop	W Richards reps	
Tir Crugybar land	D Davies, Llathigau	
Tir Crugybar footpath	Deacon of Crugybar Chapel	
Ynyssau (Derwenfawr)	Daniel Harries	
Ynyssau-issa (Pwllybaw)	David Williams	
Ynyssau Ganol (Ffynonlâs)	Thomas Davies	
Ynyssau Gate Old Toll House	Sarah Davies	
Lang Parcnewydd	William Davies	
	Parish Total Annual Rentals	£1,104.18s.7d

PROPERTY	OCCUPIER	ANNUAL RENT
LLANSTEPHAN PARISH		
Edwinsford Arms[437]	Martha Anthony	
Edwinsford Arms houses	Eliza Richards	
Use of road	Rev J Price	
Bethel Chapel	Rev D Thomas	
	Parish Total Annual Rentals	£45.5s.1d
FIELDS PART OF EDWINSFORD		
Caerhenfaes	William Jones	
Ddol-bont	Sir James Williams Drummond (68)	
Ddol-grymlin	Thomas Thomas	
Caebowlin	Thomas Davies	
	Total Annual Rentals	£123.0s.0d
	Total Estate Annual Rentals	£6,178.15s.2d

In 1914 the Derllys Estate was put up for sale but did not reach its expected price. It was sold by the executors of Sir James Hamlyn Williams-Drummond (68) on 24 March 1915 for £8,250 to John Thomas on a mortgage of £5,500 provided by the executors and subject to a yearly tenancy in favour of the sitting tenant, Percy Thomas, at an annual rent of £550 (see Chapter 8.3).

437 This was later the favourite pub of Dylan Thomas (1914-53) run by his relatives, Thomas and Catherine Thomas. It featured in his short story "A Visit to Grandpa's"

16.9 Sale of Estate Properties in 1918

As was the case with many other Estates after the Great War, including the Dolaucothi[438] and Brunant Estates, some of the Edwinsford Estate properties totalling 821 acres were auctioned for sale in September 1918. The sale took place at the Cawdor Arms in Llandeilo and fortunately many of the lots were bought by the occupying tenants[439] as follows in accordance with the wishes of Sir Jimmy Williams-Drummond (69):

Property	Acreage (ARP)	Purchaser	Sale Price £
Gulelieced ganol	57.1.30	John Williams	660
Goleugoed isaf	77.2.10	TL Edwards	1125
Glanrhyd, Crugybar	4.3.6	David Morgan	430
Glanrhyd meadow	0.0.31		withdrawn
Temple Bar house		Georgina Richards	140
Tir Crugybar	3.0.6	Mr Williams	160
Tir Crugybar field	3.1.10	Mr Williams	120
Tir Crugybar field	3.2.23	Mr Williams	100
Pigyn	5.0.24	Georgina Richards	220
Tir Crugybar field	3.3.7	TL Richards	90
Tir Crugybar 4 fields	12.0.3	Mr Williams	240
Brigend Inn		William Jones	380
Brigend field	2.0.13	Morgan Richards	85
Brigend meadow	3.1.40	JD Lewis	100
Brigend meadow	2.3.31		withdrawn
Brigend meadow	0.2.35		withdrawn
Glanrhyd field	1.0.3		withdrawn
Felin Newydd (New Mill)	16.1.12	Anthony Williams	725
Smith's Forge Penrhock	2.1.13	William Rees	200
Gilfachwen		Sold to tenant	150
Castell		John Harries	340
Penrhock field		William Rees	100
Penrhock 2 fields		Thomas Jones	120

438 David Lewis Dolaucothi and Brunant p315-325,339-345

439 Carmarthen Journal 27 September 1918

Property	Acreage (ARP)	Purchaser	Sale Price £
Bwllfa	38.3.16	Mr Davies	500
Ddollas	1.3.21	John Evans	150
Garth	78.1.22	James Jones	1250
Gilfachwen 5 fields	14.0.19	Thomas Jones	330
Ynysau Ffynnon-las[440]	99.2.5	Thomas Davies	3650
Groesfawr and Groesfach	5.1.1	Thomas Davies	150
Ynyssau Ganol	103.1.29	ET Griffiths, Glanrannell	4000
Ynyssau Gate House (Old Toll House)	0.0.36	ET Griffiths, Glanrannell Park	85
Ynyssau Issa (Pwllybaw)	157.2.13	David Williams reps	750
Ynyssau 2 fields	10.1.11	ET Griffiths	150
Goleugoed uchaf	117.3.12	David Williams	1050
Tynywaun (Albert Mount)	154.0.39		withdrawn
Tynywaun field	31.2.6		withdrawn
No 1 Church St Caio		Mr Evans	50
No 2 Church St Caio		Mr Evans	50
No 3 Church St Caio		James Morgan	90
No 4 Sextons Arms		Lewis James	200
No 5 Church St Caio		DJ Rees	50
No 5A Church St Caio		Mary Morgan	35
Cayo Inn land	1.0.17		withdrawn
Total Sold	821.2.5 approx		£18,025

440 See Chapter 28.5 which shows that the Dolaucothi Estate bought Ffynnonlâs on 1 Jan 1919

16.10 Sale of Estate Properties in 1919

A further 18 Edwinsford Estate freehold farms and small holdings totalling some 1,871 acres were auctioned for sale on Saturday 30 August 1919 at the Drill Hall in Llandeilo. According to the Sales Particulars[441] the auctioneers were Williams & Walter James of Frondeg, Llangadock; the solicitors were Morgan Griffiths Son and Prosser of St Mary Street, Carmarthen; and the Estate Agent was Lt Col Sir Dudley Williams-Drummond (76) of the Cawdor Estate Office in Carmarthen (uncle of Sir Jimmy Williams-Drummond (69) the seller). The following properties were auctioned but we do not have the sales details:

Property	Acreage (ARP)	Occupying Tenant	Annual Rent £
Trewern Fawr, Talley	104.1.16	David / Mary Thomas	£86.15s.0d
Banc Esgairnant, Talley	106.1.37	Thomas Thomas	86.10.0
Bolahaul, Talley	142.1.22	Evan Davies	77.10.0
Banc Celwydd, Talley	20.3.35	Thomas Williams	26.0.0
Glanyrafonddu Uchaf, Halfway Talley	89.2.13	Mary/John Thomas	66.0.0
Glanyrafonddu Ganol	247.1.28	Thomas Rees reps	238.5.0
Ffoslas, Cwmdu	59.2.4	William Phillips	43.10.0
Penrhiwgingen, Talley	80.3.26	Henry Davies	88.0.0
Ty Hywel, Talley	77.1.4	John/Sarah Williams	54.0.0
Banc Bach, Talley	6.0.39	John Williams	9.0.0
Banc Llanfihangel Talley	89.2.23	WR and M Thomas	63.15.0
Cwmcochiaid, Talley	61.2.18	Evan Jones	45.10.0
Cwmcerrig, Talley	119.3.19	David Thomas	98.4.0
Gelly Goedog, Talley	139.3.35	Elizabeth Davies	93.10.0
Cwmyryn, Talley	79.0.10	David Jones	54.0.0
Esgaircam, Llanfynydd	68.2.32	Thomas Thomas	51.5.0
Ty'n y Waun (Albert Mount, Caio)	185.2.27	Thomas Thomas (bought by T and J Davies for £1275)	69.0.0
Cilwenauisaf, Llansawel	190.3.38	Walter Davies	98.10.0
Total acreage for sale	1,871.1. 22		

441 NLW Edwinsford Estate archives

The Clovelly Families

17. Origins and Cary Family

17.1 Origins of Clovelly

Clovelly Dykes (SS 311234) is an Iron Age (1st century BC or earlier) hill fort on the high plateau above the village of Clovelly overlooking Bideford Bay in Devon at some 700ft above sea level; a complex series of earthworks with ramparts some 100ft apart covering more than 20 acres and one of the most impressive hill forts in Devon. It is a series of enclosures demarcated by rampant banks and ditches; the innermost enclosure is some 7ft high and the outermost enclosure is some 9ft high. It may have been built over several phases for defence as well as for the seasonal gathering of livestock and for autumn slaughter. The farms of East Dyke and Dyke Green were later built into the earthworks, ploughing has harmed the site, and the main road to Clovelly now cuts across the east side of the area.

It is thought[442] that the Dumnonii (deep valley dwellers) or Dumnones tribe lived in Dumnonia (now Devon and Cornwall) from about the Iron Age upto the early Saxon period; they spoke an early form of the Brythonic language which developed into Cornish and Welsh. They later gave their name to the county of Devon. The Romans[443] named what is now Exeter as Isca Dumnoniorum in about AD50 and we know that another Iron Age hill fort in Devon at Mount Batten at Plymouth Sound continued to be used in the Roman period. Devon was one of the last areas of the Celts to be conquered by the Anglo-Saxon invaders from the east and it was not until as late as 805 that it was formally claimed by the Saxon Kingdom of Wessex; indeed its inhabitants were called Wealcynn (foreigners) by King Alfred the Great. Cornwall was conquered a little later. Recent research[444] suggests that the original 7th century Anglo-Saxon tribal gene pool of long term resident families in Devon and Cornwall is still predominant in the population today.

The Saxons were farmers and cleared the forests as well as introducing hundreds and parish boundaries. Before the Norman invasion in 1066 "the manor of Clovelie" was part of the Saxon Earldom of Gloucester and was owned by Britric, the Saxon thane and son of Algar; he was an ambassador to Baldwin of Flanders but unwisely refused to marry Baldwin's daughter, Matilda of Flanders (c1031-83), who later became the wife of William I the Conqueror. She[445] later caused Britric to be imprisoned in Winchester where he died and his lands were confiscated and some given to Queen Matilda.

In 1083 Clovelly was being farmed and held in chief for the King by Goscelm of Exeter and this is confirmed in the Domesday Book of 1086. The Devonshire Domesday and Geld Inquest of 1083 stated that *"The King has a manor called Clovelie, which Britric held on the day on which King Edward*[446] *was alive and dead. It rendered geld* (land tax) *for three hides* (hide =120 acres). *These can be ploughed by twelve ploughs. Of them the King has one hide and five ploughs in demesne. The villeins* (tenant farmers who work on their lord's demesne lands and farm their own land and pay dues) *who have two hides and seven ploughs. There the King has 16 villeins, 11 bordars* (cottagers who work on the lord's demesne land and pay dues) *and 10 serfs* (slaves). *45 head of cattle, 15 swine, 100 sheep, and 18 goats. 40 acres of wood, 30 acres of meadow and of pasture—1 leuga in length and a half a leuga in breadth. This manor*

---

442 Ptolemy: *Geographia (cAD150)* which refers to Hartland Point as the Hercules Promontory; William Camden: *Britannia (1607)*

443 Some claim that the Romans came to Clovelly in cAD70 because of some lines in Virgil's Aeneid but this is pure speculation

444 Oxford University—Telegraph (18 March 2015)

445 Devonshire Notes and Queries 1830-40; EA Freeman: *The History of the Norman Conquest of England (1871) Vol 4 p761-4*

446 Edward the Confessor (1003-66) last King of the House of Wessex

renders 12 pounds by tale. Goscelm holds this manor to ferm and it rendered 6 pounds when he received it." So at this time there must have been a fairly substantial village located on the lands above the current Clovelly.

William II (Rufus) (1087-1100) acquired Clovelly manor following his mother Matilda's death in 1083 and then gave it with other lands (including Bideford) to Robert Fitzhamon (c1055-1107), son of Hamon the Sheriff of Kent. He was a kinsman of and loyal to Rufus and his father and was rewarded with the first Norman feudal barony of Gloucester which was one of the largest in the kingdom; he also conquered Glamorgan and became Lord of Glamorgan in 1075. On his death in 1107, leaving four daughters three of whom were nuns, the manor of Clovelly went to his daughter, Mabel Fitzhamon (1090-1157), who married Robert de Caen, 1st Earl of Gloucester (d1147) and the illegitimate son of King Henry I (ruler 1100-35). Clovelly remained in the feudal barony of Gloucester.

From about 1242 the Giffard (Gifford) family[447] occupied the manor of Clovelly as a feudal tenant of the barony of Gloucester. They were the first of the three families who have owned Clovelly over the past eight centuries. The Giffard family originated from Walter Giffard (dc1086), Lord of Longueville in Normandy, who is said to have been one of the 15 knights of William the Conqueror at the Battle of Hastings in 1066; as a reward he was granted the feudal barony of Long Crendon including over 100 manors. In 1242 Robert Giffard[448] held Clovelly[449] as one knight's fee from Sir Walter Giffard of Weare Giffard in Devon (another branch of the family). His son, Sir Matthew Giffard (d1303)[450], left two daughters who married Sir John de Stanton (Staunton) and John Maundeville respectively; between 1310 and 1324 the manor and advowson were split into two moieties (halves) although some evidence suggests that when the Giffard lands were divided Stanton inherited Clovelly where he was the lord of the manor (1316-24). His daughter and sole heiress, Matilde de Stanton, married John Crewkern of Childhey in Dorset. The population of the manor must have increased substantially since the inquest in 1083 for the Domesday Book despite plague and pestilence.

There are several suggestions by different historians concerning the ownership succession thereafter. One is that the manor of Clovelly was then sold by the family to Judge Sir John Cary MP (d1395)(101), Chief Baron of the Exchequer, although the exact date is unknown. Another suggestion[451] is that the manor was acquired by Richard Bosun from the Stantons in c1362 and then inherited by his daughter Thomazine Bosun who married the brother of Sir John Cary, Sir William Cary. Sir William died without issue in 1397 and left the manor to his nephew, Sir Robert Cary MP (102). Yet another suggestion[452] is that Sir John Cary (101) inherited the manor from Margaret Bozun, but this view is generally discounted.

The name of Clovelly has been through a number of alternative spellings over the centuries. As we have seen, it was spelt "Clovelie" in the Domesday Book 1086, and then "Clovely" in the Book of Fees 1242, "Cloveli" in 1276, "Colfely" in the Charter Rolls 1290, "Clouvely" in 1361, "Clavellegh" in 1535, "Clavelly" in 1639, and "Clavelleigh" in 1800. It is said[453] that the word originates from a Cornish name meaning "earthworks associated with Fele(c); a person whose name may survive unadorned in the ancient farms and vanished chapel called Velly." As an alternative, it is said[454] that it originates from "Velly" with the old English "Cloh" or "Clof" meaning "ravine" added. Velly[455] or Felye was the name of the semi-circular ridge above the village so named because of a likeness to the "felly" (old English "felg") of a wheel; "Clo" in the name refers to the ravine at the foot of which lies the village. It seems that the origin is not as clear as some might think.

---

447 JL Vivian(1830-96): *The Visitations of the County of Devon (1895) p159-9*

448 Tristram Risdon (1555-1640): *Survey of Devon (1811) p241*; Sir William Pole (1561-1635): *Collections Towards a Description of the County of Devon (1791) p371*

449 The first recorded rector of Clovelly in 1262 was R Gifford—see Chapter 21.1

450 Matthew Giffard held the manor at the date of the Devon Hundred Roll (Temp Edward I 1274-1307)

451 Fairfax Harrison: *The Devon Carys (1920) p52-3, 174*; Tor Abbey muniments of the Cary family; William Grigs: *A Guide to All Saints' Church Clovelly (1980 revised 2010) p3*

452 Thomas Westcote (c1567-1637): *View of Devonshire in 1630 (1845)*

453 Richard Coates: *Clovelly Devon-English Place Name Society Journal (1996) Vol 28 p36-44*

454 Sheila Ellis: *Down a Cobbled Street (1987) p53,* a wonderful well illustrated book on Clovelly

455 There is a Velly in the neighbouring parish of Hartland

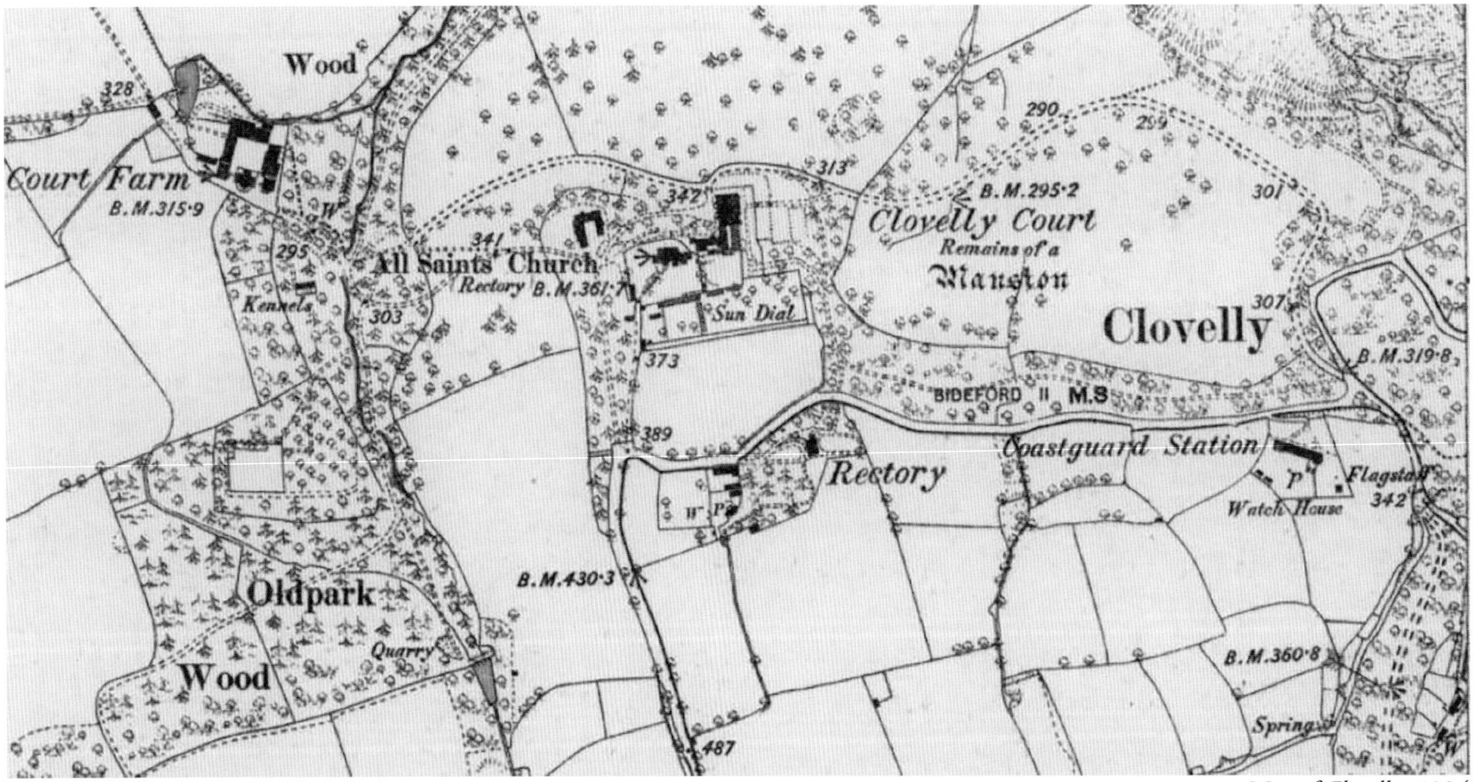

Map of Clovelly c1884

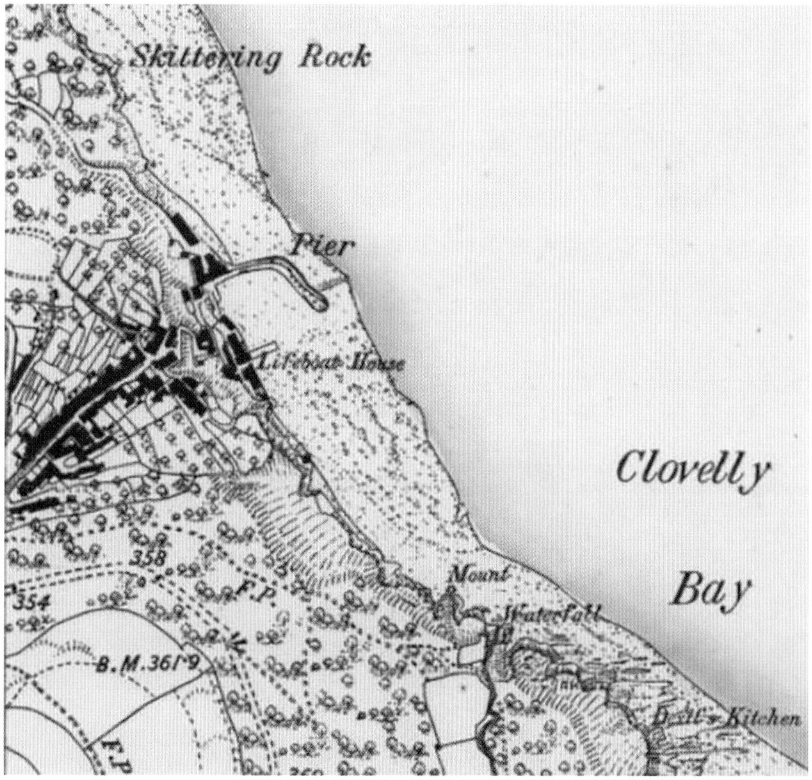

Map of Clovelly c1884

Clovelly map today

17.2 Cary Family

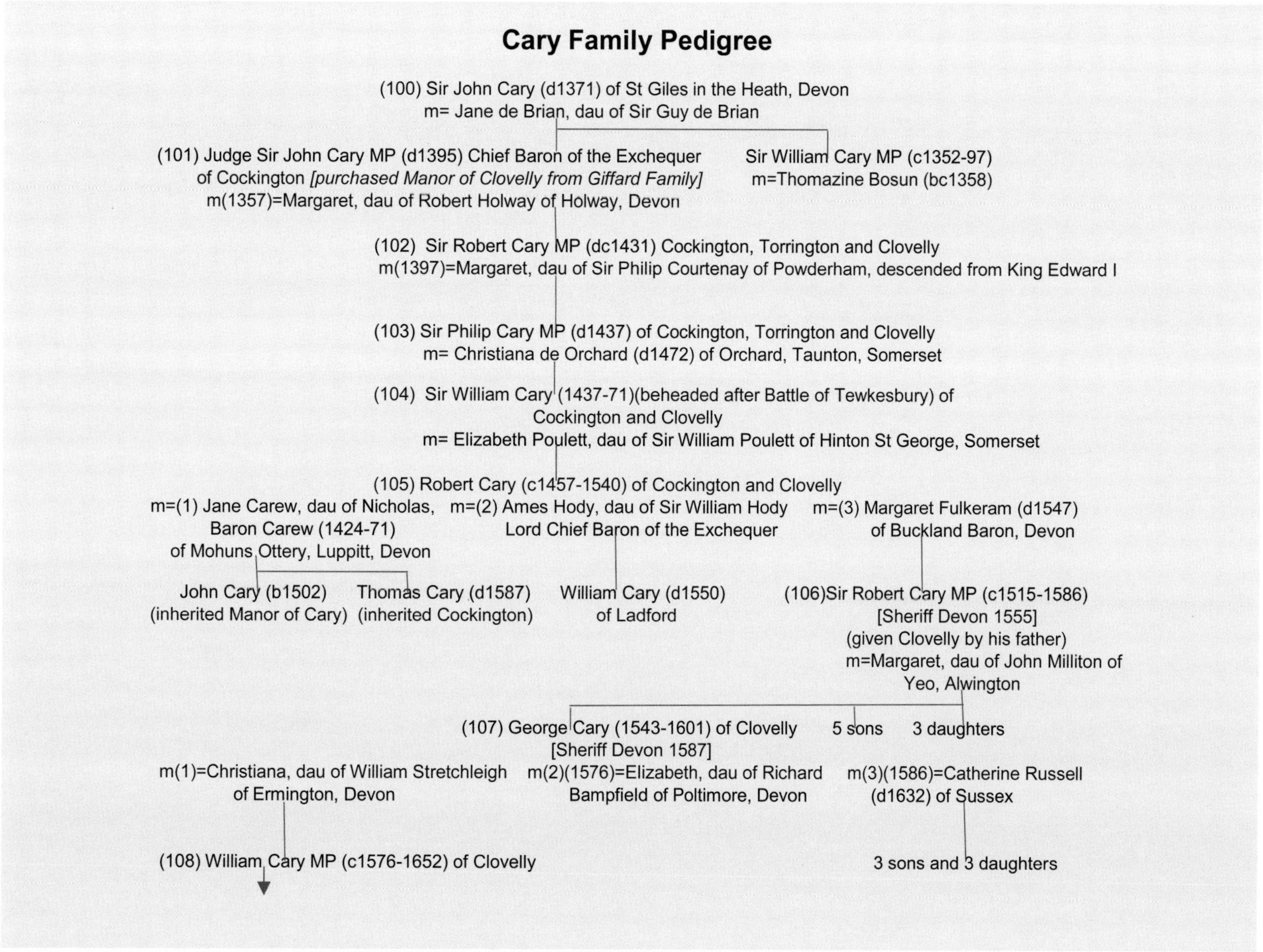

Judge Sir John Cary MP (d1395)

Sir John Cary (101) of Clovelly was the son of Sir John Cary (d1371) of St Giles in the Heath, Devon on the border with Cornwall and Jane, daughter of Sir Guy de Brian (de Brienne) of Walwyn's Castle in Pembrokeshire and Torr Bryan (Torbrian) in Devon, one of the original Knights of the Garter. Sir John served twice in 1363-4 and 1368-9 as a Member of Parliament[456] for Devon with his brother, Sir William Cary (who may have acquired Clovelly[457] through his marriage to Thomazine Bosun and left it to his nephew, Sir Robert Cary (102), in 1397). In 1374 Sir John and his uncle acquired the manor of Cockington from the widow of Sir Walter de Wodeland. He served as warden of the ports of Devonshire in 1373 and was made a commissioner of array in 1376 to help protect England against a French invasion. He supported King Richard II (ruler 1377-99) and was appointed in 1386 as Chief Baron of the Exchequer. Richard II was trying to agree a peace treaty with France in the midst of the Hundred Years' War but peace with France was opposed by the Lords Appellant. In 1387 Sir John was one of the judges who agreed that the Lords Appellant[458] were acting illegally and were guilty of treason. The King's army was defeated by the Lords Appellant's supporters at the Battle of Radcot Bridge in December 1387 and many of the King's supporters and members of his council were then impeached and executed in 1388 by the Merciless Parliament. Richard II did not recover power until 1389 and most of the Lords Appellant were themselves executed thereafter.

Sir John was condemned to death ("Sir John Cary shall be drawn and hanged[459] as a traitor and he and his heirs shall be disinherited forever") and was very fortunate not to be executed but was banished to Waterford in Ireland ("and he shall not fare forth more than two leagues from the said city") on a pension of £20 pa. So he was exiled for seven years until his death and his lands were forfeited to the Crown including the manor of Clovelly. It is thought that Sir John's seat was at Cockington or at Cary, which could have been Castle Cary in Somerset; it is doubtful if he ever actually resided in Clovelly. It is not known when he bought Clovelly from the Giffard family but it was probably before the 1380s and a junior branch of his family were seated there until 1738 as we shall see. Sir John's arms were *argent, on a bend sable three roses of the field.* He died in Waterford on the Friday before the Feast of Pentecost 1395.

Sir Robert Cary MP (dc1431) and Sir Philip Cary MP (d1437)

Sir John's son, Sir Robert Cary (102) of Cockington and Clovelly, spent much time at Clovelly during his father's exile under the watchful eye of his uncle, Sir William Cary. Sir Robert served as a Member of Parliament[460] for Devon in 12 Parliaments between 1407 and 1426. He too was a supporter of King Richard II and served as an esquire in his household. From about 1396[461] he was granted some of his father's lands which had been forfeited; his attempts to recover the family estates were further helped when the Parliament of 1398 annulled the actions of the Merciless Parliament of 1388. Then in 1399 after Richard II had been deposed, King Henry IV reversed this position and reaffirmed the Act of 1388 and granted the Cary lands to others. Sir Robert participated in a plot to oppose the King and in 1400 was found guilty but managed to escape. In 1397 he married Margaret, daughter of Sir Philip Courtenay (1340-1406) of Powderham in Devon, the son of the 2nd Earl of Devon and descended from King Edward I. The Courtenay family's influence helped him to restore his position and to recover some of the family lands. This marriage led Robert out of the influence of lawyers and men of business and introduced him to the traditions of chivalry and feats of arms.

He returned to royal favour under Prince (Hal) Henry (later Henry V ruler 1413-22); apparently Sir Robert accepted a challenge[462] of armed combat at Smithfield in London in c1402 from a knight-errand of Arragon who had challenged any man of his rank and quality. After "a long and cruel encounter" Sir Robert was victorious following which the Crown restored to Robert much of his father's lands and authorised him to assume the arms of the defeated knight in accordance with custom, being *in a field silver, on a bend sable three white roses.* A

456 HP

457 Some think that Sir William built the original breakwater in Clovelly harbour with massive boulders later extended and enlarged by George Cary (107)

458 Lord Jonathan Sumption: *The Hundred Years' War-Divided Houses (2009) p631 et seq*

459 The Devon Carys p94

460 HP

461 A Charter dated 9 September 1396 granted him Puddington and, when his uncle died, Clovelly

462 John Prince: *The Worthies of Devon (1810) p176-9*

wonderful story which could be true. In 1413 he was appointed by Henry V as escheator in Devon and Cornwall and thereafter served on several royal commissions. After his first wife's death, he married Jane (d1447), daughter of Sir William Hankford, Chief Justice of the King's Bench. Sir Robert died in about 1341 having recovered much of his father's forfeited estates including Clovelly and Cockington at neaby Abbotsham (both purchased by his father), Great Torrington, Puddington, and North Lew in Devon plus Powderham and Chivelstone in Devon which Robert had been granted for life and several manors elsewhere.

Sir Robert's only son by his first wife, Sir Philip Cary(d1437)(103) of Cockington and Clovelly, was probably educated at Lincoln's Inn in 1423 and later served as a Member of Parliament[463] for Devon in 1433, the year in which he was knighted. He married Christiana de Orchard (d1472), daughter and heiress of William de Orchard of Orchard near Taunton in Somerset. Sir Robert died on Sunday the Feast of St Tecla the Virgin in September 1437. His widow remarried Walter Portman[464] who was MP for Taunton in 10 Parliaments. Sir Robert had one son and heir, Sir William Cary (104), who was to achieve the second attainder in the family.

Sir William Cary (1437-71)
Sir William Cary (104) of Cockington and Clovelly was married twice: (1) to Elizabeth, daughter of Sir William Poulett (Paulet) of Hinton St George, Somerset, who bore him his son and heir Robert Cary (105) and possibly died in childbirth, and (2) to Anna (Alice), daughter of Sir Baldwin Fulford of Fulford Magna in Devon, who bore him another son, Thomas Cary, who had two sons: (a) Sir John Cary (1491-1552) ancestor to the Cary Viscounts Falkland, and (b) William Cary, who married Mary Boleyn (sister of Queen Anne Boleyn), and an ancestor to the Earls of Monmouth, Viscounts Rochford and Earls of Dover. Sir William died in his 34th year by execution.

Sir William supported the Lancastrian cause in the Wars of the Roses together with John Courtenay Earl of Devon. In July 1464 he fled to France and in January 1465 was attainted by Parliament for high treason and his estates were forfeited. He was captured at the Battle of Tewkesbury on 4 May 1471 when the smaller Yorkist army of some 5,000 under Edward IV decisively defeated the House of Lancaster's army of some 6,000. The Earl of Devon was killed on the battlefield, Edward Prince of Wales was executed on the spot, and other Lancastrian knights and nobles including Sir William Cary sought sanctuary in Tewkesbury Abbey to no avail. Two days later on 6 May they were dragged out and after perfunctory trials were executed. Edward IV passed through London on 21 May in triumph and Henry VI died that night in the Tower of London by order of Richard Duke of Gloucester the youngest brother of Edward IV. Sir William's body was probably recovered by his family and reburied in All Saints' Church Clovelly. In Clovelly Church there is a monumental brass[465] of a knight in armour, believed to be Sir William, set into a slate ledger stone on the floor of the chancel next to a smaller brass of his son and heir Robert Cary. His arms of *sable, three swords pilewise points in base proper pommels and hilts or* can also be seen in the church.

Robert Cary (c1457-1540) and Sir Robert Cary MP (c1515-86)
Robert Cary (105) of Cockington and Clovelly, the eldest son of his father by his first wife, was quite unlike his father. His father spent seven years in exile and died aged 34. The son was a pious, home-keeping and respected country gentleman and died aged 83. Robert was born at Hinton St George, the seat of his maternal grandfather in Somerset. He saw little of his father growing up and was only 14 when his father died. He recovered most of his father's forfeited estates in 1535 and then lived a quiet life at Clovelly serving as a magistrate and as a commissioner of array.

He was married three times: (1) to Jane, daughter of Nicholas, Baron Carew (1424-71) of Mohuns Ottery, Luppitt, Devon and they had two sons: (a) John Cary (b1502) who inherited the manor of Cary, and (b) Thomas Cary (d1567) who inherited the manor of Cockington; (2) to Ames (Agnes) Hody (Huddye), daughter of Sir William Hody (1486-1512) Lord Chief Baron of the Exchequer and they had one son, William Cary (d1550) of Ladford; and (3) to Margaret (d1547), daughter and heiress of William Fulkeram of Buckland Baron, Devon and they had one son, Sir Robert Cary MP (106), who inherited the manor of Clovelly. In 1518 he made his will

463 HP
464 An ancestor of the current Viscount Portman the owner of the Portman Estates
465 William Grigs p5

Clovelly harbour 2016

in preparation for his pilgrimage to Santiago de Compostela[466], a popular venue for English pilgrims, in 1519 the year before the Field of the Cloth of Gold. On his return he retreated back to his quiet life in Clovelly. On 12 April 1535 he settled his estate amongst the children of his three marriages with an elaborate system of cross- entails. He is believed to have died in Bristol on 25 June 1540 a staunch Roman Catholic despite the break with Rome and the dissolution of the monasteries. He died wealthy and left five sons by his three wives but instead of following the tradition of leaving his estates to his eldest son, he divided it per stirpes. The eldest John received the manor of Kegbear plus the manor of Cary for his grandsons; the second Thomas received Cockington and Chilston. The third William received the manor of Ladford. The youngest two sons received the manor of Clovelly and other lands divided between them.

His fourth son, Sir Robert Cary (or Carey) MP (106) of Clovelly, was born about 1515 and was educated[467] at the Middle Temple and practised thereafter as an eminent lawyer. He seems to have spelt his surname Cary and Carey on different occasions, which makes it difficult to distinguish him from other members of the Cary and Carey families in Devon and Cornwall. He inherited the manor of Clovelly on his father's death in 1540 and is thought to have been the first in his family whose principal seat was exclusively at Clovelly (the other lands having gone to the older sons). He showed early promise at the bar and was chosen to prepare and present to Henry VIII a report on the course of study at the Inns of Court; he also seems to have been paid £20 by Thomas Cromwell in 1539-40. He acted for several clients in Devon including neighbouring gentry families (the Carews, Fulfords and Pouletts) and in 1561 he acted in the divorce of his stepdaughter, Wilmot Yeo, so that she could marry his nephew, George Cary (Carey) of Cockington. He is described[468] as being pious, self important and without much sense of humour.

In 1548 he was a commissioner for chantries in Devon and Cornwall; in 1550 a commissioner for relief for Devon; and later a commissioner to try maritime cases. In October 1553 he was elected as the Member of Parliament for Barnstaple in the reign of Queen Mary I (ruler 1553-8) and seems to have had no strong religious convictions since he continued also to sit as a magistrate in Devon (1547-86) in the reign of Queen Elizabeth I. He served as Sheriff of Devon in 1555 and then as Recorder of Barnstaple after 1560.

In 1543 he married Margaret, daughter of John Milliton of Yeo, Alwington, Devon, who was the widow of John Giffard of Yeo. It is thought he had six sons and three daughters by her including his eldest son and heir, George Cary (107) of Clovelly. Under his will dated 15 August 1579 he asked for God's grace to make his children "profitable members of this commonwealth of England". He died on 1 April 1586 at his home in Exeter; together with other Devon gentry, juries, lawyers, witnesses and prisoners he contracted "gaol fever" at the Black Assizes of Exeter which he had been attending as a magistrate. He was buried near his parents' six poster tomb in All Saints' Church Clovelly where there is a monument in his memory confirming his year of death and containing heraldic escutcheons showing the arms of the Fulkeram, Cary, Poulett (Powlet or Paulet), Holway (Holloway), Brian (Bryan), Fulford and Milliton families[469].

George Cary (1543-1601)

George Cary (107) of Clovelly was the eldest of six sons and became a Middle Temple lawyer in 1562 like his father. He inherited the manor of Clovelly on his father's death in 1586. The following year he served as Sheriff of Devon. He was married three times: (1) to Christiana, daughter and heiress of William Stretchleigh of Stretchleigh, Ermington in Devon, who was the widow of Sir Christopher Chudleigh (1528-70). They had one son and heir, William Cary MP (108) of Clovelly; (2) in c1576 to Elizabeth, daughter of Richard Bampfield (1526-94) of Poltimore, Devon and they had no children; and (3) in c1586 to Catherine (d1632), of Sussex and they had three sons and three daughters.

George greatly improved Clovelly and the lot of his tenant mariners and fishermen by extending and enlarging a "pile" or harbour wall at Clovelly (beyond the original tidewater of boulders built much earlier) which meant there was safe anchorage at a time when the village's main

466 The Devon Carys p154. A cockleshell on English tombs was the sign of having undertaken a pilgrimage to Compostela alone, as opposed to Rome or Jerusalem
467 HP
468 The Devon Carys p181
469 Grigs p4

produce was herring fish from the Bristol Channel. The wall has been rebuilt over the centuries but it was George who had the foresight and the willingness to invest in the first such harbour for miles around. However he practically exhausted his capital in this venture to stimulate trade. In his will dated 9 August 1601 he says that it cost him £2,000 to build the pier plus the "houses, cellars, warehouses and other edifices", a very large sum at that time. He in fact built a small hamlet next to the narrow strip of shingle and the fishermen (of herring, mackerel and cod etc) added other houses up the slope which had to be terraced and cobbled with cobbles taken from the beach and laid in such a way that the rainwater flowed in the right direction to the drains; they also had to divert the Severn stream from Higher Clovelly above the cliffs since they wished to live next to their boats and their businesses. George's feudal fishing rights off the shore and his shore rights and income from the fishery trade made Clovelly a thriving community.

Clovelly and his three other manors in Devon and Somerset were tied up in the jointure granted to his third wife, Catherine, under her marriage settlement; she lived until 1632. So George provided that on his death his share of the income from the Clovelly fishery profits should be paid to his son and heir, William Cary (108), during the lifetime of his widow. Later this led to litigation.

George died on 10 July 1601. In All Saints' Church there is a monumental brass to his memory in the form of a ledger stone[470] on the floor of the chancel with a Latin inscription saying that he was a very distinguished man, a most just guardian of the peace, a very worthy patron of the Muses, a devotee of justice, lover of religion, and an example to many. This is indeed an epitaph of which to be proud.

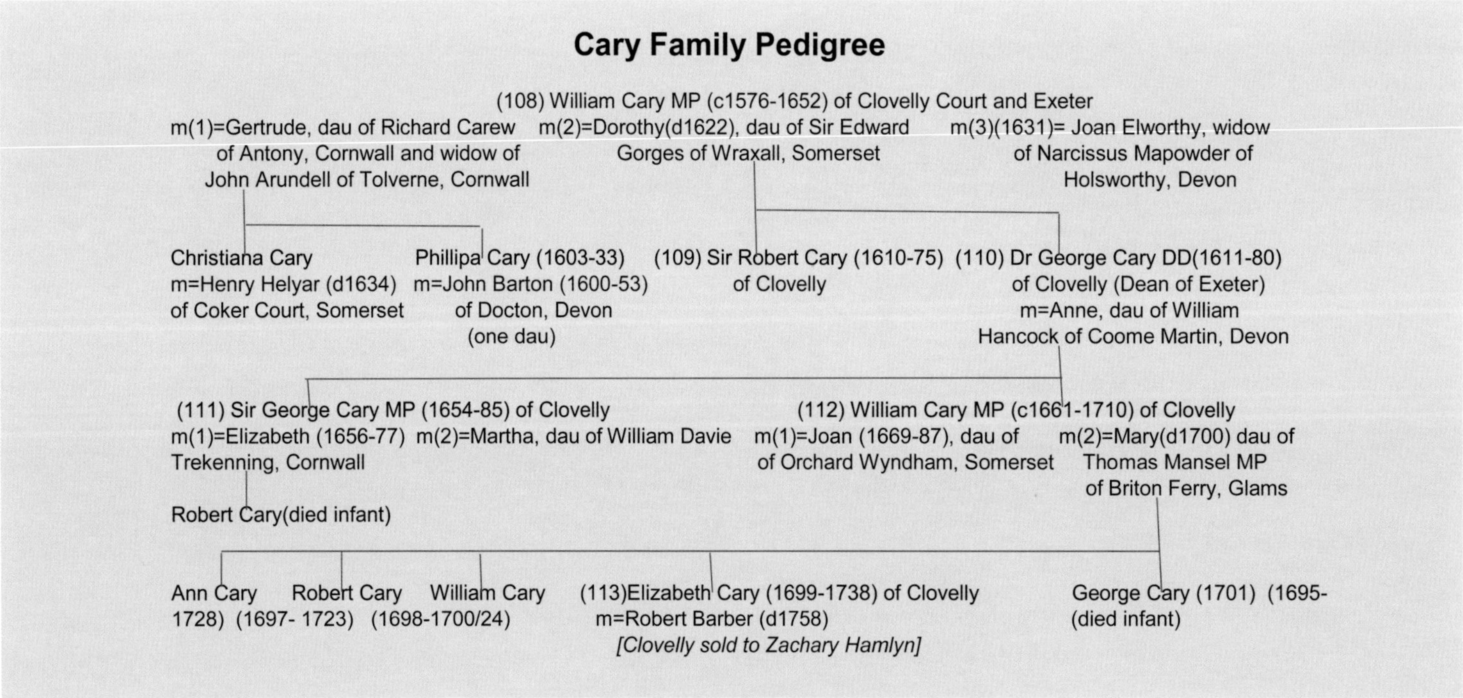

[470] Grigs p5

William Cary MP (c1576-1652)
William Cary (108) of Exeter and Clovelly Court was the eldest son and heir by his father's first wife. He was brought up at Clovelly Court and became a Middle Temple lawyer (1596) like his father and grandfather. His close family connections with the Bassets of Cornwall, the Chudleighs of Devon, and the Gorges of Somerset led to his election[471] in 1604 as a Member of Parliament (1604-11) for Mitchell (St Michael) in Cornwall. Mitchell was a rotten borough[472] village constituency and from 1547 elected two MPs (Sir Walter Raleigh was one MP in 1593 and the future Duke of Wellington in 1807). William Cary was elected with the influence of his father in law, Richard Carew, and his patron, John Arundell MP of Trerice Cornwall (1576-1654), who married his half-sister Mary Cary. William was a very bad attender in Parliament and in 1610 his excuse was that he could not attend because some pirates were threatening to burn down Clovelly Court; it seems that in March 1610 the pirate Thomas Salkeld[473] occupied and declared himself king of Lundy Island close to Clovelly and was raiding the coastline. William was granted indefinite leave of absence. His Parliamentary career was not a success because he preferred to live the quiet life of a country squire in Devon, although he did serve as a commissioner for piracy in Devon, as a magistrate (1604-43), and as a commissioner for benevolence, subsidy, sewers, assessment and array. The dashing brave exploits he is said by Charles Kingsley[474] in *Westward Ho!* to have experienced during the Spanish Armada in 1588 are pure fiction.

William was married three times: (1) in c1598 to Gertrude (d1604), daughter of the historian Richard Carew MP (1556-1620) of Anthony in Cornwall, who was the widow of John Arundell (d1598) of Tolverne in Cornwall. They had two daughters (a) Christiana the wife of Henry Helyar (d1634) of Coker Court in Somerset, and (b) Phillipa (d1633) the wife of John Barton (1600-53) of Docton[475] in the neighbouring parish of Hartland in Devon; (2) on 23 January 1605 to Dorothy (d1622), daughter of Sir Edward Gorges (1564-1624) of Wraxall, Somerset. They had four sons (including Sir Robert Cary (109) of Clovelly Court and Dr George Cary (110) Dean of Exeter) and seven daughters; and (3) on 11 June 1631 to Joan (Jane) Elworthy (dc1674)[476], widow of Narcissus Mapowder (d1628) of Holsworthy, Devon.

Although William succeeded his father in 1601, because of his stepmother's jointure over Clovelly and other manors William was not financially well off until after her death in 1632. Indeed he had to bring an action against her in 1604 to protect his inheritance. He lived at Clovelly initially where his children by his first two wives were born and then moved to live for some years in Exeter until the death of his second wife in 1622 who is buried there. He then returned to Clovelly Court. During the Civil War he supported the King but did not play any active role unlike his eldest son and heir, Sir Robert Cary (109), who held Bideford for the Royalists. In 1645 he settled most of his estate including Clovelly in entailed trust for his son, Sir Robert Cary. On 20 December 1648 he signed his will appointing his second son, Dr George Cary, as his executor and trustee to deal with the rest of his estate. After his death in 1652 there was an attempt by Parliamentarians to sequestrate the family estate but at the Restoration in 1660 his heirs had complete control over his former lands.

There is a mural[477] to his memory in All Saints' Church Clovelly on the south wall above the sanctuary rail erected by his second son George; it refers to his serving as a JP under three monarchs and dying in 1652 in his 76th year. Its Latin ending "*Omnis Caro Foenum*" (all flesh is grass) is a pun on the surname Cary. The mural bears the arms of Cary and of Gorges (the mother of his sons); the latter arms were the subject of the famous heraldic law case in 1347 of *Warbelton v*

[471] HP
[472] By 1831 it had only 23 houses and was disenfranchised by the Great Reform Act 1832
[473] He was later captured by George Eskott who handed him over to the authorities. He was hanged and Eskott received from James I a pension of 18 pence per day for life
[474] Charles Kingsley (1819-75) spent his childhood in Clovelly where his father was curate (1826-32) and then rector (1832-6)
[475] Grigs p7
[476] Grigs p7. The monument in Clovelly Church in memory of Joan Cary is not to the third wife of William Cary (108) but to Joan Cary (Wyndham) who died in 1687 and was the first wife of William Cary (112)
[477] Grigs p7

Gorges. Two of the family Knights were fighting together at the Siege of Calais and discovered that unknown to each other they had adopted identical arms. The unrelated families of Warbelton of Hampshire and Gorges of Somerset then argued that theirs was the correct arms. The six members of the Court of Honour decided that the Warbelton arms had the better title; the Gorges arms were then altered to add a red chevron (*gules*). This was important since the Age of Chivalry was at its height and in 1348 Edward III created the Order of the Garter accompanied by a lavish tournament at Windsor Castle which continues to this day.

Mural to William Cary (108)

Mural to Sir Robert Cary (109)

Sir Robert Cary (1610-75) and Dr George Cary DD (1611-80)
William Cary's eldest son, Sir Robert Cary (109), followed the family tradition by attending the Middle Temple (1629). He was a strong supporter of the Royalist cause in the Civil War and fought and held Bideford against the Parliamentarian forces as Governor of Bideford. There is a tradition that the lead was stripped from the church roof at Clovelly to make bullets to shoot at Roundheads; a possible but improbable tale. He seems to have avoided sequestration of lands although he probably had to pay substantial fines to Parliament which would have impoverished the family. He inherited the manor of Clovelly on his father's death in 1652 pursuant to the trust which had been set up in his favour. He was knighted at the Restoration in 1660. According to the monument[478] in All Saints' Church Clovelly he died a batchelor in 1675 in his 65th year having served King Charles I faithfully during the long Civil War against his rebellious subjects, served as a JP, and served as a Gentleman of the Privy Chamber under King Charles II. Sir Robert left all his estate including Clovelly to his younger brother, Dr George Cary.

Cary arms

Cary arms

George Cary (110) was born[479] at Clovelly Court in 1611 and baptised on 18 July. He was educated at Exeter Grammar School and in 1628 went up to The Queen's College Oxford (BA 1631) and later moved as a scholar to Exeter College which was more popular amongst Devonians. He then took holy orders. In 1639 his father (as patron) appointed him as rector of Clovelly, where for many years he was a "constant preacher and pastor" and held this office throughout the Interregnum despite his Royalist sympathies. In 1660 after Charles II had taken the throne he was appointed Chaplain in Ordinary to the King; he then received the honour of a Doctorate of Divinity (DD) at Oxford. He was also the parson of the rich living of St Swinthun's Church in Shobrooke near Crediton and Exeter in Devon and became the Dean of Exeter in September 1663 (possibly 1668); he seems to have lived for many years either at Shobrooke (hobgoblin brook) or in Exeter itself with his family. He was a great builder and rebuilt the parsonage at Shobrooke as well as the Dean's house in Exeter which had been ruined during the Civil War. He apparently refused the offer (*nolo episcopari*) by Charles II of the Bishopric of Exeter twice in 1666 (unknown reasons) and again in 1676 (old age). He also enlarged and partially rebuilt Clovelly Court in 1680-1 before his death.

He married Anne, daughter of William Hancock (d1625) of Coombe Martin, Devon and they had several children including Sir George Cary MP (111) of Clovelly and William Cary MP (112) of Clovelly. He eventually inherited Clovelly from his older brother Sir Robert in 1675 but seems not to have lived there himself but to have let Clovelly Court to his cousins, John, George and Anthony Cary (sons of Robert Cary of Yeo Vale, Alwington) who lived there until about 1702.

He died on 28 March 1680 aged 69[480] in Shobrooke and was buried in All Saints' Church Clovelly where his memorial monument (a typical product of the later 17th century school of Exeter based sculptors) describes him as a "Professor of Sacred Theology.....in all assemblies, guest chambers and councils he distinguished himself. In his heart, tongue and pen he was exceedingly mighty....towards the King in the most evil times he was of unbroken fidelity."

[478] Grigs p7
[479] Sheila Ellis p18
[480] Not aged 72 as suggested by some historians

Sir George Cary MP (1654-85)
Sir George Cary (111), the eldest son of the Dean, was married twice: (1) on 30 June 1676 to Elizabeth (1656-77), daughter[481] and coheiress of Peter Jenking of Trekyning, St Columb Major in Cornwall; she died aged just 20. They had one son Robert Cary who died as an infant; and (2) on 30 October 1679 to Martha, daughter and heiress of William Davie of Canonteigh, Devon; they had no children. So George had no heir.

George was knighted in 1679 the year before his father died and in 1680 succeeded to his father's estates including Clovelly. In 1681 he was elected as a Member of Parliament[482] for Okehampton near Dartmoor in Devon. This was the Oxford Parliament known as the Third Exclusion Parliament which met in Oxford from 21 to 28 March 1681 at which Charles II addressed the MPs. At the time attempts were being made to pass an Exclusion Bill to exclude the King's brother, James Duke of York, a Catholic, from succeeding to the throne. Charles II had dissolved earlier Parliaments to avoid any such Bill being passed and he did the same again. Sir George played no part and was soon replaced as MP by an exclusionist supporter.

Sir George served as Recorder of Okehampton from 1681 and in June of that year presented a loyal address signed by 230 residents thanking Charles II for his declaration upon the dissolution of the Oxford Parliament. Okehampton was granted a new charter which provided that Sir George be appointed Recorder for life. He was obviously popular with his constituents.

He died aged only 31 on 6 January 1685 according to his large mural monument[483] in Clovelly Church. He left all his estate including Clovelly to his brother, William Cary MP (112).

William Cary MP (c1661-1710)
William Cary (112), second son of the Dean, was educated[484] at The Queen's College Oxford where he matriculated (entered) on 23 March 1678 aged 16; he went on in the family tradition to the Middle Temple. He was married twice: (1) in c1684 to Joan (1669-87), daughter of Sir William Wyndham Bt MP (c1632-83) of Orchard Wyndham in Somerset. Sadly she died aged only 18 on 4 February 1887 without children and was buried in the Wyndham Chapel of St Decuman's Church in Watchet, Somerset. Her large mural monument in Clovelly Church shows the Wyndham arms; and (2) on 28 March 1694 to Mary (d1700)[485], daughter of Thomas Mansel MP of Briton Ferry, Glamorgan, who brought a large dowry of £5,000. They had three sons (William 1698-1700[486] and Robert 1697-1723[487], and George d1701 an infant) and two daughters (Ann 1695-1728[488], and Elizabeth 1699-1738) none of whom produced children. The mural monument in Clovelly Church in memory of her mother Mary, and her siblings William, Robert and Ann was erected by sister Elizabeth (113) who interestingly described herself on the mural as "the last of the family".

William succeeded to his elder brother's estates including Clovelly in 1685 although much of the estate was entailed; he is listed as being the lord of the manor in 1687 when he presented a priest to the living of Clovelly (see Chapter 21.1). Like his elder brother he served as Recorder of Okehampton from 1685 to his death, and also as a Member of Parliament for Okehampton in 1685-87 and again in 1689-95. He joined William of Orange (King William III) after his landing in England in late 1688 at the request of Parliament as James II fled to France. William was a strong supporter and a Tory by political persuasion although not very active in Parliament. In 1695 he transferred his seat to Launceston in Cornwall which he represented from 1695 to his death in 1710. He was not a good attender and in 1699 was excused for sickness reasons. In 1697 he became a freeman

---

[481] In Clovelly Church there is a memorial to her ("Libere recepi libere dedi")
[482] HP
[483] Grigs p11
[484] HP
[485] The mural in Clovelly Church states that she was buried on 6 February 1700 but her infant son George died in 1701
[486] Grigs p11 but he may have died in 1724 according to The Devon Carys p190 and have been a merchant in Bristol
[487] His ledger stone slab is on the floor in Clovelly Church
[488] Her ledger stone slab is also on the floor in Clovelly Church

of Exeter. When Queen Anne came to the throne (ruler 1702-14) he continued to support the Tory cause. He sought a paid position in government (which he failed to achieve). He wrote to Robert Harley (1661-1724) (later 1st Earl of Oxford), the Speaker of the House of Commons, saying that he was having financial problems after so many years of war and because of the restrictions of the jointure to which his estates had been subject as a result of previous marriage settlements (his second wife had died in 1700) and he needed to provide for four young children. By private Act of Parliament he was permitted in 1704 to sell entailed lands in Somerset and to resettle his Devon estates in order to pay off debts and make provision for his children.

He died in the summer of 1710 while attending Parliament and was buried at St Martin's in the Fields. His will dated September 1709 was proved in January 1711 and in it he acknowledged a debt of £800 due to John Northmore of Okehampton and a debt due to his executor John Perryman of London.

It is unclear exactly what then happened to the manor of Clovelly on his death since the entailed estate would normally have been held by trustees for the eldest son who was still alive. However we do not know whether the 1704 private Act of Parliament altered the succession in this respect. One assumes that Clovelly was held by William or Robert[489], the eldest sons, who died unmarried in 1723/4, and that it then passed to sister Anne, who died unmarried on 23 May 1728, following which it passed to her younger sister, Elizabeth Cary (113), who was the sole surviving sibling although we do not know whether she lived there. One suggestion[490] is that on Elizabeth's death in 1738 the estate was sold by order of the Court of Chancery to Zachary Hamlyn for the price of £9,426; I have been unable to verify this.

Elizabeth Cary (1699-1738)

Elizabeth Cary (113), youngest daughter of William Cary MP (112), was the only sibling to have children. She married Robert Barber (d1758)[491] of Ashmore in Dorset and they had two sons (Robert and Jacob) and four daughters (Ann, Elizabeth, Lucy and Molly). Following her death in May 1738 the manor of Clovelly was sold to the successful lawyer and businessman, Zachary Hamlyn (116) described below, although some[492] think the sale took place as early as 1724 (following the deaths of her two older brothers, William and Robert). It seems that Elizabeth was not buried in St Nicholas's Church in Ashmore, where she and her family presumably lived, and there is no mural to her memory in Clovelly Church. However her mural monument in Ashmore Church states that "she was the last of her family of the Carys of Clovelly…who descend from the ancient branch of the noble family of which was and are Cary Lord Hunsdon, Cary Lord Faulkland, Cary Lord Lepington and Monmouth, Sir Robert and Sir George Cary."

So ended over 300 years of Cary ownership of the manor of Clovelly, although as we shall see the Hamlyn family became related by blood to the Cary family.

[489] Listed as the lord of the manor—see Chapter 21.1
[490] FDWD: *Annals (1924) p12*
[491] Listed as the lord of the manor—see Chapter 21.1
[492] The Devon Carys p190

18. Later Families

18.1 Hamlyn Family

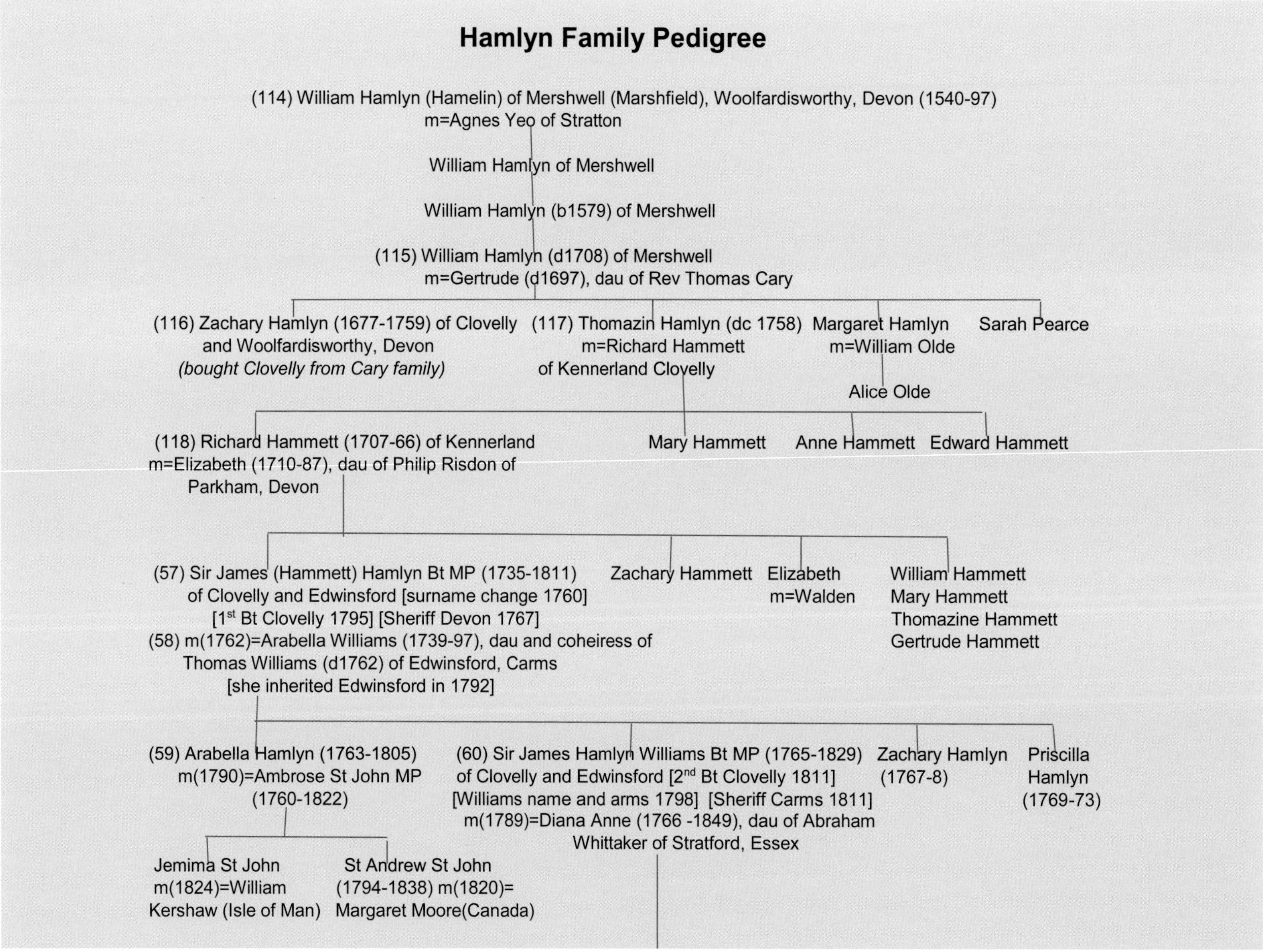

The Hamlyn family is probably descended from Hamelin[493] who is mentioned in the Domesday Book as the feudal tenant of the manors of Alwington and Broadhempston holding from a half brother of King William I the Conqueror. The family produced various branches including one living in Woolfardisworthy (known today for short as Woolsery) close to the manor of Clovelly; it is thought[494] that the first Hamlyn of Woolsery was William Hamlyn (1540-97) whose father came from Mershwell (Marshfield). William was buried in Woolsery in 1597. He married Agnes Yeo of Stratton and their son, William, had a son, also William, who was baptized at Woolsery on 21 October 1579. His son, William Hamlyn (d1708)(115), married Gertrude Cary and they are thought to have had 14 children including Zachary Hamlyn (1677-1759)(116) of Mershwell and Thomazin Hamlyn (dc1758)(117). A Robert Hamlyn was vicar of Woolsery Church (1754-81) and was presumably a relation and could have been one of their siblings.

Gertrude Cary was the daughter of Rev Thomas Cary MA, who was educated at Oxford and took holy orders, and the granddaughter of Thomas Cary of Great Torrington. She was buried in Woolsery Church on 8 December 1697 and there is a ledger stone on the floor of the chancel there in her memory; her husband William died on 19 June 1708 and is also buried there. This branch of the large Cary family of Devon and Cornwall was not it seems the branch which had held the manor of Clovelly for so long, but was related to it. So the Cary bloodline continued to flow through the veins of the Hamlyn family, who were landowners in the parish, some living at Mershwell (Marshall) and some at Kennerland.

Zachary Hamlyn (1677-1759)

Zachary Hamlyn (1677-1759) (116) is believed to have been born at Kennerland Farm in Higher Clovelly and his many siblings were brought up in the Clovelly and Woolsery area; he succeeded to Mershwell on the death of his father in 1708. He was educated at Lincoln's Inn and became a successful and wealthy lawyer and businessman. Most historians think that he bought the manor of

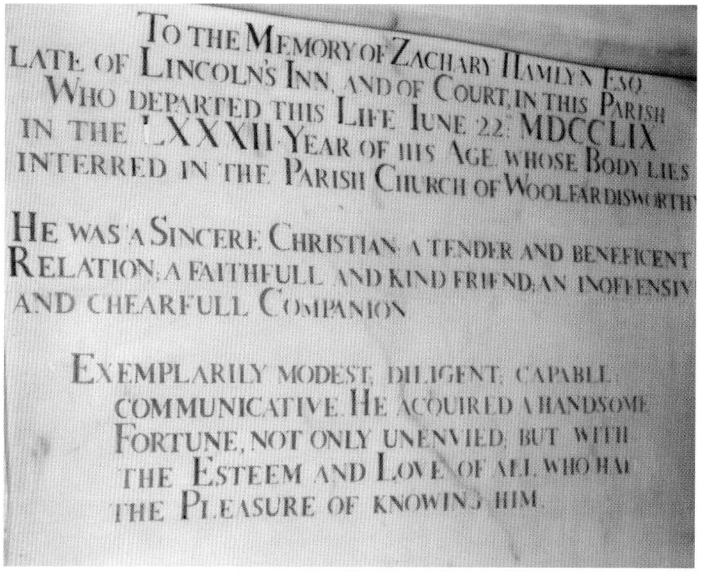

Mural to Zachary Hamlyn in Clovelly Church

Clovelly from the Cary family following the death of Elizabeth Cary (113) in May 1738, although as we have seen others[495] think he may have bought Clovelly as early as 1724 following the deaths of Elizabeth's older brothers. He lived at Clovelly Court as well as at Lincoln's Inn.

He died a rich man unmarried and without issue aged 82 on 22 June 1759. Under his will dated 17 May 1758 (proved on 31 July 1759) he appointed as his sole executor his great nephew, James Hammett (1735-1811)(57). Zachary's sister Thomazin (117) had married Richard Hammett of Kennerland close to Clovelly, and her son, Richard Hammett (1707-66)(118), and his wife had seven children of whom the eldest was James Hammett (57). In his will Zachary requested to be buried in the chancel of Woolfardisworthy Parish Church[496] without any funeral pomp or funeral sermon. He ratified the settlement he had made on 2 June 1746 leaving in trust his lands in Clovelly, Woolsery, Hartland in Devon and, interestingly, his

493 JL Vivian p483

494 Charles Worthy: *History of the Suburbs of Exeter (1892) p187-198;* Franklin Andrews: *History of the Hamlin Family (1894)*

495 The Devon Carys p190

496 Originally Holy Trinity Church being a chapelry of Hartland upto the Reformation. Now called All Hallows Church—TJ Harding: *Woolsery Church (1978 update 2006*). It contains memorials to Richard and Mary Hammett

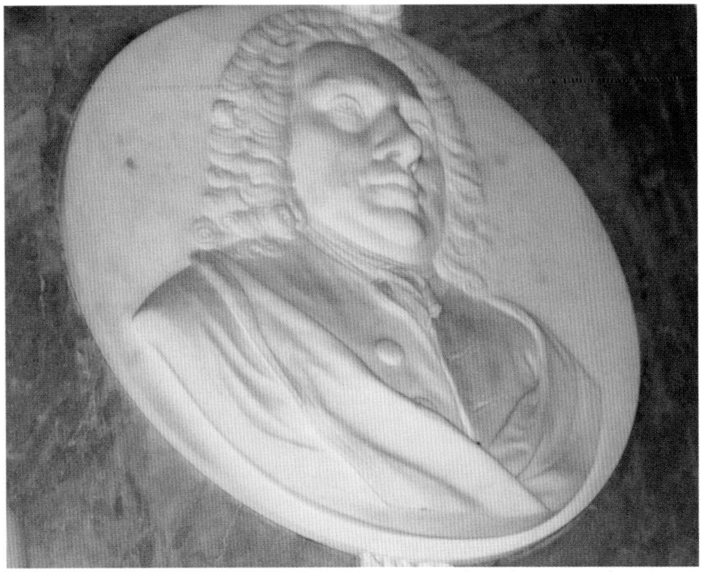

Medallion bust of Zachary Hamlyn (116)

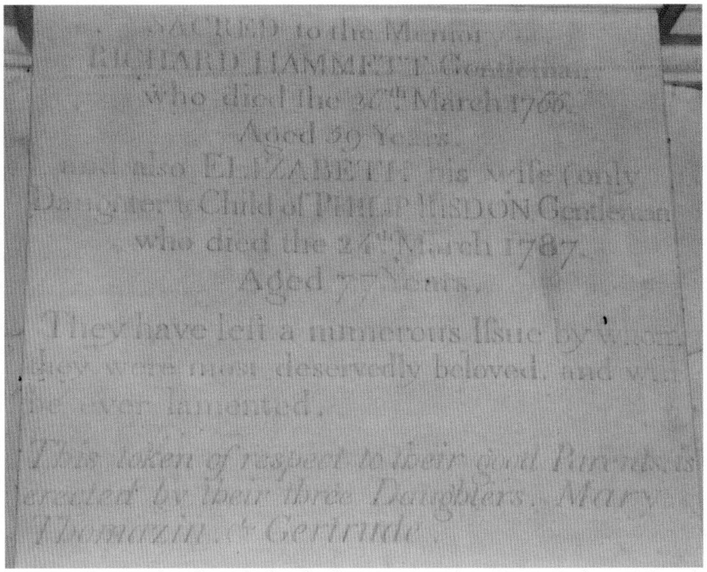

Mural to Richard and Elizabeth Hammett (118) in Woolsery Church

rectories and tithes in the parishes of Cynwyl Gaeo and Llansawel in Carmarthenshire (showing a connection with Edwinsford well before the families united through marriage) to his great nephew James Hammett. Other local lands which he had acquired he left to Anne Hammett (Richard's sister and his great niece) and her husband John Velley of Hartland. He also left land to Zachary Hammett (another great nephew); land to his niece Alice Olde (daughter of his sister Margaret); £200 to his sister Margaret Olde; £200 to his nephew Richard Hammett; £1,600 to his niece Mary Hammett; £1,200 to his niece Anne Hammett; plus annuities to his nieces Mary and Anne Hammett. He left his Chambers at Lincoln's Inn, New Square ("wherein I now live") and goods to his nieces Mary and Anne Hammett. He gave to his nephew Edward Hammett ("now living at my house at Court in Clovelly") an annuity of £6 pa for life. He left everything else including Clovelly ("and all goods….in or about my house at Court in Clovelly") to his great nephew, James Hammett, including a part share in the ship *Prince George* which had been leased to the East India Company; he had already given another share in the ship to his niece Mary Hammett.

Although Zachary was buried at his request in Woolsery Church there is a mural monument in All Saints' Church Clovelly to his memory[497] showing a medallion hanging against an obelisk with the Hamlyn arms above (*gules, a lion rampant ermine crowned or)* being the same arms as the Hamlyn families of Widecombe and Buckfastleigh. His epitaph states that "he was a sincere Christian, a tender and beneficient relation, a faithfull and kind friend, an inoffensive and chearfull companion. Exemplarily modest, diligent, capable, communicative, he acquired a handsome fortune….."

Sir James (Hammett) Hamlyn 1st Bt MP (1735-1811) and Arabella Williams (1739-97)

As we have seen in Chapter 8.3, Thomas Williams (54) of Edwinsford made his will on 21 July 1762 and died in London that autumn. His daughter, Bridget (56), then inherited the Edwinsford Estate. His other daughter, Arabella Williams (58), lived with her father and stepmother in Edwinsford, Court Derllys and their London home until her marriage on 11 June 1762, just before her father's death, to James Hamlyn (57) of Clovelly Court in Devon whom she will have met in

[497] Grigs p9

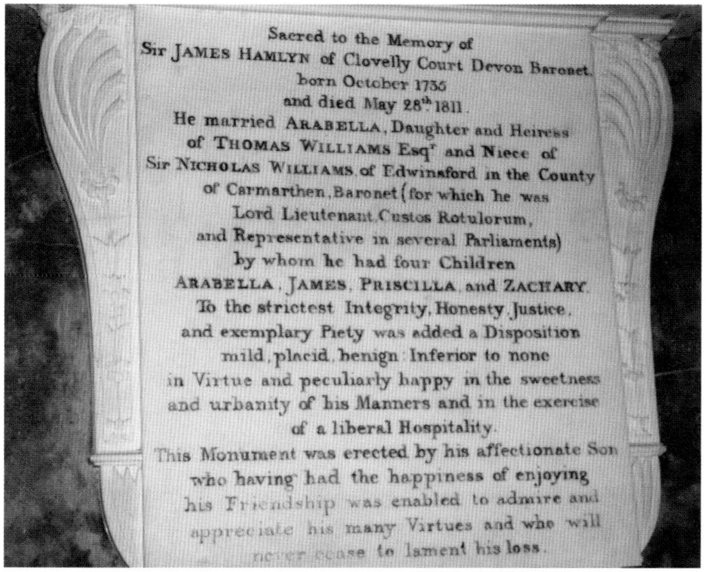

Memorial in Clovelly Church

In Memory of Lady HAMLYN
Wife of Sir JAMES HAMLYN Bart:
(Member of Parliament for the County of Carmarthen)
and Daughter and Heirefs of the late
THOMAS WILLIAMS Efqr of Edwinsford in that County
She died the 22d. May 1797 in the 58th. Year of her Age
and is interred in the Family Vault in Talley
leaving one Son and one Daughter.
Her grateful and afflicted Hufband's
laft and proudeft wifh will be, that
whenever Divine Providence fhall call him hence
his Name may be engraved on the fame Tablet
that is facred in perpetuating as much Virtue
and goodnefs as could adorn human Nature

Sir JAMES HAMLYN Husband of the Above
Born Octr. 1735 Died May 28th 1811 This inscription
is added by their great great grand Daughter
CHRISTINE HAMLYN of Clovelly Court 1890

Memorial in Clovelly Church

London society. In accordance with the terms of the settlement made by his great uncle Zachary Hamlyn, James had changed his surname from "Hammett" to "Hamlyn" by Act of Parliament in 1760 and adopted the arms of the Hamlyn family.

James Hamlyn was educated at Lincoln's Inn in 1750 and married Arabella Williams in 1762. They lived in Clovelly and London. In 1767 James served as Sheriff of Devon. On 27 January 1789 Clovelly Court was destroyed by fire along with most of the estate records, church records and family muniments and deeds; James rebuilt it in the then fashionable Georgian Gothic style.

In 1792 Arabella's sister, Bridget, died and under her father's will trust the Edwinsford Estate passed to Arabella. Bridget had owned and lived at Edwinsford with her husband for some 30 years; Arabella was only to do so for five years before her death in 1797 in her 58th year. John Swete[498] wrote in 1797 in his journal about James Hamlyn: "This gentleman was originally in the law and marrying a Miss Williams of vast fortune in Carmarthenshire, he has lately taken up the chief part

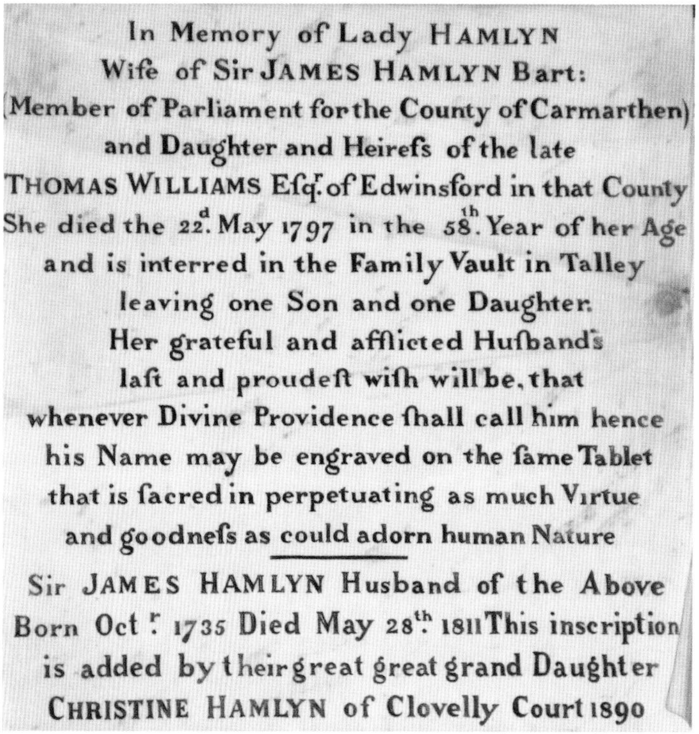

of his residence at his seat in that county." Together with Clovelly Court and its lands James and Arabella had some 14,000 acres. James had of course been born and brought up in Devon and managed the Clovelly Estate but he now took much interest in their 10,000 acre Carmarthenshire estate.

In April 1793 James stood for election as the Tory MP for Carmarthenshire and was elected unopposed. In 1796 he was reelected with only token opposition. In 1802 he retired from Parliament in favour of his son since his health was not up to the infamous contest which is described in Chapter 8.4 against William Paxton of Middleton Hall. James made no mark in Parliament and there is no record of his making any speech. He was described as "a plain downright country gentleman totally devoid of all pride and affectation."

498 John Swete: *The Illustrated Journals of the Rev John Swete 1789-1800*

Arms of Sir James Hamlyn Bt

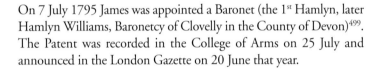

Arms of Sir James Hamlyn Bt

On 7 July 1795 James was appointed a Baronet (the 1st Hamlyn, later Hamlyn Williams, Baronetcy of Clovelly in the County of Devon)[499]. The Patent was recorded in the College of Arms on 25 July and announced in the London Gazette on 20 June that year.

On 22 May 1797 Arabella died aged only 57 and was buried in the Williams family vault in Talley. Her husband James (57) continued to live principally at Clovelly and sometimes at Edwinsford (with it seems a resident harpist[500]) while their son and heir, Sir James Hamlyn Williams Bt MP (1765-1829)(60), lived principally in Berkeley Square while occasionally visiting Clovelly and Edwinsford. On 14 March 1798 Garter King of Arms granted James Hamlyn of Edwinsford (60), Captain East Devon Militia, "only son and heir apparent the right to take the surname and arms of Williams" so that under his grandfather's will trust he was able to inherit the Edwinsford Estate. Thereafter the family surname became "Hamlyn Williams" as recorded at the College of Arms although not all members of the family always used both names as the surname.

Family letters[501] written between 1799 and 1807 evidence that there was much travelling by family members between Clovelly Court and Edwinsford often by sea and that the family complained obsessively about the state of the roads in Wales and Devon. Money was spent by the family on repairing the roads to make coach journeys more comfortable. The family would travel by horse and carriage from Edwinsford to Swansea and then take a boat to Bideford or Ilfracombe, and another horse and carriage the other end to Clovelly. This method avoided the long and arduous road journey all the way round the coast via Bristol.

Sir James had bad health in the last few years before he died in London on 28 May 1811 aged 76; his body was then brought down to Clovelly where he was buried in the family vault. In Clovelly Church there is a memorial[502] to him which includes: "To the strictest Integrity, Honesty, Justice and exemplary Piety was added a disposition mild, placid, benign; Inferior to none in virtue and peculiarly happy in the sweetness and urbanity of his manner, and in the exercise of a liberal hospitality. This Monument was erected by his affectionate son, who, having had

[499] DL Baker-Jones and others suggest he also served as Lord Lieutenant of Carmarthenshire which is incorrect, that office being held by the Rice, Johnes and Vaughan families during his lifetime

[500] Probably Mr Williams the same harpist (salary £17.15s.0d pa) who performed at Golden Grove-see Francis Jones: *Ceredigion Vol 4 (1960-3) p266*

[501] NLW Edwinsford archives; FDWD: *Annals p39-54*

[502] Grigs *p9*

Hamlyn arms

the happiness of enjoying his friendship, was enabled to admire and appreciate his many virtues, and who will never cease to lament his loss."

Sir James was followed by his son, Sir James Hamlyn Williams Bt MP (1765-1829)(60), who married Diana Whittaker (1766-1849)[503]. At Clovelly they built the celebrated Hobby Drive (being their great hobby)[504] along to the London Lodge, extended the pier in the harbour, laid out the paths in Clovelly Park, built the summer house in the "wilderness" and the cabin in the Park, and erected the Angel's Wings with carvings by their butler (from which they could see their daughter Lady Chichester's home at Youlston).

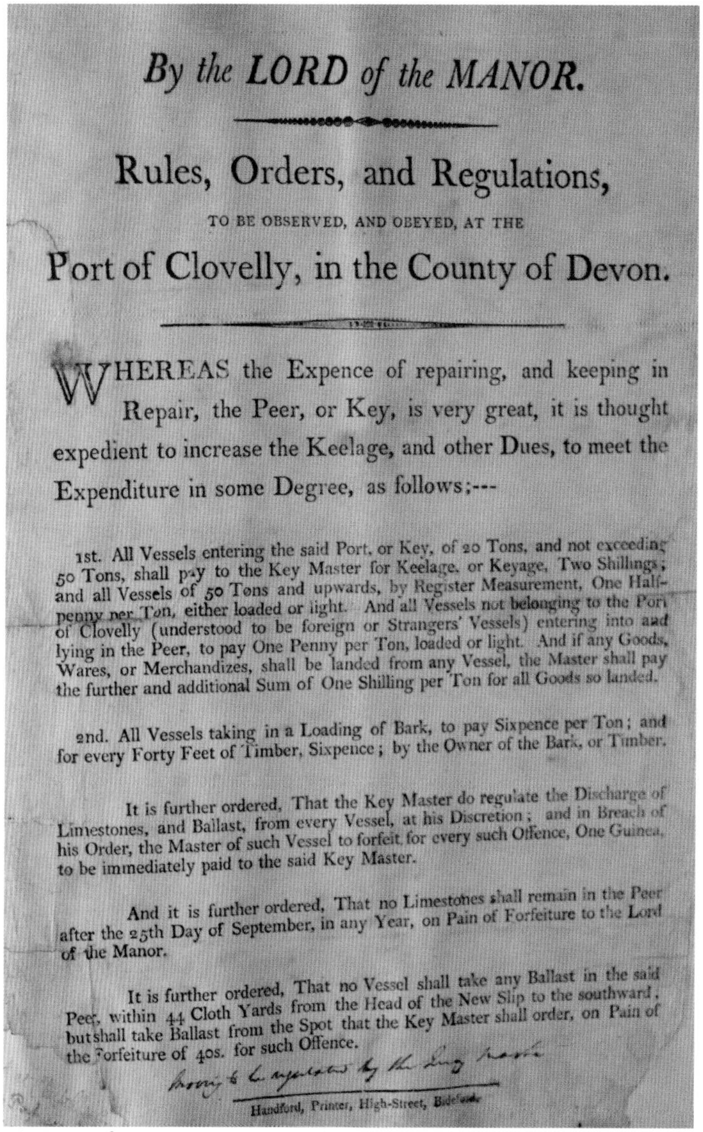

By the **LORD** *of the* **MANOR.**

Rules, Orders, and Regulations,

TO BE OBSERVED, AND OBEYED, AT THE

Port of Clovelly, in the County of Devon.

WHEREAS the Expence of repairing, and keeping in Repair, the Peer, or Key, is very great, it is thought expedient to increase the Keelage, and other Dues, to meet the Expenditure in some Degree, as follows;---

1st. All Vessels entering the said Port, or Key, of 20 Tons, and not exceeding 50 Tons, shall pay to the Key Master for Keelage, or Keyage, Two Shillings; and all Vessels of 50 Tons and upwards, by Register Measurement, One Half-penny per Ton, either loaded or light. And all Vessels not belonging to the Port of Clovelly (understood to be foreign or Strangers' Vessels) entering into and lying in the Peer, to pay One Penny per Ton, loaded or light. And if any Goods, Wares, or Merchandizes, shall be landed from any Vessel, the Master shall pay the further and additional Sum of One Shilling per Ton for all Goods so landed.

2nd. All Vessels taking in a Loading of Bark, to pay Sixpence per Ton; and for every Forty Feet of Timber, Sixpence; by the Owner of the Bark, or Timber.

It is further ordered, That the Key Master do regulate the Discharge of Limestones, and Ballast, from every Vessel, at his Discretion; and in Breach of his Order, the Master of such Vessel to forfeit for every such Offence, One Guinea, to be immediately paid to the said Key Master.

And it is further ordered, That no Limestones shall remain in the Peer after the 25th Day of September, in any Year, on Pain of Forfeiture to the Lord of the Manor.

It is further ordered, That no Vessel shall take any Ballast in the said Peer, within 44 Cloth Yards from the Head of the New Slip to the southward, but shall take Ballast from the Spot that the Key Master shall order, on Pain of the Forfeiture of 40s. for such Offence.

Handford, Printer, High-Street, Bideford

© *Hon John Rous* *Port regulations 1814*

The successors at Clovelly Court and Edwinsford to Sir James Hamlyn Bt (57) have been described previously in Chapters 8.4 and 9.3; so we now move forward to Susan Hester Hamlyn Williams (70), the eldest daughter of Sir James Hamlyn Williams 3rd Bt MP (1790-1861)(61).

[503] See Footnote 518

[504] Some claim that Napoleonic French prisoners of war were used as labourers but there is no hard evidence of this

18.2 Hamlyn Williams and Hamlyn Fane Families

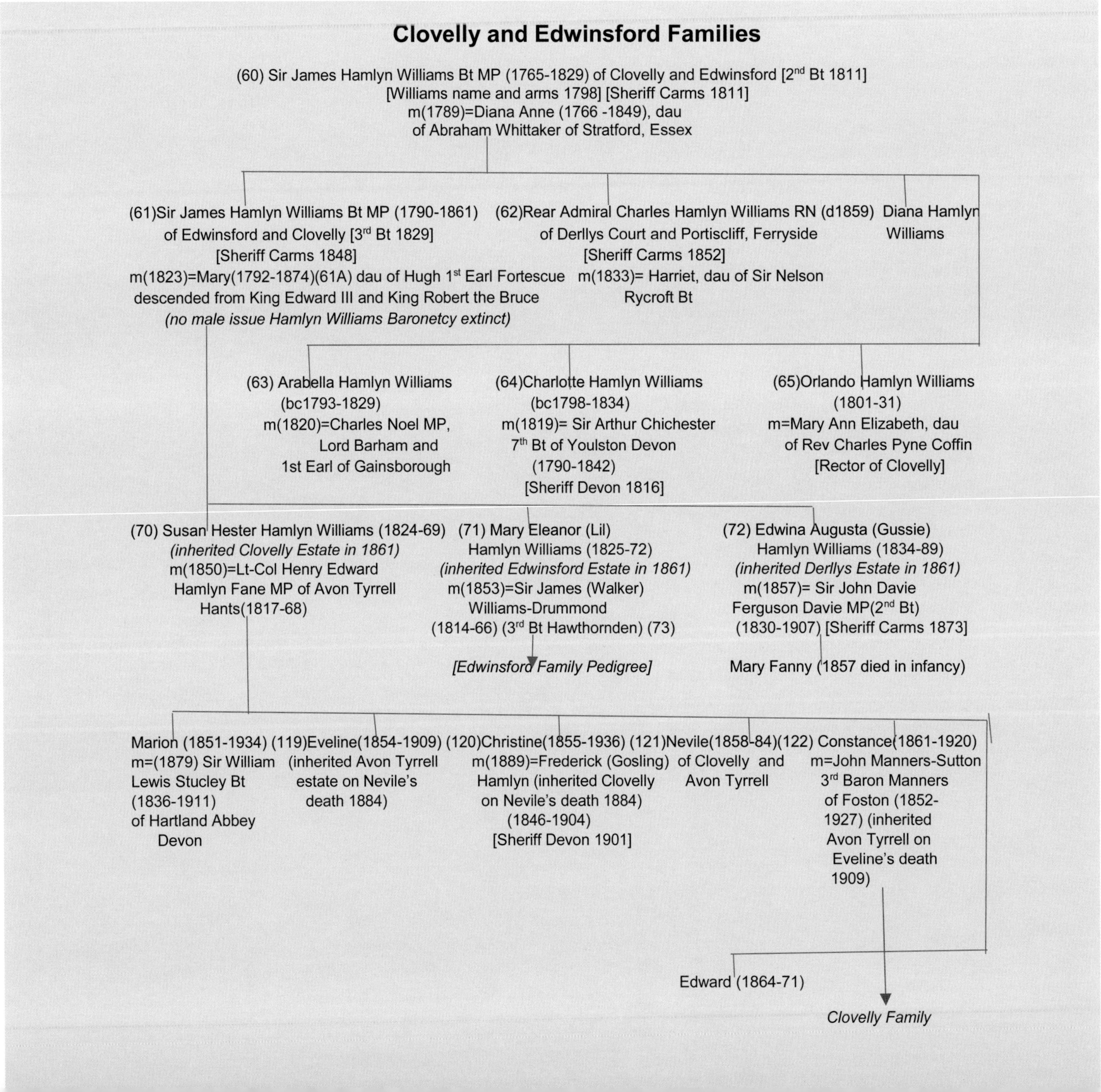

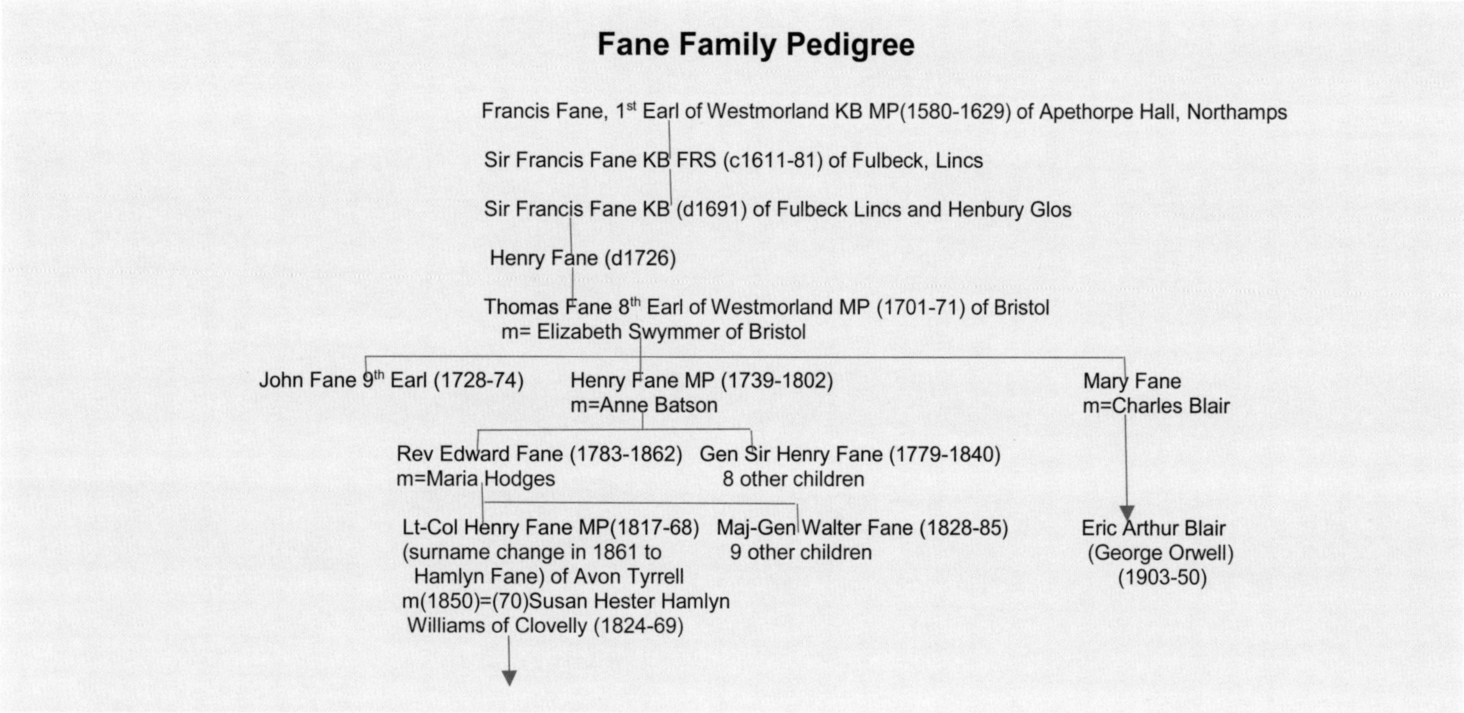

Susan Hester Hamlyn Williams (1824-69) and Lt-Col Henry Edward Hamlyn Fane MP (1815-68)

Sir James (61) married Lady Mary Fortescue (61A) and as a result their descendants at Clovelly and Edwinsford acquired an English and Scottish royal blood line as shown in the pedigrees at the end of this Chapter. They had three daughters:

(1) Mary Eleanor (Lil) Hamlyn Williams (1825-72)(71) who inherited the Edwinsford Estate in 1861 on the death of her father and is described in Chapter 9.5. She married into the Scottish Drummond family of Hawthornden Castle near Edinburgh and started a whole new chapter in the history of the Welsh Williams family of Edwinsford, which would remain close to but no longer part of the Clovelly branch of the family;

(2) Edwina Augusta (Gussie) Hamlyn Williams (1834-89)(72) who inherited the Derllys Estate in 1861 on the death of her father. She was born at Clovelly Court and married on 17 March 1857 Sir John Ferguson Davie MP (2nd Bt)(1830-1907) of Bittescombe Manor, Upton, Taunton in Somerset and of Creedy Park, Sandford in Devon; and

(3) Susan Hester Hamlyn Williams (1824-69)(70) the eldest daughter who inherited the Clovelly Estate in 1861 on the death of her father. Like her mother she was born (on 1 January 1824) at Castle Hill mansion in Filleigh, Devon, a seat of the Fortescues. She married on 9 April 1850 Lt-Col Henry Edward Fane MP (1817-68).

The Fanes were an old accomplished family with a record of Royalist support during the Civil War and high achievement in the military as well as producing generations of Members of Parliament. The Earldom was created in 1624 (arms: *azure, three dexter gauntlets back affrontée or).* Sir Francis Fane KB FRS (c1611-81), a son of the 1st Earl, was made a Knight of the Bath on the coronation of Charles I and during the Civil War served as Governor of Doncatser and Lincoln Castle; he was also a dramatist and wrote poems and his seat (purchased by his father in 1622) was at Fulbeck Hall near Grantham in Lincolnshire. His son, Sir Francis Fane KB (d1691), was also a dramatist and writer of stage plays, and a courtier in the Restoration court of Charles II. His grandson, Thomas Fane MP (1701-71), was educated at the Middle Temple (1759) and made his money as a merchant in Bristol also serving as the Clerk to the Merchant Venturers of Bristol. He married into the Swymmer family, who were wealthy slave traders in Bristol, and served as a politician and MP for Lyme Regis (1753-62), the pocket borough controlled by the Fane family. He succeeded as the 8th Earl of Westmorland on the death without issue of a distant cousin in 1762. Of his children: (1) his eldest son, John Fane (1728-74), succeeded to the Earldom; (2) one of his two daughters, Mary, married into the Blair family and one of their descendants was the famous writer, George Orwell (1903-50); and (3) his second son, Henry Fane MP (1739-1802), was a clerk to HM Treasury (1757-63) described as "very idle and careless and spending much time in the country", and then the Keeper of the King's Private Roads, Gates and Bridges as well as serving as an MP for Lyme Regis (1772-1801). In 1783 his father gave him Fulbeck Hall (which has been the seat of the junior branch of the Fane family for 400 years). One of his sons, Rev Edward Fane (1783-1862), was the rector of Fulbeck and a Prebendary of Salisbury Cathedral; he inherited the Avon Tyrrell estate in Sopley, Hampshire from his mother, Anne Batson (heiress to her wealthy banker father). Avon Tyrrell had been a royal hunting forest[505] in the 11th century, later granted to the Tyrell family in 1365, sold in 1602 and later bought by the Batson family in the late 18th century.

Edward's eldest son was Lt-Col Henry Edward Fane MP (1817-68)(70) who was born on 5 September 1817 (although his memorial in Clovelly Church incorrectly says 1815), was educated at Charterhouse and served as a Major in the 4th Light Dragoons; he had several adventures[506] overseas. As we have seen, in 1850 he married Susan Hester Hamlyn Williams (70), who inherited the Clovelly Estate in 1861 on the death of her father. By royal licence he added "Hamlyn" to his name when his wife inherited Clovelly so their surname changed to "Hamlyn Fane". In 1862 he inherited the Avon Tyrrell estate on the death of his father. He served as MP for Hampshire South (1865-8). Henry and Susan lived at both Avon Tyrrell and Clovelly Court and

Memorial in Clovelly Church

continued with their parents' strategy of managing[507] and improving both estates. This was the age of shipwrecks, piracy and smuggling so it cannot have been easy given the very few policemen in the district.

505 Walter Tyrell is said to have accidentally killed King William II with an arrow while hunting in 1100

506 Henry Hamlyn Fane: *Five Years in India comprising a narrative of Travels in the Presidency of Bengal, a Visit to the Court of Runjeet Sing, residence in the Himalayah Mountains, an account of the late expedition to Cabul and Affghanistan, voyage down the Indus, and journey overland to England (1842)*

507 Maps of the Clovelly Estate in Clovelly, Hartland and Woolsery are at the North Devon Record Office deposited by Pitts Tucker, solicitors of Barnstaple

Fane arms

Henry died at Avon Tyrrell in Hampshire on 27 December 1868 aged only 51. Susan died shortly thereafter at Clovelly Court on 19 May 1869 at the even younger age of 45 and was buried at Clovelly; a mural memorial[508] is in Clovelly Church.

Henry and Susan had six children:

(1) Nevile Hamlyn Fane (1858-84)(121) the eldest son was born on 21 November 1858, educated at Magdalene College Cambridge, and later served as a Lieutenant in the 3rd Battalion Northamptonshire Regiment. He lived at both Avon Tyrrell and Clovelly Court, both of which he inherited as a youngster when his parents died in 1868/9 so one must assume that trustees managed the estates until he gained his majority. The 1871 census return in Chapter 20 shows that Clovelly Court was being run at this difficult time by the eldest daughter Marion with the support of her aunt, Harriet Fane. Nevile died in London aged only 25 on 10 March 1884. On his death the Avon Tyrrell estate passed to his elder sister Eveline (119) while the Clovelly estate went to his sister Christine (120);

(2) Marion Hamlyn Fane (1851-1934) the eldest child and daughter was born at Clovelly Court on 5 March 1851 and on 5 February 1879 married Lt-Col Sir William (Lewis) Stucley 2nd Bt (1836-1911) at Fulbeck Church. His father, Sir George Stucley MP (1812-1900), of Affeton Castle and Hartland Abbey in Devon served as MP for Barnstaple (1855-7 and 1865-8) and Sheriff of Devon (1863) and was created a baronet in 1859. Sir Lewis served in the Grenadier Guards, and was a chartered accountant, a magistrate and a Deputy Lieutenant for Devon. He died aged 74 on 19 February 1911 without issue. Marion died aged 83 on 3 August 1934 at Holnicote and was buried at Clovelly Church;

(3) Eveline Hamlyn Fane (1854-1909)(119) the second daughter was born at Fulbeck Hall on 20 April 1854. She inherited the Avon Tyrrell estate in 1884 on the death of her younger brother Nevile; she died unmarried on 20 December 1909 aged 55 and was buried at Clovelly Church;

(4) Constance Hamlyn Fane (1861-1920)(122) is described below in Chapter 18.3;
(5) Edward Hamlyn Fane (1864-71) died in his youth; and
(6) Christine Hamlyn Fane (1855-1936)(120).

Christine Hamlyn Fane (1855-1936) and Frederick (Gosling) Hamlyn (1846-1904)

Christine (120) was born on 29 November 1855 at Fulbeck Hall in Lincolnshire, the home of her father's family, the Fanes; she was baptised in Fulbeck Church on 25 December. She and her siblings were brought up at both Clovelly Court and Avon Tyrrell by their parents who both died young by 1869 so guardians and trustees must have looked after them; probably their aunt, Harriet Fane, who is shown in the 1871 census return as living at Clovelly Court with them. Christine formed a life-long love for Clovelly which she inherited on the death of her brother Nevile in March 1884. On 11 June 1889 she married Frederick Gosling, who then changed his surname by royal licence to "Hamlyn" and devoted his life (and much of his wealth) with her to the loving care of Clovelly and their tenants. They were loved and respected by their staff and by the tenants. On rent days the tenants were given a free dinner of venison pie, beer and cigarettes to smoke; on their wedding day all the staff[509] were given new uniforms at Clovelly Court.

[508] Grigs p8
[509] Sheila Ellis p31

Frederick Gosling was born in 1846, the grandson of William Gosling (1765-1834) of Roehampton, and the son of Robert Gosling (1795-1869) and Georgina Vere Sullivan (d1879). Georgina, his mother, was the daughter of Rt Hon John Sullivan MP (1749-1839) of Richings Park, Buckinghamshire from an Irish family. In his youth John Sullivan went to India with the support of his kinsman, Laurence Sullivan, the Chairman of the East India Company and made his fortune as a merchant and then as Resident of Tanjore (1781-5); he returned to England and bought his Buckinghamshire estate. Despite many later attempts to be appointed as Governor of Bombay or Madras he failed to do so, and married into the influential Hobart family; his brother in law Robert Hobart became Governor of Madras and later Colonial Secretary and the Earl of Buckinghamshire. John Sullivan used Robert's influence to be appointed as Under-Secretary for War and Colonies (1802-4), became a member of the Privy Council (1805), and represented Old Sarum (1790-6), Aldborough (1802-6) and Ashburton (1811-8) as an MP. He died in 1839.

© Hon John Rous — *Christine Hamlyn 1876*

© Hon John Rous — *Christine Hamlyn*

© Hon John Rous *Christine Hamlyn*

© Hon John Rous *"Old one eye" 1899*

© Hon John Rous

Memorial in Clovelly Church

Gravestone in Clovelly Churchyard

Gravestone in Clovelly Churchyard

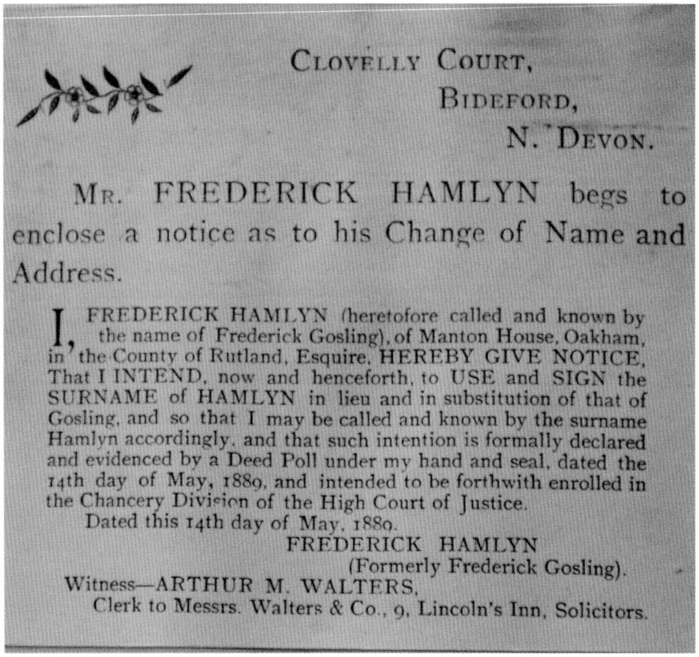

CLOVELLY COURT,
BIDEFORD,
N. DEVON.

MR. FREDERICK HAMLYN begs to enclose a notice as to his Change of Name and Address.

I, FREDERICK HAMLYN (heretofore called and known by the name of Frederick Gosling), of Manton House, Oakham, in the County of Rutland, Esquire, HEREBY GIVE NOTICE, That I INTEND, now and henceforth, to USE and SIGN the SURNAME of HAMLYN in lieu and in substitution of that of Gosling, and so that I may be called and known by the surname Hamlyn accordingly, and that such intention is formally declared and evidenced by a Deed Poll under my hand and seal, dated the 14th day of May, 1889, and intended to be forthwith enrolled in the Chancery Division of the High Court of Justice.

Dated this 14th day of May, 1889.

FREDERICK HAMLYN
(Formerly Frederick Gosling).

Witness—ARTHUR M. WALTERS,
Clerk to Messrs. Walters & Co., 9, Lincoln's Inn, Solicitors.

© Hon John Rous *1889 notice of change of surname*

© Hon John Rous
Mariners 1885 (Capt Gilly, Tom Gilly, Dick Headon, Freddy Watts, Bill Burman, Sam Whitfield, Billy Prince, Steve Headon, Billy Whitfield, Robert Badcock)

Following Christine's inheritance of Clovelly in 1884, for the next 52 years she was the "Queen of Clovelly" and with her husband cared for the village intensely. As described by one member[510] of the family: "The heritage thus bequeathed to her has been a sacred trust in the truest sense, for the village, while retaining all its ancient and unique charms, has been largely rebuilt, drained and supplied with water by her generous and zealous interest in its welfare, and the property generally improved and consolidated."

Christine continued with the improvements started by her parents and grandparents including replacing some parts of the cobbled streets and covering the previously open drains which had been the cause of the cholera epidemic in 1861, although mains water did not arrive until 1953 so before that the residents relied on wells and an old reservoir.

Christine and Frederick restored many of the cottages and farms and the initials "CH" and "FH" with the date of restoration can still be seen in the outside plaster or brickwork of many of them; most of the cottages were originally built of a stonebase from the beach with a layer of cob (earth mixed with straw and horsehair) above and some have never changed and some are thought to be 600 years old. Most cottages have steep and narrow stairs being on a slope with low ceilings and old beams; over the centuries many have been merged with the neighbouring buildings to make a larger shop or an inn or beerhouse. They built a new mortuary for the use of the parish in 1898. In 1901 they built the Memorial Fountain set in a retained wall on the cobbled main street in "honoured memory of a great Queen" to commemorate Queen Victoria. After the Great War Christine gave a plot on Mount Pleasant to the National Trust and built a cross and memorial in memory of all those in Clovelly who had given their lives including her nephew, Hon John Manners. Throughout her life Christine travelled abroad a lot and, as can be seen from the census returns for 1881 to 1911 in Chapter 19.3, she was away every Spring in those years and had a London residence. In 1929 she set up the Clovelly Estate Company to manage the estate on behalf of herself as owner and this structure has survived to this day. She acquired additional cottages during her reign as lady of the manor and, when cashflow required it, also sold some of the estate's land. Clovelly Court was partially used to house wounded soldiers during the Great War as it would be again during WW2. Between the Wars the tourists came in great numbers often on day trips by paddle steamer from Ilfracombe, walked along the Hobby Drive or hired a horse and carriage, and had Devon teas before embarking in the harbour.

Frederick served as Sheriff of Devon in 1901 and as a DL; he died on 22 July 1904. Christine carried on with her estate management until her death on 12 November 1936 aged 80. She was buried in Clovelly Church where there are two mural memorials[511] to her ("for 52 years a devoted owner of Clovelly—I dwell among mine own people—her radiant personality, the warmth and generosity of her friendship, her ever vigilant protection of the beauty and wellbeing of her beloved Clovelly and for the simplicity, sincerity and loyalty of her Christian faith"). She was a very remarkable lady, a strong Church attender, friend to all, and respected by all the residents during her 52 year reign. Her coffin lay in state in the church overnight and the whole village attended her funeral with many other friends. Her photographs and portraits are still on show in many parts of the village. She would have been a very difficult act to follow. Indeed, since Christine and Frederick did not have any children Christine's intention as regards succession was to leave the Clovelly Estate to her eldest niece, Mary Manners (1886-1904) but tragically Mary died on a visit to India at the age of 17, so she left Clovelly to Mary's younger sister, Betty Asquith (née Manners)(1889-1962)(123).

---

510 FDWD: *Annals p17*

511 Grigs p9

18.3 Manners, Asquith and Rous Families

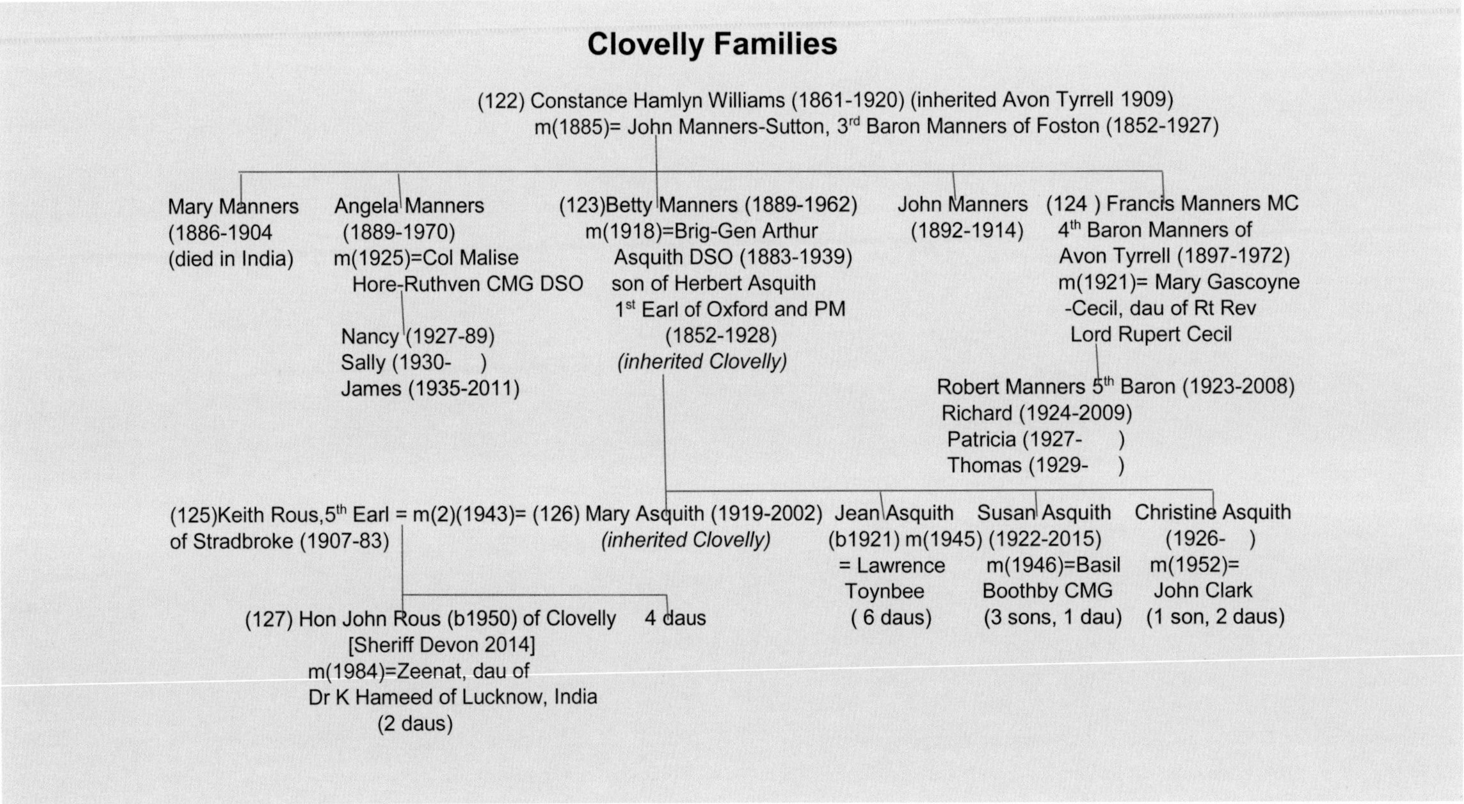

Constance Hamlyn Fane (1861-1920) and John Manners-Sutton 3rd Baron Manners (1852-1927)

Constance (122) was the younger sister of Christine Hamlyn and the youngest daughter of Henry and Susan Hamlyn Fane (70). Constance was born at Avon Tyrell on 28 September 1861 and like her siblings had to suffer the tragedy of both her parents' early deaths. On 12 August 1885 she was married at Clovelly Church to John Thomas Manners-Sutton, 3rd Baron Manners of Foston (1852-1927).

The Manners family are an interesting one. Sir Thomas Manners-Sutton (1756-1842) was the fifth son of Lord George Manners-Sutton (3rd son of the Duke of Rutland). His elder brother Charles was Archbishop of Canterbury (1805-28) and father of Charles 1st Viscount Canterbury, Speaker of the House of Commons (1817-34). Sir Thomas was a lawyer and politician and served as Lord Chancellor of Ireland (1807-27). The title of Baron Manners of Foston in the county of Lincoln was created for him in 1807. His son 2nd Baron Manners was John Manners-Sutton (1818-64) who succeeded to the title in 1842.

John 3rd Baron Manners was born on 15 May 1852 and succeeded to the title as a youngster in 1864. He was educated at Eton and Trinity College Cambridge and served in the Grenadier Guards as a Lieutenant (1877-83); he then served as a Captain in the 3rd Battalion, Hampshire

Regiment. He is best known for betting a large sum in 1881 that he could buy, train and ride the winner of the 1882 Grand National at Aintree, an extraordinary feat if he could pull it off in just four months particularly as he had not ridden many jumps before. He bought Seaman, a six year old gelding, for £1,900 from an Irish seller, Henry Linde, who did not believe he had a chance on the horse. Manners set about training with some help and entered some amateur races to gain some experience. Then three weeks before the National he won the Grand Military Gold Cup at Sandown on another horse. On the day of the National, 24 March 1882, in very poor weather and with heavy snow 12 horses started. To the astonishment of the crowd and the delight of the bookies Manners just won by a head[512]. Seaman never raced again and lived in retirement with the family and was buried in the grounds when he died. With his large winnings Manners built a new house, Avon Tyrrell, on his sister in law Eveline's estate at Sopley, Hampshire; it was completed in 1891 and had 52 rooms, 12 chimneys, four wings and 365 windows (a calendar house). It was used as a hospital during WW2 and the family later gave it to a charity for young people. Constance inherited the Avon Tyrrell estate on the death of her sister Eveline in 1909.

Constance died on 4 March 1920 aged 58. John died on 19 August 1927 aged 75 having remarried in 1922. Constance and John had five children:

(1) Mary (1886-1904) died unmarried on a visit to India on 5 February 1904 and was thus unable to inherit Clovelly as intended by her aunt, Christine Hamlyn;

(2) Angela (1889-1970) a twin was born on 15 June 1889. Before her marriage Angy aged 25 raised a hospital[513] with matron, nurses and equipment and took it to Belgium. The "Manners Hospital" in Mons was joined by Winston Churchill's sister in law, Nellie Hozier, Angy's best friend. They were captured by the Germans and thrown into prison. Angy was awarded the rare Royal Red Cross by King George V and Belgium's Queen Elizabeth medal as well as being entitled to wear the Mons Star. On 26 May 1925 she was married to Col Hon Malise Hore-Ruthven CMG, DSO (son of the 9th Lord Ruthven of Freeland and Lady Caroline Annesley Gore). They had three children: (a) Nancy (1927-89) who was killed in a car crash; (b) Sally (b1930); and (c) James (1935-2011) who retired to Hugglepit Cottage in Higher Clovelly with his wife Dron Craig after a distinguished career in reconciliation and conflict resolution;

(3) John Manners (1892-1914) who was a Lieutenant in the Grenadier Guards and was killed at Villers Cotterets in France on 1 September 1914. His aunt, Christine Hamlyn, built the memorial cross at Mount Pleasant in Clovelly in his memory;

(4) Francis Manners MC 4th Baron Manners (1897-1972) was born on 21 July 1897 and like his father was educated at Eton and Trinity College Cambridge. He fought in the Great War as a Captain in the Grenadier Guards and was mentioned in despatches and later gained the Military Cross. Because of the death of his elder brother he succeeded to the title in 1927. On 29 January 1921 he married Mary Gascoyne-Cecil (1900-94), daughter of Rt Rev Lord Rupert Cecil. Francis also fought in WW2 and served as Lt-Colonel in the 5/7th Battalion, Hampshire Regiment. They had four children: (a) Robert 5th Baron Manners (1923-2008); (b) Richard (1924-2009); (c) Patricia (b1927); and (d) Thomas (b1929); and

(5) Betty Constance Manners (1889-1962)(123).

---

512 Grand National History; Avon Tyrrell History

513 Michael Henderson: *The Adventures of Angy a Red Cross nurse at Mons (2015)*

Betty Constance Manners (1889-1962) and Brig-Gen Hon Arthur Asquith DSO (1883-1939)

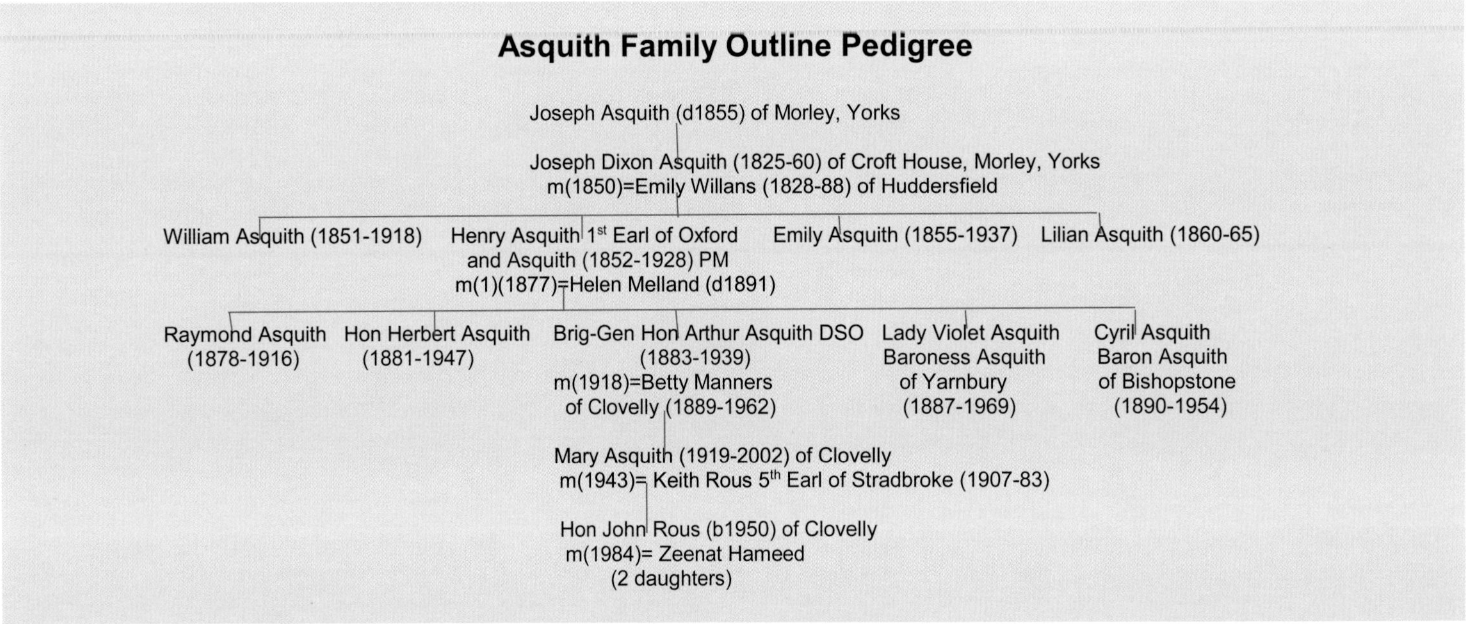

Betty was the twin of Angela born on 15 June 1889. They were brought up at Avon Tyrell in the new home built on their father's gambling winnings. On 30 April 1918 towards the end of the Great War at All Saints' Church, Thorney Hill near Christchurch she married a war hero, Brig-General Hon Arthur Asquith DSO and two bars, the son of Herbert Asquith KG PC FRS (1852-1928) who had served as Prime Minister. Herbert[514] had been educated at the City of London School and Balliol College Oxford and then gone to the Bar via Lincoln's Inn (1876) where he took silk (QC) in 1890. He served as MP for East Fife (1886-1918) and Paisley (1920-4), as Home Secretary (1892-5), as a member of the Privy Council (1892), Chancellor of the Exchequer (1905-8), and as Liberal Prime Minister (1908-16); he was succeeded as PM by David Lloyd George who held that office for the rest of the Great War. In 1925 he was created 1st Viscount Asquith of Morley, Yorks and also 1st Earl of Oxford and Asquith. His first wife Helen Melland died of typhoid on holiday in Scotland in 1891. He had several children and descendants from both his wives. Arthur's eldest son, Raymond, was a barrister and poet who was killed in action in 1916 serving with the Grenadier Guards. His second son, Herbert, also a poet served as a Captain in the Royal Field Artillery. His fourth son, Cyril, became a Law Lord. His daughter, Violet, became a Liberal politician and was made a Life Peeress in 1964. His daughter, Elizabeth, married a Romanian Prince and became Princess Antoine Bibesco. His youngest son, Anthony, became a well-known film director.

Arthur Asquith was Herbert's third son and was born on 24 April 1883. His mother died when he was only seven. He was educated with his brothers at Winchester and then went to New College Oxford and then joined the merchant firm of Franklin & Herrera who traded with Argentina. In 1914 he resigned and joined up with the Royal Naval Division, Hood Battalion (a Royal Navy land detachment and part of the Army) and was deployed to fight in Belgium; they suffered heavy casualties[515] at the siege of Antwerp, were withdrawn and sent to the Dardanelles at Gallipoli where Arthur was awarded his first DSO and was wounded. In 1916 the Royal Naval Division (63rd Division) was posted to the Western Front where Arthur commanded the 189th Brigade and was involved in heavy fighting. He was wounded again and awarded two bars to his DSO before again being badly wounded

514 Roy Jenkins: *Asquith (1964)*

515 Frank Davies and Graham Maddocks: *Bloody Red Tabs-General Officer Casualties of the Great War 1914-1918 (2014)*

© Hon John Rous Herbert Asquith PM with two of his children at Clovelly 1909

© Hon John Rous Herbert Asquith

© Hon John Rous Betty Asquith c1918

© Hon John Rous

Arthur and Betty Asquith's wedding 1918

© Hon John Rous

Betty Asquith and daughters c1934

near Beaucamp on 17 December 1917 and evacuated back to England; he was also awarded the Legion d'Honneur. His leg had to be amputated in January 1918 forcing him to give up the field as a Brig-General and transfer to serve as the Controller of the Trench Warfare Department in the Ministry of Munitions in London. Being wounded four times Arthur was very fortunate to survive the war and many of his friends, including Rupert Brooke who died from septicaemia caused by an infected mosquito bite, did not survive. After the War he served as a member of the Council of the Ministry of Labour (1918-20) and then went into business to serve on a number of boards including as chairman of Brazil Plantations, and Parana Plantations, and on the board of San Paulo Brazilian Railway Co. Following their marriage in 1918 Betty and Arthur lived in London; they moved down to Clovelly in 1936 when Betty inherited the estate on the death of Christine Hamlyn. Arthur died of Hodgkin lymphoma at Clovelly Court on 24 August 1939 aged 56.

The start of WW2 led to evacuees arriving at Clovelly and having to be housed and schooled. Clovelly Court was partially used as a military hospital. Then on 29 December 1943[516] there was a second fire at Clovelly Court (the first had been in 1789) and a great deal of damage was done; soldiers in their blue uniforms came to the rescue and many family heirlooms were saved by Betty Asquith and her sister but much of the house had to be rebuilt including a new wing.

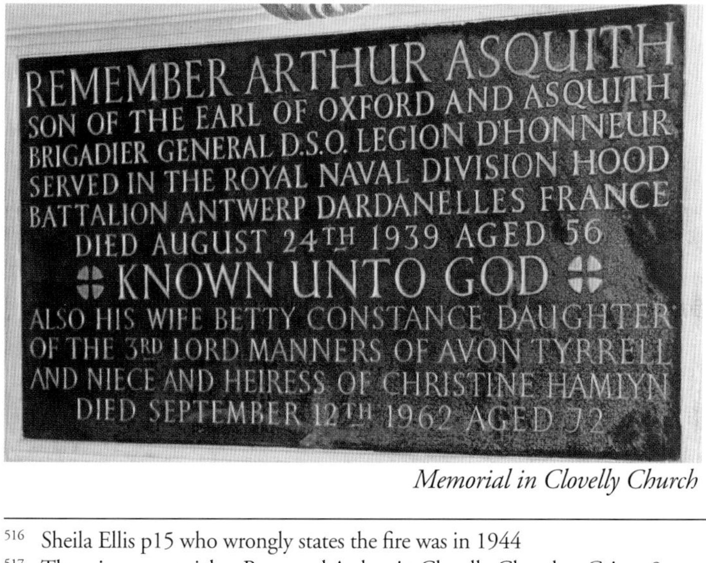

Memorial in Clovelly Church

Betty had an agent, James Hilton, to do the legwork of managing the estate for her; he had served during WW1 in the Royal Naval Division as Arthur Asquith's Adjutant and had then gone to farm in New Zealand before returning to England. Betty continued to own the estate until her death[517] on 12 September 1962 aged 72; she was buried with Arthur in Clovelly Church.

Betty and Arthur had four daughters:(a) Jean Asquith (b1921) who in 1945 married Lawrence Toynbee and had six daughters; (b) Susan Asquith (1922-2015) who in 1946 married Basil Boothby CMG and had three sons and one daughter; (c) Christine Asquith (b1926) who in 1952 married John Clark and had one son and two daughters; and (d) Mary Asquith (1919-2002) the eldest daughter who inherited Clovelly from her mother in 1962.

Stone in Clovelly Churchyard

516 Sheila Ellis p15 who wrongly states the fire was in 1944

517 There is a memorial to Betty and Arthur in Clovelly Church—Grigs p9

Mary Asquith (1919-2002) and Keith Rous 5th Earl of Stradbroke (1907-83)

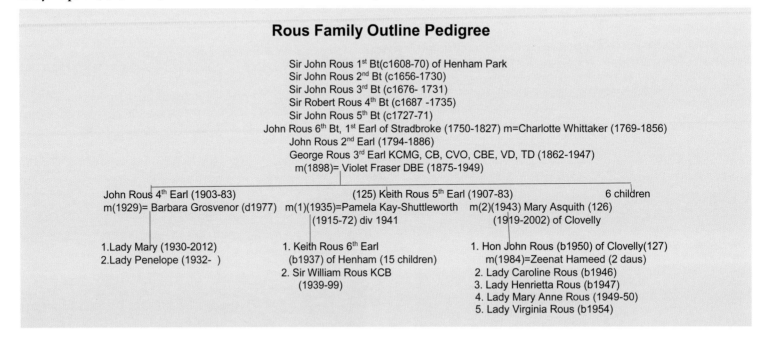

Rous Family Outline Pedigree

Sir John Rous 1st Bt(c1608-70) of Henham Park
Sir John Rous 2nd Bt (c1656-1730)
Sir John Rous 3rd Bt (c1676- 1731)
Sir Robert Rous 4th Bt (c1687 -1735)
Sir John Rous 5th Bt (c1727-71)
John Rous 6th Bt, 1st Earl of Stradbroke (1750-1827) m=Charlotte Whittaker (1769-1856)
John Rous 2nd Earl (1794-1886)
George Rous 3rd Earl KCMG, CB, CVO, CBE, VD, TD (1862-1947)
m(1898)= Violet Fraser DBE (1875-1949)

John Rous 4th Earl (1903-83)
m(1929)= Barbara Grosvenor (d1977)
1.Lady Mary (1930-2012)
2.Lady Penelope (1932-)

(125) Keith Rous 5th Earl (1907-83)
m(1)(1935)=Pamela Kay-Shuttleworth (1915-72) div 1941
1. Keith Rous 6th Earl (b1937) of Henham (15 children)
2. Sir William Rous KCB (1939-99)

m(2)(1943) Mary Asquith (126) (1919-2002) of Clovelly
1. Hon John Rous (b1950) of Clovelly(127) m(1984)=Zeenat Hameed (2 daus)
2. Lady Caroline Rous (b1946)
3. Lady Henrietta Rous (b1947)
4. Lady Mary Anne Rous (1949-50)
5. Lady Virginia Rous (b1954)

6 children

Mary (126) was born on 14 April 1919 after the end of the Great War and was mainly brought up in London before the family moved down to Clovelly in 1936 when her mother Betty inherited the estate on the death of Christine Hamlyn. On 19 July 1943 before the fire at Clovelly Court she was married to Keith Rous (125), the second son of George Rous 3rd Earl of Stradbroke and Violet Fraser DBE.

The Rous family have a distinguished history. Sir John Rous (c1608-70) was a Cavalier during the Civil War and supposedly hid in an oak tree (the Rous Oak) to escape capture. He later sat as an MP for Dunwich and was granted the Baronetcy of Henham in the County of Suffolk by Charles II in 1660 and put in control of the Cinque Ports; his country seat of Henham Park near Southwold had been bought by Sir Anthony Rous in 1544. His son 2nd Bt was MP for Dunwich and Suffolk. His son 3rd Bt was also MP for Dunwich. His nephew 5th Bt was MP for Suffolk. His son John was a racehorse owner who won the 2000 Guineas in 1815 and was MP for Suffolk. In 1796 he was made Baron Rous of Dennington, then in 1821 Viscount Dunwich and 1st Earl of Stradbroke[518]. He was succeeded by his first son, John 2nd Earl; another son, Henry Rous (1795-1877) was an Admiral in the Royal Navy, MP for Westminster, and a keen horseracer[519] and is credited[520] with the discovery and naming of the Richmond River and Stradbroke Island in Australia in 1827. John 2nd Earl served from the age of 16 with the Coldstream Regiment of Foot Guards, went to Portugal in 1812 during the Peninsula War[521] and fought at Salamanca, Burgos, Vittoria and San Sebastion, was wounded in 1815 at Quatre Bras just before Waterloo, and then transferred as a Captain to the 93rd Regiment of Foot in 1817 before retiring from the Army in 1821. He

518 Sir James Hamlyn Williams 2nd Bt (1765-1829)(60) of Clovelly and Edwinsford and John Rous 1st Earl of Stradbroke were brothers in law as a result of marrying Diana and Charlotte Whittaker respectively. Hon John Rous, the current owner of the Clovelly Estate, is a descendant of both

519 The Rous Memorial Stakes at Ascot was named after him now discontinued as well as roads in Newmarket. He also wrote “The Laws and Practice of Horse Racing”, cleared up the corruption in horseracing with Lord Derby through the Jockey Club, and introduced the handicapping formula used to this day

520 Henham Park History online

521 John Rous, Ian Fletcher: *A Guards Officer in the Peninsula: Peninsula War Letters of John Rous Coldstream Guards 1812-1814 (1992);* Nicholas Jenkins: *John Edward Cornwallis Rous*

succeeded to the title and Henham Hall in 1827 and served as Lord Lieutenant of Suffolk (1844-86).

George Rous 3rd Earl (1862-1947), son of the 2nd Earl, had a most distinguished career. He was born on 19 November 1862 and was educated at Harrow and Trinity College Cambridge (1884). He succeeded his father in 1886. From 1882 he served in the 1st Norfolk Royal Field Artillery Volunteers becoming a Colonel in 1902 and served in WW1 in France, Egypt and Palestine; in 1916 he was torpedoed by a German submarine. He was aide de camp to King Edward VII and King George V (1902-30). In 1920 he was made 15th Governor of Victoria in Australia (1921-6) and lived at Stonnington Hall in Melbourne before returning to Henham Hall to be Parliamentary Secretary to the Ministry of Agriculture and Fisheries (1928-9). He served as Lord Lieutenant of Suffolk (1935-47), Vice Admiral of Suffolk (1890-1947), as a JP, and as an Alderman and chairman of East Suffolk County Council. He was a keen Freemason and served as Provincial Grand Master of Suffolk (1902-47) and Grand Master of the Mark Masons of East Anglia (1943-47). His honours included KCMG, CB, CVO, CBE, VD,TD. On 23 July 1898 he married Violet Fraser (d1949) who was created DBE in 1927. They

Lady Charlotte (Whittaker) Rous c1796

1st Earl of Stradbroke c1796

had five sons and three daughters. In his will the 3rd Earl stipulated that his eldest son John 4th Earl (who had two daughters) should only be a life tenant of Henham Estate and that on his death it should pass to his brother Keith 5th Earl and from him to Keith's eldest son, Robert Keith Rous (6th Earl).

Their eldest son, John Rous 4th Earl (1903-83), succeeded his father at Henham Hall in 1947. On 15 January 1929 he married Barbara Grosvenor (d1977) and they had two daughters. He served as a commander in the Royal Navy, as Lord Lieutenant for Suffolk (1948-78) and as Grand Master of the Mark Masons (1973). He took exception to the provisions of his father's will and tried to circumvent it by a complex lease structure to ensure that the Henham Park estate was inherited instead by a grandson, Charles Forbes. Sadly John and his younger brother Keith Rous (1907-83)(the future 5th Earl for only four days) did not get on. John 4th Earl formulated a plan to demolish Henham Hall and this led to litigation[522] between the two brothers which ended in 1953 with the demolition of the Hall and the sale by John of its contents. He and his family moved into another home on the Henham estate. He died on 14 July 1983 and the title was inherited

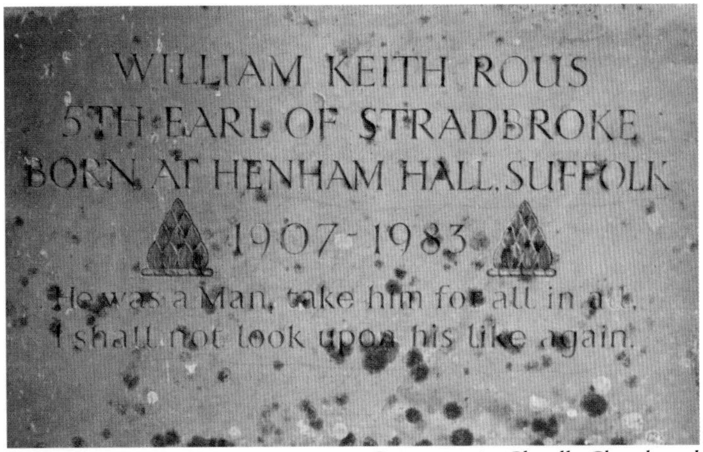

Admiral Henry John Rous

WILLIAM KEITH ROUS
5TH EARL OF STRADBROKE
BORN AT HENHAM HALL, SUFFOLK
▲ 1907-1983 ▲
He was a Man, take him for all in all,
I shall not look upon his like again.

Gravestone in Clovelly Churchyard

Stradbroke arms

JE·VIVE·EN·ESPOIR

522 Henham Park History online

© Hon John Rous

3rd Earl and Lady Stradbroke with four sons 1935

by his brother, Keith 5th Earl, described below who then died four days later. Consequently the title went to Keith's eldest son by his first marriage, Keith Rous 6th Earl (b1937); he had been sent to London in 1940 to live with his mother following her separation and later divorce from Keith (later the 5th Earl) and then to the country when their London home was bombed to live with his maternal grandmother. He was educated at Harrow until he was expelled aged 15 and then aged 19 he emigrated to Australia. In 1983 as the 6th Earl he was now faced with substantial death duties. He returned briefly to Henham and challenged his cousin, Charles Forbes, to a duel to sort out the inheritance of the Henham estate; instead of a long court case they agreed terms and Keith 6th Earl took over the 4,219 acre Henham estate and paid the death duties. By all accounts[523] the 6th Earl is a colourful and eccentric character who has some 15 children from his two wives, has successfully amassed over 25 years a 14,580 acre cattle and sheep station in Victoria which he has recently sold for some Aus $34 million, and retains his Henham Estate in Suffolk which is managed by one of his sons, Hektor Rous.

523 Telegraph (4 Oct 2002: Aussie Earl spreads panic in suburbia)and (26 July 2003: G'bye Pommies); BBC (31 Jan 2004: Auction at Aussie Earl's historic home); the Age (24 July 2003: Aussie Earl puts estate up for sale); Ipswich Star (18 Nov 2004: Aussie Earl may keep Suffolk estate); Eastern Daily Press (18 Sept 2007: Earl pays rare visit to estate); PistonHeads.com (29 July 2011: meet the Bentley Pick-up Truck); Lowestoft Journal (23 March 2011: Deal secures Latitude Festival for 15 years); the Standard (26 Feb 2015: Grand Dundonnell homestead farm on the market); Australian Financial Review (9 Oct 2016: Chinese to buy the Earl of Stradbroke's Australian farmland)

Keith Rous 5th Earl of Stradbroke (1907-83)(125) was educated briefly at Harrow before going to Geelong Grammar School in Australia when his father became Governor of Victoria in 1921. He returned with the family to England in 1926 and undertook an engineering course at the Royal Navy Engineering College Keyham (1926-31). He then served[524] on HMS Queen Elizabeth (1931-3) and other ships. In 1940 he attended the RNVR officers' training establishment at Hove before serving as First Lieutenant on HMS Amethyst (anti-submarine warfare trawler) in 1940 before taking command of that ship which on 24 November 1940 was mined and sunk in the Thames estuary; seven men were wounded but all hands were rescued by HMS Le Tiger. In March 1941 he was commanding HMS Lady Lillan (anti-submarine warfare trawler) when she was sunk by German aircraft about 75 miles west of Erris Head in Ireland. Keith went on to command HMS Lobella (corvette) in 1941 and HMS Coltsfoot (corvette) in 1941-3; he later served on HMS Corinthian (1943-4), HMS Bellona (cruiser) in 1944 and in early 1945 was posted to the RN training establishment in Torpoint, Cornwall. He was fortunate to survive with being wounded twice.

On 7 August 1935 Keith was married at St Peters' Church, Babraham in Cambridge to Pamela Kay-Shuttleworth (1915-72) and they had two sons: (a) Keith (later to be 6th Earl)(b1937) described above, and (b) Sir William Rous KCB (1939-99). They divorced in 1941 and on 19 July 1943 he was married at Clovelly Church to Mary Asquith (1919-2002)(126), the daughter of Brig-Gen Arthur Asquith and Betty Manners, who had inherited the Clovelly Estate in 1936 from Christine Hamlyn. The second marriage produced four daughters and one son, Hon John Rous (127).

In 1962 Betty Asquith died and her daughter, Mary, inherited the Clovelly Estate. Keith (5th Earl) and Mary moved to live at Clovelly Court and managed the estate while having to deal with the death duties payable on Betty's death and this involved having to sell some of the land. As we have seen, Keith inherited the title on the death of his older brother, John (4th Earl), in 1983 but only held the title for four days before he died himself. He was buried at Clovelly Church. Mary continued managing the estate initially with the help of an agent but in 1983 she asked her son, John Rous, to begin to take over the

John and Zeenat Rous 2014

[524] RNVR Officers 1939-1945 online

management of the estate and running of the Clovelly Estate Company. She died in 2002 and is also buried at Clovelly.

Hon John Rous (b1950), a tall most courteous man, was educated at Gordonstoun. After university he qualified as a chartered accountant. In 1984 he married Zeenat Hameed from the medical family of Lucknow in India; her brother is Lord Khalid Hameed CBE (b1941). John and Zeenat have two daughters. John took over the management of the Clovelly Estate full time from 1987 and moved to live at Clovelly Court with his family. He was faced[525] with a backlog of repairs, cashflow problems and a need to revitalise the tourism core business to make the future of the village viable and secure. He set about this task with professionalism and sensitivity. In 1987-8 he invested £1 million in a most impressive and large two floor new visitor centre above the village with bookshops, restaurant, and heritage centre, and commercial shops outside, which has been a great success. Clovelly village is now one of the very few privately owned villages in Britain which charges non-residents for entry; the profits help subsidise the ongoing repair of the 80 village homes many of which are 300 years old; John keeps their rents below the Devon average partly because the residents have to haul their shopping etc on sledges down the cobbled hill (the donkeys which used to be used now just give rides to children and a new John Deere tractor does the heavy lifting of beer barrels etc). John, or "JR" as he is affectionately called by all the 200 residents, is determined that the village should remain a living village, that all tenants should be full time residents (not wealthy weekenders) and happy to welcome tourist vistors, and that the timeless charm of the village and its harbour should survive. During my three day visit to the village I was left in no doubt that the residents admire and respect him as a benevolent landlord and that his strategy has worked very well indeed; like Christine Hamlyn he has adopted the belief that the heritage bequeathed to him is a sacred trust.

The estate of some 2,000 acres now comprises (a) the family trust which owns the tenanted agricultural arable land and farms in Higher Clovelly together with Clovelly Court itself and its Court Farm, and (b) Clovelly Estate Company (founded in 1929) which employs some 90 people and manages the trading side of the business including the village itself of some 80 cottages, two chapels and two pubs (the Red Lion and the New Inn) many of which are now listed plus the woodlands. The pheasant shooting on the estate is leased and some 50 days of challenging shooting takes place between mid October and the end of January with parties of 8 or 9 staying at the Red Lion next to the lovely harbour. John served as Sheriff of Devon in 2014. He shows no signs of retiring thank goodness say the residents.

Visit of Princess Anne to Clovelly 2014

525 Telegraph (16 Jan 2002: All yours, Squire)

English Royal Pedigree of Edwinsford, Clovelly and Hawthornden Families

King William I The Conqueror (1028-87)

King Edward III (1312-77)

John of Gaunt Duke of Lancaster (1340-99)
John Beaufort Earl of Somerset (1373-1410)
John Beaufort Duke of Somerset (1403-44)
Edmund Tudor (1431-56) m= Margaret Beaufort (1443-1509)

Edmund Duke of York (1341-1402)
Richard Earl of Cambridge (1375-1415)
Richard Duke of York (1411-30)
King Edward IV (1442-83)

King Henry VII (1457-1509) m=Elizabeth of York (1466-1503)
Mary Tudor, Queen of France (1496-1533) m= Charles Brandon Duke of Suffolk (1484-1545)
Lady Frances Grey, Duchess of Suffolk (1517-59) m=Henry Grey Duke of Suffolk (1517-54)
Lady Catherine Grey (1540-68) m=Edward Seymour Earl of Hertford (1539-1621)
(sister of Lady Jane Grey)
Edward Seymour, Lord Beauchamp (1561-1612)
Francis Seymour 1st Baron Seymour of Trowbridge (1590-1664)
Charles Seymour 2nd Baron Seymour (1621-65)
Charles Seymour 6th Duke of Somerset (1662-1748) of Petworth House
Lady Catherine Seymour (1693-1731) m=Sir William Wyndham Bt (1688-1740)
Elizabeth Wyndham (c1731-69) m= George Grenville PC (1712-70)(Prime Minister)
Hester Grenville (c1767-1847) m= Hugh Fortescue 1st Earl Fortescue (1753-1841)
(61A) Lady Mary Fortescue (1792-1874) m= (61) Sir James Hamlyn Williams Bt MP (1790-1861)
of Edwinsford and Clovelly (3rd Bt Clovelly)

(70) Susan Hester Hamlyn Williams (1824-69)
(inherited Clovelly Estate in 1861)
m=Lt Col Henry Edward Hamlyn Fane MP
of Avon Tyrrell, Hants (1817-68)

(122) Constance Hamlyn Williams (1861-1920)
m= John 3rd Baron Manners (1852-1927)

(123) Betty Manners (1889-1962) of Clovelly
m= Brig Gen Arthur Asquith DSO (1883-1939)

(126) Mary Asquith (1919-2002) of Clovelly
m=Keith Rous, 5th Earl of Stradbroke (1907-83)

(127) Hon John Rous (b1950) of Clovelly
m= Zeenat Hameed

(71) Mary Eleanor Hamlyn Williams (1825-72)
(inherited Edwinsford Estate in 1861)
m= (73) Sir James (Walker) Williams-Drummond Bt (1814-66)
of Edwinsford (73) (3rd Bt Hawthornden)

(68) Sir James (Joe) Hamlyn Williams-Drummond Bt (1857-1913)
(4th Bt Hawthornden) of Edwinsford and Hawthornden

(69) Sir James (Jimmy) Hamlyn Williams-Drummond Bt (1891-1970)
(5th Bt Hawthornden) of Edwinsford and Hawthornden

Scottish Royal Pedigree of Edwinsford, Clovelly and Hawthornden Families

King Malcolm I of Scotland (895-954)

King Robert I (The Bruce) of Scotland (1274-1329)

Princess Marjorie Bruce (1296-1316) m=Walter 6th High Stewart of Scotland (1296-1327)

King Robert II (1316-90)

King Robert III (1337-1406) m= Annabella Drummond (1350-1401) dau of Sir John Drummond of Stobhall (lived at Hawthornden)

King James I of Scotland (1394-1437) m= Lady Joan Beaufort (1404-45) grand-dau of John of Gaunt

King James II of Scotland (1430-60)

King James III (1451-88)

King James IV (1473-1513) m= Princess Margaret (1489-1541) dau of Henry VII

King James V (1512-42)

James Stewart 1st Earl of Moray (1531-70) Regent of Scotland

Elizabeth Stuart (1565-91) m=James Stewart 2nd Earl of Moray(1565-91)

James Stuart 3rd Earl of Moray (1581-1638)

James Stuart 4th Earl of Moray (1611-53)

Lady Henrietta Stuart (1640-1704)m=Sir Hugh Campbell 15th Thane of Cawdor (1635-1716)

Sir Alexander Campbell of Cawdor (d1697)

John Campbell of Cawdor MP (1695-1777) of Cawdor, Nairn and Stackpole Court, Pembs

Anne Campbell (d1812) m=Mathew 2nd Lord Fortescue (1719-85)

Hugh 1st Earl Fortescue (1753-1841)

(61A) Lady Mary Fortescue (1792-1874) m= Sir James Hamlyn Williams Bt MP (1790-1861) of Edwinsford and Clovelly (3rd Bt Clovelly)(61)

Princess Mary Stewart (1453-88) m= James 1st Lord Hamilton (1415-79)

James Hamilton1st Earl of Arran (1475-1529)

James Hamilton 2nd Earl of Arran (1516-75) Regent for Mary Queen of Scots

Lady Barbara Hamilton m= James 4th Lord Fleming(1534-58)

Jean Fleming (1553-1609) m=John 1st Lord Maitland (1537-95) Lord Chancellor of Scotland

John Maitland 1st Earl of Lauderdale (d1645)

John Maitland 1st Duke of Lauderdale (1616-82)

Lady Mary Maitland (d1702) m=John Hay 2nd Marquess of Tweeddale (1645-1713) Lord Chancellor Scotland

Brig Gen Lord William Hay of Newhall (d1723)

Richard Hay-Newton (d1776) m=Anne Stuart

Jane (Jean) Hay-Newton m=James Walker of Dalry, Midlothian (1743-1817)

Sir Francis (Walker) Walker Drummond (1781-1844) (2nd Bt Hawthornden)(216) m=Margaret Anne Forbes-Drummond (d1876) of Hawthornden

(70) Susan Hester Hamlyn Williams (1824-69) (inherited Clovelly Estate in 1861) m=Lt Col Henry Edward Hamlyn Fane MP of Avon Tyrrell, Hants (1817-68)

(122) Constance Hamlyn Williams (1861-1920) m= John 3rd Baron Manners (1852-1927)

(123) Betty Manners (1889-1962) of Clovelly m= Brig Gen Arthur Asquith DSO (1883-1939)

(126) Mary Asquith (1919-2002) of Clovelly m=Keith Rous, 5th Earl of Stradbroke (1907-83)

(127) Hon John Rous (b1950) of Clovelly m= Zeenat Hameed

(71) Mary Eleanor Hamlyn Williams (1825-72) (inherited Edwinsford Estate in 1861) m= (73) Sir James (Walker) Williams-Drummond Bt (1814-66) of Edwinsford (73) (3rd Bt Hawthornden)

(68) Sir James (Joe) Hamlyn Williams-Drummond Bt (1857-1913) (4th Bt Hawthornden) of Edwinsford and Hawthornden

(69) Sir James (Jimmy) Hamlyn Williams-Drummond Bt (1891-1970) (5th Bt Hawthornden) of Edwinsford and Hawthornden

19. Clovelly, Clovelly Court and Residents

19.1 Clovelly and Clovelly Court / Manor

The early history of the manor of Clovelly has been described in Chapter 17.1. It is unclear when the first manor house was built on the site of what is now Clovelly Court looking out over Bideford Bay. It is also unknown when the first Parish Church was built very closeby, although it is thought that it was probably built in Norman times and the font dates from about 1000 to 1050. It can probably be safely assumed that the first manor house, built of stone, wood and thatch, was erected sometime during the 14th century and that the Cary family as lords of the manor lived there. As we have seen in Chapter 17.2, Dr George Cary (110) enlarged and partially rebuilt Clovelly Court in 1680-1 before his death. Then in about 1740 Zachary Hamlyn (116) rebuilt the house having bought it in 1738. On 27 January 1789 Clovelly Court was largely destroyed (with the exception of one wing) by fire along with most of the estate records, church records and family muniments and deeds; Sir James Hamlyn 1st Bt (57) rebuilt it by 1793 in the then fashionable Georgian Gothic style. It was a plain white square house[526], plastered and limewashed in the local manner and incorporated parts of the house which had been damaged in the fire. He added a seven-bay wide wing. The Georgian building was redecorated internally in the style associated with James Wyatt; there were a series of beautifully elegant rooms including a wonderful Oval Hall and above it the Oval Hall Gallery with wrought iron balustrading. Above it was a dome lit by a cupola. There was a lovely dining room with dark wallpaper and lined with family portraits plus an impressive library lined with green silk and having a moulded plaster ceiling (the new wing sadly to be later destroyed in the fire in 1943). But Rev John Sweete[527] when visiting Clovelly in 1797 said: *"The old mansion of the Carys had been demolished a few years ago by an accidental fire and the present fabric had been raised by the plans of the possessor… …The front which first appeared was that of an entrance; this was altogether Gothic…Moving round to the other two fronts, I was astonished to find that the Gothic style had totally disappeared—it had given place to the fashion of modern buildings. The curve of the window had become rectangular and the circle had been squared…I was dissatisfied with this abrupt transition."*

Clovelly was described[528] in 1850: *"Clovelly, or Clovelleigh, is a pleasant village and fishing station, occupying a singular and picturesque situation, on the side of a steep rock, adjoining Bideford Bay, about 4 miles E of Hartland and 11 miles WSW of Bideford. It is one of the most romantic places in Devon, and the houses being built on the precipitous side of the sea cliff, one above the other; the main street ascends in terraces and flights of steps from the beach and pier. Clovelly is celebrated for its herring fishery, besides which large quantities of conger, whiting, hake, pollock, and cod fish are caught in the winter; and turbot, sole, plaice, gurnet and mackerel in summer. Its parish had 950 inhabitants in July 1841, besides 40 seamen who were then absent; and contains about 4,200 acres of land, mostly the property of Sir James Hamlyn Williams Bart, who is lord of the manor, and has a large and handsome seat, called Clovelly Court, erected about 1780, on the site of the ancient mansion which was destroyed by fire[529]. The views from the house and grounds are extremely grand; and above the cliffs, to the south-east of the village, are the remains of an entrenchment, called Clovelly Dykes, of a square form, and unknown origin."*

---

526 Country Life-Country Homes and Gardens Old and New-The Seat of Mrs Hamlyn (31 March 1934)

527 Todd Gray: *Travels in Georgian Devon-Illustrated Journals of the Rev John Sweete 1789-1800 (1999) Vol 3 p99*

528 White's Devonshire Directory 1850

529 In 1789 when most of the estate records were destroyed. The house was rebuilt in 1789-93 not in 1780

Clovelly Court c1831 by GB Campion

© Hon John Rous

© Hon John Rous *Terrace pre-1943 fire*

© Hon John Rous *Pre-1943 fire*

© Hon John Rous *Old library pre-1943 fire*

© Hon John Rous *Oval Hall pre-1943 fire*

Clovelly Court 2016

© Hon John Rous
Oval Hall Gallery pre-1943 fire

© Hon John Rous

Drawing room pre-1943 fire

2016

2016

2016

2016

Gardens 2016

In November 1860 Charles Dickens[530] visited Clovelly and this resulted in his description in *A Message from the Sea: "The village was built sheer up the face of a steep and lofty cliff. There was no road in it, there were no wheeled vehicle in it, there was not a level yard in it. From the sea-beach to the cliff-top two irregular rows of white houses, placed opposite to one another, and twisting here and there, and there and here, rose, like the sides of a long succession of stages of crooked ladders....Strings of pack-horses and pack-donkeys toiled slowly up the staves of the ladders, bearing fish, and coal, and such other cargo as was unshipping at the pier from the dancing fleet of village boats, and from two or three little coasting traders...No two houses in the village were alike, in chimney, size, shape, door, window, gable, rooftree, anything. The sides of the ladders were musical with water, running clear and bright...The pier was musical with the wash of the sea, the creaking of capstans and windlasses, and the airy fluttering of little vanes and sails... The rough sea-bleached boulders of which the pier was made, and the whiter boulders of the shore, were brown with drying nets. The red-brown cliffs, richly wooded to their extremist verge, had their softened and beautiful forms reflected in the bluest water..."*

Charles Kingsley[531] the novelist lived in Clovelly as a child from 1831 to 1836 while his father was the curate and then the rector of Clovelly. He described the village : *"Take the steepest hillside with which you are acquainted; let the Atlantic roll at its base; cover it with ancient trees and tangled undergrowth to its summit; suppose a brawling stream to fall in a deep and narrow channel from the heights to the shore; in your mind's eye people its banks with a straggling village of irregularly shaped lichen covered cottages, and on so sharp an incline that the base of the one is on a level with the roof of its neighbour; pave the street with miniature boulders from the shore, arranged in a series of terraces; and terminate the descent by an antique pier of wave worn stones, from which the only approach to the sea at low water is by ladders, whose perpendicular depths may well startle the inexperienced traveller; and then you obtain something which would resemble Clovelly, if it were not, indeed, unique in its singular construction and beauty and did not surpass all descriptive powers, whether of pen or pencil."*

530 The Devon Carys p178-9

531 The Devon Carys p 180. His daughter who wrote under the pen name "Lucas Malet" also lived in Clovelly for some years as the wife of another rector of the parish, William Harrison. In Clovelly Church there is a brass plate in memory of Charles Kingsley, "Rector of Eversley, Canon of Westminster, poet, preacher and novelist"

Behind Clovelly Court and next to the Parish Church is a lovely walled Victorian kitchen garden with fruit trees and glasshouses, which joins the lawns in front of Clovelly Court Great Terrace with its sweeping views of Bideford Bay.

Clovelly Court was a convalescent home for wounded soldiers in both World Wars. In 1943 there was another fire at Clovelly Court and much of one side was destroyed including the wonderful Oval Hall and above it the Oval Hall Gallery plus a lovely Library on the ground floor. The wing was rebuilt and fortunately most of the family heirlooms were saved; another original wing survived both fires.

Lodge 2016

19.2 Residents

The following table is an estimate from available records of the owners and residents (some of whom were tenants) of Clovelly Manor / Court.

YEAR	OWNER	RESIDENTS
14th Cent	Judge Sir John Cary MP and/or Sir William Cary (101)	
15th C	Sir Robert Cary MP (102)	Robert and Margaret Cary
-1437	Sir Philip Cary MP (103)	Philip and Christiana Cary
-1471	Sir William Cary (104)	Sir William and Elizabeth Cary
-1540	Robert Cary (105)	Robert Cary and family
1540-87	Sir Robert Cary MP (106)	Robert and Margaret Cary
1587-1601	George Cary (107)	George Cary and family
1601-52	William Cary MP (108)	William Cary and family
1652-75	Sir Robert Cary (109)	Sir Robert Cary
1675-80	Dr George Cary (110)	John, George and Anthony Cary, cousins (up to 1702)
1680-85	Sir George Cary MP (111)	
1685-1710	William Cary MP (112)	William and Mary Cary (from 1702)
1710-38	William Cary (to 1724), Ann (to1728) and Elizabeth Cary	Robert, William, Ann and siblings
1738-59	Zachary Hamlyn (116)	Zachary Hamlyn
1740	Clovelly Manor House rebuilt	
1759-1811	Sir James Hamlyn Bt MP (57)	Sir James and Lady Arabella of Clovelly and Edwinsford
1789	Clovelly Court burnt down and rebuilt	
1811-29	Sir James Hamlyn Williams Bt MP (60)	Sir James and Lady Diana Hamlyn Williams
1829-61	Sir James Hamlyn Williams Bt MP (61)	Sir James and Lady Mary Hamlyn Williams
1861-69	Susan (70) and Henry Hamlyn Fane	Susan and Henry Hamlyn Fane of Clovelly and Avon Tyrrell
1869-84	Nevile Hamlyn Fane (121)	Nevile Hamlyn Fane and siblings
1884-1936	Christine Hamlyn (120)	Christine and Frederick Hamlyn
1936-62	Betty Asquith (123). Clovelly Court burnt down and rebuilt 1943	Betty and Arthur Asquith
1962-2002	Mary Rous (126)	Mary and Keith Rous [John Rous managing estate since 1983]
2002-	John Rous (127)	John and Zeenat Rous

19.3 Census Returns

YEAR	CLOVELLY COURT CLOVELLY CENSUS RETURNS
1841	[Family not at home] John Kiard (60) carpenter, Mary Symonds (41), Sarah Symonds (3), Margaret Evans (22), Susan Ashton (12)
1851	**WILLIAMS: James** (60) Baronet and Gentleman born Marylebone, Lady Mary (58) wife born Devon, Mary Eleanor (25) dau, Edward (17) son born Clovelly, Henry Fane (33) son in law retired army officer, Susan (27) dau, Marion (11 mon) granddau, Ida (36) governess, Elizabeth Morgan (42) housekeeper, Mary Peters (22) cook, Charlotte Finch (26) lady's maid, Maria Peters (24) under laundry maid, Anne Dannet (38) under housemaid, Eliz Head (19) kitchen maid, Jane Piltie (19) mill room maid, James Cologate (51) coachman, James Gibbet (43) under butler, Thomas Piters (50) groom, William Cologate (19) ser, John Cologate (26) postillion, Thomas Moor (21) groom, Mary Guss (55) nurse, Mary Clows (23) lady's maid, Charles Keep (29) house ser to Mr Fane
1861	**WILLIAMS: Sir James H** (70) Baronet DL JP, Lady Mary (68) wife, Lady Drummond (35) dau, Sir James Drummond (48) Baronet, DL JP, Annabella Drummond (6) granddau, James Drummond (4) grandson, Edwin Drummond (2) grandson, Hugh Henry Drummond (1) grandson, Lady Ann Wilbraham (73) sis in law, Elizabeth Morgan (55) housekeeper, Maria Richards (29) cook, Mary Peters (34) laundry maid, Elizabeth Griffiths (31) housemaid, Emma White (26) kitchen maid, Jane Peters (29) ser, Lydia Mills (21) ser, Charlotte Vine (22) ser, Bridy Navy (29) ser, Anne Jones (24) lady's maid, Margaret Edwards (17) ser, Jane Filps (30) ser, John Micklewright (54) butler, James Colegate (62) coachman, John Colegate (35) second coachman, James Gibbitts (52) under butler, William Savage (27) footman, Thomas Parsons (17) footman, Charles Humphreys (18) footman
1871	**FANE: Marion Hamlyn** (20) born Clovelly, Harriet Fane (52) aunt, Eveline Hamlyn Fane (16) sis, Christine (15) sis, Constance (9) sis, Edward (6) bro, Emma Bacon (50) governess, Mary Harris (38) housekeeper, Mary Jennis (33) lady's maids, Lydia Mile (48) nurse, Hannah (26) lady's maid, Harriet (25) housemaid, Agnes Glover (24) housemaid, Mary Staton (17) schoolroom maid, Mary Headon (17) schoolroom maid, Jane Parsons (14) kitchen maid, William Harrison (18) footman
1881	[Family not home] William Green (56) butler, Elizabeth Webber (37) housemaid, Sybyl Steer (28) laundress, Sophia Masters (23) parlour maid, Leny Hamly (20) kitchen maid, Clara Bond (19) maid, Edward Bourne (16) hall boy, Alfred Masters (13) visitor
1891	[Family not at home in care of servants] Alice Pendry (29) upper housemaid, Louisa May (20) under housemaid, Alice Frost (33) upper laundry maid, Selina Jeffrey (23) under laundry maid, William Oke (54) garden lab
1901	[Family not at home] Alice Pendry (38) housekeeper, Sarah Frayne (20) housemaid, Lily Harris (18) housemaid, William Oke (63) gardener
1911	[Mrs Hamlyn head of house with 45 rooms but away] Susanna Blacker (31) housemaid, Emma Hobbs (22) housemaid

20. Clovelly Estate and Tenants

20.1 Tithe Apportionment Agreement 1839

Tithes, which had been payable in many countries since Biblical times, were originally paid in kind as one tenth of the produce of the land (crops, eggs, cattle, sheep, timber, fishing etc) to the local rector for payment for his services. The tithes were often stored in a tithe barn attached to the parish. After the dissolution of the monasteries in 1536 some of the land in question, having passed out of church ownership, had tithes paid to private landlords called Lay Impropriators. Over time some tithes were paid in cash instead of in kind whether or not the payer went to church, and by the 1830s this caused much local resentment generally in the country (there was a tithe war of civil disobedience in some parts of the UK) but particularly in areas of non-conformism. The Tithe Commutation Act 1836 set up a Tithe Commission charged with creating a Tithe Map of each tithe district (usually the parish), fixing a global assessment for that district then apportioning the tithe rent charge on the individual properties in that district, which was then recorded in a written agreement (some land was free of tithe due to custom or prior agreement).

In the parish of Clovelly there was one Tithe Apportionment Agreement[532] dated 25 March 1839 (prepared by JH Brimacombe the valuer and land surveyor) and made between the relevant landowners and Rev Zachary Hammett Drake, the Rector of Clovelly Parish and sole owner of all the parish tithes; the agreement provided for a new annual district payment of a total of £213.10 shillings by way of rentcharge by the landowners (principally Sir James Williams Bt) in substitution for the payment of all previous tithes.

The valuer and land surveyor surveyed all the properties in the parish and the tithe payment apportionments were calculated based on the areas of arable, meadow, woodland, moorland and glebe land set out in the Tithe Map of 1837. The total area of land the subject of tithes was estimated to be some 2,578 acres (1,322 arable, 118 meadow, 260 woodland, 800 moorland and 78 glebe). The individual quantities of land in each property were expressed in ARP measurements: acres, roods (4 roods to one acre) and perches (40 perches to one rood).

The Clovelly Estate of Sir James Hamlyn Williams (61) in the parish of Clovelly totalled approximately 3,000 acres and as stated in the Tithe Apportionment Agreement included the following (with original spellings):

OCCUPIER	PROPERTY	AREA		
		A	R	P
Sir James Williams Bt (61)	Clovelly Court, deer park, wood, wall gardens, farmyard, stables, kennels, orchard, cow close, mill pond	655	2	21
James Bartlett	Hugglefit	126	0	2
John Eddy	West Dyke	173	2	36
Henry Jewill	East Dyke	216	2	14
Joseph Budd	Clarke's House		2	1
Sir James Williams (61)	Thornery	133	0	34

532 North Devon Record Office Barnstaple

OCCUPIER	PROPERTY	AREA		
		A	R	P
Thomas Ching	Burford	140	1	2
William Cleverdon	Burford	132	3	29
Thomas Hamlyn	Stitworthy	114	3	22
John Downing	Stitworthy	105	0	36
Joseph Burrows	Heworthy	140	0	20
Joseph Burrows	Slade	65	3	33
Thomas Hartlett	Kennerland	157	0	4
William Pennington	Downland	197	2	17
Thomas Hockridge Jr	Burnstone	147	3	13
Thomas Hockridge	Burnstone	37	3	22
Thomas Hockridsge	Eastcott and Holywell	206	2	30
William Ashton	Burscott	30	2	5
William Vasser	Burscott	6	2	37
Samuel Jewill	Burscott	5	0	13
Richard Jennings	Burscott	4	1	36
John Squire	Burscott	6	1	26
Richard Prince	Burscott	6	0	3
Richard Prince	Sleera and Winkleberry	26	3	22
Thomas Jewell	Sleera	5	3	36
Thomas Lambbrook	Slade Park	2	3	5
William Jewill	Sleera	4	1	30
Richard Bunson	Sleera	2	3	37
Joseph Jewill	Wrinkleberry	8	1	3
Richard Jenkin	Wrinkleberry	4	1	5
John Squire	Wrinkleberry	10	1	23
Sir James Williams Bt (61)	Cottages and gardens inc Clovelly Village with roads, brooks and waste land	60	3	6

The Rector, Rev Zachary Hammett Drake, had glebe lands including the churchyard, rectory, meadows, farmland, gardens etc totalling some 106 acres.

20.2 Court Farm

As can be seen from the 1839 Tithe Agreement, Sir James Williams Bt (61) owned 60 acres of the village itself plus some 655 acres of the demesne land and Court Farm, which included Clovelly Court, the deer park in front, woodlands, the walled gardens, the farmyard, stables, kennels, orchard, cow close, and a mill pond.

YEAR	COURT FARM CLOVELLY CENSUS RETURNS
1841	**THOMSON: Niel** (50) yeoman, Lucretia (48) wife, Alison (14) dau, Lilly (5) dau
1851	**THOMSON: Niel** (60) farmer of 300 acres born Edinburgh, Lucretia (57) wife, Lily (15) dau, James Short (27) farm lab
1861	**HUNTON: James** (49) farm bailiff born Buckinghamshire, Mary (46) wife with 6 children
1871	**FORD: George** (64) farmer of 200 acres born Devon, Elizabeth (63) wife, Fanny (28) dau maid, Elizabeth (21) dau maid, Alice (19) dau maid, Bessie (5 mon) granddau, 1 ser
1881	**BAKER: John** (46) farm bailiff, Helen (40) wife, Ellen Bredyley (14) niece, Elizabeth Headon (23) ser
1891	**BAKER: John** (58) farmer, Ellen (50) wife, Jane (20) ser
1901	**BAKER: John** (67) farm bailiff born South Moulton Devon, Ellen (61) wife, Annie Watts (25) niece ser
1911	**SQUIRES: William** (42) cowman born Hartland, Harriet (42) with 5 children alive

Court Farm itself, which is near to Clovelly Court, was occupied by the farm bailiff for generations. In addition, there were other dwellings including Court Farm cottage, Gardiner's cottage, New Lodge, Court Stables, Home Lodge, Court Garden, Court Garage, Coachman's cottage, Snooksland (gamekeeper), Court Dairy, and Mouth Mill (cottages, adjoining the disused limekiln by the harbour, now mostly demolished), which housed other servants and employees. Part of the Court Stables and Garage are now used by the Clovelly Estate Company as their administrative offices from which the estate is managed.

20.3 The Village

The size of the estate including the village is described at the end of Chapter 18.

The population of the manor of Clovelly has changed from some 714 in 1801; 990 (1841); 787 (1881); 621 (1901); 528 (1931); 445 (1961); 390 (1976) with 158 in the village itself and 232 in Higher Clovelly; 493 (2001); and 443 (2011).

The available census returns for Clovelly Village from 1841 to 1911 show the changes in occupation of the residents during the past two centuries. Mariners and fishermen were in the majority in the early 19th century, but by 1850[533] the occupations of the residents also included carpenter, charwoman, washerwoman, pier lighthouse keeper, cordwainer, shipwright, lodging house keeper, dressmaker, general servant, tailor, butcher, bootmaker, smithy, coast guard officer, agricultural labourer, maid, beer cellar keeper, innkeeper, grocer, draper, shoemaker, surgeon, fancy dealer, boatbuilder, smack owner and coal merchant, carrier, insurance agent, schoolmaster, postmaster, victualler, and bookseller.

Today there are only six fishing families left of whom three concentrate on tourist trips to Lundy Island closeby. Sadly the traditional fishing business, which led to the harbour and pier being built centuries ago, has greatly declined. There are no more shipwrecks thank goodness but the RNLI lifeboat station (which is facing the sea along Fish Street) and dates from 1870 is still manned by volunteers and has some 10 call-outs each year on average.

Over the decades there have been several beer houses but only two licensed inns: the Red Lion which is next to the harbour at the foot of the High Street, and the New Inn which is about half way up the High Street (which is known as "Up Along" or "Down Along").

533 White's Devonshire Directory 1850

Harbour 2016

 Early 20th century

Early 20th century

High Street 2016

High Street 2016

Kingsley cottage 2016

2016

Queen Victoria fountain 2016

Memorial Cross at Mount Pleasant 2016

Shops and donkey stables 2016

Sledge 2016

Angel's Wings 2016

Red Lion

The Red Lion is a charming 18th century inn with lots of steps and corridors formed originally from merging three cottages (Nos 50-52) and has a wonderful view of the harbour and the sea; sleeping there with the noise of the sea is magical for landlubbers. It is managed most efficiently for the Clovelly Estate Company by Sally Stevens.The locals use the bar most evenings and of course visitors and shooting parties stay there and enjoy the excellent food. On my visit I was served at breakfast by a very friendly Yvonne Wills whose partner, Chris Searles, changes the beer barrels very early in the morning and is a regular in the bar in the evening. Lovely friendly people.

The Vine family shown in the census returns were mariners in 1841-6. In the 1841 census in a house on the Quay there is an innkeeper called Alice Madge (85) with four servants or visitors; this Inn may have been on or near the site of the Red Lion.

YEAR	RED LION HOTEL CLOVELLY CENSUS RETURNS
1871	**VINE: Samuel** (67) widower mariner born Clovelly, Lydia Vine (31) dau in law mariner's wife, Lydia (1) granddau, 1 ser
1881	**JONES: Susan** (32) in charge of hotel born Clovelly [No 52 Village], Susan Vine (15) niece, Lydia Vine (11) niece, Grace (9) niece, Georgina (7) niece
1891	**VINE: Lydia** (51) pub and hotel keeper, Lydia (21) dau hotel reception, Grace (19) dau, Georgina (17) dau, 2 boarders
1901	**VINE: Lydia** (61) widow hotelkeeper born Clovelly, Samuel (25) son, Elizabeth Macdonald (54) assistant, Lily Smale (21) housemaid, Eliza cook (16) ser, Lydia Burnard (31), Jack Burnard (2)
1911	**MOSS: John** (42) hotel proprietor born Clovelly, Lizzie (43) wife with 2 children alive, 1 serv, 3 visitors

Red Lion 2016

New Inn

The New Inn is a 17th century inn. Originally it was located on the other side of the High Street on the left looking down the hill and used to have stables on the right side which are now used as a bar and restaurant. Then in about 1914 three cottages (Nos 92,93,99) on the right side were merged to make what is now the inn and it was redecorated in the arts and crafts style. Today it is managed on behalf of the Clovelly Estate Company and its bar on the High Street is well frequented by residents living in the higher part of the village (those living down the High Street near the harbour frequent the Red Lion).

New Inn 19th century

YEAR	NEW INN CLOVELLY CENSUS RETURNS
1841	**SQUIRE: John** (50) inn keeper, Elizabeth (50) wife, 2 serv, 4 visitors
1851	**WHITEFEELER: Robert** (36) victualler born Clovelly, Harriet (29) wife, Henry (4) son, Mary (1) dau, 2 visitors, 1 ser
1861	**BERRYMAN: James** (33) victualler born Clovelly [7 High Street], Mary (33) wife, 1 ostler, 2 ser
1871	**BERRYMAN: James** (40) innkeeper, Mary (40) wife, 2 ser, 2 visitors
1881	**BERRYMAN: James** (52) inn keeper [11 High Sreet], Mary (52) wife, Elizabeth Colwill (32) niece maid, Sarah Harvey (21) maid, Jane Wakely (26) cook
1891	**BERRYMAN: James** (63) innkeeper [12 High Street], Mary (63) wife, Sarah Harvey (30) niece, Edwina Harvey (16) niece
1901	**BERRYMAN: James** (74) landlord innkeeper born Clovelly, Mary (73) wife, Sarah Harvey (40) niece hotel manageress, Betty Frilford (20) cook, Mary Allin (34) housemaid, Charlotte Dickson (41) visitor, Agnes Dickson (56) visitor
1911	**BERRYMAN: Mary** (86) widow proprietor deaf born Bideford, Sarah Harvey (50) manageress born Bideford, 3 serv, 7 boaders

The High Street has a number of quaint little shops and tearooms as well as the Charles Kingsley Museum and the Fisherman's Cottage. At the bottom of the hill is located the old Limekiln which was used in the 18th and 19th centuries for lime burning; lime was used by the local farmers to neutralise the acidity in the soil, for whitewashing the buildings and for making mortar for restoration. The cheap coal was shipped from South Wales and when set alight in the kiln it produced quicklime (calcium oxide), a process which could take up to four days.

As we have seen, the first harbour was built some 600 years ago by a Cary, and then extended in the 16th century by George Cary at a cost of some £2,000. The three cannons cemented into the pier as bollards are thought to have come from a Spanish Armada ship in 1588. In the 18th and 19th centuriers Clovelly was notorious for smuggling and the harbour was used together with a number of neighbouring caves to avoid detection. Clovelly's fishing trade was the core business of the village for centuries and the harbour gave essential shelter from the westerly winds; indeed the pier provided the only safe harbour along the coastline from Appledore in Devon to Boscastle in Cornwall. The tide rises by up to 32ft on this coast.

At the top of the High Street before the new Visitors' Centre there is the start of Hobby Drive along the coast, which was laid out by Sir James Hamlyn Williams 2nd Bt (60) and his wife Lady Diana between 1811-29 in accordance with the views of the Romantic Movement which embraced the beauty of nature. It is some three miles in length and visitors used to take a horse and carriage to take the air; today one walks; one could walk further along the coast as far as Westwood Ho! which is now sadly ruined by commercialism. In the other direction along the coast one can walk through lovely woodlands towards Mouthmill Cove and on the way pass Mount Pleasant, the old deer park in front of Clovelly Court, the Cabin, Angel's Wings built about 1826, the Cave, Gallantry Bower a 350ft headland, and the Lookout with fabulous sea views.

New Inn 2016

20.4 Clovelly School

The first school in Clovelly manor is thought to have been a Church Sunday School for boys set up in 1800. This was followed later by a boys' school[534] run by the rector in St Peter's Church in Providence Row half way up the High Street; this church is still owned by the estate. Christine Hamlyn established a charity school for girls financed by a £3 per annum pew rent in the Parish Church. Then in 1873 the estate provided the land for a new school which was built in Wrinkleberry near Higher Clovelly, which is quite a walk from the village. The senior school was in Bideford so pupils had to travel there. The primary school in Wrinkleberry run by the local authority closed a few years ago and the school building is now used by a free academy school, which also uses the village hall nearby and the millennium fields for sport.

Clovelly School 2016

[534] Sheila Ellis p14

21. Religion

21.1 The Parish Church of All Saints Clovelly

All Saints Clovelly 2016

Hour glass

Charles Kingsley memorial in Clovelly Church

It is thought that the first church[535] to be built on the site was 12th century Norman probably with a thatched roof; this early church had a west tower, an aisle-less nave, north and south transepts and a chancel in the shape of a crucifix. The font dates from c1000-1050 so there may well have been an earlier timber building. The church was then enlarged and rebuilt (except for the Norman tower which now houses a peal of six bells) in coursed rubble in the 13th century with huge granite pillars which are thought to have come from Lundy Island closeby; a large wagon timber roof was added which survives and a north aisle. In 1387 William Cary planned[536] to establish a college with six chaplains under a warden but this never happened. In 1699 the galleries were erected in the church by the rector William Price. Restoration was carried out in 1805, and in 1843-5 with some replastering and rebuilding of the Norman porch. In the 1860s the two great galleries and the box pews were removed, although the lovely solid oak pews we see today survived. Further restoration was done in 1884. An old 17th century sundial stands over the Norman porch and its gnomon still works when the sun is out.

Today the church is Grade 1 listed and full of stone floor slabs, monuments and memorials to the Cary and Hamlyn families who were lords of the manor and patrons of the church and appointed rectors to the living of Clovelly. Many Carys are buried in the family vault and the Hamlyn vault under the Lady Chapel is also full and closed up. The Lady Chapel contains the war memorials and closeby is the Jacobean pulpit installed in 1634 by William Cary (108) who also donated in 1635 the hour glass standing next to it, which timed the length of the sermon. The restoration and reslating of the south roof and the releading of the tower roof has recently been completed.

The lists of the known incumbents who served the church and the members of the Giffard, Cary, Hamlyn, Asquith and Rous families who were patrons and lords of the manor are:

Priests or Rectors		Patrons	
Robert Giffard	1262		
Walter de Peignton	1280	Richard Giffard	1286
Richard de Dolburghe	1308	Edith, Lady of Clovelly	1308
David Anseline	1338	John de Staunton	1338
Oliver de Staunton	1339	Sir John de Staunton and Robert de Mandeville	1339
William Payn	1362	John, heir of John de Staunton	1362
Walter Crabbe (d1396)			
Richard Loman	1397	William Cary	1397
William Penwonan (d1411)	1407		
Richard Planya	1411	Thomasine, heir of William Cary	1411
Edmund Kene (d1462)			
John Husband	1462	Sir William Cary	1462

535 The definitive histories are Sheila Ellis's wonderful book *"Down a Cobbled Street" (1987) p46-51,* and Grigs (2010). See also N Pevsner and B Cherry: *The Buildings of England-Devon (1989) p269*

536 Vatican Library 1393 document confirming the consent of Pope Boniface IX to the foundation by William Cary of a collegiate church for seven priests and 24 nuns of the Order of St Clare of Clovelly

Priests or Rectors		Patrons	
William Danyall-resigned 1503			
John Chymowe-resigned 1505	1503	Robert Cary / John Gilbert	1503
Henry Plymton (d1531)	1505		
Thomas Herle-deprived1554	1531	Robert Cary	1531
Thomas Brown	1554		
Thomas Herle MA	1559		
William Tooker-resigned 1601	1589	Queen Elizabeth I	1589
Richard Thome (d1632)	1601	Margaret Cary (widow)	1601
Walter Yeo MA-resigned 1639	1632	William Cary	1632
George Cary-resigned 1668	1639		
Oliver Naylor MA-resigned1687	1668	Dr George Cary	1668
William Prince MA (d1715)	1687	William Cary	1687
Ormond Jones-resigned 1730	1715	Robert Cary	1715
John Robbins BA (d1777)	1730	Robert Barber marr Eliz Cary	1730
Charles Hammett BA (d1782)	1777	James Hamlyn	1777
Richard Hammett MA (d1796)	1782	James Hamlyn	1782
Lewes Lewis (d1826)	1796	Sir James Hamlyn 1st Bt	1796
Orlando Hamlyn Williams BA; Charles Kingsley (curate)	1826	Sir James Hamlyn Williams 2nd Bt	1826
Charles Kingsley (d1836)	1832	Sir James Hamlyn Williams 3rd Bt	1832
Zachary Hammett Drake d1856	1836	Sir James Hamlyn Williams 3rd Bt	1836
James Chichester BA	1856	Sir James Hamlyn Williams 3rd Bt	1856
William Harrison (d1897)	1883	Nevile Hamlyn Fane	1883
Francis Philips MA (d 1899)	1897	Mrs Christine Hamlyn	1897
Thomas Simkin-resigned 1932	1899	Mrs Christine Hamlyn	1899
Philip Somers Cocks-resigned 1938	1932	Mrs Christine Hamlyn	1932
Richard Cavendish MA	1938	Hon Mrs Arthur Asquith	1938
Arthur Chandler MA	1945	Hon Mrs Arthur Asquith	1945
Peter Geake MA- resigned 1955	1952	Hon Mrs Arthur Asquith	1952
George Spinks	1955	Hon Mrs Arthur Asquith	1955

Priests or Rectors		Patrons	
Rudolph Eppingstone	1959	Hon Mrs Arthur Asquith	1959
Derek Bates	1980	Hon Mrs Keith Rous	1980
Roderick Sanders	1993	Hon Mrs Keith Rous	1993
Martin Hunnybun	1998	Hon John Rous	1998
Andrew Richardson	2001	Hon John Rous	2001

St Peter's Chapel Clovelly

The Chapel of St Peter is some 250 years old and built of stone and cob down a side lane near the New Inn halfway down the High Street. It is linked to All Saints Parish Church and is owned by the Clovelly Estate Company although its upkeep and management are the responsibility of the Anglican rector. It was first licensed by the Bishop of Exeter in 1846 for use by those residents of the village "not able to climb the hill" and walk to All Saints Church. For many years it housed the local youth club and during WW2 was used as a school for evacuees from Deptford, Peckham, Bristol and Plymouth. In 1948 it reverted to use as a chapel under Rev Arthur Chandler. Today it is simply furnished and has some lovely murals painted by a local artist, Fiona Creighton-Balfour. The Della-Robia plaque was donated by Betty Asquith, a former patron.

Chapel of St Peter 2016

Methodist Chapel

There is also a small Methodist chapel dating from about 1820 inspired by John Wesley, which is owned by the Clovelly Estate Company. It is behind the New Inn and near to St Peter's Chapel off the High Street and is adorned with flowers.

Methodist Chapel 2016

21.2 The Rectory (Parsonage)

The Rectory (or Parsonage as it was called in the census returns) housed generations of rectors and curates and their families whose livings were controlled by the lords of the manor who lived in Clovelly Court. Occupants of the Rectory included some of the rectors listed above. Rev Orlando Hamlyn Williams (65) was the brother of Sir James Hamlyn Williams 3rd Bt (61), and his successor Rev Charles Kingsley was the father of Kingsley the poet and grandfather of the wife of Rev William Harrison.

In 1680 the Rectory was probably located where the Rectory Lodge is now sited across the road from the Clovelly Court walled gardens and was probably made of stone, timber and thatch. It had[537] a hall and parlour, porch, pantry, kitchen, coal house, malting house, dairy, brew house, three piggeries, stone barn, stables plus some five chambers. Its glebeland included an orchard (0.5 acres), Berry Meadow (4 acres), Yellery (1 acre), Southern Yellery (9 acres), Northern Yellery (9 acres), meadow (0.5 acres), Barne Park (6 acres), Easter Cole (4 acres), Wester Cole (4 acres), a wood (6 acres), and Buddlemore (32 acres).

The present Rectory was built in about 1790 from rubble and stones taken from the fire in 1789 at Clovelly Court across the road. The Rectory Lodge housed the coachman and servants. By 1839 at the time of the Tithe Apportionment Agreement the rector, Rev Zachary Hammett Drake, had glebe lands including the churchyard, rectory, meadows, farmland, gardens etc totalling some 106 acres.

The Rectory was sold several years ago. The well-known actor Joss Acland[538] and his wife bought it some 25 years ago.

YEAR	THE RECTORY (PARSONAGE) CLOVELLY CENSUS RETURNS
1841	**DRAKE: Zachary** (36) Clerk, Eleanor (30) wife, 5 serv
1851	**DOLTON: Henry** (46) Curate of Clovelly born Ireland, Sophia (52) wife with 4 children, 4 serv
1861	**CHICHESTER: James** (33) rector of Clovelly, 3 serv
1871	[Family not at home] Susan Godfrey (40) dom ser, Jane Beer (19) kitchenmaid
1881	**CHICHESTER: James** (55) rector of Clovelly parish born Sherwell Devon, Jane (55) wife, Catherina (26) visitor, 3 ser
1891	[Family not at home] Thomas Boggis (74) clerk in holy orders, Frances (70) wife, Robert (27) son clerk in holy orders, Theodore Page (29) visitor lay reader, 3 serv
1901	**SIMKIN: Thomas** (41) Clergyman CoE born Rutland, Mary Smith (58) housekeeper, George Smith (31) footman, Thomas Noah (20) gardener
1911	**SIMKIN: Rev Thomas** (51) Clergman CoE, Mary Smith (68) widow housekeeper, Arthur Dixey (17) footman, Gertrude Smith (16) housemaid

Rectory 19th century

537 1680 Terrier survey; Sheila Ellis p51

538 Joss and Rosemary Ackland: *My Better Half and Me (2010)*

Rectory Coach House 2016

Public Offices

22. Public Offices

The families contributed enormously to their local communities in many different ways. This Section refers to some of the activities in which they were involved.

22.1 Members of Parliament[539]

Judge Sir John Cary (101) of Clovelly	1363-4, 1368-9	Devon
Sir William Cary	1363-4, 1368-9	Devon
Sir Robert Cary (102) of Clovelly	1407-26	Devon
Sir Philip Cary (103) of Clovelly	1433	Devon
Sir Robert Cary (106) of Clovelly	1553	Barnstaple
William Cary (108) of Clovelly	1604-11	Mitchell, Cornwall
Sir George Cary (111) of Clovelly	1681	Oakhampton
William Cary (112) of Clovelly	1685-7,1689-95,1695-1710	Oakhampton and Launceston
Sir Nicholas Williams Bt (51) of Edwinsford	1722-45	Carms
Robert Banks Hodgkinson (56) of Overton and Edwinsford	1748-54	Wareham
Sir James Hamlyn Bt (57) of Clovelly and Edwinsford	1793-1802	Carms
Sir James Hamlyn Williams (60) of Clovelly and Edwinsford	1802-6	Carms
Ambrose St John (59) of Berks and Isle of Man	1803-6	Callington
Sir James Hamlyn Williams (61) of Edwinsford and Clovelly	1831-2; 1835-7	Carms
Charles Noel, Lord Barham, 1st Earl of Gainsborough (63)	1808-14	Rutland
Gerard Noel PC	1847-83	Rutland
Sir John Davie Ferguson Davie Bt (72) of Derllys	1859-64	Barnstaple
Lt Col Henry Edward Hamlyn Fane (70) of Avon Tyrrell and Clovelly	1865	Hampshire South

539 HP; Sir John Lloyd Vol 2 p464-466

Sir Thomas Powell (1665-1720) of Broadway near Laugharne and Coldbrook Park in Monmouthshire, was created a Baronet in 1698, and served as MP for Monmouth Boroughs from 1705 to 1708 and for Carmarthenshire from 1710 to 1715; he was the grandson of Jane Williams (50)

22.2 Lord Lieutenants

1. Sir Nicholas Williams Bt MP (1681-1745)(51) of Edwinsford served as Lord Lieutenant and Custos Rotulorum of Carmarthenshire from 11 June 1736 to 1740

2. Thomas Williams (d1762)(54) of Edwinsford and Court Derllys served as Lord Lieutenant and Custos Rotulorum of Carmarthenshire from 10 March 1740[540] to his death in 1762

3. Sir James (Joe) Williams-Drummond Bt (1857-1913)(68) of Edwinsford and Hawthornden served as Lord Lieutenant and Custos Rotulorum of Carmarthenshire from 7 July 1898 to his death on 15 June 1913

The Lord Lieutenant is the monarch's personal representative in each county. Henry VIII first appointed them in the 1540s when they took over the responsibility from the Sheriffs of organising the county's militia and yeomanry against the threats of foreign invasion. The post was abolished during the Commonwealth but reinstated in 1662. Today the unpaid and non-political office involves upholding the dignity of the Crown, arranging visits of the Royal family, presenting medals and awards, recommending honours, participating in county civic voluntary and charitable activities, liaising with the military and cadet forces, and acting as chairman of the advisory committee of the local magistrates' association. The City of London is unique in that it has a Commission of Lieutenancy of which the Lord Mayor of London is the chairman and carries out the duties of a Lord Lieutenant. Many members of the families served as Deputy Lieutenants.

The Lord Lieutenant of Wales used to be the Lord President of the Council of Wales and the Marches until that body was abolished in 1689. Lord Lieutenants of each county were then appointed.

22.3 Custos Rotulorum[541]

The Custos Rotulorum was the keeper of the county records and the highest civil officer in the county being effectively the chief magistrate. The Lord Chancellor appointed people of rank to this office until 1545 and then it became an appointment by the Crown. After 1762 the Lord Lieutenant of the relevant county in Wales was also appointed the Custos Rotulorum.

Many members of the families also served on the commission as magistrates and therefore had considerable power in local administrative matters.

540 FDWD: *Annals p37*. It is possible that he was only appointed to these offices in 1746 after his eldest brother's death since the family muniments and other records are inconsistent as to the dates

541 JC Sainty: *Custodes Rotulorum*

22.4 Sheriffs or High Sheriffs[542]

Robert Cary of Clovelly	1555	Devon
George Cary of Clovelly (107)	1587	Devon
Rees Williams of Rhydodyn (41)	1614	Carms
John Vaughan of Plas Gwyn (47)	1659	Carms
Nicholas Williams of Rhydodyn (43)	1665	Carms
Sir Rice Williams of Rhydodyn (45)	1680	Carms
Nicholas Williams of Ystradwrallt, Edwinsford (49)	1698	Carms
Sir James Hamlyn Bt of Clovelly (57)	1767	Devon
Robert Banks Hodgkinson MP of Edwinsford (56)	1784	Carms
Sir James Hamlyn Williams Bt MP of Edwinsford and Clovelly (60)	1811	Carms
Sir James Hamlyn Williams Bt MP of Edwinsford and Clovelly (61)	1848	Carms
Rear Admiral Charles Hamlyn Williams of Derllys Court (62)	1852	Carms
Sir Arthur Chichester Bt of Youlston (64)	1816	Devon
Sir John Davie Fergusson Davie Bt MP (72)	1873	Carms
Sir James HW Williams-Drummond of Edwinsford and Hawthornden (68)	1885	Carms
Frederick Hamlyn of Clovelly (120)	1901	Devon
Hon John Rous of Clovelly (127)	2014	Devon

542 NLWBO; the London Gazette; HP; Sir John Lloyd 2 p456-463

Talley, Llansawel and Caio

23. Village of Talley

Talyllychau "is widely but unacceptably known as Talley (admittedly a name first recorded in 1382)" according to the Encyclopaedia of Wales[543] although no explanation is given. Fred Price[544] says the word signifies the "head of the lakes" from *llwch (llychau)* referring to the two lovely lakes in front of the Abbey, which is the most popular derivation. He adds that in older documents the name is given as Tallach, Tallaghan, Tallesch, and Tally. But confusingly a Dictionary of Place Names in Wales[545] suggests that the Welsh word derives from *tâl y llech (llechau* plural) meaning "slate, rock or stone slab" or "end of stone slabs" possibly referring to the old wall near the lower lake or to an old chapel near the village. Alternatively it suggests the word refers to a causeway between the two lakes accessing the Abbey. It adds that "Talley" is probably a mistaken abbreviation or colloquial contraction by non-Welsh speaking clerks of previously used names including Thalelech in 1222, Telechu in 1239, Tal y Llecheu in 1271, Talcheulau 1284-7, Taleleze in 1291, Tilachlargy in 1307, Tal y Lleeche in 1566, Tal y Llechau in 1710 and Talau in 1740. Talley used to be in the hundred of Maenor Deilo before it combined with Caeo. It is most famous for its Abbey described in Chapter 29.1.

Talley was a village long before monastic times and was probably a centre of Christian worship in Celtic times. In monastic times in the late 12th century when Talley Abbey was built, it owned several granges (smallholdings or hamlets farmed by canons, monks and lay brethren within a day's journey from Talley) including Gwastade near Cwmdu, Cefnblaidd in Talley itself, Trallwng Elgan near Glanrannell, Llanycrwys, Cilmaren, Brechfa Gothi, Gwyddgrug, and Manor Frwnws (Rhuddlan Teifi grange was lost to Whitland by 1208). There were also small chapels linked to the Abbey including one near Llanfihangel churchyard and another called *Mynwent Capel Crist* in the small field by the Edwinsford Arms (*rhiw fynwent fach* is the little graveyard hill). Originally Talley was in two parishes, Esgairnant and Llanfihangel Cefn Rhos, later united. There were also five administrative hamlets similar in size and name to the old granges: Esgairnant, Gwastadedd, Llanfihangel, Trallwng Elgan, and Cefnblaidd. Following the Napoleonic Wars in 1815 there was an economic slump which led to fewer jobs on the land so with the coming of the industrial revolution local familes moved to where the work was in Swansea and Merthyr. The local hamlets declined, the thatched cottages fell into disrepair, some families emigrated, and the large gentry estates slowly declined.

Historically Talley's annual Fair Day used to be held on 6 August; in the modern era the Talley Agricultural Show was first held in 1899 under the Presidency of Sir Joe Williams-Drummond, and repeated in 1900 and 1901 in September in the grounds of the Edwinsford Arms. In more recent times the Talley and Cwmdu Agricultural Shows have been replaced with an annual Talley and Cwmdu Summer Fayre (Talyllychau a Chwmdu Ffair Hâf).

Richard Fenton[546] says: *"A little further on opens the Vale of Talley or Tal y Llychau, taking its name from its situation near two Lakes, the largest near a Mile and a Quarter round, and the lesser about a Mile. The Water Lily adorn the sides. They abound with Eels, Perch and Pike. The water belongs to Edwinsford, and Fish for their own consumption, but the property besides in the Fishing is in Admiral Foley as Lord of Llansadwrn."*

---

543 Welsh Academy: *Encyclopaedia of Wales (2008) p853*

544 Fred Price: *History of Talley and Talley Abbey (1934) p5*

545 HW Owen and R Morgan: *Dictionary of Place Names in Wales (2007)*

546 Richard Fenton (1746-1821) toured Wales and wrote several journals. John Fisher edited and published these journals in 1917 as *Tours in Wales (1804-1813)*

The population[547] of Talley parish was 822 in 1801, 880 in 1811, 1084 in 1821, 1058 in 1831, 1068 in 1844[548], 1005 in 1851, 1022 in 1861, 935 in 1871, 839 in 1881, 754 in 1891, 505 in 1921, and 475 in 1931. The election boundaries have since been changed.

As we have seen the Edwinsford family played its part in the local activities of the parish. They attended and often chaired or presided over fairs, shows, shearing competitions, hedge cutting and laying competitions, ploughing matches, sheep dog trials, concerts, singing competitions and eisteddfodau.

In 1971 the village of Talley together with the two lakes was designated[549] a conservation area. The Lower Lake (nearest Edwinsford) is a nature reserve managed by the Dyfed Wildlife Trust while the Upper Lake by the Church is open to the public and is also a haven for wildlife. The mound between the two lakes might be the ruins of an old motte and bailey castle on wooden stilts. As we have seen, the canal between the lakes was created by the Edwinsford family to enable them to get to church by boat.

Map of Talley c1840

547 www.histpop.org
548 S Lewis: *Topographical Dictionary of Wales (1844)*
549 London Gazette (1 June 1971)

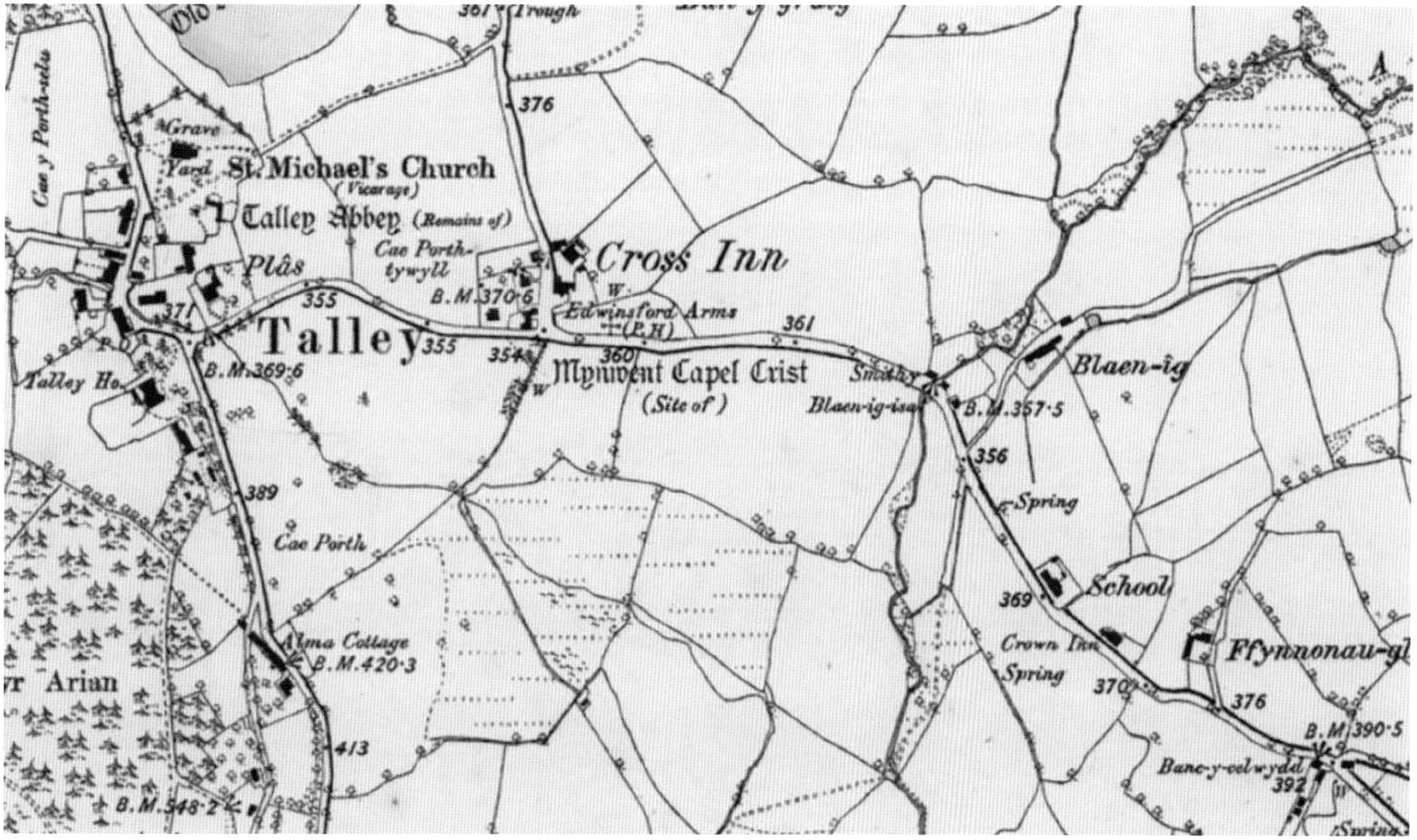

Map of Talley c1886

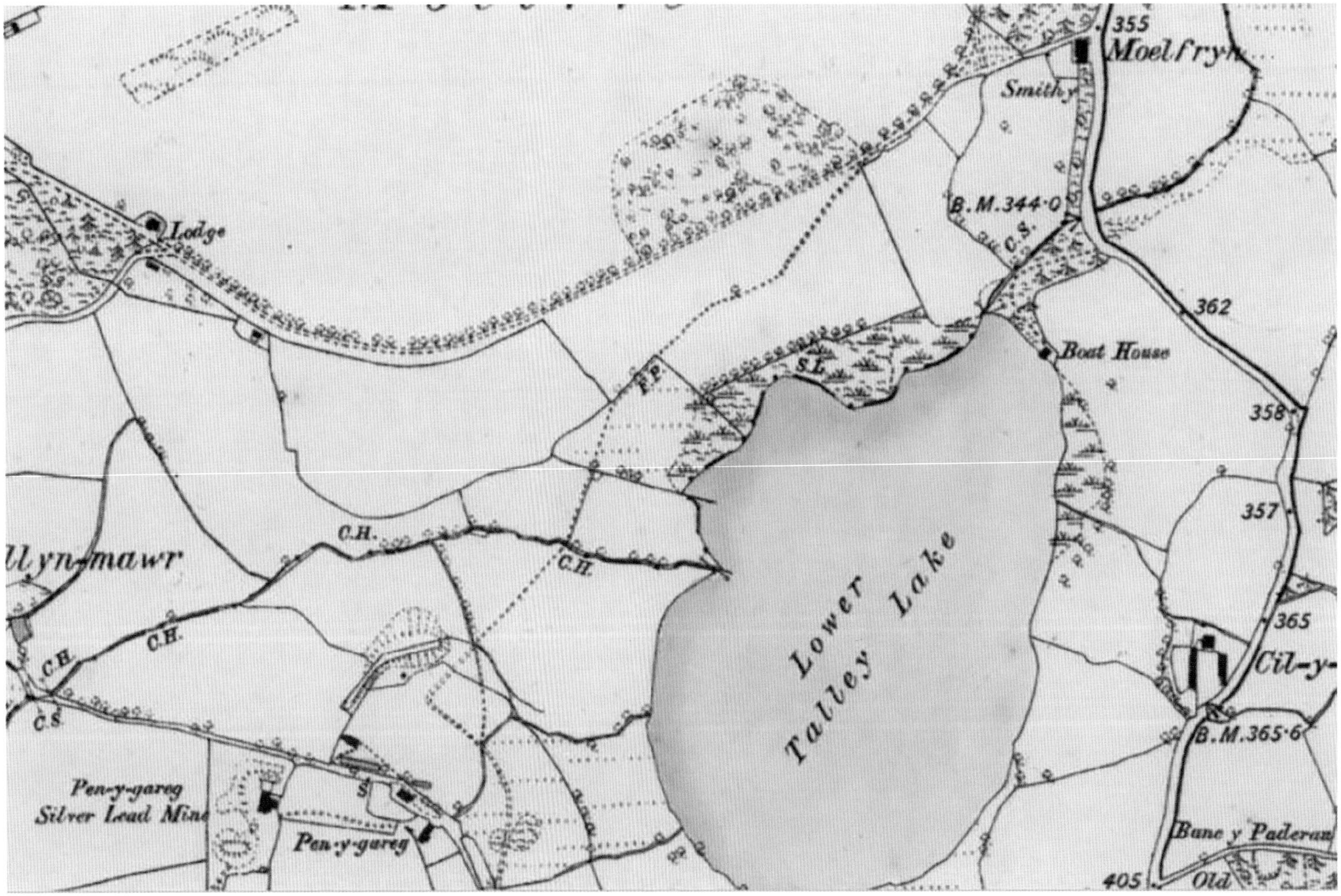

Map of Talley Lakes c1886

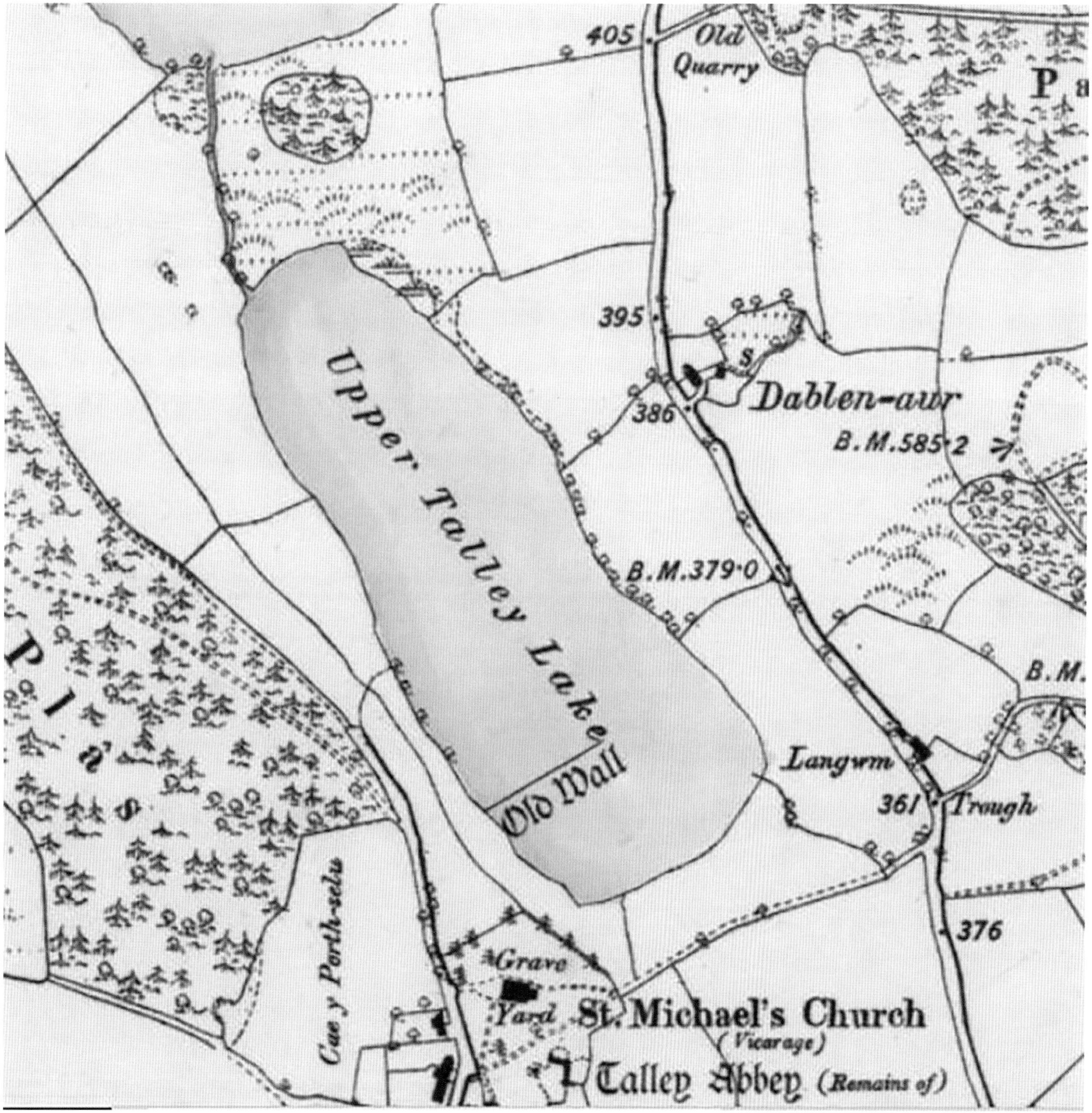

Map of Talley Lakes c1886

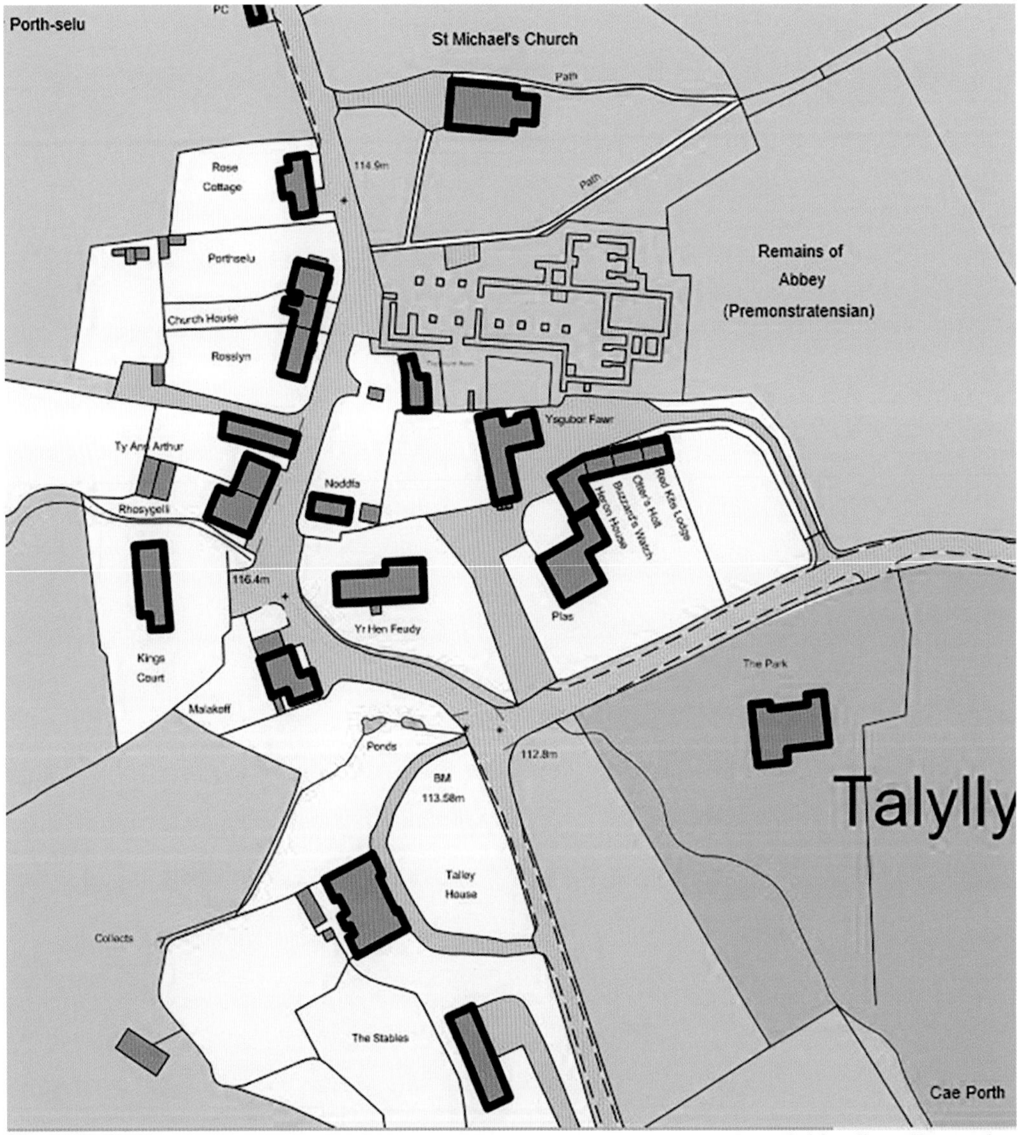

Map of old Talley village today

Talley village c1900

Talley village c1900

Talley village c1910

Talley Lakes 2016

Talley Lakes 2016

24. Selected Talley Properties

Several of the properties within the village of Talley and many of the farms outside the village have been owned by or had connections with the Edwinsford family.

24.1 Talley House [SN633326]

Talley House 2017

Talley House c1880 David and Susanne Long Price

Talley House is one of the oldest properties[550] in the old village of Talley on the corner of the back road from Talley to Cwmdu. It is possibly as old as the Abbey itself (see Chapter 29) and may be the building described in 1553 as "decayed and requireth reparation of £5." Originally it was called Ty'r Jenkin Gwynne and was part of the Abermarlais estate[551] of the Johnes family; it is thought that at that time it comprised several dwelling houses. Thomas Williams (c1620-80)(44) who served as steward of the manor of Talley is thought to have lived there.

Sir Francis Cornwallis married Elizabeth Johnes (d1720), who inherited Abermarlais on the death of her father Sir Henry Jones Bt in 1644; he owed a debt to the Williams family of Edwinsford which he settled in 1661 by transferring the property to Thomas Williams (44) and his wife Martha of Edwinsford for £860. Daniel Price (1750-1815), the agent and attorney of the Edwinsford Estate (and also the Crown's steward of Talley manor), moved to Talley from Llanwrda in 1771 and in 1777 married Elizabeth Williams (a widow and only child of John and Mary Harries). Elizabeth inherited the property in 1789 and they moved into it. They probably rebuilt much of the house. Their two sons, Thomas and Daniel, traded in Talley as attorneys together as Daniel Price & Sons. Thomas was in chambers in Llandeilo and was coroner for Llandeilo district and died at the young age of 42. The other son, Daniel Price (1788-1848), took over Talley House in

YEAR	TALLEY HOUSE TALLEY CENSUS RETURNS
1841	**PRICE: Daniel** (52) attorney, solicitor, coroner, Elizabeth (41) wife, Sarah (11) dau, David (8) son, Cicely (6) dau, Diana (2) dau, Mary (1) dau, 3 ser
1851	**PRICE: Elizabeth** (51) landed proprietor, Elizabeth (24) dau, Sarah (21) dau, Cicely (16) dau, Diana (12) dau, Mary (11) dau, Catherine (8) dau, David Davies (25) groom, Catherine Lewis (18) house ser
1861	**PRICE: Elizabeth** (61) landed proprietor born Swansea, Sarah (31) dau born Talley, Cicely (26) dau, Diana (22) dau, Catherine (18) dau, Elinor Davies (27) cook, Anne Davies (19) housemaid, Elizabeth Thomas (24) housemaid, David Morgan (28) farm ser
1871	**PRICE: David Long** (38) solicitor and landowner, Susanne (31) gentlewoman, John (1) son, Cicely (36) sis plus footman, cook, nurserymaid and maid
1881	**PRICE: David Long** (48) solicitor with 30 acres, Susanne (41) wife, John (11) son, Susanne (9) dau, Robert (8) son, Francis (7) son, Edmund (7) son, Herbert (5) son, Alan (4) son, Cecil (3) son, Sarah Moxon (23) governess, William Walters (19) footman, Anne Davies (32) cook, Rachel Thomas (27) housemaid, Sarah Beavang (16) nurse
1891	**PRICE: David Long** (58) solicitor born Talley, Susanne (50) wife, John (21) Oxford undergraduate, Robert (18) solicitor's articled clerk, Francis (17) son, Edmund (17) son, Herbert (15) son, Alan (14) son, Cecil (13) son, Cicely (55) sis, Emily Nallees (28) cook, Eleanor Griffiths (21) housemaid, William (16) footman, Elizabeth Williams (14) maid
1901	**PRICE: Susanne** (61) widow born Llandeilo, John (31) son CoE clergyman born Talley, Myfanwy (24) dau in law, Susanne (29) dau, Susanne Long Price (1) granddau, Esther Long Price (2 mon) granddau, Mary Price (24) cook, Rhoda Rees (17) nurse
1911	**PRICE: Myfanwy** (34) wife born Brecon, Susanne (11) dau born Talley, Ester (10) dau, John (9) son born Llansteffan, Barbara (5) dau, Julia (11 mon) dau, Ellen Price (27) governess born USA, Frederick Harris (19) groom, Annie Davies (17) general servant [Rev John Price Head of family absent]

550 Francis Jones: *Carmarthenshire Homes p178;* Cadw; Denzil James, Andy Gray and Arthur Davies: *Y Llychau*

551 David Lewis: *Dolaucothi and Brunant p433-5*

1815 on the death of his father; in 1821 he married Elizabeth Long (b1800) the daughter of David Long a wealthy surgeon in Swansea and they lived in Talley House with their family as can be seen on the census returns. In about 1822 they extended the property, merged it with Mynydd Cyn y Rhos nextdoor and renamed the enlarged house Talley House, the name on the Parish rate book from the 1830s. They had 13 children of whom six survived and their only surviving son, David Long Price, added his mother's surname to the family surname. The Talley estate of the family had by now grown to some 500 acres.

In 1867 the house was extended by David Long Price (1833-98)[552] who also diverted the Talley to Cwmdu back road outside so as to extend the lawn in front of the house. He was educated at the Froodvale Academy and later articled to a solicitor in Gloucester before taking his solicitors exams; he followed in the footsteps of his father and grandfather as agent and solicitor to the Edwinsford family and he also acted as agent for the Danyrallt estate. He served as under-sheriff of the county 13 times and on numerous local boards including as chairman of the Llansawel and Talley school boards, and member of the Talley Board of Guardians, as magistrates' clerk, registrar of Lampeter County Court, County Treasurer from 1886, and he conducted the first county election in 1874 under the Ballot Act. He was a fluent Welsh speaker who loved local country pursuits and wrote a History of Talley Abbey in 1879. He was a great sportsman and keen on the hounds, shooting and fishing. He served as a Captain of the 4th Corps of Carmarthenshire Rifle Volunteers, Llansawel, which was disbanded[553] in 1869 "by which time it had drunk much beer and luckily had not killed anybody".

In 1868 he married Susanne (d1905) the eldest daughter of William Peel of Taliaris Park nearby; they had seven sons and one daughter born in Talley, who were initially educated by the governess, Sarah Moxon, and later tutored in Alma Cottage by Herbert Joscelyn, the son of Rev Henry Joscelyn from Buckinghamshire; Herbert later married the daughter (1) Susanne (1871-1944) in April 1905 and the reception[554] was held at Talley House following which they took a pony and trap to Llandeilo station to get the train to Bournemouth for their honeymoon. Two of the seven sons went into the Church: (2) John (1870-1940) married Myfanwy (d1962) in 1899 and served as curate of Llanstephan and then rector of Pendine before becoming a much loved vicar of Talley from 1914 to 1940; he never wore a dog collar in his life and was a great sportsman who kept a pack of beagles and lived in Talley House with a family of six daughters and a son, who died young as can be seen in the 1911 census return (the vicar was himself one of eight children, six sons and one daughter) and (3) Francis (1874-1940) married Edith Roderick in 1902, served as a local vicar in Carmarthenshire and they lived in King's Court nearby with their family as can be seen in the 1911 census return (see Chapter 24.3). (4) Robert (1872-1930) married Margaret Rhys in 1904 and was a local authority civil servant and lawyer practising for some years in Llandovery; he succeeded his father as treasurer of Carmarthenshire County Council and during the Great War served in the Sportsmen's Battalion abroad and then took an appointment in the War Office; he died in his Surrey home. (5) Edmond (1874-1962) the other twin was a solicitor and clerk to the local magistrates' bench at Llansawel and lived at Dark Gate Lodge in Talley; his wife was the daughter of the Lewis family of Pantyresgair and they kept hens in chicken sheds at the bottom of Blaencwmrefail mountain. (6) Herbert (1875-1927) married Dorothy Payne in 1925 and had an army career serving as a Captain and Adjutant of the 1st/2nd Pembrokeshire Yeomanry. (7) Sidney (1877-1938) married Josephine Worley in 1911 and lived in Ceylon as a tea planter, made a fortune then lost it, and retired to Carmarthenshire where he died. The youngest son, (8) Captain Cecil Evelyn (1878-1915), started his military career with the Munster Fusiliers and transferred to the West India Regiment in 1900 and then the West Yorkshire Regiment in 1914; he married Mary Langford Sainsbury of Taunton in 1913 but sadly was killed near Suvia Bay at Gallipoli in the Dardanelles campaign on 7 August 1915 (he is remembered on the war memorial outside Talley Church and on the Helles Memorial at Gallipoli).

As we saw in Chapter 1,1, on Sunday 13 January 1878 Sir James (Joe) Hamlyn Williams-Drummond 4th Baronet (1857-1913) (68) reached the age of 21 and formally inherited the Edwinsford Estate in the Cothi Valley and Hawthornden Castle in Midlothian near Edinburgh. At the dinner celebrating Joe's attainment of his majority David Long Price

552 Fred Price: *Talley p31*
553 DJ Williams p160
554 Carmarthen Journal (30 April 1905)

reminded everyone that his family had served the Edwinsford family professionally for about 100 years. They were to continue to do so until the early 20th century.

Talley House today is a listed large late 18th century symmetrical house with wings added in the 1830s, having rough cast exterior walls, a three storey three window central portion, and balancing single bay two storey wings. The former wooden Doric portico has been removed as have the original fireplaces. Inside there is an early 19th century staircase with balusters and some of the rooms still retain early 19th century plasterwork. Behind Talley House and King's Court there used to be a concrete reservoir in a field owned by Talley House which supplied drinking water to the old village before the mains supply was installed.

During WW1 and WW2 the Talley House family put on concerts and dances when servicemen and women came home on leave and the village children all received small presents. The Long Price family sold the house in the 1960s and the current owner is Andrew Gray (b1961), a businessman from Cardiff, who has also served as bursar of Llandovery College (2013-15) while his wife Sarah Gray was director of development there.

Noddfa 2017

Plas (mansion) and Noddfa (refuge)
Across the road from Talley House behind Yr Hen Feudy and on the lane to the Edwinsford Arms is Y Plas. This was a farm built in 1826 from the dismantled old Abbey kitchens and bought by the Edwinsford Estate in 1828 and probably then rebuilt; a letter from Daniel Price, the agent, dated 25 March 1832 refers to the overcharging by Rees Williams, the blacksmith, for his work on the building. It is a fine listed Regency Gothic style two storey house with rubble masonry. There are the remains of the old Abbey oven and cellar and a trap door over the steps facing the Abbey is now covered up. In the early 20th century Plas farm was run by Simon Jones and his sister, both unmarried; he was the precentor in Esgairnant Chapel and a keen local historian. It ceased to be a thriving family ran farm in the 1980s. It had an L-shaped service wing which has been converted into cottages.

Plas 2017

The original Plas farmhouse was what is now called Noddfa (formerly Tŷ Isaf) and part of the old farm buildings are Ysgubor Fawr behind and near the Abbey ruins. When the Pengarreg (Pen y Garreg) silver and lead mines were operational between 1863-5 and 1885-91 near the Upper Lake on the Edwinsford Estate, some 13 miners were living in Noddfa between night and day shifts. Emma Evans lived there after WW1 and was a keen gardener who sold her vegetables and fruit to Mr Evans of Halfway (grandfather of Janet James) for the Swansea market; she died in the early 1940s and in her will left the house to Alun Morgan (Porthselu) who sold it to Eric and Gwyneth Jones. Gwyneth Jones (1933-2005)[555] lived there for some 50 years; her father served in WW1 and then delivered the post in Talley for many years following which her mother took over and used to walk about 12 miles daily. She remembers the bombing of Swansea during WW2 and the evacuees arriving from London and Swansea; children went to school carrying gas masks and a packed lunch and often had to run to the dugout in the nearby field for a drill. Many of the local men served as Air Raid Wardens, or as members of the Home Guard or the Royal Observer Corps. Gwyneth's husband was William Eric Jones MBE from the Eppynt who worked for the Forestry Commission. Gwyneth worked for 25 years in the office of the nearby Llansawel Quarry at Dinas (Pen y Ddinas) which had opened in the 1920s and employed many local men.

24.2 Malakoff House [SN633326]

Malakoff 2017

YEAR	MALAKOFF HOUSE TALLEY CENSUS RETURNS
1861	**JONES: John** (32) master tailor and draper born Talley, Elizabeth (34) wife
1871	**JONES: John** (42) tailor, draper, postmaster, Elizabeth (47) wife, David (17) nephew, John (14) nephew, Albert (8) nephew
1881	**JONES: John** (52) postman and draper, Kezia (33) wife, Luther (1) son, Sydney (3 mon) son, Morgan Lewis (22) ser, Alfred Daniel Townsend (15) shop assistant
1891	**JONES: Kezia** (42) widow postmistress draper and milliner, Luther (11) son, John (10) son, Alfred Daniel Townsend (25) ass postmaster and draper born Bristol, Mary Davies (23) ser, Thomas (17) ass [see Pretoria House 1901]
1901	uninhabited
1911	**DAVIES: John** (33) master carpenter born Llanybyther, Anne (34) wife, Mary (8) dau, Anna (6) dau, Sarah (4) dau, David (2) son, Daniel (10 mon) son

Malakoff House, which is between Talley House and King's Court and across the road from Yr Hen Feudy, was built around 1854-6 and named after the battle of Malakoff in the Crimean War; on 8 September 1855 as part of the siege of Sevastopol the French army under General MacMahon successfully stormed the Malakoff redoubt bringing the 11 month siege to an end whilst the simultaneous British attack on Russian forces at Redan to the south was repulsed. It is unknown why this property was named after this particular battle.

It was part of the Edwinsford Estate and was used as a village post office and drapers store for many years by the Jones family as the census returns reveal. It had a large shop front with a side entrance and letter box. John Jones was a master tailor whose first wife Elizabeth worked in the shop and died during the 1870s. John then remarried and his second wife Kezia assisted him; he was an elder of Esgairnant Chapel and had a Sunday school of over 150 pupils. When he died Kezia continued the business as the postmistress, draper and milliner with

[555] Gwyneth Jones: *Y Llychau*

her young family, helped by a much younger shop assistant, Alfred Daniel Townsend, who came from Bristol. Kezia and Alfred married and moved to the Cross Inn which was demolished in 1897 to be replaced with Pretoria House (see Chapter 24.10), the new village post office[556] and shop. Two of her sons, Luther and John, were living with them.

Arthur Davies[557] recounts that his parents, John and Ann Davies, were married in 1901 and went to live in Malakoff House where six children were born; in 1912 they bought and moved nextdoor to King's Court where two more children were born. Malakoff ceased to be the post office and shop and was used as a workshop by John Davies a master carpenter. In 1946 it was bought by the Davies family of Llansawel Quarry and leased to David Williams who also worked at Llansawel Quarry. David Williams bought the freehold in the 1960s and left the house to his daughter, Wendy Williams who still lives there.

24.3 King's Court [SN 633327]

King's Court 2017

[556] Denzil James*: Y Llychau*
[557] Y Llychau

YEAR	KING'S COURT TALLEY CENSUS RETURNS
1841	**MORGAN: Roderick** (54) shopkeeper, Mary (49) wife, George (17) son, Mary (15) dau, Millicent (13) dau, James (11) son, Blanch (7) dau, Jane (5) dau, Mary Morgan (21) ser
1851	**MORGAN: Roderick** (62) grocer born Conwil Gaeo, Mary (59) wife with 4 children, Rees Prosser (57) bro in law retired haberdasher
1861	**(1) THOMAS: Evan** (75) agric labourer**(2) Morgan, Mary** (68) grocer, Millicent (31) dau**(3) LEWIS: Mary** (83) agric lab
1871	**(1) THOMAS: Charlotte** (37) charwoman**(2) JONES: David** (30) draper and grocer born Talley, Mary (33) wife, Alfred Sweeny (45) lodger solicitor's managing clerk, Madeline Sweeny (12) dau
1881	**JONES: David** (39) draper and grocer, Mary (43) wife, John (9) son, Thomas (6) son, William (3) son, Mary (2) dau
1891	**JONES: David** (49) draper and grocer, Mary (53) wife, John (19) son classical scholar, William (13) son, Mary (12) dau, Mary Davies (79) mother in law
1901	**JONES: David** (59) grocer born Talley
1911	**LONG PRICE: Francis** (37) Clerk in holy orders born Talley, Edith (30) wife, Margery (7) dau, Rosemary (6) dau, Ursula (3) dau, Winifred Davies (20) servant

King's Court is set back from the road and next to Malakoff House in the old village. It was probably part of the monastic foundation of Talley Abbey across the road and is certainly one of the oldest properties[558] in the village and could date back to the time of the building of the Abbey itself (see Chapter 29). The current house which dates from about 1450 was surveyed for RCAHMW in 1992 and in 1998 following a severe storm in which the chimney collapsed revealing medieval foundations. It seems that it was a medieval hall-house with a mature three-unit plan (ie a central hall open to the roof set between inner and outer walls which were both probably storeyed). The hall would have been 21ft long and 20ft wide and thus larger than the classic timber two bay halls of the Welsh Marches. On the ground floor was an inner parlour heated by an impressive gable end hooded fireplace with voussoirs and rounded stone corbels, the hall and passageway, and a kitchen; so there were three rooms of roughly equal size. Around 1790 the house was given a partial Georgian facelift at the upper end so that the upper end (occupied by the family) and the lower end (the service quarters) had roofs of different types and levels. The lower end had a thatched roof while the upper end had a slated roof with raised eaves supported by new collar beam trusses. There were three doors at the front including a new central doorway providing an entrance to the parlour. These improvements were perhaps effected by Rev John Roberts (d1840) when the house was in effect the vicarage.

Why is the house called King's Court? Tradition suggests that this was because Henry Tudor stayed there (*Cwrt y Brenin*) in August 1485 on his way from Mill Bay near Milford Haven to meet up with Sir Rhys ap Thomas at the battle of Bosworth Field when he won the English crown; he is said to have received support from the Abbot of Talley Abbey and to have subsequently granted a tower to the church of every parish through which he travelled on his journey to Bosworth, which some of them celebrated in 1985. However there is no hard evidence to substantiate any of these claims which may well originate from those who wished to gain favour with the conquering Welsh hero whose exploits validated the long held prophesies of the medieval bards that a Welshman would successfully claim the crown of the Anglo Saxons in England. The fact that for unknown reasons an annual payment of £6 had been made for centuries by the Royal Exchequer to Talley Abbey and then its successor church up to the disestablishment of the Church in Wales in 1920 merely added to the mystique. It is perhaps more likely that the name reflects the holding of Courts Leet in the house for centuries, since under the customs of the Royal Manor of Talley the tenants owed suit and rents to the King who was Lord of the Manor, whose steward was his local representative and sat in authority at the Courts Leet every fortnight. Talley was a copyhold manor with Borough English customs (the youngest son inheriting rather than the eldest son), so the lands were held by copy of court roll and land was transferred by surrender in the Lord's Court (ie King's Court) and not by deed as elsewhere, court rolls providing a register of title. So King's Court escaped the destruction of the other parts of the monastic complex because it was the location of the Lord's Courts and administrative offices. Evidence of a Court Leet held on 22 April

[558] Dylan Roberts and Richard Suggett*: A Late-Medieval Monastic Hall-House Rediscovered CA (1999) p5-11;* Cadw

1553[559] refers to a former monastic building called a "mansion house late belonging to the said late monastery" and a "convent hall… contayneth two rooms between the roofe and the ground…a buttery and a lard-house and...a hall and a parlour called the Abbot's Chamber" with demesne lands of 13 acres of arable and meadow grounds.

In 1669[560] William John, a mercer of Talley, who occupied King's Court shop minted his own halfpenny and brass farthing, one of which is now in the National Museum in Cardiff (marked "1669 William John Mercer Talley"). In 1644 during the Civil War Parliament had ceased minting farthings and small change thus creating a huge shortage; consequently several people minted their own illegally in order that normal trade could continue.

So it seems that in the late 17th century the house was used as a shop and later as a vicarage up to 1840 and then let to tradesmen as indicated by the census returns. David Jones and his family lived there for over 30 years running a successful draper's and grocer's business, nicknamed Cloth Hall, which was transferred to Tŷ Ann Arthur when they retired in the early 1900s. One of their sons, Rev John David Jones (1871-1931), was educated at Queen's College Oxford where he read classics and then went into the Church serving as vicar of St Asaph (1900-16) and then of parishes in Bangor and Aberdovey. The Tithe map of 1839 suggests that the freehold owner was Lewis Price Jones of Glanyrannell in Crugybar. By 1911 Francis Long Price of Talley House was living in King's Court with his family as tenants of the Glanrannell Estate; the Estate auctioned the house[561] and its six acres for sale in 1917 and at that time the sitting tenant was John Davies paying annual rent of £9.

Arthur Davies[562] recounts that his parents, John and Ann Davies, were married in 1901 and went to live nextdoor in Malakoff House until 1912 where six children were born; in 1912 they moved to King's Court as tenants and then in 1917 they bought King's Court from the Glanrannell Estate at the auction for £250 and two more children were born there. Arthur was the second youngest of the eight children, the youngest being his sister who was born in 1917. His father John was a carpenter, undertaker and wheelwright (as well as the precentor at Esgairnant Chapel) and they used to keep two cows for milking, two pigs for bacon, and hens for eggs as well as a large vegetable garden with a greenhouse (the first in the village) for tomatoes and onions attached to his father's workshop. When a District Nurse, Mrs Carter, was appointed for Talley she came to live in King's Court in 1922-23 (the area doctors lived in Llansawel); her husband had been killed in the Great War and Arthur knew her two sons well; one of them Vernon lived in Llandyssul where his mother moved after a few years in Talley and Arthur remembers them coming to stay in King's Court for their school holidays from Maesteg, the village in which they lived. Arthur married Mair from Cwmdu in 1937 at Esgairnant Methodist Chapel, Talley and their daughter, Margaret, was born in King's Court. In 1939 the family moved to London and Margaret spent some time during the war years at King's Court and went to Talley school. Mair died aged 88 a few years ago and Arthur went to live with his daughter in Newtown, Powys.

Charles Field and his wife bought the house some time after WW2 and sold it to John Davies and his wife in 1963; they sold it in 1985 to Alison and Simon Mostyn who lovingly restored it. Today this listed medieval house with Georgian façade has four bedrooms upstairs, and plenty of exposed timbers, stone walls plus an inglenook fireplace, large drawing room, hall and kitchen downstairs. Outside it has mature gardens, a stable, kitchen garden, a paddock and a stream. In June 2015 the Mostyns moved to the west country and sold the house[563] to Andrew and Kate Hill from Manchester.

---

559 Francis Jones: *Carmarthenshire Homes p178*

560 Alun Morgan

561 I am grateful to Andrew Hill for showing me the Auction Particulars

562 Arthur Davies: *Y Llychau*

563 Strutt & Parker sales particulars

24.4 Swan Inn (Rhosygelli) (moorland of the wood) [SN 633327]
At the end of the 18th century there were four inns in Talley: the Edwinsford Arms, the Cross Inn across the road, the Crown Inn, and the Swan Inn. Today they are all closed.

Rhosygelli and Tŷ Ann Arthur nextdoor are thought to have been one house originally called Tŷ Mawr which was taken down and rebuilt in 1817 as two properties. The house nearest to King's Court was called the Swan Inn or Swan House. It was run by a number of innkeepers. During the 19th century several residents of the Swan Inn baptised[564] their children and are recorded in the register of baptisms for the parish. These included Hannah (1857) the daughter of Anne and Lewis Henton; Sarah (1853) and William (1856) the children of Anne and John Lawday; seven children of Margaret and Thomas Evans between 1861 and 1869; and three children of Mary and John Jones (innkeepers) between 1875 and 1877. Francis Jenkins, a shoemaker, lived there with his wife Anne and two daughters, Rachel (b1880) and Sarah Jane (b1882), before they moved to Swansea in the 1880s. At the beginning of the 20th century the Inn was run by David Lewis and his daughter Annie Jane; David's brother farmed at Maesllan in

Rhosygelli (left) and Tŷ Ann Arthur (right) 2017

564 Pat Edwards: *Y Llychau*

YEAR	SWAN INN (RHOSYGELLI) TALLEY CENSUS RETURNS
1841	**DAVIES: John** (41) innkeeper, Jane (41) wife with 5 children, Daniel Davies (29),1 ser
1851	**WILLIAMS: William** (72) victualler and labourer born Llansawel, Mary (66) wife, Thomas (21) son
1861	uninhabited
1871	**MICKLEWRIGHT: Sarah** (56) innkeeper's wife, Alice (27) dau
1881	**JENKINS: Francis** (30) shoemaker, Anne (27) wife dressmaker, Rachel (8 mon) dau, Mary Murray (16) ser
1891	**LEWIS: David** (41) innkeeper, Rachel (39) wife, Annie (5) dau
1901	**LEWIS: David** (51) publican and farmer, Rachel (49) wife, Annie (15) dau barman
1911	**LEWIS: David** (60) licensed victualler born Llangathen, Rachel (59) wife, Annie (25) dau

Llansawel. In 1918 the owners of the Swan, Susanne Long Price and her son John of Talley House, let the property to another of her sons, Francis Long Price, who was living nearby in King's Court. In 1920 they sold the house for £250 to David and Annie Lewis who were the resident publicans. When her father David died in 1932, Annie sold the house to John Daniel Rees for £225 and the licence was surrendered[565]. John Rees died in 1939 and his wife Annie lived there until her death in 1945 when the property was inherited by Frederick Morris Rees of the Post Office in Cwmdu and his wife Adeline.

In 1955 William and Jennie Davies retired from farming at Gellicefnrhos, bought the Swan for £500 and renamed it Rhosygelli (the last and first syllables of their former farm). He was an elder at Esgairnant Chapel. At the same time the stables owned by Swan House were sold to the owners of Tŷ Ann Arthur next door. William and Jennie renovated the property and moved in during October 1956.

Esmond and Caroline Gale sold the house in 2003 to Ian and Cerys Moir.

Swan Inn early 1900s. Annie Lewis 2nd from left

[565] Betty Williams (née Thomas) from Glanyrafon Ddu Uchaf was nicknamed Betty Swan because she spent so much time there

24.5 Tŷ Ann Arthur (Ann Arthur's house) [SN633327]

YEAR	TY ANN ARTHUR (SHOP) TALLEY CENSUS RETURNS
1841	**EVANS: John** (29) tailor, Anne (23) wife, David (4 mon) son
1851	**EVANS: J** (39) shopkeeper and master tailor born Llanfynydd, Anne (33) wife born Llansawel, Margaret (6) dau, Anne (5) dau, Jane (4) dau, Thomas (1) son, David (3 mon) son, 2 serv
1861	**EVANS: Anne** (43) draper grocer and postmaster born Llansawel, Esther (18) dau dressmaker, Margaret (16) dau, Thomas (11) son, David (10) son, William Chapman (25) lodger photographic artist
1871	**THOMAS: Joseph** (72) farmer of 8 acres and grocer born Llansadwrn, Anne (53) wife, Esther Evans (28) stepdau school mistress, David Evans (20) stepson tailor
1881	**THOMAS: Joseph** (84) shopkeeper and farmer, Anne (63) shopkeeper's wife
1891	**DAVIES: Daniel** (50) builder and shopkeeper, Margaret (44) wife, David (9) son, Evan (8) son, Margaret (5) dau, Anne Thomas (15) ser
1901	**DAVIES: Daniel** (60) draper and grocer born Llandyssul, Margaret (54) wife, Evan (18) son grocer's ass, Mary (15) dau
1911	**DAVIES: Margaret** (64) widow shopkeeper grocer and draper, Evan (28) son relieving officer, Mary (25) dau

As stated above Tŷ Ann Arthur and Rhosygelli (formerly the Swan Inn) are thought to have been one house originally called Tŷ Mawr which was taken down and rebuilt in 1817 as two properties. The house[566] nearer the Abbey was called Tŷ Ann Arthur although who she was is unknown save that in her will dated 1731 she donated a horse valued at 20 shillings and a chamber pot to her two sons.

John Evans, a master tailor, and his wife Anne and children lived there, but he died young and she then continued running the shop as postmistress, draper and grocer. By 1871 she had remarried a man much older than herself, Joseph Thomas, while her daughter was a schoolmistress and her son was training as a tailor. One of her sons, David Evans, married Jane and their son, William Edward Evans[567], was born in the house in April 1880. He worked for the GWR and then in the Great War fought as a Private with the 26th Battalion, Royal Fusiliers; he was killed on 10 October 1916 near Courcelette on the Somme aged 36. He is remembered on the Thiepval Memorial in France and on the war memorial in Talley Churchyard.

By 1891 Daniel Davies (d1909) and his wife Margaret had taken over the thriving shop; she ran the shop and baked bread. He was a successful builder with a workshop on Water Street and in 1899 built Aelybryn for £275 and also rebuilt Esgairnant Chapel. Margaret was one of nine children of John and Esther Griffiths of Cwmdu who ran the post office in that village. In 1918 Rev Francis Long Price (who had rented King's Court up to 1912 and later lived at Pistillgwynne) was given Tŷ Ann Arthur which he later sold in 1920 to Margaret Davies, a widow and the tenant, for £250.

Daniel and Margaret Davies had three children: (a) Caradog (Evan) Davies, who was a great musician and served and was injured in WW1 in Turkey. He died in 1957 aged 74; (b) Mary Davies, who kept the busy shop going with their mother initially and then after her death aged 89 in 1935 by herself with some help from Caradog until Mary's own death in 1962 aged 76; and (c) David Davies who was the bank manager of Barclays in Ammanford. In addition to groceries they sold ironmongery items, paraffin, clothing and paint. Mary also served teas in their living room for all who attended funerals. Mary left Tŷ Ann Arthur to Brenda Allen who lived in Hereford. In 1963 Brenda Allen sold the house to John Richard and Nansi Pinches of the Edwinsford Arms for £1,625. In 1971 they sold it to Roger Flaherty of Gowerton for £4,400. In about 1975 Roger and Elizabeth Flauherty were members of the South Wales caving club; they are remembered for saving the life of a dog which had fallen down the shaft of the Pengarreg silver mine by the Upper Lake.

In 1977 Roger Flaherty sold the property to Esmond and Elizabeth Gale of Llanwit Major. In 1983 they also bought the stable at the end of the barn from Jennie Davies of Rhosygelli. Then in October 2003 the Gales sold to Selby and Caryn Le Roux for £187,000; they

566 Denzil James and Arthur Davies: *Y Llychau*. I am also most grateful to Angela Hastilow for allowing me to use her research

567 Pat Edwards and Talley History Group: *Y Llychau*

renovated the barn and made it part of the house by adding a conservatory in between. In 2008 the area was designated a conservation area. In October 2011 Selby and Caryn Le Roux sold the house to Ian and Angela Hastilow.

24.6 Belle Vue (Rhoslyn: moorland by the lake) [SN633327]

Rhoslyn 2017

Church House 2017

YEAR	BELLE VUE (RHOSLYN) TALLEY CENSUS RETURNS
1841	**WILLIAMS: William** (35) carpenter, Sarah (40) school mistress, Elinor (9) dau, Thomas (8) son, 1 ser
1851	**WILLIAMS: William** (49) carpenter born Talley, Sarah (53) school mistress, Thomas (17) son carpenter, 1 ser
1861	**WILLIAMS: William** (59) builder, Sarah (63) school mistress, Sarah Griffiths (43) housemaid
1871	**WILLIAMS: William** (69) carpenter, Elizabeth Jones (27) ser
1881	**DAVIES: John** (81) auctioneer and accountant born Conwil Gaeo, Jane (83) wife, Jane Lawday (50) dau, David Davies (51) son accountant
1891	No entry
1901	**BEYNON: Ann** (72)
1911	(1) **WILLIAMS: William** (74), Margaret (64) wife (2) **REES: Mary** (53)

This house is next to Tŷ Ann Arthur and was originally known as Belle Vue (View). It was part of the Edwinsford Estate. William Williams, a carpenter, and his wife Sarah, who taught in Talley school, lived there with their family for nearly 40 years. At the beginning of the 20th century another William Williams and his wife Margaret lived there and after William's death Margaret continued to reside there. Llewellyn Christmas Williams, who had been out of work started his own public transport bus service in 1926, the year of the General Strike. It later became known as LCW Motors[568] and ran the first service to Lampeter, Llanybydder and Llandeilo many times daily; he was a hard worker and first class mechanic. Then two sisters from Pantyresgair bought the house and renamed it Rhoslyn.

In 1992 John and Nancy Walford moved into the house having lived nextdoor in Church House since 1989; they bought it from Mrs Morgan Kirby who retired to Llandeilo. John was the lay reader at Talley Church for many years.

568 Gwyneth Jones: *Y Llychau*

Church House
Church or Abbey House was built between Porthselly and Rhoslyn as a one storey school academy on land provided by the Edwinsford Estate. The tutor was Rev Thomas Phillips from Bancyfelin.It had a resident keeper, Han Evans, for some years who lived in a small annexe on the side. Later Abner Gerwyn Bassett lived there with his widowed mother.

24.7 Porth Selu / Selly / Selim (watch gate)[SN 633327]

Porth Selu 2017

Porth Selly (spelt over the years in numerous different ways including Porth Selu, Porth Selim, Portsely and Portselyf) is located next to Church House in the row of three dwellings opposite the Abbey ruins. Originally Porth Selly was on the site of the west gate of the Abbey. The property was part of the Edwinsford Estate.

John Jones and his wife Sarah, who were tailors and dressmakers lived there for nearly 40 years and had 10 children of whom four died in infancy. John Morgan[569], a carpenter on the Edwinsford Estate, who lived at Brocyn asked for consent to marry the daughter Catherine and

YEAR	PORTH SELU/SELLY/SELIM TALLEY CENSUS RETURNS
1841	**JONES: John** (40) tailor, Sarah (35) wife, John (13) son, Margaret (9) dau, Anne (6) dau, Elizabeth (2) dau
1851	**JONES: John** (57) master tailor born Llanfynydd, Sarah (48) wife, Mary (26) dau dressmaker, John (22) son journeyman tailor, Margaret (18) dau dressmaker, Anne (15) dau, Eliza (6) dau, Catherine (3) dau
1861	**JONES: John** (62) master tailor born Llanfynedd, Sarah (60) wife laundress with 2 children and 1 lodger
1871	**JONES: John** (72) tailor, Sarah (71) laundress, Catherine (28) dau laundress, John Morgans (28) son in law wheelwright, David Evans (15) grandson
1881	**DAVIES: William** (34) schoolmaster, Elizabeth (33) wife and two sons
1891	**THOMAS: Elizabeth** (33) charwoman
1901	**THOMAS: Elizabeth** (48) charwoman born Llansawel
1911	**THOMAS: Elizabeth** (59) widow laundress

this was granted on condition that he built a house. He did this by first renting a plot next to and beyond Porth Selly from the Edwinsford Estate and then building Rhos (now Rose) Cottage on it by working in his evenings with a friend who was a builder; it cost him £12. (see Chapter 24.8).

Griffith Morgan (d1951) lived in the house in the early 20th century. He[570] was a tall strong character and a strict disciplinarian and backbone of Esgairnant Chapel; he would preach against the evils of drink and criticise the holding of noisy dances held in the Church Hall opposite his house. He was a carpenter by trade who was also the local pigkiller. He married a much younger wife, Edith (d1959), a seamstress and had two sons, Alun (d2000) a local historian[571] who acted as the caretaker of the Abbey for many years, and Trefor who served in Egypt during WW2; Trefor had a cheerful personality and had three sons, two of whom were doctors and the other a dentist, and one daughter

569 Denzil James: *Y Llychau*
570 Brenda James p74-6
571 Alun Morgan gave a fascinating historical lecture about Talley in the Edwinsford Arms in 1992 and I have used the contents of his lecture which are kept by the Talley History Society

who was a stockbroker. Alun worked in the local quarry and married Gwyneth whose parents lived at the Plas; they had one daughter who became a teacher and she still lives in Pontyclun. Alun continued to live at Porthselu until his death in 2000.

The house was sold in 2001 after Alun's death and resold in 2009 as a holiday cottage. The current owners live in the Gower.

24.8 Rose Cottage (Rhos) (moorland) [SN633327]

YEAR	ROSE COTTAGE (RHOS) TALLEY CENSUS RETURNS
1881	**MORGANS: John** (37) carpenter born Talley, Catherine (32) wife with 3 children, George Evans (53) lodger solicitor's clerk
1891	**MORGAN: John** (46) carpenter, Catherine (43) wife, Henry (12) son, Edith (11) dau, Morgan (7) son, Alice (3 mon) dau
1901	**MORGAN: John** (56) carpenter and builder born Talley, Catherine (53) wife, Alice (10) dau
1911	**MORGAN: John** (66) widower carpenter, Alice (20) dau

Rose Cottage is located at the end of the road and opposite the church. Its origins have been explained in Chapter 24.7. It was part of the Edwinsford Estate. It was built in the late 19th century when John Morgan (d1928) asked for consent to marry Catherine Jones of Porth Selu. He started building in around 1868 and completed the job in 1872 using the stone from the ruined Abbey across the road. In 1872 there was a 60 year lease on the property. His wife Catherine lived there with him and their children until she died in the early 1900s. He continued there until his death and his daughter was able to buy the house from the Edwinsford Estate for £150 in 1932. During WW2 child evacuees were sent to Talley and went to the local school; Rose Saunders was one such evacuee who spent some of the war years living at Rose Cottage and she well remembers Simon Jones and his sister, whom she called Uncle and Auntie.

The house remained in the family until 1995 when it was sold to Ms Jacqueline Hays. Since then the house has been substantially renovated, the original workshop next to the house has been demolished and the house extended. In 2000 Dennis Boyes joined Jacqueline at Rose Cottage and they married in 2006; Dennis served as a churchwarden at Talley Church. In 2009 they moved to live in France. In 2011 Jackie and Derek Nash from Llansawel bought the house and have lived there since then having previously run the Brunant Arms in Caio.

Rhos c1900. John Morgan, Catherine and family

Rose Cottage 2017

24.9 Dark Gate Lodge [SN 635326]

This property was originally called Porth Tywyll and was so called because on this site once stood the south gate to Talley Abbey. It was part of the Edwinsford Estate and the house is thought to have been built in the 1840s. Nearby in the field there used to be a fulling mill called *Felinyparc* which stood until the mid 20th century and is mentioned in a 1661 deed under which the Edwinsford family acquired Talley House and lands; the water to power the mill wheel came from a leat from behind the Edwinsford Arms and down to the mill.

There were several different tenants during the 19th and 20th centuries. Edmond Long Price (1874-1962) of Talley House lived there as can be seen from the census return; he was a solicitor and clerk to the local magistrates' bench at Llansawel and lived at Dark Gate from the early 1900s; his wife was the daughter of the Lewis family of Pantyresgair. During WW2 a number of evacuee children stayed there. Mrs Long Price died in 1986 having spent some 10 years in a nursing home. Following her death the house was sold in 1986 to Michael and Siân Corcoran who have lived there ever since with their family.

Dark Gate 2017

YEAR	DARK GATE LODGE TALLEY CENSUS RETURNS
1841	No entry
1851	**JONES: Rev David Lewis** (49) curate of Talley born Cards, William Beynon (33) lead miner, Elizabeth Beynon (42) cook and housekeeper
1861	**(1) LLOYD: Magdalen** (33) dressmaker **(2) WILLIAMS: Thomas** (63) agric lab, Mary (56) wife, Sarah (3) granddau**(3) BEYNON: William** (44) lead miner, Anne (32) wife with 2 children, Evan Williams (19) bro in law carpenter
1871	**WILLIAMS: Evan** (29) wheelwright born Llandeilo, Sarah (24) wife and 2 children
1881	**(1) LLOYD: Magdalene** (58) dressmaker **(2) THOMAS: William** (72) retired carpenter, Sarah (56) wife
1891	**(1) LLOYD: Magdalene** (69) retired dressmaker **(2) LEWIS: Rachel** (69) retired milliner
1901	**SELLICK: James** (28) bootmaker born Taunton, Mary (37) wife born Talley, Edith (13) niece
1911	**PRICE: Edmond Long** (37) solicitor born Talley, Sarah Hughes (48) general housekeeping servant

24.10 Pretoria House [SN 635326]

YEAR	PRETORIA HOUSE TALLEY CENSUS RETURNS
1901	**TOWNSEND: Alfred** (35) assis accountant born Bristol, Kezia (53) wife postmistress and shopkeeper born Llandissilio, Luther Jones (21) stepson bootmaker's apprentice, John Jones (20) stepson post office ass, James Gill (17) ass, Frank Smith (14) ass, Mary Davies (34) dom ser [see Malakoff House 1891]
1911	**TOWNSEND: Alfred Daniel** (45) assistant overseer of account, Kezia (65) wife sub postmistress, Luther Jones (31) stepson shoemaker, John Jones (29) stepson drapers assistant, Mary Davies (40) servant, Frederick Oakley (17) apprentice post office clerk, Herbert Eastap (14) apprentice post office clerk

This property is on the site of the old Cross Inn thatched cottages on the corner of the crossroads off the main Crugybar to Llandeilo road which goes through the village. The site was part of the Edwinsford Estate. No doubt the house was named after the city in South Africa whose surrender to the British was accepted in the Boer War on 5 June 1900 by Field Marshal Earl Roberts VC accompanied by Lt General Sir James Hills-Johnes VC[572] of the Dolaucothi Estate (and neighbour to the Edwinsford Estate).

Although the house is today on a bend with a turning to the old village and the Abbey ruins it seems clear that there used to be a (cross)road[573] from the bend past what is now the village notice board across the field called Cae y Porth and meeting the old Talley to Cwmdu mountain road; a road probably used in the past by drovers and referred to as the Old London Road (called *Heol Llundain*) by David Long Price in his book on Talley in 1879 and apparent from the 1839 Tithe map.

As we saw in Chapter 24.2, Malakoff in the old village was used as a post office and drapers store for many years by the Jones family. John Anthony Jones (d1881) was a master tailor whose first wife Elizabeth (a cook at Edwinsford Mansion) also worked in the shop and died during the 1870s. John then remarried and his second wife Kezia (d1931) assisted him. When he died Kezia continued the business as the postmistress, draper and milliner with her young family helped by a much younger shop assistant, Alfred Daniel Townsend (d1912), who came from Bristol and also served at one stage as one of the valets in Edwinsford Mansion. By 1901 they had married and moved up the road to the purpose-built Pretoria House[574], which had been erected on the site of the former old Cross Inn thatched cottages demolished in about 1897. Alfred was clerk to the Parish Council and chief clerk in the Cawdor Estate office for many years. Kezia continued with their business of post office and shop[575] and two of her sons, Luther and John, were living with them. The so-called Townsend Stores also had petrol pumps and had just the right location for a thriving trade. Luther Jones was a shoemaker and worked with James Davies at Aelybryn next to the Crown Inn. His brother Sydney Gordon (John) Jones, known to all as Jack Post, had been a packer with Lewis Lewis in Swansea and had to return home because of ill health; he took over the business at Pretoria House when his mother died at a ripe old age a much loved and respected lady. Jack was the first person in the village to have a car, a black First Ford Type with a canvas top supported by tubular steel; Brenda James recounts that on one occasion the car left the road, turned over three times and landed upside down on its canvas top with all the passengers escaping without serious injury. On Sundays Jack would take the elderly vicar, Rev John Long Price, in his wheelchair to church with his dog Lavender. The family ran a taxi service during the 1930s. Jack's son, Devonald, and his wife Rowena inherited and ran the business; Devonald served in the RAF throughout WW2. Devonald and Rowena retired as postmaster and postmistress in 1983 (after 21 years' service) and in 1986 (with 18 years's service) respectively and were presented with Post Office long service certificates; the post office was then transferred to a room in the Edwinsford Arms across the road which was run by a Mr and Mrs Fletcher. Rowena later moved into a home.

In 2014 the house was bought by David Ince, who lives on the edge of the village down the lane opposite Esgairnant Chapel and he renovated it before letting it to tenants.

572 David Lewis: *Dolaucothi and Brunant p205.* Pretoria Cottage on the Dolaucothi Estate was also renamed accordingly

573 Wyn Edwards: *Y Llychau (Nov 2016) and https://journals.library.wales/view/2919943/3003931/19*

574 The Edwinsford Estate accounts for 1903 (see Chapter 16.8) still referred to this property as the Old Cross Inn

575 Brenda James p44-5

Pretoria 2017

Post Office c1900

Cross Inn Cottage

Cross Inn Cottage beyond Pretoria House, also part of the Edwinsford Estate, was home to many tenants over the decades including a Mr Baggott[576] who took groups to the seaside in his lorry before the LCW Motors bus service started; the seats were wooden and hard and must have been very uncomfortable. Evans the saddler also lived there. Ebenezer Davies, son of Thomas and Elizabeth Davies[577], who lived there enlisted in WW1 and joined 15th Battalion of the Welsh Regiment (Carmarthen Pals) in 1916 which had famously captured Mametz Wood in July 1916 at great cost; he was wounded near Ypres and died of his wounds on 20 February 1917 aged 38. He is buried at Mendinghem Military Cemetery in Belgium and remembered on the war memorial in Talley Churchyard. Peggy and John Williams have been the most recent owners.

Pretoria corner 2017

Painting of the Cross Inn, Cross Inn Cottage, Abbey View and the Edwinsford Arms c1890

---

576 Brenda James p17

577 Pat Edwards and Talley History Group: *Y Llychau*

24.11 Abbey View [SN 636327]

YEAR	ABBEY VIEW TALLEY CENSUS RETURNS
1871	**EVANS: Dafydd** (28) teacher born Talley, Jane (28) wife, Henry Fulford (50) lodger gamekeeper, Richard Fulford (26) draper's assis
1881	**EVANS: Dafydd** (38) elementary schoolteacher, Jane (38) wife, David (3) son, William (11 mon) son, Elizabeth Gwynne (58) lodger former cook
1891	**EVANS: Dafydd** (48) schoolmaster, David (13) son, William (10) son, Mary Jones (21) ser
1901	**THOMAS: William** (36) schoolmaster, Margaret (31) wife, Margaret (6) dau, Elizabeth (4) dau, Evan (3) son
1911	**THOMAS: William** (46) elementary school teacher born Llanboidy, Margaret (41) wife, Margaret (16) dau, Elizabeth (14) dau, Evan (13) son, David (6) son, John (3) son

Abbey View is located next to Cross Inn Cottage opposite the Edwinsford Arms across the road. It was part of the Edwinsford Estate and the home of the village schoolmaster for many years. Following the Thomas family the tenancy went to the Williams family[578]. Richard Williams was a carpenter and cabinet maker, son of Thomas Williams an elder at Esgairnant Chapel. Richard moved to work in London and Cardiff before joining the army in 1914. He was badly wounded at the Somme and invalided home; in the 1930s he was an instructor at Treglog Camps for the unemployed near Llansawel. Richard married Mary and had two daughters, Gwladys and Doris Williams, and one son Basil. Doris married Albert Lewis of Manchester, a schoolmaster in Hereford and after his death, Doris returned to Abbey View.

Carol and Peter Jones were the next owners for about 12 years (1995-2007) before they moved to Llandeilo. Then in 2007 John Rees and Dawn Masters bought the house; it has an extension behind, a lovely well kept garden and vegetable plot, and an impressive view of the Abbey by the lake across the fields behind, hence the name of the property.

Abbey View (right) and Edwinsford Arms (left) 2017

[578] Brenda James p43-4

24.12 Edwinsford Arms [SN636327]

Edwinsford Arms c 1900

Edwinsford Arms 2017

The Edwinsford Arms was built around 1830 as an inn with stables, barns and farmland to cater for travellers; it was part of the Edwinsford Estate across the road from Abbey View and Cross Inn Cottage. It is listed and described as an imposing Regency inn with neo-classical allusions. A similar building is marked but not labelled in the same location on the 1838 Tithe map (and some consider this was the old Cross Inn) but confusingly[579] on other old maps is shown separately. My guess is that the old Cross Inn was in the thatched cottages on the corner and later demolished for the new Pretoria House whilst the Edwinsford Arms remained as now on the other side of the road, all on Edwinsford Estate land. The property also included a small farm.

Next to it in a field called *Mynwent Capel Crist* (Christ's chapel graveyard) there used to be a burial place[580] and small chapel linked to the Abbey and also an adjacent well with the same name.

The Davies family were tenant innkeepers there for over 40 years before Henry Micklewright from Clovelly arrived in about 1880 to take over the licence; he was obviously well known to the Edwinsford family who presumably asked him to move there from Devon and he may have been the son of John Micklewright, the butler at Clovelly Court in 1861 (see Chapter 19.3). The inn was used by the agent of the Edwinsford Estate to entertain the tenants and as we have seen from Chapter 1.1 was used for hosting dinners to thank local tenants and residents when members of the Edwinsford family attained their majority or married. It was also a popular meeting place for local societies (eg the Talley Agricultural Society[581]) and for the local hunts which would often meet in the road outside (see Chapter 15.3). In the late 1880s John and Elizabeth Griffiths from Alma Cottage (see Chapter 24.13) took on the tenancy and after their mother died in 1898, the son David (d1957) and his two sisters Margaret (d1929)

---

579 Dyfed Archaeological Trust historic environmental record

580 Royal Commission: *An Inventory of the Ancient Monuments in Wales and Monmouthshire (1917) p264;* Brenda James p5

581 Carmarthen Weekly Reporter (27 May 1907)

YEAR	EDWINSFORD ARMS TALLEY CENSUS RETURNS
1841	**DAVIES: David** (26) innkeeper, Anne (46), Rachel (20), Anne (12), John Evans (10), Thomas Evans (8)
1851	**DAVIES: John** (57) inn keeper and farmer of 60 acres born Conwil Gaeo, Jane (53) wife with 4 children, 3 serv, 1 visitor
1861	**DAVIES: John** (61) innkeeper farmer auctioneer and registrar of births deaths and marriages for Talley, Jane (64) wife, Daniel (22) son, plus 3 serv
1871	**DAVIES: John** (71) innkeeper farmer and auctioneer born Conwil Gaeo, Jane (74) wife, David (41) son accountant, James Lewis (49) visitor auctioneer and 2 ser
1881	**MICKLEWRIGHT: Henry Arthur** (31) innkeeper born Clovelly, Harriet (35) wife, Elizabeth Westell (20) niece housemaid
1891	**GRIFFITHS: Elizabeth** (52) innkeeper, Margaret (23) dau, Agnes (22) dau, David (15) son, Rosabella (8) dau, Emma Rees (56) boarder
1901	**GRIFFITHS: David** (25) licensed victualler, Margaret (33) sis, Sarah (32) sis
1911	**GRIFFITHS: David** (35) law student born Talley, Margaret (42) sis hotelkeeper, Sarah (41) sis, Edwin Philipps (36) visitor teacher

and Sarah (d1938) ran the inn with an old war veteran running the farm for them.

David Ellis Thomas[582] remembers growing up there in the early part of the 20th century with creeping stretching shadows and candles in his back bedroom before electricity arrived, dreaming of ghost monks from the ruined Abbey, and seeing out of his window two men pulling the carcass of a cow with five legs which frightened the family. The room next to the bar was called the Squire's Room because people from Edwinsford Mansion and sometimes the Long Prices too would use it and when they were seen all the residents would hold their hats in their hands to show respect.

In 1988 Gary Williams (b1935) and his wife Diane (b1948) and the General Manager Stewart Williams (b1962) took over the pub. In 1989 planning consent was granted to convert the pub into a residential dwelling and they planned to refurbish and extend it to provide a 20 bedroom hotel with a recreation and leisure club open to local residents including a gym and swimming pool. However this never happened. In about 2001 the property was bought by a Mr Brown who left it to his two sons; they transferred the licence from the inn to a barn behind and changed the user of the inn to residential. The barn was then used as a restaurant. In 2008 a planning application was made by the Brown brothers to redevelop the site by converting the house from a residential dwelling back to a pub, converting the restaurant behind the house back into two houses, and building seven houses on the carpark. These plans were strongly opposed by the residents despite being recommended by the planners (subject to the owners financially supporting a local playing area and local education services). Again these plans never came to fruition. The house was by now in some disrepair and the barn and former restaurant have been for sale for many years. In 2015 Lloyd Gregory (a builder) and his wife Emily Ashdown (a paediatric medic) bought the listed house and are restoring it as their home.

The Edwinsford Arms is featured on a giant Millenium Tapestry which took three years to complete; it measures 5ft x 4ft and was created by 13 local stitchers to commemorate the new 21st century. It hangs in St Michael's Church in Talley.

[582] David Ellis Thomas: *Y Llychau*

24.13 Blaenug Issa Forge (leading lower forge) [SN639327]

Blaenug Issa mid 20th century

2017

YEAR	BLAENUG ISSA FORGE TALLEY CENSUS RETURNS
1841	**LEWIS: Thomas** (80) blacksmith, Mary (70) wife, John Davies (20) blacksmith
1851	**GRIFFITHS: William** (38) blacksmith, Elinor (38) wife with 6 children
1861	**GRIFFITHS: William** (49) blacksmith born Llanybyther, Elinor (49) wife, Eliza (23) dau dressmaker, David (20) son blacksmith, Mary (17) dau dressmaker, Elinor (14) dau, Peter (7) son
1871	**GRIFFITHS: William** (59) general blacksmith and farmer of 7 acres, Eleanor (58) wife, Peter (16) son law clerk, Margaret (22) dau dressmaker, Eleanor (19) dau dressmaker, Jonathan Williams (20) general smith
1881	**GRIFFITHS: William** (69) blacksmith, Eleanor (68) wife, Eleanor (29) dau dressmaker, Peter (27) son solicitor's clerk, Thomas (15) grandson blacksmith journeyman
1891	**GRIFFITHS: William** (78) blacksmith born Abergorlech, Margaret (41) dau, Peter (37) son solicitor's clerk, Mary (12) granddau
1901	No entry
1911	**GRIFFITHS: Morgan (38)** blacksmith born Llandebie, Margaret (39) wife

Blacksmiths were major contributors to the rural economy. They made the essential handtools which all farmers needed before the tractor and mechanisation arrived. They made scythes, sickles, billhooks, spades, shovels and hand shears as well as much larger implements such as ploughs, harrows, carts and gamboes. They shod the working horses (and the oxen and cattle who used to do the ploughing before them) and they shod for the drovers on their way to the marts in England. Many did the work of farriers, coopers, saddlers and wheelwrights. Every village used to have its own blacksmith with the noise of the anvil hammering and the forge heard by all, but most blacksmiths were unable to compete with mechanisation and disappeared after the Great War.

Blaenug (Blaenig) Issa is located about 150 yards along the road from the Edwinsford Arms bend towards Llandeilo. It is an early 19th century single storey rubble built former forge with a slate roof. Next to it is a former single storey cart house of similar age. Before WW2 there were no other houses between the Edwinsford Arms and these buildings. Both buildings were part of the Edwinsford Estate and are now listed.

As we saw in Chapter 14.11, Thomas (Tomos) Lewis (1759-1842)[583] was apprenticed as a smithy to the Thomas family at Moelfryn Forge on the Edwinsford Estate for over two years. He had been born in Cwm Cynwal near Hafod Bridge on the Lampeter to Llanwrda road, lost his father when he was only 13 and then helped his mother on the farm. He worked at Moelfryn and then moved to set up his own business in Talley in about 1801 although we do not know in which building initially; it was only later that he moved to Blaenug Issa next to the stream which was needed for his work. His first wife was a maid at Edwinsford Mansion. He was a strong character, morally and physically, tall (6ft 3ins), a hard worker and good craftsman and also became a specialist on clocks and sometimes a dentist as well as a herbalist. He was a strong believer in education and life-long learning, studied Latin and Greek, was a strong supporter of Methodism and played an important role as an elder at Esgairnant Chapel nearby. He will always be remembered for his hymn writing including his famous and immortal hymns *Wrth gofio'i riddfannau'n yr ardd* and *Caed ffynnon o ddŵr ac o waed* which are sung in hundreds of Welsh services. Apparently he destroyed all his compositions thinking they were valueless and it was Richard Thomas, one of his deacons, who remembered them and wrote then down for posterity. He died in Talley on 14 September 1842 aged 83 and was buried in the parish churchyard; his second wife Mary Howell died on 2 March 1860 aged 90 and is also buried there.

583 J Morris: *Hanes Methodistiaeth Sir Caerfyrddin (1911) p257;* DG Griffiths: *Centenary of Thomas Lewis CA (1942) Vol 1 p15-9*; Fred Price: *Talley p32*; T Griffiths, Alun Morgan, Sharon Meek and Pat Edwards: *Y Llychau*

In the 1840s Griffiths Williams, a smithy from Llansadwrn and believed to be a son in law or other relative of Thomas Lewis, had three sons and the eldest came to work with Thomas in Talley and thought of the old man as his grandfather. He was known as William (Wil) Griffiths according to the old Welsh tradition of adopting the first name of one's father as one's surname. Wil had lived at Yr Hen Efail, Cefnblaidd but then moved to live at Blaenug Issa and took over the forge for the next 50 years with his wife Eleanor (Elinor) and their eight children: (1) Thomas (b1836) married Eizabeth George of Llansawel and later took over Penny Forge as the blacksmith; (2) Elizabeth (1838-98) married John Griffiths a farmer of Talley and they lived at Alma Cottage before moving to the Edwinsford Arms, which their children took over on Elizabeth's death in 1898; (3) William (b1839) a corn merchant married Mary Griffiths of Cwmdu and they lived at Ivy Cottage; (4) David (b1841) married Margaret Rees of Llandebie and they set up a smithy in Llandebie where they lived; (5) Mary (b1844) married David Phillips of Talley a relieving officer and they lived at Langwm; (6) Margaret (b1848) died young; (7) Eleanor (b1850) married David Morgan and took over the Crown Inn (see Chapter 24.15); and (8) Peter (1855-91) who was a law clerk.

Wil Griffiths' grandson, Morgan Griffiths, took over the forge and was the last smithy to work at Blaenug; he can be seen boarding nearby at Blaenug farm in the 1901 census before he married. He retired in the 1950s. He and his wife Rachel had two sons, Llewelyn and Thomas, and one daughter Mair. Morgan Gof, as he was called, attended Esgairnant Chapel like his forbears. The dwelling nextdoor has been modernised and was owned by Thomas Lewis Griffiths, great great grandson of the hymnwriter; Thomas served in the Royal Navy during WW2 and was awarded the DSM for gallantry.

Gravestone of Thomas and Mary Lewis in Talley Churchyard

24.14 Blaenug (leading) [SN639327]

YEAR	BLAENUG TALLEY CENSUS RETURNS
1841	**THOMAS: James** (45) auctioneer, Sarah (45) wife, Mary (25), John (15), Han (13), 1 ser
1851	**(1) THOMAS: John** (25) farmer, Anne (26) wife with 2 children, 2 serv **(2) WALTERS: J** (35) lead miner, Mary (34) wife, son (10)
1861	**THOMAS: John** (34) farmer born Talley, Anne (35) wife, David (12) son, Rachel (10) dau, Thomas (6) son, Sarah (1) dau, Joseph (60) father in law, and 2 serv
1871	**THOMAS: John** (45) farmer of 40 acres, Anne (45) wife, Rachel (19) dau, Thomas (15) son, Sarah (11) dau, Elizabeth (7) dau, Mary (2) dau
1881	**THOMAS: John** (55) farmer of 55 acres, Anne (56) wife, Sarah (23) dau, Elizabeth (18) dau, Mary (12) dau
1891	**THOMAS: John** (64) farmer, Anne (65) wife, Elizabeth (27) dau, Mary (22) dau, Joseph (99) father in law retired farmer
1901	**THOMAS: John** (74) farmer born Talley, Elizabeth (37) dau, Mary (32) dau, John Evans (26) farm ser, Morgan Griffiths (28) boarder blacksmith
1911	**THOMAS: Elizabeth** (47) agriculture born Talley, Mary Thomas (42), John Evans (32) ser

Blaenug (Blaenig) is a farm up a lane behind Blaenug Issa and was part of the Edwinsford Estate. As can be seen from the census returns the Thomas family were tenants for many decades. As we saw in Chapter 9.3, in 1805 David Thomas was the bailiff of the Edwinsford Estate living in Blaenug. In 1902 when Charles Caryl Clifton, son of Lady Madeline Williams-Drummond (67), returned from the Boer War, John Thomas (aged 75) living at Blaenug being the oldest tenant on the Edwinsford Estate was given the honour of presenting the address to him from all the local tenants and residents and welcoming him home.

Blaenug 2017

24.15 Crown Inn (Ardwyn (on a hill) or Old Inn) [SN 640325]

YEAR	CROWN INN TALLEY CENSUS RETURNS
1841	**DAVIES: William** (29) innkeeper, Mary (30) wife, Lewis Davies (4), Margaret Price (20) ser
1851	**JONES: Evan** (35) victualler, Sarah (24) wife, Eleanor (40 dau, David (1) son, Jane mother
1861	**JONES: Evan** (44) lead miner and innkeeper, Sarah (35) wife and 3 children
1871	**JONES: Evan** (55) innkeeper born Talley, Sarah (47) wife and 3 children
1881	**LEWIS: David** (31) innkeeper born Llangathen, Mary (26) wife, John (4) son, Jane (1 mon) dau
1891	**MORGAN: David** (38) innkeeper, Eleanor (40) wife, Eleanor (4) dau
1901	**MORGAN: Eleanor** (49) innkeeper, Eleanor (14) dau, Janet Williams (20) boarder school teacher
1911	**MORGAN: Eleanor** (60) licensed victualler born Talley, Eleanor (24) dau

Ardwyn 2017

This building is located after Talley School on the road out of Talley towards Llandeilo; it is adjacent to Aelybryn, the old shoemaker's house and home of James Davies. It was one of the four inns in Talley for many decades, all now closed. It had several innkeepers as can be seen from the census returns. Eleanor Morgan shown in the 1891-1911 census returns and married to David Morgan was the daughter of Will and Eleanor Griffiths of Blaenug Issa Forge nearby.

Morgan Morgans, who lived there in the late 19th century, served in WW1 and afterwards became the headmaster of Talley school from 1920 to 1950. His son Glyn served during WW2 but suffered serious illness whilst in the Middle East.

Later the house was renamed "Ardwyn". More recently Peter Griffiths, a pharmacist and nurse, and his wife bought it in about 1998 and renamed it "Old Inn". Since their separation Peter has lived there alone.

Across the road by the junction is Bancelwydd farm and opposite at the junction of the road to Llansadwrn there used to be a small grocer's shop where an old lady called Anne sold sweets.

Aelybryn

Daniel Davies (d1909) of Tŷ Ann Arthur was a successful builder with a workshop on Water Street who built Aelybryn for £275. Aelybryn was bought by James Davies, a cousin of the family at Tŷ Ann Arthur, who kept a cobbler's shop there with his son for many years. His son Jack (known as Jack Jim) was the first owner of a motorbike in the village and he ran a Raleigh bicycle agency from his shop. Jack's son, Stanley, took over the business but later decided to become the manager of the Llansawel Co-op. Stanley's sister, Betty, emigrated to Melbourne.

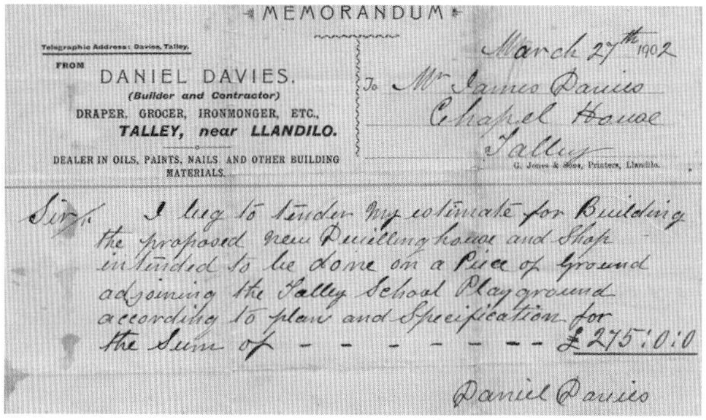

MEMORANDUM

Telegraphic Address: Davies, Talley.

FROM DANIEL DAVIES.
(Builder and Contractor)
DRAPER, GROCER, IRONMONGER, ETC.,
TALLEY, near LLANDILO.
DEALER IN OILS, PAINTS, NAILS AND OTHER BUILDING MATERIALS.

March 27th 1902

To Mr James Davies
Chapel House
Talley

G. Jones & Son, Printers, Llandilo.

Sir, I beg to tender my estimate for Building the proposed new Dwelling house and Shop intended to be done on a Piece of Ground adjoining the Talley School Playground according to plan and Specification for the Sum of - - - - - - - £275:0:0

Daniel Davies

Daniel Davies' estimate 1902

24.16 Bolahaul (Fronhaul) (hillside of the sun) [SN657326]

YEAR	BOLAHAUL CENSUS RETURNS
1841	**EDWARDS: John** (31) farmer, Anne (33) wife, William (3) son, Elizabeth (1) dau, 3 ser agric labourers
1851	No entry
1861	**RICHARDS: John** (31) widower farmer born Talley, Mary (27) sis housekeeper, Ebenezer (15) bro with 2 ser
1871	**RICHARDS: John** (40) farmer of 174 acres born Talley, Mary (37) wife, with 6 children and 2 ser
1881	**THOMAS: David** (32) farmer with 147 acres, Margaret (33) wife, Evan (1) son and 3 servants
1891	**THOMAS: David** (42) farmer born Llansadwrn, Margaret (45) wife, Evan (11) son, Thomas (8) son, Jane (4) dau, Anne (3) dau, David (1) son, John Williams (20) ser, Mary Davies (19) ser, Jane Davies (14) ser
1901	**THOMAS: Thomas** (18) farmer born Talley, Jane (14) sis, David (11) bro, Maria Davies (33) dom ser, Albert Welch (16) ser
1911	**DAVIES: Evan** (41) farmer born Llansadwrn, Margaret (42) wife, Phillip (8) son, Elizabeth (7) dau, Annie Maud (5) dau, David (1) son, William Davies (22) servant waggoner

This farm is located on the backroad from Talley to Llansadwrn. It was part of the Edwinsford Estate as can be seen in Chapter 16.5 and the farm of 142 acres (with the tenant Evan Davies in occupation at an annual rent of £77.10s) was sold by the estate at the 1919 auction; it is described then as "a dwelling house with parlour, kitchen, backroom, dairy and four bedrooms with outbuildings of a cart house with store overhead, stable and two stalls and two loose boxes, cowshed for 15 cowties and two food walks, young cattleshed, two calf cribs with servants bedroom over. All Carnarvon slated. Barn and pigstyes with corrugated iron roofs."

Daniel Evans[584] and his brother Jack of Bolahaul served in the army during WW1. Daniel fought at the Somme in 1916 and was awarded the Military Medal. He also served in the Royal Observer Corps during WW2. David Rogers, who later farmed at Bolahaul, also served in the army in France during WW1. During WW2 evacuee children used to visit Jack Bolahaul to have their hair cut. One evacuee[585] remembers sitting on a chair in the kitchen one summer day when a huge rat scurried past the open door. Jack stopped, fetched his shotgun, waited for the rat to return and then shot it.

The property was bought by Albert Williams' father and was let to Mr and Mrs Furminger; later it was left empty for a while until Albert and Glynis Williams swapped their home with their son Lyn.

Cliff and Georgina Williams bought the farm in 2013. Cliff is a farmer and builder and is also the Huntsman of the Cwrtycadno Hunt (see Chapter 15.3); we see him making his daily trip to the hounds near Pumsaint with his white terrier in his pickup who keeps the hounds in order. Georgina has horses for dressage and is an equine chiropractor.

Fronhaul 2017

[584] Pat Edwards and Talley History Group: *Y Llychau*
[585] Geoffrey Whitlock: *Y Llychau*

25. Village of Llansawel

As we saw in Chapter 1.3, originally Llansawel was in the lower division of the hundred of Caeo comprising the hamlets of Edwin's with Glynn, and Wen with Ganol[586]. The name Llansawel or Llansawyl is probably derived from the 6th century St Sawl or Sawyl, an early form of Samuel. Sawyl Benuchel, the brother of Dunawd or Dunod Fyr and Cerwydd, was the son of Pabo Post Prydyn and a Welsh chieftain. He married Gwenasedd, daughter of Rhain Rhieinwg, by whom he became the father of the famous St Asaph (d596). St Sawyl is the Patron Saint of Llansawel. The Parish Church of Llansawel, St Sawyls, seems always to have been ecclesiastically attached to St Cynwyl's Church in Caio village in Cynwyl Gaeo.

Before the late 19th century Llansawel was an active market town with drovers driving their cattle, pigs, sheep and other animals through on their way to the markets in England. There were at one time eight public houses or inns and, as can be seen from the census returns, residents included blacksmiths, corn millers, dressmakers, doctors, grocers, a postmaster, police officers, tailors, carpenters, shoemakers, wheelwrights, waggoners, charwomen, labourers, schoolteachers, and maidservants etc. In 1801 the population[587] of the parish numbered 731, in 1811 (849), in 1821 (919), in 1831 (1024); in 1841 (983); in 1851 (1,051); in 1861 (1003), in 1871 (883), in 1881 (944); and in 1891 (898). During the 20th century the population halved as farms could no longer afford to employ workers and servants, the Edwinsford Estate was divided and sold off, and youngsters left to work in the cities thus reducing the population in 2001 (413); and in 2011 (438) of whom 47.9% could speak Welsh.

On 25 July 1688 by Letters Patent[588] King James II granted Sir Rice Williams (45) the right to hold a Market in Llansawel "every Friday in every week through the year forever" and two Fairs or Holydays in Llansawel on 15 July and 12 October annually.

These dates were later altered and thereafter fairs were traditionally held in Llansawel on the first Friday after 12 May, on 15 July, on 23 October and on the first Friday after 12 November, but these have long been discontinued. Since about the 1920s the village has held its own Annual Show usually in the second week in September; for some years it was held on Beili Ficer Farm land (near to where the clay pigeon shooting takes place) but in recent years it has been held on the Castle Green field and later in the Village Hall and the field behind Penybont.

As with other local parishes the percentage of residents attending a church or chapel today has decreased very markedly compared with a century ago, the local school has recently had to close, and only two of the original public houses are still open for business. However the local community remains vibrant and the Llansawel Village Hall, which was built in 1957 is well used for various activities by a number of community groups thanks to the voluntary work of a few public spirited residents.

Llansawel map c1840

---

586 S Lewis: *A Topographical Dictionary of Wales (1844);* Fred Price: *History of Llansawel p15-18;* Sabine Baring-Gould*: Lives of British Saints*

587 www.histpop.org

588 NLW Edwinsford Estate archives

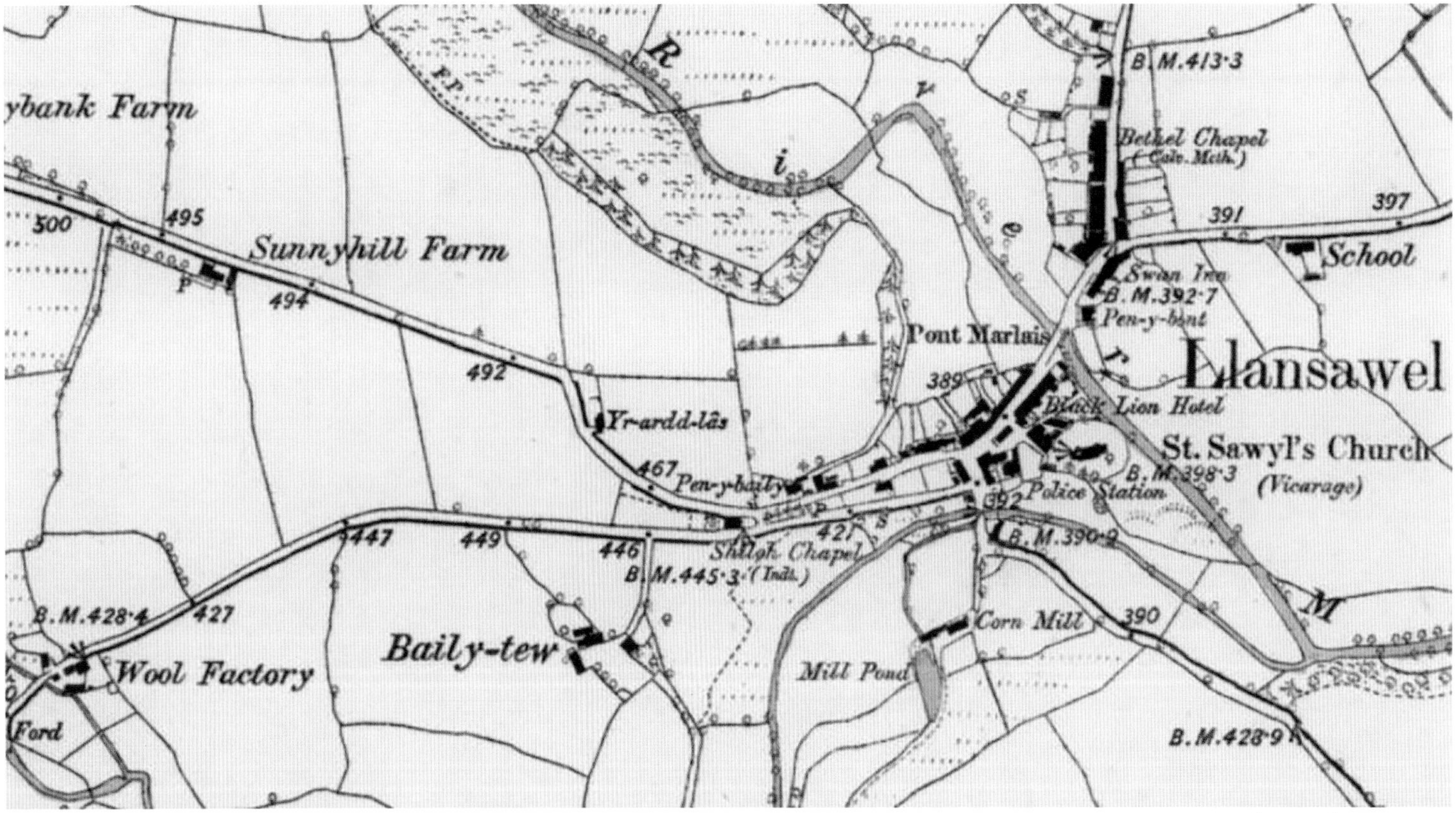

Llansawel map c1886

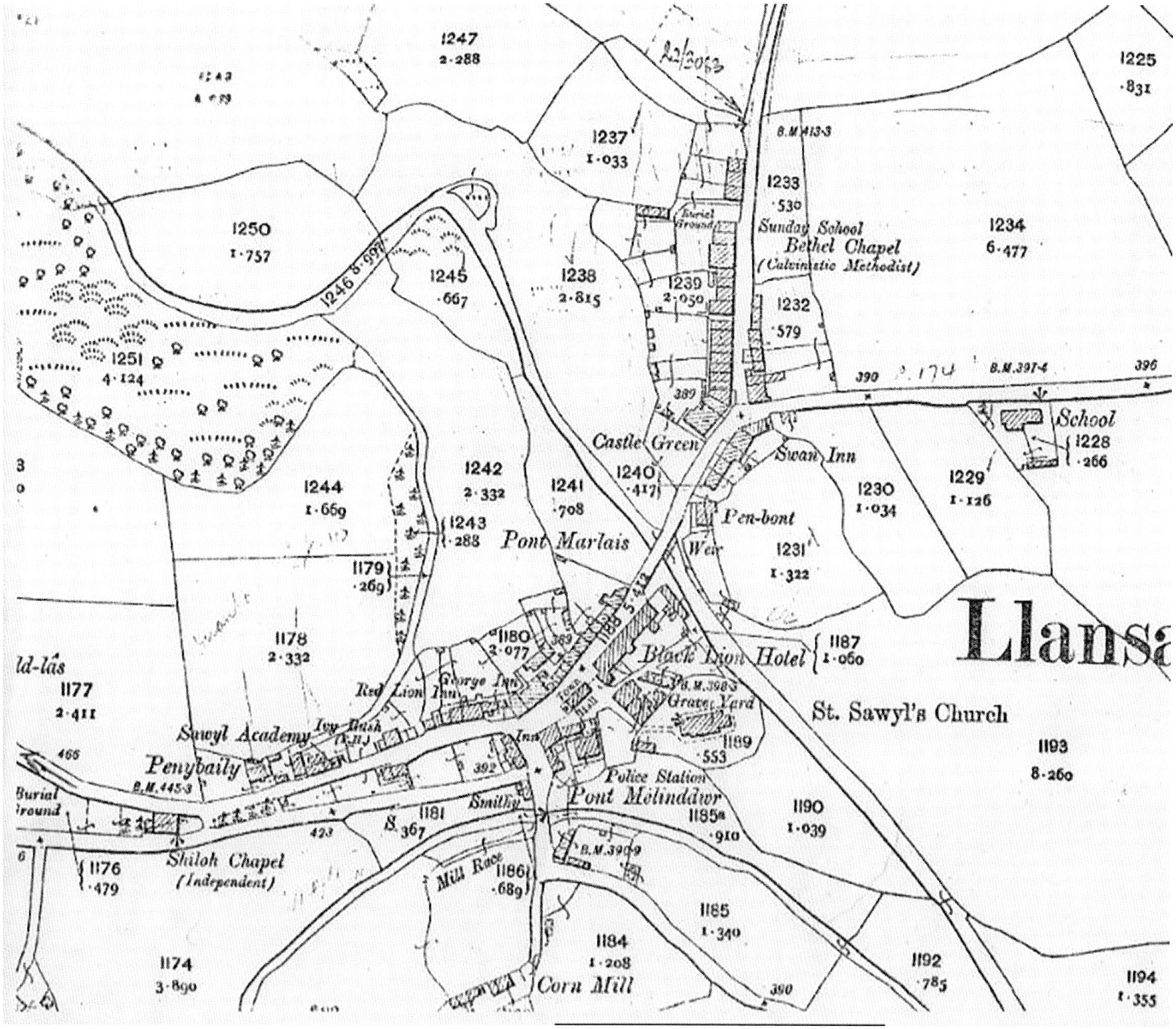

Llansawel map c1920

Melinddwr river bridge 2017

Marlais river bridge 2017

Village Hall 2017

19th century

19th century

c1900

26. Selected Llansawel Properties

As can be seen from Chapters 16.5 to 16.10, the Edwinsford Estate owned several properties in the parish of Llansawel for generations; some were sold in 1918-19 and the rest in the 1970s when the estate was divided up. The following properties include some which were owned by the estate.

26.1 Ffynnongrech (undulating or wavy spring) [SN643345]

This farm which used to be in the parish of Talley and is now in the parish of Llansawel is located up a lane near the turning to Edwinsford off the Crugybar to Llandeilo road.

It was owned by the Edwinsford Estate. In about 1641 when he attained his majority, Thomas Williams (44) inherited this and other farms from his father's estate under the "Borough English" tenure system applicable in Talley whereby the youngest son inherited. At a Court Baron of the Manor of Talley (see Chapter 35.1) held on 26 June 1736 the property, then copyhold, was surrendered by Lloyd Williams Esq of Talley for a fine of seven shillings to the Lord of the Manor (the Crown) and consent was granted by the Steward, Sir Nicholas Williams, and the jurors who signed signifying their consent.

In the 1813 Edwinsford Estate accounts the tenant was John Parry, who is also listed in the 1841 and 1851 census returns and in the 1841 Tithe Apportionment Agreement as the farmer of 79 acres. David Davies took on the tenancy in the 1850s; he married Elizabeth who died young leaving three sons, William, Thomas and David. He then married[589] Margaret Rees (née Jones) who had been widowed aged 36 on the death of her husband Evan Rees; of her children Peter was a

Ffynnongrech 2017

[589] Rita Butler: *Y Llychau (March 2010)*

YEAR	FFYNNONGRECH CENSUS RETURNS
1841	**PARRY: John** (55) farmer, Ann (22) dau, Elizabeth (17) dau, 2 serv
1851	**PARRY: John** (67) farmer of 76 acres born Talley, David Davies (31) son in law, Elizabeth (24) dau, Mary (3) granddau, John (1) grandson, 3 serv
1861	**DAVIES: David** (43) farmer born Pencarreg, Elizabeth (39) wife with 5 children, 4 ser
1871	**DAVIES: David** (54) farmer of 50 acres, Margaret (45) wife, William (14) son, Thomas (11) son, David (9) son, Mary Rees (13) stepdau, Joshua Rees (11) stepson and 2 ser
1881	**DAVIES: David** (63) farmer of 99 acres born Pencarreg, Margaret (54) wife, David (18) son, Mary Rees (23) stepdau, David Thomas (18) ser
1891	**DAVIES: David** (75) farmer, Margaret (65) wife, Mary (34) dau, David (28) son, Rees Williams (19) ser, Elizabeth Evans (18) ser
1901	**DAVIES: David** (38) farmer born Talley, Mary Rees (43) sis, Eliza Evans (19) serv, John Williams (16) ser
1911	No entry

tailor who was apprenticed locally before going to London and having a successful career in that trade, and Mary and Joshua lived with them at Ffynnongrech. Mary later ran the farm with her half brother David Davies and two servants as evidenced in the 1901 census return. Eleanor Davies is shown as the tenant in the 1903 estate accounts; she might have been the wife of David Davies the son.

I suspect that the farm was sold by the Edwinsford Estate in the 1970s. In the 1990s the farm was owned by June and Sid Heaton with their daughter Loraine and her husband Mike Makowski. They reared goats and produced confectionery and milk products for people who are intolerant to cows' milk under the brand "Kid Me Not". They ran the farm for about 10 years and then sold it in late 2013 and went to Norfolk. The new owners, Suzy and Michael Cushing, had a flock of sheep on their 50 acres and Suzy has horses for dressage. They converted one of the old barns into three flats which they let. Michael sadly died and Suzy continues with her sheep and horses.

26.2 Porth Factory (Tegfan) [SN613362]

Old Porth Factory 2017

This wool factory was located to the west of Llansawel on the Abergorlech road and was part of the Edwinsford Estate as was its neighbouring Baileytew farm and indeed most of the farms between Llansawel and Abergorlech. Porth means a gateway and at one time there used to be a toll gateway on the road by the river. The old woollen mill still stands and, although the waterwheel no longer survives, the leat which ran from the river past the mill can still be seen. The newer house behind is called Tegfan. The smallholding has been used as a dog and cat kennels for more than 25 years; the old mill building is now used as an office and storage shed. Its local family history is most unusual.

Despite Llansawel being a hotbed of Methodism in the 19th century no fewer than 41 clergy were produced by its families, who were mainly brought up as Welsh speaking non-conformists and yet were ordained into the Anglican Church. The Davies family of Porth Factory produced 10 of these priests.

YEAR	PORTH FACTORY LLANSAWEL CENSUS RETURNS
1841	**DAVIES: Thomas** (25) wool carder, Eleanor (25) wife, Thomas (3) son, Martha (1) dau, Elizabeth Jones (10)
1851	**DAVIES: Thomas** (39) carder and spinner of wool born Cilycwm, Eleanor (37) wife with 5 children, David Rees (24) journeyman carder, 2 ser
1861	**DAVIES: Thomas** (50) wool carder, Eleanor (47) wife with 8 children, David Evans (20) wool spinner, Thomas Jones (15) wool carder
1871	**DAVIES: Thomas** (61) wool manufacturer, Eleanor (57) wife with 3 children and 1 ser
1881	**DAVIES: Eleanor** (67) wool spinner, Eleanor (29) dau spinner, Mary (25) dau maid
1891	**JONES: Joseph** (36) wool manufacturer and cabinet maker, Eleanor (39) wife, Anne Jones (21) ser
1901	**JONES: Joseph** (46) woollen manufacturer born Llansawel, Eleanor (49) wife, Eleanor (9) dau, Thomas Owens (57) wool skinner, Anne Evans (30) ser
1911	**JONES: Joseph** (56) woollen manufacturer, Eleanor (59) wife, Eleanor (19) dau

As can be seen from the census returns the Davies family were wool carders[590]. Thomas Davies (1812-73) and his wife Eleanor Davies (1814-91) were pillars of the local Bethel Methodist Chapel in Llansawel (see Chapter 29.4). Thomas was born in Cilycwm, the son of David (b1777) and Rhucama Davies of Cwmrhaiad. Eleanor was born in Pencarreg and they were married on 23 May 1837 in Pencarreg Parish Church. They had nine surviving children all of whom attended Bethel Methodist Chapel yet four of their sons were ordained as priests[591] in the Church of England (who have become known as "the four apostles of Llansawel"):

(1) Rev Thomas Davies (1838-1914) born in Abermangoed[592] near Cwrt y Cadno, studied at Froodvale Academy and St David's College Lampeter, and then served as curate at Ystradgynlais before getting a living as vicar in 1868 at Bettws Evan Newcastle Emlyn, then at Llangen Whitland for 23 years and finally at Troedyraur in 1905;

(2) Rev Evan Alltud Davies (1842-1910) born in Llansawel after the family had moved there in 1841, became a schoolmaster at Gwauncaegurwen for three years before starting his career in the Anglican Church, becoming a deacon in 1870 and a priest in 1872 as a "literate" (meaning a priest who had attended neither a university nor a theological college) in the Swansea area then becoming a vicar in Llangennech followed by Cwmamman (Garnant) in the Amman valley. He married Bridget Roderick (1842-86) by whom he had eight children and then Isabella Cashbourne (1841-1909). His generosity included giving food and clothes to tramps and gypsies;

(3) Rev Daniel Sawelian Davies (1847-1911) was educated as St Bees' College Cumberland (which offered a two year cheaper theological course), became a deacon in 1878 and a priest in 1880, served as a curate in Llandyssul then moved to Llanybri near Ferryside where he stayed from 1904 until his death. Two of his sons followed him into the ministry: (a) Rev Latimer Davies (b1883) who was rector of Oxwich (1918-24) and then of Ilston in the Gower (1924-55), and (b) Rev Charles Davies (1886) who was educated at St David's Lampeter, then served as curate at Llanddewi Ystradenny (1917-25), vicar at Garth in Breconshire (1925-44) and vicar at Vaynor (1944-50);

(4) Rev John Davies (1854-1922) baptised as a methodist and then rebaptised by his elder brother in 1876 at Llangan church. He served as deacon in 1877 but failed his exams and did not become a priest until 1882, later becoming a vicar at Llanilltyd (1884-1903) and then at Vaynor;

(5) Martha Davies (1840-1904) is described on her grave at Bethel Chapel "she opened her hand to the poor and stretched forth hands to the needy". Lady Madeline Williams-Drummond (67) used to ask her to make Sunday dinners for the local poor and pay her to do so.

590 Dr Roger Brown: *The Followers of Jeroboam The Son of Nebat—A Study of the Clerical Members of the Davies-Williams Family of Llansawel (1983).* I am grateful to Dr Brown for providing me with this private publication

591 James Morris: *Hanes Methodistiaeth yn Sir Gâr (1911)* ("all the Factory sons, four in number, became priests of the Church of England. The four were reared on the breasts of old Bethel church and they speak reverently of her")

592 David Lewis: *Family Histories p171-5*

She married David Williams (1823-82) of Tyissa Llansawel, a draper and grocer and then postmaster in Llansawel; she took over as postmistress until her death in 1904. She was his third wife (his second wife was Mary Peters the daughter of the Edwinsford coachman). David was the son of Charles Williams (1793-1873), an itinerant tailor who also acted as landlord of the George Inn from the 1830s to 1860s; another of his sons Rev Daniel Williams (b1834) was also an Anglican vicar as was one of his grandsons, Rev Charles David Williams (1851-86) who sadly became an alcoholic and emigrated to America abandoning his family; the latter's grandson, David Williams, was a chaplain to the RAF (see Chapter 28.8).

David Williams died in 1882 having switched from his Anglican Church upbringing to his wife's Bethel Methodist Chapel where he served as an elder and treasurer; his wife Martha took over the business of grocer, draper and postmistress and used to deliver the Llansawel mail on horseback to the outlying farms. She died in 1904 and her funeral in Llansawel Parish Church (not at her Bethel Chapel) was attended by her four Anglican vicar brothers as well as by the great and the good including Sir James and Lady Williams-Drummond of Edwinsford. David and Martha had four children: (a) Rev Thomas Alfred Williams (1870-1941) who served as a curate at St Peter's Carmarthen, then at Golden Grove and later became the Dean of Bangor. His son Rev Charles Williams (d1973) was a Canon of Chichester, and his daughter Martha married Rev Mervyn Daniel a Canon of Bangor; (b) Rev Evan Daniel Williams (1879-1951) who became the Archdeacon of Cardigan; (c) Eleanor who married Rev Michael Williams a Methodist minister at Cilfynydd; and (d) Sarah Agnes Williams who married Caxton Davies, a printer at the Welsh Church Press in Lampeter, and succeeded her mother as postmistress of Llansawel;

(6)-(7) Anne Davies (b1850) and Mary Davies (1854-63) both of whom died young; and

(8) Eleanor Davies (b1852) who married Joseph Jones (1849), a draper of Ammanford, and took over the woolcarding factory at Porth in Llansawel from her mother as can be seen from the census returns.

It is unclear why so many bilingual nonconformist sons of Llansawel converted to be Anglican priests. Motives may have included a more secure employment and a desire for social progress; perhaps the family could only afford for the eldest son to be educated at St David's Lampeter or a theological college, so the second son became a Methodist minister and the third took over the farm tenancy which was not uncommon.

"The Four Apostles" of the Davies family

26.3 Llansawel (Sawel) Mill [SN619362]

YEAR	LLANSAWEL MILL CENSUS RETURNS
1841	No entry
1851	**WILLIAMS: David** (34) miller and farmer of 5 acres born Llansawel, Mary (28) wife with 4 children, 3 serv
1861	**WILLIAMS: John** (31) miller, Sarah Jones (31) housekeeper, Thomas Davies (10) ser
1871	**EVANS: James** (32) miller born Llansawel, Sarah (32) wife with 3 children
1881	**DAVIES: William** (52) farmer of 86 acres and miller born Llansawel, Margaret (47) wife, William (22) son Calvinistic methodist preacher, Elizabeth (20) dau, John (11) son, Maggie (7) dau, Margaret Davies (74) mother in law
1891	**DAVIES: David** (29) miller born Llanybyther, Elizabeth (30) wife, William (2) son, Margaret (84) mother in law, Margaret Davies (16) boarder ser
1901	**DAVIES: William** (70) corn miller, David Williams (38) son in law, Elizabeth (39) dau, William (12) grandson, Davy (6) grandson, Margaret (4) granddau, Mary Evans (13) dom serv
1911	**DAVIES: David** (49) corn miller born Llansawel, Elizabeth (50) wife, Willie (22) son waggoner, Margaret (14) dau, Oswyn (5) son

Before the 20th century there were many working water powered woollen mills and corn mills which were used by Estate employees, tenants and other residents of the area. Llansawel Mill was on the Edwinsford Estate and on the left just before the bridge over the river entering Llansawel on the B4337 road from Talley. Originally it was a thatched longhouse which was replaced with a two storey millhouse the remains of which can still be seen although the waterwheel behind it has gone; the outline of the old mill pond in the field above also remains although the leat has been infilled.

In 1810 the rent roll states that Llansawel Mill and land totalled 4 acres and 35 perches in area and the value was £32.

Fred Price described how millers[593] used to prepare the corn by means of *brenan* (quern) and *odyn grasu* (drying kiln). Initially mills had no drying kilns nearby and all the corn had to be dried at home. The last outdoor drying kiln in use in Llansawel Parish was at Cilwenau-isaf as late as 1845 under the supervision of Michael Pentalog (Michael y Gât). On a gently sloping ground there was made a hollow three yards long, two yards wide and two yards deep which was cut similar in shape to a trench for potatoes (*clâdd tato*). Two planks were placed at right angles to each other with their ends resting on the surface outside the hollow. These served to support the sticks which were placed regularly over the kiln until covered. Over the whole, clean straw was laid upon which the corn was placed to be dried. Underneath and at the lower end of the kiln, the fire was placed so that the heat and smoke went under the straw contrivance above. One man looked after the fire, which was generally of furze and brushwood. He always kept by him a tub of water and a straw wisp or a mop to regulate the force of the fire. He kept moving the corn continually to obtain even drying with a short-toothed wooden rake, and when ready the corn was raked off the straw into a large canvas, and was then fit for the mill. Instead of straw some covered the kiln with what was called *carthen rawn, carthen odyn* (kiln cloth or haircloth). It was said by the old people that corn dried after the old fashion makes sweeter bread than that dried in the modern brick kilns of the mills.

The Llansawel Mill was a corn mill which had a leat drawing water to a waterwheel from a millpond above the millhouse fed from a stream coming down the hill from Penlan and then emptying into the river via another leat (this can be seen on the 1886 map). In the days of a bartering economy when rents were paid in kind rather than in cash, the mill toll was the mechanism by which millers were paid. Farmers took their corn to the mill for grinding into flour after having been dried at home or by *odyn grasu* and the miller was paid in kind with bread or other produce. The miller's capacity for taking toll became a proverb: *Fel y melinydd am y doll* (as able as the miller gathering toll). The modern form of virtual currency (bitcoins and others) is reinventing the old customs.

Mills were dangerous places in which to work. The millers at Sawel Mill were: (a) Moses Harris in 1810 followed by (b) John Lloyd (Jack Llwyd)

[593] Fred Price: *Llansawel p42-45*

in 1844, whose daughter aged 21 was tragically killed in the mill in 1846 whilst engaged in *malu Cynnos Harri'r Castell* (meaning unknown) and was buried in Crugybar, (c) David Williams by 1851, (d) John Williams (late Pengelly) by 1861, (e) James Evans by 1871, (f) William Davies by 1881, whose son John aged 13 was killed in the wheels of the mill in 1883, and (g) his son David Davies by 1891, whose son Daniel aged only 3 fell into the millpond and was drowned in 1896.

In April 1894 the Royal Commission on Land in Wales and Monmouthshire met in Llansawel School and later in the Town Hall to take evidence from the landowners and residents including tenants. Thomas Davies of Tynycwm (Chairman of the Llansawel School Board) gave evidence on behalf of the neighbouring farmers complaining about bad housing for tenants etc. He described Llansawel Mill as a "low thatched house, leaking, no proper loft, no windows or ventilation, and no partition up in the sleeping place, and yet obliged to use it for sleeping for both sexes. It is not the worst, but it is near enough for you to see it if you will come over, it is on the Edwinsford Estate." The commissioners under the chairmanship of Lord Carrington GCMG inspected the mill and described it as a disgraceful hovel, a description accepted by Sir Francis Dudley Williams-Drummond (76), the brother of Sir James Williams-Drummond (68) the owner of the Edwinsford Estate and himself the Land Agent for the Cawdor Estate. It seems that shortly afterwards the Edwinsford Estate sold the mill to the Davies family tenants, no doubt as a result of the embarrassment of its condition.

David and Elizabeth Davies continued to own the property known now as Sawel Mill when it ceased to be a mill; David died aged 90. Today their grandson, Alun aged 80 (b1936) who was born there, and his wife Mairwen have a smallholding and live in a rebuilt house there. Alun and Mairwen have four sons, Ieuan, Roy, Afion and Eirian, who live close-by or in the area; a cousin Cynfryn Davies farms at Cilgawod in Caio (See Chapter 28.13).

Old Mill which replaced the former thatched millhouse 2017

26.4 The Old Forge Llansawel [SN619364]

We have already seen from the forges at Edwinsford and Talley how important blacksmiths were to the local economy. Every village and hamlet needed to have their services. They made the essential handtools which all farmers needed before the tractor and mechanisation arrived. They made scythes, sickles, billhooks, spades, shovels and hand shears as well as much larger implements such as ploughs, harrows, carts and gamboes. They shod the working horses (and the oxen and cattle who used to do the ploughing before them) and they shod for the drovers on their way to the marts in England. Many did the work of farriers, coopers, saddlers and wheelwrights. They worked closely with the carpenters and wheelwrights in making wheels for the carts and putting iron tyres on them. They made horseshoes, nails, axes, pitchforks, hammers, hog's rings, hay knives, chains, gate hinges, as well as making parts of boots and shoes for the cobbler. Many blacksmiths apprenticed their own sons to carry on their trade and some took on other apprentices usually for only board and lodging.

This forge was owned at one time by the Edwinsford Estate. Fred Price[594] writing in 1898 says he has "pleasant recollections of William y Gôf who was loved and respected by all. He was also an experienced dentist, one that relieved many a person from pain, after going through the ordeal of having the tooth extracted". He added that "the village smithy was a rare place for gossip on autumnal and wintry nights, for, true to the instincts of his calling, the smith knew all the gossip; and the din of hammer on anvil gave zest to the conversation, which was always breezy or bellowsy, or savoured of the hard ring of iron."

Fred Price goes on to comment that "the present smithy (in 1898) is much superior to the old low thatched building of former years". In the Edwinsford Estate accounts for 1903 shown in Chapter 16.8 Smith Forge house is listed as then being occupied by John Thomas. We know that the smithy continued up to the mid 1950s. It was occupied as a home by a Scottish family called Heath from 1982 to about 1989 and then left empty until it was bought in 1992 by the current owner, James Somerfield, who is disabled and affectionately known in the village as "Jim Sticks". It is now known as the Old Forge Cottage and is close to the bridge over the river near to the site of the old Sawel Mill.

Old Forge Cottage 2016

Llansawel Forge c1910 (the trap belonged to the Swan Inn)

[594] Fred Price: *Llansawel p11.* This may be the old grey-bearded William Thomas to whom DJ Williams p328 refers in c1891

26.5 Police Station [SN619364]

YEAR	POLICE STATION LLANSAWEL CENSUS RETURNS
1861	No entry. 2 PCs lodging at Angel Inn
1871	**(1) SAER: James** (26) Police Constable, Anne (25) wife and 2 children **(2) EVANS: Henry** (25) Police Constable, Esther (21) wife and 2 children
1881	**(1) ROBERTS: Thomas** (26) Police Constable, Sarah (27) wife and 2 children **(2) MORGANS: Philip** (31) Police Constable, Eleanor (27) wife, Frederick (7) son
1891	**(1) REES: William** (43) Police Constable, Mary (52) wife, William (14) son born Cilycwm **(2) THOMAS: James** (32) Police Constable, Ann (28) wife and 3 children
1901	**HARRIES: John** (49) Police Sergeant, Mary (50) wife, Elizabeth (8) adopted dau, Joseph Beynon (23) Police Constable
1911	**ANDREWS: Frederick** (35) Police Constable, Elena (33) wife, Mary (17) niece

For many years there were no police officers in the area and the magistrates would nominate farmers to act as constables. In 1850 the Parish Vestry[595] and local ratepayers signed a memorial requesting Quarter Sessions to disband the local rural police force to save money and "relieve your memorialists from the support of a force which renders them no service". This was ignored and, as can be seen from the census returns, a Police Station was built about 1864 across the road from the Old Forge.

26.6 Town Hall (Old Court House) [SN619364]

Old Town Hall 2017

The Town Hall is a rubble built 19th century, slate roofed building with a stone flight of stairs at one end to the first floor. It was owned by the Edwinsford Estate and is listed in the 1903 estate accounts as being let to the County Council for the holding of Petty Sessions. The building was divided so that the upper floor with its entrance up the steps could be used as a public meeting hall for parish council meetings, for the holding of magistrates' meetings and court hearings, as an auction room and as a general function room. The ground floor was let to a number of different tradesmen listed in the census returns including John Myles Jones, a saddler and harness maker who was also a newsagent, bookseller and general dealer. From around 1869 the local school, which had been started in the church vestry, moved to the Town Hall so some 40 children aged 5 to 13 were taught in one room (15ft by 35ft) by one teacher with the help of two monitors and a pupil teacher. The school had to close or even meet on Saturdays when the Hall needed to be used for other purposes. Fortunately the new school opened in 1876 as described in Chapter 30.2.

595 Fred Price: *Llansawel p61*

YEAR	TOWN HALL LLANSAWEL CENSUS RETURNS
1841	**(1) MORGAN: Mary** (40) pauper, Sarah (15) dau, Anne (10) dau **(2) THOMAS: Rees** (55) agric lab, Anne (55) wife, Mary Williams (75)
1851	**(1) THOMAS: Rees** (65) agric lab, Anne (64) wife baker, Mary Williams (89) mother in law, Anne (10) lodger **(2) MORGAN: Mary** (49) baker, James Jones (31) lodger carpenter
1861	**(1) JONES: James** (36) carpenter **(2) JAMES: William** (52) tailor, Margaret (56) wife bakeress, Lettice Davies (86) mother in law retired innkeeper
1871	**(1) JAMES: William** (64) tailor and baker, Margaret (65) wife, Maryanne (7) granddau **(2) JONES: James** (42) carpenter, Margaret (39) wife and 4 children
1881	**(1) JONES: Margaret** (49) carpenter**,** William (12) son, David (10) son, John (6) son, Sarah Davies (87) lodger **(2) JONES: John** (33) saddler and harness maker
1891	**(1) JONES: John** (43) saddler and harness maker **(2) JONES: Mary** (22) charwoman, John (16) bro, Mary (8) niece, Sarah (4) dau
1901	**EVANS: Margaret** (68)
1911	**JONES: William** (50) harness maker, Jane (43) wife, Ann (10) dau

For many decades in the 20th century the upper floor continued to be used as a magistrates' court for the parishes of Llansawel, Cynwyl Gaeo and Llanycrwys but was closed in the 1970s as a court house (see Chapter 35.2). Today it is a private dwelling.

Old Town Hall Square 19th century (George Inn on the left)

YEAR	TOWN HALL SQUARE LLANSAWEL CENSUS RETURNS
1871	No entry
1881	**HARRIES: Daniel** (42) accountant, Margaret (40) wife plus 7 children and 3 boarders
1891	uninhabited
1901	**GRIFFITHS: William** (30) blacksmith, Rachel (23) wife, Mary (1) dau
1911	**GRIFFITHS: William Thomas** (40) blacksmith born Llansawel, Rachel (33) wife, Mary (11) dau, Florence (9) dau, William (7) son, James (6) son, Simon (4) son, Goronwy (2) son, Sarah (1) dau

Published by permission of The National Library of Wales *Llansawel Post Office 1885 in main street*

October 1959 water delivery to village outside Swan Inn L to R: Mrs James (Corner House), Claudia Evans (Heddfan), Tegwen Davies (No 8), Mary Davies (Llwynhelig), Mrs Williams (Llyscerdd), Mrs Thomas (Swan), Irene Williams (Glynawel), Mary James (Pantygawen), Mona Bayford (Bethel Terrace)

26.7 Public Houses

There were eight public houses in Llansawel at one time, although there are no census returns for the Pelican Inn which was in Church Street. The number of inns reflects the business brought to the village by the drovers during the 18th and 19th centuries. The four Friendly Societies in Llansawel used to meet at the George Inn, the Angel Inn, the Red Lion and a female society at the Swan Inn, but they had all disappeared by the end of the 19th century. Formerly it was also the custom[596] in this area for farmhouses to brew their own beer from the malt from their own barley.

Ivy Bush Inn [SN619364]

YEAR	IVY BUSH INN LLANSAWEL CENSUS RETURNS
1841	No entry
1851	**GRIFFITHS: William** (38) publican and carrier, Mary (35) wife, David (2) son, Anne James (19) lodger dressmaker
1861	**GRIFFITHS: William** (48) innkeeper and carrier born Llansawel, Mary (45) wife with 4 children and 1 lodger
1871	**GRIFFITHS: Mary** (53) publican
1881	No entry
1891	**GRIFFITHS: Mary** (73) innkeeper, Lettice Jenkins (19) ser
1901	uninhabited
1911	**LEIGH: Ann** (39) innkeeper, Mary (30) sis dressmaker, Nellie (27) sis dressmaker, Annie (10) niece

The Ivy Bush was on the Llansawel to Abergorlech road on the right going up the hill from the Angel Inn corner near the Sawyl Academy. William Griffiths shown as the innkeeper in 1851 was formerly at the Red Lion in 1841. He and his wife remained at the Ivy Bush for more than 30 years.

Angel Inn [SN619364]

YEAR	ANGEL INN LLANSAWEL CENSUS RETURNS
1841	**JONES: John** (40) butcher, Charlotte (35) wife, Margaret (8) dau, John (5) son, Mary (2) dau, 1 ser
1851	**JONES: John** (51) victualler and farmer of 139 acres, Charlotte (46) wife, 3 children, 2 serv, William Evans (24) Police Officer lodger
1861	**JONES: John** (61) innkeeper and farmer of 29 acres born Conwil Gaeo, Charlotte (55) wife, Mary (22) dau, Margaret (3) granddau, Hannah Davies (28) maid, John Davies (23) Police Officer boarder, James Colegate (31) Police Officer boarder
1871	**JONES: John** (72) innkeeper and farmer, Charlotte (67) wife, Charlotte (18) granddau, Sarah (12) granddau, Mary (8) granddau, Margaret Jones (13) granddau
1881	**JONES: Charlotte** (76) farmer of 26 acres and innkeeper, Margaret Evans (48) dau, Sarah Evans (20) granddau, Mary (18) granddau, Johnny (12) grandson
1891	**EVANS: Margaret** (59) widow innkeeper born Llansawel, Charlotte Jones (87) mother widow, Lewis Jones (25) son in law tailor, Mary Jones (28) dau, Thomas Jones (4 mon) grandson, Charles Thomas (40) bro in law labourer
1901	**GRIFFITHS: Mary** (65) innkeeper, Eleanor (32) dau, Margaret (24) dau
1911	**GRIFFITHS: Mary** (75) widow innkeeper, Eleanor (42) dau, Margaret (34) dau

The Angel Inn was owned by the Edwinsford Estate. It is located on the corner where the main street meets the Talley to Llanybydder road. In the 1903 estate accounts the tenants are named as Margaret and William Griffiths, although the tenant innkeeper on the 1901 and 1911 census returns is listed as Mary Griffiths. They followed the Jones family who had the tenancy for some 50 years and passed it to their daughter Margaret Evans. Mary Griffiths was related to the blacksmith family of Talley. Today the inn remains a cosy pub with an inglenook fireplace and friendly atmosphere.

[596] DJ Williams p40

Angel Inn 2017

Red Lion Inn [SN619364]

YEAR	OLD RED LION LLANSAWEL CENSUS RETURNS
1851	**(1) DAVIES: Daniel** (32) agric lab, Anne (30) wife with 3 children **(2) JONATHAN: David** (39) lab, Anne (43) wife with 4 children
1861	**(1) Williams: William** (31) cooper, Sarah (25) wife, David (1) son**(2) JONES: David** (48) labourer, Sarah (26) dau, Jonathan (24) son, Lettice (9) dau
1871	**(1) JONES: David** (57) lab, Sarah (34) dau, Thomas (3) grandson**(2) JAMES: David** (52) carrier, Margaret (50) wife with 2 children and 2 grandsons
1881	**(1) JAMES: David** (62) carrier, Margaret (61) wife, James (15) grandson, Evan (13) grandson **(2) DAVIES: Joseph** (41) waggoner, Margaret (38) wife and 6 children
1891	**(1) DAVIES: Catherine** (68) charwoman, Mary (25) dau, Jane (23) dau, Rachel (6) granddau, John (3) grandson**(2) JAMES: David** (72) carrier, Margaret (70) wife, Evan Evans (23) grandson carrier,
1901	(1) **DAVIES: Catherine** (71) charwoman, Anne (42) dau, Mary (34) dau dressmaker, Rachel (18) granddau, John Morgan (13) grandson(2) **EVANS: Evan** (33) carrier, Margaret (39) wife, Rachel (4) adopted dau
1911	No entry

The Old Red Lion which was an Inn in the 18th century was next door to the Red Lion Inn; the latter was located on the Llansawel to Abergorlech road on the right going up the hill from the Angel Inn corner just before the Ivy Bush Inn. Charles Williams who was a tailor as well as an innkeeper held the tenancy for more than 20 years. His successor, David Davies the innkeeper in the 1881 and 1891 census returns, was also a tailor, draper, breeches maker, and maker of leggings to order according to his advertisements and traded from Ivy Cottage; "Dafydd the Red Lion" as he was called was the tailor for numerous local families.

YEAR	RED LION LLANSAWEL CENSUS RETURNS
1841	**GRIFFITHS: William** (25) agric lab, Mary (25) wife, Anne (2) dau
1851	**WILLIAMS: Charles** (56) victualler and tailor, Daniel (16) son, Amelia (14) dau, James Rees (18) journeyman tailor
1861	**WILLIAMS: Charles** (66) tailor and innkeeper, Sarah (66) wife, Amelia (24) dau
1871	**WILLIAMS: Charles** (76) publican, Catherine Davies (29) ser
1881	**DAVIES: David** (38) tailor, draper and innkeeper, Mary (41) wife, David (17) son, Jane (15) dau, Walter (12) son, Thomas (10) son, Louisa (8) dau, Mary (7) dau, Priscilla (5) dau, Margaret (10 dau, Eleanor (6 mon) dau
1891	**DAVIES: David** (49) tailor draper and innkeeper born Llanybyther, Mary (35) wife, Jane Philipps (35) dau, Watkin (22) son tailor, Priscilla (15) dau, Margaret (11) dau, Eleanor (10) dau, John (7) son, Catherine (5) dau
1901	**DAVIES: Mary** (46) licensed victualler, Kate (15) dau dressmaker, Margaret (21) stepdau dressmaker, David (37) stepson tailor, George (12) grandson, Thomas (11) grandson
1911	No entry

During the 20th century the Red Lion eventually became a branch of the Carmarthenshire Farmers Co-operative Society[597] which ceased trading in the late 1990s and the building is now a private residence.

[597] David Lewis: *Family Histories p90-1*

George Inn [SN619364]

YEAR	GEORGE INN LLANSAWEL CENSUS RETURNS
1841	**WILLIAMS: Sarah** (45) publican, Mary (25), Sarah (12), Elizabeth (10), Daniel (7), Amelia (5), Eleanor (2), 1 ser, 2 lodgers
1851	**SIMON: John** (36) victualler and blacksmith born Llansawel, Elizabeth (39) wife, William (7) son, John (5) son, Mary (2) dau, Esther Jones (25) ser
1861	**SIMON: John** (46) innkeeper, shoeing smith and sexton, Elizabeth (49) wife with 4 children and 1 serv
1871	**SIMMS: Elizabeth** (59) licensed victualler, Elizabeth Davies (10) ser, Rachel Davies (89) charwoman
1881	**SINNION: Elizabeth** (70) innkeeper, Mary Davies (8) granddau, John Thomas (54) cattle dealer, Thomas Robinson (42) cattle dealer, John Owen (46) millwright, Esther Davies (37) needlewoman
1891	**JAMES: Thomas** (35) tailor and innkeeper, Mary (36) wife, Hannah (12) dau, Evan (9) son, Mary (7) dau, Margaret (5) dau, Thomas (1) son, David Jones (73) widower
1901	**HALL: Charles** (40) coachman, Mary (43) wife, Phoebe James (21) stepdau dressmaker, Evelyn (15) stepdau, Edith (13) stepdau, Harold (11) stepson
1911	No entry

The George Inn was located on the main road through Llansawel near the Red Lion and opposite the Angel Inn corner (see photo in Chapter 26.6). Sarah Williams shown as the innkeeper in the 1841 census was the wife of Charles Williams who was running the Red Lion Inn in the 1850s to 1870s; it looks as if the wife started innkeeping in the 1840s when her husband was tailoring and then he took on the Red Lion with her help. The Simon family then took on the tenancy and the wife, Elizabeth, continued with it until the 1880s (I suspect that the surnames Simms and Sinnion were clerical errors for Simon).

Black Lion Inn [SN620364]

Black Lion 2017

The Black Lion was owned by the Edwinsford Estate and is located in the main street through the village of Llansawel. It was probably built in the early 19th century and altered around 1907 as stated on the outside of the end nearest to the Old Town Hall. In the 1838 Tithe Apportionment Agreement the tenant is listed as John Davies; David Davies, who is probably the same person, is listed as the tenant in the 1841 and 1851 census returns and his wife Mary continued with the tenancy. Later Henry Rumbold held the tenancy for over 20 years and is also listed in the 1903 estate accounts as the tenant of Penrhiw as well as the Black Lion; those accounts also show that part of the Black Lion was rented by the Parish Council together with the Black Lion hearse house.

The Black Lion was the venue for tenants' dinners provided by the Edwinsford family from time to time. It was also the venue for the holding of Courts Leet (see Chapter 35.1) and for the annual payment of chief rent to the monarch as Lord or Lady of the Manor. Tenants would also attend at the Black Lion to pay their rent to the agent for the Edwinsford Estate on the traditional rent days. Today the inn remains a welcoming pub with character which has been updated. It is well attended and is where the Llansawel and District RFC met. It also sells milk, bread and essentials in the absence of a village shop. The post office closed some time ago and the residents now rely on a mobile post office van.

YEAR	BLACK LION INN LLANSAWEL CENSUS RETURNS
1841	**DAVIES: David** (50) innkeeper and farmer, Mary (25), John (2), Margaret (10 mon), 6 lodgers
1851	**DAVIES: David** (59) innkeeper, auctioneer and farmer of 120 acres born Llansawel, Mary (36) wife born Talley, John (18) son, Margaret (10) dau, David (6) son, Mary (4) dau, Anne (2) dau, 6 serv, 2 lodgers
1861	**DAVIES: Mary** (46) innkeeper and farmer, Margaret (20) dau, David (18) son enumerator, with 3 children, plus 4 lodgers (civil engineer, inland revenue collector, land drainer, land drainer) plus 3 servs (carter, ostler and housemaid)
1871	**HARRIES: Daniel** (32) farmer and innkeeper born Caio, Margaret (31) wife with 4 children and 2 servs
1881	**RUMBOLD: Henry** (40) farmer of 66 acres and innkeeper born Bath, Annie (45) wife, Sarah Morgans (8) niece, Eliza Davies (24) maid, Jane Williams (15) maid, John Colgate (57) postboy
1891	**RUMBOLD: Henry** (49) farmer and hotelkeeper born Bath, Annie (54) wife, Margaret Williams (19) ser, Hannah Evans (13) ser
1901	**RUMBOLD: Henry** (54) farmer and innkeeper born Gloucester, Jane Davies (33) niece housekeeper, David Davies (18) postboy, Sarah Leigh (25) dom serv
1911	**GRIFFITHS: Jane** (42) widow hotelkeeper and farmer born Talley, Isabel Rumbold (8) dau, Maggie Evans (21) ser, Lizzie James (25) ser, Daniel James (23) farm labourer, Sam Cumming (65) farm labourer

Cart and Horses Inn (Reform Inn)

YEAR	REFORM INN LLANSAWEL CENSUS RETURNS
1841	**DAVIES: Thomas** (60) publican, Amelia (60) wife with 3 children
1851	**DAVIES: Thomas** (71) publican born Cards, Amelia (70) wife David (4) grandson

YEAR	CART AND HORSES INN LLANSAWEL CENSUS RETURNS
1871	**JENKINS: John** (36) innkeeper born Llanwenog, Eleanor (32) wife with 5 children and 1 ser
1881	No entry
1891	**JENKINS: John** (56) butcher and innkeeper, Eleanor (53) wife, Sarah (17) dau, John (13) pupil teacher
1901	No entry
1911	**JENKINS: John** (76) widower innkeeper, Sarah Davies (37) dau helping in the inn, Nellie (12) granddau, Ellis (10) grandson, Margaret (8) granddau, John (7) grandson, James (5) grandson, David (2) grandson, Hugh Jones (33) visitor

Thomas Davies was the publican in 1841 and 1851. Later the Inn was renamed the Cart and Horses and John Jenkins[598] was the innkeeper for over 50 years; his father was Deio Jenkins the butcher. He and his wife Neli had five daughters and three sons. Neli ran the inn and had three cows and a pony outside while John received commission for dealing for others in cattle, sheep. pigs etc at marts.

598 DJ Williams p48-66 whose family were close friends of John Jenkins

Swan Inn [SN621364]

YEAR	SWAN INN LLANSAWEL CENSUS RETURNS
1841	No entry
1851	**EVANS: Daniel** (62) victualler born Llanybyther, Lettice (50) wife, David Lewis (24) lodger shoemaker
1861	**THOMAS: David** (30) publican and carrier born Llanybyther, Mary (27) wife with 2 children, Thomas Thomas (21) lodger woollen weaver
1871	**JONES: Jane** (35) innkeeper, Mary (7) dau, Thomas Price (70) boarder
1881	**DAVIES: Thomas** (37) innkeeper and carrier born Llansawel, Elizabeth (41) wife and 5 children
1891	**JONES: Richard** (29) wool skinner, Margaret (32) wife innkeeper, Elizabeth (10) dau, Margaret (7) dau, Mary (1) dau, Catherine (1 mon) dau
1901	**DAVIES: James** (26) innkeeper, Sarah (29) wife, Evan (3) son, Isaac (1) son, Mary (6 mon) dau
1911	**DAVIES: James** (38) innkeeper and farmer born Llansawel, Sarah (39) wife (6 children 4 still alive), Evan (13) son, Mary (10) dau, Johnnie (8) son, Hannah (6) dau

Old Swan Inn 1891

The Swan Inn is located on the corner of the main street which branches into the road which goes north out of the village past Bethel Chapel to Esgairdawe. It was probably built around about 1840 and retains its original frontage. It has the old stables and carthouse on one side and on the other side is Swan Fach, which may itself have been part of the inn at one time.

There have been several innkeepers over the decades. Thomas Davies on the 1881 census was also a carrier. His successor Richard Jones was a wool skinner while his wife ran the inn, and his successor James Davies is said to have had a wonderful singing voice. In the mid 20th century Megan Jones ran the inn for many years. John Mcmurray was the publican for about 10 years (1987-97) and then Colin and Carol Hayward bought the pub in 1997. Colin served in the Royal Marines and then ran his own engineering business. He was the publican until 2002 when he decided to convert it into a private residence with his wife Carol, a nurse for over 48 years. A lovely couple who would help anyone.

Old Swan Inn 2017

26.8 Castle Green [SN621364]

Castle Green is located opposite the Swan Inn. It dates from about 1845 and was an important gentleman's residence. It was probably built by Morgan Jones, the proprietor in the 1851 census. For many years it was painted brown but has been white for a long time. It has a two storey wide stuccoed face with a symmetrical five window front, central wooden portico and doric columns. The rubble built rear has a two storey later 19th century extension. The interior includes a slightly curving early 19th century stick baluster staircase with fine plasterwork in the rooms. Fine early 19th century railings are in the front. It is a fine example of an early Victorian gentleman's residence which has been well maintained. It has land behind and a lake.

It is now listed and was the home and surgery of the doctor in Llansawel for many decades during the 19th and 20th centuries; he was the nearest doctor for some miles around. During the past 150 years there have been two well-known local murders which directly involved the doctor in Llansawel; indeed the second murder was of the doctor himself.

Castle Green 2017

YEAR	CASTLE GREEN LLANSAWEL CENSUS RETURNS
1841	No entry
1851	**JONES: Morgan** (34) landed proprietor, Elizabeth (30) wife, Elizabeth (2) dau, Evan Price (29) boarder draper, Anne Rees (18) ser
1861	**(1) WILLIAMS: John Evan** (24) GP **(2) JONES: Morgan** (44) road surveyor and farmer born Llansawel, Elizabeth (40) wife born Tretower with 2 children, 1 housemaid
1871	**JENKINS: Evan** (29) FRCS Edin and Lon born Llandyssul, Elizabeth (22) wife, Thomas (1) son and 2 ser
1881	**JENKINS: Evan** (39) surgeon, Elizabeth (32) wife and 5 children and 3 servants
1891	**EVANS: Thomas** (32) GP, Joyce (37) wife, Marcus (4) son, Bilton (2) son, Jane (1) dau, Charles (2 mon) son, Lettitia Davies (18) ser, James Phillips (18) stableboy, Sarah Jones (15) ser
1901	**EVANS: Thomas Jones** (42) surgeon born Llanwenog, Joyce (47) wife, Mary (16) dau, Jane (11) dau, Florie (7) dau, Eric (6) son, Rees Rees (26) ass surgeon, Catherine Davies (24) dom ser
1911	**PRICE: John Thomas** (33) physician and surgeon born Anglesey, Jane (21) wife, John (7 mon) son, George Taylor (25) coachman, Mary Thomas (17) dom serv

Murder of Judge John Johnes of Dolaucothi (1800-76)

The various accounts in the press, at the inquest and in later reports[599] of the murder of Judge John Johnes on Saturday 19 August 1876, which so shocked the neighbourhood and indeed the whole of Wales, contain some inconsistencies. However most, although not all, of the basic facts are clear.

John Johnes aged 76 was enjoying his retirement at Dolaucothi Mansion busy with numerous cultural activities and continuing to run his estate. His butler Henry Tremble had come from County Wexford with Charlotte Cookman (one of the Judge's two daughters) and her husband Charles to Dolaucothi in about 1859 having served Charles

Judge John Johnes

well in Ireland as a stablehand. After Charles's death he had been employed for 17 years by John Johnes as a coachman, gamekeeper and later as the butler. Tremble had met Martha Davies (b1844) a maid at Brunant Mansion nearby and married her in 1862 just before she gave birth to their first child Bessie. In 1867 Tremble and Martha took over the Sextons Arms in the village of Caio opposite the lychgate of the Parish Church of St Cynwyl while Tremble continued to work at Dolaucothi; Martha was not a success as an innkeeper and seems to have taken to the drink and consequently lost her tenancy. Tremble's employment at Dolaucothi and his relationship with John Johnes had deteriorated to such an extent that the judge had given him notice to quit expiring on Saturday 19 August 1876. Tremble and Martha had earlier applied to John Johnes for the vacant tenancy at the Dolaucothi Arms in Pumsaint, but had been turned down given their history at the Sextons Arms, and John Johnes had decided to give it to John Davies the licensee of the Caio Inn in Caio village. Tremble may have thought that he had been promised the tenancy and was very angry. On 15 August he wrote his will so his later actions were clearly premeditated.

Charlotte Johnes's first hand account[600] (very fortunately her sister Betha was away) after she had recovered some four months later is in her Journal:

"Dolau Cothi—Friday December 29, 1876

Here is a long and terrible interval—on the morning of the 19th August last, I went after breakfast to the library to see dear Papa as usual, talked to him for a few minutes chiefly about the Aneroid which he had just bought and the difference between it and the Barometer….then I went out to the kitchen to order dinner—-in passing the Diningroom door saw Henry Tremble the Butler standing reaching across as if to remove the Silver Tray (the one presented to Papa on his resigning the County Court Judgeship in 1861) he was to leave his service on that day by his own desire[601] and I had told him to put the Plate on the Diningroom table for me to count over—-This man or rather fiend had been a trusted servant in this house for seventeen years and had lived besides with my Husband from the time he was a boy helping with the stables (his father a man from Liverpool

[599] Charlotte Johnes's Journal in NLW Dolaucothi archives and CA (1970) p108; CRO; Western Mail, Carmarthen Journal and Llanelly Guardian reports; Fred Price: *Caio p65*; Herbert Lloyd-Johnes CASJ (1956) Vol III p10; Bob Hinton*: South Wales Murders p1-20;* Bethan Phillips: *The Lovers' Graves p41-55;* Susan Beckley; *A Devil who Cared for his Own CH (1982) p78-81*

[600] NLW Dolaucothi archives; CRO; Lynn Hughes: *Carmarthenshire Anthology p181-4*

[601] In fact he had been given a week's notice to leave

having rented a cottage on the Monart estate from Mr Cookman)—except for a short interval and had never received anything but the utmost kindness from us all throughout—I went to the Kitchen found Margaret Davies the Cook was not there, turned back as far as the passage door to the yard, when I saw Margaret coming in from the Larder with three jugs in her hand from which she had been bottling Rasberry Vinegar. I spoke to her for a minute then walked with her into the Kitchen, as I got just to the middle of it, at the end of the long table opposite the window I heard a hurried step which made me turn round facing the door when I saw Henry Tremble with a large breech loading gun in his hand, take up his stand on the mat at the passage door, opposite the Kitchen door. He raised the gun to his shoulder, took deliberate aim said "Take that for your persecution of me" fired at me. I saw the fire come out of the muzzle of the gun I turned suddenly round and the whole charge entered my back and down the thigh, I fell on my face towards the scullery door, fortunately escaping the fire and cock of the boiler, the muzzle of the gun must have been about 7 or 9 feet from me I think. How long I lay insensible I know not, but I was lifted up, laid on a mattress on the Kitchen floor where I fainted several times, and after the Doctor came I was about 3 o'c carried upstairs to the Colton room, where the dreadful wound was poulticed.....it was a cowardly deed, but far worse than this deed was done before[602] *he came to shoot me the murderer went into the Library and deliberately shot to death our beloved Father, the fiend fired two*[603] *shots, the first not taking effect, into his body. Cottie (Lady Wilkinson who was staying with them) and Jane Jenkins the housemaid, hearing the shots, rushed in, darling Papa said "I am dying, Henry Tremble shot me, mind he is taken." He was sensible and very calm he never uttered a harsh word even against his brutal murderer, he did not pass away for about an hour, and he died as he had lived all his life, a Saint, with a blessing on his lips, his last words were "God bless my children and I know He will bless them." He asked for me and said I must be wounded as I was not with him....he was the most virtuous, honourable man that ever lived, who was old and broken down, weakened by a long illness of two years' duration but "I will avenge saith the Lord."*

It seems that Arthur Sturdy, a young footman, had seen Tremble collecting a gun from the strongroom and loading it presumably to shoot game. After the first shot Lady Wilkinson (wife of an archaeologist) and the maid Jane Jenkins rushed into the Library where they found Judge Johnes sitting in his chair with a large wound in his stomach and some of his intestines hanging out. They then heard another shot from the kitchen where they found Charlotte lying wounded on the floor and the maid Margaret who had fainted in shock. Someone went off on horseback to fetch Dr Evan Jenkins of Llansawel but by the time he arrived at about 11.45am the Judge was dead. Charlotte's wound in her bottom took two months to heal up and she was confined to her bed for three months.

Meanwhile Tremble went to the kennels where he cruelly shot three farm dogs and threatened Benjamin Jones the gardener and Thomas the waggoner who ran for cover. Tremble then walked to Caio village about one mile away. He called at the Caio Inn with a view to killing the publican, John Davies, in revenge who fortunately was not there. Davies had been given the licence to run the Dolaucothi Arms instead of Tremble and Tremble wanted to kill him. Not finding Davies, Tremble next made his way down the street and threatened PC Daniel Davies who ran off to summon help. Tremble next met William Morgan a retired resident and told him what he had done and told him to fetch a doctor. He then made his way towards his own home, Myrtle Cottage, next to the Post Office and opposite the King's Arms and met his daughter Bessie and asked her to take a written message (his will) to Rev Charles Chidlow in the vicarage. He then met JH Williams outside Myrtle Cottage and said: "I have shot Mr Johnes like a dog......I have done my duty...they thought they could tread upon my neck because I am an Irishman." He then entered his own home Myrtle Cottage and threatened his wife who fled with the children. PC Phillip Morgans returned with PC Daniel Davies (under the command of Superintendent Durnford who was setting up roadblocks around Dolaucothi). William Morgan then returned and tried to persuade Tremble to give himself up to the Police but was told he would never disgrace his family by being hung. His daughter Bessie was permitted to enter the cottage and give Tremble a glass of water which she did before exiting in tears. For some time Tremble held the Police at bay until he shot himself; they found him upstairs with one shot discharged into his chest and a loaded pistol on the table and he died a few minutes later at about 1.30pm.

[602] Charlotte seems not to have heard the shot which killed her father

[603] It was probably only one shot since the other was used to shoot her before Tremble was seen reloading his gun to shoot the dogs

At the inquest[604] on Judge Johnes held on Monday 21 August, Charles Lloyd of Brunant (1829-87) was the foreman, and Rev JA Williams of Caio, Dr Evan Jenkins (Llansawel), Arthur Sturdy (footman) and Jane Jenkins (housemaid) and others gave evidence. The verdict was wilful murder. The verdict at the inquest on Tremble, aged 36, was suicide. At the inquest Rev Charles Chidlow revealed Tremble's will which his daughter Bessie had delivered to him. It made no mention of his wife Martha (whom he might have planned to kill) and asked the vicar to use the monies in his National Provincial Bank account in Carmarthen to look after his children by paying £30 to £40 per annum to Bessie on their behalf; he also said that there would be some £8 in his pockets. It is a mystery how Tremble could have saved such substantial sums given the modest wages he would have had received.

In accordance with the coroner's warrant and as usual in cases of suicide, Tremble was buried in Caio graveyard at about 10.30 pm on the same day, 21 August, in silence and without a religious service. Two months later the local residents dug him up because they did not think it right for the body of the murderer to lie in the same graveyard as that of the victim and took his coffin to Llandulais in Breconshire and buried it there in an unmarked grave. The residents of Llandulais did not take kindly to this when they discovered the truth so they dug up his body during the night, carried it back to Caio on a gambo and dumped it on the pathway in Caio graveyard with a note of explanation. It was later reburied in an unmarked grave; few people are buried three times.

Margaret Davies, the cook at Dolaucothi, was rewarded with an engraved gold watch for her help in saving Charlotte; she later married John Evans, Headmaster of Cilycwm School from 1887 to 1922.

Murder of Dr Glyn Jones of Llansawel

I remember my father first telling me as a small boy about the murder at Blaenrhisglog[605] in Cwrt y Cadno in 1916 when he was just 12 years old and how frightened he and everyone was of the murderer on the run in the area. The press[606] understandably dealt with these events rather sensationally but the facts speak for themselves.

Thomas Davies and his wife Jane took over Blaenrhisglog Farm (SN 697466) at the top of the Rhisglog or Fanagoed valley in Cynwyl Gaeo some time before the 1891 census which shows them living there with their son David (Dai).

Thomas Davies aged 77 had been ill in bed for a week with heart problems so his wife Jane called the doctor. On 13 July 1916 Dr Rowlands of Lampeter arrived at the farm to be met in the farm yard by David Davies aged 32 who was the son of Thomas and Jane; he was holding a rifle and said to the doctor "If you don't stand back I will shoot you". The doctor thought he was joking until David put the rifle to his shoulder, took aim and pulled the trigger but the gun did not go off, so the doctor beat a hasty retreat. Dr Rowlands reported this incident but no action was taken on the advice of the Deputy Chief Constable until first hand evidence could be obtained. Sadly this did not happen before the tragic events of 15 July. On 15 July Thomas Davies was in a worse condition and his wife called the doctor in Llansawel by telegram. Dr Glyn Jones aged 47 from Castle Green in Llansawel who had only arrived to practise in the area 18 months previously came to Ffarmers in his car driven by his chauffeur Mr Scribbins and walked the rest of the way from the village to the farm "as was his custom". When he arrived at the farm at 1pm he was met in the farm yard by the son David, who gave evidence that he had told the doctor "there was enough vagabonds like him going about the country poisoning people. He raised his hands and on the impulse I fired at him. I was getting up with no intention of any harm; he gripped me and struggled. Another shot went off accidentally. He turned round on his knees and started struggling again. As he was coming at me I struck out blindly. I started off to the shore to get away. I came back to get his purse to have some money. I went towards Aberystwyth. I came back home afterwards but ran away when I saw the Police".

The mother Jane said in the trial that she was in the house and heard a shot so she rushed outside and saw Dr Jones and her son struggling violently. Both had hold of the gun. The mother tried to pull her son away from the doctor but the gun went off and hit the doctor. Both the son and the doctor then got up and fought with fists, the doctor

[604] Aberystwyth Observer 26 August 1876

[605] David Lewis: *Family Histories p310-6*

[606] Carmarthen Journal

fell over, the son picked the gun up and then using the butt end of the rifle battered the prostrate doctor about the head and body unmercifully and his skull was badly fractured. The son then said goodbye to his mother, threw the body of the doctor over a hedge into the field and ran off across the hills. The mother ran down to the next door farm Tyllwyd and told Tom Williams to fetch help. He told the local blacksmith to call the Police so he rushed to Ffarmers, met the chauffeur who was concerned at the time the doctor had been absent and PC Rees was informed. At 3.15pm PC Rees and PC John Thomas from Llanwrda went to the farm where they found the body. The skull was broken and parts of it were missing; there were two pools of blood and several pieces of bone nearby.

The Police description of David Davies was that "he was rather peculiarly attired. He is a single man, 33 years of age, 5ft 8ins or 9ins in height, with fair hair and moustache, and of proportionate build. Dressed in a brown jacket and breeches without gaiters, grey socks and grey cap and very likely there are bloodstains on the clothes". From daylight on Sunday 16 July there was a search of the surrounding countryside with a posse of Police with two trained bloodhounds and with many farmers and others turning out to assist; the photograph of the 11 local farmers and two Policemen with rifles and shotguns shows in the backrow (left to right) a PC, Police Inspector, Jack y Gof (blacksmith), Tom of Troedyrhiw, Howell Jones of Glanmeddyg, Tom Williams of Tyllwyd, David Tom Edwards of Aberbranddu and a PC.

The posse of Police and local farmers at Blaenrhisglog 1916

In the front row there are David Davies of Gwndwnmawr, Dai Davies of Llandre, Will Davies of Tanlanfawr, Robin Edwards of Cefngarros and Tomos Davies of Cwmgerwyn. The search went on during Tuesday and then on Wednesday night the fugitive was seen arriving at his home Blaenrhisglog but bolted when he saw the police, and the posse went after him but to no avail. Then on the Thursday he was seen at 2.30pm coming from Llanwrtyd to Clarwen by two PCs who hid behind rocks and then sprang at him and brought him to the ground. The fugitive struggled to get the carving knife he had hidden in his jacket but the PCs managed to handcuff him and he was then charged with murder. He was taken by car to Llandeilo and then by train to Carmarthen Jail pending his trial.

David Davies at Llandeilo Station

Shortly after these events the ill father Thomas Davies died at home in his bed and at his inquest the jury returned a verdict of "death from natural causes probably heart failure". The funeral of Dr Glyn Jones took place at Llansawel on 20 July 1916 in the presence of a large gathering. In addition to his widow and the chief mourners, there were present Mr Scribbins the chauffeur, Sir James Hills-Johnes of Dolaucothi and other well known local landowners.

The trial of David Davies for wilful murder was held at the West Wales Assizes at the Shire Hall in Carmarthen at the end of October 1916 before Mr Justice Lush with a jury. Evidence was produced to the effect that the accused suffered from delusions, that he thought someone was coming to the farm to poison his father and that people were poisoning their cattle. The medical officer at the prison said that he thought the accused was of unsound mind. The prosecution argued that he was sane and had given statements quite rationally after being arrested. After deliberating in private for only 15 minutes the jury returned to the Court and the Foreman said to the Clerk of Arraigns: "We find him guilty but insane". The Judge then committed the accused to "be detained as a criminal lunatic until His Majesty's pleasure is known".

So in the middle of 1916 Thomas Davies died of natural causes, his son David was sent to Broadmoor and Bridgend Hospital as a lunatic guilty of murder, and the local doctor Glyn Jones was murdered. What the newspapers do not reveal is that many years later in about 1959 after David Davies had been released from prison, he returned to visit his old home and the graveyard at Bethel Chapel in Ffarmers, which must have caused quite a stir.

Ownerships

The property was leased by the various doctors from the freehold owners in the 19th and early 20th centuries. In 1892 Elizabeth Rees (née Jenkins) the owner of the house married Rev Thomas Rees of Oswestry; she became a widow and in 1909 sold the property to Mrs Louisa Davies (wife of Rev David Davies of Rumney) and Miss Edith Jones in equal shares for £500. In 1924 the two lady owners (who were probably sisters) sold on to David Jones a farmer of Llanwrda for £600; the tenant at this time was Dr William Richards. David Jones died in 1939 and left the house to his grandson, David TGP Jones, a Police Officer in Birmingham; the tenant in occupation was Dr Richard Hall. In 1941 David Jones sold to Mrs Dorothy Burniston, the wife of the resident Dr James Burniston. Then in 1943 she sold to Evan Harries of Brondeilo, Crugybar for £900. Evan Harries died in 1951 and left the house to his wife Mary Harries. Mary died intestate in 1959 and the property passed to her two brothers, David Harries and Evan Harries. In 1967 the two brothers sold to Mrs Beatrice Newton-Dawson of Guildford for £3,500. In 1970 she onsold to Canon and Mrs Howard Williams of Llanelli for £5,200.

In 1987 Mr and Mrs Forward bought the house for £58,000 and sold it in 2009 to the current owners, Esdaile (Dale) Hudson (b1937) and his wife Jenni. Dale was born in India into a traditionally military family and educated at Sherborne and Sandhurst. He served in the 2nd KEO Goorkha Rifles for 10 years (1956-66) in Malaya and Borneo and then trained to be an artist. Since 1972 he has painted full time and exhibited in many galleries both in the UK and abroad as well as restoring period furniture.

26.9 Baileyvicar / Beili Ficer (vicar's enclosure) [SN632369]

Fred Price[607] suggests that Baily Vicar used to be an ancient palace in the 15th century and that Sir D Thomas Bt lived there and was Sheriff of Carmarthenshire in 1524. There seems to be no hard evidence for this and we have no idea who Sir D Thomas was; he could not have been a baronet since that title was not created until the 17th century. We do know that this farm has been the largest in the Llansawel area for generations and its spellings have included Baily Vicar, Beilificer, Beili Fier, and Bailey Vicar. In the Llansawel Rent Rolls[608] for James I (1603-25) Morgan Thomas is stated to pay rent of jd (1p) for Bayli r Vichar. In 1670 the house had four hearths. During the 18th century it became a farmhouse[609] and during alterations made in 1830-35 certain parts of the interior and the very fine entrance door of the 1550-80 period were taken away and installed in the new 19th century mansion at Glanyrannell where they remain.

Beili Ficer 2017

[607] Fred Price: *Llansawel p78*
[608] Mee (1891) p87
[609] Francis Jones: *Carmarthenshire Homes p8*

YEAR	BAILEYVICAR (BEILI FICER) FARM LLANSAWEL CENSUS RETURNS
1841	**EVANS: Theodorus** (60) farmer, Jane (50) wife, Sarah (25) dau, Daniel (20) son, Mary (15) dau, 4 serv agric lab
1851	**MORGAN: William** (43) farmer of 293 acres born Llanfynydd, Sarah (32) wife, Thomas (18) cousin draper, Mary (10) cousin, 7 serv
1861	**HARRIES: Evan** (41) farmer of 300 acres, Jane (40) wife with 5 children, 4 serv
1871	**HARRIES: Evan** (50) farmer of 300 acres born Caio, Jemima (26) dau, Daniel (23) son, William (21) son, Margaret (18) dau, Rachel (16) dau, Jane (13) dau, Evan (12) son, Kate (9) dau, Mary (7) dau, David (3) son and 2 ser
1881	**HARRIES: Evan** (60) farmer of 330 acres employing 5 men, Evan (22) son, Jemima (37) dau, Catherine (18) dau, Mary (16) dau, David Thomas (13) grandson, Thomas Evans (21) ser
1891	**HARRIES: Evan** (69) farmer, Jemima (47) dau, Evan (31) son, Mary (26) dau, David (22) grandson, David (36) nephew, Margaret Williams (23) ser, James Davies (17) ser, Thomas Jones (18) ser
1901	**HARRIES: Evan** (82) farmer born Caio, Jemima (59) dau housekeeper, Esther Thomas (19) granddau dairymaid, Margaret (17) granddau ser, John Harries (23) nephew cowman, Roderick Williams (19) ser, Daniel Williams (12) ser
1911	**THOMAS: John** (53) farmer born Llandeilo fawr, Jane Jones (31) dau, Margaret Thomas (27) dau, William (24) son, Mary (18) dau, Daniel (14) son, Simon Jones (7) grandson, John Harries (38) farm ser, Thomas Davies (24) farm ser

The first known family were the Morgan family, descended from the house of Edwinsford. Morgan Thomas referred to above was Sheriff of Carmarthenshire in 1618 and was succeeded by his son James Morgan. A later James Morgan married Mary Protheroe of Nantyrhebog and after he died she married William Combey. She died in 1685. The next family were also called Morgan (unrelated) and they moved to Upland near Carmarthen. Later Thomas Mainwaring lived there (1696-1709) followed in 1725 by Lewis Price. His descendant, Evan Price (1821-96), the son of Thomas and Mary Price, was born there on 4 October 1821. His parents[610] farmed there in the early years of the 19th century and were much respected for their kindness and honesty. His father, Thomas Price (b1791)[611], was the son of John and Margaret Price of Tyllwydd, Cwrt y Cadno[612] and was a cattle dealer as well as a farmer selling to drovers; his mother was the daughter of Evan and Sarah Evans of Y Plas in Talley. Evan was educated at the Froodvale Academy and acted as the local Liberal Party Agent for many years being nicknamed "Gladstone Bach". He married an English girl from Stroud, Eliza, and they had two sons, Fred (1862-1947) and John (b1865), and two daughters, Marian (b1859) and Ada (b1866).

In 1849 Evan (known as Price Bach y Siop)[613] bought and opened a drapers and grocers shop (Glynsawyl House, now Sawyl House) in Llansawel in the main street not far from the Post Office. Evan served as treasurer of the Llansawel Highway Board (1861-86) and as assistant overseer for the poor of the parish (1866-96). He was involved with setting up Llansawel School in 1871 and served as clerk until 1875. He was buried in Llansawel Churchyard. His elder son, Fred Price (1862-1947), the well-known historian was born in Llansawel and educated at Llansawel School and then at Sawel Academy, which had been established in the old Parish Schoolroom by Rev Jonah Evans (see Chapter 30.2). He then went to Swansea and in 1893 married an English girl, Rebecca. Fred is described in the census returns as an accountant and land valuer employed by the tax office. Their eldest son, Evan Emrys (1897-1971), was born in Swansea and was a teacher there; their second son, Wesley Owen (1903-83), was an electrical engineer and married. In 1898 Fred published his *History of Llansawel* later to be followed by his *History of Caio* (1904) and *History of Talley* (1934). He also produced a literary index of the publications of the Hon Society of the Cymmrodorion which won a prize at the National Eisteddfod. He died in Swansea in 1947.

610 Fred Price p69-71

611 DJ Williams p76 states that Thomas Price's sister, Jane (b1797), was a pillar of the Baptist cause at Bethel Cwmpedol and the great grandmother of DJ Williams. Jane Price was closely related to Daniel Price, the solicitor of Talley House (see Chapter 24.1)

612 David Lewis: Family Histories p317-320

613 DJ Williams p76

During the 19th century the farming families on this 300 acre farm included Evan Harries who was there for over 40 years. During the 19th century the Glanrannell Estate nearby at Crugybar acquired the farm; in 1917 they auctioned it for sale although the Thomas family continued as tenants. William Thomas, shown in the 1911 census, took over the tenancy from his father John Thomas, and his son John also took on the tenancy until 1964 when he bought the freehold. His sons, Alfor and Elwyn Thomas, now aged 64 and 63, were born on the farm and inherited it. They are both unmarried and have farmed there all their lives. They did not want to sell the farm to a larger enterprise and preferred to continue as a sustainable entity. So in 2010 they decided to continue farming a smaller acreage of their farm and a young first generation farming couple, Sion and Claire Williams, took on a 10 year tenancy of the remaining 255 acres; they have also since bought a smaller farm nearby. They have a mixed flock and are applying the latest technology and ideas; this includes rearing Aberfield sheep under contract to Innovis, Aberystwyth, with Aberfield embryos being implanted into mule and texel mule ewes, which is showing very successful results.

27. Village of Caio

The origins of the village of Caio are described at the end of Chapter 1.3.

The Cothi and Tywi valleys are renowned not only for their tradition of hymnology and singing but also for their history of droving (see Chapter 33). In Caio there were no fewer than six public houses (compared with the 28 in Llandovery in 1830) catering for the drovers and others: the Sextons Arms was opposite the lychgate to the Parish Church, the Square and Compass Inn (which probably had a freemasonry connection), the Plough and Harrow and the Caio Inn were at the entrance to the village, the King's Head Inn now renamed Brynrannell was opposite the Post Office, and the Brunant Arms is the only surviving inn today. It is said that some of the drovers stayed overnight at a farm called Llundain-fach Esgairdawe in Caio and that the stream running through the farmyard was christened *Y Tafwys* (the River Thames). Caio provided blacksmiths, food and lodging, a chapel as well as the Church, and fairs for the dealers and pedlars; in short it was ideal for a stop on the long way to Barnet Fair or Smithfield Market. Along the route in Cilycwm there is still a water course on the side of the main street where the cattle and sheep could drink. Blacksmiths and farriers did a good trade wherever the drovers stopped overnight and a common name for such spots was "Cwm Pedol" (horseshoe valley) as in Ffarmers where of course the Drovers Arms tavern was well used. The Brunant Arms in Caio and the Drovers Arms

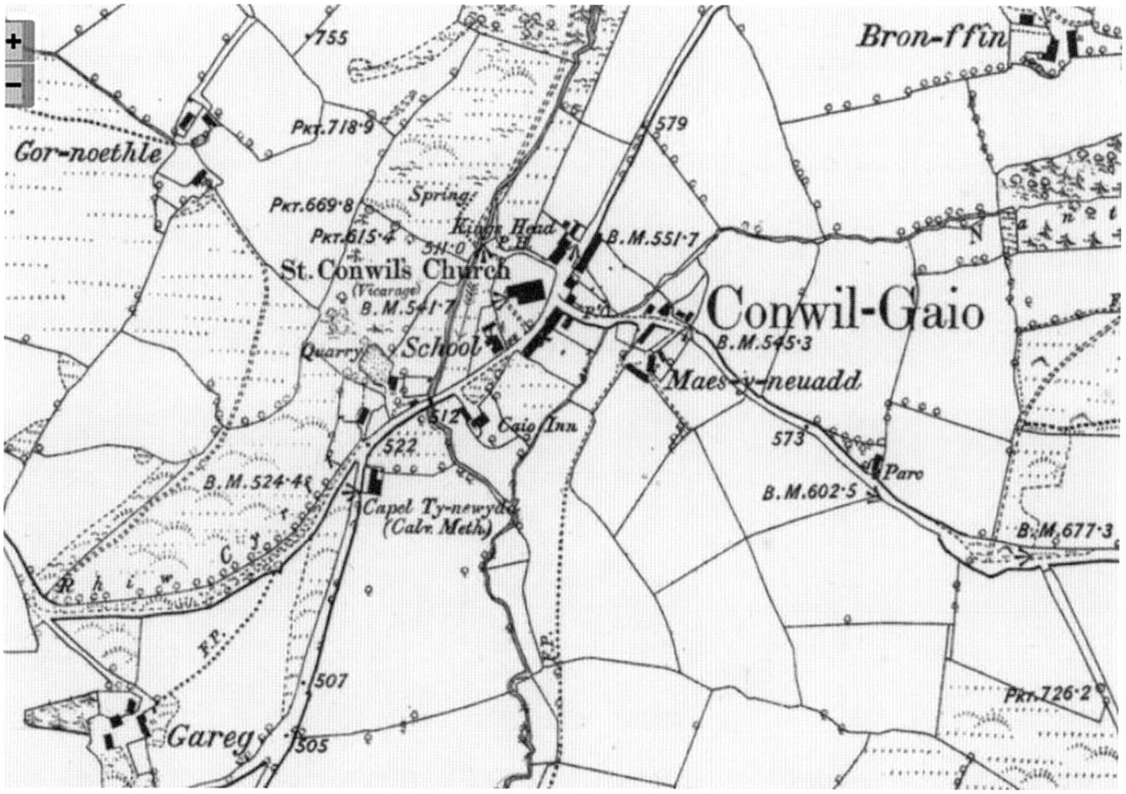

Map of Caio c1886

Caio Village 19th century

Caio Village 2011

in Ffarmers were both part of the Brunant Estate while the Dolaucothi Arms in Pumsaint was part of the Dolaucothi Estate. Most of Caio village and surrounding farms were part of the Edwinsford Estate including the post office and the cottages in Church Lane (in which No 4 was the Sextons Arms) as well as the Caio Inn.

Every Parish used to have its fairs and Saint's day festival when visiting traders and dealers would attend to join in the merriment with the local inhabitants. They would take place at the centre of the Parish at the Llan. T Gwynn Jones in his *Welsh Folklore and Folk Custom (1930)* tells us in relation to the local Saint's Day that: *"The Festivals were generally held on Sundays, but often began on Saturday and continued until Tuesday. The proceedings included contests in leaping, running, hurling, wrestling, cock-fighting and football playing. In the latter contest, players of two parishes would be opposed, and the losers had to supply the winners with beer. Relics of the Saints were carried in procession in some places....intoxication and fighting seem to have been general at these meetings in the 18th century....Rivalry and competition were prominent elements in the Gwylmabsant, which is the reason, perhaps, that to this day there is little chance for anything—religion, education, literature, music, drama, art or sport——to thrive in Wales except on lines of competition."* There would be bear baiting, bull fights, cock fighting, pole vaulting, weight throwing, the tug of war and other sports for the crowds and there is evidence of this for example at the Llandovery and Lampeter Fairs. In the days before pews in the Parish Church it would be common for the Church to be used rather like a Village Hall is used today and for many community activities to take place either in the Church itself or outside in the graveyard.

It is thought that in the 17th century there was a fair or market somewhere in Wales about four days out of seven which means that there were about 520 weekly markets held in the eight principal towns of Carmarthenshire. At these fairs and markets tenant farmers would sell their produce and pedlars would hawk their wares as well as bring news from elsewhere. Local inns and alehouses would also be the centre of social discourse.

Sometimes these fairs would be held on the same day as the cattle fairs which were also important because cattle, sheep, pigs and horses were bought and sold and drovers would attend. After the arrival of the railways these animals could be more efficiently transported by rail and many markets were located close to the railway stations.

The Carmarthen Fair held on 14 November each year was a big event and farm servants used to be given a week's holiday to attend and that week was the annual start date for a farm servant's year. There were also horse fairs at Llanybydder and of course the famous Dalis Fair at Lampeter for horses in front of the Black Lion Hotel.

Marts were held regularly in all the large towns and these gradually replaced the old system of farmers selling direct to dealers and often losing out on the best price. Llandovery for example had many fairs regulated by its Royal Charter but only started its regular livestock mart in 1912. Gradually the farmers saw the benefits of auctioneers dealing with the buying and selling of animals and obtaining the best market prices for them. During the Second World War this system of open trading had to be suspended but it was restored afterwards and has survived ever since. The railway of course has helped too although many cattle and sheep continue to be transported by lorry. There were also small livestock marts at Pumsaint and Felin Newydd in Crugybar up to the Second World War. Many farmers especially in remote areas would sell livestock to visiting dealers who would visit the farms and make an offer on the spot.

Fairs[614] were traditionally held in Caio three times a year on 30 May, 21 August and 6 October and Caio fairs were amongst the largest in Wales being arranged to suit the dealers and drovers with six inns and plenty of food and accommodation to cope with the visitors. Blacksmiths met the dealers to shoe the cattle. Fairs would involve much entertainment, many stalls, pageants and parades, with music and alcohol which would not have been appreciated by non-conformists and the temperance societies.

In the 1920-30s most of the men worked on the farms or in the Dolaucothi Goldmines and then for the Forestry Commission. Some worked on the roads as "lengthmen" or as repairers. None of the houses had mains water or electricity. There were very few cars and no buses so journeys to Lampeter meant walking to the main road, although

[614] Fred Price: *Caio p77*; LCTA p162

provisions were delivered by the P&D Co-op lorries and travelling salesmen came round from time to time. Children who passed the scholarship exam (11+) weekly-boarded in Llandovery from the age of 11, 12 or 13; they often lodged with someone with whom their parents had family connections or who were former neighbours. In the parish of Cynwyl Gaeo there were telephones only at Pumsaint and Caio Post Offices and at Dolaucothi, Brunant and Glanrannell.

In 1989 the villagers of Caio held a fair and dressed up in contemporary costumes. In the same year a floral festival was held in the Parish Church depicting well known local historical figures including Dafydd Jones and Morgan Dafydd (drovers and hymnologists), Timothy Richards (the missionary who went to China), Nurse Jane Evans (who worked with Florence Nightingale), Nansi Jones from Crugybar (probably the first woman to take part in a religious service in Wales), Dr John Harries (the wizard from Pantcoy), and Roger Williams (founder of the State of Rhode Island). In 1994 a special fair was held celebrating the 75th anniversary of what is believed to have been the last fair held in Caio although some think the last one was held in 1934. I remember it being a great success with everyone dressed in Victorian costume, Ieuan Williams of Abermangoed re-enacting the ballad singers in front of the Caio Post Office who used to attend the old fairs and bring news, and a hog roast for the hungry attendees.

28. Selected Conwil Gaeo Properties

As can be seen from Chapters 16.5 to 16.10, the Edwinsford Estate owned several properties in the parish of Cynwyl (Conwil) Gaeo over recent centuries around Caio and Crugybar; in the main they were sold in 1918-19.

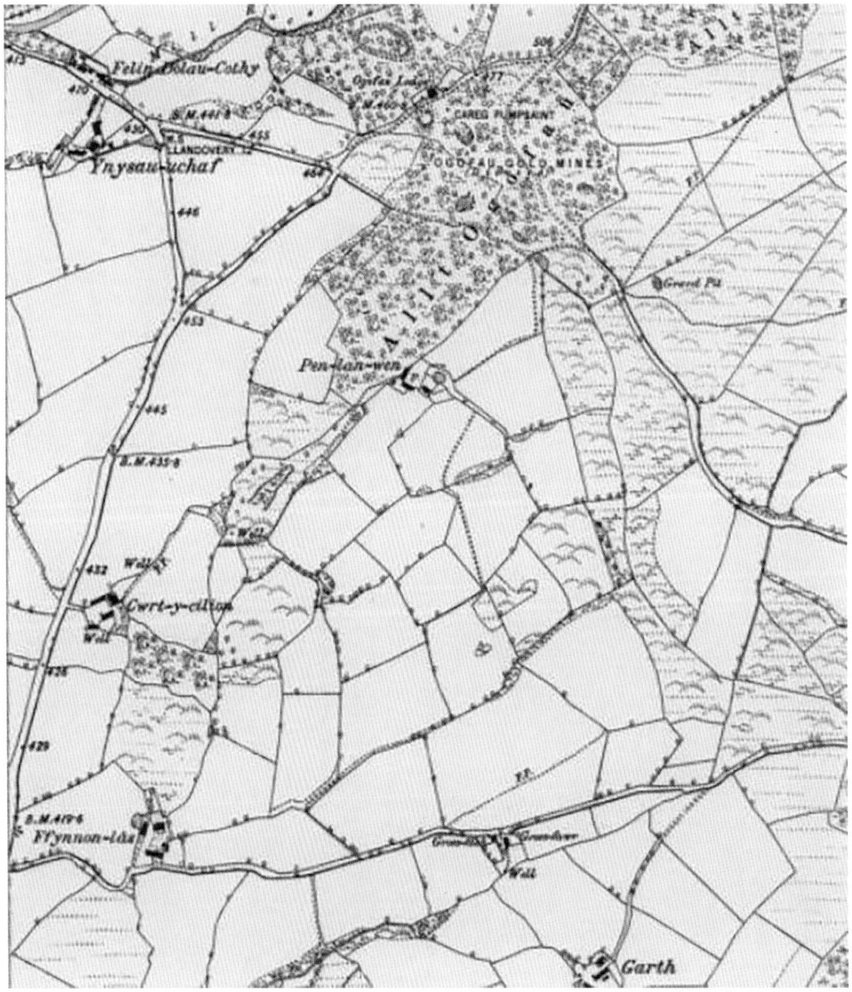

Pumsaint to Bridgend road map c1886

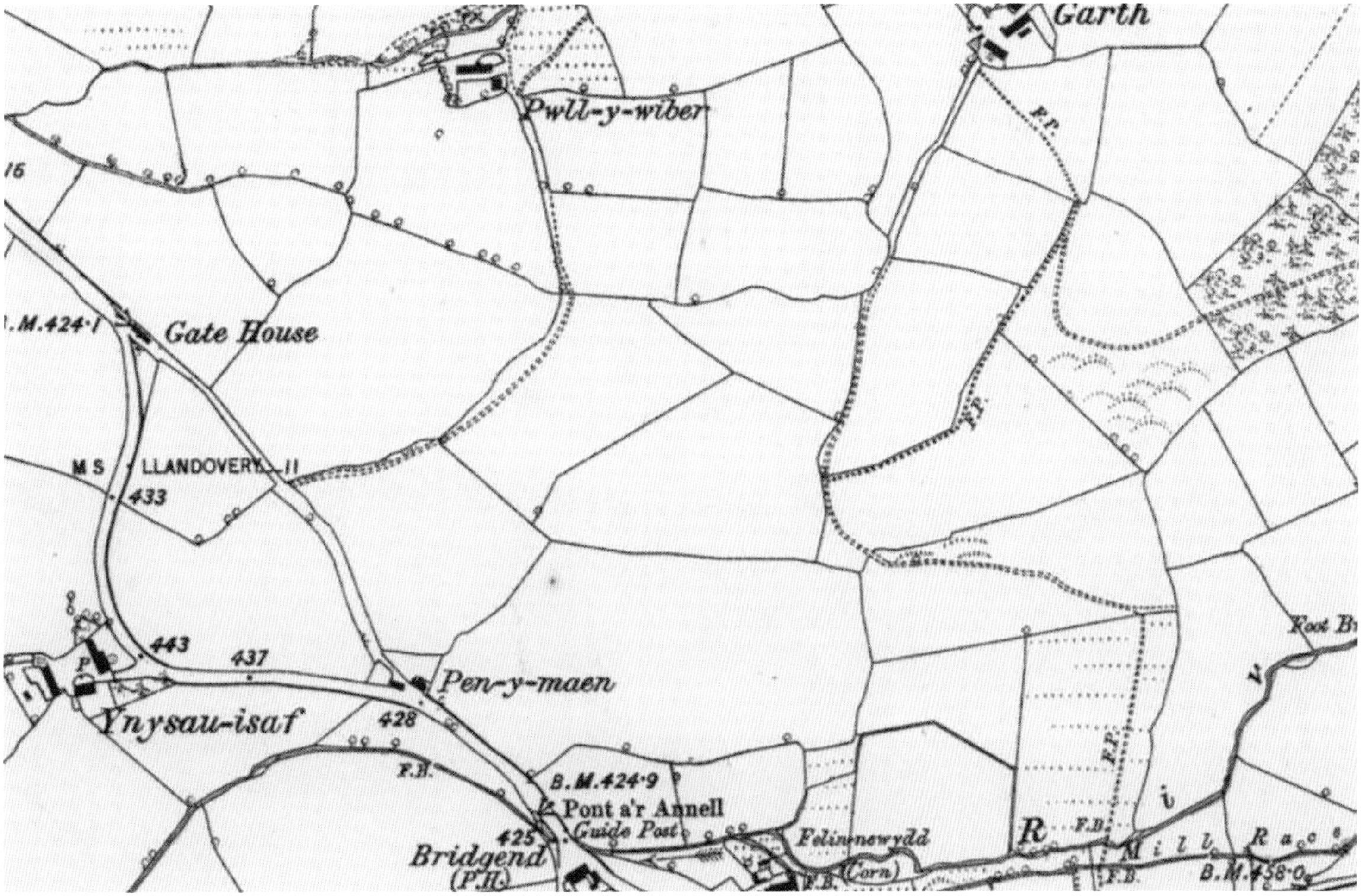

Bridgend road map c1886

28.1 Abernaint Fawr (mouth of the large streams) [SN646355]
This farm was owned by the Edwinsford Estate for generations and is located on the Crugybar to Talley road on a steep hill which used to be difficult for traffic in the winter before salting was used. It used to be in the parish of Talley but is now part of Crugybar. In the 16th and 17th centuries it was the seat of a cadet branch[615] of the Edwinsford family who adopted the surname of Price. We saw in Chapter 6.2 that James Price, the fourth son of Rhys ap William (39), was living there when he married Elinor Gwynne of Taliaris in 1589 and that one of their sons, William Price, was living there in 1621 and was Purse Bearer to the Earl of Northumberland. Thomas Price living there in 1740 was the last of his line, but the property remained as part of the Edwinsford Estate.

In the 1813 Edwinsford Estate accounts it is shown as occupied by David Williams as tenant who is also shown on the 1841 census and in the 1841 Tithe Apportionment Agreement as the tenant of 128 acres. The Williams family continued as tenants but the farm increased to 200 acres according to the census returns. By 1891 there is no census entry which suggests that there was a change of tenant after Anne Williams had perhaps retired. The tenant in the 1901 and 1911 census returns is shown as Thomas Evans who is also listed in the 1903 estate accounts; he was married to Jane Williams who was born in Abernaint and the daughter of the previous tenants, David and Anne Williams.

The Williams family from Builth took on the tenancy and later bought the freehold during the 1970s when the Edwinsford Estate was divided

Abernaint 2017

[615] Francis Jones: *Carmarthenshire Homes p4*

YEAR	ABERNAINT FAWR CRUGYBAR CENSUS RETURNS
1841	**WILLIAMS: David** (35) farmer, Mary (75) mother, 4 serv
1851	**WILLIAMS: David** (29) farmer of 200 acres born Talley, Anne (34) wife with 5 children, 6 serv
1861	**WILLIAMS: DAVID** (38) farmer of 200 acres, Anne (46) wife with Mary (18) stepdau and 6 children, Thomas Williams (18) ploughman, Thomas Powel (35) visitor local preacher of the Independents
1871	**WILLIAMS: David** (50) farmer of 200 acres born Talley, Anne (54) wife, William (25) son, Jane (20) dau, John (17) son, Margaret (9) dau with 2 ser
1881	**WILLIAMS: Anne** (63) farmer of 200 acres, Sarah (27) dau, Margaret (19) dau, David Lewis (19) ser, Thomas Davies (14) ser, Rachel Jones (21) ser
1891	No entry
1901	**EVANS: Thomas** (47) farmer, Jane (50) wife, Davie (16) son, John (10) son, Jane Dicks (22) ser, William Hudson (18) carter, Joseph Sestener (15) cowman
1911	**EVANS: Thomas** (57) farmer born Caio, Jane (61) wife (5 children 3 still alive) born Abernaint, David (26) son born Cwmyrin Caio, James Morgan (19) serv waggoner born Blaenwain Caio, George Haskins (23) cowman, Margaret Morgan (17) serv

and sold; John Francis the auctioneer was offering some 27 farms of the estate for sale at a total cost of about £800,000 at that time. DJ Williams, father of Malcolm Williams (b1963) who has farmed there for 24 years, died in 2016 aged 88 and his widow died in 2017. Malcolm married Llinos Williams (b1971) of Llwynceiliog[616], Cwrt y Cadno and they now farm Abernaint with some 200 acres. They have three children, Harri (b2002), Tomi (b2005) and Molly (b2013).

Abernaint Fach, which was a one storey longhouse, had tenants in past years but not in living memory. It is now in ruins and is located to the south of the farm.

28.2 Ddyfadfa (sheep path) [SN653415]

YEAR	DDYFADFA PUMSAINT CENSUS RETURNS
1841	**THOMAS: Lettice** (61), Thomas (35), Daniel (40), Mary Williams (20), John Lloyd (14)
1851	**JONES: Jane** (39) widow plus 5 sons (Thomas, David, Daniel, John, James), Mary Saunders (19) ser
1861	**JONES: Jane** (47) farmer, Thomas (25) son, David (22) son, Daniel (18) son, John (12) son, 1 ser
1871	**JONES: Jane** (56) farmer born Llansawel, James (30) son, Daniel (27) son, Elinor Evans (17) ser
1881	**JONES: Daniel** (36) farmer of 65 acres, Jane (32) wife, Daniel (2) son, Daniel Jones (18) ser
1891	**JONES: Daniel** (43) farmer, Daniel (12) son, David Williams (30) ser, Jane Jones (20) niece
1901	**JONES: Daniel** (55) farmer born Caio, Hannah (47) wife, Dan (21) son
1911	**JONES: Daniel** (67) farmer, Hannah (57) wife, Dan (30) son, P Jones (19) nephew postman

This farm is located opposite the old tollgate house outside Pumsaint on the Lampeter road. In the 1813 estate accounts the farm is shown as owned by the Edwinsford Estate and occupied by John Thomas. By the time of the 1841 Tithe Apportionment Agreement it was occupied by Lettice Thomas who was probably his wife farming 92 acres. It was spelt "Dudadfa", then "Dyfadfa" of "Ddyfadfa".

The Jones family who followed the Thomas family farmed there for several decades well into the 20th century. By the time of the 1903 estate accounts the farm had been sold by the Edwinsford Estate to the Methuens of Llystroiddyn closeby. Around 1920 William Williams (dc1950) took over the tenancy of the farm. He was born at Blaenrhisglog and married his sister in law following the death of his brother who was her husband; he worked in the coal mines before returning to take on a farm tenancy at Caegwyn, Harford, and then moved to be the tenant of Ddyfadfa. Later he bought the farm from

[616] David Lewis: *Family Histories p188*

the Llystroiddyn Estate. He had three daughters and one son, Samuel Williams (b1911), who was the youngest. Samuel and one of his sisters farmed Ddyfadfa until they retired and sold the farm in about 1955. Samuel lived in a cottage in Crugybar for a while until his niece, Anne (née Boobyer), married Heddwyn Jones; Samuel bought them a small farm Derlwyn, Harford and they looked after him there until his death in about 1993. Anne later inherited a farm Maesionydd in Ffarmers. Anne's son Justin married Eirlys Evans of Penarth Uchaf, Pumsaint and they lived in Maesionydd. Anne also had two daughters, Gwyneth and Lynwen. Gwyneth, married Alun Richards of Ynysau (Cwrtycilion) son of Gwynfor and Bethan Richards of Tegfryn, Pumsaint; Gwyneth is a physiotherapist at Lampeter surgery and has three children.

Evan Jones and his wife Margaret, who both died about 1923, took over the tenancy of Cefncoedmawr, a farm on the Dolaucothi Estate close to Ddyfadfa, in 1902. Their son David farmed with them. Their grand-daughter Sarah (b1902) married Tom Jones (1907-94) from Harford who took over that farm and they retired in 1972. By all accounts Tom was a man of wit; on one occasion he was fishing after dark and when approached by a water bailiff who asked his name, he replied "John West"! He was a big man who used to enjoy visiting all the local farms for a chat in the evening. When he retired he went to live with his daughter Ceinwen.

Tom and Sarah (Sallie) had one daughter Ceinwen (1933-2016) who was born at Cefncoedmawr. Ceinwen married Merfyn Davies from Crugybar Post Office in 1955 and they farmed at Ddyfadfa from 1955 (when they bought it following the retirement of Samuel Williams) until Merfyn's death in 1988. Ceinwen continued to farm there until 1992 when she moved over the road to a nice new bungalow next to the tollgate house which she had built on part of her farm land. Ddyfadfa was then farmed by her son Gareth Davies and his wife Sue; following Gareth's tragic early death Sue continued to farm there with her partner, Tom Herbert from Gwarcoed Esgairdawe, who very sadly died of cancer in 2016. Ceinwen had a wonderful memory and it was a delight to speak to her before her death in 2016. Sue continues to farm Ddyfadfa and is a lovely person much admired by all who know her. Today the farm is some 65 acres in size with an additional 60 acres on the hill across the road.

Ddyfadfa 2017

28.3 Ynysau Uchaf (upper river meadows) [SN658403]
There have been no fewer that six properties called "Ynysau" beside the Llanwrda road just outside Pumsaint; four of them have at some stage been owned by the Edwinsford Estate. In earlier times[617] the name "Llawr Ynyssau" was used and the family pedigree recorded by Lewys Dwnn[618] is headed "Plwyf Gynwil Gaio, Llawr Ynysse". It is thought that at least one of the Ynysau farms was home for five generations from the late 15th century of a minor gentry family descended from Jestyn ap Gwrgant, the last Welsh Prince of Glamorgan. David ap Jenkin was followed by his son John, and his son Morgan ap John of Llawrynyssau married Elen, daughter and coheiress of William Rees Morgan of Rhydodin (Edwinsford).

Ynysau Uchaf farm is located outside Pumsaint by the bridge opposite Dolaucothi Mill (Felindolau). For centuries it was part of the Dolaucothi Estate[619] owned by the Johnes family who passed it to the National Trust in the 1950s.

The Davies family tenants followed the Williams family at the farm. Both were in occupation for several decades in the 19th and early 20th centuries reflecting how settled the farming industry was at that time. The backbone of the farm like so many others in the Cothi valley was dairy with the milk being made into butter and used for rearing calves and pigs upto the 1930s followed by a period of selling milk to the Milk Marketing Board. This ended in the 1980-90s when the farms started to sell their milk quotas and their dairy herds to concentrate just on sheep and in some cases breeding cattle.

John Davies took over the tenancy in the late 1870s and was followed by his son Albert who retired to live near Llanfair ar Bryn, Llandovery in 1941. Another Davies family then took over the tenancy.

David Davies (1869-1936)[620] from Brynglas in Llanddewibrefi and his wife Anne Jones (1870-1933), the daughter of Evan Jones (1844-78) and Margaret Jones (1850-1921) of Aberbranddu, farmed at Gwndwnmawr. They had two sons:

(1) David Davies (1890-1952) who married Sarah Ann Powell (1901-83) from Noyadd Blaenduhonw, Maesmynis, Builth Wells in November 1929 and settled at Gwndwnmawr, David's parents having retired and moved to Trebeddau. David and Sarah had two children: (a) Glyn (b1930) who was born in Gwndwnmawr and (b) Elizabeth Ann (Bethan)(b1933) who was born in Garthynty to where the family had moved in 1932. The family moved to Abermangoed in 1943 and then to Llandre in May 1947. In 1952 following the death of his father David, Glyn took over the running of Llandre with his mother. Glyn married Doris Davies (b1941) in 1960 and they retired from Llandre to their house in Lampeter in 1987 following which their son Huw (b1963) and his wife Sheila Powell (b1963) took over the National Trust tenancy; and

Ynysau Uchaf 2016

617 Francis Jones: *Carmarthenshire Homes p199*
618 Dwnn Vol 1 p241; NLW Alcwyn Evans Ms 12356 p719
619 David Lewis: *Dolaucothi and Brunant p319-325*
620 David Lewis: *Family Histories p153*

YEAR	YNYSAU UCHAF PUMSAINT CENSUS RETURNS
1841	**WILLIAMS: Thomas** (35) farmer, Anne (35) wife, William (13) son, Mary (11) dau, Thomas (9), John (7) , David (5), Elizabeth (3), Anne (7 mon), 4 serv
1851	**WILLIAMS: Thomas** (47) farmer of 231 acres born Conwil Gaeo, William (23) son, Thomas (19) son, John (17) son, Mary (21) dau, Elizabeth (12) dau, Anne (10) dau, Timothy (3) son, 2 serv
1861	**WILLIAMS: Thomas** (57) farmer born Caio, Mary (30) dau, David (24) son, 4 serv
1871	**WILLIAMS: David** (35) farmer of 150 acres born Caio, Mary (19) wife and 4 ser
1881	**DAVIES: John** (41) farmer of 200 acres born Caio, Jane (41) wife, Janet (19) dau, Benjamin (17) son, Jemima (15) dau, James (13) son, Margaret (11) dau, David (9) son, Sarah (7) dau, Albert (3) son, Edith (8 mon) dau, David Thomas (20) ser
1891	**DAVIES: John** (51) farmer, Jane (51) wife, Jeanette (28) dau, John (26) son, Mia (25) dau, Maggie (21) dau, David (18) son, Albert (120 son, Edith (10) dau
1901	**DAVIES: John** (61) farmer, Jane (61) wife, Margaret (30) dau, David (28) son, Sarah (25) dau, Albert (22) son
1911	**DAVIES: John** (70) farmer born Caio, Jane (70) wife (9 children alive), Maggie (38) dau, Albert (31) son, Bill Dawson (40) farm serv

(2) Evan Davies (1892-1959) who married Elizabeth (Lizzie)(1894-1959) from Garthynty nextdoor where they farmed until they moved to Llandre in 1932 with their two children, David (Dai)(1912-77) and Nell (1917-86). Evan and Lizzie retired and moved to Brynglas in Pumsaint in 1946. Dai married Sarah (Sallie) Anne Jones (1916-2004) while his sister Nell married Sallie's brother, David Tom Jones, who was born at Ddeunant in Cwmann but farmed at Gwladeithau over the hill from Llandre, so a brother and sister of the Davies family married a sister and brother of the Jones family. Dai and Sallie moved to Ynysau in 1941 and shared the house and farmwork with Albert Davies (from a different family) until Albert and his sister retired around 1946 when Dai took on the tenancy. Initially they employed a live-in fulltime farmworker John Jones who married Gina Jones who later lived in Caio, then Aneurin James of Cwmpriddfa Caio followed by three brothers, Eric, Emrys and Glyn George from Pantiauau, Llansawel (Glyn George now owns Ynysau Isaf), then Aelwyn Evans from Llanllwni, Sid Mason now of Bryndolau, and Leonard Jones of Abermangoed Mill. The maids included Blanche Davies of Tynant Ffarmers, Gwladys Morgan of Bryneglwysfach Pumsaint, Beti Rowlands of Taliaris, Lil Bolton of Gwarnoethle, and Gwladys's sister Yvonne. In the 1950s they also employed Tegwyn Williams (now of Cwrtderi) who was living in Felindolau opposite and with his wife Iris later took on the National Trust tenancy at Dolaucothi Home Farm[621].

Dai and Sallie had two children: (a) Eiddwen (b1944) who married Edward Morgan and farmed at Nantybwia near Carmarthen where they produced the Nantybwia cheese, and (b) Arwyn (b1949) who went to Llandovery College and is a most charming and amusing man whose interests include singing and playing in his own local band (Free Beer). He married Jill from Reading who had come to work at the Dolaucothi Arms in 1977 for a family who had come from Rhodesia and had the tenancy. Arwyn took over the farm tenancy in 1975 when his father had health problems (and later died aged 64) and he and Jill retired in September 2016 to live near Llandovery; I and several hundred friends and neighbours attended the traditional huge farm sale. So ended 75 years of the second Davies family's tenancy. Arwyn, who farmed 200 acres with 650 ewes was a key member of the National Trust Dolaucothi Farming Group[622] of seven sheepfarmers who since 2003 have won several national best lamb awards.

Arwel Jenkins from Llanybydder (who is also a mechanic) and his partner Gail Lewis (a land agent consultant) from Llanidloes took over the tenancy in October 2016.

[621] David Lewis: *Family Histories p130-2*

[622] David Lewis: *Family Histories p133-4*

28.4 Ynysau (Cwrtycilion) [SN658397]

This farm is located next to Ynysau Uchaf but its farmhouse is on the other side of the main road. It was owned by the Methuens of the Llystroiddyn Estate in 1891 who had the sporting rights and who also owned Penarth (222 acres)[623] and Penarth Fach across the Cothi river; it is unclear for how long they had owned it before that. When the river was high it was often difficult to cross and had to be attempted on horseback which was more convenient than the journey round by road via Pumsaint which took much longer. The Llystroiddyn Estate was sold during the 1920s.

David Evans and his family lived there from about 1938. He was a car owner and on one occasion was travelling towards Pumsaint from the Bridgend Inn and turning right into his farm when he collided with someone who was overtaking him and there was a serious accident. A grand-daughter of the family was Ceridwen Thomas (1925-2000), a cousin of the William Evans family of Erwhen[624], who was evacuated from London in 1939 to live with her uncle and aunt Mr and Mrs Jack Timothy, became head girl of Lampeter School and in 1946 married Dai Williams[625] of Brynteg, Cwrt y Cadno. David Evans died in 1939 following which his wife continued farming until 1946 when she sold the farm for £3,000 to John and Mona (née Lloyd) Richards of Blaenwaun, Ffarmers (some locals still call the farm Ynysau Richards). John and Mona's son, Gwynfor, and his wife Bethan took over the farm and lived there until 1998 when they retired and sold it to Stephen and Mair Cavanhagh of Cilycwm (now separated but running the farm in partnership). It is now a farm of some 70 acres with a small flock of ewes plus cattle and milking cows which are also grass fed on their Cilycwm farm.

YEAR	YNYSAU (CWRTYCILION) CENSUS RETURNS
1841	**EVANS: Daniel** (55) farmer, Anne (55) wife, Margaret (20) dau, 4 serv
1851	**EVANS: Daniel** (60) farmer of 70 acres born Pencarreg, Mary (49) wife, 3 serv
1861	**EVANS: Mary** (59) farmer with 4 serv
1871	**DAVIES: Mary** (42) wife farmer of 75 acres born Caio, Annie (5) dau, Eleanor (4) dau with 3 ser
1881	**DAVIES: Daniel** (59) farmer of 74 acres, Mary (52) wife, William (14) nephew and 4 servs
1891	**DAVIES: Daniel** (69) farmer born Caio, Mary (61) wife, Ellen (24) dau, Daniel Evans (1) grandson, Elizabeth Evans (18) ser, John Morgans (20) ser, John Evans (16) ser
1901	**DAVIES: Nellie** (30) farmer, Daniel Evans (11) nephew, John Jones (27) ser, Ann Thomas (19) ser, John Edwards (14) ser
1911	No entry

Ynysau Cwrtycilion 2017

[623] Francis Jones: *Carmarthenshire Homes p145*. Penarth uchaf, ganol and fawr had been sold to the Edwinsford Estate in 1636-9, but later sold onto the Llystroiddyn Estate
[624] David Lewis: *Family Histories p343*
[625] David Lewis: *Family Histories p215*

28.5 Ynysau Ganol (Ffynnonlâs) [SN659394]

This farm is next to Cwrtyceilion on the north side of the main Pumsaint to Llanwrda road. It was owned by the Edwinsford Estate for generations. It is listed in the 1813 estate accounts when John Edwards is shown as the tenant; he was probably the father of the David Edwards shown in the 1841 census. It is also listed in the 1903 estate accounts as occupied by Thomas Davies (shown in the 1901 census), and at the 1918 auction the estate sold the farm of 99 acres for £3,650 to the tenant, Thomas Davies[626]. However something went wrong with the sale because the title deeds show that on 1 January 1919 the farm was sold to the Dolaucothi Estate[627]. The Edwards, Williams and Davies families had been tenants for more than a century.

Griffith Davies, son of Thomas Davies, and his wife then ran the farm as tenants (known as Ynysau Davies) and later retired to the neighbouring farm, Godregarth. Griffith was followed by David Davies from Esgairdawe (no relation) and his wife who took on the tenancy; they later retired to Felindolau on the Dolaucothi Estate in 1953 (after the existing tenant Isaac Williams died) and they died fairly soon afterwards. They had three children: (a) Gwyneth (who married Danny Powell, who in his early days was a gardener for Major Marshall in England before he bought Brunant, and then farmed at Cefntelych Lodge), (b) Beryl (who married Emyr Griffiths a lorry driver with D Lloyd & Sons), and (c) Elwyn (who discontinued farming and became a bus driver in Ammanford).

Rees Edwin Evans and his wife Martha (Mattie) from Babel, Llandovery then took over the tenancy of the farm, which was owned by the Dolaucothi Estate, and they later bought the freehold on 29 September 1960 from Hilda Lloyd-Johnes to whom it had been left by her husband, Herbert Lloyd-Johnes, on his death in 1958 (he had already given most of the Dolaucothi Estate to the National Trust).

Ffynnonlâs 2017

626 Carmarthen Journal (27 Sept 1918)

627 David Lewis: *Dolaucothi and Brunant p263*

YEAR	YNYSAU GANOL (FFYNNONLAS) CENSUS RETURNS
1841	**EDWARDS: David** (25) farmer, Mary (25) wife with 4 children, 5 serv
1851	**WILLIAMS: Walter** (47) farmer of 107 acres born Conwil Gaeo, Mary (42) wife with 3 children, 4 serv
1861	**WILLIAMS: Walter** (58) farmer, Mary (53) wife with 3 children, 2 ser
1871	**WILLIAMS: Walter** (68) farmer of 109 acres, Mary (61) wife, Thomas (25) son, Margaret (26) dau, Walter (2) grandson, Elizabeth (1) granddau with 2 ser
1881	**WILLIAMS: Walter** (76) farmer of 112 acres born Caio, Mary (71) wife, Thomas (33) son, Walter (12) grandson, John Evans (18) ser, Anne Connell (23) dairymaid, Anne Davies (13) ser
1891	**WILLIAMS: Thomas** (43) farmer born Caio, Anne (35) wife, Walter (87) father, Joseph Edwards (17) ser, Mary Evans (20) ser
1901	**DAVIES: Thomas** (52) farmer, Anne (48) wife, Sarah (18) dau, David (16) son, Lizzie (12) dau, Griffith (9) son, Willie (7) son
1911	**DAVIES: Thomas** (63) farmer born Llandeilo, Anne (59) wife (5 children all alive), Sarah (28) dau, David (26) son, Lizzie (21) dau, Griffith (19) son

Mattie was the sister of Sallie Davies of Ynysau Uchaf. Rees and Mattie had two daughters: (a) Esme (b1942) a much respected headteacher at Caio School and chairman of the local magistrates' bench who married Daniel (Dan) Jones (b1938) from Blaenau-Caio[628] and they live at Llaindeg very close to Ffynnonlas, and (b) Edwina also a teacher. In 1975 Rees retired and sold the farm to MK Thomas and Munro Rees from whom the current owners, Mr and Mrs Robert Rees, inherited it; they have a son Gavin and a daughter Anna.

28.6 Ynysau Ganol (Derwenfawr: large oaks) [SN 657392]

YEAR	YNYSAU PUMSAINT CENSUS RETURNS
1841	**JAMES: James** (70) farmer, Anne (65) wife, James (20) son, 4 serv
1851	**JAMES: James** (80) farmer of 103 acres born Talley, James (31) son, Catherine (32) dau in law, David (4) grandson, William (1) grandson, 4 serv
1861	**(1) JAMES: James** (41) farmer of 103 acres born Caio, Catherine (43) wife, David (14) son, William (11) son, 3 serv **(2) DAVIES: Thomas** (30) agric lab, Margaret (28) with 2 children, David (69) father former miner [Ynysau Fach]
1871	No entry
1881	**JAMES: James** (61) farmer of 102 acres, Catherine (64) wife, Anne (35) dau, David (33) son, Ann Davies (18) dairymaid
1891	**JAMES: James** (71) farmer born Caio, Catherine (74) wife, David (45) son, David Davies (16) ser, Jane Jones (31) ser, Mary Lewis (17) ser
1901	**HARRIES: Daniel** (54) widower farmer born Llansawel, Evan (20) son, Daniel (17) son, Margaret Rees (28) ser
1911	**HARRIES: Evan** (31) farmer born Talley, Margaret (31) wife, John Halley (36) serv, Charlie Piper (25) serv, Elizabeth Thomas (16) ser

This farm is across the road from Cwrtycilion. It was owned by the Edwinsford Estate for many years; it could be one of the Ynysau properties listed in the 1813 estate accounts in Chapter 16.5.

As we saw in Chapter 9.6, on 21 February 1889 when Sir Joe and Lady Madeline Williams-Drummond (68/67) returned to Edwinsford after their honeymoon, James James as the oldest tenant on the Edwinsford Estate was given the honour of presenting them with a silver chandelier as a wedding present from all the tenants.

In the 1903 estate accounts the farm is listed as occupied by Daniel Harris who is shown in the 1901 census return. The Harries family followed the James family as tenants. Daniel Harries died in 1911 and

[628] David Lewis: *Family Histories p373*

was succeeded by his son Evan. He and his wife had a daughter Marjorie Mary who died aged 15 in 1928; a lovely white marble sculpture of an angel over her grave is near the main door at Caio Church. The family moved to Bryneira, Llandeilo and the mother and her sister (who died in 1942) are also buried at Caio.

In December 1918 the Edwinsford Estate sold the freehold of the farm of 103 acres including Ynysau Gate (the Old Toll House) to Evan Griffiths of Glanyrannell Park (who had bought much of the Glanyrannell estate in 1917 at auction) whilst retaining the rights to gold, silver and minerals (see Chapter 16.9); he died in 1920 and his widow sold the farm in 1921 to Evan George Harries, the tenant, for £4,262.

Evan Harries sold the farm in 1926 to David John Davies of Pencarreg for £3,900. John Davies and his sister employed two fulltime farm workers; one was David Williams of Glancothi who later worked for the Forestry Commission and married Nancy Williams who died in childbirth in 1951. At this time the farm (known as Ynysau Davies) was a 100 acre productive farm of easily worked flat land with regular crops of grain and roots, although the mainstay was dairy given the huge call for milk from the cities and easy rail goods travel. John Davies was a tall good looking man and an elder at Pumsaint Methodist Chapel who led the hymn singing with a deep melodious bass voice at the time of the ministries of Rev TH Creunant Davies and Rev Idris Jones who also had the pastorate of Cwrt y Cadno Chapel. John retired to Aberaeron in 1948 when he sold the farm for £5,535.

Roscoe and Elin Lloyd from Llanybyther were the buyers. Elin was from Abermeurig, Talsarn and a grand-daughter of Dan Jenkins, headmaster of Llanycrwys School[629]. Roscoe set up a grass drying plant where the timber yard is now located. They had two sons (a) Evan

Derwenfawr 2017

[629] David Lewis: *Dolaucothi and Brunant p23, 408;* Alan Leech*: Dan Jenkins (2011)* a famous headmaster of three schools, supporter of Welsh in the curriculum, singer, organiser of concerts and eisteddfodau, recorder of poetry and folk songs, publisher, writer and beekeeper

Stallion doors

(d2016) who set up a Volvo distribution agency in Aberystwyth and then was the owner of Lloyd Motors in Aberaeron now run by his daughter, and (b) Ifor who took over from his father the Derwen Welsh cob stud at Pennant near Aberaeron; the stud farm was started at Ynysau and the stallion stalls survive as do the high stallion doorways in the barn. Both sons were good bass singers and blue medal winners at the National Eisteddfod. In 1963 Roscoe and Elin sold the farm for £29,980 to Major Ralph Yule and his wife Patience; he was a retired army major who lived in Herefordshire and employed bailiffs to run the farm for him; they included the Childs, Glyndwr James, and Yandell families. In 1974 Major Yule sold the farm in various lots; Tegwyn Williams of Dolaucothi bought one lot of 20 acres on which he built Cwrtderi; John Lewis of Cefncoedmawr (now Godregarth) bought another lot; another lot was sold on which the timber business is now located; and the farmhouse with four fields of 16 acres was bought by Bob and Ethel Lewis, who had returned to the UK from teaching in Canada. They sold in 2003 to the current owners of the farmhouse, David and Theresa Ford, a very friendly couple from Towcester.

28.7 Ynysau Gate (Old Toll House) [SN658388]

YEAR	YNYSAU GATE (OLD TOLL HOUSE) CENSUS RETURNS
1841	**EVANS: Evan** (40) blacksmith, Anne (35) wife, Margaret (4) dau
1851	**DAVIES: Lewis** (57) lab on turnpike road, Mary (52) wife, David (12) son, Thomas (8) son
1861	**DAVIES: Lewis** (66) county road lab born Llanarth, Mary (62) wife, Anne (4) granddau
1871	**(1) DAVIES: Mary** (71) annuitant with dau (36) **(2) DAVIES: David** (32) tailor, Sarah (28) wife and 2 children
1881	**DAVIES: David** (42) tailor and draper born Pencarreg, Sarah (38) wife, 5 children, Mary Davies (46) ser
1891	**DAVIES: David** (52) tailor, Sarah (47) wife, Linda (12) dau, Celia (7) dau, Mary Davies (55) ser
1901	**(1) DAVIES: Sarah** (58) charwoman, Elizabeth (65) sis **(2) DAVIES: Mary** (66) charwoman
1911	**(1) DAVIES: Sarah** (68) serv, Elizabeth Harries (76) **(2) DAVIES: Mary** (75)

This property was originally two houses one of which was used as a toll house for the turnpike trust which upkept the road and was similar in shape to the old toll house the other side of Pumsaint (see Chapter 37.1); in those days the main road went past the front of the house and over the hill to the Bridgend Inn. The property is listed in the 1903 estate accounts as being owned by the Edwinsford Estate and the tenant was Sarah Davies; it is unclear when it was acquired by the Edwinsford Estate. As can be seen from Chapter 16.9 the property was sold at the 1918 Edwinsford Estate auction to Evan Griffiths of Glanrannell Park for the sum of £85. He died in 1920 and his widow sold the property together with Derwenfawr in 1921 to Evan George Harries, the tenant of Derwenfawr, although it continued to be occupied by tenants. One of the tenants in the late 1940s and early 1950s was the Bartlett family; Mr Bartlett worked in Llandeilo and used to travel on the early bus to work, but they then moved to the Llandeilo area. It was then left empty for several years.

In 1956 Evan George Harries sold the freehold property consisting of two small cottages with 36 perches (40 perches to the acre) to Roscoe and Elin Lloyd. In 1963 the Lloyds sold to Major Ralph Yule and his wife Patience, who onsold in 1974 to Mrs Patricia North for £1,800. Alan North her husband had a nautical background and he merged the two cottages into one, renovated them and added a number of nautical features including some porthole windows. He died in 2001 and in 2002 Mrs North sold the house to Anne Francis, a very nice Irish nurse who had been working in London and she has lived there ever since.

Ynysau Gate 2017

28.8 Ynysau Isaf (Pwllybaw: a very muddy farmyard) [SN657386]
This farm is located on a sharp bend on the Pumsaint to Llanwrda road just before the Bridgend Inn. It was owned by the Edwinsford Estate. Timothy Davies was the tenant for over 30 years in the mid 19th century. In about 1880 his daughter, Harriet Davies, married Rev Charles Williams, the son of David Williams (1823-82) a draper and postmaster in Llansawel. Sadly Charles[630] drifted into drink and as a result was suspended from his curacy in 1882 and eventually emigrated to America where he died in about 1886. His wife Harriet moved back to live with her father at Ynysau Isaf with her three children (later moving to Bwlchcefnseth): (a) Annie died in her nineties in 1973; (b) David died in 1953 leaving two sons; and (c) Timothy was educated at Llandeilo County School and Aberystwyth University before teaching. He served in 5th Battalion South Wales Borderers as a territorial and then enlisted in 1916 in the Glamorgan Royal Engineers obtaining a commission in 1917 with the Royal Garrison Artillery. He was wounded at the battle of Cambrai and died of his wounds on 5 April 1918 aged 34 and is buried at Varennes Military Cemetery. He is named on the War Memorial in Pumsaint and in Caio Church.

This farm is listed in the 1903 estate accounts as being owned by the Edwinsford Estate and occupied by David Williams, who remains the tenant in the 1911 census return. By the time of the auction in 1918 the farm of over 157 acres is in the hands of David Williams's personal representatives so he must have just died as a tenant; the farm was sold at the auction by the Edwinsford Estate for £750, although the estate retained the mineral and quarry rights over the land.

After David's death his daughter Sarah Jane (1897-1954) and her husband William Morgan (1891-1963) took over the running of the farm. Their two children, Moelwyn (1931-2014) and Violet (1935-2002) inherited the farm and never married. They retired to Glynborthyn House in Crugybar in 1997 when Glyn and Louvain George from Llansawel and Llanwrda bought the farm, which is some

Ynysau Isaf 2017

[630] I am grateful to Dr Roger Brown for this background (see Chapter 26.2 on Porth Factory, Llansawel)

YEAR	YNYSAU ISAF (PWLLYBAU) CENSUS RETURNS
1841	**MORGANS: Mary** (30) farmer with 5 children, 5 serv
1851	**DAVIES: Timothy** (43) farmer of 140 acres, Anne (39) wife with 7 children, 3 serv
1861	**DAVIES: Timothy** (52) farmer of 140 acres born Cards, Anne (49) wife, David (24) son born Llanddewibrefi, plus 6 children
1871	**DAVIES: Timothy** (63) farmer of 165 acres born Cards, Anne (60) wife, Thomas (29) son, James (24) son, Harriet (22) dau, Hannah (20) dau, Anne (6) granddau, Mary Thomas (17) ser
1881	**DAVIES: Timothy** (72) farmer of 136 acres, Anne (69) wife, James (35) son, Hannah (29) dau, Ann (18) granddau
1891	No entry
1901	No entry
1911	**WILLIAMS: David** (53) widower farmer, David (23) son, Tom Morgan (23) nephew waggoner, Mary (20) dau, Willie (17) son, Bessie (16) dau, Sarah Jane (15) dau, Tom (11) son

135 acres in size with a further 21 acres of woodland; they have some 300 ewes and 58 suckling cows plus followers. Glyn and Louvain have a son Hugh (married to Jennifer), who jointly farms with his parents, and a daughter Eleanor (b1970) who farms with her husband Gary Lewis (b1964) at Cefncoedmawr[631] on the Dolaucothi Estate.

On the farm's hilltop overlooking the village of Crugybar stands the old Pigyn Quarry[632] whose quarry rights had been retained by the Edwinsford Estate. Between 1916 and the mid 1930s the quarry was leased to Carmarthenshire County Council and worked continuously to produce stone for road repairs; some 20 men were employed who lived in a hut in a field next to the Bridgend Inn nearby. A steam boiler powered two drilling machines which made the holes into which was placed dynamite. The rocks were moved down the hill in trams running on a simple railway and then crushed and graded for size, and taken away by steam engine for use.

28.9 Bridgend Inn [SN662385]

YEAR	BRIDGEND INN CRUGYBAR CENSUS RETURNS
1841	**(1) JONES: William** (24) shoemaker, Margaret (25) wife, John (11 mon) son **(2) DAVIES: John** (68) tailor, Mary (65) wife, Mary Jones (5)
1851	**JONES: William** (34) shoemaker, Margaret (36) wife with 4 children
1861	**JONES: William** (45) innkeeper born Cilycwm, Margaret (46) wife, John (20) son, Anne (16) dau, Elizabeth (11) dau
1871	**JONES: William** (54) innkeeper, Margaret (55) wife
1881	**JONES: William** (64) innkeeper, Margaret (65) wife, John (40) son, William (11) grandson
1891	No entry
1901	**JONES: William** (31) innkeeper, Janet (31) wife, John (6) son, William (5) son, Margaret (2) dau
1911	**JONES: William Lewis** (41) innkeeper born Caio, Janet (41) wife (5 children 3 still alive), John (16) son, William (15) son, Margaret (12) dau

This Inn is located at the turning to Crugybar off the main Pumsaint to Llanwrda road. It was owned by the Edwinsford Estate for many decades and is listed in the 1903 estate accounts as occupied by William Jones as tenant, who is shown in the 1901 census return. At the 1918 auction the estate sold it to the tenant, William Jones, for £380. His son William worked at the Crugybar Post Office in his youth and then farmed at Tŷ Newydd, Crugybar; he was a deacon at Crugybar Chapel and retired to Minyrafon in Crugybar.

The Inn has been through numerous owners. In the 1940s it was kept by Mrs Keen, the daughter of Mr Davies of Glanfano, Ffarmers who was the headmaster of Ffarmers' School; she had formerly managed the Royal Oak, Pumsaint. In the 1950s it was kept by an English couple, the Barrets, who later received planning consent to build a petrol filling station across the road (the Bridge End Garage) on a site

631 David Lewis: *Family Histories p140*

632 Malcolm Beeson and LCTA: *Llandovery and its Environs (1994) p195-6*

previously used as a livestock market despite there already being closeby the New Mill (Felin Newydd) Garage. The Bridge End Garage was later bought and converted into a Downs Home Store selling gas and heating equipment; it was run by Wyn Lloyd and his partner who both died in 2017 and is currently for sale; Wyn died in an accident when his car ran over him.

The Inn was very popular in the 1960s and 1970s and even had an extension built but in recent years it has gone downhill and has been for sale and closed for some time.

Bridgend Inn 2017

28.10 New Mill (Felin Newydd) [SN664385]

For centuries all rural communities depended on cornmills which were powered by waterwheels either in the local stream or river or in a leat from the river or a millpond built for the purpose; indeed the Romans probably brought the idea to Britain and locally to the Pumsaint area when they started mining for gold. Cornmills were essential to produce sufficient flour in the quantities required locally. Perhaps the most famous cornmill in Cynwyl Gaeo was Felin Newydd at Crugybar which is next to the River Annell and until recently was one of the last surviving water mills in Wales in working order. It was originally part of the Glanrannell Estate but by 1585 had become owned by the Edwinsford Estate[633]. The early mills would have been built of wood and later of stone. The first mention[634] of "the mill of Glanyrannell" is in 1670 and by 1725 it was called "y Velin Newydd" and it is thought that the current building is the "new mill" built at that time on the site of the previous mill. In 1810 the mill was renovated and upgraded so that it had two pairs of high quality millstones from France with the latest new processing machinery and large wooden gears with a 12 foot diameter waterwheel fed by a mill pond with its water drawn down a leat from the river. Local residents would bring their grain to the mill and it could take an hour for one sack (114 kg) to be milled or much longer if the grain had first to be properly dried. The miller was paid by a toll of a percentage of the meal produced from the grain rather than in cash.

The millers have included Rees Williams (c1744-60) whose rental was "£12 and four fatt pullets at Christmas"; David Thomas (1793); John Daniel (1813-1830s listed in the 1813 estate accounts) with a rental of £38; John Davies (1836); James James (1836-7); his widow Elizabeth James (1837 and listed in the 1841 census); and then the Edwards (1851), Davies (1861), Williams (1871), and Davies (1981-1905) families listed in the census returns (some of the last Davies family's children emigrated to Patagonia). In 1905 Anthony Williams became the tenant and it was he who bought the freehold with 16 acres of land from the Edwinsford Estate at the 1918 auction for £725. Anthony Williams' son, David (b1906), took over the mill and produced oatmeal and wheatmeal for human consumption as well as for animal consumption upto the mid 1950s when electricity arrived; he then concentrated on animal feed until he retired in 1970. David

YEAR	NEW MILL CRUGYBAR CENSUS RETURNS
1841	**JAMES: Elizabeth** (50) miller, Margaret Thomas (20), Thomas Thomas (15), Mary Davies (30)
1851	**EDWARDS: Edward** (31) miller of 14 acres born Cards, Margaret (30) wife, Thomas (3) son, Thomas Thomas (26) bro in law cattle drover
1861	**DAVIES: John** (53) farmer and miller born Talley, Mary (57) wife with 7 children
1871	**WILLIAMS: John** (40) miller and farmer of 12 acres born Llansawel, Jane (38) wife, John (11) nephew with 2 ser
1881	**DAVIES: Daniel** (63) miller and farmer, Mary (64) wife, Sarah (24) dau, John (7) grandson
1891	**DAVIES: Daniel** (73) corn miller born Llansawel, Mary (75) wife, John (18) nephew, Joice Price (24) ser
1901	**DAVIES: Mary** (86) born Caio, Daniel (52) son corn miller, Elizabeth (13) granddau, Jane Thomas (33) ser
1911	**WILLIAMS: Anthony** (33) miller and farmer born Caio, Esther (31) wife, John (10) son, David (5) son, Annie Davies (29) visitor serv

and his wife Martha (Mattie) had four children: (a) Minwel Tibbott a graduate at Aberystwyth University who was a curator at the National Museum at St Fagan's; (b) Meurig an art teacher in Ruthin who committed suicide; (c) Elfyn a local clerk who was unmarried and lived in Llandeilo; and (d) Myra Leyshon who was a librarian and emigrated to Canada some 40 years ago.

In 1980 the mill was sold to David Clarke who milled flour for sale locally. In 1986 Malcolm Beeson bought the mill and restored it to working order as well as converting the milking parlour into a tearoom and crafts shop and another outbuilding into a workshop for local craftsmen to demonstrate their trade to visitors in the summer. He also built a wildlife pond and nature trail in the meadows. At one stage in the 1990s thousands of visitors were coming to see the old mill in working order and producing fine wholemeal flour for sale in the local

633 Malcolm Beeson and LCTA: *Llandovery and its Environs (1994) p199-205*
634 NLW Edwinsford archives

health shops. In 1999 the mill was sold to Jo and Chris Maple who closed the mill to the public; they sold the property in 2004 to Dr David and Gill Ashton. David is a forensic pathologist and haematologist, and Gill used to be a nurse.

David Williams's brother, John (b1901), and his wife Nan established a garage, the New Mill Garage, in the 1920s opposite the Bridgend Inn selling petrol and motorbikes. He also repaired clocks, was a barber and ran a taxi service; it was a valuable and popular service station for over 40 years. The garage was later taken over from Nan Williams by the Povey family who added a general store which also sold food, fruit, cigarettes etc. The petrol station has been closed since 2016 when the Poveys retired.

Felin Newydd and wheel 2017

28.11 Garth (Garthbyr) (headland of the enclosure) [SN 666393]
This farm is located on the back road from near Caio to Ynysau Ganol. It was part of the Edwinsford Estate for decades. In 1740 a circulating Welsh school visited Garth (see Chapter 30.1).

The Williams family shown in the 1841 census were tenants for some 40 years, and were followed by the Morgans and Lewis families. Thomas Davies and his wife Elizabeth are shown as tenants in the 1901 census and listed in the 1903 estate accounts. Thomas was the brother of Mrs Ann James (1876-1959) of Aberdâr[635] and the son of John Davies of Tyllwyd, Cwrt y Cadno[636] and thus the great uncle of Vincent James (b1934)[637]; Elizabeth (b1874) was the illegitimate daughter of Mary Davies of Glanrhyd[638], Aberdâr, who was the sister of Rees Davies (1852-1930) the ancestor of the Troedybryn, Ffarmers Davies family[639]. Thomas and Elizabeth married in 1894 and moved to be tenants at Garth but perhaps they could not meet their rent payments because they moved to farm at Cwmgerwyn Uchaf a farm of 219 acres of poor land in the upper Annell valley, and in the 1920s moved to Cwmcrych[640], Pumsaint. They had a large family of 10 children many of whom went to England: Will became a foreman with the Forestry Commission; Elizabeth married Tom and had a son who became a jet aircraft test pilot and was killed in a flying accident after WW2; Jennie was a housemaid at Llandre in 1926 and had an illegitimate daughter Blodwen whose father was named in a court case in Llansawel as Tom Davies of Glanrannell Farm.

By 1911 James Jones had become the tenant of Garth and in the 1918 sale auction the farm of 78 acres was sold to him by the Edwinsford Estate for £1,250. His son James inherited and ran the farm until about 1950; he married a daughter of William Williams of Ffrwdfal Lodge who died young leaving a daughter, Morfydd, who worked as a barmaid at the Dolaucothi Arms for many years. Morfydd married Tom Cleminson who worked for the Forestry Commission and the National Trust and they lived at Ogofau Lodge until about 1990.

YEAR	GARTH CENSUS RETURNS
1841	**WILLIAMS: William** (35) farmer, Anne (35) wife, Daniel (10) son, Thomas (8) son, David (6) son, 4 serv
1851	**WILLIAMS: William** (45) farmer of 132 acres born Conwil Gaeo, Anne (46) wife with 6 children, 2 ser
1861	**WILLIAMS: William** (56) farmer, Anne (57) wife, Thomas (28) son, David (25) son, Mary (22) dau, John (11) son, David Davies (23) boarder school master
1871	**WILLIAMS: William** (65) farmer of 120 acres born Caio
1881	**MORGANS: Daniel** (51) farmer of 75 acres born Llanycrwys, Martha (50) wife, Thomas (26) son, Eleanor (13) dau, Eleanor Jenkins (15) ser
1891	**LEWIS: Thomas** (34) farmer born Cilycwm, Alice (29) wife, Thomas (8) son, Amy (6) dau, Daniel (3) son, Amy (1) dau, Mary Davies (15) ser
1901	**DAVIES: Thomas** (27) farmer born Caio, Elizabeth (27) wife, John (6) son, Thomas (5) son, David (3) son, Margaret (4) dau, Mary (1) dau, Mary Williams (37) ser, Anthony Allen (85) postman born Llandovery
1911	**JONES: James (63)** farmer born Conwil Gaeo, Hannah (67) wife (6 children 5 still alive), Mary (38) dau, Hannah (26) dau, James (24) son, David Thomas (62) ser

A Smith family bought Garth from James Jones the son and lived there until about 1970 when they sold to the Jacob family; Maureen Jacob the daughter married Mansel Lewis and they are tenants at Pentwyn[641], Cwrt y Cadno. Mr Jacob died around 2000 and his widow moved to Cellan and sold the farm of some 19 acres to Mr and Mrs Bowles from Hampshire; the remaining land was sold to two of her daughters and sons in law, Maureen and Mansel Lewis of Pentwyn Cwrt y Cadno,

635 David Lewis: *Family Histories p244*
636 David Lewis *p318*
637 David Lewis *p221*
638 David Lewis *p233*
639 David Lewis *p422*
640 David Lewis p137
641 David Lewis p226

and Heulwen and Idris Evans of Pantycoubal Gwernogle. In 2003 Mr and Mrs Bowles applied for planning consent to convert the farmhouse and buildings from agricultural use to residential accommodation for educational courses for up to 32 disadvantaged children. The local residents led by Liz Spencer of Brynhyfryd nearby strongly objected and, despite a recommendation from Carmarthenshire County Council planning officers to grant such consent, were successful in persuading the planning committee to refuse it. Mr and Mrs Bowles moved to Hampshire in 2009 and let the farm of some 19 acres; the farm has recently been sold.

Garth 2017

28.12 Garreg (rock) [SN672396]

This farm is located on the backroad from Pumsaint to Caio. It was owned by the Edwinsford Estate. In the 1823 estate accounts the tenant is shown as Joseph David and the Thomas family took over from him and lived there for over 40 years. In the 1903 estate accounts the occupier is stated to be the personal representatives of David George who took over the tenancy in the 1870s and must have died around 1902. His son William took over the farm. This family is probably related to Trooper William John George of Glynteg, Caio who was on home leave during WW2 and became ill and died; his name appears on the war memorial in Pumsaint. The family are also related to the George family of Ynysau Isaf.

Although this property is not listed in the 1918 sale auction of some of the Caio properties owned by the Edwinsford Estate, it seems

Garreg 2016

YEAR	GARREG CAIO CENSUS RETURNS
1841	**THOMAS: William** (45) farmer, Miriam (45) wife, Margaret (16) dau, Anne (15) dau, Gwenllian (15) dau, Joice (10) dau, Anne Beynon (2), 3 serv
1851	**THOMAS: William** (59) farmer of 66 acres born Conwil Gaeo, Miriam (59) wife, Anne (25) dau, Gwen (25) dau, 2 serv
1861	**THOMAS: William** (69) farmer, Miriam (69) wife, Gwenllian (35) dau, 3 serv
1871	**THOMAS: Margaret** (36) farmer of 150 acres born Llansadwrn with 3 ser
1881	**GEORGE: David** (46) farmer of 120 acres, Jane (40) wife, Mary (14) dau, William (12) son, Jane (5) dau, Ann (3) dau, William Jones (21) ser, Anne Lloyd (23) ser, Thomas Williams (10) visitor
1891	**GEORGE: David** (57) farmer, Jane (51) wife, William (21) son, Jane (15) dau, William George (14) ser, Anthony Allen (70) lodger
1901	**GEORGE: David** (67) farmer born Llansawel, Jane (61) wife, Isaac Davies (15) ser, Mary Jones (16) ser, Anthony Allen (85) boarder postman
1911	**GEORGE: William** (41) farmer born Llansawel, Jane (71) mother, May (18) dau, Ida (11) dau, Annie (8) dau, Cyril (5) son, William Jennings (17) ser, Anthony Allen (97)

probable that it was sold during the early 20th century to the Dolaucothi Estate. Capt Armitage, the land agent for the Dolaucothi Estate during the 1940s and 1950s, lived in it. It has been occupied by National Trust tenants ever since including the Barnard family; Mrs Barnard later moved to live in Pumsaint Chapel House (Preswylfa) and is the sister of Mrs Jean Rees (the wife of Garnet Rees of Thomas Rees & Son). Other tenants included the Du Pauvre family and the Johnston family; Brian Johnston now lives in Caio and has a painting and decorating business with his father Phillip.

The former farm's land has long been farmed by others including Bevan Williams of the Forge and now Goronwy Jones of Gwarnoethle, Caio.

28.13 Cilgawod (Cilygawad) [a retreat from a rain shower] [SN687398]

This farm is located on the hill overlooking the village of Caio on the Caio road to Porthyrhyd. It was owned by the Edwinsford Estate for generations. In the 1813 estate accounts the tenant is listed as Rees David who had a number of other tenancies. By the time of the 1838 Tithe Apportionment Agreement the tenant of 91 acres was William Lloyd who is shown in the 1841 census. In the 1903 estate accounts the tenant is John Davies who is also listed as the tenant in the 1901 and 1911 census returns. The property is not listed in the sale auctions

Old Cilgawod Farmhouse 1993

YEAR	CILGAWOD CAIO CENSUS RETURNS
1841	**LLOYD: William** (55) farmer, Mary (50) wife with 4 children, Rees Davies (75)
1851	**WILLIAMS: Daniel** (29) farmer born Conwil Gaeo, Elizabeth (24) wife, Timothy Jones (4) stepson illegitimate, 1 ser, 1 visitor
1861	**JONES: John** (58) farmer born Llanwrda, Mary (53) wife born Caio with 3 children
1871	**WILLIAMS: Evan** (34) farmer of 215 acres born Caio, Gwenllian (45) wife, Margaret (7) dau, William (6) son, Thomas (3) son with 2 ser
1881	**PRICE: David** (35) farmer of 120 acres, Martha (33) wife, Jane Jones (20) ser
1891	**PRICE: David** (45) farmer born Llanwrda, Martha (43) wife, William Bowen (19) ser, Jane Lewis (24) ser
1901	**DAVIES: John** (45) farmer, Sarah (47) wife, Mary (24) dau, William (22) son, Sarah (8) dau, Elizabeth (6) dau
1911	**DAVIES: John** (64) widower farmer born Caio, Mary (34) dau, Thomas (30) son, Rachel (26) dau, Sarah (18) dau, Maggie (10) dau

of 1918 and 1919 but was probably sold by the Edwinsford Estate to the Forestry Commission in the 1930s when the latter bought land in the area and employed a number of men who had previously worked at the Dolaucothi Gold Mines; the Forestry Commission then planted larch along the hilltop and let the farming land to tenants.

About the time of the start of WW2 David Rees Davies (1910-44) and his wife Margaret (1912-99) moved to farm at Cilgawod as tenants of the Forestry Commission. They had two children: (a) Gerwyn Davies (1936-72) who was educated at Caio School and Llandovery School, suffered badly from asthma and died aged only 36, and (b) Beryl Davies (b1943) who was born in Cilgawod and married Cynfyn Davies (b1942) one of 12 children of the Davies family of Llansawel (his father Oswyn Davies was related to the Davies family of Llansawel Mill as shown in the 1911 census return in Chapter 26.3 and he was a mechanic who also worked at the mill). Cynfyn's brother, Kenyon Davies, worked for the Forestry Commission and farms at Brynare[642] with his wife Judith.

After the death of David Rees Davies in 1944 aged only 34 his widow Margaret continued as the tenant at Cilgawod and during the 1970s bought the freehold of the farm of some 50 acres. Beryl and Cynfyn inherited the farm and bought additional land so that today the freehold farm is about 90 acres in size, although they also rent additional land nearby. Their only son, Alun Davies (b1979), is a highly regarded and successful local builder who built a new house for his parents and has rebuilt and extended the original farmhouse where he now lives. He has a daughter Delun (b2007) from his first marriage and another daughter Gwenllian (b2015) with his partner Vicki Jones from Crickhowell. A much respected and hardworking family.

[642] David Lewis: *Family Histories p293*

28.14 Post Office (Manchester House) Caio [SN675398]

Before the 19th century letters were delivered by hand via drovers or errandboys or by coach mail. It is thought that an early form of post or letter office was first opened in Llandeilo in about 1750 in George Street and was run by David Gwilliam. The famous John Morgan (Jac y Post) who was born about 1770 carried letter bags for some 60 years between Llandeilo and Carmarthen.Then the railway arrived in Llandeilo in 1857 and brought the mail from London and Cardiff. In Llandovery the first Post Office dates from about 1764. On 19 December 1835 only a couple of miles outside Llandovery on the road to Brecon the Gloucester to Carmarthen Royal Mail coach plunged 120 ft down the embankment into the river and was destroyed. The coachman Edward Jenkins was drunk and travelling at about 14 mph; fortunately no one[643] was killed. There is a Mail Coach Pillar in stone commemorating this accident on the side of the road which was restored in 2016.

In 1840 the Queen Victoria penny post stamp started and letters were weighed and it cost the same amount to send a letter irrespective of distance. In Pumsaint during the 18th century the Dolaucothi Arms and the coach house were focal points for letter deliveries by coach and the important mail road from Llanwrda to Lampeter was also used by the drovers. By the mid 19th century there was a Post Office in Pumsaint. Mail would be delivered on horseback or later by bicycle. The mail used to come from Llanwrda to Pumsaint where people would collect it by horse and trap or on foot. John Thomas (1838-1905) ran the local postal service to Pumsaint. John Davies and his mother ran the Pumsaint Post Office; he died in the 1890s aged only 50 or so. He was followed by Richard Jones (d1930) of Frondeg who ran the Post office and shop with his brother David Jones (d1932) of Bronhuan. They were very successful and built Frondeg and Bronhuan in 1909. The telephone exchange for Pumsaint was installed and had to be manned 24 hours per day. The Pumsaint post was sorted at the Post Office and a number of postmen delivered locally on foot, by bicycle or on horseback. Gerallt Morgan, son of Jim Morgan of Dolaucothi Farm and Pretoria Cottage, and his wife Daphne bought the Post Office and shop in Pumsaint when Mrs Mary Evans (the widow of Tom Evans, brother of Mrs Jane Williams of Llystroiddyn) retired and sold it in the 1960s. The Post Office closed after Gerallt's death in 2005.

YEAR	MANCHESTER HOUSE (POST OFFICE) CAIO CENSUS RETURNS
1871	uninhabited
1881	**MORGAN: James** (31) draper, grocer and ironmonger, Mary (28) wife, Elizabeth Thomas (20) ser
1891	**MORGAN: James** (38) draper, grocer, postmaster, Mary (34) sis, William Fairburn (22) assis
1901	no entry
1911	**MORGAN: James** (57) grocer and draper born Caio, David Evans (18) assistant

In Caio there was a Post Office at Manchester House for many years in the late 19th century which was also a grocers, drapers and general store run first by a Mr Andrews and then from the 1870s by James Morgan up to the Great War. John Thomas (John the Post) lived in the Chapel House in Caio and for many years he delivered the local post in the Caio area before the Second World War. The Post Office was acquired by the James family who were descendants of Thomas James[644] of Abermangoed; for many years Evan James and his son Peris James (d1999) were the postmasters followed by Peris' daughter. Peris James played in the Swansea rugby team which beat the South Africans on their 1953 tour. He died in 1999 and the post office and shop has sadly been closed for many years.

In recent years there have been a number of local postmen and women who deliver in all weathers; John Vanlandewyck from Llandeilo who is a very friendly and hard working man has delivered in the Cothi and Rhisglog valleys for the last 23 years or so and always has time for a chat; his partner covers the Crugybar area. Postmen and postwomen continue to provide an essential local and social service to rural communities.

643 Passengers included Col Sackville Gwynne of Glanbran Cynghordy, and David Lloyd Harries a Llandovery solicitor. The coachman was fined £5 plus costs

644 David Lewis: *Family Histories p172,187*

Before the telephone arrived messengers would deliver urgent telegrams in towns via the local Post Office but this was a much slower business in the countryside. When the telephone arrived the only public kiosks were in the Post Offices or in the main villages for many years so people would have to run or drive to them when there was an emergency or need to call the fire brigade or the ambulance. The first private telephones were installed in Edwinsford Mansion, Dolaucothi Mansion and in Brunant. The first public telephone[645] in Caio was installed in the Post Office on 22 May 1911 and the postmaster used to call people to the phone; the first public phone in Pumsaint Post Office was installed 12 years later on 29 June 1923. Later red public kiosks were erected but most of these have been taken away now because all houses have had their own private phones for many years.

Ieuan Williams singing at the Caio Fair outside Caio Post Office 1994

[645] Peris James: *LCTA (1994) p162*

28.15 Caio Public Houses [SN 675398]

There used to be six public houses in the village of Caio. Census returns for five survive. After the drovers had ceased coming through Caio in large numbers in the 19th century trade dwindled and six pubs could not survive. Only the Sextons Arms and the Brunant Arms were still operating in the 1930s and today only the Brunant remains a public house. Sadly today many of the pubs in Carmarthenshire and elsewhere are for sale.

YEAR	SEXTONS ARMS (4 SEXTON/CHURCH STREET) CAIO CENSUS RETURNS
1841	**REES: David** (55) tailor; Mary Rees (50) wife plus five children
1851	**REES: DAVID** (65) tailor; Mary Rees (63) wife
1861	**REES: DAVID** (75) tailor; Mary Rees (72) wife plus one servant
1871	**TREMBLE: MARTHA** (28) wife Innkeeper born in Pembrokeshire; Elizabeth (8) dau; Suzannah (3) dau; Charles (1) son; Alice (5 months) dau [**Henry Tremble** (30) the husband and father was the butler living in Dolaucothi Mansion who murdered his employer Judge John Johnes in 1876]
1881	**WILLIAMS: JANE** (38) licensed victualler plus sister and nephew
1891	**EVANS: WILLIAM** (35) shoemaker and innkeeper; Elenor (37) wife milliner plus four children and Benjamin Jones (16) shoemaker apprentice
1901	**JAMES: JAMES LEWIS** (31) innkeeper; Jane (34) wife plus six children
1911	**JAMES: JAMES LEWIS** (41) butcher and innkeeper; Jane (44) wife plus eight children

The Edwinsford Estate owned many of the farms surrounding Caio as well as the properties in Church Street as shown in the 1903 estate accounts in Chapter 16.8. The Church Street properties included the Sextons Arms; most were sold by the estate at the 1918 auction often to the sitting tenants. Tim James and his sister Maggie were the last to run the Sextons Arms as a public house; they also provided the milk for Caio school and the village.

YEAR	KING'S HEAD CAIO CENSUS RETURNS
1841	**DAVIES: Daniel** (35) publican; Elizabeth Davies (30) wife
1851	**EVANS: WILLIAM** (24) victualler and butcher of 60 acres of land; Martha Evans (25) wife plus one daughter, two servants and one visitor
1861	**EVANS: WILLIAM** (34) Innkeeper; Martha Evans (35) wife plus five children and one servant
1871	**MORGANS: JAMES** (52) shopkeeper and innkeeper; William (28) son cattle dealer; James (23) son draper plus two servants
1881	**MORGAN: JAMES** (64) chemist, druggist and innkeeper; William (37) son cattle dealer plus one servant
1891	**MORGAN: JAMES** (71) innkeeper; William (43) cattle dealer plus one servant
1901	**GEORGE: WILLIAM** (31) innkeeper; Mary Ann (29) wife plus three children
1911	**DICKS: WILLIAM** (60) labourer; Mary (65) wife plus two children and two grandchildren plus one visitor

The King's Head (now renamed Brynrannell) is opposite the Post Office and Myrtle Cottage. After the Great War the local policeman resided there rather than in Pumsaint where the officers were later stationed. The first police house was built just outside Pumsaint in the 1950s when PC 40 Ben Phillips moved there from Cilycwm; prior to that PC Rees had lived in Frondeg in Pumsaint near the Chapel upto the mid1940s before retiring to Llanllwni. A number of officers lodged with Miss Sarah Thomas at Gwynant, Pumsaint until the Police Station was built in the 1950s.

After WW1 William Williams, a plasterer and tiler, lived in the King's Arms after it had ceased to be a public house; he was the father of Watt Williams who with his brother Dai worked for the National Trust as general builders and plasterers along with William Jones (1880-1963) and his son Gwilym Jones (1917-79) of Tynyllwyn[646] who were carpenters and undertakers. The Williams family had worked for both the Edwinsford Estate and the Dolaucthi Estate. Watt's son,

[646] David Lewis: *Family Histories p147*

Caio 19th century

Former Sextons Arms 2011

King's Head Inn 19th century

Brunant Arms 2011

Peter Williams (d2015), was the manager of the WD Lewis store in Pumsaint until his retirement; he did a great deal for local charities including the Llandovery Hospital, and was a regular across the road in the Brunant Arms in Caio. He walked for miles at weekends over the hills and was a wonderful raconteur with a pint of Guinness in his hand and would often grow a long white beard and then cut it off annually for charity. A great character whose portrait is in the Brunant Arms.

YEAR	BRUNANT ARMS CAIO CENSUS RETURNS
1841	**LLOYD: ANN** (50) publican plus two children and three lodgers
1851	**EVANS: JOHN** (36) victualler and sadler; Jane Evans (39) wife plus two children and servant
1861	**JONES: MARGARET** (32) Innkeepers wife plus one sister and daughter
1871	**JONES: JOHN** (30) Innkeeper; Martha Jones (29) wife plus son William (1) and one servant
1881	**FULFORD: HENRY** (61) innkeeper; Mary (53) wife
1891	**JONES: THOMAS** (48) carrier and innkeeper; Elizabeth (55) wife plus two servants
1901	**JONES: THOMAS** (59) innkeeper
1911	**JONES: MARY** (56) widow innkeeper plus one child visitor Sold by Brunant Estate in 1918 to Mary Jones (tenant)

The Brunant Arms on the corner of Church Street was owned by the Brunant Estate until the auction of the estate in 1918. It survives as the only public house in the village today. There have been several owners and publicans since 1918. The current owner is Justin Jacobi and the current publicans are Jan Slee and her son Chris Reeve who are delightful people and provide a great service to their customers including the pensioners, the local darts teams, and local groups.

YEAR	CAIO INN CENSUS RETURNS
1871	**DAVIES: JOHN** (56) Innkeeper and saddler; Anne Davies (58) wife plus two sons and two daughters
1881	**JONES: THOMAS** (38) timber carrier and innkeeper; Elizabeth (47) wife plus one servant
	No more entries

Caio (Cayo) Inn was at the entrance to the village down a lane on the right past the Chapel and owned by the Edwinsford Estate. In the 1903 estate accounts the tenant is shown as Lewis James. It seems that it ceased to be a pub in the 1880s. In the 1918 auction the pub was put up for sale but withdrawn; it was probably sold not long thereafter.

YEAR	SQUARE AND COMPASS CAIO CENSUS RETURNS
1841	**JONES: WILLIAM** (35) carpenter; Hannah (30) wife plus five children plus three visitors
1851	**JONES: WILLIAM** (47) carpenter; Hannah (46) wife plus eight children
1861	**JONES: TIMOTHY** (32) carpenter and farmer; Mary (32) wife plus one daughter, three boarders and two servants
1871	**WILLIAMS: SARAH** (70) agric labourer's widow; Margaret Thomas (11) grand dau
1881	**WILLIAMS: SARAH** (70) agric labourer's widow
	No more entries

This pub was also at the entrance to the village and its name suggests that it had masonic connections. It seems to have ceased to operate as a pub before the census in 1841.

I have been unable to discover where the Plough and Harrow was located.

29. Religion

29.1 Talley Abbey

Over the centuries the Edwinsford family had close connections with the Abbey and later the Parish Church in Talley; the family's burial vault is in the Abbey grounds and after it was closed members of the family were buried in the family burial plot in the churchyard. Several members of the family are remembered in the church with mural memorials and several served as churchwardens.

The origins of Talley are explained in Chapter 23. Talley Abbey was for centuries the most famous and most important building in the area; its exact history[647] is uncertain. Most historians consider that there had been a religious site at Talley for many centuries before the monastic revival of the 11th and 12th centuries. As we have seen in Chapter 4.5, Rhys ap Gruffydd (1132-97)(13), known as The Lord Rhys, who was effectively ruler of South Wales (Deheubarth) was an ancestor of the

Early 20th century

647 Sir William Dugdale: *Monasticon Anglicanum (1817-30) Vol 4 p161-6;* David Long Price*: Talley Abbey- Archaeologia Cambrensis (1879) p161-187;* Stephen Williams: *Excavations at Talley Abbey (1892 lecture);* Edward Owen: *History of the Praemonstratensian Abbey of Talley- WJO Archaeologia Cambrensis (1893-4)*; Sir John Lloyd Vol 1 p154,336-343, 347-9,352-3, 356, Vol 2 p270; Fred Price: Talley; BH St J O'Neill: *Talley Abbey- Min of Works (1946);* Cadw (1992); Glanmor Williams: *Carmarthenshire Monasteries in the 14th and 15th Centuries CA (1959) p138-151*; JF Jones: *Talley Abbey Traditions CA (1963) p190*; Thomas Lloyd: *Carmarthenshire and Ceredigion p378-81*; Talley History Soc: *Y Llychau*

Abbey and church 2017

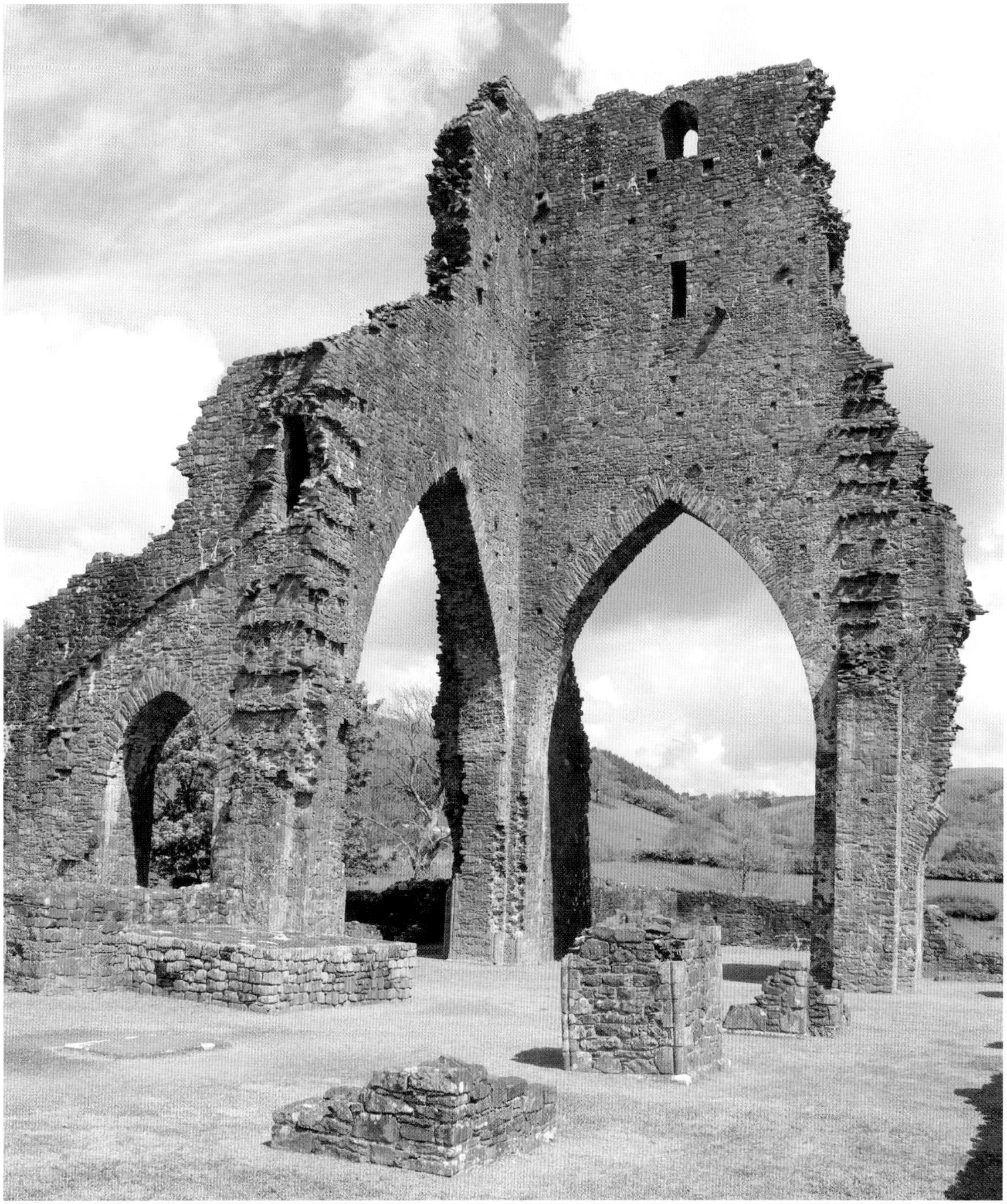

Abbey ruins 2017

Tudor royal line and of the Edwinsford family. As a great benefactor and patron he supported Cistercian abbeys at Whitland (*Alba Domus*) (founded near Haverfordwest in 1140 by monks from Clairvaux and then moved to Whitland in 1155), at Strata Florida (*Ystrad-Flur*)(founded in 1164), and at Llanllyr (founded 1180) as well as priories at Llandovery and Cardigan. In about 1184-5 he founded the monastery at Talley for the Premonstratensians (the Order of Canons Regular of Prémontré, also known as the Norbertines or the White Canons). This Roman Catholic Order had been founded in 1120 by Saint Norbert near Laon in Picardy. Norbert was a friend of Saint Bernard of Clairvaux and so his Order's way of life was modelled on Cistercian lines, but the Norbertines were canons regular not monks so in undertaking their duties within the parish they behaved much more like Augustinians and also wore a white cassock, a rocket, a long white cloak and a white cap. The canons were mostly laymen bound by vows of poverty, chastity and obedience, but they did not preach, confess or exercise any spiritual functions. The Order came to England in 1143 and eventually had some 35 monastic houses throughout Britain; in about 1184-5 the Order started at Talley, the only Premonstratensian Abbey in Wales and in an ideal place for agriculture and fish farming in the two lakes; there is some doubt as to whether the canons in fact farmed to the same extent as the Cistercians, although we know that the Abbot stipulated in the leases that tenants had to pay certain dues in cereals, livestock and dairy produce thereby ensuring the continuation of agrarian operations.The Abbey was dedicated to the Virgin and St John the Baptist and was generally known as the Monastery of our Blessed Lady of Talley. There is no evidence that there were ever any canonesses at Talley.

The Lord Rhys endowed much of the tithe income from Llandeilo Fawr[648] to the new Order at Talley together with the church at Llandyfeisant, lands in Ystrad Tywi and the chapel of St David at Dinefwr. However between about 1197 (just after the death of the founder The Lord Rhys) and 1202 the jealous Abbot Peter of the Cistercian Abbey at Whitland induced several of the canons at Talley to join his monastery at Whitland and become monks; he then succeeded in forcibly ejecting all the canons at Talley and seizing their property (described by Gerald of Wales in his *Speculum Ecclesiae* as "high handed proceedings against a poor house of canons"). This led to the dispossessed canons walking to Canterbury to complain to Archbishop Hubert Walter (d1205) who found in their favour and ordered all their property to be returned to them. Whitland did not comply and the matter was referred to Rome; after costly litigation Talley recovered its land but lost the fertile grange of Rhuddlan Teifi and had to accept some less valuable land in exchange. In 1208 King John by Patent Roll granted lands to Talley Abbey and in 1215 Abbot Gervase of Talley was elected Bishop of St Davids; he confirmed the appropriation of the churches of Llandeilo Fawr and Llanegwad by Talley. Talley fared badly during the warfare which ended with the conquest of Wales in 1282; in 1278 Edward I took Talley into royal custody because of its poverty. In 1284 he placed Talley under the jurisdiction of Wellbeck, the chief of the English Premonstratensian houses at Wellbeck Abbey in Nottinghamshire, and the native canons at Talley were expelled[649] to make room for "others of the English tongue who are able and willing to observe the religious life". In 1291 the income of Talley was only £8.16s.6d per annum compared with over £2,600 at Strata Florida and £1,200 at Whitland. In 1271 the great grandson of The Lord Rhys, Rhys Fychan ap Rhys Mechyll, was buried at Talley. In 1291 the Abbey seems to have been under the patronage of Rhys ap Maredudd (executed in 1292) the son of Maredudd ap Rhys Gryg (d1271) and a Welsh rebel and descendant of The Lord Rhys. In 1332 Talley obtained several gifts of lands in the parishes of Llansadwrn, Llansawel, and Cynwyl Gaeo, and the grange of Carreg Cennen. Talley also had several granges (smallholdings farmed by canons, monks and lay brethren within a day's journey from Talley) including Gwastade near Cwmdu, Cefnblaidd in Talley itself, Trallwng Elgan near Glanrannell, Llanycrwys, Cilmaren, Brechfa Gothi, Gwyddgrug, and Manor Frwnws (Rhuddlan Teifi grange was lost to Whitland by 1208).

Then followed the Black Death which must have effected the canons and the residents of the area causing much poverty. In about 1380 Abbot Rhys requested that the monastery be taken into royal custody and in 1382 King Richard II issued a commission to enquire into the Abbey's financial position and the repair of the buildings due to "the negligence of previous Abbots impoverished by corrodies". In 1391

[648] William Strange: *The Early Medieval Community at Llandeilo Fawr CA (2012) p9*

[649] HM Colvin: *The White Canons in England (1951)* p237-8

the commission was renewed and instructed to ensure that the property of the Abbey be restored to it without delay. In 1410 the Abbey was described as "despoiled, burned and almost destroyed" by the English and Welsh armies after a decade of war. In 1429 a confirmatory charter was issued to the Abbey (the original charter is lost). In 1430 Abbot Dafydd requested that Talley be taken into royal custody (for the third time) and another special enqiry was made into the wastage of the Abbey's possessions. In 1485 the Abbot is supposed to have been influential[650] in assisting Henry VII on his journey from Milford Haven to Bosworth when he stopped off in Talley, although there is no hard evidence of this.

The *Valor Ecclesiasticus* of 1535, an audit of all monastic lands prepared by Thomas Cromwell for Henry VIII, stated the Abbey's annual income to be £136 (£153.1s.4d in some sources). The Abbey was closed in the first phase of suppression of the Dissolution of the Monasteries since its annual income fell far below the threshold of £200 as did that of Whitland and Strata Florida. The estate and possessions of the Abbey were taken into the Crown's hands under the jurisdiction of the Court of Augmentation and the King became Lord of the Manor in succession to the Abbot. In about 1545 the lands were leased to Sir Thomas Jones MP (1492-1558) of Abermarlais (a member of the Johnes family of Dolaucothi). Thereafter the lands of the Royal Manor of Talley were let out and managed by stewards who acted as chief agents of the Lord of the Manor maintaining records and presiding over its courts; Richard Muckleston (1580-1638) is named as the steward[651] at a Court Leet held in the reign of James I and we know that during the 19th century the Long Price family of Talley House acted as stewards of the manor.

From the available sources the Abbots of the Abbey included: Abbot Iorwerth (Gervase) (d1229) who resigned in 1215 when he became Bishop of St Davids; Abbot G (1215-29); Abbot Gruffudd or Griffin (1239); Abbot E (1281); Abbot Simon (1284); Abbot Rhys ap David (1343-4); Abbot Thomas de Pagliam (1347); Abbot Rees ap Yevan (1380-3); Abbot William (1397-99); Abbot Morgan (1409-16); Abbot Morgan (1426); Abbot David ap Yevan (1430); Abbot Lewis (1435); Abbot David (1463-93); Abbot David (1504-18); Abbot David ap Yevan (1519); and Abbot Rhydderch Jones or Roderic Johns (1522-36) who received an annual pension of £24. The last Abbot at the time of the dissolution had seven monks with him. The seal[652] of Talley Abbey was found in a Norfolk churchyard in 1894 and is now in Norwich Museum.

Following the dissolution in 1536 the nave and presbytery of the Abbey were preserved and used as the parish church until 1773 when a new parish church was built nearby using the stones of the Abbey; indeed much of the village was built from the same source. Today the Abbey ruins are all that remain. In 1933 the guardianship of the ruins was entrusted to the commissioners of HM Works and today this responsibilty has been assumed by Cadw. The Edwinsford family vaults which have been closed remain among the ruins; two vaults were used by the family. The older was marked with a square block of masonry set against the Northern wall, the upper part of which was later removed down to the original level of the Church, and the newer was

Edwinsford family vault and old vault in the background 2017

650 Lynn Hughes p100-2 (William Samuel: *Llandilo and its Neighbourhood 1868*)
651 Archaeologia Cambrensis (1894) p206
652 Sir John Lloyd Vol 1 p342

Slab over newer vault 2017

marked with a slab of stone covering the entrance. The last member of the family to be interred in the vault was Lady Mary Hamlyn Williams in 1874.

The suggestion[653] that Talley Abbey had an enormous bell weighing 72cwt which was carried to Carmarthen in 1772-3 and is now in Exeter Cathedral[654] seems to be erroneous not least because none of Exeter's archives reveal anything about this. Following the dissolution and later during the Civil War period a number of relics from the Abbey were given by the Abbot or vicar to the Johnes family of Dolaucothi (at that time the pre-eminent family of the area) including the altar piece (which is now in St Davids Cathedral), a lovely Ikon of Elijah (also now in St Davids), a beautiful chain and clasp of pure gold which had been ploughed up in an estate field and worn by the canons of Talley, and other relics which are in Carmarthen Museum.

The original ambitious plan was to build an abbey at Talley on Cistercian lines with a magnificent eight arched aisled nave (in fact it ended up with only four bays), crossing and presbytery. Excavations show that the length of the building was to have been 226 ft long (compared with 213ft at Strata Florida), with a nave 143ft long, a nave and aisles 62ft broad, transepts 112ft long and 29ft broad, a square of the tower of 29ft and a presbytery 44ft long. But it seems clear that although Talley Abbey was planned to be one of the largest monastic churches in Wales, the actual building was one of the plainest and the architecture was simple. The reason was cost which is why the original plans were downsized, and builders had to be content with local quarried stone (from Llansawel) and materials probably erected with local labour rather than by expensive stonemasons; the building reflected the poverty of the foundation and its initial problems and expensive litigation with Whitland.

In 1710, on the instructions of the Archbishop of Canterbury, the Archdeacon of Carmarthen, Edward Tenison, conducted a Visitation of 62 local parishes. The notes[655] of the Visitation concerning Talley Church being part of the former Abbey state: *"The Church 150 foot in length, & in breadth & height proportionate. The floor uneven, the walls want rendering, & the windows glazing, & the standards of all the windows to be either replac'd, or new ones put in their room. No Table of degrees. Mr William Davies Minister. Mrs Cornwallis's salary is but 8£ a year notwithstanding the Tyths to her are worth about 100£ a year. The Act against Swearing is not read. Some of the Parishioners when they hear of a strange Preacher go to the Presbyterian Meeting, but for the most part they come to Church, & none of them do constantly frequent the Meeting.*

653 Fred Price: *Talley p21*
654 Rev VGM Scott: *The Bells of Exeter Cathedral*
655 G Milwyn Griffiths NLWJ (1974-6)

Here are two reputed Papists, John Weston & his wife. The Impropriator finds bread & wine at Easter & at all other times for the Communion. Communicants at Easter about 50, at other times 10 or 12. Families about 140. Poor that can read about 20. The Clark cannot read, he is old & therefore continued. The Ivy at the west end of the Church, the Elder & other Trees growing on the top of the south wall between the west end & the cross Ile, the Ivy & trees growing on the top & on other parts of the wall, the Ivy & other Trees that cover the greatest part of the south wall from the Cross Ile (the walls whereof are fallen down) to the east end, the Ivy & large Ashes growing on the north wall & battlements between the east end & the north cross Ile, & the Ivy on the west side of that Ile, & the trees & Ivy that cover a great part of the north side of the Steeple, & the Ivy, Elder, Yew, & other plants of great stature growing out of the north wall from near the bottom so as in a manner to cover it from the cross Ile to the west end, & the Ivy & trees growing over the windows & extending themselves to the top of the Church should be wholly rooted up & the walls repair'd & new pointed. The fence of the Churchyard should be repair'd. The Sculls & bones lying above ground in great heaps in the Church should be buried in the Churchyard, Prayers every Sunday. Sermons qu?" It is clear from these notes that the building was in a very bad state of repair, which may explain why in 1772 it was decided to build a new one using the stones of the Abbey.

During the Middle Ages the Abbey would almost certainly have had an infirmary[656] for the sick and dying. Monastic houses were also the burial places of choice for members of Welsh ruling houses and some dying, sick or wounded lords entered monasteries and assumed the habit of the order early to prepare themselves for death. Whilst each local commote usually had a physician (*meddyg*) and the Physicians of Myddfai (*Meddygon Myddfai*) practised in the area for some five centuries upto 1739, the monks at Talley would also have helped the sick without being general physicians themselves.

Both Strata Florida Abbey and Talley Abbey have memorials claiming that the Welsh poet, Dafydd ap Gwilym, is buried in their grounds.

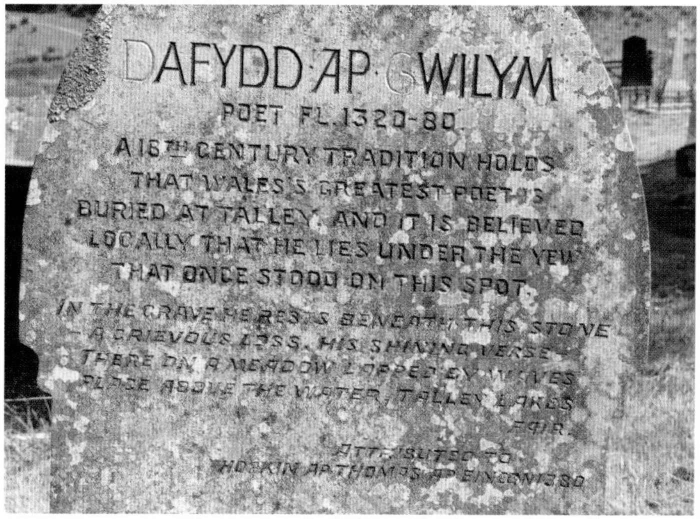

Memorial to Dafydd ap Gwilym in Talley Churchyard

There is no definitive proof of his burial place and indeed we do not even know when he was born or died; historians guess he lived from c1315/20 - 1350/70[657], or 1340-70[658], or 1320-80 being his dates on the memorial in Talley Churchyard erected in 1984 on the site of the yew tree under which he is supposed to have been buried, or that he died in 1368 as mentioned[659] in a poem. Dafydd ap Gwilym was one of the finest Welsh medieval poets who invented a new metre verse form, the *cywydd*, based on rhyming couplets. Strata Florida's claim is based on a poem by Grufudd Grug and a book by William Owen Pughe[660] as well as a memorial erected by the Hon Society of Cymmrodorion in 1951. Talley's claim is based on a book of burial places of poets dating from 1600 by Thomas Jones of Tregaron[661], and a local tradition of long standing that Dafydd retired to live in the Abbey and died there. None of the evidence is compelling and like most good legends no one will ever know the truth. The Talley Abbey ash tree[662] which is some seven metres in circumference at its base is located within the old monastic grounds about 300 yards from the Abbey; its age is uncertain.

---

656 David Stephenson: *The early Physicians of Myddfai in context CA (2013) p38-45;* Red Book of Hergest; Morfydd E Owen: *Meddygon Myddfai CA (2011) p30-43*

657 Welsh Academy: *Encyclopaedia of Wales (2008) p190*

658 National Dictionary of Welsh Biography

659 Lynn Hughes p99 (poem of c1380 attributable to Hopcyn ap Tomos ab Einion)

660 WO Pughe: *Barddoniaeth Dafydd ap Gwilym (1789)*

661 Also known as Twm Siôn Cati (c1530-1609) an outlaw and a genealogist

662 Archie Miles: *Heritage Trees Wales (2012)*

29.2 The Parish Church of St Michael's and All Angels, Talley

Talley Church 2017

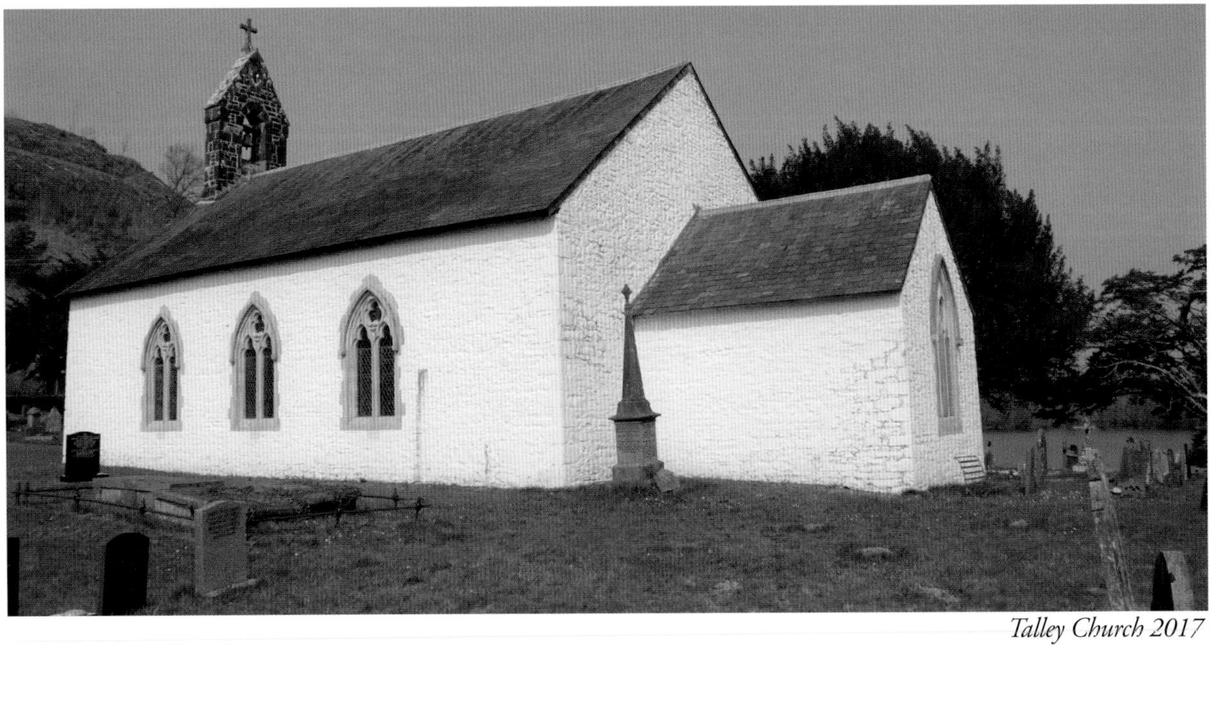

Talley Church 2017

Talley Church 2017

Talley Church 2017

Edwinsford family burial plot

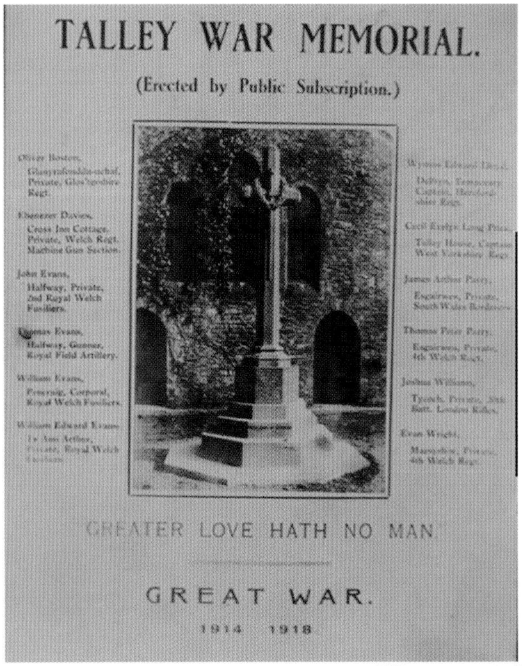

TALLEY WAR MEMORIAL.

(Erected by Public Subscription.)

[illegible],
[illegible], Private, [illegible] Regt.

Ebenezer Davies,
Cross Inn Cottage, Private, Welch Regt. Machine Gun Section.

John Evans,
Halfway, Private, 2nd Royal Welch Fusiliers.

Thomas Evans,
Halfway, Gunner, Royal Field Artillery.

William Evans,
[illegible], Corporal, Royal Welch Fusiliers.

William Edward Evans,
[illegible], Private, Royal Welch Fusiliers.

[illegible],
[illegible], Temporary Captain, [illegible] Regt.

Cecil Evelyn Long Price,
Talley House, Captain, West Yorkshire Regt.

James Arthur Parry,
Esgerwen, Private, South Wales Borderers.

Thomas Peter Parry,
Esgerwen, Private, 4th Welch Regt.

Joshua Williams,
Tycoch, Private, [illegible] Batt. London Rifles.

Evan Wright,
[illegible], Private, 4th Welch Regt.

GREATER LOVE HATH NO MAN.

GREAT WAR.

1914 1918

War memorial

The state of repair[663] of the Abbey by 1710 was very poor as we have seen from the Visitation notes. The Impropriator to whom the tithes were paid, Elizabeth Cornwallis (d1720) of the Johnes family of Abermarlais[664] and Dolaucothi and the wife of Sir Francis Cornwallis (d1675), was not willing to spend sufficient funds to repair the church which was part of the demolished Abbey, nor did the churchwardens, Morgan Thomas and Richard Rees, have the funds to do so. In 1772 it was agreed that a new church should be built using the stones of the Abbey; the foundation was laid on 20 April 1773. Rees John was paid 8s.6d for hauling large beams in the tower of the Abbey. Lewis John was paid 8s.6d for taking care of 3,608 lbs of lead, iron crests and brick tiles; Nicholas John hauled the lead to Carmarthen for £1.6s.6d. David Jones and Sylvanus Lloyd were appointed trustees authorised by the Bishop's Court to manage the building of the new church just north of the Abbey ruins; the cost of obtaining this authority was £3.11s.0d. In dismantling the Abbey many bones of the dead were unearthed and buried in the churchyard by David Davies who was paid 1s.6d for doing so.

The new church was dedicated to St Michael[665] and All Angels; St Michael is one of the four Archangels venerated in Christianity, Islam and Judaism who is the patron of Israel and medicine. His feast day is Michaelmas Day on 29 September.

The new church[666] consists of a broad aisleless nave with a small narrower chancel, the exterior built with rubble masonry and squared quoins. Initially it may have had a double-gabled roof as shown in a watercolour painting by Elizabeth Long Price in the early 19th century, although this was later replaced with a pitched slate roof which survives to this day. In 1787 John Zacharias was paid £2.15s for painting the top of the church and whitewashing the interior. In 1801 Mr Watkins, the singing master, was paid £2.2s for coaching the inhabitants to sing psalms. In 1832 John Jones of Moelfre a tiler was paid £3 for repairing the lead gutters and whitewashing the church inside. In 1840 the churchwardens approved the construction of a new boarded wagon ceiling of Russian red deal in the nave which cost £40. The church was extensively restored in 1863 and again in 1874-6 when the original medieval style gallery at the west end was removed to accommodate the three windows in the west wall and to give more room for the choir; at the same time a gabled bellcote was installed and an 8 day clock added to the internal north wall donated by Mrs Morgan of Capelhir Cwmdu. She also donated the church bell in 1886.

Inside the church there is a wonderful set of 1773 oak box-pews in three ranks with fielded panels; each box-pew on the north side of the nave is numbered for the Edwinsford family at the front, the Long Price family behind them (whose children carved their names in the wooden panels) and estate retainers (originally pew rents used to be paid to the church); in previous times the Edwinsford family pews had a fire to keep them warm. The font dates from the late 18th century being a Bathstone bowl on a pedestal. In Victorian times electricity was installed.

In the parish of Talley there was one Tithe Apportionment Agreement[667] dated 28 September 1838 (prepared by William Morgan of Llansawel the valuer and land surveyor) and made between the relevant landowners and Rev William Thomas Nicholls of Glandulas, the Lay Impropriator and sole owner of all the parish tithes; the agreement provided for a new annual district payment of a total of £300 by way of rentcharge by the landowners in substitution for the payment of all previous tithes. Rev Nicholls was the patron of the benefice of Talley being the heir of Ven Thomas Benyon, Archdeacon of Cardigan, who had bought the tithes from the Johnes family of Abermarlais.

Following the Great War a memorial for the dead was erected at the front of the west end of the church costing £220 paid for by public subscription; details of those named are included on www.laugharnewarmemorial.co.uk.

In 1920 the church became part of the Church in Wales on disestablishment. During WW2 dances were organised in the Church

663 Fred Price: *Talley p21-3*; Parish Register dating from 1634; Cadw; Articles by the Talley History Society and John Walford in Y Llychau

664 David Lewis: *Dolaucothi and Brunant p433-5*

665 Lady Jane Williams: *Angels (2006)*

666 Faculty for building 1772 NLW; BH Malkin: *The Scenery, Antiquities and Biography of South Wales (1807) p467;* Carmarthen Journal *(15 Aug 1862, 20 May 1892);* The Architect (27 May 1892)

667 CRO and NLW

Hall (the old school room) in support of those serving in the armed forces. A major restoration of the church costing some £300,000 was carried out in 2005-6. On Sunday 30 September 2013 a special service led by the Area Dean, Rev Ian Aveson, was held to commemorate the 240th anniversary of the building of the church.

The incumbents and vicars[668] of Talley Church are believed to have included: William Davies (-1688); Evan Jones (1725-48); David Jones (1748-83); John Lewis (1783-1801); Thomas Morgan DD (1801-52); David Thomas (1852-54); Thomas Thomas (1854-71); Howell Howell (1871-73); David Rees (1873-89); James Hugh Lloyd (1889-1903) who supported missionary work in China and Japan; John Alban Davies (1903-14); John Long Price BA (Lincoln College Oxford) (1914-40); AP Williams (1940s-1950s); Rev Thomas (1950s); Rev Evans (1960s); Canon Hywel Jones (1970s); Cyril Jones (1981-94); Ryland Oliver (1995-9); Canon Joanna Penberthy (1999-2010); and Delyth Bowen (2011 briefly).

John Long Price (1870-1940) the son of David Long Price, the agent and solicitor to the Edwinsford Estate, married Myfanwy in 1899 and served as vicar of Talley from 1914 to 1940; they lived in Talley House (see Chapter 24.1) with a family of six daughters and a son who died young. John died on 5 March 1940 aged 70.

Canon Jo Penberthy who served as vicar (1999-2010) was later elected as Bishop of St Davids in 2016, the first female Bishop of the Church in Wales.

In the early years of the current century the vicar of Cynwyl Gaeo had three parishes in his benefice, St Cynwyl Caio, St Sawyl Llansawel and St Michael and All Angels Talley. These were contained within the Rural Deanery of Llangadog and Llandeilo, being part of the Archdeanery of Carmarthen within the Diocese of St Davids. Later Abergorlech was added as well. Since January 2015 the group of churches has been part of the Bro Dyfri Ministry Area of 15 parishes each with its own church in the Archdeanery of Carmarthen. Lay readers are licensed to administer communion and in the benefice to maintain regular church services assisted by occasional visiting clergy; in Talley the lay reader used to be John Walford for many years who served the community very well. The current acting curate since 2016 is Rev Delyth Wilson.

29.3 The Parish Church of St Sawyl, Llansawel

As we have seen from Chapter 1.3, St Sawyl[669] is the Patron Saint of Llansawel. The Parish Church St Sawyl, seems always to have been ecclesiastically attached to St Cynwyl's Church in Caio village in Cynwyl Gaeo. The original church[670] of mud, stone and thatch was probably erected in the 6th century when Sawyl Benuchel was in the area. The actual date of the building of the current church is unknown but was probably during the 13th century and has since been altered, repaired and restored on a number of occasions. It is referred to in Pope Nicholas IV's (1288-91) *"Taxatio Ecclesiastica"*, and in the Charter of Talley Abbey of 1331 we find reference to "the Church of Saint Cynwil with the chapels of Llansadwrn and Llanwrda, and Pistillsawyl and Llanpumsaint, and others to the same (church) belonging...." So it seems clear that Talley Abbey (Talyllychau), founded by Rhys ap Gruffydd (The Lord Rhys)(1132-97)(13), owned Cynwyl Gaeo with its three chapelries of ease, Llansawel, Llansadwrn and Llanwrda (the latter two being separated and given their own benefices in the 13th century).

The church is situated within an oval churchyard immediately south of the River Marlais and close to the River Melinddwr. The original 13th century building had a nave and chancel and the tower was added in the 15th century and unusually bears the coat of arms of Henry VII above the west door; this may suggest that Henry VII when he supposedly passed through Llansawel in 1485 and stayed in King's Court (Chapter 24.3) promised to make the parish independent civilly (but not ecclesiastically) and its name was changed from Pistyll Sawyl to Llansawyl. The church is constructed of mixed local rubble stone and consists of a three-bayed chancel, three-storeyed west tower, and a single aisle. Slates were put on the roof at the start of the 19th century and the church was restored in 1884-7 and the tower in 1890 by Rev Charles Chidlow at a cost of £1,491; red sandstone and oak wood was used and much of the cost was borne by the Edwinsford family. The gallery was removed and a new roof put on, new seats and pews and a

668 Fred Price. I am also very grateful to Mrs Janet James (who often plays the organ) for her research

669 WN Yates: *The Age of the Saints in Carmarthenshire CA (1973) p67-8* suggests caution in this dedication

670 Fred Price: *Llansawel p16*-25; Rev Daniel Thomas; Carmarthen Journal (26 Aug 1887); 1887 plans for restoration, Gloucester Record Office D2970/115

St Sawyl, Llansawel 2017

new pulpit were added, and the inside walls were plastered and bigger windows replaced the old ones. The vestry in the churchyard was once used as a schoolroom but is now disused. In 1890 a lovely stone reredos depicting the good shepherd with the 10 commandments engraved on its sides were added behind the altar by Sir James and Lady Madeline Williams-Drummond (68/67) in memory of their parents (a member of the Edwinsford family was nearly always a churchwarden). Inserted in the wall on the right side of the entrance is a 19th century square stone stoup or benitier for holding holy water in which worshippers dipped their fingers and cross marked their foreheads before entering the church, while the stone font is inserted into the left hand west wall which is most unusual. The church is one of the very few to have a Maltese Cross on the roof. Unusually it also has two leper windows,

St Sawyl, Llansawel 2017

while the senior church in Caio has none. Significant repairs were carried out in 2000 by Rev Jo Penberthy and the tower had to be restored.

In 1710, on the instructions of the Archbishop of Canterbury, the Archdeacon of Carmarthen, Edward Tenison, conducted a Visitation of 62 local parishes. The notes[671] of the Visitation concerning Llansawel state:

"A Chapel to Cynwyl Gaeo. The Churchyard wall to be repair'd. The tiling of the Chancell to be mended. The Ashes & plants growing on the buttress on the north side of the Chancell to be destroy'd. The windows to be glaz'd. The floors to be made even. The floor is rais'd in some places about 2 foot higher than it was at first, as appears by the Chancell floor laying so much lower. The Clerk says that earth had been brought out of the Churchyard to raise the floor of the Church for the sake of new graves. The Bible imperfect. No Canons, no Homilies, no Table of Degrees. The Minister's House that was on the Glebe here is dropt down. He promises that it shal be built up next Summer, & that a Certificate of it's being built up shal be put into Mr Harvard's hand to lay before My Ld Bishop, at or before Midsummer next. Prayers read once a Sunday. [f.70] Sermon once a month. Catechize in Lent. Act against swearing not read. Here are about 40 Presbyterians. Bread & Wine at Easter found by the Clerk.

671 G Milwyn Griffiths NLWJ (1974-6)

Communicants at Easter about 40. Families about 100. Poor that can read abt (sic) 20. Four Hamlets belong to it & 2 Churchwardens. This Account from the Minister."

As can be seen from the Edwinsford tithe books described in Chapter 16.2, local residents had to pay tithes in cash or in kind for centuries. By the early 19th century the traditional payment of tithes[672] to the Church and to Lay Impropriators (in the case of Cynwyl Gaeo and Llansawel parishes being the Edwinsford family) caused much resentment particularly amongst mainly non-conformist local inhabitants. This resulted in the Tithe Commutation Act 1836 which established the Tithe Commission (see Chapter 37.2). Traditionally Church Rates were payable by residents ranging from a halfpenny to two shillings despite the church not providing any educational services to the poor children of the parish other than at Sunday school.

Parishioners who breached Canon Law would find themselves before the Bishop's Court in Carmarthen. Offences included tithe evasion (the rector or vicar was entitled to 10 per cent of the produce annually), defamation (speaking ill of a parishioner), clandestine marriage (marrying without the knowledge of the clergy), usurpation of the parish church seat (the right to be buried under or near the family seat), brawling (creating a disturbance in church or the churchyard), neglect of duty (by ordained priests,or sextons or clerks) and jactitation of marriage (falsely declaring that a parishioner was married). Parish parochial problems were many and unusual. For example when John Davies of Caio died he died having been excommunicated for keeping swine in the churchyard, so his body could not be buried there; undaunted his family bribed Thomas Gwynn of Talley to carry out the burial service in Caio Church, which since the sexton would not provide the key, involved breaking a window to gain entry. The result was that the vicar reported the event to the Bishop and the Bishop's Court then also excommunicated Thomas Gwynn.

Llansawel Parish Church remained an integral part of the Church of England until disestablishment in 1920 when the Church in Wales was set up. When Henry VIII dissolved the abbeys and monasteries in 1536 he never parted with Caio or Llansawel so the reigning Sovereign continued to nominate the incumbent vicars of both parishes. The incumbents of the parish are believed to have included:

	David Glyne	1838 July	David (Daniel) Prytherch (Price)
1401	David ap Jenu	1846 Aug	George Howell
	John ap Llu (Llewellyn)	1851 June	Henry Jones Davies
1487 Feb	Morgan David	1873 Dec	Charles Chidlow
1488 Jan	David Morgan	1898 Jan	Henry Lloyd
1517 Jan	David, Abbot, Talley	1914	Griffith Jones
1554 Aug	David Llu	1929	Daniel Thomas
	Hugh Morgan	1970	BJ Hywel Jones
1560 June	Thomas Morgan	1981-94	Cyril Jones
1685	William Price	1995	Ryland Oliver
1726 May	Lewis Evans	1999-2010	Joanna Penberthy
1762 June	Leyson Lewis	2011	Delyth Bowen (briefly)
1784 Sept	Eliezer Williams		
1820 June	William Morgan		

672 David James: *Parish Life Eighteenth Century Style CA (2009) p54-60* for examples of tithing

After the Civil War Oliver Cromwell procured an Act of Propagation in 1649 to expel clergy from livings where there had been immorality and irregularities; as a result in 1650 Rev George Prichard[673] of Llansawel was "sequestrated for malignancy, insufficiency and refusing the engagement."

Rev Henry Thomas was curate at Llansawel in 1754-62. Then Leyson Lewis, who first served as curate, served as vicar; he was a relative of Thomas Lewis a solicitor in Llandeilo to whom the Stradey Park estate in Llanelli was left by his client, Mrs Mary Anne Mansel, the last surviving member of the Mansel family who died childless in 1808. In her honour he changed his family's surname to "Mansel Lewis" and his successors now own Stradey Castle, a new mansion which was built in 1855 on the estate.

Some of the incumbents did not actually live in or near Caio and Llansawel and relied on their curates. For example Rev Eliezer Williams (1754-1820), the son of Rev Peter Williams (1723-96) of Carmarthen (Methodist cleric and author of the "Welsh Commentary on the Bible"), was born at Llandefeilog in 1754, went to the Free Grammar School in Carmarthen and then to Jesus College Oxford in 1773-5, was ordained in Oxford in 1777, taught at Wallingford grammar school, served as a naval chaplain on HMS Cambridge and then as a tutor to the children of Lord Galloway and in 1784 was presented with the living of Caio and Llansawel. However, he resided in London until 1799 and in 1805 accepted the living of Lampeter; he did not actually reside in Caio or Llansawel or within 100 miles for the 21 years from 1784 until he came to Lampeter in 1805. In Lampeter he started a grammar school to prepare young men for holy orders which later became the foundation for St David's College in 1822. He died on 20 January 1820 and is buried at Lampeter.

Rev Henry Jones Davies from St David's College Lampeter was vicar (1851-73), a JP, described as a typical country gentleman who was a good preacher noted for his short and pithy sermons; initially he was a Congregational Minister before he became an Anglican. He was buried in Caio Churchyard and a marble tablet is in the church porch to his memory. He was succeeded as vicar by Rev Charles Chidlow (1873-97) who was educated at Jesus College Oxford, a staunch churchman, scholar, and historian with an active interest in agriculture who introduced *magnum bonum* potatoes locally (known as *tato'r ffeirad*: the vicar's potatoes).

Rev Daniel Thomas, who was the vicar from 1929 to 1970, was formerly an Oxford don with a mind of his own; when the Bishop instructed vicars not to take part in Chapel services, at the next Chapel funeral service he told the minister in charge that he would be taking part in the service and walked upto the pulpit to announce the hymn. He also invited Chapel members to take communion in his Church. He had an unrivalled knowledge[674] of local genealogy. His wife Dr Ferguson was the local GP and took surgeries in the vicarage; they raised their children, Henry and Elsbeth, in Caio and later Elsbeth followed her mother as a local GP.

Rev Jo Penberthy who served as vicar (1999-2010) was later elected as Bishop of St Davids in 2016, the first female Bishop of the Church in Wales.

In 1919 the residents of the parish raised funds to help pay for the tablet in Llansawel Church to commemorate those residents who had died in the Great War.

Until January 2015 the churches of Caio, Llansawel, Talley and Abergorlech were a benefice in the deanery of Llandovery. Since then the group of churches has been part of the Bro Dyfri Ministry Area of 15 parishes each with its own church in the Archdeanery of Carmarthen. Lay readers are licensed to administer communion and in the benefice to maintain regular church services assisted by occasional visiting clergy. Rev Delyth Wilson is since 2016 the current acting curate.

Beating the Bounds

The centuries old custom of "beating the bounds" is a pagan tradition[675] taken over by the Christian church; it might even derive from a festival celebrated in honour of Terminus, the Roman God of landmarks. In England the custom dates from Anglo-Saxon times and

673 Fred Price: *Llansawel p22-3*
674 DJ Williams pxvii
675 David Lewis: *Beating the Bounds (2003) City of London Livery News p14*

is mentioned in the laws of King Alfred the Great. When maps were rare and most parishioners could neither read nor write, it was common under the jurisdiction of the ecclesiastical courts for a priest, his churchwardens and his parishioners to perambulate the parish boundaries with young boys who would beat the parish border-stones often with willow or birch wands. Sometimes the boys would be themselves whipped or held upside down and had their heads bumped on a marker-stone or tree to make them remember the event and the boundary-markers (particulary where the open field system was used) for the benefit of the next generation. Hymns would be sung and hence the reference in many parishes to the Gospel Oak.

The ceremony usually took place every third year on Ascension Day or during Rogationtide (the priest would ask (rogare) for divine blessings), hence providing an opportunity to pray for a good harvest free of plague and for protection and blessings, to reassert the boundary rights of the landowners, and to enable everyone in the parish to have a celebration. Checking the boundaries of each parish prevented encroachment by neighbouring parishes, ensured that the correct parish paid poor relief to the correct residents, and avoided unnecessary disputes between parishes about income raising through tithes and the entitlement to raise rates. There was often a feast and in Henry VIII's reign the occasion had become an excuse for much revelry. Elizabeth I and Cromwell each tried to ban it unsuccessfully. Samuel Pepys says in his diary entry of 23 May 1661…. "it pleased me to see the little boys walk up and down in procession with their broom-staffs…"

In Carmarthenshire the custom used to be quite common and is still adopted for example in Laugharne[676] where the "Common Walk" takes place every three years on Whit Monday when the residents led by the Portreeve and officials of the Court start at the Town Hall at 6am for a 24 mile walk round the boundaries in accordance with their rights under their 13th century Charter. In Beaumaris in North Wales a similar custom takes place led by the Town Mayor but only every seven years. I can find no reference to when this custom died out in Llansawel and Talley.

29.4 Calvinistic Methodists (Presbyterian Church of Wales)

Bethel Cavinistic Methodist Chapel, Llansawel [SN621365]

The Edwinsford family were Anglicans but supported religious freedom and the local chapels which were attended by some of their tenants and employees.

During the 18th century no fewer than 17 Englishmen were appointed Bishops of St Davids and the Anglican Church was hostile to the Welsh language and to using Welsh in education. This helped start the Welsh revival in 1735 at Trevecca with the conversion of Howell Harris. One of the oldest Methodist meeting-houses was at Soar in Cilycwm[677] founded in 1740. William Williams of Pantycelyn (1717-91)[678] was converted by and joined Harris. John Wesley visited Sir Gâr in 1763, and in 1765 Harris, Williams and Daniel Rowlands spent five days in Llansawel. The early Methodists remained in the Anglican Church although this became more difficult after time and gradually there were disagreements over the speed of reform, the moral standards of the Anglican clergy and the perceived injustice and oppression by the hierarchy. Other non-conformist denominations spread and on average in Wales at this time a new chapel was being built every eight days. Eventually after the majority of Anglican priests refused to marry and baptise Methodists the latter established a separate Church in about 1811. The Methodists adopted the use of the term elder (*blaenor*) for their lay leaders rather than deacon (which in the Anglican Church is a minister below the rank of Bishop and Priest) while the Baptists and Independents adopted the term deacon since they were not so closely related to the Anglican Church.

In Llansawel and the surrounding area the Calvinistic Methodist farmers started meeting in private farmhouses or in the open. Howell Harries, Daniel Rowlands and William Williams sometimes came on horseback to preach in the area. There is much doubt as to which was the first Calvinistic Methodist chapel in Wales to be built. Some historians think it was the chapel attended by William Williams and his family called Tŷ Newydd (the New House). Some think it was a chapel built in Builth Wells in 1847 called "Alpha". Local residents of

676 JI Thomas: *A Laugharne Mixture (Lynn Hughes p44)*

677 Sir John Lloyd Vol 2 p205 says the inscription of 1740 is not conclusive

678 In about 1748 William Williams married Mary (Mali) Francis, daughter of Thomas Francis of Penylan in Llansawel and they had eight children. He also taught briefly in Llansawel after losing his curacy in Llanwrtyd and Abergwesyn. He wrote over 800 hymns in Welsh and 200 in English and travelled thousands of miles on horseback to preach

Bethel Chapel 19th century

Bethel Chapel

Llansawel argue that at Quarterly Meetings held locally at Abergorlech on 4 September 1744 and later at Porthyrhyd on 3 October 1744 it was decided to build a "house in Llansawel for religious purposes, such as preaching, teaching school etc" and that this was built around 1746-9 on the road to Esgairdawe up the hill from the Swan Inn. The answer perhaps[679] is that the chapel in Builth was the first to be called a "chapel" and that while the Methodists remained part of the Anglican church they did not wish their meeting houses to be called chapels. In 1743 the members at Llansawel numbered 40 and had increased to 180 by 1898. In 1801 the first Sunday school was started at Bethel. In 1829 the chapel[680] was enlarged and partially rebuilt and altered and renovated in 1904 by David Jenkins of Llandeilo. It still retains its lovely wooden pews and woodwork with its three sided slightly curving timber gallery. A tablet states *"Bethel Chapel y Trefnyddion Calfinaidd. Adeiladwyd yn 1749. A Ail adeiladwyd yn 1809. Ac A Adnewydd yn 1904"*. A two storey 19th century vestry is attached and there is also a rubble single storey former stable next to the vestry. The interior of the chapel is wholly from the 1904 renovation.

The graveyard next to the chapel was donated by Evan Jones of Cardiff, and his brother David Jones of Alltrycloriau donated the gate and paid for the wall. The land across the road for the new cemetery was donated by James Thomas of Maesllan in 1932 and he was the first person to be buried there on 9 December 1933 when the land was consecrated.

The preachers (pastors and all Reverends) at Llansawel[681] have included: Robert Salmon (1867-73), D Byron Lewis (1874-80), James Morris (1881-92), David Jones (1893-98), David Hughes (1902-5), Daniel Jones (1908-13), J Ellis Williams (1915-19), Daniel Nicholas (1924-29), Stephen Jones (1931-54), Hartwell Morgan (1956-60), Richard Evans (1961-65), Henry Roberts (1965-67), J Howell Evans (1969-82), Robert JO Griffiths (1984-87), Haydn Richards (1989), and Casi M Jones (1992-97). Prior to 1867 Rev BD Thomas of Llandeilo and Rev William Jenkins (d1868) were overseers of the chapel. Since 1997 itinerant and guest preachers have been shared with other local chapels.

As described in Chapter 26.3, despite Llansawel being a hotbed of Methodism in the 18th and 19th centuries no fewer than 41 Anglican clergy were produced by its families[682], many of whom were brought up as Welsh speaking non-conformists and yet were later ordained into the Anglican Church. As Fred Price said Bethel "has fed the church better than the church itself." The Davies family of Porth Factory produced ten of these priests, which must be some sort of record.

From the incomplete records which are still available the elders (blaenoriaid) at Llansawel Chapel have included: James Davies (Ffosgotta), Jonah Williams (Trawsgoed)[683], Mark Penrhiwcarne, David Thomas (Pantiauau), William James, Thomas Davies (Porth Factory, the father of the "four apostles of Llansawel"), William Peters (Iron Gate), William James, Evan Evans (Blaenwaun), David Williams (Post Office), John Davies and Daniel Davies (Ffosgotta), David

---

679 Fred Price: *Llansawel p26-7;* Rev James Morris (Minister at Llansawel)*: Hanes Methodist Sir Caerfyrddin 1911*

680 Carmarthen Journal (21 Nov 1902); The Architect (24 April 1903); Welshman (2 June 1905)

681 I am very grateful to Mrs Betty Williams of Cilgwyn, Crugybar (elder and secretary) for this information and for her helpful assistance on this section

682 Dr Roger Brown: *The Followers of Jeroboam The Son of Nebat—A Study of the Clerical Members of the Davies-Williams Family of Llansawel (1983)*

683 Uncle Josi to DJ Williams p110

Williams (Felinwaun), James Williams (Penybont)[684], Isaac Davies (Bwlchyddinas), Rees James (Bethel Terrace), John Williams (Pistyllgwyn), William Davies (Pantiauau), John Jones (Penlan), David Jones (Esgair), DB Evans (schoolmaster), David Evans (Tanlan), James Thomas (Maesllan), Joseff Jones (Porth Factory), John Davies (Rhydcymerau), ET Griffiths (Glanrannell), David Davies (Glynmarch), Tom Davies (Ynys), David Jones (4 Bethel Terrace), Gwernwy Richards (Castle Green), John Morgan (Island), John Thomas (Nantgwyne), Thomas Thomas (Maesllan), William Jones (schoolmaster), Eneck Davies (8 Castle Terrace), James Davies (Blaenresgair), John Griffiths (Pantdderwen), John Thomas (Penybont), Griffydd Rogers (Bancyglyn), Simon Griffiths (Geryllan), Idris Williams (Glynawel), DT Davies (Bryngwyn), Leonard Evans (Parkyrhos), Evan Davies (Trewaun), Terwyn George (Crudyrawel), DT Davies (Cilcennen), Bryn Thomas (Rhiwlas), Glyn Jones (Eirlyn), Tegwyn Jones (Marlais), Gilmour Morgan (Maesycoed), Gerwyn Davies (Blaenresgair), and Elizabeth Williams (Cilgwyn, Crugybar). The latter two are the current elders. My great grandfather, Thomas Davies of Nantmawr Ffarmers and Goilandew Llandeilo (1838-1913), was also an elder and is buried with his wife Margaret of Llethyrbledrig, Llansawel (1843-84) in the old graveyard.

In the early days each family by farm or cottage would donate an annual subscription which would financially help the chapel and would also guarantee that family its own pew. By tradition each family would sit in their own pew or pews. Today Llansawel Chapel has about 30 members of whom less than 10 are regular attenders; this is the experience of many local chapels.

I have described[685] the Calvinistic Methodist Chapels in Caio, Pumsaint and Cwrt y Cadno elsewhere.

Esgairnant Calvinistic Methodist Chapel, Talley [SN643324]

Around 1739-42[686] a Mrs Mary Griffiths (d1785) of Glanyrafondduganol was one of many staunch supporters of the Methodist movement in the Talley area and she hosted numerous private prayer meetings in her house to which preachers would come; meetings were also held at Maerdy Isaf; she was the founder of the Griffiths charity for the poor among Methodists. When she died she left her carriage to Daniel Rowlands to help him in his journeys throughout Wales. In 1793 a Mrs Jane Lloyd of Pantyresgair donated a house called Esgairnant for members to hold services in and this continued for some 12 years; this is located on the road from Talley to Llandeilo just outside Talley. In 1806 she gave the house with some land on which to erect a chapel. The cost of building the chapel in 1806 was £180; in 1828 the chapel was enlarged at an additional cost of £180. In 1858 a gallery was added at a cost of £125, and later the vestry was built. In 1878 a small dwelling house was built on the original plot and named Esgairnant. In 1899 the whole building was taken down by Daniel Davies, a building contractor of Tŷ Ann Arthur of Talley (see Chapter 24.5), and the cost of renovation was £420; the architect was probably David Jenkins of Llandeilo whose did a similar job at Cwmdu Chapel in 1883. The moneys were raised by Rev JD Evans from members and donors with some borrowings; the debt was paid off by 1922. The chapel is unusual because one faces the congregation when one enters the building. There is a small two storey vestry next to the chapel. Inside the chapel is a three sided timber gallery, an inset clock on marbled cast iron columns, raked pews, and a raised timber pulpit.

The Ministers (pastors and all Reverends)[687] who have served at Esgairnant have included: Rev John Jones (1873-80); Rev Isaac Morgan (1885-89); Rev James Morris (1889-93); Rev JD Evans (1893-1933) from Abermeurig who lived in Cilwern with a Mrs Davies as housekeeper, always wore a bishop-style black hat and organised the concert in the chapel on Christmas night; Rev E Alun Thomas (1942-45); Rev Stephen Jones (1948-54); Rev Hartwell Lloyd Morgan (1956-60); Rev Richard John Evans (1961-64); Rev Henry

---

684 Uncle Jemi to DJ Williams p108

685 David Lewis: *Family Histories p25-7*

686 Rev James Morris: *Hanes Methodistiaeth Sir Caerfyrddin (1911) p257*; DG Griffiths: *Centenary of Thomas Lewis CA (1942) Vol 1 p15-9;* Brenda James: *Fond Memories of Talley (1994) p72-80*; Gwyneth Jones of the Talley History Society: *Y Llychau (2006)*

687 I am very grateful to Mrs Janet James of Dolwerdd, Halfway (elder) for this information and for her helpful assistance on this section

Esgairnant Chapel 2017

Roberts (1965-67); Rev J Howell Evans (1969-82); Rev Robert J Owen Griffiths (1984-87); Rev Haydn Richards (1989); and Rev Casi M Jones (1992-97). The chapel acquired a marriage licence in June 1872.

From the incomplete records which are still available the elders (blaenoriaid) at Esgairnant Chapel have included: Dafydd Harry (Glanyrafondduganol); Rhydderch Siôn Hugh (Nantyrhogfan); Morgan Rhys (Capel Hir); David Morgan (Maerdy); Thomas Lewis the blacksmith of Blaenug Issa who famously wrote the hymn *Wrth gofio'l riddfannau'n yr ar*dd (see Chapter 24.13); John Thomas (Cwmsidan); John Thomas (Wern); Rhydderch Evans (Cwm); Edward Thomas (Cwmsidan); Lewis Hopkin (Gellicefnrhos)(d1871); John Thomas (Cwmsidan)(d1878); Rhydderch Evans (Cwm)(d1844); William Richards (Felinwaun)(d1846); Thomas Thomas (Cilyllynfach)(d1860); Thomas Thomas (Glanyrafondduganol) (d1863); Rhys Thomas (Coedhirion); John Anthony Jones (d1881); John Thomas (Wern); Thomas Rees (Glanyrafondduganol); W Davies (Cilwern); Thomas William (Wernfawr); JD Thomas (Plasnewydd); Griffith Morgan (Banc, Porth Selu); Simon M Jones (Plas, Rose Cottage); John Davies (Gellicefnrhos); J Sellick (Bancelwydd); David Evans (Cwm); John Davies (King's Court); Joshua Davies (Blaenug); DJ Morgan (Cilyllynfach); Morgan Morgans (Ardwyn) the Headteacher[688] at Talley School; Parry Reynolds (Dolwerdd); Alun Morgan (Porth Selu); Morgan Davies (Bancelwydd, Langwm); William Davies (Gellicefnrhos, Rhosygelli); Vincent Davies (Glanyrafondduisaf, Talybont); Idris Davies (Gellicefnrhos); Aneurin Morgan (Cilyllynfach); John Jenkins (Maerdy Uchaf); and Mrs Janet James (Dolwerdd).

688 Brenda James remembered him with great affection

Griffiths memorial in Talley Churchyard

Today the members number some 31 and regular attendees number less than 10. In 1956 Esgairnant celebrated its 150th anniversary and in 2006 its bicentenary at which its last minister Rev Casi Jones preached.

29.5 Independents

The first group of non-conformist worshipers[689] in Cynwyl Gaio parish met at Crugybar. The exact date that the Chapel was established is not known although there was a chapel there in 1662. During the reigns of Charles II and James II the worshipers (a mixed group of Independents and Baptists) were cruelly persecuted. They therefore moved to Bwlchyrhiw and like the Independents at Cefnarthen used the caves in the area to worship in secret. There is an area at Bwlchyrhiw that is called Craig yr Eglwys. The Independents and some Baptists returned to worship at Crugybar in 1688 when William III and Mary came to the throne. Many of the Baptists stayed at Bwlchyrhiw or Glynyrefail as it was then called.

Stephen Hughes (1622-88) is generally thought to be the preacher that motivated the establishing of Crugybar Chapel. Vavasor Powell (1617-70) and Rees Prytherch (1579-1642) are also connected with the cause in its early days. The first Chapel was located by the side of the road from Talley where the lane turns in towards the present Chapel. By 1763/1765 the third Chapel was being built but at the present location [SN 657377]. The plaque on the Chapel wall notes that the present Chapel was built in 1765, rebuilt in 1837 and renewed in 1883. Crugybar is the mother of most of the other Independent Chapels in the area. In 1690 some members from Crugybar formed the chapel in Ffaldybrenin at Crofftycyff. A branch of Crugybar was started in Bwlchyffin in 1864 but sadly was closed by 1971. Some of the other chapels that have their roots at Crugybar are Carmel and Ebenezer, Llansadwrn, Tabor Llanwrda and Shiloh Llansawel.

Shiloh Chapel, Llansawel [SN618363]

Shiloh Independent Chapel in Llansawel stands at the top of the hill on the junction of the road from the village to Abergorlech. After the great religious revival of 1849 attempts were made to buy some land on which to build a chapel, but this was not achieved until 1867 on a site near Penybailey. The Edwinsford Estate owned most of the surrounding land in that area but I have been unable to discover if the site of the chapel was ever part of the estate. The £550 cost of the chapel[690] was raised from subscribers including members of the Crugybar Chapel, Rev Evan Jones of Crugybar and Rev Jonah Evans of Llansawel. In 1868 the foundation stone was laid and it opened in

689 For a history of nonconformity see Glanmor Williams: *Nonconformity in Welsh History CA (1994) p33-42*
690 Fred Price: *Llansawel p29*

Shiloh Chapel 2017

October that year after £400 had been raised; the remaining debt of £100 had been paid off by 1872.

The preachers (pastors) (shared with those at the mother chapel in Crugybar) have included Rev Evan Jones (1834-1877); and Rev DB Richards (1877-1927) assisted by Rev Jonah Evans who was ordained in 1870; Rev Jonah Evans (1836-96)[691] opened a school in Llanybydder in 1861 and then moved to Llansawel in 1866 as a preacher; he is famous for having established a grammar school in 1875 in the church vestry and then building the Sawyl Academy in 1884-6 very close to the Chapel on the hill into Llansawel where he also lived (see Chapter 30.2). Subsequent preachers at the chapel have included Rev DM Lloyd (1928-42); Rev T Glenville Rees (1943-87); Rev Alan John (1988-94); Rev Aled Jones (1995-2000) and Rev D Huw Roberts (from 2002).

Ebenezer Apostolic Church, Halfway [SN647307]

Many non-conformists who met in neighbouring homes for prayer meetings in the area south of Talley near Halfway and Cwmdu decided just before the Great War to build their own church. David Evans of Glanyrafonddu Isaf bought the old Smithy forge and some land on the junction to Cwmdu off the main Talley to Llandeilo road from John Philip Griffiths of Cwmdu Inn in 1913. The members from the Providence Chapel in Cwmdu converted the old building and built a new Ebenezer Church. Stones were carried from the river nearby, bricks were sourced by Jack Evans from Llandybie quarry, and Stephen Bowen a building contractor from Llandybie erected the building. Services started in 1914 although the official opening took place on 24-26 April 1915. District and local ministers (pastors)[692] have included Caleb Price, John Evans, Ernie Williams, Owen Roberts, Gordon Wright, Jacob Harries, Jim Mcinley (1978-85), Eric Horley (1985-92), John Morgan (1992-2009), Eric Horley (2009-17) who has just retired with his wife Diana after very long service , and Ian Hughes (2017-) ex Royal Navy who has just moved to Halfway from Llanelli with his wife Megan. The Church celebrated its centenary in September 2013.

Ebenezer Church 2017

[691] Rev T Mardy Rees: *Notable Welshmen 1700-1900 p446.* Rev Jonah Evans wrote the *Memoir of the Rev E Jones (Crugybar) (1883)*

[692] I am very grateful to Eric Horley (Halfway) and to Laverne Anamelechi (Luton) for this information

29.6 Baptists

The first Baptists in Wales were Arminian (rather than Calvinistic) in Radnorshire although an earlier Baptist Chapel was started at Olchon in Welsh speaking Herefordshire as early as 1633. The Calvinistic Baptists started at Ilston in Gower about 1649. The first Baptist Association meeting in Carmarthenshire was held on 19 January 1651 in Carmarthen. Records indicate that there was a mixed gathering of Baptist and Congregationalist worshippers at Crugybar in 1662. Due to the cruel persecution of the non-conformists, those who did not conform with the established church fled to Bwlchyrhiw and worshipped there secretly in a remote and safer region in a cave near Craig yr Eglwys. They also worshipped at Crofft y Cyff, a farm in the parish of Llanycrwys.

By 1688 the persecution was gradually dying down, so the Congregationalists returned to Crugybar, but the Baptists stayed at Bwlchyrhiw. The first Chapel at Bwlchyrhiw [SN 729464] was built in 1717 just on the Cilycwm side of the parish boundary and people used to travel long distances to worship secretly in safety. It was built in an area of wild magnificence where Twm Siôn Cati used to roam in his day. The chapel was known at first as Glynyrefail, since a smithy's workshop stood nearby, where earlier meetings had been held. A Cardiganshire preacher, Thomas David Evan, was the first Minister and for many years after 1730 he crossed the hills from Llanddewibrefi on horseback to preach to a small congregation of farmers and shepherds without much success. Dissenting meeting-houses and chapels in Wales were built which replaced the private houses formerly used for worship and these served large but relatively poor rural communities. By 1715 many Independent and Baptist chapels had been built and Ministers supplemented their income by holding schools.

Aberduar Llanybydder, the mother church, effectively sponsored branches at Bwlchyrhiw and at Bethel in Ffarmers as well as elsewhere. Bethel Chapel [SN 667453] was built in 1741 on the current car park side of the road to serve the farming and local community, the baptism pool being just below in the river by the bridge. The first chapel had a thatched roof and was built by Thomas Morgan Thomas, father of Rev Joshua Thomas (1853-1916) who was Minister at Bethel and Salem Caio for 25 years and is buried at Bethel, a distinguished Baptist historian. Salem Caeo and Seion Rhandirmwyn were built in 1829, but four years later Bethel and Salem were united and Bwlchyrhiw and Seion relinquished their connection with Bethel.

The Salem Caeo Baptist chapel [SN 649423] built in 1829 near the Great Oak on a 999 year lease was under the joint ministry of Rev Thomas Thomas and Rev Timothy Jones for many years. Salem's best known members have included Dr Timothy Richard (1845-1919), the missionary who was born in the old smithy in Ffaldybrenin, and his nephew, Timothy Richard Morgan born in Llandre in 1861 who was ordained in 1887 and ministered for 56 years.

The Baptist Register publication in 1794 records 1,907 members in Sir Gâr county. By the 1851 religious census 77% of those who attended chapel or church in Sir Gâr attended a chapel and only 23% went to church (but only 39% of the total population attended either). The religious census of 1851 records for Bethel Ffarmers (Cwmpedol) that there was space for 150 free, 160 other and 50 standing; that 244 adults and 56 scholars (children) were present at the morning service and that the average for the year was 200 adults and 80 scholars at the morning service.

In 1853 Bwlchyrhiw and Seion Rhandirmwyn reunited with Bethel and Salem Caeo. At this time the chapels were very well attended and generations of Welsh children learnt to read their mother tongue. In 1859 a great religious revival swept the country and there were 407 members of Bethel and Salem in 1860. Fred Price tells us that in 1901 there were 122 members at Bethel and that a Sunday school was held in various farm houses in the area. At the movement's height the Welsh Baptists had some 190,000 members, but today this number has declined to less than 20,000. Today Bethel Chapel has about 43 members and an additional 18 who contribute financially but less than 10 regular attendees at the services.

The Baptists did not have a place of worship in Llansawel or Talley, although in 1823 Christmas Evans and Daniel Davies, the blind preacher from Swansea, visited Llansawel[693] and while on horseback preached to a large audience in the street outside the Angel Inn and then dined inside.

693 Fred Price: *Llansawel p30*

Providence Baptist Chapel[694] in Cwmdu was built near the Inn, shop and Post Office. The original chapel was built in 1789. It is a tall whitewashed building fronted by a small burial ground and was rebuilt, refitted and restored in 1839, and renovated again in 1883 by David Jenkins[695] of Llandeilo. Inside it has a three-sided gallery with a panelled front on marbled cast iron columns. In its early years it had some 180 members but regular attendees today number less than 10. The baptism pool is in the stream across the road where in 1859 some 46 people were baptised. In 1939 when Rev Price Evans was the minister about 2,000 people attended a two day preaching festival there of the Baptist Conference of Carmarthenshire and Ceredigion.

29.7 Quakers (Religious Society of Friends)

As we saw in Chapter 6.2 Morgan ap Rhys of Rydodyn was the third son of Rhys ap William (dc1582). He married Catherine, daughter of David ap Lewis ap Rhys ap Philip of Builth. They lived in Talley parish and he inherited Tyr Bryngwyn from his father. They had five children, Lewis, William, Sioned (Jenet), Maud and Rees (42), whose son, David (ap) Rhys Williams (bc1660), is probably the member of the family who emigrated with the Quakers (members of the Society of Friends) in 1693 to Philadelphia County in Pennsylvania. The Quaker movement had been formed during the Civil Wars.

The Welsh[696] constituted an early and important element of the population of provincial Pennsylvania and played a conspicuous part in the founding of the colony. Emigration from Wales to America was due primarily to religious motives and the early Welsh immigrants were mostly Quakers (Friends) although there were also some Welsh Baptists, Presbyterians, and Anglicans or Episcopalians. Many Welsh families accepted the offer by a fellow Welshman, William Penn, to escape oppression and seek a new life in the New World where they could retain their language and distinctive customs. Indeed many of these Welshmen belonged to the gentry and were men of means. A Welsh committee visited William Penn in London in 1681 to negotiate the purchase of tracts of land in Pennsylvania and their leader, John ap John, was the effective founder of the Society of Friends in Wales as well as the founder of the Welsh Tract in Pennsylvania. These 40,000 acres of land were to be a Welsh Barony with self government and were located in a fertile region north of Philadelphia. The first ship arrived on 13 August 1682 and the next in November 1683.

David Rhys Williams (c1660-1714) was probably born at Rhydodyn or nearby. He is thought to have married Katherine Harry (c1660-c1700) in about 1685. They emigrated to Pennsylvania and brought with them a Certificate of Removal from Llandeilo Friends Meeting dated May 1693 which is recorded in Radnor MM:

"To All Whom It May Concern,
Where as our Deare and Honest Frind David William his wife and family Late of the Parish of Llandilo vaur in the county of Caer Marthinyom is Intendinge to take his voyage for Pennsylvania God Willing. These are therefor to Certifie That he lived in This Country Peaceably and honestly And of good report amonst his Neighbours; And that he left his Native Country for noe ill deed. And as upon Consideration of his faithfulness and Integritie to the truth and its Servic for divers years in his Native Country as a living member of the Suffering Body whereof Christ is the head; we therefore have thought it meete and noe less than an Incumbent duty Lying Upon us to recomend him to you as such as is worthy to be received. And with earnest breathings unto the Lord in his Behalfe for his Safe arrival unto you. We therefor recomend this as our Brother's Testimony. From yor Frinds in the undecevable truth of God. Att Llanstephan the 26th day of the 3rd month (May) 1693.
Attested......"

David (described as a gentleman) and his family arrived in Pennsylvania in 1693. In 1697 he built the Spring Mill in Whitemarsh on the Schuylkill River and a home next to it. This Mill may have been the oldest in Pennsylvania and years later it supplied flour to General Washington's troops in Valley Forge. David was a member of the Haverford Meetings and held weekday meetings at his Spring Mill home. Later David helped found the Plymouth Meeting, which in 1715 was combined with the Gwynedd as the Gwynedd Monthly Meeting.

Katherine died before 1701 and David then married Mrs Mary Rhodes Maulsby (1662-1709) on 30 January 1704 in Philadelphia. He wrote

[694] Jack Thomas, Cwmdu 2003
[695] Western Mail (3 May 1907)
[696] Wayland F Dunaway: *Pennsylvania History (1945) p251-267*; Thomas Allen Glenn: *Welsh Founders of Pennsylvania (1911) Vol I p217*

his will in September 1714 naming his children by Katherine as Isaac (1688-c1735), Joseph, Rees (1686-c1750), Phebe (1692-1716), Esther (b1695), and Jenis (1690-1720). He also had by Mary a son, Joseph (1705-55). David died on 11 November 1714 and he and Mary are buried in Plymouth Meeting Friends Cemetery in Montgomery (formerly Philadelphia) County, Pennsylvania.

Joseph Williams (1705-55) married Sarah Griffith (1707-73) from Radnor MM, Chester County, Pennsylvania; their son, David Williams (1730-89), was born in Lower Merion Twp in Philadelphia County (now Upper Merion, Montgomery County) and their daughter was Catherine Williams Dunwick (1740-1813). David married Anne Thomas (1730-1805) in about 1748 near Uwchlan, Chester County. In October 1762 Anne was admitted to the Fairfax MM (Monthly Meeting). They are both buried in Potts Cemetery, Hillsboro, Loudoun County, Virginia near their Hillsboro farm, which was sold in 1815 to the Thompson family. Their children included William (1747-86), Margaret (1758-1835) and Israel (1740-1813).

There were Quaker communities in Llanddewibrefi and Llandeilo up to the end of the 19th century with their Friends Houses. In addition near New Inn by Salem Heolgaled off the Talley to Llandeilo road there used to be a Friends House and small walled burial ground upto the mid 20th century. The burial ground[697] remains although the gravestones have been removed.

29.8 Church of Jesus Christ of Latter-Day Saints (Mormons)

The LDS Church or, informally the Mormon Church, is a Christian restorationist church which is considered by its followers to be the restoration of the original church founded by Jesus Christ. Today it has some 15 million followers. It was first organised by Joseph Smith in 1830 in New York; it moved to Ohio in 1831 and then to Missouri in 1833. Following Smith's murder in 1844, Brigham Young led the followers to Nebraska and then in 1847 to Utah where their headquarters are in Salt Lake City. In 1890 Utah was admitted as a US state and in 1904 the church president Joseph F Smith disavowed polygamy.

By 1847 missionaries were sent to Europe to gain new converts. They arrived in Llansawel in 1849[698] and created quite a stir by their open air preaching and teaching. They baptised many people in the river. Thomas Thomas of Pantmawr and Daniel Davies of the Old Red Lion (shown in the 1851 census with his wife Anne and three children-see Chapter 26.7) were converted and went to Utah with their families. An old soldier, William Jones, of Garnwen followed with his family. Daniel Lewis[699] of Caio (b1834), son of Joseph Lewis and Mary Morgan (born in 1797 and died in Llansawel in 1847), was baptised in Caio Church on 9 December 1834 and later converted and was baptised as a member of the Mormon Church on 16 October 1854 and sailed for America on 18 April 1856. As a missionary he later revisited Wales (1885-7) and his met his cousin Jane Davies in Llansawel in 1886. The records[700] show there were some 42 members of the Llansawel Branch of the British Mission for 1849-55 including residents of Pantmawr, Penlan and the Red Lion Inn in Llansawel and Elizabeth Williams and Jane Thomas of Cilgawod in Caio.

In 1848 Dan Jones, an early Welsh convert, returned to America with 250 Welsh converts many of whom became the foundation of the Mormon Tabernacle Choir. John Parry, another Welsh convert, organised a choir as early as 1849. Today the 360 voice Mormon Tabernacle Choir is famous internationally.

---

697 Rev Gomer Roberts: *Cloc y Capel (1973) p71-4*

698 Fred Price: *Llansawel p30;* TH Lewis*: The Mormons and Brechfa CA (1959) p27-9 and Y Mormoniaid yng Nghymru*

699 I am grateful to Gregg and Trudena Fager for this information. Daniel Lewis was Gregg's great great grandfather

700 history.lds.org

30. Education

30.1 Background

In 1698 the Society for the Promotion of Christian Knowledge (SPCK) was formed by some Anglican laymen to spread knowledge. This also included translating religious books into Welsh. With the great help of Sir John Philipps (1666-1737) of Picton Castle Pembrokeshire and of John Vaughan of Derllys Court Carmarthenshire, it also aimed to set up SPCK charity schools in every parish with the help of the local clergy. Several SPCK schools were established in Carmarthenshire including in Llandeilo and Llandovery in the early decades of the 18th century. Additional charity schools were set up by non-conformists, but the great majority of Welsh children still received no education.

As we saw in Chapter 8.3, Thomas Williams of Edwinsford (1693-1762)(54) married Arabella (d1728), the daughter of John Vaughan (1663-1722) of Court Derllys in Merthyr parish just west of Carmarthen, by his wife Elizabeth Thomas (d1721) of Meidrim near to Merthyr (the sole heiress of her own mother's Protheroe estate at Hawksbrook in Llangynog). Arabella and her two sisters were the co-heiresses to the Derllys and Hawksbrook estates and also inherited the Derwydd estate on the death of their uncle Richard Vaughan MP in 1724. Her youngest sister and co-heiress was Bridget Bevan (1698-1779) known as Madam Bevan, who was born at Derllys Court and on 30 December 1721 married Arthur Bevan MP (1689-1743) at Merthyr Church.

Madam Bevan[701] continued her father's interest in philanthropy and education by financially supporting Rev Griffith Jones (1683-1761) the rector of Llanddowror who married the sister of Sir John Philipps. With the help of Sir John and of Madam Bevan he set up the concept of "Circulating Welsh Charity Schools" in Wales "for all comers to learn to read and be supplied with books and taught gratis". The schools were open to all ages and most were conducted in Welsh. After he died Madam Bevan continued with the work and it is estimated that there were over 6,000 schools with about 300,000 scholars (pupils) of all ages attending, a very considerable achievement. She died in Laugharne in 1779 leaving £10,000 to the schools, but her relatives disputed her will and eventually after 30 years of Chancery litigation the money, which had by then grown to over £30,000, was released in 1804 to the educational purposes intended by her.

In 1740 a circulating school visited Garth in Cynwyl Gaeo and Rev E Jones, curate of Caio, and later Rev Leyson Lewis wrote to thank Griffith Jones for the great work the school was doing in the parish. In 1740 a circulating school was started in Llansawel with 48 pupils increasing to 64 in 1742 and to 84 in 1743 and then decreasing to 33 by 1745. The first schoolmaster in Llansawel was David Jones from Llanwenog in Cardiganshire.

The infamous Royal Commission Report of 1847 into non-conformist schools by three arrogant English barristers stated that the Welsh language was the curse of Wales: *"the Welsh language is a vast drawback to Wales and a manifold barrier to the moral progress and commercial prosperity of the people. Because of their language the mass of the Welsh people are inferior to the English in every branch of practical knowledge and skill"*. The Commissioner says in the Report about the village school in the vestry in Llansawel Churchyard: *"I visited this school on November 2nd; it is held in the churchyard in a ruinous old building, the roof of which in windy weather is dangerous from the looseness of its tiles. The master had been three quarters of a year at Ffrwd Vale. He seemed a well-meaning, civil, and kind young man. His desk contained a few tattered maps of his own providing. Lady Mary Williams[702] pays him £5.10s per annum, for which sum 18 scholars to be taught. Eight of the children in school could read fairly well. Average attendance 50. Income from school pence, £18. Subscriptions and donations, £5.10s. Master's age, 29; formerly a farm servant. I found both this parish and Cayo in charge of a single curate, who resided in Cayo. I, unfortunately, twice failed in meeting the Rev George Enoch, curate of this parish (Cayo) and Llansawel—once on the 22nd of October, when I called, and again on the 1st of November at Llansawel, where I had written requesting him to meet*

[701] Peter Stopp: *Griffith Jones of Llanddowror CA (2016) p52-67*

[702] Lady Mary, the wife of Sir James Hamlyn Williams 3rd Bt MP (61)

Madam Bevan

me, but he was otherwise engaged." This Report which commented so harshly on the morality and intelligence of the Welsh people led to a furore and the three volumes became known as the Treachery of the Blue Books (*Brad y Llyfrau Gleison).*

The Education Act 1870 made the English school system compulsory in Wales, Welsh was outlawed in schools and any child using it was made to wear a board hung round their neck saying "Welsh Not"; were it not for the Chapel Sunday schools it is possible that many children would not have been literate in Welsh at all. Welsh speakers declined from 49.9% of the population (1 million out of 2 million) in 1901 to 19% in 2011 (the population is now 3 million) up from 18% in 1991 so the tide is slowly turning principally due to the compulsory learning of Welsh in schools (about 16% of children are now taught in the medium of Welsh). Interestingly more than 10% of Welsh speakers were not born in Wales. The majority of the local population are fully supportive of the success in this policy of expanding the use of Welsh so that bilingualism becomes more and more common. Just as important however is that in a small country it is necessary to raise the general standard of secondary and tertiary education to assist economic growth; recent Welsh administrations in Cardiff seem to have failed to achieve this so far and the standards of school education in Wales continue to fall short of those in the other parts of the UK.

What is interesting from the 1891 and 1911 censuses is that they showed which languages the local residents of each dwelling could speak. Very few were bilingual and the great majority could only speak Welsh, although the youngsters could speak both languages because by now they were learning English at school under the new compulsory education rules. Prior to the middle of the 19th century many were illiterate as can be seen from their marks on birth and death certificates.

As Fred Price noted in his *History of Caio* in 1904: *"the inhabitants of this parish cherish a most ardent attachment to the land of their birth, and still cling with wonderful tenacity to the language of their remote ancestors. It is the language selected by the persons who wish to reach the hearts of their fellows; it is the language used by the people in their times of trouble and of triumph"*. Whilst the number of Welsh speakers has decreased since 1904 the sentiment expressed by Fred Price still holds good.

I have described Caio School (1869-2012), Cwmcothi / Cwrt y Cadno School (1877-1971), Ffarmers School (1877-2008) and Llanycrwys School (1878-2008) elsewhere[703]; sadly they have all now closed.

30.2 Llansawel

In Llansawel a circulating school started in 1740; this *Ysgol râd* (Welsh charity school) survived from 1740 to 1805. Then in 1805 the Parish Register[704] evidences that Evan Jones, a mason, was authorised to erect a schoolhouse in the churchyard (the vestry) of 24ft in length with two large windows at a cost of £31. 10s; it was a small single storey building, rubble built with a slate roof and a chimney stack. It was used for a parish school for many years (1805-71) as well as for the headquarters of the 4th Company of the Carmarthenshire Rifle Volunteers. The school was in keeping with other local parishes where during the early 19th century chapel schools and Sunday schools were held in the local chapels or in the vestries. The first Sunday school in Llansawel was started by the Methodists in various farmhouses and then at Bethel Chapel in 1801.

703 David Lewis: *Family Histories p36-52 and Dolaucothi and Brunant p403-408*

704 Fred Price: *Llansawel p63*

Old School in Churchyard 2017

Old Sawyl Academy building 2017

Rev Jonah Evans came to Llansawel in 1866 as a preacher and in 1875 decided to start a grammar school to prepare bright students for the ministry. By 1869 the school previously run in the church vestry had moved to the Town Hall so Jonah Evans, a Congregational Minister, started his Sawyl Academy[705] in the old parish schoolroom in the vestry. Later he fell out with the vicar and by then had raised the funds to build the new Sawyl Academy building which was completed in 1886. The building stands on the hill between the Angel Inn and Shiloh Chapel and has a stone plaque saying "Sawyl Academy 1884, JE". He lived in the building and taught there until his death aged 55 in 1896; at one time there were some 40 to 50 pupils and the academy became one of the most successful in training young men to prepare for both conformist and non-conformist colleges. Jonah's daughter, Mrs Elizabeth Morgan, then lived there for many years and her niece, Dorothy Evans, the daughter of Jonah's son, Rev Tom Eli Evans, lived with her. Rev Tom Eli Evans was a minister at Cefnarthen, Pentretygwyn and Halfway Chapels for many years. Dorothy Evans kept house for her father after her mother died; she moved to Llansawel after her father's death and was a very keen musician. On her death the house passed to her friend and neighbour, Sadie Jones, who passed it to her son, Alun.

The masters of the old parish school included: SJ Bird (1835); John Jones, Maesllan (1836); Peter Davies (1850); Edward Williams; Thomas Jones, Plough Llandovery; Rev William Jenkins (d1867); David Davies, Glan Cynllo (d1867); John Parry, Froodvale; Rev Jonah Evans; Daniel Thomas; A Kier; ADJ Davies; Rhys Edwards; and DB Evans.

After the Education Act 1870 the School Board of the parish was formed in 1871 under the chairmanship of Cyril Davies JP of Froodvale. The Llansawel School[706] moved from the vestry in

705 Fred Price p35-6

706 Evan Price (Price Bach y Siop) was involved with setting up the new Llansawel School and served as clerk from 1871 to 1875-see Chapter 26.9

December 1869 to the Town Hall (which continued to be used for other community meetings) with some 62 children and the teachers collected fees (school pence) from the children who attended; initially Lady Williams of Edwinsford paid the fees for the poorest children. Fees in 1873 were sixpence a week for the oldest children and two pence for infants, later reduced to four pence and one penny. In October 1874 a Dames' School was opened opposite the Town Hall. On 12 June 1876 Llansawel School moved to a new purpose built building[707] on the edge of the village on a site acquired by compulsory purchase for £40 from Maesllan and the number of pupils was about 90. Additional sportsfields were similarly acquired from Maesllan in 1915 for £70 and 1947 for £150.

The headteachers[708] have included: William Franklin (1869-72); James Kerr (1873-4); Arthur Hubert (1874-6); Edward Preece (1876-8); William Jones (1913-53) who catered for evacuees from London and Swansea during WW2 and retired one year after the school was briefly elevated to include a secondary school section; Arthur Trevor Davies (1953-63) formerly headteacher at Caio School; Miss Sheila Lewis (1963) who briefly filled in after the sudden death of AT Davies; Hiram Gwynn Jones (1963-72) formerly headteacher at Cwmbach School; Morlais Dyfnallt Owen (1972-4) who had to deal with the alterations following the closing of the secondary school section and who wrote an unpublished Historical Survey of the Parish of Llansawel in 1974 ; Brynmor Jones (1974-81); Mrs Myfanwy Phillips (1982-9) known as Fanw (sister of the undertaker Denzil Williams) who was born in Llansawel and attended the school as an infant and junior and died in 2015 aged 85 much respected by several generations of local residents; Aled Gravell (1989-94); Lyn Edwards (1994-2005); Mrs Lesley Walters (2005-12); and Aled Jones Evans (2012-14) the headteacher of Carreg Hirfaen, Cwmann.

The school was emptied of pupils and teachers in the summer of 2014 and was formally closed by Carmarthenshire County Council in April 2015. Ysgol Cylch Meithrin, a playschool for two to five year olds, started in 1974; they were tenants of one of the school's outbuildings and also had to move in 2015 and are now temporarily housed in a large portakabin in the grounds of the Village Hall. Plans to convert

Former Llansawel School 2017

the school building into a community centre are currently being considered by the County Council.

Formerly up to WW2 pupils generally left school and completed their education at age 14 unless they were obviously very bright and their families were able to finance their secondary schooling in Llandovery, Llandeilo or Lampeter which would often involve weekly boarding coming home at the weekends. Sadly many potentially bright children were still prevented from reaching their potential. The school leaving age was later increased to 15 but it was not until the Education Act 1944 that it became compulsory for all children to attend secondary school. Today most secondary pupils travel to the new school just outside Llandeilo or to Lampeter School.

[707] CRO and school log

[708] CRO and school log; I am very grateful to Bill Davis for his help with this information

30.3 Talley

The Talley Parish register[709] records that in 1705 a request was made for a school. In 1739 it was said that a petty school was kept by Mr Griffies Evan Jones, Minister, and in 1748 that "our Minister keeps a public school." In 1782 the Vestry arranged to build a schoolhouse and in 1782 Peter Davies is said to have kept a school and the Vestry allowed him a grant to pay the rent. In 1788 William Jones, the village schoolmaster, was allowed a grant to pay the rent for a room. In 1802 the Vestry agreed to build a school on part of the churchyard; John Phillips and John Rees Jones were employed to carry out the job by June 1803 "at a cost of 1s.8d per perch." This was a small single storey rubble built building, formerly limewashed, with a slate roof and an attached shed; it is now listed. William Lloyd was the schoolmaster in 1829 and Roderick Morgan in 1839. In 1842 there was an election to choose the schoolmaster and John Jones won the contest against Thomas Williams; the curate David Lewis Jones refused to accept the result so the Vestry had to reoccupy the building in order to enforce the result. In the Education Commissioners' Report of 1847 it is stated that Talley school is one of the SPCK charity schools set up by Madam Bevan and that pupils in the day school number 43, in the Church Sunday school 67, and in the Nonconformist Sunday schools 125.

Talley School 2017

Old School in Churchyard (Church Hall) 2017

In 1871 a School Board was formed and the first members were David Long Price of Talley House, Thomas Rees of Glanyrafonddu, John Morgan of Cillynfawr, David Williams of Abernaint, David Thomas of Llwyncynhwyra with John Griffiths of the Edwinsford Arms as clerk. The first headteacher was Dafydd Evans (d1893) of Cwmdu, who was also secretary of the Abbiessau Club held at Tŷ Ann Arthur and of the Oddfellows Club held at the Edwinsford Arms. The new School was built on its current site near the old Crown Inn (Chapter 24.15) in 1876-7.

Headteachers[710] at Talley School have included Dafydd Evans, Mr Thomas, Morgan Morgans (1920-50), Elwyn Morgan, Brin Davies, Basil David, Mrs Mary Young, Andi Morgan (1990-), Mrs Pauline

709 Fred Price: *Talley p27-8*

710 I am very grateful to Mrs Janet James for her research

Roberts Jones, Elfed Wood, Mrs Elizabeth Howells, Roy James (also head of Teilo Sant Llandeilo), Mrs Christa Richardson, and Miss Alana Walker

During WW2 evacuee children to Talley had to be educated. Initially classes for them were held in Esgairnant Chapel vestry but then the teacher died and the children were moved to Talley School where Morgan Morgans (nicknamed *Mishtir* the Welsh name for master) was the headteacher and Miss Sarah Lewis was the infant teacher. In addition Joan Williams (née Evans)[711] from Swansea was employed to teach; she remembers weekly boarding at Dark Gate Lodge with the Long Price family and marrying Harvey Matthews in 1945 with a wedding dress borrowed from Doris Williams of Abbey View. Morgan Morgans[712] was an outstanding head, excellent teacher, strict disciplinarian, and pillar of the community by all accounts.

The school was used for many years for adult evening classes. Women were taught needlework and the men woodwork and there were also basketmaking classes taught by William Williams of Pengarreg during the 1930s.

Today Talley Primary School is one of the few in the area to survive despite attempts by Carmarthenshire County Council to close it and is much appreciated by the parents and local community. It has a most supportive parents' and teachers' association.

30.4 Jesus College Oxford

Very many eminent Welshmen had studied at Oxford for generations before Hugh Price, Treasurer of St David's Cathedral, petitioned Queen Elizabeth I to set up another college in the University. This would be the first Protestant college to be founded at the University of Oxford since 1555 in the reign of Queen Mary when Trinity and St John's colleges had been founded as Roman Catholic colleges. The letters patent dated 27 June 1571 make it clear that the intention was to promote the classics and the Anglican religion, a college for future churchmen. The Queen had been excommunicated by the Pope the year before and the awful memories of Popery in the time of Queen Mary were still fresh; it had not been long since Bishops Latimer and Ridley had been burnt at the stake in Broad Street, Oxford. David Lewis (no relation to the author) was the first Principal having previously been Principal of New Inn Hall, which took a lot of Welsh lawyers as did All Souls; he was then a High Court Admiralty Judge (he is buried in a private chapel in Abergavenny Parish Church). There was a strong Welsh element in the powerful group behind the foundation of the college. Indeed Jesus College seems to have been intended to divert bright Welsh graduates away from remunerative legal careers in London and encourage them to promote the Anglicanism of the Elizabethan church settlement in the provinces including naturally Wales. Later on the establishment of new good grammar schools in Brecon, Abergavenny, Bangor, Beaumaris, Carmarthen, Cowbridge, and Ruthin led to an increase in well educated students who wanted to come to Oxford and to Jesus in particular.

Literally thousands of Welshmen have received their university training at Jesus, many from Carmarthenshire[713]. Dr Griffith Lloyd (d1586) of the Lloyd family in Cardiganshire was the second Principal from 1572 to his death in 1586. Several other Principals of the College have come from Sir Gâr: (a) Dr Francis Bevans (Principal from 1586 to 1602) from Cynwyl Gaeo;(b) Dr John Williams DD(1550-1613)[714],whose family came from Llether Bledri in Llansawel and was connected by marriage to the Vaughans of Golden Grove, entered Oxford in 1569, was a Fellow of All Souls by 1579, Professor of Divinity (1594-1613), became Principal of Jesus (1602-13), Vice-Chancellor in 1604, and then Dean of Bangor in 1605; (c) Dr Griffith Powell BCL (1561-1620), whose family were descended from the Edwinsford[715] family and came from Prysg Melyn and Penylan in Llansawel, matriculated at Jesus College in 1582, was elected a Fellow in 1589, became the

---

711 Mrs Joan Matthews Williams of Ontario Canada: *Y Llychau*

712 Brenda James p23 et seq. Brenda's brother, Jack Roberts of Blaennant and Ffaldybugail (now aged 90) well remembers Morgan Morgans with affection.

713 JNL Baker: *Jesus College Oxford (1971)*; Brigid Allen: *The Early History of Jesus College Oxford 1571-1603*; Prys-Jones: *Vol 2 p99-111*; AG Prys-Jones*: Carmarthenshire and Jesus College Oxford CH (1962) p16-25;* Fred Price*: Llansawel p13*

714 Dr Roger Brown: *The Followers of Jeroboam The Son of Nebat—A Study of the Clerical Members of the Davies-Williams Family of Llansawel (1983) p52.* Dr John Williams and Dr Griffith Powell were two of the many clergy in the Anglican Church produced by the families of Llansawel (see Chapter 26.2)

715 Dwnn Vol I p 223-4; Francis Jones: *Carmarthenshire Homes p159,167*

Jesus College Oxford 2016

Jesus College Oxford

Principal (1613-20) and left his estate of £648 to the college; (d) Dr Francis Mansell (1579-1665) from Muddlescombe, Kidwelly (Principal three times from 1620 to 1621, from 1630 to 1648, and from 1660 to 1661) and a descendant of the family of Sir Rhys ap Thomas KG (see Chapter 6.1) who left all his estate to the college; (e) Dr John Lloyd (1638-1687) from Pendine (Principal from 1673 to 1687) who served as Vice-Chancellor (1682-5) and briefly as Bishop of St Davids in 1686; (f) Rev Edmund Meyrick (1636-1713) who was born in Bala, a kinsman of the Vaughans of Golden Grove and closely connected with Sir Gâr, became a vicar at Eynsham and then at Llangathen in 1665 and at Carmarthen and then Treasurer of St Davids in 1690 and when he died in 1713 in Carmarthen he left much of his estate to educate Welshmen at Jesus. His memorial can be seen on the north wall of the chancel in St Peter's Church, Carmarthen where he is buried in the vestry under a massive stone slab; (g) Dr William Jones (1676-1725)[716] from Ferryside (Principal until 1725); and (h) Dr Thomas Pardo (1687-1763) from Kidwelly (Principal from 1727) who also served as Chancellor of St Davids.

Another famous alumnus[717] of the college is Roger Williams (1604-83) who might have been born in Maestroiddyn-fawr in Cynwyl Gaeo, the son of William Williams. The Dictionary of National Biography suggests that many historians now think he was born in London the son of James Williams (d1621) a merchant tailor. He was a scholar of Sutton's Hospital (Charterhouse), won an Exhibition to Jesus College in 1624 then became a clergyman but fell out with the established church. In February 1631 he set sail with his wife on the "Lyon" from Bristol to Boston Harbour in America where he taught and preached Puritanism. He was forced to leave his family when a warrant for his arrest was issued and he fled to the town of Providence, Rhode Island where he founded a colony; "inflexible integrity, undaunted courage, and prompt decision marked all his conduct." In 1851 some of his American descendants visited Caio to see his birthplace and to meet some of his relatives then living in Ynysau.

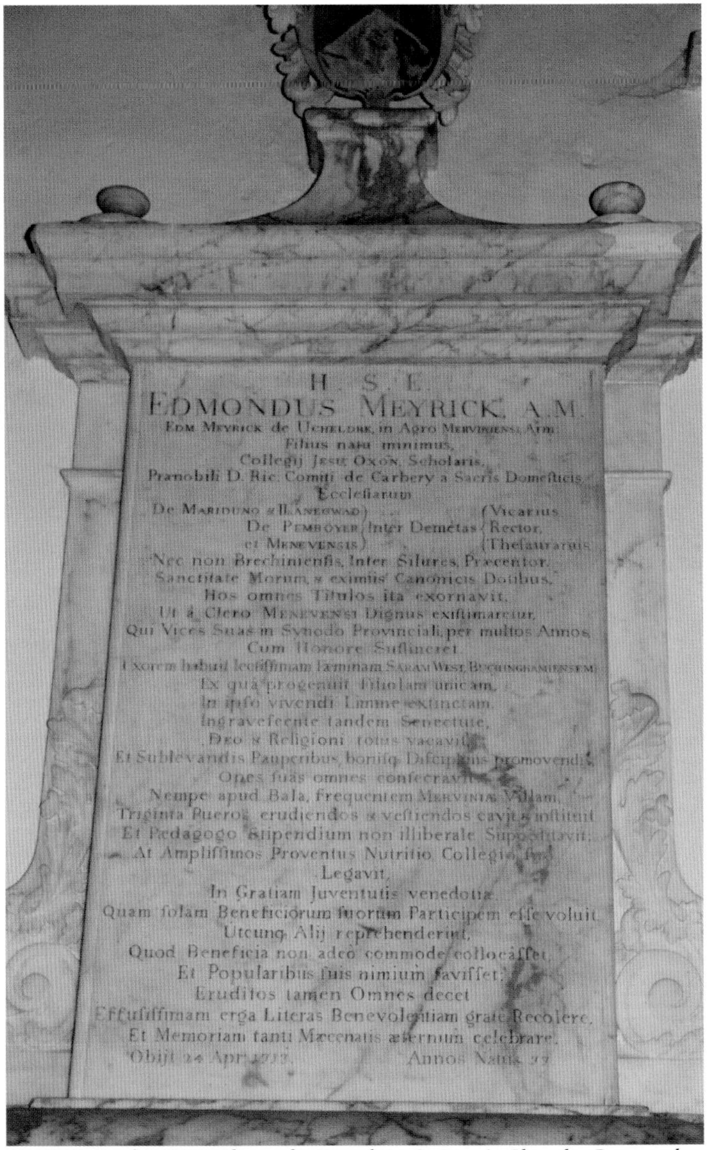

Memorial to Rev Edmund Meyrick in St Peter's Church, Carmarthen

[716] CA (1941) p61

[717] Francis Jones: *Carmarthenshire Homes p128*; Fred Price: *Caio*

Many sons of the Vaughan family (later the Earls of Carbery) of Golden Grove went to Jesus College as did many clerics including Vicar Rhys Prichard (1579-1644) of Llandovery. Many Welshmen[718] attended other Oxford Colleges too.

In addition to the Principals from Llansawel referred to above, in the surrounding parishes a number of members of resident families have attended including my father, TPM (Tommy) Lewis (1904-89), from Brynteg Farm on the Dolaucothi Estate who was there between 1922 and 1926; he won a Meyricke Exhibition for Welsh students in 1922 of £50 per annum without which he would not have been able to go and after graduation spent his working life in the Malayan Education Service. Professor John Cayo-Evans (1879-1958) of Blaenau-Caio in Ffarmers (nephew of my great grandfather, Thomas Lewis), went to Ffarmers School and then had a brilliant academic career at Jesus taking a triple first before going to India in the Indian Education Service. Rev Jack Strand Jones (1877-1958)(nephew of Thomas Lewis's wife) from the Evans family of Llwyncelynmawr in Ffarmers is described in the History of Jesus College as having had a brilliant rugby career in 1899 when he played at centre and then in the two following years at full back ("at least as good a full back as Oxford ever had"). He went on to play for Wales at fullback three times in 1902 and twice in 1903 winning on all fivc occasions and also winning the Triple Crown in 1902. He was then ordained in 1903 and went abroad to spend his clerical life in India and on retirement became a farmer near Lampeter before retiring to Pyllaucrynion, Cwmann, a house with a magnificent view. He also served as President of the Lampeter RFC.

[718] Dr R Brinley Jones: *All the Welshmen Abiding and Studying in Oxford (1986);* Dr R Brinley Jones: *Rhamant Rhydychen (2016)*

31. Community Life

31.1 Background

Life in the Welsh countryside has changed enormously during the past 100 years or so and far faster than during the preceding centuries. In the 17th and 18th centuries the vast majority of the local population in Carmarthenshire relied on the land and on what they grew and made for themselves. In order to make ends meet most families would have been farmers or labourers with the women also carrying on some local trade such as spinning, weaving or stocking knitting and doing whatever was necessary to keep the family unit alive; there was no time for leisure. The population was made up of the landed gentry (some 2% who controlled most of the land and ruled the community); yeomen, free-holders, tenant farmers, craftsmen and tradesmen (some 60-70%); and about 25% who were in the poor or pauper category with no land and only able to sell their services. The Church of course also owned much land and had influence accordingly through tithe and glebe lands. In 1670 some 20% of the population could not afford to pay the hearth tax of one shilling half yearly on each hearth in their possession and were thus classified as paupers in receipt of alms from the parish. Even the gentry in Carmarthenshire were not that rich compared with others and only five Carmarthenshire families out of 37 in the whole of Wales had lands worth £1,000 per annum in income which was the requirement to receive baronetcies from King James I.

By the time of the 19th century the vast majority of inhabitants in the Cothi valley area were born and lived in the locality hardly ever needing to stray more than a few miles. Travel was difficult with poor roads and not enough bridges. The education provided to children was non existant or woefully inadequate. Many inhabitants were still very poor indeed and the parish was under a legal obligation to raise a poor rate to feed the poor; the overseers administered poor relief to the numerous paupers who in some parishes had to wear special badges to prove that they were entitled to relief in that parish. The older children in the ever increasing number of large families were sent for financial reasons at a young age to be servants, maids or apprentices at other farms as we can see from the census returns; many children died very young and malnutrition, fevers, consumption, tuberculosis and smallpox killed many. It is little surprise that non-conformism prospered in this environment.

The gentry families at Edwinsford, Dolaucothi and Brunant were the leading landowners often serving as Sheriffs of the county, as magistrates and Deputy Lieutenants, strong supporters of the Parish Church where they were buried, often Welsh speaking and supportive of their non-conformist generally Liberal tenants, and important employers in the area. As we have seen the importance of religion as a vital social glue in the community cannot be overemphasised. Before non-conformity arrived every family attended their local Parish Church from time to time and members were christened, married and buried there; today families are still traditionally Church or Chapel although attendance at either is very much reduced (except for marriages and burials) and sadly there might come a time when one or more local chapels will have to be sold and converted into homes as has happened in other parts of Wales. Village halls in Talley, Llansawel, Pumsaint, Crugybar and Ffarmers, community singing, young farmers' clubs, foxhunting, shearing competitions and local agricultural shows help to retain the sense of community spirit, although the ease of 21st century travel and the influx of other nationalities into the area during the last 75 years has inevitably resulted in great social change in the rural community.

The strong social bonds in the community traditionally derived from the culture of the Welsh family and in its traditions and heritage. The great majority of local inhabitants lived very similar lives with no real class divide, speaking only Welsh as their mother tongue, many being illiterate, going to the same chapel and Sunday school, walking to their local school in Llansawel, Talley, Caio, Crugybar, Cwrt or Ffarmers, probably leaving that school aged 14 and then working on their family farm, becoming a servant at a neighbouring farm or starting an apprenticeship as a blacksmith, carpenter or whatever. Very few had the opportunity to achieve a better education or leave the area to prosper elsewhere, although there are some notable exceptions. Neighbourliness, hospitality, an open house and mutual support reflected the social mores of that time; fortunately much of this approach to life continues. With industrialisation came movement of workers and many moved from the countryside to the cities, mines and railways.

31.2 Occupations

The census returns reveal that inhabitants had such varying occupations or descriptions as: farmer, agricultural labourer, farm servant, shepherd, maid servant, coachman, gamekeeper, farm bailiff, butler, cook, footman, governess, parlourmaid, nurse, housekeeper, housemaid, ladies maid, dairymaid, kitchenmaid, groom, cowman, waggoner, gardener, carpenter, blacksmith, manager of the gold mines, Minister, dressmaker, tailor, cobbler, woodman,cattleman, cattle dealer, schoolmaster, shoemaker, carter, mason, stockingsmaker, woolenweaver, stocking knitter,seamstress, grocer, molecatcher, charwoman, chapel cleaner, school cleaner, district council water inspector, miner, horsedealer, lodger, lodger relief of the parish, millwright, corn and flour merchant, smithy, goods messenger, strawmaker, scholar (meaning a child at school) , errandboy,and sadly, bastard or adopted or foster child, and pauper. When the last 2011 census return is made public in a hundred years time the occupations and descriptions will be very different indeed.

31.3 Farming

Farming has always involved very hard work and in the Cothi valley has been based primarily on animal husbandry rather than cereal cultivation although prior to the 20th century mixed farming was very common. Sheep and cattle were the primary providers of meat, dairy products, wool and leather. Pigs, geese and chickens were also important in the food chain, and of course horses (usually with English names) were essential to the running of the farm with the sheepdogs (always with Welsh names) helping the farmer and the shepherd. Generally speaking before the First World War the pastoral rural economy was largely self sufficient. The farm provided almost everything that the average inhabitant required. Local blacksmiths, carpenters, tailors, dressmakers, cobblers and saddlers provided their products. Visits on market day to Llansawel, Talley, Llandeilo, Lampeter or Llandovery provided the other products which every farm needed. Each field on every farm had its own name.

Many farmhouses and cottages before 1800 were part timber and part stone with thatched or rushmade roofs. The very poor lived in hovels with earthen floors and walls made out of earth, straw and dung with grass and rushes on top and with no windows; their animals would be housed in the same dwelling with a dividing timber wall so the smell and living conditions must have been awful. The most important factor which decided the location of a dwelling was the water source be it a spring, well or stream.

During the early 1800s many of the farms were built often next to or near existing dwellings which were dismantled. Although we cannot be certain, it is quite possible that some of these farmhouses particularly on the higher ground were originally built as *tŷ-un-nos* (houses built in one night). Under this tradition squatters would arrive at some suitable site at night and erect an abode with just earth and wood and a straw or rush made roof, light a fire in it so that smoke came out of it before daybreak and then argue that by law they had the legal right to that hovel as well as to the surrounding land as far as an axe could be thrown from the door.Of course they had no rights in law at all but possession being nine-tenths of the law (particularly if you do not know or care what the law is or cannot afford to find out) resulted in many squatters remaining on the sites and gradually replacing their hovels with stone made dwellings. In this way some areas of common land were effectively illegally enclosed and this resulted in disagreements with landowners and nearby tenant farmers and the poor who had previously used the sites.

The Edwinsford Estate built a number of new stone and slate farmhouses for their tenants during the early 1800s in slightly different styles replacing the former thatched longhouses. A farm dwelling would typically have a kitchen at the back containing a Welsh dresser; a parlour in the front with a small fireplace, almost unused and principally for visitors and the Minister, and containing the best china and the family bible; a large livingroom with an open fireplace containing a fire which never went out and from an oak beam hung an iron bar with a hook for the kettle to boil plus hooks from which hung hams and thick slices of bacon, pieces of beef, some game, salted black, nets of shallots and ropes of French onions, baskets of various sizes, a couple of pigs' bladers full of lard etc; next to the fire was the traditional baking or bread oven and the heavy irons on the floor for ironing clothes after they had been washed by hand and mangled; and a pantry with gauze wire on the open window to act as a coolroom before refridgerators were invented. Naturally there was no electricity and no running water in the house and the tŷ-bach was at the bottom of the yard. The bedrooms were upstairs (one with a chest for the linen) and the servants either slept above the side kitchen or above the cattle in the cowshed (the loft stable). The yard in front of the farmhouse contained a large barn on one side with a second floor at one end and at the side there used to be a water wheel to power some of the machinery. The cowsheds and stables were on the other side of the yard. Only in the 1960s did electricity arrive when the diesel engine (often in the barn) was at last removed which provided power for the lights and for shearing etc.

31.4 Community Co-operation

Farming used to require a community and cooperative effort at certain times of year since no ordinary farmer had all the necessary machinery and implements required. No cash payments were involved under this bartering system with an exchange of labour and produce; farmers and their servants would help each other out at haymaking, at the corn harvest, at sheep shearing, potato picking and whenever a large workforce was required. The bull or boar was lent out, expensive farm machinery was borrowed, carts and gambos (a long two wheeled cart) were borrowed, cottagers (those living in cottages with little land) would give their labour to farmers in return for produce such as potatoes or fruit, the blacksmith would make a scythe, sickle, billhook, spade or other handtool in return for produce etc. Other local craftsmen such as tailors, cobblers, coopers, wheelwrights, saddlers, masons, rope makers, thatchers, weavers and corn millers all participated in this system which made the rural economy work very well for a long time.

Then after the First World War the rural economy began to change. The setting up of the Milk Marketing Board resulted in many farmers concentrating on their milk production with a good cheque at the end of every month to help the cashflow, milk churns were collected every morning from each farm and over time Jerseys and Friesans became more popular than the traditional Welsh Blacks and dual pupose shorthorns. Farmers could no longer afford the wages for the usual two or three farmhands they had traditionally employed, and such farmhands were attracted by better wages in the coal and tin mines or by going to industrial jobs in England. So gradually fewer people stayed on the land or in the locality of the Cothi valley, farmers farmed their land with the help of their wives and sons without any servants and farming gradually became less labour intensive particularly after the Second World War with new machinery replacing the traditional horsepower. But milking is a thing of the past for the majority of farmers in this area today; the daily lorry to collect the milk churns has gone, the milk quotas have been sold and most of the farmers concentrate on their sheep and their silage, although some are still also involved in stock rearing.

Today each farm can cope on the whole very well without the farmer's need for help from a large number of neighbours except on rare occasions. Many local farmers now hire contractors for the large jobs, for silage making on that farm's pre-agreed day every year (subject to the weather), for shearing, for ploughing fields and grass reseeding, for cutting the hedges in the late summer etc. The result of this of course over time has been the end of the need for the local blacksmith, carpenter, saddler, cobbler etc whose services or products can now be easily acquired and more cheaply, albeit now in a cash not a barter economy, from the urban retail outlets in Llandeilo, Lampeter, Llandovery or Carmarthen. The local shop, which used to be a centre of social discourse, is no more and the days of the local Post Office are numbered. Many farmers have other jobs and interests, some lease out farm cottages, some lease out machinery, and some are in haulage or forestry businesses. Sadly many sons and daughters brought up on local farms have decided it is easier and more lucrative to get jobs elsewhere. One good result however has been that the standards of animal husbandry and farm efficiency and production have risen greatly with the increase in the standard of living for farmers and other local inhabitants over the last 50 years in particular. Farming has certainly changed; environmental conservation, the gradual loss of subsidies and the UK's exit from the European Union will force many to diversify and seek new opportunities including in forestry, windpower projects, larger farms, specialised products, tourism etc.

Smithy at Plasnewydd

Hedgelaying and ditching

Alexander Walnychi dipping at Tŷcerrig c1950s

Brynteg shearing c1910

Raking at Waungoch, Cwmdu 1941

Haymaking between Talley Lakes and Langwm 1943

32. Farming Calendar

The typical annual farming calendar a century ago in the Cothi valley would have involved:

(a) Spring: lambing, all outside in the fields, would take place on each farm between early March and late April depending on when tupping (mating) had taken place 25 weeks before; there would have been no scanning of ewes as happens today to determine which ewes had twins or triplets with additional food for the latter, and the average number of lambs born would have been about one lamb per ewe compared with about 1.7 lambs per ewe today; finishing any ploughing which had not been completed in the previous late autumn, which would have involved a horse plough usually with a pair of horses (a century before that a team of oxen would have been used); then harrowing also with a pair of horses; around Easter time sowing of oats and barley would have been done either by hand or a seed drill; the potato fields would be manured with dung from the dungheap after ploughing and this would be done by using a horse and cart to dump several large mounds at intervals round the field following which the manure would be spread by fork; liming of fields would also take place if not completed the autumn before and the collection of lime could involve a journey to Llanwrda railway station or an all day journey by horse and cart to the lime kilns[719] near Llandeilo; then the planting of seed potatoes in rows by hand from a sack worn round the waist; the milking cows and stock cattle which had been kept in during the winter were let out into the fields and were always delighted to get to the fresh grass although of course the milking cows returned to the cowshed twice every day for milking by hand. Today the great majority of farmers do much of their lambing indoors in sheds sometimes with the help of trainee vets, everyone has suitable fields for silage, no one plants potatoes and very few have any arable crops other than for rotation purposes.

(b) Summer: all the sheep would have been collected from the mountain fields and brought down to the river for washing; then the big shearing day on each farm would take place with community help from neighbours and a slap up midday dinner round a large table which was a matter of great pride for the farmer's wife; later there was the dipping of all the sheep usually in a special sheepdip to kill all the maggots and other pests; haymaking took place and again involved a huge communal effort for each farm, repaid by the farmer helping to do the same on his neighbours' farms; the days of a row of farmers scything and reaping in unison across a hayfield with the women following as binders were gradually replaced with horsedrawn mowers, rakes and binders, and today of course combine harvesters can do the work of several men in very quick time indeed; the pitching of the hay onto a horsedrawn gambo to take to the haybarn (there was no silage in those days) and the carting into the barn also involved very hard work; for those farmers who had cereal oats or barley crops, the harvesting in August was equally hard work involving the community helping in the fields to cut, reap, rake, stack the sheaves, and cart them to the barn and if necessary to build round ricks outside with sheaves on top to keep off the rain. The local agricultural shows usually took place after harvesting. Today contractors tend to do most of the shearing and haymaking which are no longer communal activities; silos and silage have taken over from the old form of haymaking.

(c) Autumn: at the end of the summer and during the autumn farmers would take some of their lambs to market locally or in Llanwrda (next to the railway station which would take them to England), Llandeilo, Lampeter and Llandovery and hopefully receive the price they sought or they would have to take them home again (before those days many were driven by the drovers to markets in England); oats and barley were threshed usually in the barn with a thresher powered by a horse walking round a circle or by a waterwheel and then taken to the mill; potato picking took place and was often a communal activity (I remember "potato week" when the pupils in school went home to help

[719] DJ Williams p294-8 describes scores of lime carts in procession from May to July on the Llandeilo to Llansawel road

in the fields) followed by sorting the potatoes for sale and for seeding the following year. Besides sickness, reasons for absences of pupils from local schools included harvesting, planting and picking potatoes, shearing, collecting acorns, barking, and beating on shoots at the Edwinsford Estate. Today some farmers continue to sell their lambs at marts[720] while others take their lambs direct to nearby abattoirs such as Dunbia at Llanybydder from July to late autumn; farmers who rear cattle for stock breeding tend to sell them at marts in Llandovery, Tregaron or Brecon and they are then fattened up elsewhere; the cutting up of wood for the winter was also completed at this time of year. Today hedging usually takes place in September and often by contractors.

(d) Winter: hedging and ditching were usually jobs for the early winter months; sales of lambs continued; the purchase of new rams had to be completed before tupping usually in October and November; the annual killing of pigs took place before Christmas followed by their salting and curing and then pieces would be hung from the ceiling of the kitchen on hooks; Christmas was a time for eating geese or turkey and when the children visited each dwelling for a "*calennig*" present. Children had to make sure they arrived at the door of the relevant farm between 12 midnight on New Year's Eve and 12 midday on New Year's Day (*dydd calan*) in order to receive their present; otherwise they missed out according to tradition.

[720] DJ Williams p42 recounts how unscrupulous dealers took advantage of farmers when times were bad

33. Drovers

The Cothi and Tywi valleys are renowned not only for their tradition of hymnology and singing but also for their history of droving. For centuries between the Middle Ages and the coming of the railways around 1900 the innumerable tracks through the heart of Wales were drovers' roads; they were trodden by tens of thousands of Welsh Black cattle, sheep, geese and even pigs driven at an average of 2 mph to the markets of London to be later fattened up over the winter or on good green grasslands during the summer. The noise of the shouting drovers[721] on horses with corgi dogs could be heard for miles and often the procession of animals was half a mile in length. Dafydd Jones (born 1711) the 18th century drover/hymn writer[722] of Cwmgogerddan in Caio likened the souls coming before the Lord on Judgment Day to the cattle converging on his native village of Caio; he was a gifted hymn writer and translator of English hymns into Welsh. The numerous Drovers' Arms on the various routes from Wales to England each have their own histories. In the early days taverns in Wales tended to be just ordinary houses and often very close to the village church with the blacksmith's forge not far away. As we have seen at one time there were eight inns in Llansawel and six in Caio which were well used by the drovers.

Many people used to join the drovers for security; Nurse Jane Evans, who is commemorated by a plaque in the chapel at Caio, went along with the drovers in order to find work in London as one of the "Welsh gardening women" and later joined Florence Nightingale's nurses in the Crimea. Drovers (porthmon) needed a licence, were not allowed to work on the sabbath but were quite well rewarded; in the 19th century the average labourer was paid 1 shilling a day in winter and 1s 6d in the summer for working from 5am to 8.30pm; a drover received about 3s a day and a bonus of 6s when he reached his destination. They were also important as sources of news and information and the senior ones were entrusted with carrying money and documents to London; the excellent Museum in Llandovery explains that the Black Ox Bank which was started in Llandovery (and later became part of Lloyds Bank) avoided the risks of transporting money; anyone wanting a drover to deal with a financial transaction in London could deposit the money in the bank in Llandovery, and the drover then paid the London bills in cash out of the sums he realised on the sale of the cattle or sheep. Naturally there were some rogue and dishonest drovers and many were treated with scorn but there were many who were honest and played an important part in the economic life of the area. The last drover[723] in Llansawel was Dafydd Cilwennau who often drove cattle and sheep to Barnet Fair in the early 20th century.

---

721 Shirley Toulson: The Drovers' Roads of Wales (1977); Richard Moore-Colyer: *Welsh Cattle Drovers (2006)*

722 Fred Price: *Caio p47*

723 DJ Williams p250-2

34. Local Festivals, Fairs and Shows

Every parish used to have its fairs and Saint's day festival when visiting traders and dealers would attend to join in the merriment with the local inhabitants. They would take place at the centre of the parish at the Llan. T Gwynn Jones in his *Welsh Folklore and Folk Custom (1930)* tells us in relation to the local Saint's Day that: *"The Festivals were generally held on Sundays, but often began on Saturday and continued until Tuesday. The proceedings included contests in leaping, running, hurling, wrestling, cock-fighting and football playing. In the latter contest, players of two parishes would be opposed, and the losers had to supply the winners with beer. Relics of the Saints were carried in procession in some places....Intoxication and fighting seem to have been general at these meetings in the 18th century....Rivalry and competition were prominent elements in the Gwylmabsant, which is the reason, perhaps, that to this day there is little chance for anything—religion, education, literature, music, drama, art or sport——to thrive in Wales except on lines of competition."* There would be bear baiting, bull fights, cock fighting and other sport for the crowds and there is evidence of this for example at the Llandovery and Lampeter Fairs. In the days before pews in the Parish Church it would be common for the church to be used rather like a village hall is used today and for many community activities to take place either in the church itself or outside in the graveyard.

I have not discovered to what extent the common annual festivals and traditions in most rural areas often in or near the llan and Parish Church of the Celtic Saint were celebrated in Llansawel, Talley and Cynwyl Gaeo before the influence of non-conformism. In many rural areas in Britain including parts of Wales some of the old pre-Christian or Celtic customs survived for centuries including:

- Plough Monday (the first Monday after Twelfth Night, 6 January, the start of the new agricultural year when labourers went round the parish dressed up in women's costumes asking for money and pulling a plough;
- Candlemas Day (2 February to bless candles in the church and when people would visit each other and sing carols);
- 14 February (St Valentine's Day when gifts, cards or letters would be exchanged between lovers);
- Shrove Tuesday (the last day before the start of Lent when pancakes were eaten, pancake races took place, and cock throwing was common);
- Ash Wednesday (the first day of Lent);
- 29 February (Leap Year Day when once every four years ladies could by custom ask their partners to marry them);
- St David's Day (1 March when the Welsh wear leeks. This may originate from the custom of the Welsh wearing leeks when they fought against the Saxons or it might refer to the Welsh archers at Crécy who followed this practice);
- Lady Day (25 March a quarterday when rent was often paid and being the Spring equinox);
- 1 April (All Fools' Day);
- Easter Day (the oldest feast in the Christian Church and usually special cakes and eggs were given to friends and family). By tradition in Wales daffodils would be placed on family graves on Palm Sunday a week before Easter Sunday;
- Easter Monday (with lots of festivities to rejoice in after Lent including men lifting women up horizontally three times);
- Beating of the bounds (at Rogationtide about 40 days after Easter when the parishioners walk round the boundaries of the parish with the vicar; originally it was to teach the children in the absence of maps where the boundaries were so that they could teach their children and to make the point they were often bumped against well known local marks so that they did not forget. Fights often ensued if villagers from separate parishes met on their common boundaries). I have participated in such events in my former parish in the City of London;

- May Day (the first day of summer with village festivities, Maypoles and dancing);
- Ascension Day (the fifth Thursday after Easter);
- Witsun (the seventh Sunday after Easter with fairs, pageants and excursions);
- Midsummer Day (24 June the summer solstice and another rent quarterday);
- August Feast (on about 12 August for all the shepherds);
- Harvest Festival and Feast (in September with much merriment and rejoicing and around the autumn equinox);
- Michaelmas Day (29 September and another rent quarterday);
- Halloween or All Hallows' Eve (31 October when people generally stayed at home playing games such as apple and candle biting while some children paraded the streets with Jack o' Lanterns made out of swedes or turnips);
- All Saints' Day and All Souls' Day (1 and 2 November and when people would collect soul cakes for the souls of the dead and have bonfires);
- Guy Fawkes Night (5 November with the usual bonfires and fireworks);
- St Thomas's Day (21 December when women would visit houses asking for flour before Christmas called "Thomasing" or "gooding");
- Christmas Eve (24 December with a midnight mass);
- Christmas Day (25 December being the winter solstice and another rent quarterday with festivities, cards, carol singers, decorations, stockings and a family feast which survived the abolition of Christmas by Oliver Cromwell in the mid 17th century);
- Boxing Day (26 December when boxes of gifts were distributed and often men wearing a mare's headdress would visit their neighbours for a drink in the Mari Lwyd custom, and hunting would occur); and
- New Year's Eve (with church bells ringing in the New Year followed the next day by the children visiting their neighbours for "*calennig*" money).

It should be remembered that in 1752 the Church of England adopted the Gregorian calendar, so many of the above dates changed by 11 days (the so called lost 11 days). Many of these festivities and customs then changed as a result of non-conformism and the Methodist Revivals; so hymn singing, choirs, eisteddfodau, the cymanfa ganu, Sunday schools, prayer meetings and in particular the temperance movement resulted in much change to a rural society. Today some of the traditions and festivities still survive albeit in a rather different form. Local customs which have long died out included sending bidding letters for wedding gifts to be reciprocated later, holding a *cwrw bach* evening at which home brewed beer would be drunk and songs sung with neighbours, and attending a corpse in candle light the evening before the burial followed by a wake afterwards.

It is thought that in the 17th century there was a fair or market somewhere in Wales about four days out of seven which means that there were about 520 weekly markets held in the eight principal towns of Carmarthenshire. At these fairs and markets tenant farmers would sell their produce and pedlars would hawk their wares as well as bring news from elsewhere. Local inns and alehouses would also be the centre of social discourse.

Sometimes these fairs would be held on the same day as the cattle fairs which were also important because cattle, sheep and horses were bought and sold and drovers would attend. After the arrival of the railways these animals could be more efficiently transported by rail and many markets were located close to the railway stations.

The Carmarthen Fair held on 14 November each year was a big event and farm servants used to be given a week's holiday to attend and that week was the annual start date for a farm servant's year. There were also horse fairs at Llanybydder in mid July and of course the famous Dalis Fair at Lampeter in early May in front of the Black Lion Hotel.

Marts were held regularly in all the large towns and these gradually replaced the old system of farmers selling direct to dealers and often losing out on the best price. Llandovery for example had many fairs regulated by its Royal Charter but only started its regular livestock mart in 1912. Gradually the farmers saw the benefits of auctioneers dealing with the buying and selling of animals and obtaining the best market prices for them. During the Second World War this system of open trading had to be suspended but it was restored afterwards and has survived ever since. The railway has helped too although many cattle and sheep continue to be transported by lorry. There were also small livestock marts at Llanwrda, Pumsaint and Felin Newydd in Crugybar up to the Second World War. Many farmers especially in remote areas would sell livestock to visiting dealers who would visit the farms and make an offer on the spot; this tradition lasted into the 1960s at some local farms.

As stated in Chapters 23, 25 and 27 Annual Fair Days used to be held in Talley, Llansawel and Caio, which were later replaced with Annual Agricultural Shows.

Talley Agricultural Show 1900 – Thomas Evans

35. Local Justice

35.1 Manorial Courts

In Anglo-Saxon times in England justice was administered by the local lord subject to the local customary laws with trial sometimes by combat, ordeal or compurgation. The Normans introduced trial by jury made up of 12 local freemen. Manorial courts were feudal and seignorial courts with jurisdiction only in the local manor; there were three types. Courts of the honour, also known as duke's court (*curia ducis*) or soldiers' courts (*curia militum*) were made up of the senior free tenants who owed the lord knight service and also acted as an appeal court for the junior manorial courts. Courts Baron dealt with disputes involving the free tenants. Courts Customary (or halmot courts) dealt with unfree tenants. In addition Royal Courts had wider jurisdiction, such as Courts Leet and View of Frankpledge, where the lord paid a fee to the Crown.

By the early medieval times the Lord of each Manor had jurisdiction over his tenants and bondsmen and the Court Baron would dispense justice in non-criminal matters. The Lord of the Manor might also dispense justice in criminal matters if he was granted by the Crown the prerogative right of "view of frankpledge". Under this system created by King Canute of Denmark and England before the Norman invasion, every man had to be part of a Hundred (ten households) which put up a surety in money for good behaviour and were responsible for producing in court any man who had misbehaved, failing which the headman known as the chiefpledge or tithingman was responsible for the fine. By the 15th century frankpledge was superseded in most areas by local constables operating under Justices of the Peace.

In Llansawel, Talley and Cynwyl Gaeo the old Welsh Laws of Hywel Dda applied until the mid 13th century and thereafter the manorial courts[724] took over. The Court Baron met to hear cases involving manorial rights, the customs of the manor and its boundaries. The Court Leet would meet with juries to hear minor criminal cases (serious crimes were dealt with by the Hundred Court with the Sheriff (the shire-reeve) presiding on his circuit (tourn) and later by the King's Justices); often both Courts would meet together. The Court Leet (leet meaning an area of jurisdiction) would take pledges such as oaths by freemen to keep the peace and deal with breaches by tradesmen in the quality and measuring of food and drink for sale (rather like weights and measures inspectors).

Courts Leet had a jury of local freehold tenants and elected officers including a Steward or seneschal (appointed by the Lord of the Manor as his chief agent and the judge), a Bailiff (who would make arrests and organise court meetings), a Constable (to ensure proper behaviour during court meetings), an Aletaster (to check the quality and measures of ale and wine sold locally),a Bread Weigher (to ensure the freshness and weight of the bread sold), a Fleshtaster (to ensure the freshness of meat sold locally), Affeerers (who assessed the fines payable), the Hayward (who was responsible for enclosures and fencing of common land), the Surveyor (who oversaw all roads and highways), the Macebearer and the Town Crier where relevant.

Courts Leet lost their local importance over the centuries although their legal criminal jurisdiction was only abolished as late as 1977[725]. A few still survive to deal with local customary issues. In the City of London the Court of Husting and the Court of Grand Wardmote to hear complaints from electors continues to meet as do three Courts Leet for the three Manors of Southwark being Guildable, King's, and Great Liberty. In Laugharne[726] they maintain one of the last surviving medieval corporations under their 13th century Charter with the Portreeve (acting as the Town Mayor) wearing his traditional chain of gold cockle shells appointed annually on the first Monday after Michaelmas at the Big Court, attended by the aldermen and burgesses. They hold a Court Leet half yearly dealing with minor criminal cases

---

724 RR Davies: *Lordship and Society in the March of Wales 1282-1400 (1978);* RR Davies: *Baronial accounts, incomes and arrears in the later Middle Ages, Economic History Review (1968) p211-29;* Helen Watt: *Welsh Manors and their Records (2000)*

725 Administration of Justice Act 1977 s.23 and Sch 4 which permitted some dealing with customary matters to continue

726 RH Tyler: *Laugharne, Local History and Folklaw (1925); George Tremlett: Laugharne Corporation Founded AD 1290 (2007)*

and a Court Baron every fortnight dealing with civil matters and the administration of their open field system of medieval strip farming. In practice most Courts Leet were superseded by the Justices of the Peace and then by modern magistrates' courts.

As described in Chapter 24.3, it is probable that the name of King's Court in the old village of Talley reflects the holding of Courts Leet in the house for centuries, since under the customs of the Royal Manor of Talley the tenants owed suit and rents to the King who was Lord of the Manor, whose steward was his local representative and sat in authority at the Courts Leet every fortnight. Talley was a copyhold manor with Borough English customs (the younger son inheriting rather than the eldest son), so the lands were held by copy of court roll and land was transferred by surrender in the Lord's Court (ie King's Court) and not by deed as elsewhere, court rolls providing a register of title. So King's Court escaped the destruction of the other parts of the monastic complex in Talley because it was the location of the Lord's Courts and administrative offices. Evidence of a Court Leet held on 22 April 1553 refers to a former monastic building called a "mansion house late belonging to the said late monastery" and a "convent hall" with demesne lands of 13 acres of arable and meadow grounds.

The following is an example[727] of the business of a Court Baron held in Talley in 1736 relating to the transfer of copyhold lands for which a fine of seven shillings per property was paid to the Lord of the Manor for consent (with original spellings):

Lordshipp and Manor of Talley

At his Majesties Court Baron held for the Mannor of Talley and Lordship the Twenty Sixth Day of June One Thousand Seven Hundred and Thirty Six Before Sir Nicolas Williams Baronet Steward there:

To the which Court came Lloyd Williams of Talley Esq and Desireth Leave and Licence of the said Lord of the said Manor and Lordship to surrender by the verge all those several coppyhold messuages tenements and lands with their appurtenances commonly called and known by the several names of Tyr Doleglyson, Tyr Ffynnon Grech[728], Tyr Carreg Llwud......in the same Lordship of Talley to such use or uses intents purposes and limitations as the said Lloyd Williams Esq shall by his last will and testament in writing declare limit and appoint To have and to hold all and singular such lands.....unto the said Lloyd Williams Esq and his heirs and assignes for ever according to the custom of the said Manor

To which the Lord of the said Manor and his Steward granted Leave and Licence to surrender the said lands and payeth the Lord of the said Manor for a fine Seven Shillings for each tenement and is admitted Tenant in the presence of us Suitors

Thomas Brookes	Howell Price	Thomas Price
William Davies	James Price (Deputy Steward)	Lewis Evans

Seal of Sir Nicolas Williams (Steward there)

[727] NLW Edwinsford archives

[728] See Chapter 26.1

In Cantref Mawr the Commote Courts of Caeo[729] used to meet thirteen times per annum on a Tuesday in the 13th century dealing with local minor issues. Later on the Courts Leet took over. The sovereign remained the Lord of the Manor and Courts Baron and Courts Leet met for centuries to deal with minor issues.

A typical example of the resolutions and presentments made by the jurors of the Court Leet in Cynwyl Gaeo in the 19th century provided for the forfeiture of stray animals, a mortuary fine on death (heriot or *ebediw*), and a fine on the purchase of a property and on a marriage, all for the benefit of the Lord of the Manor in accordance with long custom.

Lordship of the Manor of Cayo in the County of Carmarthenshire 3 February 1887

The Court Baron and Court Leet, View of Frankpledge and Law Day of her Majesty the Queen, Lord of the Lordship or Manor held at the dwelling house of James Morgan in Cayo within the said Lordship or Manor on Thursday 3 February 1887

Court Baron

The following free tenants were sworn in as Homagers, namely Mr David Williams of Llandre and Mr Thomas Lewis of Brynteg.
The following free tenants were sworn in as Affeerors, namely Mr David Edwards of Aberbranddu and Mr David Evans of Bwlchygilwen.

Court Leet, View of Frankpledge and Law Day

The following free tenants were empanelled to act as Jurors:

Mr James Morgan, King's Head (Foreman)
Mr Daniel Davies, Frongoch
Mr John Jones, Llwynceiliog
Mr David Evans, Bwlchygilwen
Mr David Williams, Llandre
Mr John Morgan, Pantyronen
Mr Thomas Lewis, Brynteg
Mr David Edwards, Aberbranddu
Mr Rees Davies, Cadwgan
Mr William Evans, Sextons Arms
Mr John Williams, Ddollas
Mr John Evans, Glanfrena

Appointment of Officers

Mr Daniel Price, Abermangoed was appointed Beadle, Bailiff and Pound Keeper for the Parish of Cynwyl Gaeo for the year

Resolutions and Presentments

1. That one ewe, one wether and one lamb being strays in the possession of the Bailiff to be forfeited and affeered and valued at 15 shillings
2. That on the deaths of Charles Lloyd of Brunant and Rice Watkins of Troedrhiw a mortuary of 10 shillings for each tenement is due to the Queen as Lady of this Manor according to the custom of this Manor
3. That a fine of 10 shillings be due on the purchase of Ffynongrech[730] by David Williams
4. That a leather wit of 10 shillings be due on the marriage of Annie Morgan eldest daughter of William Morgan a freeholder residing in this Manor.

Signed — Thomas Lloyd
Deputy Steward

729 Sir John Lloyd Vol 1 p226
730 David Lewis: *Family Histories p288-9*

Lampeter[731] was governed by a Court Leet for decades which met twice annually at Michaelmas and Easter on a day appointed by the Lord of the Manor (who was the squire at Peterwell for many years). At the Michaelmas Court the jury, who were selected and sworn in by the Steward, chose a Portreeve and Beadle to be sworn in for the ensuing year. The Portreeve used to act as the chief magistrate before the 1820s; the Town Clerk was the Steward appointed by the Lord of the Manor, who in practice controlled what was going on. The only method of acquiring the freedom of the borough and thereby being appointed a burgess (and thus able to vote in elections) was by presentment of the jury at a Court Leet; the first recorded was in 1615 and by 1832 there were 254 burgesses able to vote and use the town common for grazing without fee. Everyone else had to pay a fine for grazing their animals and had to use the Lordship mill for grinding their corn. The Court Leet fined defaulters and those commiting minor offences, ensured that weights and measures were correct, ensured that the streets were kept clean, were responsible for the whipping post and stocks in the High Street, and managed the fairs and markets. It also ensured that the Lord of the Manor received due payments when a freeholder or member of his family married, or bought property, or died. The corrupt appointment of burgesses to vote at elections became so bad (particularly in the time of Sir Herbert Lloyd Bt of Peterwell) that in 1814 the town was granted a new Charter by George III, and in 1884 Lampeter was made a municipal borough with another new Charter which entitled it to elect a Mayor, four aldermen and 12 councillors; the first Mayor was William Jones of Glandenys and Thomas Lloyd solicitor was elected one of the new aldermen. The Court Leet and Lord of the Manor thereby lost their purpose and the Town Council took over.

Aberystwyth was governed by a Court Leet[732] until the Municipal Corporations Act 1835.

35.2 Justices of the Peace and Quarter Sessions

Most market towns like Llandovery which had Royal Charters were authorised to discharge local justice through Hundred Courts where bailiffs and local burgesses would bring criminal cases unless they were serious felonies in which case they had to be dealt with in the principal county town at Carmarthen.

When King Edward III established the office of Justice of the Peace in 1361, he appointed Sheriffs to represent him in every English county and also chose local landowners to be Justices; they dealt with licensing, weights and measures, and vagrancy as well as with petty crime. This system did not apply to Wales however until new Acts passed between 1535 and 1543 provided for Wales to be united with England under the Act of Union, for the separate lordship marcher and Crown lands to be abolished, for JPs to be appointed for the whole of Wales by the Lord Chancellor, and for the establishment of Quarter Sessions and the Great Sessions[733]. Initially each county was allowed eight JPs, but in practice Carmarthenshire had 25 in 1581 and by the 18th century it had over 100.

At one stage in Carmarthenshire there existed several different types of jury[734]. At the Assize Courts for very serious cases there would first be a County or Borough Grand Jury responsible for deciding whether or not the case should be tried at all and these jurors tended to be MPs, gentry and JPs. At the actual trial there would be Petty jurors who generally were middle class farmers. Then for other cases heard at County or Borough Quarter Sessions there would again be a Grand Jury to decide whether the case should go to trial and if so the Petty jurors would hear the case. In the 19th century the qualification for serving on County Quarter Sessions Grand or Petty juries was owning property of £10 per annum in freehold or rents, or £20 under long leases in England and 60 per cent of such sums in Wales. In the case of Borough Quarter Sessions Grand and Petty jurors had to be burgesses of the borough. Welsh juries were often very unreliable in practice; this may have been partly because many jurors did not understand English and therefore the evidence, and partly because they felt a guilty verdict would reflect very badly on their own locality and community.

---

731 WJ Lewis: *History of Lampeter (1997) p14-20*

732 George Eyre: *Aberystwyth Its Court Leet 1690-1900 (1902)*

733 Sir John Lloyd Vol 1 p209-41

734 Francis Jones: *Ave Atque Vale CH (1972) p5-30;* Richard W Ireland: *Putting oneself on whose Country? Carmarthenshire Juries in the mid 19th century CH*

The Justices of the Peace met four times a year to conduct their courts at Quarter Sessions and in addition to their judicial functions they were responsible for the civil administration of the county. In practice nothing happened unless these unpaid administrators, all of whom were gentry, agreed; they were in effect the precursors of the County Councils. Quarter Sessions were abolished in 1971 when the new Crown Courts were established for serious crime.

Rural police forces did not really start until the mid 19th century and the local parish constable usually dealt with all the petty crime. For many years in Llansawel, Talley and Cynwyl Gaeo parishes there were no police officers and the parish vestry nominated and appointed so many of the farmers as fit and qualified men to act as constables without fee[735] or reward. Cases were generally dealt with at the courts held in Llandovery Town Hall where petty sessions and the County Courts were held. Judge John Johnes of Dolaucothi would often sit there as well as at Carmarthen Assizes on the more serious offences; life in the prisons[736] for those defendants who were given custodial sentences and in the workhouses[737] was very grim indeed. Minor crime such as theft, drunkenness, assaults, poaching, selling short measures in pubs and alehouses, and traffic offences involving horse and traps and bicycles etc were dealt with by the Justices as they are today. Local Magistrates' Courts were held at one time in Llandovery, Llandeilo, Llansawel (where many of the cases from the parishes of Cynwyl Gaeo and Llanycrwys were heard), sometimes in the Dolaucothi Arms in Pumsaint, and in Ammanford as well as Llanelli and Carmarthen.

The Justices used to be the large landowners and many members of the Edwinsford, Dolaucothi and Brunant families served as such over the centuries. Women were not allowed to be JPs until 1919. Since WW2 JPs are appointed from all parts of society and women and men are probably equal in numbers on most benches. The magistrates' courts in Llandeilo and Llansawel closed in the 1970s. The Court house at Llandovery closed in about 1998 and was converted into a library and the one at Ammanford closed in December 2011 so all minor crime is now dealt with by Justices sitting in Llanelli or Carmarthen. Carmarthenshire now has a single unified bench and the Dinefwr Bench on which the JPs resident locally used to sit has been subsumed.

---

735 Steve Dubé: *Mr Plod's Road to Recognition CA (2012) p87-94*

736 E Vernon Jones: *Twelve Months in a Victorian Gaol CH Vol XVIII p28-50*

737 DJ Evans: *Before It's Forgotten-Workhouse Days Remembered CH Vol XV p81-88*

36. Local Parish Administration

The gentry and wealthier farmers, the clergy and the schoolmasters generally helped the community by looking after the poor, overseeing the parish constable, and generally dealing with local problems in the parish. The parish overseer, constable and the surveyor effectively ran the local day to day administration of the parish, kept their own rate books and accounts and reported to the Court Leet and to the JPs in Quarter Sessions, who had considerable administrative powers. The overseer was responsible for operating the Poor Law[738] in the parish, which since Elizabethan times had been financed by a Poor Tax from property owners; parishes were legally obliged to care for the paupers. In practice parish vestries did pay sums to paupers living in the parish, although in 1828 the Talley Parish Vestry "ordered that no pauper be relieved who keeps a dog." The ecclesiastical affairs of the parish were handled by the churchwardens and the parish clerk.

The Reform Act 1832 led to the gradual democratisation of local and parish government with JPs (mainly local gentry and squires) losing their former local government powers. Local Boards of Guardians were given responsibility for public health given the frequent outbreaks of cholera and scarlet fever from which many died and for the local workhouse and the poor. In 1894 parish councils were introduced under the Local Government Act 1894 for every rural parish to be elected by the local electorate and to be responsible for many local issues and generally for local administration. Carmarthenshire County Council had the powers to enforce local government under the 1894 Act.

Workhouses and Gaols

Apart from the obligation on parishes to cater for the poor or paupers there was also a responsibility to deal with vagrants and tramps. Criminals were incarcerated in common gaols which up to the 19th century were dreadful places full of disease. Houses of correction or workhouses were set up as early as the 16th century and were intended to stop able-bodied tramps and vagrants from obtaining poor relief and made them work for their board and lodging. Sometimes the distinction between gaols and workhouses became blurred even after imprisonment for debt was abolished by the Debtors Act 1869.

In 1836 many of the parishes in Carmarthenshire including Llansawel and Talley elected 20 men to the Board of Guardians[739] of the newly formed Llandeilo Fawr Poor Law Union which then built the workhouse in Ffairfach designed to accommodate 120 inmates. Families were split up and paupers usually either entered the workhouse or starved which is why they were so feared. In 1901 William Simon of Llansawel was the master of the workhouse and his inmates included: Daniel Harries (aged 63 labourer of Cayo), David Davies (aged 71 draper of Talley), Rachel Ann Jones (aged 12 of Llansawel) and Hannah Jones (aged 10 of Llansawel). It was not until 1929 that local councils took over control of the former workhouses. The Ffairfach workhouse building was not demolished until the 1970s.

The Carmarthen County Gaol records for 1845 show that prisoners spent many hours each day chained on the treadwheel; treadwheels were a deterent and usually performed no useful purpose although a few sometimes did raise water from a well or ground corn. Prisoners were often put in leg irons or straight jackets. If they misbehaved they would be put in the refractory dark cell on bread and water. Crimes ranged from very serious crimes leading to transportation as a convict to being drunk and disorderly, refusing to break stones, leaving one's family to claim poor relief from the parish, and refusing to maintain bastard children.

---

[738] DJ Davies: *Guardians of the Needy Found Wanting CH (1982) p54-69*

[739] Dr Geoff Hooker: *Llandilofawr Poor Law Union 1836-1886 thesis (2013)*; Llandeilo Fawr Union 1836 CA (1962) p91-3; Hywel Jones: *Y Llychau*

The Carmarthen Workhouse was still functioning as late as just before the Second World War. Mr DJ Evans was appointed a Porter by the old Board of Guardians in 1929 at an annual salary of £52 plus £5 for hair cutting and shaving plus living in quarters and free coal and light. He has written that the staff comprised the Master and Matron, the Porter, a female nurse, a cook and four maids to look after 100 inmates plus another 100 tramps or vagrants who were admitted each week into the casual wards.

Every inmate had to work for long hours, the regime was very strict and the institution was in many respects self sufficient. Food was limited with one slice of bread with margarine and some tea for breakfast and evening meal, and mainly soup and bread for midday dinner. Inmates cut wood, worked in the vegetable gardens, broke stones and did other chores to warrant their board and lodging. Travelling tramps would often work for one day and be allowed to sleep for two nights in the sleeping block; they would then move on to the next workhouse in a neighbouring town. More than a third of casuals were Irish often ex-servicemen who did casual work in the area. On discharge from one workhouse they would be given a "bread and cheese" ticket which they could exchange for food at appointed shops in another town. The nearest workhouses were in Llanelli, Ffairfach (Llandeilo) and Lampeter. The idea was that casuals should not be allowed back to the same workhouse within a month of last discharge but in practice this did not always work out since they were not allowed to sleep on the streets.

37. Toll and Tithe Riots

37.1 Rebecca Riots

During the 17th to 19th centuries many Welsh families emigrated to America via ports at Bristol and Liverpool. Quakers and Baptists went because of religious persecution after the Restoration in 1660. Others followed during the next two centuries in search of a better life because of poverty, the level of taxation including the unjust payment of toll charges and tithes, enclosure of common land, the setting up of workhouses, and the unjust system of justice controlled by the gentry.

Since 1555 the responsibility for the repair and maintenance of local roads was that of each parish. Every inhabitant had to work unpaid for six days each year on the local highways under the supervision of the local parish Surveyor, also unpaid, who enforced this obligation via the JPs in Quarter Sessions. If a parish did not upkeep its roads a presentment for neglect of road repairs was heard by the Court of Great Sessions in Carmarthen and the parish fined accordingly with each inhabitant having to pay. The position was made even worse after 1788 when the Llandovery and Lampeter Turnpike Trust[740] was established by Act of Parliament. Several similar trusts were set up in Carmarthenshire sponsored by landlords as trustees with local support from gentry, clerics and wealthier tenants to take over a particular stretch of road, maintain it and charge tolls for the traffic along it. There were nine such trusts in Carmarthenshire controlling some 330 miles by 1800. They were intended to supplement not replace the local obligation of the parish to maintain its roads.

The tolls charged by the Llandovery and Lampeter Trust initially were 3d for each horse drawing, 1d for each horse not drawing, the full toll for the carriage of coal; half the toll for the carriage of lime, and the full toll for use of less than 300 yards of the turnpike road. The number of toll gates was more of a problem than the amount of each toll and there was no legal limit. The trusts borrowed too much money, charged very high tolls, and worst of all some trustees effectively sold their tolls by auction to the highest bidder every year; this meant that the trustees received a monthly fixed payment for doing nothing while the purchasing toll-farmer collected the tolls for himself and often neglected his repairing obligations. Consequently many trusts became insolvent, the roads were unrepaired and yet the local parishes remained responsible for maintaining their roads unpaid.

It is thus perhaps unsurprising that, following a number of very poor harvests between 1837 and 1841 with rents increasing, tithe payments, poor rates and these turnpike road tolls which resulted in great poverty adversely affecting all families, protests and riots took place particularly in the rural areas during the "Hungry Forties". There were four tollgates on the roads outside Llansawel at Michael's (Tŷ Meichel), Charing Cross gate, Porth Factory gate and Penny Forge gate; two outside Pumsaint at Pentre Davies and Ynysau gate; and at least one on the road from Talley to Llandeilo as well as the Cefen Trysgod gate in Llandeilo, so in practice it was impossible to drive a horse and cart to market without paying a toll (although attempts were made to use the drovers roads to avoid the tolls). The famous Rebecca Riots[741] started in Pembrokeshire in May 1839 when a group of men on horseback disguised in women's clothes burnt a tollgate. During the riots Judge John Johnes of Dolaucothi Mansion wrote *An Address to the Inhabitants of Conwil-Caio* dated 16 August 1843 appealing to them not to join in the illegal meetings or to attack the tollgates.

By 1843 the authorities under the command of the 4th Lord Dynevor and Colonel Love reporting to the Duke of Wellington had to send in the troops assisted by the Metropolitan Police (created in 1829) and the new Carmarthenshire police force[742]. They swept through South Wales including Carmarthenshire and came to Llansawel[743] where they destroyed Michael's gate[744] twice (an onlooker Twmmi Davies of

740 Anthony HT Lewis: *The Early Effects of Carmarthenshire Turnpike Trusts 1760-1800 CH (1967) p41-54; LCTA: Pages from the History of Llandovery (1975) Vol 1 p402-7*

741 Named after Rebecca in the Book of Genesis Chapter 24, verse 60

742 JF Jones: *Carmarthenshire Rural Police Force CA (1962) p45-8*

743 TH Lewis: *The Rebecca Movement in Carmarthenshire CA (1943) p6-15*; Pat Molloy: *And They Blessed Rebecca (1983) p264;* Fred Price: *Llansawel p3*

744 DJ Williams p30

Clynmarch was forced to set light to the gates himself while the tollgate keeper, John mab Deio Josi, who was lame and decrepit was terrified); they also destoyed Penny gate next to Penny Forge on the Llansawel to Crugybar road (Hannah Evans was the tollgate keeper).

By the end of 1843 some 250 tollgates had been destroyed in Wales including one in Llandeilo which became a military station for two years and one at Pumsaint[745] on the road to Lampeter called Pentre Davies gate on Thursday 6 July 1843 (the tollgate keeper was Mary Davies aged 65 living with her daughter Mary Davies aged 30). A few of Rebecca's daughters were caught as a result of local paid informers and some were transported to Australia after a trial which had to be held for safety reasons in Cardiff well away from the relevant areas. Following a Royal Commission a new turnpike road act was passed to correct the many defects in the former system, tolls were reduced and County Road Boards took over from the former hated turnpike trusts. The riots ceased by 1844.

37.2 Tithe Riots

The payment of tithes[746] to the Church and to Lay Impropriators (in the case of Cynwyl Gaeo and Llansawel parishes being Sir James Williams Bt of Edwinsford) caused much resentment particularly amongst mainly non-conformist local inhabitants. This resulted in the Tithe Commutation Act 1836 which established the Tithe Commission which created tithe maps for each tithe district (usually the parish) in the country. In the case of Llansawel, Talley and Cynwyl Gaeo this led to new Tithe Apportionment Agreements in 1838-41 between the tithe owners and the local landowners and a new annual rentcharge in lieu of the former tithe payments, which in practice was passed on by landlords to their tenants.

Resentment continued over the following decades. In 1886 tithe riots started again in Wales and there was much civil disturbance when the authorities tried to distrain goods of tenants for payment of arrears of tithe rentcharges. Parliament then passed the Tithe Act 1891 which

Former Tollgate at Pumsaint 2016

[745] The gate, posts and rails were completely destroyed at night; HT Evans: *Rebecca and Her Daughters (1910) Ch 8*

[746] See David James: *Parish Life Eighteenth Century Style CA (2009) p54-60* for examples of tithing

made the landowner alone responsible for the payment of tithe rentcharges and made void any future contract between a landowner and his tenant for the payment of such rentcharges. In practice however landlords continued to try to recover such payments from their tenants.

By the early 1900s many farmers all over the country were finding it very difficult to survive and resented the payment of rentcharges dressed up as rent or some type of tax. Many refused to pay and thousands were threatened with court orders and distraint of their goods and animals by bailiffs. Attempts by bailiffs to get auctioneers to sell their animals and goods led to civil disobedience with the police called in to keep the peace; tithe rebels would blow a tithe horn to warn everyone of the approach of a bailiff attempting to distrain. Whilst there were disturbances in Carmarthenshire I have found no evidence that they directly affected the parishes of Llansawel, Talley or Cynwyl Gaeo to any great extent.

In the case of the Edwinsford Estate the annual tithes[747] were paid by the tenants in the Edwinsford Arms for Talley tenants and in the Black Lion for Llansawel tenants until about 1920 and every tenant received a free pint of beer.

Rebecca and her daughters—Illustrated London News 1843

[747] DJ Williams p230

Index

Welsh names in patronymic form are listed under their first names. Surnames and place names are listed alphabetically. In order to avoid confusion, for some people I have stated their date of birth or death or pedigree number (stated in the pedigrees at the front of this book) in parenthesis after their names.

Aim as high as the sun

Arduus ad solem **εἰς ἥλιον σπευστέον** **cyfuwch â'r haul bo'r nod**